# Master of Airpower

# Master of Airpower

General Carl A. Spaatz

By David R. Mets
The Aerospace Education Foundation
and
The Air Force Historical Foundation

PRESIDIO

*To the airmen who fought and flew with General Spaatz.*

Copyright © 1988 by Air Force Historical Foundation/Aerospace Education Foundation

Published by Presidio Press
505 B San Marin Drive, Suite 300
Novato, CA 94945-1340

This edition printed 1997

**Library of Congress Cataloging-in-Publication Data**

Mets, David R.
    Master of airpower/David R. Mets
    p.      cm.
    Bibliography: p. 406
    Includes index.
    ISBN 0-89141-317-0 (hardcover)
    ISBN 0-89141-639-0 (paperback)
    1. Spaatz, Carl, 1891–1974. 2. Generals—United States—Biography. 3. United States. Air Force—Biography. 4. Aeronautics, Military—United States—History. I. Title.
UG626.2.S66M48 1988
358.4'0092'—dc 19
[B]                               88-5427
                                     CIP

Printed in the United States of America

# Contents

| | | |
|---|---|---:|
| Acknowledgments | | vii |
| Chapter I | An Airman's Roots | 1 |
| Chapter II | The Great War | 21 |
| Chapter III | Pursuit Aircraft and Military Aviation | 39 |
| Chapter IV | Bombers and the Depression Thirties | 75 |
| Chapter V | Going to War | 105 |
| Chapter VI | Reversing the Tide in the Mediterranean | 139 |
| Chapter VII | Winning Air Superiority over Western Europe | 175 |
| Chapter VIII | The Tactical Exploitation | 219 |
| Chapter IX | The Strategic Exploitation | 255 |
| Chapter X | An End and a Beginning | 289 |
| Chapter XI | Creating the Air Force | 311 |
| Epilogue | | 333 |
| Author's Acknowledgments | | 341 |
| Notes | | 344 |
| Bibliography | | 406 |
| Index | | 417 |

# Acknowledgments

## THE AEROSPACE EDUCATION FOUNDATION AND THE AIR FORCE HISTORICAL FOUNDATION

*Master of Airpower* was written under the auspices of the two foundations in furtherance of their efforts to perpetuate the history and heritage of military aviation and aerospace operations. The foundations and the author are grateful for the continuing support of their memberships in this biographical effort.

We also wish to make particular note of and express special appreciation to the Eighth Air Force Historical Society and the Eighth Air Force Memorial Museum Foundation for their demonstrated confidence in the production of the book and their generous financial support which assured the writing of the manuscript.

We are indebted to many individuals who provided countless hours of dedicated work and assistance in researching, writing, editing, and preparing the manuscript for publication. We particularly commend Mrs. Carl A. Spaatz; Irene W. McPherson; Col. Louis H. Cummings, USAF (Ret.); John Schlight; Col. John A. Frisbee, USAF (Ret.); Col. Kenneth Bixler, USAF (Ret.); Mrs. Lillian B. Dempsey; and Mrs. Jeanne Collier.

JAMES M. KECK
Lieutenant General, USAF (Ret.)
President
Aerospace Education Foundation

JOHN B. MCPHERSON
Lieutenant General, USAF (Ret.)
Past President
Air Force Historical Foundation

# Chapter I

## AN AIRMAN'S ROOTS

The summer of 1974 will long remain etched in the memories of Americans who experienced it. Abroad, the United States was approaching the climax of a two-decade involvement in Vietnam. The front page of the *Washington Post* for July 14, 1974, was covered with crises. One column told of two desperadoes who were holding hostages in a District courthouse, demanding an airplane to flee the country. Another described the contempt findings against a police strike in Baltimore. The lead story reported: "Culminating 18 months of investigation and hearings that constituted the most intensive congressional inquiry into alleged White House corruption in American history, a unanimous Senate select Watergate committee called for major reforms to prevent a recurrence of the Watergate affair."

That July 14th also was the day this country lost a great man, Gen. Carl Andrew Spaatz, graduate of the United States Military Academy at West Point, air pioneer, outstanding operational commander in World War II, and first Chief of Staff of the United States Air Force. He died at the Army's Walter Reed Medical Center in Washington, D.C.

A memorial service, conducted by a longtime friend, Chaplain Charles Carpenter, was held for him in the chapel at nearby Andrews Air Force Base. After the service, the casket and the funeral party of family and pallbearers were flown to Colorado by Air Force jet, and General Spaatz was laid to rest in the Air Force Academy cemetery.

The youngest children in the party had not known their grandfather as a general. Spaatz retired from military service in 1948, and the young-sters had never seen him in uniform. Was this their kindly, bird-watching grandfather for whom the troops formed alongside the airplane at Andrews Air Force Base? Was it for this peaceful man that the Air Force Academy cadets sang the "Battle Hymn of the Republic"? What had he done during his eighty-three years on this earth that such homage was being paid him? What had his life meant for the United States Air Force and for his country?[1]

The Spaatz grandchildren were not the only ones who might have asked these last two questions. Among the major combat leaders of World War II, Gen. Carl "Tooey" Spaatz was the least known outside the military. He was a genuinely modest man who abhorred ostentation and rejected offers from publishers to write his memoirs. Such books, he thought, were apt to be self-serving, or at least so regarded. In any event, if he agreed, he would have to write honestly. Inevitably that would hurt some people he liked and admired but with whom he had disagreed on strategic, tactical, moral, or ethical grounds.

At the time of his death, there were tributes from civilian and military leaders here and abroad. Typical were the words of Sir John Slessor, Marshal of the Royal Air Force: "He had an uncommon flair for the really important factor in any issue. . . . Tooey was one of the relatively few Commanders on either side in World War II to whom can honestly be applied that much overworked word, 'Great.' "[2]

That view was shared by Field Marshal Sir Michael Carver, chief of Britain's Defense Staff and editor of *The War Lords: Military Commanders of the 20th Century*. From a list of some hundred nominees, Sir Michael selected forty-three on whom short biographical essays were written by civilian and military historians. Among the forty-three were but five airmen. The only American air commander was Carl Spaatz, whose essay was done by Alfred Goldberg, chief historian in the Office of the Secretary of Defense.[3]

Any assessment of Spaatz must begin with the understanding that he was "his own man." Neither Marshall, nor Eisenhower, nor Arnold or Portal, not even Churchill, overawed him; he regarded himself unselfcon-sciously as their peer in the art of making war. Nevertheless he did not have the mental arrogance characteristic of many self-made men. But he had strength and force of character—enough to deal on equal terms with other leaders who were strong and stubborn also. And yet Spaatz was a man of genuine modesty and diffidence. There was a sturdy no-nonsense quality and an unmistakable professionalism about him that could not help but impress. His modesty did not inhibit his capacity to command because he knew his own mind and made free to speak it when necessary.

More than a decade later, a conference on air leadership, sponsored by the Air Force Historical Foundation, considered as possible models for leadership the military careers of Gen. Carl Spaatz and of Rear Adm. William A. Moffett, chief of the Navy's Bureau of Aeronautics in the 1920s. Spaatz's methods and achievements were presented by the author of this book and by Dr. I. B. Holley, Jr., of Duke University. The conferees agreed unanimously that Tooey Spaatz justly deserved his reputation for genius in the organization and command of great air forces. Almost unanimously they felt that Spaatz's career, extending from the early days of military aviation through two World Wars and culminating in his selection as the first chief of staff of the newly independent United States Air Force, was not a model to guide aspiring young officers.[4] This apparent paradox sets some parameters for a study of command as exemplified by Carl Spaatz, taking into account the unique combination of character, personality, experience, and world events by which his years of service were shaped.

## Ancestral Roots

On the 14th of March 1865, the mayor of the town of Eberfeld issued in the name of the King of Prussia a passport to Carl Spatz[5] and three members of his family—his wife Juliana Amalie Busch Spatz, his daughter Julie, who was three, and Auguste, not yet a year old. Their destination was shown as Philadelphia, the duration of the passport one year, the declared purpose to visit family members in America.[6] Carl Spatz never went back.

The reason for Spatz's emigration to the New World is not recorded. He left behind a family of solid middle-class accomplishment. His father was in the fabric dyeing business and the family was related to the famous Krupp manufacturers through Juliana.[7] Family recollection holds that he was a bit of a maverick,[8] a nineteenth-century liberal, not much at home in a Germany then being driven toward unification under the hand of Bismarck. It may well have been so, for Carl was educated at the College of Berlin, had been in the printing business, had traveled widely in Europe, and was said to be fluent in several languages.[9]

Carl and Juliana settled for a time in Philadelphia. Soon after they landed, on November 25, 1865, another child, Charles B. Spatz, was born. Carl worked in the printing trade for five or six years before moving to the Pennsylvania Dutch village of Boyertown, about forty miles northwest of Philadelphia. In 1871 he bought a newspaper, which he built into a substantial force in the community and a factor in Pennsylvania politics. Even today, the German flavor of Boyertown is inescapable, though milder than when Carl was publishing the *Boyertown Democrat,* subsequently known under his son, Charles B., as the *Berks County Democrat* and now, no longer in the family, as the *Boyertown Area Times.* At first, the paper was published entirely in German. During the 1870s, Carl began to set the first four pages in German and the last four in English. Later, the order was reversed, and by 1910 only a small column among the back pages was in German.[10]

Carl died prematurely in 1884, leaving his family and the paper in the hands of his son, Charles B. Spatz, then nineteen. Charles, though not as well educated or experienced as his father, inherited Carl's aptitude for writing and speaking. He was active in community affairs, was a stalwart Democrat, and was twice sent to the Pennsylvania legislature.

The Boyertown area was, and still is, populated largely by people of German extraction and of the Mennonite or Lutheran faith. The Spatzes belonged to the Reformed (Lutheran) Church. The *Berks County Democrat* of Charles' day reveals the editor as a liberal, by the standards of his time, who shared the main values of his German-Protestant neighbors. The work ethic was strong among them and the editorial pages of the paper are replete with homilies on the virtues of honesty and manual labor. Also apparent is a strong utilitarian bent and a stout commitment to law and order.[11] At the same time, editor Spatz salted it with a wry sense of humor that was passed on to his son, Carl Andrew.

After three years as an editor, Charles apparently felt well enough established to take a wife, Anne Muntz of Reading, Pennsylvania, who also was of German extraction. They were married on January 17, 1889.[12] Their first-born was a girl, Flora, the second Carl Andrew, who arrived at the end of June 1891. Following Carl were Ruth, Frederick, and Anne. In personality, at least, Carl Andrew favored his quiet mother. Music played a prominent role in the family's life, with Flora at the piano while Carl accompanied her on the guitar.[13]

When Charles Spatz was elected to the Pennsylvania Assembly in 1896, he took Carl to Harrisburg with him to serve as a page. Charles introduced a resolution on the second day of his first session, proposing to recognize the belligerent rights of the Cubans in the rebellion against their Spanish masters.[14] There now was greater concern for foreign policy on his editorial pages than one would expect in a small-town newspaper before World War I. Carl, as the elder son, was put to work around the journal's plant, where he was exposed to at least a limited view of the world beyond our shores. He was known as Pennsylvania's youngest linotype operator.[15]

Carl graduated from Boyertown High School in June 1906, just before his fifteenth birthday. There is not much evidence that he and the school influenced each other to any great degree. He did not stand out in the academic, athletic, or social life of the institution, perhaps because of his self-professed laziness. Public secondary schools in the area were limited to two or three years at that time and were not geared to preparing students for college. Carl was sent to Perkiomen Preparatory School at nearby Pennsburg in the fall of 1906, where his career as a student remained undistinguished except in one respect. His conduct record foreshadowed the one he was to establish at West Point. Offenses included throwing apples and water from windows and repeatedly "bumming" to visit town at night.[16]

When his father was seriously injured in the Boyertown Opera House fire of January 1908, Carl returned from Perkiomen to help run the paper. In addition to Charles' serious injury, one of the paper's employees had been killed in the fire and another quit in the aftermath. Until Charles was back on his feet, Carl and one other employee did the work formerly done by four men. Carl handled most of the mechanical and some of the editorial tasks, while his colleague did the reporting and some of the editing. It is difficult to know which writing was Carl's, but the quality and quantity of the paper's content was not much different from the standard fare of the *Berks County Democrat*. At any rate, the experience must have been both educational and maturing.

Sometime in 1909, when his father was fully recovered, Carl was free to resume his preparation for college, this time at the Army-Navy Preparatory School in Washington, D.C.[17] His motivation for wanting to attend a service academy probably was largely economic. The family's financial condition during the first decade of the century was somewhat precarious. They lived in a small building that still stands at 41 East Philadelphia Avenue in Boyertown. It served as family quarters, editorial offices, and printing plant. There were constant appeals in the paper for payment of accounts in arrears and, one suspects that Charles was rather lenient with friends and acquaintances. Moreover, Charles' mother—Carl's grandmother—lived for twenty-six years after her husband died, and there were five children in the family, three in boarding school at the same time.

The details of Carl's appointment to West Point are blurred and do little to clear up the matter of the original motivation. Although the family had no military tradition, Charles was a close friend of Maj. Thomas Rhoads, then personal physician to President Taft and later surgeon general of the U.S. Army. Some accounts say that Rhoads proposed the idea and urged Charles to send his older son to the academy.[18] Another version has it that Charles had a good chance to win election to the U.S. Congress but gave way to another Democrat in the field when the latter promised he would appoint Carl to West Point in return.[19] In any case John H. Rothermel was elected to Congress, and Carl was duly appointed to West Point, arriving there on March 1, 1910.[20] His was the last class that would report in March.[21]

Later on, in the 1920s, after Carl had graduated from West Point and was well established in the army, Charles and Anne were prosperous enough to build a substantial home that still stands on 6th Street in Boyertown.[22]

## West Point

Many of the greatest generals in American military history came from the West Point of Spaatz's era: Eisenhower, Bradley and Arnold among them. The class after Spaatz's, which had a greater proportion of men who reached the rank of general than any other in history, became known as "the class the stars fell on." This is partially explainable by the fact that the normal thirty-year career for the classes of 1914 and 1915 spanned two world wars, when promotions were accelerated. The argument about whether West Point and the other academies make profound changes in the character of their students continues.[23] Spaatz would be a disappointing case study for those who argue that they do.

The initial impact of the academy on Spaatz was negative and on the 20th of March, 1910, he submitted his resignation.[24] While the precise reason is not clear, it is known that Carl was far from enchanted with West Point when he first arrived. He later told his wife that he wanted to leave because of the "indignities of those first awful days of hazing."[25] His father's friend, Thomas Rhoads, dissuaded Carl from leaving.

The first days at the academy, called "Beast Barracks," were well calculated to turn the most benign man into a crocodile. In Spaatz's years the management of both the discipline and honor systems was largely in cadet hands. This was thought to be an essential feature in providing leadership training. Still, it led to recurrent problems with hazing. Though some of the worst excesses had been repressed before 1910, the idea that an ordeal must be imposed to test the manliness of the novice remained strong in the corps of cadets, and the practice was far from eliminated when Carl arrived.

Countless reports from all periods of his life suggest that Carl A. Spaatz was never kindly disposed to what lately has been known as "Mickey Mouse," which was in abundance during "Beast Barracks." Even seventy-two years later, his wife has testified that he was not very "military."[26] His conduct record at the academy was dismal and did not improve as he moved to the upper classes. In fact, he was still marching punishment tours on graduation day.[27]

Spaatz's offenses at West Point were generally of two kinds. The first reflected a casualness towards the demands of good order and discipline. On August 31, 1910, for example, he was put on report for failing to clean his rifle bore properly and for "Trifling during Gymnasium, 1015AM." Carl's other offenses may be taken as evidence of a disposition to challenge the system. Cases of this sort include "combining with other cadets for the purpose of raising a sum of money to wager on results of the Army-Navy game,"[28] or the incident in which he was acquitted of the charge of possessing liquor on the post. (According to Gen. Robert Walsh, who was there at the time, he was guilty but escaped on grounds of a technicality.)[29]

Given the stringency of the program, the typical plebe would try to remain as inconspicuous as possible. Anything that made him stand out was bound to result in pain of one sort or another. Carl Spaatz was unfortunate in this regard—he had freckles of monumental proportion and his hair was red. His boyhood nickname, "Boz," was replaced by "Toohey," because he bore a striking resemblance to an upperclassman named F. J. Toohey. This new nickname would stick with him the rest of his life, though it was later corrupted to "Tooey."[30]

West Point was the first engineering school in the United States and one of the first in the world. During Spaatz's time there it still clung to the century-old educational system that had been installed after the War of 1812. The curriculum focused on mathematics and experimental science. A key feature was the use of small classes of eleven or twelve students. Preparation for class centered on intensive study for daily, graded recitations by each cadet.[31] A large part of the system was designed to build character. This concentration on daily recitation of mathematics for grades was done as much for its perceived moral value as for academic or utilitarian benefits. It was thought that the self-discipline resulting from such rigors was an essential trait for officers. The work load was made deliberately heavy and the environment kept austere in the belief that challenges build character and that a shared ordeal creates loyalty and *esprit de corps*.[32] Obedience, loyalty, and discipline were central features of the system.

Spaatz was a fair student, graduating with a class standing of 57 out of 107, in the lower half of his class.[33] This final standing, however, is deceptive. His write-up in the yearbook, *Howitzer,* suggests that he might have stood far higher had he been so inclined:[34] "It is his indifference to tenths [the competitive struggle for high grades]—and demerits as well—that keeps him from standing high in the class." Despite the tinge of undergraduate humor that usually infuses such statements, the item in this case is substantiated by other evidence. He stood in the top half of his class in every mathematics course, of which there were many. These were considered the toughest academic hurdles. During his freshman (plebe) year, Spaatz stood in the middle of his class. By the end of his sophomore (second class) and junior (third class) years, he had moved solidly into the top half of his class.

A cadet seldom was dismissed for academic reasons during his last year, a practice that was at times conducive to relaxation. Unfortunately for those who let up, the academic subjects during that last year carried a far greater weight than did those of earlier years, as did military subjects such as conduct, drill regulations, and leadership. Spaatz's record took a turn for the worse after his junior year, and he plummeted from a rank of 39 to 98 during the last year. Only nine men were behind him in his senior year's work, but some would interpret that (not always with tongue in cheek) as an indication that only nine were more efficient in achieving the same outcome with less effort.[35] In the end, his best course was chemistry, with French next, and mathematics third. His lowest grades were in hygiene, law, and conduct. In the classrooms of West Point, Carl Spaatz demonstrated two things. First, he could learn difficult material in either the sciences or the humanities. Secondly, he possessed a certain nonchalance from the outset of his military career.

His years at the academy did little to change Spaatz's character.

His personality when he graduated was fundamentally the same as it had been when he entered. He was gregarious and a lover of the outdoors as a boy, and remained so throughout his life. He was unflappable as a cadet and as a general. There is virtually no evidence of anger on his part while on the job, and his family is unanimous in stating that he never lost his temper at home.[36]

Carl attended the academy when smoking and drinking were held to be moral defects. This ethical code permeated the institution: smoking was permitted only at very limited times and restricted to areas generally out of sight; drinking resulted in dismissal. Even card playing was looked upon as evil, and it carried twice the number of demerits assigned to unauthorized smoking.[37] The military academy failed to purge any of those three "sins" from Carl Spaatz's character. He became known far and wide as a poker player (although a bad one) during his active duty years and whiled away his days of retirement at the Army-Navy Club in Washington playing a little bridge and a lot of poker.[38] Though all accounts hold that liquor never got the better of Carl Spaatz, many testify that he always had a glass of scotch and soda at his side during these games and was capable of considerable consumption without an apparent effect on the quality of his game.[39] Nor did he ever manage to break the cigarette habit, continuing it to the end of his days.

As for personal appearance, West Point did have some effect on Spaatz. He kept himself trim throughout his life and always made a neat appearance in public (except for the "50 mission crush" on his garrison cap, which was a symbol of USAAF independence.)[40]

Another of the values shared by most West Point graduates is a personal loyalty to friends that goes beyond the American norm. Spaatz possessed this trait in full measure. He made a set of friends at West Point that lasted for decades, among them Brehon B. Somervell, John H. Jouett, George Stratemeyer, Thomas Lanphier, Ralph Royce, and Sheldon Wheeler. Spaatz's roommate, Carl E. Fosnes, was assigned with him to Schofield Barracks in Hawaii when they graduated. Though Tooey had not yet met his future wife, Ruth, one of her cousins, Roger B. Harrison, was also in his class.[41] Of 107 graduates, twenty-six retired as generals. Oddly, twelve of them came from the top half of the class while fourteen, including Spaatz, came from the lower half. The top man in the class retired as a colonel, as did most of the rest who reached retirement, including Lester Lampert who graduated at the bottom.[42] The class of 1915 had an even better record of promotions; as a cadet

Spaatz formed some important acquaintances there, the two most prominent being Omar Bradley and Dwight Eisenhower. Joseph McNarney, Ralph Cousins, Charles Benedict, Henry Miller, and Hubert Harmon were also in that class, and they went into the air arm to figure importantly in Spaatz's life.[43] The man most important to his later career, Henry "Hap" Arnold, had graduated from West Point before Spaatz arrived.

Spaatz and Eisenhower knew each other at West Point, but the depth of their friendship at the time was exaggerated later on. Eisenhower was a prominent cadet and Spaatz must have noticed him; Spaatz was president of the Dialectic Society (a spoofing dramatic group that staged the "Hundredth Night Show") which brought even a quiet man to attention. In addition, the two men were similar in height, so they marched close to one another in ranks. Out of World War II would come the legend that the two had been pals at West Point. Their close friendship actually had its beginning in the African campaign of 1942–43.[44]

Carl Spaatz emerged from West Point with no consuming aspiration to generalship but with an ambition to become an aviator. His desire to fly was kindled by an event that took place early in his cadet days. In the spring of 1910, *New York World* offered a ten-thousand dollar prize to the first aviator who could fly down the Hudson River from Albany to New York City. Glenn Curtiss, early aviation pioneer, was determined to win it. After a reconnaissance trip upstream on a riverboat, Curtiss brought his entourage to Albany in May. It took him several days to prepare and to overcome his unease about flying conditions along the river.[45] On Sunday morning, the last day of May, 1910, he took off. As he winged southward, a special railroad train running along the east shore escorted him; aboard were his wife, mechanics, and a host of reporters. The day was a splendid one, and the grand adventure proceeded without incident until Curtiss ran into the venturi tube created by the mountains that arise on both sides of the river at West Point. He reported:[46]

Everything went along smoothly until I came within sight of West Point. Here the wind was nasty and shook me up considerably. Gusts shot out from rifts between the mountains and made extremely rough riding. The worst spot was encountered between Storm King (adjacent to West Point on the north) and Dunderberg, where the river is narrow and the mountains rise abruptly from the water's edge to more than a thousand feet on either side. Here I ran into a downward suction that dropped me in what seemed an interminable fall straight down, but which as a matter of fact was not more than a hundred feet or perhaps less. The atmosphere seemed to tumble about like water rushing through a narrow gorge. At another point, a little farther along . . . one blast tipped a wing dangerously high, and I almost touched the water. I thought for an instant that my trip was about to end . . .

Earlier he had remarked:[47]

All along the river, wherever there was a village or town, and even along the roads and in boats on the river, I caught glimpses of crowds or groups of people with their faces turned skyward, their attitudes betokening the amazement which could not be read in their faces at that distance.

One of those amazed faces turned skyward was that of nineteen-year-old Cadet Carl Andrew Spaatz. Only ninety-two days into his military career, he was at a turning point that he would remember forever, for it was then he decided to be a flyer. The immediate outcome of that last day of May was fame and ten thousand dollars for Glenn Curtiss. The long-term effect was a lifelong devotion to aviation for Carl Spaatz, whose fame still lay in the future.[48]

## Hawaiian Interlude

A new lieutenant's first assignment after graduation from West Point was determined by his class standing. The elite of the class went into the engineer corps. It is doubtful that Spaatz was interested in going immediately to another school, as an engineer must, even if his class standing were high enough. Spaatz himself later implied that he was more interested in flying than in a military career.[49] Before being assigned to flying school, a young officer was required to serve at least one year in a basic combat branch. By a process of elimination, Spaatz headed for the infantry, determined to move on to flying school at the first opportunity. His first post was an enviable one—he was sent to serve with the 25th Infantry at Schofield Barracks in Hawaii.[50] Carl, his roommate from West Point, Carl E. Fosnes, and another classmate, Sheldon H. Wheeler, were all assigned to Schofield Barracks, arriving there in October, 1914.

The tranquillity of life at Schofield Barracks was in odd contrast to what was going on in other parts of the world. Europe was aflame, and Mexico was experiencing the agony of a long revolution. During

Tooey's graduation leave, Austria's Archduke Ferdinand fell to the shots of Princips in far-off Serbia, igniting the First World War. Foreign offices in Europe were in a frenzy for a month before the "guns of August" spoke.

Just before Tooey got to Hawaii, von Schleiffen's plan had failed, by the narrowest of margins, to conquer France. Though Spaatz could hardly know it, this campaign was the first in history to be influenced by airplanes (balloons had been used as early as the wars of the French Revolution). The Allies' aerial reconnaissance had discovered a gap developing between the wheeling armies of the German right flank that allowed them to counterattack and win the Battle of the Marne. By the time Spaatz arrived in Hawaii, the two sides were rapidly extending their field fortifications northward until their flanks rested on the sea. They settled into bloody trench warfare which, during the next four years, would decimate a generation of young men on both sides—an experience so searing on the consciousness of western civilization that it was to influence Spaatz's life in myriad ways.

Although America's first reaction was to proclaim neutrality, the atmosphere at home was not as quiet as it was in the islands. Woodrow Wilson was not as neutral toward the Mexican Revolution as he was toward the European war. The Panama Canal was finally opened that summer. A crisis with Mexico had been brewing all year, and American marines had landed at Vera Cruz. The U.S. government that summer changed its support from its former favorite in the Mexican Revolution, Venustiano Carranza, to Pancho Villa. After yet another switch, it was Pancho Villa against whom America's first combat air unit would fly.

If Tooey looked upon his first assignment as little more than a temporary way station on the road to pilot school, he was not outspoken about it. That would have alienated the career infantry officers who surrounded him. He did receive good marks from his company commander.[51]

When an officer was accepted for flying school he could expect to receive "The Lecture" from his commanding officer. Essentially it was a raking over the coals for the misguided soul who was demonstrating such poor judgment as to put his life and career at risk in a part of the army that didn't have much of a future. The commander of the 25th Infantry was Colonel Kennon, a tall, handsome, impressive officer. When Tooey and his friend Sam Wheeler were summoned to his office for "The Lecture," they were surprised and relieved when the colonel got out of his chair, extended both his hands, and said, "My boys, if I were your age, I'd be doing the same."[52]

One of the most important events of the year at Schofield Barracks for the 24-year-old Lieutenant Spaatz was meeting a teenaged girl, Ruth Harrison, daughter of a cavalry colonel.[53] Col. Ralph Harrison and his wife, Edith, were fairly conservative, even for that day, and the young people never went anywhere after dark unaccompanied. According to Ruth Spaatz, she and Tooey once went to a dance and, when the chaperone got lost, Tooey took Ruth home alone. Their appearance at the door shocked her mother, especially since it appeared that Lieutenant Spaatz had imbibed an alcoholic beverage. This incident, to her, only emphasized the belief that these young pilots were wild young men who spent all their time tinkering with and attempting to fly ridiculous machines of questionable usefulness, when they should, instead, be settling down to the serious military business of the Army. As time went by, however, Edith began to know and like Tooey and the two developed a remarkable rapport; he called her Miss Edith and was quite devoted to her.[54]

Many friendships were developed during Spaatz's academy years and his first assignments. The realities of life were brought home to him also. Just before he left for flying school in October, 1915, Spaatz faced for the first time the death of a friend. His partner in undergraduate escapades and roommate at West Point, Carl Fosnes, took his own life. This marred what otherwise would have been a joyous occasion for Tooey and Sam Wheeler, who departed together for the Air Service's only flying school, in San Diego, California.[55]

## Winning His Wings

For a few years after the Army bought its first airplanes, training was purchased from the manufacturer along with the machines. Henry Arnold, for example, learned to fly with the Wright brothers at Dayton.[56] Soon after Arnold got his wings, the Army organized its own flying school at College Park, Maryland, and he went there to complete his qualification as a military aviator. Needing better winter flying weather, the College Park school migrated to Augusta, Georgia, for a time, but even that far south the flyers ran into snow, ice, and floods. In the meantime, Glenn Curtiss had set up an operation at North Island in San Diego. The weather there, aside from morning fogs, was ideal for flight training year-round. Several years before Spaatz arrived at North Island, Curtiss had invited some flyers from College Park to San Diego for the winter. As a result, the Army set up a permanent school there to avoid the semiannual moves and to minimize the amount of training time lost to weather.[57]

During Spaatz's seven months at North Island, the school was in a state of flux, and its personnel were facing multiple crises. Several types of aircraft were used, none of them very dependable and all difficult to maintain in safe condition. One of the chief tensions at the school was a continual need to deal with death. At the end of 1913, for example, the school's "mortality rate . . . had been extremely high—eighteen percent, or one death for every 5,806 miles flown."[58] Further, the lease to the airfield was lost. The Army was determined to make North Island its permanent training center, but the owner of the land, the Coronado Beach Corporation, realizing the great potential of the site, substantially raised the price when the Army tried to buy it. The company served notice that it intended to evict the flying school in March, 1916, just before Spaatz was to graduate.[59]

Nevertheless, it was an exciting time for Spaatz to be getting into aviation. World War I was stimulating rapid change in aviation technology in Europe and even in America, though America was not yet involved in the war. The North Island community was at that time the center of army aviation, though a small flying detachment existed in the Philippines. During the summer of 1915, just before Spaatz arrived, the 1st Aero Squadron left North Island for Fort Sill, Oklahoma, to develop tactics for artillery spotting and reconnaissance. The squadron was soon to become involved in combat on the Mexican border.[60]

The aviation environment into which Spaatz now moved was made up of a group of thirty-four students and eight instructors.[61] Many of the early pioneers in American aviation were connected with the school, and new ideas were in the air. Some aerial record was broken almost daily. When asked at the Air Force Academy many years later to identify the individuals who most affected his career, Spaatz named his instructor at North Island first.[62] This was Oscar Brindley, a civilian, who was one of the heroes from the infancy of flying. The same month that Tooey departed Hawaii, Brindley had set a new record for seaplane distance flying.[63]

By the time Spaatz got to North Island, things had improved a bit for trainees—though it still was an insecure life. Those were the days when students could not be married, and when one was promoted to captain, he was thought to be past his prime for flying and sent back to his original branch of the service. The law provided that student pilots receive an additional 25 percent of their base pay as flight pay; junior military aviators got 50 percent and military aviators got 75 percent.[64] No more than fifteen officers could be qualified for the latter rating. Relatively speaking, flight pay constituted a more substantial portion of the flyer's income than it does today, a contributing factor to the growing tensions between the flyers and the ground officers of the Army.

Oscar Brindley thought Spaatz was well enough qualified to solo after a total of fifty minutes in the air. Fifty minutes is an astonishingly brief time by today's standards (about ten hours are normally required), and it was short even then. Tooey wrote home expressing his exhilaration, and his father passed on his feelings to the readers of the *Berks County Democrat.*[65]

At San Diego, Spaatz learned as much about the general field of air power as he did about flying. The United States Army had converted from "pushers," like the Wright airplane, to "tractors" (aircraft whose propellors pulled them along.) It was also in the process of equipping its planes with a standard control system which has been in use ever since, with the ailerons and elevators controlled by hand through a stick or wheel and the rudders moved by foot pedals. The ground school at North Island included courses in engine maintenance, airframe construction, and meteorology.[66] Frequent forced landings in those times made it necessary for the pilot to be his own mechanic; he had to know aircraft systems thoroughly and be able to repair his plane far away from tools and line technicians.

These years were seminal ones for new ideas on air power, and one of the centers for such thinking, perhaps the paramount one, was the flying school at San Diego. Spaatz was exposed to new concepts being considered and tested there. Parachutes, for example, were used successfully in experiments, although their routine use lay far in the future. Tests were also being conducted to develop air-to-ground radio communications. This research had a practical application: the 1st Aero Squadron at Fort Sill was working with ground artillery units by spotting their shots and adjusting fire.[67] In Europe strides had already been made in that direction, but a major difficulty was communication between the spotter in the air and the battery commander on the ground. Sometimes the spotter planes would buzz the site of the guns and the pilot would drop messages, but that slowed the process and reduced the rate of fire. This procedure was particularly poor for fleeting targets. On the western front, spotters in tethered balloons often talked with the gunners by telephone. While balloons served some useful purposes in the static warfare of France, they could not match the flexibility of airplanes which was essential for mobile warfare. Sometimes gunners sent messages to flyers by laying out panels or flashing lights on the ground. Since this method was far from satisfactory, experiments to devise better communications were given top priority at North Island.[68]

There seemed to be no limit to the imaginations of the flyers at North Island. The airmen were experimenting with dropping bombs from aircraft and testing bomb sights. They were even involved with the Navy in attempting to develop tactics for locating minefields from the air.[69] The flyers also tried to use drogue parachutes to brake their aircraft (wheel brakes had not yet been installed).[70] The chutes, incidentally, did not prove successful, and for several more years, until wheel brakes were perfected, it was not uncommon for landing aircraft to run out of runway. Much later, with the advent of the jet age, the very high landing speeds of the first generation of jets reintroduced the problem, and the Air Force supplemented brakes with parachutes.

While Spaatz's friends from West Point were his contemporaries, at San Diego, he added to his list of acquaintances some of the older flyers who were to play an important part in developing the air arm. Oscar Brindley had a decisive influence on him, but Brindley was killed in an airplane crash in 1918.[71] Before Spaatz graduated from North Island, Frank P. Lahm, one of the first (some say *the* first) army airmen to fly an airplane, and a distinguished leader of the air arm for many years, became the school's secretary.[72] Spaatz could hardly have avoided knowing Lahm, as the school secretary was central to the training life of the base, and Lahm already enjoyed considerable renown. Herbert A. Dargue and B. Q. Jones, both somewhat senior to Spaatz, and both to become prominent during the 1930s, were also on the flying school's staff. Tooey just missed meeting Hap Arnold, the man who was later to become his friend and mentor. Arnold arrived at the San Diego base a week or two after Spaatz graduated.[73]

By May, 1916, then, Spaatz had finished the flying school, been exposed to a host of new ideas about flying and airpower, and made some important new friends. He pinned on his junior military aviator wings and headed for Columbus, New Mexico, and the 1st Aero Squadron, which was supporting Pershing's ground forces against Pancho Villa.[74]

## The Punitive Expedition

In the spring of 1916, Woodrow Wilson was neutral in neither thought nor deed when it came to Mexico. By then, the United States was again supporting Carranza against other contenders for power in the revolution. Villa was out of favor, and on March 9 he attacked the town of Columbus, New Mexico, killing seventeen Americans. In retaliation, Wilson ordered the U.S. Army to pursue Villa across the border. The commander of the expedition was Brig. Gen. John J. Pershing, and the 1st Aero Squadron, under Capt. Benjamin Foulois, became part of his force.[75]

Pershing knew that communications in northern Mexico would be difficult. There were few roads and railroads, and telegraph lines were continually being cut by roaming bandits and enemy troops. He wanted the squadron's eight Curtiss JN-3 "Jennies" to act as liaison planes to help him with that problem. In addition, hoping to benefit from the experience of aircraft in the European war, he gave the squadron a reconnaissance mission—to look for the enemy and for friendly units whose whereabouts had become unknown. Secretary of War Newton Baker specifically prohibited the air arm from undertaking offensive operations.[76]

Following Villa's attack on the town, Foulois deployed his outfit from its home station at Fort Sam Houston in San Antonio to the base at Columbus. When he tried to move it to Mexico, to set up a forward operating location (FOL) at Casas Grandes, the trouble began. All eight of his 90-horsepower Jennies took off from Columbus around sunset for Casas Grandes on the 19th of March, but none arrived at their destination that night. Only one or two of the pilots had flown at night before, and the aircraft were not equipped for night flight.[77] In the gathering darkness Foulois and a few of the aircraft landed at a place about halfway to their destination. The rest were scattered about northern Mexico. The one that fared best was an aircraft that had engine problems during take off and returned to Columbus for repairs. It made the trip without incident during daylight hours the next day. Fortunately, only one plane and no pilots were lost during the move.

The squadron spent a fruitless month in Mexico. Maintenance in the high desert was a nightmare, and supply was not much better. The reconnaissance effort came to naught—it was too difficult to tell friend from foe from the air. Villa's men knew that any airplane they saw belonged to the "gringos" and consequently went into hiding long before an American party sent to investigate suspicious groups could arrive. The squadron's only success during the month was in locating a friendly column that was out of touch so that a supply train could be sent to it. The aircraft performed the liaison mission a bit better, but even there their potential was limited by the 90-horsepower engines which could not carry them over the numerous high passes.

Living conditions at Columbus were bad enough, but to the south they were appalling. The aviation section had not yet developed satisfactory flight clothing, and the pilots suffered particularly at night from the cold. In March and April the weather was still bad in Mexico because the terrain was so high. Moreover, because the climb and payload capabilities of the Jennies were limited, the pilots could not carry much in the way of tools or survival gear. There were also problems with the airplanes. The laminated wooden propellers split apart in the arid climate when the glue holding them together dried up. This cost one airplane and the severe damage of several more. By April 20th, the squadron had become so weakened that Foulois was ordered to take it back to Columbus for new airplanes. Only two of the original eight were still flying, and as soon as these planes landed in Columbus they were declared not airworthy. By almost any measure, the mission was a failure. Foulois and his men returned to the United States greatly discouraged.[78]

When Spaatz arrived in June the squadron was maintaining a forward operating location at Pershing's division headquarters in Mexico with one or two aircraft there most of the time. The Jennies had been replaced with new Curtiss R-2 tractors. Although these new planes experienced many of the same propeller problems as the JN-3s, they did have 160-horsepower engines compared with 90-horsepower. Even with this improvement, conditions were still primitive, and Spaatz received a good baptism, flying aircraft under field conditions.[79]

It was another time of learning. The pilots did not trust the new Curtiss R-2s any more than the Jennies, and they did not venture very deeply into Mexico with them. The unit had also been supplied with machine guns and bombs, and was manufacturing some of the latter in the squadron shops at Columbus. They received new cameras and flew aerial photography trials with good results. The flyers learned much about logistics. Special trucks were assembled at Columbus to carry spare parts and tools for the aircraft. Through drastic measures, the propeller problem was solved. At first, metal propellers were tried, but they were too heavy for the engines and could not develop sufficient revolutions per minute to carry the weight. Then a large humidor was built, and at the end of each flight the propeller was removed from the crank shaft and stored in it until the next mission. That worked well enough, but was too cumbersome. Finally, a manufacturer set up a propeller shop at Columbus. By producing propellers in the dry climate in which they were to be used, the problem of splitting was overcome. Before the summer was gone, the squadron was even testing a twin-engine Curtiss, but it, too, was inadequate—though the pilots liked the idea of two engines.[80]

During an interview at the Air Force Academy in 1968, General Spaatz was asked to identify the most satisfying experience of his air force career. He initially said that it was commanding the 1st Pursuit Group, but then added:[81]

> and joining the 1st Aero Squadron at Columbus, New Mexico, and the Pershing Expedition to Mexico was probably, looking back, very satisfactory—if not the most satisfactory—period. Of course at that time we were all young and somewhat irresponsible, so that we enjoyed our work and we enjoyed our play at the same time. Later on, we enjoyed our work less and played less.

By June, the weather had improved sufficiently to make camp life more pleasant. Spaatz had his guitar with him, and there was a good deal of laughter and song around the campfire. He composed a song for the purpose, "The Punitive Rag," which he was still playing in World War II days and beyond.[82] On the first of July he was promoted to first lieutenant.[83]

It is not clear how close Carl Spaatz was to his commander, Benjamin Foulois. Their time in the squadron overlapped by three months, and there is documentary evidence that Foulois knew Spaatz.[84] Concerning that period, Foulois later wrote:[85]

> In short, I realized that I was thinking about a ground battle (the Pershing expedition) from the vantage point of the sky. Although I had forced myself to think this way previously, I found that I was doing it subconsciously now. It is this third-dimensional point of view of ground events that sets the airman apart from his earth-bound colleagues. Experienced pilots always have it. Only rarely is anyone whose life is tied to the ground so gifted that he can truly assess military situations with the omniscience of the flier. This difference has long separated the men of the air from their counterparts in the Army and Navy.

Spaatz added to his store of lifetime friends during the punitive expedition. Howard Davidson was there, and they became friends. Millard Harmon already was known to Spaatz for he had been in the class of 1912 at the Military Academy. And two of Spaatz's classmates were in the squadron: Sam Wheeler and Ralph Royce. Spaatz was destined to cross paths with Foulois many times again, and his future boss in France, Mike Kilner, was also in the 1st Aero Squadron. Edgar Gorrell, another airman who was to be prominent in the Great War, was at Columbus, as was Herbert Dargue. Dargue had moved from Rockwell Field to Columbus and was a key figure in the Army's air arm until he was killed at the beginning of World War II in a plane crash enroute to the Pacific.[86] Spaatz met Pershing, too, and in fact seems to have made a pest of himself trying to get the general to go for an airplane ride (which he never did). Pershing told Spaatz, "Young man, when I want to fly, I'll order you to take me up."[87] Pershing never again figured prominently in Spaatz's career, though their paths crossed once or twice in France.

Foulois left the squadron in September but Spaatz stayed on until November. At the end of 1916 Spaatz was sent to San Antonio to join a new squadron. Partly because of the experiences of the punitive expedition, Congress appropriated $13,281,660 for army aviation in August, and the Aviation Section of the Army was growing rapidly.

So were America's interests in the European war. The world was approaching a watershed that was to have a profound impact on the development of Carl Spaatz. During Spaatz's tour in San Diego, the British had lost fifty thousand men in the first hours of the Battle of the Somme. During the Mexican expedition, Erich von Falkenhayn tried to end the war by bleeding the French army white over the fort at Verdun; and soon decision-makers in Berlin were preparing to resume unrestricted submarine warfare against the suppliers of their European enemies, a move that would help to bring the United States into the war.

# Chapter II
## THE GREAT WAR

Stunned by the air fiasco in Mexico, Congress in the summer of 1916 increased appropriations for the Army's air arm. The Aviation Section of the Signal Corps began a rapid expansion, and Carl Spaatz was caught up in the change. In November, he left the 1st Aero Squadron for San Antonio, where he joined a newly formed squadron, the 3rd.[1] This was one of five new squadrons that were being added to the two existing ones—the 1st on the Mexican border and the 2nd in the Philippines.[2] By that winter, opposition to the preparedness program was evaporating, and the factors limiting the expansion were now personnel and equipment rather than money. Most of the commanders and key staff officers for the growing Aviation Section had to come from the regular army, either from the 1st Aero Squadron or from among the handful who were assigned to headquarters or were on detached duty.

Not only was it necessary to train large numbers of new flyers, but it was also imperative to improve the skills of those aviators already on board. Until then, military aircraft had been used by the United States only for liaison and observation. By the time Spaatz got to San Antonio, however, it was clear from experiences in the war in Europe that military planes would have to perform an additional role—air-to-air combat to protect observation aircraft and discourage enemy reconnaissance and artillery spotting. The United States Army had prohibited aerobatics as too dangerous. Aerobatics was an essential element of air combat, however, and it became necessary to make up for the dearth of aerobatic training for the rated Army flyers. The Stinson family had opened a flying school in San Antonio in 1914 to train Canadian aviators on a private contract basis. Marjorie Stinson had been teaching aerobatics there for several years. The Army contracted with the school to train three of its pilots, Spaatz among them. He became one of the Army's first flyers trained in aerobatics, receiving instruction from one of America's premier women flyers.[3]

No sooner had Spaatz arrived in San Antonio than he encountered Ruth Harrison's mother at the officers' club. Colonel Harrison had been transferred to Fort Sam Houston after Tooey left Hawaii. Mrs. Harrison promptly reported his presence (and his elevation to the rank of captain) to Ruth, who was then in Berkeley at the University of California. She met Tooey when she came home on vacations. They dated (Ruth was now twenty and no longer required a chaperone) but gave no serious thought to marriage. In May, after the Germans resumed their unrestricted submarine campaign and the United States declared war, Spaatz was transferred from the 3rd Aero Squadron to the 5th, as its commander.[4] It seemed clear that he would soon be going overseas.

On the 26th of July, he called Ruth and proposed that they get married—that day. He explained that he had received orders to depart for France, and it was then or never. Ruth agreed. She later said that it seemed at the time a perfectly natural thing to do, but after having raised three daughters of her own, she could understand her parents' shock when she broke the news. Tooey and Ruth almost missed being married on the 26th, arriving at the judge's office in San Antonio just after it closed. The clerk informed them that they could still be married at Floresville, some miles away, since that office closed an hour later. They arrived there just in time, were married, and had two weeks together before Tooey left for France.[5]

By midsummer, the Aviation Section had surpassed its goal of seven squadrons and was forming additional ones as rapidly as possible. Spaatz was placed in command of one of these, the 31st Aero Squadron, and was assigned at the same time as officer in charge of yet another, the 33rd, for the trip to Europe. The squadrons left San Antonio by rail on the 11th of August and arrived in Jersey City three days later—only to spend a week at Fort Totten awaiting embarkation. They boarded the S.S. *Baltic* on August 22 and sailed the next day.[6] The crossing was not as difficult as many other wartime voyages. The *Baltic* was a modern passenger liner that had not been converted to a troopship; the officers had private staterooms and the soldiers were in accommodations far superior to those found on the typical troop-carrying vessels. As they got under way, Spaatz's second squadron, the 33d, received its own commander, Thomas Bowen, who had served on the Mexican border. Another passenger, much senior to both, was Col. Frank P. Lahm, an American pioneer in both lighter-than-air craft and in airplanes.

The *Baltic,* relatively fast, steamed to Halifax in three days. There she lay at anchor for ten days awaiting the assembly of a convoy. Musical sessions and boat races diverted the men, and some shore leave was allowed. On Thursday, September 6, 1917, the anchors were weighed, and the convoy headed for England. Music and boxing continued as diversions after the convoy put to sea, and the thought of German submarines, then not far from the peak of their unrestricted campaign against Allied shipping, kept the passengers on edge and rumors alive. There were even rumors that the hoists for the ship's ammunition had been sabotaged. Lifeboat drills were held, and all hands were required to carry their life preservers about the ship wherever they went. After dark the portholes were blacked out, and smoking was not permitted on deck.

When the convoy was nearing its destination, a U-boat was sighted and depth charges dropped. The passengers on the *Baltic* heard a loud thud below decks just as the ship heeled in a radical turn and all, including the captain, thought a torpedo had struck. Passing debris from previous sinkings added to the speculation. It was soon discovered that the vessel was undamaged—the thud had merely been the effect of a depth charge dropped by one of the escorts.

On Sunday, the 16th of September, the *Baltic* berthed in England.[7] Ten days later Spaatz was in France, assigned to the Headquarters, Department of Instruction, of the American Expeditionary Force (AEF). He did not remain long at the headquarters, however. In November, he was transferred to the Third Instructional Center (3d AIC) at Issoudun, 130 miles south of Paris, which was being organized.[8] He remained at Issoudun for the next nine months.

## At Issoudun

Spaatz's arrival in France coincided with Germany's renewed submarine warfare campaign and the Communist revolution in Russia. These two events gave the German armies on the western front a second wind, the former by slowing down American reinforcements and the latter by freeing a million German soldiers to join the battle before American power could be felt. Three years of warfare in the west had produced an impasse; each side was developing newer and bloodier weapons and tactics in an attempt to break through the enemy's defenses. Among these weapons was a rapid and continuous succession of faster, more powerful airplanes, and Spaatz's job was to help train pilots to support the American troops who soon would be arriving in large numbers.

When the United States entered the war, the Army had fewer than two hundred pilots, none of them ready for combat. The major American emphasis during the first year, therefore, was on training. Only two flying schools were in existence, the one at San Diego and another at Mineola, on Long Island, New York. The Army developed a flying training program of four phases. Students first attended ground school for a few weeks at a university in the United States. They then went to primary flight training, either at home or in France. The final two phases, advanced and combat flying, were conducted overseas. These latter "finishing schools" (today called combat crew training) could not be set up in the United States, since neither planes nor experienced pilots, all of which were foreign, could easily be brought from Europe. The overseas finishing schools were specialized by mission: pursuit, bombing, and observation.[9] Issoudun was designated as the advanced pursuit school and also provided primary instruction for many cadets.

European airmen had already developed a specialized pursuit role using single-seat airplanes with synchronized guns and with a performance edge over reconnaissance and artillery spotting planes. The demand for this specialized air superiority mission had arisen first among the soldiers on the ground rather than among airmen. Experiments had already taken place to develop weapons and tactics that could blind the enemy's prying aerial eyes and reduce the effectiveness of his gunfire by driving off his spotters.[10] At first, aviators carried small arms on their missions, but this proved ineffective. Experiments with a second man in the aircraft to handle the gun reduced speed to the point where the interceptor could not overtake reconnaissance or spotting planes. For a time, machine guns were mounted on the top wing of the aircraft and fired over the propeller. The pilot had to point the entire aircraft at the enemy. This worked but ruled out clearing jammed guns, which was vital in a day when machine guns were not reliable.

Finally, a Frenchman, Rolland Garros, developed a method in which the gun could be fired through the rotating propeller with only a small percentage of the rounds hitting the plate-protected blades. When Garros went down in German territory, his invention was discovered and improved upon: Anthony Fokker devised a mechanical synchronizer that permitted the rounds to pass through the propeller arc without hitting the blades. The Germans, in turn, lost to the Allies an aircraft equipped with a synchronizer. It was promptly copied, and the Germans lost the advantage they had temporarily gained. This was the equipment Spaatz had to work with after his arrival in France.

As soon as he signed in at Issoudun he was put in charge of the school and the base. According to engineering officer, Eddie Rickenbacker, the previous commander, Capt. James Miller, was relieved by Pershing when he failed to salute the general during a visit. Spaatz was made commander in Miller's place.[11] He could not have viewed the move as much of an opportunity: Issoudun was universally referred to as a "mudhole."[12] A construction squadron had been rushed over from the United States several months earlier and was building the base from nothing. One of its first tasks was to erect quarters so the men could move out of tents before winter set in. Another was to lay down an eleven-mile railroad from the town of Issoudun to the empty field where the base was to rise. A few French airplanes had arrived in October, but the first attempt to fly one was aborted when its wheels stuck in the mud and the plane went over on its nose.[13]

By November several tarpaper barracks had been thrown together, each heated only by an old stove. Cadets were trucked to town periodically for baths. There were neither paved streets nor sidewalks, so the students were turned out to build duckboards over the mud. To make the challenge for Spaatz all the greater, students began arriving before the airplanes and instructors.

Spaatz remained as commander for a hectic month. At the end of November, Lt. Col. Walter G. Kilner, two years ahead of him at West Point and his squadron mate on the Mexican border, took over as commander, and Major Spaatz became the Officer in Charge of Training, the second most important position on the post.[14]

The curriculum that Carl Spaatz managed was originally patterned after the French program, but it was gradually modified as Americans gained experience in the war. At first the instructors were French, but they gradually were replaced by Americans who were retained at the school after graduation. A series of satellite fields surrounded the main airdrome at Issoudun. Each of these provided a different phase of flying instruction, and each had its own commander and training officer who reported to Kilner and Spaatz. By the end of Spaatz's tour, ten such fields were in operation, not counting the one the students called "Field Thirteen"—the base cemetery.

A student moved from field to field for various phases of training. At the first field he learned to steer a plane on the ground and work the complicated throttles. To ensure that none would inadvertently leave the ground, the planes' wings were clipped. Appropriately, the students dubbed them "penguins." At his second stop the student learned to solo in French Nieuports. He then moved on to a different type of Nieuport whose shorter wingspan made it more difficult to fly. In the next phase he learned to fly the plane that only recently had been retired from combat, the Nieuport 15. This was the fastest and the most difficult of the trainers to master. The final test came at the aerobatics field. Here the student flew against an instructor in a similarly equipped Nieuport with a gun camera aboard. His work was critiqued after they landed and the film was examined.[15]

Flying in these early days, even during training, was dangerous. During Spaatz's nine-month stay at Issoudun, forty-nine students moved on to "Field Thirteen" as a result of crashes.[16] These losses bore heavily on Spaatz's conscience, and a search for ways to reduce this rate became one of his major preoccupations.[17] He was not very successful. Pursuit was inherently dangerous, and the fatality rate at Issoudun remained at a level five times that of the bombardment and observations schools.[18] In July 1918, it appeared some progress was being made when the death rate decreased to .53 deaths per thousand hours of flying time. The following month, however, seventeen students were killed, a record high rate of 1.35 per thousand hours.[19] Kilner, in his final report, showed a high regard for Spaatz and viewed the accidents as inevitable in that type of work.[20] All told, about one out of nine students in the pursuit school was killed in training, the same rate as the British,[21] whereas in the bombing and observation schools the number was but one out of fifty.[22] The chief of the AEF's Air Service, Maj. Gen. Mason Patrick, noted the problem in the same way and suggested, without success, that it might be alleviated somewhat by using parachutes as the Germans were doing. It would be a long time before the air arm developed a flying safety program to remove death from the category of a daily occurrence.

Fatalities and accidents were not the only problem Spaatz faced at Issoudun. The morale of both students and instructors was lowered by factors largely outside his control. Cadets received their wings and commissions when they completed primary flight training. Those who came to Issoudun for primary training had been at the head of their classes in ground schools back home; their classmates, who had not done as well, went on to flight training in the United States. The school at Issoudun was just being set up, but those in the United States were fully operating and the lower-ranking cadets at home were completing their training and being commissioned, while Spaatz's students had yet to fly and were doing hard labor in the mud of France.[23] The cadets hardly considered this a reward for their superior performance.

The American instructors' morale was impaired by their inability to get to the front. Once classes began to graduate, instructors were chosen from among the top graduates on the theory that, having more recently been students themselves and being closer to the age of the students, they would relate better to the fledglings than would pilots with line experience. The "old men," it was believed, were too impatient to permit cadets to make any mistakes in flight, yet it was through mistakes that the best learning occurred. Since most graduates were anxious for the glory and prestige that accompanied fighting "the Hun" at the front, they viewed the instructor assignment as punishment.

Spaatz tried several measures to mollify them. He permitted instructors from other fields to fly occasionally at the aerobatics field as "aggressor" pilots against students about to graduate. This practice helped somewhat to boost morale—except when an instructor encountered a student so good he could not be shaken from the mentor's tail.[24] He also attempted to alleviate the problem by assigning instructors to temporary tours with frontline units.

Discontent persisted, however, made all the more difficult because Spaatz shared the instructors' sentiments. One of his more imaginative officers, Eddie Rickenbacker, was so valuable as engineering officer that Spaatz strenuously resisted his entreaties for release. Finally, Rickenbacker, who at the time was suffering from a severe head cold, persuaded the flight surgeon to put him in the hospital for several weeks. When he emerged he pointed out to Spaatz that his assistant had done a perfectly acceptable job in his absence and his own presence was not essential. Spaatz relented and released Rickenbacker for the gunnery school and the front, where he went on to become America's leading ace in the war.[25]

Another of Spaatz's problems was equally intractable, and it, too, has its counterpart today: standardization. There were thirty-two different types of airplanes at Issoudun,[26] seventeen different models of the Nieuport alone.[27] The array of engines was not as diverse, but it was equally bewildering because there were two completely different types, rotary and nonrotary. Although most of the thousand airplanes at the school were of French manufacture, some were of English design and American manufacture. Many of the supply and maintenance documents were in French, and some measurements were in the metric system while others were in the English system—conversions were not easy. Since America's production program was slow in gearing up until near the very end of the war, and since it did not produce some types of aircraft, there was no easy solution to these problems. Maintenance and supply men, and the pilots as well, had to learn some French and become familiar with two systems of measurement.[28]

When Issoudun was fully operational it carried more than 30,000 different items in its warehouses to service this collection of heterogeneous equipment. Shortages were frequent, and the supply system was so cumbersome that often parts had to be manufactured in the shop on the field because it took too long to requisition them.[29] Spaatz never claimed any fluency in foreign languages, but with the supply and maintenance complications at the 3rd Aviation Instruction Center (and with the fact that his instructors at first were all Frenchmen) his two years of French at West Point proved useful.

Commanders and section heads at the satellite fields complained continuously of a lack of discipline and of the low quality of some of the human resources they had to work with—officers as well as enlisted men.[30] The air arm was already gaining a reputation for lax discipline, and many reports reflected it, especially those coming from former infantry officers such as a 1914 classmate, Maj. Thomas Lanphier. Lanphier noted repeatedly that the air officers did not understand as well as did their brothers in the trenches that war was a deadly serious business. He and others recommended that not all pilots be made officers, for they did not understand the importance of good discipline. Rather, a separate category should be established for pilots and observers; they would be paid like officers because of their technical prowess, but would not have the prestige and authority that goes along with "real" officership.

Similar complaints were lodged in these reports regarding the enlisted men. The concern was that the mere possession of stripes earned by a man because of his mechanical aptitude did not make him a competent noncommissioned leader. The proliferation of stripes, it was argued, diluted the prestige and authority of the "real" NCOs. The proposed solution was similar to the one suggested for the flyers: pay the enlisted technicians for their special technical expertise, but reserve the stripes for the first sergeants, mess sergeants, supply sergeants, and other enlisted section and shop leaders. This issue was to have a long future.

In May 1918, Kilner was transferred to headquarters and Spaatz once again became Issoudun's commander. To cite the problems Tooey faced at the 3d AIC, as both training officer and commander, and to remark on those that were not solved, should not obscure his achievements. Before the winter was over the administrative inertia of the Army had been overcome, and Secretary of War Newton Baker was allowing graduating cadets at Issoudun to be commissioned with dates of rank commensurate with those of their classmates in the United States. Living conditions on the base had improved considerably. By Thanksgiving, 1917, the students had enjoyed a turkey dinner, and by January they no longer had to be trucked into town to the public baths, for hot showers were available.[31] Early in the new year students were reporting that the food had improved and even that a piano had been placed in the barracks. The rail spur from town, known as the "Hula Hula and Snake Railroad," had been finished early, and by summer 1918 most of the roads on the main base were paved and the barracks put into respectable condition. The shops and warehouses were substantial and impressive. A large hospital was in place and an experimental flight surgeon's unit was in operation studying the new science of aviation medicine. A group of German prisoners of war had been detailed to help with the construction of the field, and some Chinese laborers had been recruited from Shanghai and brought to France where they figured prominently in the construction and maintenance of the installation. The Red Cross had developed a strong presence at the main field and was holding dinner dances. There was even a military band at the main field.[32]

Spaatz was instrumental in putting the center's growing pains behind it. During a visit in March, General Pershing noticed the striking contrast to what he had witnessed six months earlier. At that time, construction was far behind schedule and the first airplane had just arrived. Now the field put on a show for the general and for Secretary Baker who accompanied him. A formation of one hundred planes passed by in review. Spaatz and two other pilots treated the dignitaries to an aerobatic and dogfighting demonstration which pleased not only the visitors but also General Foulois, now the Chief of Air Service, A.E.F.[33] Earlier, Pershing had complained that the officers of the AEF Air Service were "good men running around in circles."[34] But now most of the incompetents had been weeded out, and the survivors had settled down into an effective training organization. By war's end, 1,839 men had passed through Issoudun for advanced training, 829 of whom stayed on and went through the pursuit school. Of these, 627 went into combat against the German air force, the remainder becoming instructors. The combat record of Issoudun's pursuit graduates was creditable.[35] The AEF lost 289 aircraft and 48 balloons in the war while destroying 781 enemy planes and 73 balloons.[36]

## At the Front

Two major functions of military leadership are organizing forces for conflict and leading them in battle. At Issoudun, Spaatz had been concerned mainly with the first of these. In the summer of 1918 it was decided that he should go back to the United States to bring the stateside training program for pursuit pilots into line with the realities of the war. Although he had spent several days at the front the preceding February with the 11th Wing of the Royal Flying Corps, he had no combat experience. Despite the promise of the First Army's Chief of Air Service, Billy Mitchell, that he would give Spaatz command of a unit at the front when he returned from the U.S., Tooey protested that the war might be over by then. Mitchell relented enough to permit him three weeks or so with a Spad squadron in the 2nd Pursuit Group.[37]

Earlier that year, the German commander Ludendorff, employing new tactics and soldiers transferred from the eastern front, seemed to find the solution to the problem of penetrating the defensive strength of the Allied trenches. Employing specially selected personnel in storming units, the Germans probed for the Allied soft spots and went through them, leaving the strong points to be mopped up later. Once the advance had gone some miles, however, the Allies had the advantage of servicing their troops with intact communications lines. The German offensives that spring and early summer ran out of steam even though they did achieve penetrations that had seemed impossible earlier in the war.[38] By the time Spaatz joined his combat unit, only a large German salient at St. Mihiel remained.

Foch approved a plan by Pershing for an American offensive against this salient, but Pershing agreed to limit the exploitation to flattening the salient rather than pushing on toward Metz and points east. Foch wanted the bulk of the U.S. forces to disengage in time to turn north for another offensive scheduled for late September through the Argonne Forest. The U.S. First Army would have to finish its work on the salient in a couple of weeks.[39] These weeks coincided with Spaatz's abbreviated combat tour.

For the St. Mihiel offensive, Pershing had three American corps and a French colonial corps. His air chief for the First Army, Brig. Gen. Billy Mitchell, had as his air resources a total of 1,481 aircraft, the majority of which were from Allied armies—the French, Portuguese, and Italian, plus the cooperation of Air Marshal Hugh Trenchard's RAF Independent Air Force. Among these forces were one pursuit wing containing two American pursuit groups and one fighter group from the French army. Also in that wing was a bombardment group. The First Pursuit Group was also a part of Mitchell's order of battle. Pershing's plan was to send one American corps against the western face of the salient, two others against the southern face, and to use the French colonial corps against the apex. While the French held the German forces in place, the converging American troops would join up in the east to cut off the enemy's escape route.[40] Once the salient had been flattened, the American First Army would break off the offensive and deploy its forces across the rear of its own position for the Argonne attack.[41]

The way Billy Mitchell used his planes in the Battle of St. Mihiel did not forecast the ideas for which he was later to sacrifice his career. The air forces were divided into two parts: those dedicated to the ground units and directly subject to the orders of the ground commanders, and others centrally controlled, receiving their daily operations orders directly from Mitchell. This centrally controlled force might seem a precursor of the airmen's desire for an independent air force, but it was actually an idea that had been used earlier by the French. Even ground officers supported it as they recognized the need for air superiority over the front and the need for central control to achieve the mass necessary to maintain it. For the most part, it was the reconnaissance and artillery adjustment units that were assigned to the ground units and the pursuits and bombers (of which there were few) that were held in a centrally controlled force.[42]

In preparation for his combat tour, Spaatz spent a week or so in mid-July attending the gunnery course run by the French at Cazaux.[43] In August, he was ordered from Issoudun, initially to the 1st Pursuit

Group on the western face of the salient.[44] He stayed there only three days before moving on to the southern face, to Toul, which served as the base for the 2d Pursuit Group. The 2d Group was commanded by Davenport Johnson, who had been in the class of 1912 at West Point and also in the 1st Aero Squadron when it was chasing Villa in Mexico.[45] The commander of Tooey's squadron, the 13th, was one of America's aces, Charles Biddle. Biddle had graduated from Princeton in 1911 and after the war gained additional renown as a lawyer and author. It was understood from the outset that Tooey was there temporarily only to gain combat experience and that Biddle would remain in command notwithstanding Spaatz's seniority.[46]

Spaatz was permitted nearly two weeks to get used to his new surroundings and to fly the Spad before the battle began. Most of his squadron mates were newly recruited officers, in the Army only for the duration; one, Howard Stovall, was to become a friend for life. Becoming accustomed to the Spad was no problem for Spaatz. He had been flying a bewildering variety of Nieuports for almost a year. The Spad was a sturdier airplane, did not have the touchy rotary engine, and was a later-generation pursuit plane in an age when technology was advancing so rapidly that one generation made a substantial difference.

Mitchell's still-conservative approach to airpower was reflected in the mission he gave his pursuit units. Though they were controlled by an airman at the highest level, Mitchell used them in a way that conformed to the most conservative tenets of the infantrymen. In his general mission statement he emphasized what already was becoming an article of faith within the air arm, that airpower is inherently an offensive—not a defensive—instrument:[47]

> Our Air Service will take the offensive at all points with the object of destroying the enemy's air service, attacking his troops on the ground, and protecting our own air and ground troops.

These bold words about the destruction of the enemy's air arm would have fit well into his later thinking, but their force was weakened by the specific missions he assigned to his pursuit units in 1918. The main work of the 2d Pursuit Group was to set up "barrages" of pursuit airplanes over the battlefield to prevent any intrusion of enemy aircraft and to protect in a general way the observation aircraft and balloons working below. It was also directed to attack any enemy balloons that showed themselves in the sector to which the group was tied.

When Mitchell's battle orders were translated into operations orders, however, the force of the word "offensive" was diminished by the inclusion of geographical limits in which the pursuit planes were allowed to operate. Davenport Johnson's group, the one with which Tooey was flying, was ordered to set up a "barrage" patrol from daybreak to dusk, but was prohibited from venturing more than five kilometers ahead of the infantry units on the ground—in effect an air alert that would be viewed by latter-day airmen as an inefficient defensive waste of air resources that are inherently offensive in character.[48] The same order required that the group provide close escort for the observation aircraft. When the reconnaissance and artillery spotting units demanded it, the pursuit airplanes were to remain in close proximity to their charges, thereby beginning any battle with German pursuits at a great disadvantage.[49] The pursuit units were also given a collateral mission of reconnaissance, though that was the main business of the squadrons assigned to the ground formation commanders.

During his weeks at Toul, Spaatz had his first brief brush with bombers. All nineteen bombers in the American air arm were stationed there. In theory, Mitchell could have used them in rear areas against targets only indirectly related to the battle on the ground. However, the targets they actually struck were not far beyond the enemy's lines, and all were directly related to the battle.[50] These missions today would be classified as "tactical" and described as "interdiction." True strategic bombing still lay in the future.

The weather for the first two or three days of the St. Mihiel offensive was bad, ruling out large formations, inhibiting both bombing and reconnaissance, and limiting aerial work to single-ship operations. Still, all the units were able to get some planes into the air. The 2d Pursuit Group flew sixteen patrols during the twenty-four-hour period ending at 7:00 P.M. on the 12th of September, the first day of the offensive. The 13th Squadron accounted for twenty-five sorties without losses, though one or two men were missing from the other squadrons in the group. There was some limited contact with the enemy and not much else to report.[51]

The weather on the second day was no better. That afternoon Spaatz flew in one patrol composed of eight aircraft and led by Lt. H. G. Armstrong. It was no more eventful than those of the previous day, though they did see one enemy aircraft poke its nose up through the clouds but turn around and descend when its pilot spotted the American formation. Armstrong's flight was relieved in the barrage by another led by L. J. Dickinson Este, which saw a good deal more action. This flight of five was "jumped" by seven Fokkers, and a dogfight ensued. The Americans claimed to have shot down three of the seven Germans, but they returned without one of their number, Lieutenant Converse.[52] The engine on Converse's Spad quit in the middle of the battle, but he was unsure whether it had been hit by enemy fire or had just suffered a mechanical failure. He landed near enemy lines and was taken prisoner by an Austrian unit and later turned over to the Germans.[53]

By the 14th, the weather was clearing and the ground units had already achieved most of their objectives. Captain Biddle led the first patrol of the day. The Germans had brought up reinforcements, and the Americans on the ground were heavily engaged. Biddle reported that his flight tangled with four Fokkers and requested confirmation that it had shot down two of them. Three of his Spads were missing, however.[54] Another, piloted by Lt. Charles Drew, was shot down. Wounded in the arm and leg, he came down near the German positions and was captured.[55] By day's end, Biddle's squadron had flown twenty-two sorties, engaged the enemy numerous times, lost four pilots, and claimed two enemy victories.[56]

Spaatz's baptism of fire came the following day, Sunday the 15th. Visibility was much improved as he took off at 9:00 A.M. in a flight of seventeen Spads led by Lt. Howard Stovall. In the next two hours, the flight sighted seventeen Fokkers. Fourteen of the Spads were engaged in two different battles, one at 10:10 A.M. and the other at 10:30 A.M. Nine German single-seaters were encountered in the first battle. Stovall fired 125 rounds at four different aircraft and claimed one had gone down. In the general melee, Spaatz was able to get his sights on two of the Germans, fired fifty rounds at each one and claimed to have shot down one. Twice during the fight his guns jammed, but both times he succeeded in clearing them. By the time the two forces disengaged, the Americans were well scattered. Spaatz flew to the rendezvous location, to find only one other Spad there, that of Stovall.

Together, they returned to the combat area and discovered five more Fokkers. They then spied two other German planes circling at a higher altitude. Stovall dove on the five below while Spaatz remained above flying cover against the Germans at the higher level. Stovall's pass at the lower aircraft was ineffective, and since the two were running low on fuel they had to return to Toul. They landed with two hours of flying time under their belts.[57]

Not a week after Tooey had shot down his first Fokker, his squadron, the 13th, was transferred as a part of the redeployment to a field at Belrain, about forty miles to the northwest of Toul.[58] The mission of the pursuit groups remained much the same as before: to stay close to the troops on the ground, to make the air over the battlefield safe for Allied reconnaissance and artillery-spotting planes and unsafe for those of the enemy, and, if possible, to aid in collecting intelligence. This was to be done by keeping airborne a set of patrols composed of large pursuit formations and, if demanded, by providing escort for the observation aircraft operating over the battlefield. Finally, they were to shoot down whatever enemy balloons appeared.[59]

Spaatz's temporary duty orders lasted long enough to permit him to make the morning patrol on the first day of this last offensive. Enemy resistance on the ground was much more stubborn than it had been at St. Mihiel, and that was reflected in the fight in the air.[60] Mitchell later wrote that the American forces were unable to dominate the air to the extent they had during St. Mihiel.[61]

At daybreak on the opening day of the offensive, the 26th, Biddle led two formations out to battle, Spaatz among them. Almost immediately they encountered seven German Fokkers and a melee ensued. The dogfight gradually drifted over enemy territory. During the battle, Spaatz twice managed to get on the tail of Fokkers and shoot them down. In the course of doing so, however, he may have fallen victim to a vice of new pilots on the front and become too engrossed in his quarry to "check six" (keep an eye out behind him for enemy planes). He wound up with two German aircraft on his tail and was having trouble shaking them off. At this point, Biddle led a flight down against Spaatz's antagonists and "shot them off his tail." Spaatz, having been preoccupied with the battle and with his own survival, had overstayed his time above enemy territory. Too low on fuel to make it back to Belrain, he stretched it as far as he could, then crash-landed in no-man's-land. His Spad was wrecked, but fortunately he came out of it without injuries—and thankfully the first voices he heard were French. Certainly he had had more than enough excitement for his last day at the front.[62]

The squadron commander of the 13th wearily summed it all up:[63]

Once more [it is] the same old story of a man forgetting that there is any danger other than that which may come from the machine which he is attacking. This is, of course, much the lesser danger. In this fight we had everything in our favor and there was no reason why anyone should have gotten in trouble if they would only not get carried away with themselves. It is splendid the way these boys will sail in and fight, but no amount of warning seems to teach them the necessary caution if they are to live long at the game. Only bitter experience teaches them, and that is dearly paid for. The man who was being pursued by the Fokkers which I drove off was a major [whom Biddle nowhere names] temporarily attached to the squadron to get some practical experience. He got it all right. He is an extremely nice fellow and I am glad to say he got safely back to our lines. . .

Billy Mitchell, however, was impressed and promised to recommend Spaatz for the Distinguished Service Cross, the citation of which contained not a trace of the criticism Charles Biddle had leveled at the incident.[64] Back in Washington, Ruth Spaatz read in the *New York Times* of an unnamed flyer who reported downing three planes—"two Germans and my own." On reading it, she guessed, rightly, that the unnamed pilot was her husband.[65]

## An End-of-Tour Report

By October World War I was almost over. For Carl Spaatz it *was* over. On the 5th, he left Europe aboard the S.S. *Northern Pacific* for the United States and his task of improving the flying training program there. Equally important for Spaatz's future were the command and combat experience he had gained in Europe, and the airpower ideas he had come in contact with there.

Tooey had made a lasting impression on both students and staff at Issoudun.[66] The memories of practically every cadet included the "German" major as the nemesis of all the innocents. Edward P. Curtis remembered him that way even though they later became close friends, as did Charles D'Olive[67] and John Francisco Richards II.[68] George Kenney, later to become MacArthur's airman in the Pacific and a four-star general, never forgot that Spaatz had laid some demerits on him at Issoudun.[69] When Spaatz became commander of the 3d AIC for the second time, he chose Charles C. Benedict to succeed him as training officer.[70] They were to meet again. Tooey's West Point classmate Tom Lanphier turned up in mid-summer 1918; he was to remain in the Air Service and Air Corps through the twenties and to return to service in World War II. Hiram Bingham, already prominent before the war as a Yale professor and explorer, was dressed down one day by Spaatz for making an unauthorized flight.[71] He succeeded Spaatz as commander of the training base and was to become a U.S. senator in the 1920s. Spaatz's path also crossed those of some of the prominent aces of the war: Eddie Rickenbacker, Douglas Campbell, and Frank Luke. Quentin Roosevelt, Theodore's son, came through Issoudun on the way to his death at the front.[72] Frank O'D. Hunter, who was to figure prominently as a fighter commander with Spaatz in World War II, was also at Issoudun. Leigh Wade, who would gain fame as one of the round-the-world flyers in 1924 and who would come back to active duty in World War II, worked for Spaatz as an aerobatics instructor and commander of one of Issoudun's satellite fields.[73] Gen. Mason Patrick, who was to play an important role in Spaatz's life when Patrick became chief of the Air Service and, later, of the Air Corps, knew him at Issoudun.

One of the strongest early influences on Spaatz was exerted by Billy Mitchell, who personally arranged Spaatz's reassignment in the fall of 1918. This, coupled with Mitchell's role in allowing Spaatz his temporary stay at the front and in sponsoring his decoration,[74] shows that the First Army's air chief recognized potential in the flyer.

Although Spaatz's direct experience in the war had been limited to fighter planes and their tactics, he could not help absorbing other ideas about how aircraft could be used. The American Expeditionary Force had a small bomber contingent commanded by a fellow veteran from the Mexican war, Edgar Gorrell. Although this contingent of Bréguet bombers did not participate in strategic bombing, the seeds of later ideas on such bombing existed in the AEF's bomber headquarters. Strategic bombing was not then well defined. In a vague way, the term was interpreted as bombing targets away from the battlefield. For the most part this meant attacks against the nodal parts of the transportation system leading to the front and against masses of men and materiel in the rear areas. Although they were never used, Gorrell's office assembled some target folders looking toward campaigns in the interior of Germany against industrial targets.

These early ideas about using airplanes against targets not directly connected to the battlefield gave rise to two schools of thought concerning who should control air resources. Some airmen, Gorrell among them, saw a need to concentrate aviation assets under one commander for independent operations against the basic sources of the enemy's strength. Other airmen, and some soldiers, thought that military aviation was best divided into two parts. Observation and artillery-spotting planes should belong to the individual commanders of the ground units they served. Other air assets, principally bombers, should be centralized and directed by the theater commander or his air deputy. The French and British had established precedents for such centralized units, and General Pershing had gone along with the idea—thus Gorrell's command. Lest the airmen begin thinking of themselves as independent from the army, however, Pershing rejected their word "strategical" for the organization and insisted on calling it "GHQ Reserve."[75]

This idea of an independent bombing mission, and a separate air unit to perform it, formed the core of much of the controversy that took place after the war. The number of regular military airmen in World War I was small, and such issues formed the agenda of their professional discussions. Carl Spaatz had become acquainted in the war with the ideas of strategic bombing and of an independent air arm, and he carried these ideas into the peacetime world.

# Chapter III

## PURSUIT AIRCRAFT AND MILITARY AVIATION

The decade of the twenties was an important one in the education of Maj. Carl Spaatz. At Issoudun he had struggled with the problems of an air commander in an era where money was plentiful but time was short. During this decade, as commander of the 1st Pursuit Group, he was to encounter the same set of problems, but now time was plentiful and money short. Spaatz continued his airpower education as one of Billy Mitchell's pupils and began to learn the ways of Washington. His four years in the capital on the air staff of Gen. Mason Patrick and Gen. James Fechet gave him insights into the styles of bureaucracies, into the high-level organizations of national security, and into ideas about how airpower might be used in campaigns independent of the Army and Navy. Meanwhile, he continually gave fate its chance by repeated tests of his skill *and* luck as an aviator in a time when flying was still in its infancy.

While Tooey was in France, Ruth had not returned to college, but rather had indulged her fascination for the theater. Moving to New York, she had a brief association with the professional theater. She joined a troupe to put on shows for the soldiers and sailors, an experience she claimed was delightful for the performers, though perhaps not for the soldiers. Sometime during that summer of 1918, she received a letter from Tooey saying he would soon be home. He could not say when or for what reason, because of censorship, but Ruth went to Washington to be there when he arrived. She hoped to get involved in some volunteer work at Walter Reed Hospital, but the great influenza epidemic was already causing thousands of deaths, and spouses of soldiers overseas were not allowed to take the risk. Consequently, she passed the short time remaining before Tooey got back working in a government office.[1]

Tooey arrived from Europe in mid-October, but the hectic wartime pace did not slacken for him and Ruth. The original intent had been to assign him permanently to the training section of the Air Service Headquarters in Washington, after some temporary duty as an adviser to pursuit training programs at Arcadia, Florida, and San Diego, California. The plan went according to schedule for only the first few weeks. By the 11th of November, he and Ruth had been to Arcadia and were enroute by train to San Diego. As they pulled into the station at El Paso, Texas, the crowds in the streets were going wild. The war was over![2]

The Spaatzes got into San Diego the next day and found Rockwell Field equally jubilant. The flyers there celebrated by passing in review over the city with 212 airplanes. Back at Issoudun, one pilot allegedly celebrated the armistice by putting his tired biplane through three hundred consecutive loops.

At San Diego, Spaatz started out as pursuit adviser to the school at Rockwell Field,[3] but during the spring was put in command of the Western Flying Circus. Washington was mounting another Liberty Loan drive, supporting it with flying circuses. These aerobatic groups moved about the country by train, assembled their aircraft, did stunts for the crowds, then tore down the equipment and traveled by train to the next site. The Flying Circus was on the road for but a few weeks. When it ended, Spaatz was sent off to Fort Worth, Texas, where he commanded Taliaferro Field for several months. He then moved to the Presidio in San Francisco as assistant to Henry (Hap) Arnold, the Department Air Service Officer.[4]

While Tooey and Ruth were being moved back and forth between Rockwell, Fort Worth, and San Francisco, things were hardly more stable in Washington. After leaving France, Billy Mitchell had orders to become the Director of Military Aeronautics, the highest uniformed position in the Air Service. By the time he got home, however, the job had been abolished and Maj. Gen. Charles Menoher, an infantryman who had commanded the Rainbow Division in the war, had been assigned the new top position, that of Chief of the Air Service. Mitchell was given an important assignment, however, as head of the Training and Operations Group.[5]

At the same time, Congress was considering a series of proposals to create a Department of Aeronautics and a separate air force. While Congress debated, Mitchell hatched a promotional scheme, the Transcontinental Reliability Test, a race to stir up public interest in aviation. General Menoher saw some merit in the plan as a field test and approved it. The plan was ambitious, involving about eighty Air Service aircraft. One group departed from the Presidio at San Francisco in October 1919 and flew to Mineola, Long Island, while the other passed in the opposite direction between the same two terminals. Though Spaatz had suggested a safer southern route, Washington persisted in promoting the northern course, which it justified as breaking ground for potential airline routes through larger population centers.

To go that way, however, spelled trouble for the flyers. They had to climb to far higher altitudes. Until the eastbound group passed Cheyenne, Wyoming, the terrain was mountainous, with few emergency landing fields. There was only one multiengine airplane in the race, a Martin bomber designed for, but never used in, the war. It crashed before it finished its westward trip. All the others were open-cockpit, uninstrumented relics from the Great War including Spads, SE-5s (British-designed fighters), and even some captured Fokkers. Spaatz was fortunate. He flew one of the modified wartime DH-4s with two cockpits, which was a bit safer than some of the earlier versions. There were but sparse navigational aids, and the few fields enroute were poorly marked and undeveloped. Air Service officers were deployed in advance to the chosen landing fields, but communications were so primitive that their coordination with the pilots and the Air Service headquarters was almost nonexistent. The selection of the northern route also made bad weather more likely. Indeed, the weather turned out to be abominable.[6]

Some of the incidents during the race reflect the character of aviation in 1919. First Lt. B. W. Maynard, the overall winner, attracted considerable attention by carrying along his pet German Shepherd, Trixie. One would think that Maynard's mechanic might have objected to riding in the rear cockpit with an animal that size, but, in the end the sergeant benefited. In the cold October weather, Trixie turned out to be a fine cockpit heater.

Another DH-4 pilot used a clever tactic for adjusting his aircraft's center of gravity in flight to prevent a noseover on the landing. As he approached the Presidio's airfield, he ordered his rear cockpit man out of his seat to straddle the fuselage and slide back towards the tail. The movement of his weight to the rear would help to hold down the tail as the wheels dug into the soft ground. Unfortunately for the cockpit man, the pilot missed his approach and went around for another try. The poor man in back had to straddle the fuselage during the climb out and second circuit around the landing pattern. In the end they landed safely, and the DH-4 did not wind up on its nose![7]

After many bad hours on the way across the continent, Spaatz got his DH-4 to Long Island before any of the other airplanes in the eastbound group. His mother and father were waiting anxiously below on the field at Mineola. Unfortunately, Tooey landed at the wrong airfield. He noticed his error immediately and took off again for the right place. But it was too late and the best he could achieve was second place, landing only a fraction of a minute behind the winner.[8]

The flyers had many harrowing experiences. About a third of them never finished the race. Before it was over, there were nine deaths and many other accidents that did not involve fatalities.[9] Spaatz and the others who had completed the eastbound heat recommended that they return through El Paso, but again Air Service Headquarters refused. The flyers at Mineola then suggested that the return trips be made by rail, but Washington specified a round trip by air—allowing the flyers to do it on a voluntary basis. Accordingly, Spaatz and his colleagues departed in their planes from Mineola and arrived first at Buffalo. One of the other pilots, Lowell Smith, came staggering in with an airplane that could go no farther. Smith persuaded Tooey to give up his DH-4, which he flew back to San Francisco while Spaatz finished the trip by rail.[10] The Transcontinental Reliability Test did not lead to the creation of a separate air force, nor did it build enough public confidence in flying to induce an immediate growth in the airline industry. It did, however, portend great things for air travel.

The rest of Spaatz's time as Arnold's assistant in San Francisco was occupied with routine peacetime affairs. They were responsible for providing forest fire patrol to the U.S. Forest Service[11] and border patrol against gun runners from Mexico.[12]

The delightful interlude at San Francisco ended rather abruptly as a result of congressional action in the summer of 1920. The legislators passed a law whereby officers with temporary wartime promotions reverted to their permanent ranks. It applied to everyone in the Army except those who had won their military aviator ratings in action at the front. As a consequence, Colonel Arnold became Captain Arnold while Major Spaatz remained a major. Arnold was immediately promoted again to major, but his date of rank was more recent than Tooey's, so he prepared to turn his job over to his assistant—some seven years his junior. Spaatz would have none of it. He went immediately to Gen. Hunter Liggett, their boss, and arranged a transfer for himself to Mather Field, leaving Arnold in charge in San Francisco.[13]

The stay at Mather was only temporary; after two months, the Spaatzes were off again for San Antonio. They spent a year there while Tooey served as the commander at Kelly Field and then as the Air Service Officer for the 8th Corps Area at Fort Sam Houston. Finally, in the fall of 1921, Spaatz was given command of the 1st Pursuit Group at Ellington Field just south of Houston, Texas—a post into which he quickly settled and long after remembered as one of the most rewarding in his entire career.[14]

## The 1st Pursuit Group

For the first several years after the war, the 1st Pursuit Group was the only pursuit unit in the Air Service. The outfit's primary mission was unit training for combat readiness. This was difficult, however, because in America combat training did not generate any sense of urgency. Some in American politics held that there would be no more wars; others scoffed at that notion but insisted the U.S. would never again participate in wars overseas.

Another major function of Spaatz's group was to provide training for the reserve aviators who lived in the unit's area. In addition, since Spaatz's was the only pursuit unit in the country, it became the locus of tactical development and testing for its specialty. There was little new equipment available to them, however. The United States was left with a large surplus at war's end, and there was strong pressure to use it up before any new materiel was purchased by a Congress ideologically bent on reducing expenditures and taxes. As a consequence, the Spads, SE-5s, and Liberty engines remained with the Air Service long past their prime.[15]

Because of the group's uniqueness, Spaatz developed a close working relationship with both tactical and strategic thinkers at the Air Service Tactical School at Langley Field, Virginia, and with the leaders of the technical and logistical part of the Air Service, the Materiel Division at McCook Field, Dayton, Ohio. In many ways he became the focal point between the technical, the operational, and the academic currents swirling about the Air Service. These other officers often leaned heavily on his experience, and he certainly added greatly to virtually every dimension of his own military education.

In the 1st Pursuit Group, Spaatz had working for him many of his wartime acquaintances as well as several airmen who would play an important role in his future. Among them was Monk Hunter, an ace in World War I with nine victories and later the commander of the 8th Fighter Command in World War II. Byrne V. Baucom, who had shot down six German aircraft, was also with Spaatz at Ellington. John Cannon and Claire Chennault had not been aviators in World War I but were outstanding at Ellington.

Commanding a group of exuberant pursuit pilots had its rewards and also its problems. The town of Houston (it was scarcely a city in 1921) did not offer much in the way of excitement, so some of the more venturesome spirits at Ellington made their own. One night an officer with a large black moustache (according to witnesses) amused himself by driving down a main street knocking over the "wooden policemen" placed at intersections during night hours. The next morning an angry chief of police arrived at Ellington Field. He was greeted by the adjutant, Capt. Charles Letchell, who ushered him into the C.O.'s office. Immediately upon closing the door, Letchell rushed to locate Monk Hunter and barked, "Don't ask any questions—just shave off that damned moustache—and *fast*." In the meantime, Major Spaatz was doing his best to mollify the irate police chief, inviting him to attend officers' call, where he could observe all the officers on the post and perhaps identify the culprit. When that proved nonproductive, the major suggested that the chief might care to look over the noncommissioned officers. Spaatz thoughtfully assigned Capt. Frank O'D. Hunter as his escort officer. And that, so far as is known, was the only time the dashing Monk Hunter was ever seen without his famous black moustache.

On another occasion, a group of boisterous officers, occupying a stage box, disrupted a performance at the local vaudeville theatre. This outrageous affair was witnessed by some of Houston's leading citizens, so a report immediately reached the highest military authority in Texas. Ruth was visiting her family at Fort Sam Houston in San Antonio when the storm broke. Her father was, at that time, adjutant general at Corps Area Headquarters, and was, of course, incensed at such behavior by officers of the United States Army. He announced sternly, "Tooey should have the lot of them court-martialed." Tooey, however, managed to dissuade the commanding general from taking such drastic action, and meted out some lesser form of discipline.[16]

Military budgets in the twenties were very austere and often presented problems at base level. When pilot John Cannon fractured his skull in an airplane accident, Spaatz ordered a civilian ambulance to take him to the hospital some twenty miles away. When the 1st Pursuit Group put in for reimbursement of the $20 ambulance fee, the 8th Corps Area surgeon in San Antonio refused to pay it because army ambulance wagons had been available and he thought the horse-drawn vehicles were sufficient. Spaatz argued that the injury was too serious for such rough transportation, but to no avail. In the end, the money had to come out of the pockets of the officers in the group.[17]

Spaatz had been at Ellington only a few months when orders came to move the group to Selfridge Field near Detroit. The outfit had been at Selfridge before, until 1919, when it moved south because of problems with drainage on the landing strip and with the acquisition of the land. These problems had since been cleared up. In addition, since Selfridge was only twenty miles from Detroit, the source of most aircraft engines, it was deemed advantageous to have one of the Air Service's groups nearby. The move took place in the summer of 1922.[18]

Until then, unit moves had normally been made by rail. Such had been the case, for example, with the Western Flying Circus. But the redeployments to the Argonne after the Battle of St. Mihiel, and other organizational moves, stimulated an interest among the officers of the Air Service in unit mobility. According to some airmen, one of the lessons of the war was that each air unit should fly its own planes during a move and have enough organic motor transport to enable it to move the entire ground personnel and equipment in one phase.[19]

In pursuance of the concept of mobility, the 1st Pursuit Group was ordered to make the move by flying its aircraft from Houston to Michigan. Spaatz wanted to improve the redeployment's training value by having the ground elements move to Selfridge by truck convoy to simulate wartime conditions, but he could not get approval and they followed by train.[20] Even at that early date, the move was slightly complicated by what was to become a perennial problem: the Texas congressional delegation inquired as to the necessity of the move away from Ellington. The Air Service persisted in making the change, however, and Spaatz took off with his convoy of Spads and DH-4s at the end of June.

The group set out with twenty-one airplanes—fourteen Spads and the rest SE-5s and two-place DH-4s—and encountered the usual difficulties. Two of the young flyers wandered away from the rest and were lost for a time, but eventually showed up. Another taxied his craft into a "gas house" and clipped both wingtips on one side. The damage was quickly repaired in the field, and he was able to continue on in the wake of the others. One airplane had to make repeated forced landings for an overheating engine until the problem got so bad over Ohio that it could go no farther. After Spaatz and the rest landed at Selfridge, they sent back a plane with a new radiator. The repairs were made, and even this downed aircraft got into the new base only a day behind schedule. The remarkable thing about the move was that there had been no aircraft lost and no deaths or injuries—this in stark contrast to the Transcontinental Reliability Test. The success of the move added to Spaatz's reputation as a "doer."[21]

Before he got to Selfridge, Spaatz received warnings from three sources of the rough conditions there: the Sixth Corps Headquarters in Chicago, the Chief of the Air Service in Washington, and the two officers already stationed at the base.[22] The First Group was assigned to the Sixth Corps, which was responsible for operations, maintenance and supply of the base, and unit training. The Office of the Chief of the Air Service, on the other hand, was to provide technical guidance, individual training for flying personnel, and supplies of materiel peculiar to aviation. Spaatz had two bosses. His short-term professional future lay in the hands of a general in Chicago, but his long-term prospects were controlled by General Patrick in Washington.

From Lieutenant Brenneman, one of the two officers stationed at Selfridge, Tooey learned that the heating plant in the commander's quarters had been broken since the previous winter, that there were no heating units in the rest of the quarters on the field, that the roofs of most of the buildings leaked, that the landing field was unusable for four months of the year because of standing water, that there was no commissary, that there was an officers' club but with no furniture, that the barracks also did not have furniture, and that the hospital was without medical equipment. Aside from that, the lieutenant reported that the field was in good shape. All the buildings had been repainted the previous summer and the place looked good. Moreover, relations with the local civilian community were excellent. The townspeople got along quite well with the military men at the base—both of them![23]

The Air Service officer at the 6th Corps Headquarters in Chicago had little encouragement to add. He informed Spaatz that the water system at the field was in operation, but the plumbing in the quarters had been disconnected. Most quarters had not been occupied for several years. The 6th Corps, he said, would be doing everything it could to help, but he warned that the group should expect some difficulties in the beginning. The base was serviced by an "excellent wagon road and a dilapidated railroad spur."[24] The word from Washington was hardly any better: "Do not deceive yourself," wrote Maj. Herb Dargue, "about the amount of work that is to be done at Selfridge. The quarters need a tremendous amount of work and for a while you will not be able to do any flying at all."[25]

Fortunately, the move from balmy south Texas was made in June, so there was time to make some preparation for the bitter winter to come, on the shores of Lake St. Clair. The quarters, which had been thrown together during the war, were little more than beaverboard shacks. The only heat came from a potbellied stove in the living room, and the kitchen was equipped with a very large, coal-burning stove and a very small old-fashioned icebox. Housekeeping under these circumstances was almost impossible, so nearly everyone took their meals at the club. The efficient mess officer had miraculously acquired some modern kitchen equipment and a good cook.

The club, which had been stripped and abandoned for many months, presented a challenge to the young women of the 1st Pursuit Group. But in the tradition of Army wives, dating back to frontier days, they put their talents to work and transformed a vast, barn-like room into a warm, cheerful meeting place. Bright curtains and cushions were fashioned by clever fingers, quartermaster furniture was refinished, bookshelves were built and filled, pictures were hung, and money was raised for a rug, a second-hand piano, and the all-important Victrola (there was no TV then and only rudimentary radio). By September the club was, if not a proper one, an adequate one.[26]

Notwithstanding all the pessimism coming at Spaatz from every direction, the situation was much better at the outset than it had been at Issoudun, and the scale of the job to be done (and its urgency) was far less than he had encountered in November, 1917. The cross-country flight had been wearing on the Spads, and a good bit of maintenance work had to be done on them. Once the troop trains arrived, the greater part of the group was turned out to get the field in shape for the coming winter. Then, to top it off, Spaatz was informed that Selfridge had been selected as the site for the 1922 International Pulitzer Air Races, which would be held in mid-October, just three months ahead.[27]

Spaatz had the field ready for the races, which came off with no fatal accidents or serious injuries. The outcome was all the sweeter for Spaatz in that the Air Service walked away with the honors in the presence of Generals Patrick and Mitchell and Secretary of War John W. Weeks. These military leaders were brought into contact with some of the leading lights of the Detroit automobile world at the dance that Spaatz and his officers arranged during the races in honor of General Patrick.[28] The chief was pleased, of course, but he did not go overboard with praise. Five days after the races were over, Spaatz got a letter from him:[29]

> . . . There is a matter about which I intended to speak to you before leaving Detroit. I was told that on several ocasions (sic) when officers under your command had been invited to social affairs, dinners and the like, they had been inexcusably late . . . I think it would be well for you to impress upon your officers that they should not render themselves liable to charges of such breaches of decorum . . .

No one had died or even been hurt in the races, but it *was* hard for Spaatz to get his pursuit pilots to dinner on time!

Once the disruption caused by the Pulitzer races had passed, Spaatz turned to the real business of the group: training and tactical development. The air arm lacked a fully developed set of operating procedures and any tactical doctrine, and Tooey set about to fill the void.

One of Spaatz's early innovations was to equip his pilots with parachutes. Toward the end of the war, the Germans had started using parachutes to good effect, an example that impressed Allied flyers. General Patrick had recommended their use in his final report on the war,[30] but this had yet to be done. Selfridge was not far from Dayton, and Spaatz went outside normal supply channels and informally arranged for all his pilots to fly through McCook Field to be fitted with parachutes.[31]

Spaatz also increased the range of his aircraft. The problem in pursuits was that adding fuel tanks to increase the range also increased drag and thus, fuel consumption. In the fall of 1922, the group's Spads were replaced with new Boeing Thomas Morse aircraft.[32] The range of this new craft was limited, and it fell to the only pursuit group in the service to help find ways to improve it. The new airplanes were equipped with bomb racks, and the group acquired some auxiliary gasoline tanks that could be suspended from the racks. They were installed so that they could be jettisoned from the cockpit once the contents were consumed or when contact was made with enemy aircraft. Spaatz tested the system in 1924 and was elated with the results. Drop tanks extended the planes' endurance to about five hours, a substantial increase for the time. Aircraft manufacturers started incorporating the idea in their new pursuit designs, and soon the army wrote it into the specifications for new aircraft proposals.[33]

Selfridge's location in the snowbelt made it ideal for other experiments with equipment for the pursuit planes. Spaatz's unit did the field testing for ski-equipped planes, that the nearby Materiel Division was developing, and made recommendations for improvement. In addition, the 1st Pursuit Group gained valuable experience in maintaining and operating gasoline engines in frigid conditions.[34] This proved to be a step towards enabling the World War II air arm to work effectively in arctic regions.

Throughout his time at Selfridge, Spaatz was involved in the development and testing of new ideas for airplanes. He was periodically ordered to temporary duty in Washington or at McCook Field as a member of committees to write specifications for new aircraft or to consider other technical problems.[35]

Beside his contributions to technical and tactical developments, Carl Spaatz was deeply involved in personnel policies and practices during this period. Frequently he was a member of examining boards for aspirants for regular commissions and applicants for flying schools, and he helped to develop curricula for these schools. He had a hand in retaining some people he deemed worthwhile when it seemed they would be lost to the service. He played a part in the founding of customs and standards of discipline in the Air Service, as it was beginning to differ from the Army. He also helped formulate flying safety standards for both equipment and training that would reduce the number of flyers lost through injury and death.

At Selfridge Spaatz had to contend with a host of personnel problems. When he brought the 1st Pursuit Group up from Texas he had to detach some people to Kelly Field in San Antonio, Texas, to man the pursuit school there. In the process he lost ten officers and a hundred enlisted men. By the time the group settled at Selfridge, Spaatz found himself short two hundred enlisted men. As the Army was in the midst of one of its many interwar periods of austerity, higher headquarters had no men to send him and could not get authority to let him recruit them himself. The 1st had as much trouble with desertions as any other outfit, and it was a situation to which Spaatz found no easy solution.[36]

Spaatz's problems with his officer force were equally intractable.

The ceiling imposed by Congress on the number of officers was very low, and the appropriations were never enough to reach that ceiling. The peacetime complement of the group was supposed to be one hundred officers, and at least fifty were necessary to man two squadrons so that one could be used against the other in unit training. However, the number of officers assigned was usually below twenty-five, and the shortage was never overcome while Spaatz remained in command.[37]

The 1st Pursuit Group could get new pilots only from the limited output of the pursuit branch at Kelly Field. Spaatz's man at Kelly, Capt. B. V. Baucom, was convinced that the nonpursuit pilots among the leaders of the school were prejudiced against his program and followed policies that reduced its effectiveness. He complained that his officers were continually siphoned off for other duties and that the support of his program was insufficient to keep up with his schedule. Moreover, though Spaatz's was the only pursuit group in the Air Service, many of the graduates of Baucom's program were posted to other assignments— such as composite groups at overseas locations in the Philippines, Hawaii, and Panama that had pursuit planes.

To further reduce available personnel, the accident rate in the training programs was still substantial, and even at Selfridge, the Air Service was suffering its losses.[38] Frank Hunter, for example, crashed in November 1924 and was out of action for many months with a broken back. On the day of his accident, Hunter's wing man had been Capt. Burt E. Skeel. In less than a year, Spaatz was writing to Skeel's father about his son's death.[39] On top of those losses, there was the continual need to fill quotas for training spaces in various technical schools and the Air Service Tactical School and to provide personnel for work at the headquarters in Washington. Though Spaatz finally managed to get his enlisted strength up to the mark, he was never able to come close to the authorized number of officers.

The Army's air arm had a reputation for lax discipline that had started even before World War I and lasted through World War II and beyond.[40] To some extent, it was deserved. As Spaatz had demonstrated with his conduct record as a cadet, he was not much disposed toward a rigid interpretation of regulations. Moreover, his officer force contained the high-spirited people attracted by flying pursuit planes. By the time the group got to Michigan, the 18th Amendment (prohibition) was in force. Nonetheless, it was more or less an open secret that liquor was in use on the base at Selfridge, and the complaints were loud enough to attract the attention of the chief in Washington. In response to General Patrick's inquiry, Spaatz admitted that he did permit the consumption of alcohol in the Officers' Club, but he thought it was good policy— otherwise his men would go off base for their recreation. This would create more trouble than if their indulgence were confined to the station, where Spaatz could keep an eye on it. Coming from some men, that kind of response would have been seen as defiance, but General Patrick chose to believe that Spaatz was a man of such integrity that he had the courage to be completely candid even where the truth was bound to be unpleasant.[41] It is quite clear that Spaatz from cadet days forward was not averse to drinking, and there is no reason to suppose he was any more prepared than the rest of society to go on a crusade to enforce prohibition.

Even matters having to do with uniform came to be subjects of conflict between the air arm and the ground army. The flyers complained that the old, high-collar military uniform was impractical for the Air Service. Because of the constant need to "clear" the airspace around one's aircraft, the pilot had to keep his head moving continuously. The result was that the starched liner of the high Army collar would chafe the skin and cause bleeding. Similarly, the Army garrison cap was a cumbersome thing for pilots crammed into the tiny cockpits of the day. They took to removing the wire grommet inside the rim of the cap to make it easier to put into small spaces in the airplane. This was such an annoyance to the Army that Spaatz had to require all his officers to sign a form stating they understood that grommets were not to be removed.[42] One is entitled to wonder how serious Spaatz was about this form. Two weeks earlier in a letter to Lt. D. G. Lingle, who was working in Patrick's office in Washington, Spaatz remarked:[43]

> After careful consideration, the job of Air Officer of the Third Corps Area does not appeal to me at all. My disposition would be ruined if I were in the immediate vicinity of a bunch of old Army officers every day of the year.

A perennial problem for air commanders was the young pilots' temptation to "buzz" people on the ground. On one occasion, the 1st Pursuit Group received a more serious complaint from a bridge construction company. This time, the aggrieved party got the pilot's airplane number, making it possible for Spaatz to identify the culprit. The pilot-sergeant had come so low over the workers laboring high above the water that the foreman had difficulty in preventing the men from jumping. Spaatz informed the company that he had taken disciplinary steps. The low-flyer was grounded for only two weeks.

A more persistent adversary was a wealthy landowner, Mr. Henry B. Joy, whose property lay adjacent to the field boundary. His estate had existed on the shore of the lake before flying started at Selfridge, and he was upset by the airplanes' noise. He complained directly to General Patrick in Washington and threatened to take up the matter with Congress. Since his place was so close to the landing field, it was impossible to eliminate the noise completely, and it was always one man's word against the other's as to how high a particular plane was flying. Spaatz could do little more than revise his landing patterns to avoid that side of the field, preach to his men about the problem, and issue more orders against bothering his neighbor—but it appears that Joy was not an easy man to satisfy.[44]

Carl Spaatz's handling of these problems led to two serious blows to his prospects in the Army. The first had to do with Joy's complaints, which ultimately got all the way to the secretary of war. The fact that his planes were alleged to be flying over Mr. Joy's land did not seem to bother the powers to a very great degree—though Spaatz was told that if the measures he had taken to prevent a recurrence were not success-ful, the failure would reflect unfavorably on his leadership. What bothered the secretary more was Spaatz's action in connection with a confrontation coming after the squabble with Joy. At this time theft of government property had become a major problem at Selfridge Field, and extra surveil-lance was set up. A sentry, misunderstanding orders, arrested some civilians outside the borders of the base after threatening to shoot. For this, Spaatz received a reprimand from the secretary that remained in his files.[45]

The second blow was even more serious, and it, too, arose from human failings. His finance officer, 2d Lt. Howard Farmer, had been gambling and drinking excessively for many months before the issue came to a head in the spring of 1924. A shortage in his accounts was discovered, and he was convicted by court-martial for the embezzlement of approximately $16,000, dismissed from the service, and sentenced to five years imprisonment at Fort Leavenworth. When Spaatz left Self-ridge, he had yet to hear the end of the Farmer case.[46]

From the fall of 1921 to September 1924, while Carl Spaatz com-manded the 1st Pursuit Group, the material and human factors occupied much of his time. Nonetheless he remained involved throughout this time in developing ideas about tactical and strategic doctrine and about the proper organization of American airpower. As the commander of the only pursuit group in the force, technical and doctrinal ideas found their natural focal point in his office. He was well-known throughout the service and carried on a voluminous correspondence on the subject of airpower ideas and doctrine.

One of the more important sources of these ideas was Billy Mitchell. Mitchell's relations with General Menoher had been stormy from the beginning. By 1921 the volatile airman's agitation for a separate air force and air mission had stirred up so much controversy that the air chief demanded he be relieved as his assistant. When this was refused, Menoher resigned and returned to the ground components of the Army.[47] He was replaced by Maj. Gen. Mason Patrick, with Mitchell as his assistant.

The assistant air chief made frequent visits to Selfridge. He was courting the charming Betty Miller who would become his second wife, and she lived in Detroit. In his role as a visiting dignitary, Mitchell was far from self-effacing. A correspondence he had with Spaatz about his visits suggests a medieval duke visiting one of his barons. With obvious self-assurance, Mitchell would dash off a note announcing a visit to Selfridge. Would Spaatz get in touch with one of the manufacturers in Detroit and arrange to have a car available for the general's stay? Would he make sure it was big and fast? The one the general had at home would do 80 mph on the straightaway. Would Spaatz be good enough to check on the arrival of the general's horses at a private stable in Detroit? Would he send down a few enlisted men to help the general's groom take care of his mounts? Would he make sure there was a nice, quiet room in the hotel in Detroit saved for the general?

Still, Mitchell took these inspection trips seriously. He had been impressed with Spaatz during the war and spent much time with him at Selfridge. They flew together exploring the border areas, and Mitchell attended social affairs on the base. It is clear from Mitchell's correspondence that he and Spaatz had serious conversations not only about the housekeeping of the group and the day-to-day administrative problems, but also about the use of airpower in war. Mitchell's confrontation with the establishment was gradually coming to a head during this time, and Spaatz got a substantial grounding in the ideas on organization and employment for which Mitchell was campaigning.[48]

Spaatz was personally well known to most of the faculty members of the Air Service Tactical School (ASTS) at Langley Field, Virginia. He was the most authoritative operational voice on pursuit, a subject central to the curriculum of the school. He was frequently contacted for his views on various doctrinal and technical points. A faculty member, Harvey Cook, wrote frequently to Spaatz during the winter of 1922–23, working with him on the coordination of a pamphlet the latter had developed which was being perfected for the purpose of becoming Air Service doctrine.[49]

Spaatz was involved in the exchange of ideas by yet another route in his correspondence and personal contact with people at the Pursuit School in San Antonio. His connections with the head of the school, Captain Baucom, were extensive, and he visited Kelly Field for conferences on training that involved doctrinal discussions with the leaders of the other schools at the field. Spaatz had, in fact, been asked by the head of the attack branch to critique his draft of the manual for ground support tactics.[50]

Finally, Spaatz had frequent business at nearby McCook Field. As a member of many technical committees and boards, he became involved in the doctrinal and organizational implications of the decisions being made. Since Air Service was small and the membership of these groups was drawn from all its parts, there was necessarily cross-fertilization of ideas during the proceedings.[51] Through all of these affiliations, Spaatz had a hand, to varying degrees, in shaping the Air Service's early ideas on such roles as attack, coastal defense, pursuit, and airlift.

Attack aviation (today called close air support), which directly supported ground groups, was prominent among air missions in the closing days of World War I and was encouraged by the ground officers in the Army. Spaatz's pursuit planes were equipped with bomb racks, and an important concern during his stay at Selfridge was the acquisition of a bombing range where his pilots could practice the art in safety. Though the direct support of ground combat formations was not a primary function of the 1st Pursuit Group, this attack role was included as a subsidiary mission. Writing the manual on that subject was assigned to Maj. Lewis Brereton, who had done his flying in the Great War in observation units. When he had completed a draft of the proposed manual, he sent it to Selfridge for Spaatz's comments.[52]

By the early twenties, the state of public opinion was such that it was impolitic to try to justify military expenditures based on a hypothetical foreign war. One could only speak of defense in the most restrictive sense of the word. Fortunately for the Air Service, a case could be made for the effectiveness of future airpower in the mission of coastal defense. It was all the more appealing to the political authorities because Billy Mitchell built his argument for the assignment of this mission to the air arm largely on the grounds that it could do the job more economically, as well as more effectively, than could surface ships.[53]

Spaatz absorbed these ideas through his close relationship with Billy Mitchell. General Patrick, too, was involved in the debates, and he was in the habit of sending résumés of his thoughts and arguments to all his group commanders. Through them, Spaatz remained abreast of the latest thinking on Air Service matters not directly related to his own area. One example of this occurred in late 1922. The annual report of the commanding general of the Hawaiian Department, a ground officer, was excerpted, and Patrick added his endorsement commenting upon it for the officers under his command. The basic report was very keen on the use of aircraft as an extremely effective mobile reserve for defending the coasts of the Hawaiian Islands; Patrick's endorsement made much of this as a substantiation of the need for a clearer definition of responsibilities for the defense of the coasts of the continental United States and for increased funding for planes and personnel for the Air Service to handle the mission.[54]

Spaatz's forte during this period, however, remained his understanding and promotion of the pursuit role of aircraft. One widely shared idea was that airpower was inherently an offensive, not a defensive, instrument. Another was that the prerequisite for performance of all the other missions was the achievement of air superiority, which could be gained only by the offensive use of pursuit aircraft in air-to-air combat.

During the winter of 1922–23, Billy Mitchell ordered the preparation of manuals for pursuit, attack, observation, and bombardment. Ordinarily, these manuals would have been written at the Air Service Tactical School, but that institution was understaffed in the 1920s. Air Service Headquarters made Spaatz primarily responsible for preparing the initial draft of the manuals on pursuit.[55] In this work, Spaatz received assistance from Capt. Frank Hunter and from Capt. H. W. Cook at the Air Service Tactical School.[56]

One idea stressed in the preparation of these manuals was cooperation. It was derived directly from World War I experience when air-to-air encounters tended to degenerate into an anarchy of numerous one-on-one dogfights. In the last year of the war, the emphasis on both sides was increasingly on unified action by ever-larger units. Nearly all pursuit pilots involved with doctrine in the immediate postwar years insisted on the importance of maintaining unit discipline in combat.[57]

A perennial doctrinal issue had been the manner in which pursuit aircraft should provide escort protection for bombers and reconnaissance aircraft. During the war, the bomber and observation pilots demanded that their escorting single-seaters fly close to the airplanes they were protecting. Pursuit pilots were reluctant to do this for it usually meant they would begin any combat on the defensive, from a low speed (no more than that of the bombers), and from an altitude lower than that of the adversary—all serious disadvantages in air-to-air fighting. In their doctrinal writings, Spaatz and Cook attempted to brand close escort as a "defensive" use of pursuit and thus make it undesirable.[58]

While the 1st Pursuit Group was at Ellington, the 8th Corps area commander in San Antonio wrote Spaatz's efficiency report. Maj. Gen. J. L. Hines said that he knew Spaatz well, that he was an excellent and conscientious officer. Only two marks on the report were lower than the others: "Tact" and "Military Bearing and Neatness." Spaatz's last efficiency report at Selfridge was written by the 6th Corps area commander, Maj. Gen. Harry Hale. It was prepared several months after the Selfridge finance officer had been court-martialed and while Spaatz's reprimand over the incident was being processed. Nonetheless, Hale rated Spaatz an above average officer, but with reservations about his administrative abilities.[59]

Spaatz and his old West Point friend George Stratemeyer debated via mail for some time about whether they should ask for the Engineering School at McCook Field or the Air Service Tactical School at Langley, Virginia, as their next assignments. One thing they did agree on was that they wanted to go to the same school together.[60] Spaatz did not seem to have a strong preference, but in the end asked for the school at Langley. At the last minute, Stratemeyer got the chance to extend his tour in Hawaii for a year, and he took this rather than go to Langley.[61]

## Academic Interlude

Professional military schools, in the 1920s as now, were important stepping stones in the careers of regular military officers. For aviators in the twenties, the first level of schooling was at the Air Service Tactical School (later the Air Corps Tactical School) at Langley Field, Virginia. The second step, in mid-career, was the Command and General Staff

School at Fort Leavenworth, Kansas. The eleven-month course at Langley was devoted largely to tactical and technical subjects,[62] and it reflected official War Department doctrine on the role of aviation in the Army. Immediately after World War I, the views of most air officers and their colleagues in the ground arms were similar. Both groups appreciated the need for air superiority before either could exploit its own particular weapons. As a consequence, the school emphasized the role of pursuit aviation, and little was said about bombers.

By the time Spaatz got to the school in mid-1924, however, the airmen's ideas had begun to diverge from those of the soldiers. The example of the independent Royal Air Force in Britain, Billy Mitchell's agitation and successful bombing tests against battleships, and perhaps even the writings of the Italian airman Giulio Douhet, had begun to push unofficial opinion at Langley away from its official concentration on fighters and towards bombers and a more offensive attitude.

The War Department's General Staff and the faculties at the Army's other professional schools, on the other hand, steadfastly maintained that the aircraft were only an auxiliary, although a very useful one, to the main combat arms—the infantry, cavalry, and artillery. The airmen had been disappointed by Congress's failure to create a separate air arm immediately after the war. The case had been lost on the grounds that creation of a third service would increase the uneconomical duplication of functions within the armed forces. At Langley, during Spaatz's time, airmen were beginning to think they could overcome these objections by justifying a separate service on the grounds that air forces had a mission clearly independent of those of the Navy and Army—that bombers could bring the war to the enemy far from the struggle on the surface and only indirectly related to it. Further, they thought they could deflate the duplication argument by backing the creation of a third service, but simultaneously reducing the number of departments in the national security apparatus to one: a Department of Defense that would fulfill the functions of both the Navy and War Departments as well as new ones related to independent air operations.[63]

Even in those early postwar years, though, the airmen understood the care they must exercise in advocating an independent, "strategic" bombing mission. Secretary of War Baker had already asserted in 1919 that any notion of attacking cities and industries not immediately involved in the ground battle was inhumane and too barbaric to be contemplated as American policy. He was supported in this attitude by public opinion, and America's airmen generally shared the values of their parent society.[64] The independent mission that would justify a separate existence for the air arm, therefore, had to be one that did not entail the bombing of cities. They believed they had found it in the concept of aerial defense of the coasts against invaders. This was the issue that would lead to substantial conflict between the Air Service and the Navy. If Spaatz had not already been fully instructed on the subject by Mitchell during his many visits to Selfridge, he certainly received a full dose of these notions from his comrades at the Air Service Tactical School.[65]

The academic schedule at the school was less extensive, and probably less rigorous, than it became in later times. Typically, classes were held only in the mornings, the afternoons being devoted to flying and other activities. Judging from the handwritten diary Spaatz kept for part of his stay at Langley, a good deal of time was available for tennis, golf, reading, bridge, poker, and exploring the shores of the Chesapeake.[66] There was little hesitancy to disrupt studies, and the students frequently were called to Washington to testify before congressional committees. Spaatz traveled twice to the capital during the winter and spring of 1924–1925, first to testify on another bill being considered to create a separate air force, and then before the Lampert Committee, which had been convened by the House to investigate the problems of aviation in general.[67] This "Select Committee of Inquiry into Operations of the United States Air Service" had been established in the spring of 1924. It began hearings in October 1924 and called Spaatz and several others up from the school early in 1925. Billy Mitchell also testified before the committee in such harsh terms that he was transferred from the capital. Spaatz, though still a major, was bold enough to tell the lawmakers that the United States was not ready for war in the air and that the official doctrine of the War Department made it impossible to build the capability for effective independent air operations.[68]

At the school Spaatz was reunited with many of his wartime flying companions. Oscar Westover was the commandant and Thomas DeWitt Milling was his assistant. Although Spaatz had known Milling in France, and cited him as one of the most influential people in his life, it is probable that Milling's real impact on Spaatz came at Langley. Earl Naiden, Lewis Brereton, Joseph McNarney, and Harvey Cook were also on the faculty.[69] Naiden and McNarney had been at West Point with Spaatz, one class behind him. Brereton had gone to the Naval Academy, but Spaatz may have known him in France where he gained some fame as an observation pilot and commander. Other students who, then or later, influenced Spaatz were Jacob Fickel, Walter H. Frank, Clarence L. Tinker, James Chaney, and Charles C. Benedict.[70] Spaatz received a serious blow at Langley when Benedict was killed in an airplane accident. Benedict had married one of the Red Cross girls who had been at Issoudun, and they were living wih their children at Langley at the time of his death. He met his fate by colliding with a balloon, and both Tooey and Ruth witnessed the crash.[71]

Another major distraction for Carl Spaatz at Langley was the aftermath of his Selfridge finance officer's court-martial. There was ample evidence that Spaatz had been insufficiently vigilant. He had been aware of Lieutenant Farmer's involvement in both gambling and drinking some time before the man's embezzlement was uncovered. Yet, contrary to regulations, he had accepted the man's word that he would discontinue his vices. The possibilities for disciplinary action against the former Selfridge commander ranged all the way from a court-martial to merely dropping the case. In the end, Spaatz received a reprimand, and a severe one:[72]

> . . . It appears that while you were Commanding Officer at Selfridge Field, Michigan, on learning that Lieutenant Howard Farmer . . . was gambling, instead of suspending his function and requiring him to turn over all public funds . . . you elected to take his pledge that he would not gamble . . . Your duties under it (the applicable Regulation) are clear . . . Your disregard of these regulations was so flagrant as to indicate either dense ignorance of your duties . . . or a presumptuous setting of your opinion against those of your superiors. Even did regulations permit you to handle this case according to your own ideas, your judgment was bad and your action futile . . . it was well known in the post that Lieutenant Farmer was drinking heavily . . . a competent commanding officer would, in light of the facts which you knew . . . have ascertained the true conditions and taken proper steps to protect the Government . . . Your administration of your duties . . . at Selfridge Field . . . does you no credit and calls for severe censure.

Strong words. It is little wonder that Spaatz considered leaving the service to set up a flying business in St. Augustine, Florida.[73] Yet the fact that the commander of the Sixth Corps, Area Maj. Gen. Harry G. Hale, a ground officer and Spaatz's tactical superior for the 1st Pursuit Group, seemed willing to drop the matter,[74] and that General Patrick had Spaatz assigned to his office shortly after, indicate that his service reputation was by then strong enough to escape a much worse fate. Moreover, when Milling wrote his efficiency report, though citing Spaatz as an "average" performer, he added: "An excellent officer in every respect. Would prefer to have him as a Pursuit commander to anyone else that I know."[75] Also strong words.

## In Washington

Carl Spaatz's arrival in Washington during the summer of 1925 coincided with a period of unusual turbulence for the Air Service. The secretary of war, Sinclair Weeks, upset by Mitchell's testimony before the Lampert Committee, had transferred him to San Antonio. The outspoken airman's legacy, however, remained strong among his many disciples in the capital. Since the war, Mitchell had been pushing the idea of a separate air arm with its own distinct mission through a series of public relations campaigns designed to win over the public to his way of thinking. In 1919 he had conceived the Transcontinental Reliability Test. Two years later he organized the successful bombing test which sent the captured German battleship *Ostfriesland* to the bottom of the ocean.[76] Through all of this he had written a series of books and articles that kept the controversy alive. Despite investigation by several congressional committees and executive boards, however, results for the Air Service had been meager. A minor advance was made in 1920 with the passage of the National Defense Act, which raised the Air Service to a branch within the Army equivalent to the infantry, cavalry, and artillery. The Lassiter Board, in 1923, had called for a substantial buildup of the air arm, but it could neither recommend any radical reorganization nor appropriate money to achieve the buildup. The Air Service was staggering along with fewer than a thousand officers and proportionately few dollars and enlisted men—though it had plenty of airplanes and engines, leftover from World War I.[77]

When he arrived on the air staff, Spaatz was assigned as chief of the Tactical Units Section in the Training and War Plans Division, whose chief was Maj. H. Conger Pratt.[78] The Lampert Committee was still deliberating, and its conclusions were expected momentarily. Its mere existence, however, stimulated the fear in both the administration and the War Department that if something were not done about airpower problems, Congress might take the matter into its own hands and pass legislation that was not to the liking of either the president or the general staff[79]—such as creating a separate air force.

Even in San Antonio Billy Mitchell was not easy to repress. Two events relit the fires as soon as the summer was gone. The U.S. Navy's dirigible *Shenandoah* was lost on what was essentially a public relations mission in early September, and immediately after that a Navy airplane went down trying to make a flight from the West Coast to Hawaii. These accidents gave Mitchell the chance he was looking for to make statements so outrageous that the establishment could not avoid court-martialing him—thus giving him yet another chance to bring his views on airpower before the public eye.[80]

Soon after Mitchell's statements, President Calvin Coolidge announced the formation of the Morrow Board to consider America's military aviation problems. Dwight Morrow, a friend of the president, was a man of sterling reputation, as were most other members of the board.[81] Many of the airmen thought the board's composition was "stacked" against change, and some felt that its purpose was to take the wind out of the sails of the upcoming Lampert Committee Report, which promised to be more radical than the establishment desired. Some also felt that Coolidge's goal in announcing the move before the decision to court-martial Mitchell was made public was to upstage Mitchell, who was thought to be in search of a pulpit from which he could preach the sermon of airpower to the entire country.[82]

The Morrow Board did in a month what the Lampert Committee had been working on for a year and a half! It had available to it the transcripts of the testimony given before the congressional committee. Further, it examined around one hundred people in person, many of them prominent airmen—including Mitchell himself. All the airmen cited the need for an independent air mission in their testimony to both groups, and before the Morrow panel Mitchell demanded that an independent air force be created and all the services be subordinated to a department of defense. General Patrick and his subordinates in the Air Service (including Carl Spaatz) were not ready to go that far in their public testimony to the board. What they supported at that moment was an arrangement similar to the U.S. Marine Corps, within the Navy Department, which is subordinate to the War Department, though not to the Army General Staff. They hoped that this autonomous air corps would enjoy a separate budget and a separate promotion list. Neither the War Department nor the Navy, however, was ready to admit that airpower could have a decisive independent mission. Consequently, both were diametrically opposed to Mitchell, and even to the more moderate position of Patrick and his followers.

The War Department felt that the inferior promotion situation for airmen was acceptable in light of their higher income derived from flying pay. The ground soldiers further argued that the uniform complaint was a false issue, since the flyers were already authorized to wear flight suits when involved in operations. They further asserted that the creation of another service would lead to duplication and to a lack of responsiveness to the air support requirements of the ground commanders. Neither the soldiers nor the sailors were prepared to admit Spaatz's assertion (shared with most of the other airmen) that the next war would begin with an air battle. The limited range of aircraft, they held, would prevent any such opening battle between air forces.[83]

By every account, the tactics of Dwight Morrow during Billy Mitchell's testimony were supremely effective. Mitchell began by reading from the pages of his newly published book, *Winged Defense*,[84] hoping to stimulate questions and contradictions that would lead to dramatic arguments, which would be reported by the press with the desired effect. The members of the board chose to hold their tongues, permitting Mitchell to drone on and on with dreary effect.[85] His performance during the nearly simultaneous court-martial was a little better, since his press coverage did paint him somewhat in the light he desired—as a martyr. In the end, most of his supporters in the Air Corps would say later that although his ideas were sound, his tactics did more harm than good. Arnold, who had by then been reassigned from San Francisco to Patrick's air staff, was present at both the board meetings and the court-martial. He was Mitchell's most stalwart supporter, yet, in *Global Mission,* which was published in the late forties, he admitted that his hero really had not advanced the cause of airpower that much, and that America did about as well as she could at the time, for the obstacles to the development of airpower really were technical and budgetary.[86] In later years, both Ira Eaker and Carl Spaatz were in the minority who would still assert that Mitchell had done more good than harm.[87]

Spaatz was one of the people on the air staff who helped Mitchell prepare his case. According to Ira Eaker, Mitchell, Spaatz, Eaker himself, and several others would gather at Billy's apartment after the end of each day's proceedings to discuss the prospects and tactics for the next day.[88] When Spaatz's turn came to testify at the trial, he sounded radical enough to gain a prominent notice on the front page of the *New York Times*,[89] and his remarks certainly did nothing to please the War Department and its General Staff. His reputation as a daring and outspoken advocate of airpower enjoyed a boost from the trial not only because of the effectiveness of his own testimony, but also from the *Times* reporter's flair for the dramatic:[90]

> Again the defense scored point after point when Major Carl Spaatz, a West Pointer and one of the outstanding heroes of the American World War Air Service, took the witness chair and swore that the policy of the War Department is . . . such as to retard the organization and development of the aerial defense of the nation. There has been in the army service, he testified, no bombing operations for two years, while, as for equipment, the big majority of the airplanes owned by the army are obsolete, obsolescent or of little serviceable use.
>
> Recommendations to the War Department for the improvement of the service, he declared, for the most part had up to now gone unheeded. Out of more than 1,800 airplanes carried on the army list . . . (he said) that about 400 are standard machines. Of these 400 standard, he added, 237 were inherited from the war . . . there are . . . sixty-nine modern machines of which sixty are being used in the training service, leaving nine for use against an enemy. There is not, he declared, a single pursuit airplane equipped for war-time service.
>
> Major Spaatz . . . was complete master of himself and his answers were always prompt and to the point. The crowds . . . roared on one occasion when he got his ''I do'' into the record before Colonel Moreland could frame an objection.
>
> ''So you believe,'' Mr. Reid (defense counsel) asked, ''that the organization of the tactical units of the Air Service is being retarded by the War Department?''
>
> Colonel Moreland leaped to his feet, but he was not quick enough. Before he could utter a word Major Spaatz's ''I do'' rang through the room.

These comments and others from the same testimony are cited again and again among the memoirs and oral histories of Spaatz's contemporaries of the Air Service. He already had a considerable renown for courage from his World War I exploits, and that characteristic is repeatedly cited as his strongest point in his efficiency reports of those times. Perhaps the opposite side of that coin is a category labeled on the efficiency forms as ''tact,'' which was equally consistently rated as his least strong virtue. Whatever the effects of the trial and associated events for Mitchell, Arnold, and airpower, Spaatz's status as a courageous spokesman for airmen received a great boost.

Two weeks before the issue of the Lampert Report and about a month before the announcement of the verdict of the Mitchell trial, the Morrow Board made public its recommendations. The board gave what now must be perceived as "lip service" to the needs of the air arm and recommended a major five-year expansion program. Congress, however, never appropriated the money to reach the stated goals. The board also recommended that the name of the air arm be changed to "Air Corps" to avoid the notion that a "service" existed to support the other, real, combat arms. Some considered it a cosmetic change of no substance, but from the bureaucratic point of view it was a smart move on Coolidge's part, and it defused criticism in the press and the Congress. The combination of the prestige of the board and the promise of expansion to come was enough to calm the waters—all with no increase in the federal budget, and with what the War Department perceived as a restoration of some discipline in the air arm.

The Lampert Committee reported a couple of weeks after the Morrow Board published its findings. It was much more radical and more in tune with what the airmen would have liked than were Morrow's recommendations. The legislation which followed in the spring of 1926 favored the notions of the Morrow Board rather than the desires of Congress's own Lampert Committee. The air arm remained solidly a part of the Army, subject to Army discipline and its officers competing directly with those of the ground forces for promotion. Its budgeting was to remain integrated with that of the Army. It was to receive its operational direction from the Chief of Staff of the Army.

In another two weeks the verdict in the Mitchell trial was announced. Mitchell was found guilty as charged and subsequently resigned from the Army. Arnold, who was even more outspoken than Spaatz, got in trouble soon afterwards over some related activities and was "exiled" to command an observation squadron at Fort Riley, Kansas.[91] Spaatz's closest friend, Ira Eaker, has explained that he was able to rise in the esteem of his Air Service colleagues and yet not suffer the wrath of the War Department only because his testimony was a bit less radical than that of Arnold and Mitchell and, as he was junior to both, his statements were not deemed as threatening to those in high places.[92]

Coolidge and the Morrow Board have often been painted as reactionaries with little understanding of the problem.[93] But even Arnold came to see that the future of airpower depended on developing long-range bombers and not on the immediate reorganization of the air arm in its relation to the War Department.[94]

The War Department has often been portrayed as inherently hostile to aviation in the twenties and as the very nemesis of Billy Mitchell and his followers. Yet even before the Morrow Board submitted its recommendations for a buildup of Army aviation, the department had already been devoting a disproportionately large share of its small budget to its air arm. Like any other organization, the department had to protect its functions if it were to maintain its organizational health. The General Staff was quite aware that if the aviation branch were starved, chances were good that an aggressive Navy would be able to monopolize the coastal defense mission and therefore justify a larger share of the budget for itself. Whatever the General Staff's vision of aviation's future strategic utility, it had solid grounds for paying more attention to the needs of the Air Service than, say, of the cavalry, which the Navy was not challenging.[95]

If Carl Spaatz still needed any instruction in airpower theory, the air staff, in the fall of 1925, was an ideal school. The need to prepare his own testimony for distinguished audiences and to assist in preparing Mitchell's case before the court helped him consolidate and articulate the ideas he had developed during World War I, at Selfridge, and at the Air Service Tactical School. In the three years after the trial, Spaatz continued in the Training and War Plans Division. Mason Patrick remained Chief of the Air Corps for the first two of these years and was succeeded by James Fechet. When Mitchell had been sent off to San Antonio in the spring of 1925, Lieutenant Colonel Fechet was brought to Washington to take his place. Spaatz must have met him in the early twenties, for Fechet, who had had a substantial career as a cavalryman before he moved to the Air Service in 1917, commanded Kelly Field for the first several years of the twenties. In any event, they had served together under Patrick for two years before Fechet took over. Spaatz and Fechet seemed to enjoy a mutual respect. The latter was not a West Pointer. He was one of those who got into aviation late in the game and were sometimes resented by aviators who had spent their entire career in flying. But Fechet seemed exempt from that.[96] When Fechet stepped up, Foulois was brought to the headquarters to take the assistant chief's position—and, of course, Spaatz had known the latter well ever since the 1916 operations on the Mexican border. Though Arnold had been shipped out to Kansas under a cloud, most of the rest of the group remained in Washington, and they seem to have been congenial company for Spaatz. Eaker was still there, of course, and a new man, Elwood Quesada, had come aboard to serve as General Fechet's aide.

The next few years were more tranquil for Spaatz than the recent past. The airmen had had their day in court and lost. Perhaps the example made of Mitchell, and to a much lesser extent Arnold, had the effect that Coolidge and the War Department desired. The outcome of the agitation was the Air Corps Act of 1926, which was accepted by the airmen as the best that could be expected for the time being. It contained several incentives for the airmen but fell far short of their ultimate goal. The name of the Air Service was changed to the Air Corps, two additional brigadier general slots were authorized, and a new position, Assistant Secretary of War for Air, was created, although without stipulated authority or responsibility. A five-year expansion program was written into the act. The new goal would be 1800 "serviceable aircraft." To fly these, there would be 1,518 officers and up to 2,500 cadets who would be supported by sixteen thousand enlisted men.[97]

Spaatz and his colleagues settled into the routine of running a peace-time service. Now at the vortex of things, Spaatz began to have more frequent contacts with people not involved in the pursuit end of the Air Corps, and he continued all his old relationships as well. His job entailed a good bit of travel, and he also became involved with periodic maneuvers and air races.[98]

Spaatz, as Chief of the Tactical Units Branch, was now on the receiving end of complaints from the field. The perennial problems had to do with the need for good airplanes and especially the shortage of gasoline. Appropriations being what they were under Presidents Coolidge and Hoover, Spaatz could do nothing to solve these problems for the units. His usual response was the familiar one pleading for patience and asking that the operations people do the best they could with the material available.[99] The expansion promised in the Air Corps Act of 1926 was hard to perceive by those in the field.

As Chief of the Tactical Units Branch, Spaatz had much to do with the selection and improvement of bases for tactical aircraft. The pursuit group was well established at Selfridge, and the bombers had found permanent homes at Langley Field in Virginia and at March Field in California. The observation units were attached to ground organizations and consequently spread across the United States. The attack aviation establishment, however, had yet to find a permanent home. While Spaatz was in Washington, this issue was being debated, and if he needed any more indoctrination to the logistical aspects of basing after his work at Issoudun and Selfridge, he acquired it during these negotiations. For a time, Galveston, Texas, was the leading candidate since bombing and gunnery ranges were easy to find along the Texas shore, the flying weather was generally good, and water transportation up to the base area was possible. However, the hurricane threat prevented its selection.[100] Finally, Barksdale Field in Louisiana was chosen.[101] Spaatz had a role in decisions about many other bases as well, even those overseas since they, too, were partly under the jurisdiction of the Air Corps—although the real power still was with the ground commanders in the respective geographical areas both at home and overseas. These activities forced Spaatz to think of the long-range interests of the air arm.[102]

Though Spaatz was assigned to the Training and War Plans Division and his specialty was to work with tactical units, he remained involved in logistical decision-making, especially with regard to the development of material for pursuit functions. The conventional wisdom held that a pursuit plane was subjected to such great forces during air combat that only the truss-like structure of a biplane's wings could stand the stress. A mono-wing pursuit plane, it was thought, was out of the question. The bomber, on the other hand, did not perform such violent maneuvers, so did not need the same wing strength. Bombers, therefore, were built as monoplanes earlier than were fighters. The consequence was that the larger airplanes had a speed advantage that was thought to make air-to-air interception impossible. The pursuits suffered so much drag from the wing bracings and their unretractable landing gear that they would no longer be able to catch the bombers before they had to return to base for gasoline.[103] The doctrinal conclusion at the time was that daylight, precision, unescorted bombing was feasible, a conclusion that would be tested in the coming war.

The design of pursuit planes did not change radically in the late twenties, and Spaatz was largely concerned with such routine matters as removing the fabric from the center section of the upper wing to improve the pilot's visibility[104] and designing parameters on the life span of pursuit plane components.[105] Real progress in fighter design had to await improvements in technology in the next decade and for the stimulus of the threat to world peace.

During the latter part of Spaatz's Washington tour, the Air Corps focus was slowly shifting from pursuit planes to bombers as the key to successful war in the air. Spaatz was involved in this metamorphosis only peripherally. Not only did technology favor bomber development, but the bureaucratic imperatives were also pressing in the same direction.

Billy Mitchell had rested so much of his case for the coast defense mission on the economies to be realized by assigning it to the air arm that his successors had to do what they could to substantiate his arguments. In isolationist America, with a self-perception that the U.S. was more humane than the decadent countries of the Old World, any thought of bombing cities was out of the question as a justification for a larger slice of the budget. The strategic argument for the shift to bombers, therefore, had to be made on the basis of their value as coastal defenders.

The biggest part of Mitchell's argument on economy had to do with a not altogether valid comparison of the cost of battleships versus airplanes. But another part of the issue, and one that Mitchell probably did not make enough of, was that there were two oceans to be defended. Even with the Panama Canal, surface ships could not go from one coast to another rapidly enough to provide the defense thought necessary. The implication was that the Congress would have to buy two navies where only one air force would suffice, because, with its superior mobility, the air force could move from one coast to another in time to meet any threat. This notion was at the root of many of the record-setting flights that took place during the interwar period. The round-the-world flight of 1924 was but one example.[106]

The Air Corps' claim to the coastal defense mission was also the wellspring of such other current notions as the forming of a General Headquarters (GHQ) air force, the development of lighted airways, the establishment of emergency airfields, and extending the range of aircraft. Spaatz had been involved in some of the airways development work and in the Transcontinental Reliability Test flight before he got to Washington. In the late twenties, he took part in many maneuvers that were performed for the same purposes. He was most often engaged in the planning of such missions, but also flew in a few of them and helped analyze the results when they were over.

In early 1927, Spaatz wrote to Lewis Brereton, the commander of the 2d Bombardment Group, about some upcoming maneuvers. He remarked on the possibility of concentrating a large formation of bombers at Wright Field prior to the commencement of the maneuvers, suggesting that both coasts could be defended by one air force from one central location. He also directed that Brereton send along a transport with the bomber formations on their upcoming deployments, again indicating concern with air mobility and the need to service both coasts.[107]

Another way in which the Air Corps of the twenties tried to win public support was to participate in air races and attempt to better world flying records. The U.S. Navy was usually the team to beat at these events. It had been so at the Pulitzer races at Selfridge in 1922, and it was so at the National Air Races of 1926. Working at Air Corps headquarters during the latter event, Spaatz became involved in the technical preparations for the competition.

The Air Corps had learned that the Navy was secretly installing a V-1400 high-compression engine in the P-1 it intended to enter. The Army reacted by installing a similar engine in a P-2 at the Materiel Division's field in Ohio. Shortly before the races, Spaatz wrote to John Curry at Dayton to caution all involved in the operation to treat the engine with care since it was the only one available to the Air Corps. A pilot from the Pursuit Group at Selfridge was chosen by lot to fly in the race; he was to pick up the Air Corps entry at Dayton and fly it to Philadelphia where the races were being held. Spaatz cautioned that the engine was the air arm's only hope of beating the Navy, and the pilot was to be carefully instructed to nurse it along all the way to Philadelphia.[108]

Not only did Spaatz help plan for the race, but he served as commander of the Air Corps troops temporarily assigned to support the race.[109] The Army had enjoyed considerable success as hosts of the Pulitzer races in 1922—no serious accidents or fatalities occurred and they had captured the prizes for most of the flying events. Unfortunately, at the National Air Races in 1926, the Army did not get the same kind of glory. Though the weather did not cooperate, the week was a gala event for Philadelphians. The races took place at the Model Farms Flying Field outside the City of Brotherly Love, and the spectators were treated to all manner of civilian races, parachute jumps, and even to a visit by the Navy's great airship, the *Los Angeles*. The final event, and principal one for the military services, was one for pursuit ships of standard design— eliminating any entities built solely for speed. Sadly for Spaatz and his people, all their care before the race did not result in victory, for the first place was taken by Lt. C. T. Cuddihy of the United States Navy. It was small consolation that Air Corps pilots took the next four places before another sailor or marine crossed the finish line.[110]

In the fall of 1928, Ira Eaker proposed to Spaatz that the Air Corps attempt to set a new world endurance record in air-to-air refueling, at the same time testing the endurance and reliability of aircraft, engines, and flight crews.[111] Air refueling had been done before. The barnstormers of the era had gone beyond that to actually transferring people from plane-to-plane while in flight. The Air Service itself had tested the refueling idea in 1923, and it had worked well enough then to establish an endurance record of thirty-seven hours.[112] Spaatz was immediately taken by the idea of setting a new record and carried it to the chief, General Fechet, who approved it on the provision that the equipment and methods be tested and proven before the force was deployed to the West Coast for the attempt. The test was to take place in January, and since a week or so of good weather would be required, southern California was about the only part of the country that could be counted upon— and suitable bases existed there.[113]

Necessary modifications were made to the receiver airplane, named the *Question Mark,* a standard Fokker trimotor, and to two "nurse" aircraft, standard Douglas biplanes used for transport work by the Air Corps. The work was done at the Middletown Air Depot near Harrisburg, Pennsylvania, and the planes were flown to Bolling Field at the capital for last-minute checks. These were completed in mid-December, 1928, with General Fechet himself aboard the *Question Mark* (the Fokker trimotor) and everything checked out properly. The crew of the receiver aircraft and one refueling crew flew the planes to Rockwell Field, San Diego, California. There they passed the holiday season training another refueling crew and making preparations for the test. Spaatz was the commander and organizer during the planning phase and all through the execution of the mission. The crew of the *Question Mark* included Ira Eaker, Elwood Quesada, Harry Halvorsen (all of whom became generals in World War II), and S. Sgt. R. W. Hooe, the flight mechanic.[114]

The flight was launched early on the morning of New Year's Day, 1929, and for the next seven days shuttled back and forth between San Diego and the vicinity of Los Angeles. Public relations was one of the undeclared missions, and the Air Corps fliers attempted a refueling on the first day over the Rose Bowl game, which provided as large an audience as could be hoped for in those pretelevision days. According to General Eaker, Spaatz came close to "streaking" the crowd in a parachute. The fuel was transferred from the Douglas biplanes to the Fokker through hoses that had recently been replaced. The new item was one of smaller diameter and, consequently, the automatic shutoff valve at the lower end could not be adapted. Spaatz's job was to stand in a midships hatch at the top of the plane with half his body out in the slipstream to catch the hose and place it into a funnel-like arrangement aboard the *Question Mark*. The valve in the tanker airplane was then turned on, and the fuel fed into the receiver.

The problem was that the turbulent air around the Rose Bowl caused the two aircraft to separate, yanking the hose from Spaatz's hands. Without the shutoff valve, the high octane aviation fuel in the hose doused him to the skin. Spaatz ripped off his clothes and had his body rubbed with oil in the hope of preventing serious burns. If the oil did not work, Spaatz said, he would bail out to get medical aid. He ordered the crew to continue the mission. All went well, so the refueling continued with Spaatz again up in the hatch clad only in his parachute.[115]

Numerous "hook ups" were achieved during daylight and darkness, and food and equipment—even storage batteries—were lowered to Spaatz while he stood in the hatch of the airplane. Weight was a serious concern; it was kept as low as possible so the pilots could maintain altitude with minimum power settings and conserve the engines. Aircraft radios had been under development for a long time by 1929, but the *Question Mark* did not have one. General Eaker later explained that the radio they might have used weighed several hundred pounds with its batteries— too much for a plane whose empty weight was barely over 5,000 pounds.[116]

Nonetheless, the *Question Mark* remained in communication with the ground through visual means. The aircrews used hand signals and flashlights, and the ground support organizations devised an elaborate set of panel signals that were laid out on the ground. Further, two airplanes were equipped as blackboard aircraft. Their sides were painted black, messages were chalked on them, and they were flown alongside the *Question Mark,* whose crew in turn would climb up through the hatch and chalk a response on the blackboard that had been painted on top of their wing. They also resorted to the old World War I method of dropping a message bag with a streamer attached. The crews on the ground replied by sending letters in the food containers that were lowered from the tankers.

Though the communications were primitive, some of the other equipment and techniques used on this flight have a modern ring about them.[117] For example, the new tanks installed in the Fokker for the mission were equipped with dump valves, something that was incorporated into all large aircraft, not just tankers and bombers, after World War II. These valves allowed the pilot to lighten the aircraft rapidly by ridding the plane of its extra fuel in case of an in-flight emergency. Another example is the refueling technique. The Douglas refueling planes were an older vintage than the Fokker and could not fly as fast. As the fuel was transferred to the receiver, it became heavier and was consequently brought closer to its stalling speed. Since the Douglas biplanes were incapable of going any faster in level flight, they began a gradual descent which enabled the *Question Mark* to increase its speed enough for safety and still remain "hooked up"[118]—a procedure identical to that used in the 1950s when the bomber force had already been modernized with high-speed jets while the tankers were still driven by propellers.

In some ways, Sergeant Hooe was the most daring of the crew, for it fell to him to go out on the trapeze. Catwalks had been built from the fuselage out to the under-wing engines so that in-flight maintenance could be performed. On the seventh day of the flight, the left engine began acting up. Hooe was sent out to see what he could do to repair it. He had actually removed the rocker box cover from cylinder number eight on that engine, when the officers in the cabin decided they could not maintain altitude on the two good engines long enough for him to finish the job. They called him in and proceeded to land after 150 hours in the air—breaking every endurance record in existence, even those for balloons and zeppelins.[119]

Spaatz's comments on the tactical lessons learned from this flight are significant, and they constitute a solid prediction of what was to come, not in his time, but after World War II. First, Spaatz concluded that air-to-air refueling on a routine basis was practical and safe—in fact he made it sound easy. The skeptic would have pointed out that his test was done in a benign climate under good weather conditions (for the most part). Some things would not have worked in the frigid temperatures of northern climes or higher altitudes; nor would things have gone smoothly in harsher weather conditions. Still, when the need arose, air refueling did indeed prove to be a practical proposition. Second, Spaatz predicted that air-to-air refueling would permit the bomber to take off with a much smaller fuel load, thereby increasing safety, permitting a heavier bomb load, and extending the range of the attacking aircraft. In fact, he asserted that the tactic would remove the range limitations from bombers altogether.[120] These ideas were later implemented by the Strategic Air Command and have proved, since World War II, highly effective in providing bomber and fighter range data for war planning.

In his final report on the mission, Spaatz also remarked that the refueling practice could be applied to pursuit, attack, observation, and commercial aviation as well. But the degree to which he concentrated on long-range bombing says something about the way his mind was moving on the eve of his reassignment to take command of a bombardment group. Elsewhere in the report he alluded to the significance of in-flight refueling for transcontinental and transoceanic flight, but he did not explicitly connect these things with bombing. It would have been a small leap, however, to put them together and go beyond mere coastal defense bombing to the notion of achieving the nation's political objectives through an attack on the vital centers of an enemy's industrial system.

After being in Washington for nearly four years, in the spring of 1929 Carl Spaatz got his orders to move on. One of the leading pursuit experts in the Air Corps, he was ordered to San Diego, where his flying career began, to take command of a bombing outfit: the 7th Bombardment Group at Rockwell Field.

# Chapter IV

## BOMBERS AND THE DEPRESSION THIRTIES

Carl Spaatz's professional direction shifted during the 1930s. Until then, he was recognized as one of the deans of the world of pursuit pilots, and pursuit planes were still considered the mainstay of war in the air. He took command of one of the Air Corps' few bomber units just at the time research was producing the first big bombers with long range and large load capacity and the idea was taking hold that daylight bombers could find and destroy vital centers of the enemy's military and industrial power. In the ensuing years, he helped develop the theory that airpower could cheaply and effectively defend the U.S. against seaborne threats. During the thirties, Spaatz also served again near the seat of power during the airmail crisis (when the army served briefly as the mail carrier for the U.S. Postal Service), and he became an important figure at Langley Field, home of the General Headquarters (GHQ) Air Force and its premier flying unit, the Second Wing. This new air force was, in embryonic form, the organizational expression of the evolving long-range bombing ideas, and the wing at Langley was the first in the Air Corps to receive the new B-17 Flying Fortresses, the technological expression of the same ideas.

### Rockwell and March

Tooey and Ruth arrived in southern California just before the onset of the Great Depression, but their personal world was largely insulated from the suffering it caused. Spaatz had been dabbling in the stock market throughout the twenties, and seldom more than in 1929. Yet he was able to report a profit on his market transactions for that year, though most of his stocks showed a loss.[1] His parents were still in Boyertown, and his mother visited California shortly after Tooey and Ruth settled in at Rockwell. Anne Spaatz, who was 65 years old, was bold enough to go for a ride with her son in an open cockpit, fabric-covered biplane.[2]

Life in California held many diversions. San Diego was close to Mexico's Agua Caliente and its legal liquor and gambling. The Spaatzes frequently went there to entertain friends visiting from the more austere world of Washington and the rest of the country.[3] The population of California then was rather thin; hunting and fishing in the Sierras and in Mexico were good.[4] When the daily routine did not permit expeditions to the wilds, the officers played squash, as Spaatz had had courts constructed at both Rockwell and March Fields. In this, he had the active support of General Foulois, himself a squash buff, and the sport reached the stage where officers at Rockwell, and later at March, were making exchange visits for tournaments with athletic clubs up and down the West Coast.[5]

The first two Spaatz children were Katharine and Rebecca. While the family was in California, the Spaatzes had their third daughter, naming her "Carla" after her father (Carl A.). It was a good life for Tooey and Ruth; they were only indirectly disturbed by the economic storms racking American society and still less troubled by the puffs of clouds beginning to appear on the international horizon.

Carl Spaatz knew when he was sent to Rockwell that his stay was likely to be short. The flying weather around San Diego was benign, North Island had ample space for flight operations and buildings, the post was well served by both water and land transportation, the field was so located as to allow its planes to meet any seaborne threat, and the city of San Diego was nearby to provide for the needs of the air corps community. The trouble was that the base was too good—so good that the Navy and the Army had been competing for its ownership for many years. Lately, they had been sharing the airfield, but the requirements of both services had become so great that the ground and airspace were becoming overcrowded. Because North Island is adjacent to an excellent deep-water harbor (along a coast that has very few of them), the Navy had a powerful argument on its side. Because the Army's air arm had founded the installation, tradition was on its side. The Air Corps held out until the Navy came up with funds to build a replacement airdrome.

After much negotiation, a new wing was set up at March Field, Riverside, California, to incorporate both the 7th Bombardment Group and a pursuit group. This entailed a good deal of reorganization and building at March. Much of Spaatz's time in the subsequent four years was consumed in the logistical aspects of moving a large air unit, building a new base, and creating a new organization, the 1st Bombardment Wing, to oversee both groups.[6] After more than two years in San Diego, Spaatz brought his group to March in the latter part of 1931. Having served under Patrick and Fechet in Washington, when the controversy with the Navy was at its height, the experience in San Diego did nothing to reduce his perception of the sister service as an adversary.

Though Carl Spaatz was now a continent away from the technical decision-making centers at Washington and Dayton, Ohio, he nonetheless remained deeply involved in that aspect of the air arm's work. He participated frequently in the servicewide pursuit and bombardment boards that selected new equipment and sought solutions for old problems.[7] As commander of one of the Air Corps' few tactical units, he was sought out for his technical advice—and as the 7th Bombardment Group and the 1st Bombardment Wing both contained pursuits, he was considered an authority on both bombers and pursuit aircraft.[8]

In January 1933, for example, Spaatz was a member of the Pursuit Board that met at Wright Field in Dayton, Ohio. Also attending were many who were to gain fame in World War II: George Brett, Millard Harmon, Hal George, Frank "Monk" Hunter, and Claire Chennault.[9] The board was looking into the question of whether escort planes were needed for penetrating bombers. It concluded that research and development should proceed along parallel lines: creating a two-place, long-range fighter to accompany the bombers and improving the capabilities of the bombers to defend themselves, even turning the bomber airframe into a battle plane wholly devoted to the defense of the other planes in the bomber formation. The board's report recommended developing these battle planes with two gunners firing upwards, and two more shooting downwards, and installing turrets to improve the gunnery. It explicitly cautioned, however, that the emphasis on improving the bombers and creating battle planes should not divert the Air Corps from the simultaneous development of long-range, fast fighter planes to support bomber formations. There was a good deal of concern about the need for escort fighters in 1933, long before anyone had a glimmering that radar was a possibility.[10] Spaatz advised George Brett that the members of the board should put up a stalwart defense of their ideas.[11]

Throughout this tour in California, Spaatz was involved in the day-to-day problems with airplanes, both pursuits and bombers, of a passing generation. When he arrived in California, his unit was being reequipped with Boeing P-12 pursuits, a good airplane, but one of the last fighters of the biplane-fixed landing gear designs. He did most of his flying in it, and was involved in the problems that remained with the plane when it reached the tactical units. For one thing, the oil cooling system, which was fine in more northern climes, proved inadequate in warmer southern California. The problem was resolved by the simple expedient of cutting additional louvers into the access panels covering the engine compartment. Other minor problems were experienced in integrating a new and larger machine gun, and in the installing of cowlings to improve the air flow around the cylinder heads.[12] On the 4th of January, 1932, Spaatz made rather more dramatic changes to at least one pursuit plane. While making a crosswind landing at Santa Monica, he wrecked his airplane. An investigating committee attributed the accident to materiel failure—one of the axles had given way on touchdown.[13]

The bombers of Spaatz's units were even more troublesome. The squadrons included both old Keystone LB-7s and newer Curtiss Condor B-2s. The Keystones had been brought on line in the mid-twenties, equipped with Liberty engines left over from World War I. Though the Air Corps staff in Washington was well along in its planning for more modern bombers, the Keystone was a fabric-covered biplane with open cockpits and fixed landing gear.[14] The 7th Bombardment Group had the later versions with radial engines, but they were not much better than the old Martin bombers Billy Mitchell had used against the *Ostfriesland* in 1921. The Keystones were a constant headache to the group commander. As Spaatz reported:[15]

> We have five of the Keystone bombers on hand. So far we have been unable to keep more than one or two in commission out of the five. On the other hand, out of the nine B-2s on the field, nine of them are in commission practically all of the time.

Sudden unexplained fires were one of the Keystone's problems. On the 14th of September 1929, one of them burned mysteriously while on the ground at Los Angeles. The Air Corps grounded all the bombers until new exhaust stacks were installed, but that did not solve the problem. On the 21st of December of the same year, another Keystone went up in smoke at the home field for no known reason—it was being washed at the time it ignited.[16]

Spaatz and his pilots preferred the Condor. Not that its design was radically advanced over that of the Keystone, for it, too, was a fabric-covered biplane with fixed landing gear and open cockpits. Its only distinctive feature was the inclusion of extra cockpits at the aft end of the engine nacelles—lonely perches for two gunners guarding the regions behind the plane.[17] The things that appealed to the pilots of the 7th were its mechanical reliability and the ease with which it could be flown. Spaatz regretted that the Air Corps had not bought more Condors, for he thought they could penetrate enemy airspace with relative impunity at high altitudes in daylight. When a new Boeing B-9, with retracting landing gear and one wing, passed through March in the fall of 1931, Spaatz considered it a precursor of things to come.[18]

Notwithstanding the advances that had been made in airframe and engine design, airplanes were still not very reliable. Crashes posed a continuing problem for Spaatz. October 8, 1929, was, for him "one of those days." While one of his pilots was flying a pursuit aircraft to San Francisco, its engine died. Fortunately, the pilot was able to glide to a safe landing on a dry lake bed. He repaired the engine himself, but when he tried to take off, he ran into some soft sand and nosed over, damaging the plane. Another lieutenant took off in a Keystone bomber with a repair crew and parts. Instead of rescuing the downed airman, Spaatz found that now he had, in addition to the pursuit plane, a wrecked bomber in the sand of the dry lake. Courage was mustered for a third try, and the group's transport plane was sent up with more people and parts. This time the Fokker got in and out safely. The pursuit was repaired and flew out under its own power, but the Keystone had to be dismantled and sent home by truck.[19]

Two weeks later, one of his lieutenants hit a boundary light with his propeller, on the field at Reno, Nevada, as he was on his way to the runway for takeoff. He judged that no damage had been done so he followed the rest of the squadron into the air. He was wrong. Soon after he was airborne, the propeller separated from the aircraft. The plane was high enough to glide back to the field, but the runway was already occupied by the next aircraft. The pilot set his plane down on the turf and another pursuit was stranded away from home.[20]

According to the unit historian, two days later another pursuit pilot in one of the P-12s invented a new maneuver. He had just landed and was accelerating for another takeoff when a plane taxied across his nose at right angles. He made an instant right turn, and, in so doing, put his airspeed below that at which the plane could fly. As a result, "Lieutenant Israel was not injured, except for a slight laceration of the chin, but he will go down in aviation history as the originator of a new maneuver—a cartwheel in a P-12."[21] Doubtless the group commander was not as amused as the historian. Nor were the bomber pilots immune from accidents. On the 4th of March, 1930, one of them gave the home field spectators a thrill by landing with one wheel dangling from his Keystone. The pilot was not injured, and there was enough left of the airplane to repair.

During these years in California, Spaatz made some major contributions to developing areas of air-to-ground communications and command and control. During World War I, reconnaissance, artillery spotting, and coordinated pursuit action were severely handicapped by the primitive state of communications. Even at sea, during the Battle of Jutland, airpower could not play much of a role because it lacked air-to-surface communications and a reliable command and control organization to integrate the airplanes and zeppelins into the overall effort. As late as 1929, suitable aircraft radios were unavailable for the *Question Mark*'s flight. During the years immediately following that flight, the application of radio to military air operations and the development of command and control procedures and organizations were major preoccupations of Spaatz. At March Field he acquired a Fokker transport plane to serve as a command post and equipped it with the necessary radios. The equipment was capable of operating either while the Fokker was airborne or while it was parked at a forward location during maneuvers or combat. A desk was built into the aircraft so the commander could attend to the problems of command without the distractions of flying the airplane at the same time. On missions, the lead plane in each formation was equipped with radios, and the lead pilot used a system of hand signals to transmit the commander's orders to the other planes. Spaatz seems to have been one of the leaders in this development for as early as 1930, when the chief of the Air Corps, General Fechet, came to the West Coast for maneuvers, the 7th had already outfitted one of its Keystones as a command post. Fechet utilized it to control his forces while in-flight and even from the ground.[22]

Spaatz's tenure in California in the early thirties was marked by a further cementing of his relationship with Henry Arnold. Following his banishment from Washington to Fort Riley, Kansas, Henry Arnold had attended the Command and General Staff College for a year before being transferred to the Air Corps' Materiel Division at Wright Field in Ohio. Throughout this period, Spaatz and Arnold remained in touch through the mails and whenever their paths crossed on maneuvers or other travels. Learning in the summer of 1931 that Spaatz's 7th Bombardment Group would soon vacate Rockwell and take up a new station at March Field, Arnold began negotiations to have himself assigned to the new base. As a part of that effort, he asked Spaatz to put in a good word for him with General Foulois.[23] The negotiations succeeded and Arnold moved to March to become the base commander while Spaatz remained in command of the 1st Bombardment Wing. That meant that Spaatz, the tactical commander, was again subordinate to his old friend Hap Arnold, and they remained together at March for another year and a half. There were other old acquaintances at March, such as Ira Eaker, and two new faces that would become important later in his career: Joseph McNarney, one of his group commanders whom he had known at West Point, and William Tunner, a new lieutenant whose first assignment was March.

Spaatz's attitude toward discipline became a bit tougher during this time. His preferred methods of leadership still favored using the carrot more than the stick, but his trusting attitude towards Lieutenant Farmer at Selfridge had had near-terminal effects on his reputation as an effective commander. Now, although he still preferred the gentle approach, there was evidence that he had learned from the Farmer incident and could be tough when he thought the situation demanded it. One story illustrating this has to do with a group of lieutenants under his command who had developed the habit of getting "socked in" by the weather on Friday nights—close to some pleasure resort. One Friday night, when the usual message arrived describing the horrid weather at the other field, Spaatz climbed into his own plane, flew to the place, and left his calling card on the windshields of the lost fledglings before he winged back to Rockwell without meteorological impediment.[24]

Mrs. Spaatz has also said that Tooey did learn something from the Selfridge case,[25] and there are other signs of a sterner hand in the Rockwell-March period. In the spring of 1930 Spaatz became so exasperated with the performance of the captain commanding his headquarters detachment that he gave him an unsatisfactory efficiency report—something that was rare then and from which it was difficult to recover.[26] In another case, he took the trouble to write to a friend at Boeing Airlines to rescind the recommendation for employment he had written on one of his former officers who had since lost Spaatz's esteem.[27] On another occasion, he wrote to the commander of another unit to report unacceptable conduct on the part of one of the latter's officers and to suggest an investigation.[28]

Controlling his officers' drinking behavior was still a troublesome part of Spaatz's command duties. When General Patrick six years earlier had asked for an explanation of reports that excessive drinking was going on at the officers' club at Selfridge, Spaatz did not trouble to deny it. His approach then was to tell the general that he would rather have his officers drinking on the base where he could keep an eye on them than out in the civilian community where anything might happen. Though it was in the midst of the prohibition era, Patrick had accepted that. Now, in 1930, Spaatz was faced with the same problem again— with the repeal of prohibition still three years away.

The problem was a little tougher now because it had become public. An aviation magazine with offices in Los Angeles, *Western Flying,* had published an editorial entitled "Officers, But Not Always Gentlemen." The thrust was that Air Corps officers were discrediting the entire aviation community by their unruly conduct in public. The article included the words: "Taking a sociable drink with a friend or friends in private is one thing; getting drunk and making a general ass of one's self in public is quite another." The writer named neither units nor particular officers, but the implication was that Spaatz's group, the closest large Air Corps unit to Los Angeles, was involved.[29] General Fechet wrote on the 19th of August asking for an investigation and a report. Spaatz's response this time was more cautious. For a time, he considered demanding space in the magazine for a rebuttal,[30] but in the end decided it was better to avoid a public debate.[31] He closed the issue by telling the editor of *Western Flying* that it was deemed inappropriate for a junior commander to make a public response, and if one were to be made, it would have to come from Air Corps headquarters in Washington.

Aircraft accidents were still a common occurrence in those days, although the pilots often walked away from them. Flying commanders had to be able to handle frequent deaths, while controlling their own grief. It fell to Spaatz as the commander to try to ease the pain of parents and widows and do what he could to see that the dependents were provided for. William R. Casey came to the 7th Bombardment Group as a pursuit pilot shortly after Spaatz took command. Before the summer was gone, the young lieutenant married Muriel Anderson of Los Angeles.[32] In the fall of 1930, Spaatz found himself trying to build a fire under the bureaucracy so that the widow, Muriel, would start receiving her dependent's compensation.[33] Such things were never routine, of course, but an even tougher blow was in store for Spaatz. During a Pursuit Board meeting in January, 1933, his close friends Monk Hunter and Hugh Elmendorf demonstrated a new two-place pursuit airplane to the rest of the board. Near the end of the demonstration, Elmendorf stalled the airplane and it went into a violent spin. Hunter delayed perhaps longer than he should have, but bailed out in the last minute and escaped with a broken back. Elmendorf went down with the plane.[34]

The 7th Bombardment Group and the 1st Bombardment Wing had to share the personnel difficulties under which the entire Air Corps labored. The emphasis on government economy did not lessen after the coming of the depression, and Spaatz was faced with a continual struggle to keep his units manned with competent officers and enlisted men. His problems were in no way different from those experienced by the tactical commanders when he had been on the Air Staff, and now that he was in a tactical command, the Air Staff gave him the same answers he had recited many times to others. On one occasion, Spaatz's people went to San Francisco to raid the personnel of Crissy Field at the Presidio. The commander there, Capt. Walter F. Kraus, complained vehemently at the want of ethics on the part of Spaatz's mess officer, who was trying to lure away some cooks. Kraus complained that the Rockwell party had promised promotions to his men if they would reenlist and practice their culinary arts in the Rockwell kitchens. Particularly painful to Kraus was the fact that one of them did indeed go to Rockwell when he reenlisted at the end of his "hitch." Spaatz quickly answered the complaint by agreeing with Kraus on the matter of ethics and promising to prevent a recurrence—but even were he inclined to do so, there was nothing he could do to return the lost cook.[35]

Carl Spaatz's contribution to airpower theory is more evident when he was the commander of bombing units on the West Coast than during any other part of his pre-World War II career. This was a time when airpower theory and doctrine were changing rapidly. Though the corporate wisdom of the Air Corps, and Spaatz along with it, was moving towards the notion that "the bomber would always get through," the idea that it could not do so unassisted never disappeared completely. Earlier, General Patrick and the entire Air Corps establishment had based their case for independence on the notion that airpower could defend the coasts of the U.S. more effectively and economically than could any other instrument. Throughout the twenties, neither the Congress nor the U.S. Navy could be sold on that proposition. During 1931, however, new men were appointed to the offices of both Chief of Staff of the U.S. Army and Chief of Naval Operations: Douglas MacArthur to the former and William V. Pratt to the latter.[36] The appearance of this new blood among the decision makers at the apex of both services broke the deadlock.

At the time of the Spanish-American War, the citizens of the great ports on the American East Coast put up a cry for the stationing of the Navy's capital ships at the entrance to their harbors for protection against the Spanish fleet. This appalled the Navy, for it flew in the face of the primary teachings of Alfred Thayer Mahan—that the main battle fleet must be kept concentrated, that it must be used as an offensive weapon, that its target first and foremost was the destruction of the enemy's fleet. The main battle fleet could not be deprived of its flexibility by being tied down to the defense of any particular geographical point. That function was to be left to the Coast Artillery.[37]

The advent of the airplane complicated the issue. Now the Army had a reach out to sea that far exceeded that of the Coast Artillery. It would also have a claim to a much larger share of the federal budget were it able to justify the defense of the coasts with aircraft. The Navy faced a dilemma. If it adhered to traditional doctrine, it could not contest the Army's growing claim on a greater proportion of the defense budget. The issue remained unsettled through the twenties. When Pratt became Chief of Naval Operations, he decided to stand by traditional naval doctrine and concluded an agreement with MacArthur in January, 1931. All naval aviation would be attached to the fleet and would move with it. The Army would be responsible for the coastal defense mission, thus allowing the Navy the mobility it required to fight an offensive war. For a time, that settled things. Pratt was unable to carry the rest of the Navy along with him, however, and the agreement was dependent upon his tenure in office.[38] The Army Air Corps finally had an agreed-upon mission which did not offend the pacifist and isolationist sentiments of America and which could easily be used as justification for the development of long-range heavy bombers.

In November, 1932, one of the group of instructors at the Air Corps Tactical School most deeply involved in fashioning strategic bombing theory, Kenneth Walker, wrote to Spaatz asking his advice on the ideal organization for airpower in light of the changing roles of bombers and pursuit planes. Walker gave a special insight to Spaatz's function in all of this when he wrote:[39]

> We have considerable difficulty in coming to any conclusions here at the school. As we feel that you, without question, will be the guiding hand in this particular development, your reactions will be of great assistance in giving us a fresh point of view.

That comment is particularly significant because it shows that Spaatz had the reputation as a man of action who could be assigned a practical task and be counted on to get it done with a minimum of fuss. Spaatz never had a tour as an instructor at any of the professional schools and did not spend a great amount of time writing for publication as did his friends Mitchell, Arnold, and Eaker; yet the people at the formal center of Air Corps doctrine-making came to Spaatz for advice with more than the usual amount of respect. He had a continuous input of ideas to the technical center of the Air Corps, at Wright Field, through participation in various board meetings and through the mails. He also influenced the Air Corps people assigned to the Army's Command and General Staff College at Fort Leavenworth, again through the mails.[40]

There was as yet little discussion about attacks on enemy population and industrial centers, and much of the bomber talk focused on the notion of coastal defense. Still, the trend of Spaatz's thought, and that of the Air Corps establishment, can be gleaned partly from ideas expressed in his correspondence. One element was the growing conviction that the bomber would be able to penetrate enemy airspace in daylight without escort protection, or in the words of Spaatz:[41]

> Normally, at low altitudes, i.e., altitudes below 15,000 feet, penetration of attack and bombardment (aircraft formations) into enemy territory will be shallow unless protected by pursuit. At altitudes above 15,000 feet observation from the ground becomes difficult, and above 20,000 feet bombardment airplanes can make deep penetrations without pursuit protection.

He wrote in a similarly confident tone to his friend Jan Howard at Wright Field:[42]

On days when sufficient ceiling can be obtained and with the supercharged motor, a bomber of the B-2 type can make a very deep penetration during daylight with, I believe, comparative safety at altitudes above 20,000 feet. I am advancing this thought to you, particularly since present disarmament plans indicate the possibility of very little increase in the number of our combat airplanes, and we may be forced, in order to obtain sufficient striking power, to go to much larger airplanes . . .

Nowhere in his correspondence is there allusion to the bombing of cities. In one of his most complete statements of his view of airpower during the early thirties, Spaatz wrote to Walker:[43]

There undoubtedly will be three stages in the progress of a war. In the first stage, hostile ground or naval forces will not have gained contact and air forces only will engage in action. In the second stage, hostile [surface] . . . forces will gain contact . . . and will engage in the initial battles in conjunction with air forces. In the third, . . . hostile ground forces will remain in contact and a stabilized situation will develop . . .

    To meet the threat in the first two stages will require an Air Force fully manned, fully trained, and fully equipped *prior* [author's emphasis] to the outbreak of hostilities . . . The missions required in the initial stages should determine the organization, equipment, and training of our Air Force in peacetime . . . Hence, in the first stages of a war, we must be prepared to meet aerial attacks emanating from carrier bases and from land bases.

    . . . A summation of all of these factors [range factors] indicates that our aerial striking force must have a range of 1,000 miles to meet the carrier threat.

    The Gulf of St. Lawrence area will be the most probable location where an enemy can establish his forces . . .

    . . . Proper dispersion and camouflage on the ground by the enemy may result in less damage to their air force if attacked on the ground than would result in an aerial engagement in which we concentrate our fighters against the invading aircraft.

Spaatz went on to discuss the types of aircraft needed to fulfill the functions and the types of organizations into which they would be incorporated; he concluded that six multipurpose wings would be necessary to protect both coasts and our northern border. Three more would be required for Hawaii, Alaska, and Panama—but the Philippines, he seemed to imply, could not be defended. A divergence between German and U.S. naval thought on the one hand, and U.S. Army Air Corps theory on the other, was apparent in Spaatz's attitude toward ground support (attack) aviation. He suggested that the attack function could be fulfilled by pursuit planes whose primary function was air superiority. (Both the U.S. Navy and the Luftwaffe developed aircraft and organizations especially dedicated to the ground attack role.) Artillery spotters and tactical reconnaissance aircraft would be needed only in the third phase of the war and could be drawn from the National Guard once mobilization began.[44]

If the Air Corps was obsessed with the strategic bombing idea, Spaatz did not show it in the early thirties. He hedged his confidence in bombing by anticipating some of the problems that would later be encountered and some of the ways in which attacking bombers could be opposed. He argued that one of the four principal functions of the multipurpose wing would be to escort the attacking force in warding off enemy pursuit and antiaircraft artillery attacks.[45] Further, he held that bomber formations, if they could be located (radar had not yet been invented), could be successfully attacked from the rear and the flanks, but not from dead ahead. His wing had been experimenting with some success with pursuits bombing the shadows of bomber formations flying across the desert. The idea was that pursuit aircraft could fly above enemy bomber formations and on the same course. They would remain out of the range of the bombers' machine guns and could at leisure release their missiles with time fuses to burst among the bombers, scattering shrapnel in all directions.[46] He worried also that night interceptions might be possible after all. Having read in the open literature of British experiments in that area, Spaatz was concerned enough to write to Air Corps headquarters trying to get some intelligence on the subject.[47] Finally, he was much concerned about the disappointing inaccuracy of his aerial gunners, implying that fighter escorts would indeed be needed.[48]

The ideas not found in Spaatz's correspondence with his colleagues are also important. There is no mention of industrial bombing, of morale bombing, nor of the vital targets to be found in the enemy's economic network. The war envisioned in the early thirties was never in Europe or the Far East—it was always in and around North America.

At the tactical level, in Spaatz's correspondence at least, there is not much about target selection or about the development and effects of bombs—but that is understandable, given the absence of the idea of attacking industry. Similarly, there is little about the need to gather industrial intelligence—in fact, there is little attention to intelligence at all. The concern with the development of air mobility, though, carried over from the twenties.

In the early thirties, the high point each year for the air staff, for tactical commanders, and for the entire Air Corps came during the annual maneuvers. This was the closest, short of war, that airmen could come to testing the validity of their theories about air power. The scenarios on which the maneuvers were based were constrained, of course, by the establishment's incomplete view of what future war would be like. Budget limitations further distanced maneuvers from reality. Finally, the participants were quick to find enough ambiguities to permit constructions of outcomes that favored their own particular services. Notwithstanding these faults, the maneuvers were worthwhile because they gave those who were to be the high commanders in World War II some practical experience in handling moderately large organizations in the field and in discovering in advance some of the problems that would arise once hostilities began. The staffs benefited from the drills they had in planning for deployments and employment even though the exercises seldom approximated real war.

The scenario of the joint Army-Navy maneuvers in the summer of 1930 provided that an attacking naval force would be equipped with three aircraft carriers (the *Langley,* the *Saratoga,* and the *Lexington*) with full complements of aircraft, and a group of battleships. Their mission was to attack the harbor of San Francisco. The defenders had some small naval ships, submarines, and Coast Guard cutters to provide seaborne patrol around San Francisco. The Army's antiaircraft artillery around the harbor was also included. The core of the defense, however, was Spaatz's 7th Bomb Group, which was considerably outnumbered by the aircraft of the aggressor fleet.[49] The Air Corps kept its forces dispersed at a number of airfields around San Francisco.

Carriers had been used in maneuvers before, but the two big ones, the *Lexington* and the *Saratoga,* were new ships and their utility or tactics in war was still an open question. The defenders planned to absorb the first attack from the fleet's aircraft and then shadow the attackers back to their ships. When the blow came from the Navy, the umpires declared that six of the defenders' aircraft were gone. The remainder were launched and caught the aircraft carriers with their planes on deck and with no appreciable air defense aloft. The Air Corps escaped without any theoretical losses, and the mock attack was deemed devastatingly effective. All the forces "destroyed" on the first day were resurrected for the second day. Again, the defenders discovered the aggressor ships and delivered decisive attacks against minor opposition.[50]

At the critique held after the "battle," Spaatz discounted the remarks of the Navy partisans as "their usual alibi about unnatural situations."[51] He was aglow with enthusiasm about the power of his group against carrier threats. One of the lessons of the maneuver, he said, was that naval forces could not successfully attack major shore installations defended by air forces unless they were prepared to accept a suicide mission for their air elements. This was so, he argued, provided the air commanders had the strength of will to use their planes aggressively against the carriers instead of defensively patrolling the air above the protected target. Two additional keys to success for coastal defenders were the use of radio for command and control and the dispersal of defending aircraft to many bases to compound the problem of the aggressor air forces. The latter, Spaatz said, was a major advantage of land-based aviation: it could be directed to recover at any of numerous potential bases, while the seaborne flyers were tied to their ships. Moreover, the carriers could launch and recover just one airplane at a time while whole formations could depart and land at shore bases simultaneously.[52] Post-Pearl Harbor hindsight makes Spaatz's evaluation seem overly optimistic and perhaps a little naîve. Later in the Second World War, however, carrier forces were seldom enthusiastic about approaching a shore defended by the Luftwaffe or the Japanese air forces before those forces had been grievously weakened.

## Return to Washington

Spaatz left California in June, 1933, with his service reputation in fine shape. In a final effectiveness report Hap Arnold characterized him as: "One who can do any job given him. He is an officer who can fill any Air Corps office, group, or wing command, or staff position and fill it to the satisfaction of everyone."[53] The bond between the two men was growing stronger.

When Spaatz arrived in Washington at the end of the month, he was assigned to a key position: head of the Operations and Training Division of the Office of the Chief of the Air Corps,[54] one level up from the office in which he had served when he first came to Washington eight years earlier. Though his responsibilities were steadily increasing, a promotion was not forthcoming, and he continued into his sixteenth year as a major. His office was responsible for writing unit training directives, preparing training manuals of all sorts, writing the plans for the annual maneuvers, monitoring the execution of operations plans, making recommendations on the acquisition and distribution of combat aircraft to the units, and coordinating Air Reserve programs.[55] Much of the work was the same as it had been under Patrick: explaining to the field commanders why they could not have more men, money, and airplanes. There was greater emphasis on all-weather flying techniques and on long-range navigation (over water), training the Air Corps for its new duties derived from the MacArthur-Pratt agreement. During Spaatz's tour there was also much greater emphasis on the development of large bombers of very long range[56] and a growing concern over what other nations were doing, though discussion of industrial bombing was still absent from the correspondence going in and out of his office.

Spaatz's arrival in Washington coincided with an initially almost imperceptible, but gradually growing, buildup of the armed forces. The new president, Franklin D. Roosevelt, had once been Assistant Secretary of the Navy and had a reputation as a naval buff. Appropriations for new ships had been low through the twenties because of limits set on naval building by the various disarmament agreements, but the Congress and the presidents of the time had never brought the Navy up to treaty limits. Now, Roosevelt, partly as an unemployment relief measure, applied new funds first to building up the sea service to agreement limits and then, after the treaties' expiration in 1935, to even higher levels, responding to growing threats in Europe and the Far East. The growth of these threats also helped win more funds for the Air Corps.

Spaatz was plunged immediately into the issue of how the air arm should be organized. The Army had been wrestling with this question since the First World War. During the war, airmen wanted to assign to the operational control of ground unit commanders only those aircraft dedicated to battlefield reconnaissance and artillery spotting. They wanted to keep the rest in a centrally controlled "strategical" organization to be used for independent operations against the enemy air force and his rear areas. The ground Army had been concerned about these independent tendencies among the airmen, and General Pershing himself had purged the word "strategical" from unit titles. Instead, agreeing that there would be benefit in holding some aviation under centralized control, he assigned it the title of "General Headquarters Reserve." From the outset, therefore, there was agreement between the airmen and soldiers that some advantage was to be derived from centralized control of air units. The problem arose in deciding specifically how those centralized units would be used. Though that issue was not resolved in the twenties, a "General Headquarters Air Force" was included in the war plans. The implementation of such an organization, however, was to be undertaken only after the outbreak of war. At that point the air units would come directly under the control of the theater commander.

In 1933, as Spaatz arrived on the air staff, an Army board under Gen. Hugh Drum was considering this question of air organization and recommended that the General Headquarters Air Force idea be implemented during peacetime. Though some tactical units would be left under the control of the corps area commanders, the bulk of combat aviation would be assigned to this GHQ Air Force. They would be directly under the operational control of the chief of staff during peacetime and under the theater commander after the onset of hostilities.[57]

In the summer of 1933, the General Staff of the Army asked the Air Corps to study the role of this potential GHQ Air Force and to revise the basic training regulation governing the use of air elements in the new coast defense mission. This order was to occupy much of Spaatz's subsequent two years in the capital. The assistant chief of the Air Corps, Oscar Westover, was the senior official responsible for developing the plans, but the detailed work fell to Spaatz's office. The first plan sent by the Air Corps to the General Staff was rejected. The soldiers thought that the airmen had not related their supporting air plan to the parent war plan and suspected that their purpose had been to devise a scheme to increase appropriations for the Air Corps.[58]

In addition, the Office of the Chief of Air Corps in general, and Spaatz's Training and Operations Division in particular, were unable to make much headway in revising the basic air doctrinal document (Army Training Regulations 440–15). Admiral Pratt had retired in the summer of 1933, and the future of the Air Corps' coastal defense mission was too tenuous to permit confidence that a new regulation would live long enough to justify the cost.

## The Airmail Fiasco

Progress on plans and recommendations for a basic air doctrine was interrupted during the first half of 1934 when the Air Corps became involved in carrying the mail. Early in the year, President Franklin Roosevelt was told by his advisors and by Senator Hugo Black that the airmail contracts that had been let during the Hoover administration were illegal—

that they had been awarded to a few of the biggest airline operators through collusion and the effect was to squeeze small companies out of business. In those early years of civil aviation, the airmail business was a substantial part of the whole, and winning such a contract usually made the difference between prosperity and bankruptcy. President Roosevelt was advised that cancellation of the contracts would be both legal and proper, but he was also advised to delay action until June, to give the government time to negotiate new contracts. The president would have none of it, and he sent Assistant Postmaster Harlee Branch to investigate whether the Air Corps could carry the mail and whether the job could be undertaken without delay.[59]

General Foulois, the Air Corps chief, met with Branch early on the 9th of February. The proposition was laid before him in the utmost secrecy, and he asked for permission to call in some of his assistants to help evaluate its feasibility. When the call came to the Munitions Building, it was for Lt. Col. James E. Chaney, Foulois's executive officer, and Carl Spaatz, head of the Operations and Training Division. Spaatz was out, so Foulois directed that Capt. Edwin House be brought along. The three Air Corps men studied the problem for two or three hours, and then Foulois assured Branch that the Air Corps could indeed carry the mails and could commence operations within "a week or ten days."[60]

Foulois had consulted neither his military superior, Gen. Douglas MacArthur, nor his chief operations subordinate, Maj. Carl Spaatz. He had undertaken a major commitment for the Air Corps with little reservation. At about the same time, President Roosevelt was holding a cabinet meeting at which the airmail contracts were discussed. At that caucus, Secretary of War Walter Dern, also without consulting anybody in the Army, assured Roosevelt that the Air Corps could carry the mail. That same day, the president issued the order to cancel the contracts and to have the Army carry the mails commencing on the 19th of February, just ten days away. It occurred to Foulois late in the day that he should have kept his superiors informed, and he sought an appointment with General MacArthur's deputy, Gen. Hugh Drum. It was not soon enough, however, for MacArthur first heard of the president's action through the media. The chief of staff was not greatly upset, though; he said he would help Foulois, but that it was the latter's "ball game." Foulois was also cautioned that no Army money could go into the effort.[61]

The period that followed was not a shining hour for the Air Corps.

Its aircraft were designed for combat, not for carrying the mail. As combat in those days was largely confined to daytime and fair weather, the Army airplanes were not equipped for adverse weather and night flying. Moreover, they did not have the payload capacity that the airliners had, and there was a serious lack of experienced pilots.

Foulois appointed his assistant, Brig. Gen. Oscar Westover, to command the airmail effort and assigned Spaatz to run the operation. Spaatz had little to work with. It was decided to avoid disrupting the professional schools and the training programs of the Air Corps, but that is where the most experienced fliers were. The line units were composed largely of young reserve lieutenants just out of pilot school engaged in getting a year or two of flying before returning to civilian life. Compared to the airline pilots, their experience level was low, and few of them knew much about flying in bad weather. Some last-minute attempts were made to fill these gaps by sending the Air Corps' few instrument flight instructors around to the various airmail stations to give crash courses to the young pilots, but that could not take the place of formal training and practice.

To make matters worse, the Army started carrying the mail on the 19th of February, in the depth of winter. The weather that year was far worse than the norm, and from the outset the Army fliers suffered from a rash of accidents. The crashes, as bad as they were, were highly magnified in the press and in the halls of Congress. The political atmosphere was particularly bitter: the Republicans in Congress and substantial portions of the press were looking for ways to criticize the president. The airlines were smarting, too, and they had some powerful voices that were quick to find fault with the Army's operation of their former routes. Eddie Rickenbacker voiced the concerns of his airline colleagues, and Charles Lindbergh added his protests to the clamor. From the outset, Foulois tried to emphasize to his people the priority of flying safety, but the combination of vile weather and the inexperience of his pilots led them into traps, and the accidents continued. Finally, the political heat got so great that President Roosevelt called Foulois and MacArthur to the White House for a dressing down and demanded that the Chief of the Air Corps conduct further operations only with the maximum concern for the safety of his crews. It was a bad hour for Foulois.[62]

During the second week in March, General Foulois ordered a halt to operations while he sought ways to reduce the risk. He toured some of the airfields, with Spaatz as his pilot, to seek out ways to improve flying safety. The rules for dispatching pilots were stiffened, and some of the least experienced were taken from the line, while others were restricted to flight in daytime or ideal nighttime conditions. After a week, Foulois returned to Washington and ordered resumption of the operation. Though two more deaths occurred after the standdown, things began to go much more smoothly. That was partly due to the improving weather as spring wore on. But the stiffer regulation of flights and the growing experience level of crew members also helped.

By then, though, the decision had been made to return the job to the commercial operators, and the Army ended its involvement by the first of June. Twelve lives had been lost, and many airplanes had been wrecked. The boast was made that not one piece of mail had been lost, but the Army carried only a fraction of the amount that had been handled by the airlines before February, and the cost for doing so was substantially higher.[63]

For Benjamin Foulois the airmail operation was bad news; for the Army Air Corps the outcome was somewhat beneficial; for the airlines, the result in the long run was all to the good. It seems fair to charge General Foulois with making hasty commitments without sufficiently checking his facts. He had a full measure of the air arm's legendary "can do" spirit and it got him into trouble on more than one occasion.[64] But Secretary of War Walter Dern had also assured the president that the task could be done handily, and he did so without checking his facts with Foulois, MacArthur, Spaatz, or anyone else.[65] Still, there were voices urging the president to move with caution while the decision was being made. Instead, he forged ahead. When the results turned sour, President Roosevelt called in MacArthur (who had had no voice in the decision) and Foulois and heaped criticism on them. Soon afterward, Foulois became the subject of a congressional investigation into the award of aircraft construction contracts. He retired in 1935 and was replaced by his deputy, Oscar Westover.

There is room to suppose that Westover was selected because the General Staff thought he might be less troublesome than his predecessor. He had spent his first decade of service in the infantry,[66] which gave him a lower status among airmen than the "early birds" like Foulois and Arnold, who were in aviation from the beginning. Moreover, Westover was reputed to have deplored the antics of the more radical officers around Mitchell in the early twenties, and he made a big issue of loyalty at the outset of his service as chief of the Air Corps.[67] While all of these qualities probably recommended him to the ground segment of the Army, reports from airmen suggest he was less than popular among his own men.[68]

For the Air Corps, the airmail fiasco did have some positive effects. Foulois later claimed that the airmail experience was an excellent test of air corps capabilities. The weaknesses he had been complaining about were proven, and Congress loosened the purse strings to provide funds for the building of a respectable air force. Another favorable outcome was the convening of the Baker Board, which gave decisive support to reorganizing the Air Corps.

The airlines, of course, benefited. They subsequently retrieved their contracts and airmail remained for a long time one of the pillars of their prosperity. Mail was never again carried on Army aircraft.

Spaatz did not share in the setback suffered by his boss. He did learn a good deal about public relations and about survival in Washington. Possibly the experience contributed to his growing reputation for being tight-lipped and cautious enough not to make hasty commitments like the one that had put Foulois between two grindstones.

## The Baker Board

A more or less typical administrative response to difficulties, then as now, was to appoint a board or commission to consider the problem. The airmail difficulties were no exception. After failing to recruit Charles Lindbergh or Orville Wright for the task, the War Department appointed its ex-secretary, Newton D. Baker, to head a board that would consider the defects and take up the issue of air organization raised by the Drum Board. General Drum himself was the executive vice chairman of the Baker Board. Though his influence on the outcome was important, some prominent airmen were appointed to the board as well: Jimmy Doolittle, General Foulois, and Edgar Gorrell. The nonmilitary members were leaders from academe and government.[69]

The general conclusion of the Baker Board report, issued in mid-July 1934, was that air power could not be decisive in independent action in war. It further concluded that there was no immediate air threat against the United States nor any realistic prospect of surface invasion by any probable combination of enemies. Consequently, it recommended that air power continue to be organized as a part of the Army and that the Drum Board's proposal to create a peacetime General Headquarters Air Force be adopted.[70] Foulois signed the majority report, and only Jimmy Doolittle filed a minority statement, advocating creation of an independent air force immediately. Even Doolittle's report stated that if the independent air force proved to be not feasible at that time, the majority's recommendation should be implemented. Much of aviation literature since has condemned the Baker group for its conservatism and lauded Doolittle for his independence of mind.[71] Notwithstanding the unwelcome statements about the limitations of independent air action and the criticism of excessive partisanship on the part of the Air Corps, most airmen embraced the board's recommendation to create a peacetime GHQ Air Force "as a step in the right direction."[72]

The Baker Board's recommendation to activate the GHQ Air Force revived the earlier interest in developing a basic doctrinal statement. This time, however, the initial draft of the new doctrine was prepared in the War Plans Division of the Army General Staff rather than in Spaatz's office. Its sponsor was Brig. Gen. Charles E. Kilbourne. Though his draft was in for a rough ride at the Air Corps Tactical School, and has sometimes been painted as a reactionary document, it did compromise the hard-line Army ground position in favor of some of the airmen's ideas.[73] Kilbourne's draft asserted that a decision in war could only be obtained on the battlefield; this implied that the infantry was "the queen of battle" and that all other combat arms and support branches were auxiliary. Still, the War Plans Division draft allowed the GHQ Air Force some independent missions: the defense of the coasts, the air defense of rear areas, and other roles beyond the influence of the ground forces. The General Staff's version of air doctrine made it clear, however, that the primary mission (after the establishment of air superiority) was direct support of the ground forces.[74]

A pillar of the airmen's arguments had been the notion that the first phase of any war would be an air battle—that the air forces would have to grapple with one another from the outset, before the armies and navies could be mobilized and moved into fighting position. The corollary was that while the surface arms could depend on a cadre that would be the nucleus of much larger forces mobilized from civilian sources, the air force would have to be maintained at its full combat strength continuously to be able to move instantly against any unexpected threat that might develop.[75]

Since Douglas MacArthur had become chief of staff, the Army had moved, to some degree, towards the airmen's view of the use of airpower and of the way in which the U.S. might be confronted with war. It had conceded that an air phase of the war would precede contact between surface forces and that the direction of the GHQ Air Force and the selection of targets might be left to the air commander during that phase. This was reflected in Kilbourne's initial draft of Training Regulation 440–15, which envisioned the kinds of targets to be struck in the air phase as being mostly military. It did allow that civilian population centers might be attacked, but only in retaliation for enemy attacks on American cities.[76]

General Kilbourne's paper was sent to the various divisions of the General Staff, to the Air Corps Tactical School, and to the Office of the Chief of Air Corps. Spaatz prepared a critique of the document for General Foulois's executive officer. He feared that the new training regulation would retard the development of strategic bombing doctrine and technology because of its emphasis on the direct support of ground forces. Spaatz argued that there was insufficient recognition that the geographic position of the United States probably meant the air phase of any war would be longer than it would be for countries with more powerful land neighbors. He feared that the War Plans Division's view of the GHQ Air Force "might militate against the continued development of the ultra long-range bomber." Though Spaatz did not advocate an attack on enemy cities by U.S. forces, his commentary did reflect the most advanced thought being preached at the Air Corps Tactical School when he wrote:[77]

> The first hostile blows will probably not be struck at our coasts but by air against our heart, i.e., against centers of industry, of transportation, of finance, and of the government itself. Such attacks would come over the seas but not necessarily on them and from land bases which our Army cannot reach or our Navy cannot approach without the grave risk which would attend the employment of sea-based aviation and seacraft against land-based aircraft.

Criticism by the Air Corps Tactical School was equally spirited along the same lines, and it opposed the statement of the War Plans Division that independent air operations could not by themselves be decisive in war.[78]

In the end, the new version of Training Regulation 440–15 did not respond to the objections of the most radical airmen. It remained much the same as when Kilbourne had first written it, recognizing that there could be independent missions for the GHQ Air Force, but insisting still that air power's primary role was to support the ground combat arms which would be decisive instruments in any war. The new regulation envisioned different methods of command and control according to the phase of the war being fought. In the "strategical" phase, that is, before the ground arms of the two sides had gained contact, the GHQ Air Force commander would get his mission started in general terms and then be free to choose his own targets. Later, once the armies were firmly in contact on the ground, the theater commander would give detailed instruction to the airmen on target selection. It was this latter feature which caused some resentment among the fliers.[79] As chief of the Training and Operations Division of the Air Staff, Carl Spaatz was at the vortex of this doctrinal activity and responsible for preparing many of the Air Corps position papers on the subject. He helped move the Army in the direction of the airmen's goals, but he could not go as far as he would have liked because the "ultra long-range" aircraft that might substantiate his theories were not yet flying.

## Back to the Classroom

In the summer of 1935, Spaatz was becoming impatient with life in the capital, even to the point where he was looking forward to his new assignment to attend the Command and General Staff College.[80] Spaatz was never an enthusiastic student and had long avoided going to the school at Fort Leavenworth, Kansas. By 1935, however, the two-year course was being shortened to one year and that made the thought of attendance less intolerable to him. Still, on the eve of his departure from Washington, his enthusiasm for the future of airpower was substantially greater than his optimism about attending the professional schools of the Army. He privately remarked to his friend Arnold: "I am going to Leavenworth not because I expect it will do me any good, but primarily because I am ordered there and secondarily to get away from here [Washington]." In the same letter, he discussed the B-15 bomber, which was then being developed, and closed with the words: "Airpower is going to be an entirely different thing than what we have visualized in the distant past and in the future is going to justify our most rosy dreams."[81] Whatever the frustrations of the airmail crisis and the struggles to develop a founding doctrine for the GHQ Air Force, Spaatz's hopes for independent airpower remained strong.

Spaatz left little trace of his year at the Command and General Staff School, for no thesis or papers of his have been preserved. George

Stratemeyer and Lewis Brereton, both old friends, were on the staff at Leavenworth when he arrived. Hoyt Vandenberg, who had been about a decade behind Spaatz at West Point and was later to succeed him as the Air Force's chief of staff, was a classmate at Leavenworth. It may be that Spaatz did not do much to hide his lack of enthusiasm for the school.[82] He emerged with the grade of "very satisfactory." Only one student in his class got a lower rating.[83] Spaatz's final efficiency report recommended against his selection for either high command or general staff duty. That was serious enough to elicit the remark that: "The Faculty Board considered the general character of work to warrant unfavorable entries (to the efficiency report)."[84] Whatever the judgment of the soldiers at Leavenworth, their comments did not seem to hurt Spaatz with the Air Corps establishment—they may, in fact, have helped. Upon graduation, Spaatz, who had been promoted to lieutenant colonel while a student, received a choice assignment. He was sent to Langley Field as executive officer to the commander of the 2d Wing of the new GHQ Air Force. Whatever the root of the difficulty at Leavenworth, Carl Spaatz nonetheless landed on his feet.

At Langley, Brig. Gen. H. Conger Pratt was commander of both the 2d Wing and of the base, one of the largest in the Air Corps. Pratt left the running of the base to Spaatz while he concentrated on the tactical unit. Spaatz was well acquainted with the kinds of problems faced by a base commander from his experiences at Rockwell, Selfridge, and March Fields. Since Langley was the host base not only for the 2d Wing but also for the headquarters of GHQ Air Force, Spaatz's burdens were complicated by the presence of so many Air Corps senior officers. Also, the proximity of Langley to Washington meant that he had to cope with many distinguished visitors. Fortunately, the Air Corps soon managed to name a separate commander for the base, Col. Walter Weaver, allowing Spaatz to give all his attention to the 2d Wing.[85]

The headquarters of the GHQ Air Force was commanded by Frank Andrews, who was given the temporary rank of major general. The Spaatzes and the Andrews lived on the base not far from one another. The girls of both families were about the same age, so Tooey's acquaintance with one of the rising stars of the Air Corps was on both an official and social plane.[86] It is conceivable that the General Staff saw in Andrews some of Westover's pliability. He had been Westover's classmate at West Point and had spent time in the cavalry before he won his wings. He had been in Germany during the Mitchell agitation of the early twenties,[87] and though he ultimately became friends with Mitchell,[88] Andrews was not as closely identified with him as were Spaatz and Arnold. Col. Hugh Knerr, Andrews' chief of staff at Langley, thought the General Staff was mistaken in thinking that Andrews would be more pliable than Foulois and Billy Mitchell had been.[89]

If Andrews and Westover were seen as "safe" options by the General Staff, the same could not be said of many of the airmen who made up the initial cadre of GHQ Air Force. In addition to Spaatz, there were others who had been around Mitchell during the twenties. George Kenney was assigned to the headquarters staff. Hap Arnold was given command of the West Coast Wing (the 1st) of Andrews' command and a jump in rank of two grades. Follett Bradley, like Hugh Knerr, a Naval Academy graduate, was also on the staff. Knerr had some reputation for being a maverick (and so perceived himself).[90] Robert Olds was there, too, as the commander of the 2d Wing's elite bomber group. Because of a wide disparity in rank and age, Spaatz did not have close relations with a relatively new man assigned to Langley, Curtis LeMay, who was beginning to attract attention as one of the pioneers in long-range, over-water navigation.[91]

As executive officer of the 2d Wing, Spaatz functioned as an extension of General Pratt. The organization included bomber, pursuit, and reconnaissance groups. Spaatz was involved in the personnel, intelligence, operations, and supply functions of all of them. Though procurement of new aircraft in the early thirties had never satisfied the airmen or reached the goals Congress had established in the twenties, the Air Corps did get more in the way of new equipment and additional men than did any other combat branch of the Army. During the Foulois era, the B-17, B-15, and B-19 projects were funded—something that could never have happened without at least a modicum of cooperation from above.[92] Spaatz, then head of Foulois's Training and Operations Division, had a key role in planning all those projects, and now was on hand at Langley when the most important one, the B-17, reached fruition, and Fortresses were delivered to the 2nd Bomb Wing. In fact, Spaatz himself was aboard the first Fortress to land at Langley in early 1937.[93] The Air Corps was able to obtain only thirteen B-17s in this first increment, but for the airmen, it was a case of love at first sight. Before testing was completed, and even though the prototype had crashed, the Air Corps recommended to the General Staff that a substantial order be placed with Boeing. The General Staff would not go further than the thirteen aircraft.[94]

The Air Corps was fortunate to get even these, since two years earlier the program had nearly collapsed. The ground branches of the Army had been starved for money and people in order to build up the Air Corps, and their situation was becoming desperate. Admiral Pratt retired, the Navy withdrew its agreement, and the coastal defense justification for the long-range bomber mission was no longer secure. Moreover, much of the foundation for the Air Corps' desire for long-range heavy bombers was based on speculation. The First World War had done more to substantiate the importance of aviation as an auxiliary to ground forces than to make a case for strategic bombing. The "lesson" that the General Staff and other ground soldiers thought they saw in the wars going on in China, Ethiopia, and Spain was that high-altitude-level bombing was ineffectual. The bombing of Madrid, they thought, had effects just the opposite of those intended. On the other hand, in Spain especially, small aircraft working in close support of the troops seemed to be deadly. These notions were shared by the new chief of staff, Malin Craig. Thus, after the first thirteen Fortresses were delivered to Langley, the program came to a halt. The new emphasis was on small airplanes, which were deemed better for the direct support of troops in the field than the B-17 and other large aircraft. Finally, the General Staff argued that the national policy of the U.S. was so clearly defensive, and the long-range heavy bomber was so clearly an offensive weapon (and had been so identified at the World Disarmament Conference a few years earlier), that the acquisition of such bombers would emit an entirely erroneous signal to foreign powers.[95]

Still, the thirteen Fortresses were enough to start building an experience base for training, logistical, and technical improvement programs that would make the B-17 one of the pillars of the U.S. Army Air Forces throughout World War II. Further, they helped keep the problems of the Air Corps before the public eye and served to refine the ideas that would govern the application of strategic airpower in the war to come. In February, 1938, for example, a flight of B-17s from Langley flew a goodwill mission to Argentina for the inauguration of Dr. Robert M. Ortiz as president, and in May, Andrews sent a flight of three Fortresses far out to sea to intercept a simulated enemy invader, the Italian liner *Rex*. The interception was nominally a part of the spring maneuvers, but one of the airplanes had a battery of radio journalists aboard and the trip received a good deal of attention in the press—just as intended by Ira Eaker, then serving at Air Corps headquarters in a public relations position.[96]

These missions did more than just keep the B-17 and the Air Corps before the public eye. The technology and techniques of over-water navigation were being improved, and important modifications were made to the aircraft as a result of their service testing. When the initial requirements for the B-17 were established, the Air Corps did not demand much in the way of defensive armaments, believing that the airplane would be so fast that fighters could not catch it. Thus, there was no reason to weigh down the craft with excessive defensive armament when the same weight of bombs would enhance the Fortresses' primary mission.[97]

When measured in new ideas, the Langley tour was no more than a finishing school for Carl Spaatz. The notion that the "bomber would always get through" seemed to be confirmed by the extent to which the B-17 exceeded the performance of the B-9 and B-10 of the early thirties. The heavy bomber was seen first as a means to attack enemy seaborne invasions and then as a means of reinforcing outlying possessions like Hawaii and Panama.

Another idea reinforced for Spaatz during his Langley assignment was that everything possible must be done to enhance the mobility of tactical air forces. Thus, the air arm of the Army was divided into two branches: the GHQ Air Force for combat, and the Air Corps for support, including individual training, research and development, supply, and the like. Organization at the lower level within the GHQ Air Force was also divided into combat and support forces, into wings and bases. The mission of the wings was to fight; the mission of the bases was to replenish and maintain the fighting forces.[98] As Carl Spaatz was involved in both dimensions of this work, while acting commander of the Langley Base and as executive officer of the premier tactical wing, he gained firsthand experience with this concept of organization.

This notion that the separate functions of preparing force for war and employing force in war be placed in different organizations had led to open controversy within the Army. At the time the GHQ Air Force was conceived, Benjamin Foulois strongly recommended that it be put under the chief of the Air Corps for the sake of unity of command among the airmen in peacetime. The General Staff disagreed, arguing that the whole idea was a wartime plan and, therefore, the GHQ ought to report to the Army chief of staff in peacetime and to the theater commander during hostilities. It has been suggested that the General Staff took this position precisely to keep the air arm divided within itself, thereby making it easier to manage.[99] If that were the intent, it was a clever move of bureaucratic politics. The dilemma was that by providing for unity of command during war, the Army practically guaranteed that there would be conflict within the Air Corps during peacetime. The arrangement made the commander of the GHQ Air Force and the chief of the Air Corps both subordinate to the General Staff and on an equal plane. Yet the flow of materiel and personnel for the former was controlled by the latter.

The arrangement stimulated a good deal of argument between Andrews and Westover. When Westover was killed in an air crash at the Burbank, California, airport in the fall of 1938, the unity of command problem did not go away. Hap Arnold, Spaatz's close friend and patron, was chosen to replace Westover. Although Arnold had been a good friend of Andrews, both were ambitious men and both were popular enough to have substantial followings within the air arm. Since the new Army chief of staff, Malin Craig, had been the corps' area commander under whom Arnold had served in California, Hap was better acquainted with him than was Andrews.

Finally, at the end of Andrews' tour at Langley in the spring of 1939, the General Staff was persuaded to place the GHQ Air Force directly under the chief of the Air Corps and thus put almost all of its functions under a single commander—Hap Arnold.[100] That occurred at the time of a changing of the guard at Langley. Hugh Knerr, Andrews' chief of staff, had retired in 1938. Andrews himself reverted to his permanent rank of colonel and was transferred to San Antonio. He had committed the sin of speaking out too strongly in a speech, on January 16, on the deplorable combat status of the air arm. His pronouncements were at odds with assurances given to the president by the secretary of war, Harry H. Woodring. Delos Emmons, who had taken command of the 1st Wing at March when Arnold came back to Washington, now moved up to command the GHQ Air Force. Many of the initial cadre had already departed when the commander was replaced.

Though they could not know it, the two years the Spaatzes spent at Langley would be the last time they would live on an Air Corps base. They were pleasant years, the last before Europe erupted in war. In off-duty time there was tennis, sailing, and golf (the course was in nearby Yorktown and was actually built on part of the battlefield). There was frequent socializing, usually ending in intense discussions of the needs of the newly established GHQ Air Force, commanded by the much-admired Frank Andrews. In addition to the usual post activities, Walter Weaver, the C.O., asked Ruth to form a dramatic club, and some excellent talent was discovered. Capt. Dudley Hale and his wife Anne were soon known as the Lunts of Langley Field, and Bill Kepner, the future head of the Fighter Command in England, proved to be a fine dramatic actor.

It was at Langley that Tooey's wife and daughters talked him into changing the spelling of his name to Spaatz. The correct pronunciation of the name is "spahtz," but it too often became "spats," which had irritated Ruth and the girls for years. It didn't bother Tooey, but Ruth knew that one branch of the family in Europe spelled the name with two a's, and she hoped the unusual spelling would alert people to the correct pronunciation, without changing the identity of the name. Bob Olds had recently changed his name from Oldys, and he sent Ruth to the lawyer in Hampton who had helped him. Fortunately, the legal procedure was simple, for Tooey had stated he would have nothing to do with the project if it entailed a court appearance! So the spelling change became official, and Ruth reports that it indeed helped, especially for Tattie, who was off to Sweet Briar College that year. Beckie at this time was spending five days a week at Miss Turnbull's School in Norfolk and coming home for weekends. Six-year-old Carla (Boops) was the only resident child the last year at Langley.[101]

But the pleasant years of peacetime were coming to an end as war clouds gathered over Europe. Immediately after Arnold became chief of Air Corps in the fall of 1938, he "borrowed" Spaatz from Langley to work with him in Washington on a temporary basis. In early 1939, the transfer was made permanent when Spaatz was assigned to the Plans Division of the Office of the Chief of Air Corps, later becoming the division chief.[102]

# Chapter V

## GOING TO WAR

When the Spaatzes left Langley and moved to Washington in January 1939, they moved into an old house in Georgetown with a view towards buying and remodeling it. That plan did not work out because the place was part of an estate tied up in litigation, but they were happy there for a couple of years.

Their oldest daughter, Katharine (''Tattie''), was planning to go to Europe that summer to begin a year of study at the Sorbonne, in Paris, France. She was on the point of leaving when her father came home for lunch one day—an unusual thing for him. Although he seldom put his foot down about anything with his girls, he forbade Tattie to make the trip on the grounds that he felt war was imminent in Europe. Tattie's professor at Sweet Briar scoffed at Spaatz's notion, but Spaatz was adamant and refused to let her go. The second daughter, Rebecca, was attending a private school in Norfolk, Virginia, and she had remained behind to finish the school year. Already she was showing her bent for music, and the following year, she entered the Peabody Conservatory in Baltimore, Maryland. The youngest, Carla, was only seven and attended Mrs. Cook's School on Massachusetts Avenue, Washington, D.C. (now the Sheridan School).[1]

Technology almost caught up with Carl Spaatz that winter. Just as he got to Washington, the Air Corps flight surgeons were introducing a new device for measuring the condition of flyers' hearts: the electrocardiograph. The machine brought down Tooey's old friend and mentor from Issoudun days, Mike Kilner. It identified a heart problem that caused his retirement just as the war was coming on. For a time it looked as though it might happen to Spaatz as well. He was grounded in January, but things on the Air Staff were so hectic then that he could not be rounded up for a complete evaluation until March. After he spent a week at Walter Reed Army Hospital in Washington, the doctors decided that the cardiogram had merely identified a heart murmur that Spaatz had probably had all his life. He escaped Kilner's fate and was restored to flying status.[2]

Heart murmur notwithstanding, Spaatz still was frequenting the squash courts. But the hectic pace in the Munitions Building interfered with his game more and more. Nor was there much time for family recreation or visits to the group in Boyertown.[3]

The Spaatzes' settling-in this time was more or less permanent. There would be many trials and tribulations and detours along the way, and several changes of residence, but the nation's capital would serve as the family's home base for the rest of Tooey's military career and for his retirement as well.

## Prelude to War

The main activity of Arnold's Air Staff between 1939 and 1941 was organizing for war. Spaatz, by virtue of his positions as chief of the Plans Division and later chief of the Air Staff, was necessarily involved in the day-to-day work of trying to acquire the wherewithal and to put it into the hands of people trained to use it. The principal issues that occupied him during those years were continuation of the Air Corps commitment to the heavy bomber as the main air instrument, the debate on whether unescorted heavy bombers could penetrate enemy airspace in daylight, the amount and kind of equipment that would have to be allocated to support of the growing armies, and the need to provide the British with materiel while conserving enough of it to train and build American defense forces in the event that the English went under.

When Spaatz got to Washington, the Nazi threat was beginning to be recognized by a large segment of the U.S. electorate, though the isolationists were still very strong. Within the past few years Germany had remilitarized the Rhineland, invaded Austria, destroyed the Treaty of Versailles, rearmed itself, intervened in the Spanish Civil War, and finally, in September 1938, taken over Czechoslovakia's heavily German Sudetenland by agreement at Munich. Though the Roosevelt administration still spoke words of peace, it had begun a rearmament program with the hope that the economic and financial muscle of the United States would be enough to head off participation in any new world war. Just two months after the Spaatzes arrived in the capital, Hitler's pretense of German national reunification was exposed when the Nazis took over the remainder of Czechoslovakia—the first of Hitler's conquests that could not be represented as merely the gathering of Germans under the flag of the fatherland.

At the time, the U.S. Army was the least prepared of the U.S. Armed Forces. Its numbers were low, its arms were few and old, and its doctrine was traditional. It did have some elaborate mobilization plans, but the pressure necessary for their implementation had not yet arisen. The Navy was somewhat better off. It had resumed ship building in the previous six years, some of those ships were coming on line, and its carrier and aviation doctrines were more advanced than were those in other navies. The Army's Air Corps was somewhat better prepared than its parent organization. It had a modern and well-articulated doctrine of employment. Though there were some serious defects in its procurement programs for men and in some categories of attack and fighter aircraft, the Air Corps had a good bomber, the Flying Fortress. And Spaatz was experienced in both flying and managing it. There also was another good heavy bomber in the works—the B-24 Liberator, which was to become the running mate of the B-17. Several medium bombers were being developed, but the air corps lagged in fighters of all types and especially in long-range escorts. Although the P-47 Thunderbolt was in the design stage, the heavy bomber was at the very core of the air arm's theory of the employment of airpower.

The B-17 had recovered from a close brush with death the previous year. In the summer of 1938, Malin Craig had been persuaded that the B-17 should be dropped altogether from future procurement in favor of smaller bombers. That caused a good deal of consternation within the Air Corps, but then Hitler came to the rescue at Munich.[4] There he had humiliated France, then deemed the world's greatest land power, and Great Britain, whose Navy was clearly far superior to that of Germany. It was widely perceived that he had achieved great political gains by threatening to use his superior air force.[5] Roosevelt's reaction was to set in motion a massive preparedness program, emphasizing air power. A little later, he sent a delegation to an inter-American conference in Lima, Peru, with instructions to work for an international approach to hemispheric defense. The Declaration of Lima was duly issued, proclaiming the common interest in such a defense and the intention to cooperate toward that end. This political decision at the highest levels resurrected the B-17 program. Now, greater funds became available for the Air Corps, and the expansion of the declared mission from coast defense to hemispheric defense provided near-perfect justification for the restoration of the long-range bomber program.[6]

Suddenly it was no longer a question of money, but rather one of time. By October 1938, the problem had changed from getting the maximum number of airplanes and people for a small amount of money to generating the greatest amount of airpower in the shortest possible time from the material and human resources available to the United States, no matter what the cost. The first step was to prepare a detailed expansion program for presentation to Congress, and Arnold put his staff to the task. Two days before Carl Spaatz officially assumed his new duties as chief of the Plans Section of the Executive Division, Office of the Chief of Air Corps, President Roosevelt went to Congress with the defense program.[7] The new scheme called for the creation of industrial capacity to produce 10,000 airplanes a year, with the capability of doubling that output. It also included provisions for expanding units, airfields, and training programs. Notwithstanding the limitations of the air force in January 1939, the political decision had been taken that opened an awesome vista for the airmen.[8] Spaatz stepped in as head planner at this critical moment.

As breathtaking as the airpower vista was, it would have to be built on the existing Air Corps. In January 1939, the Air Corps was not far removed numerically from where the Luftwaffe had stood in 1935 when the latter's existence was first acknowledged. The Air Corps had about seventeen hundred airplanes on the line, but many of them were training or obsolescent aircraft. It had eight hundred or so that were classed as fit for combat, but there were only fourteen four-engine bombers, the primary instruments, in the whole force.[9] By way of contrast, just before its onslaught against Poland later that year, the Luftwaffe had four thousand good airplanes.[10] The aircraft had all been tested in Spain and, after 1937, had been proven superior to the Russian planes then in use. The majority of the German planes were bombers, though there were some good fighters. All were dedicated to cooperating with the Army, even though the Luftwaffe was organized as a separate air force with a coordinate status with the ground forces and Navy.

At the time President Roosevelt addressed Congress on the need to build a great air force, the Army Air Corps contained but 20,000 officers and men. The officer corps was headed by a contingent most of whom had experienced combat in France (though Arnold himself had not). The majority of them had also gone to the Air Corps Tactical School and to the Command and General Staff School or the Army War College. The training center at Randolph Field, Texas, was capable of producing 750 new pilots a year. Arnold felt that by going to shift work that output could be doubled.[11] Fewer than 2,000 of the Air Corps personnel were pilots. Practically none of the officers below the rank of major had any combat experience, and these were the people who were flying and heading the tactical units.

Hitler struck again in September, 1939, this time against Poland. The Polish air force was caught asleep on its fields, and the Wehrmacht's great pincer movements eliminated the Polish ground forces in a matter of days. Russian soldiers marched in from the east to ingest their half of Poland, and then turned to annex the Baltic states and seize parts of Finland. For a time that winter, the world was in the calm eye of the hurricane, but when spring came, the Germans burst forth with fury into Norway, Denmark, and then France. The rapid fall of the French army sent shock waves around the world. The Japanese increased their effort to make the most of the West's troubles. American complacency, born of her sheltered position behind two oceans, withered. The collapse of France was so rapid that even the Germans seemed a little bewildered by it. It was several weeks before they were able to collect themselves for the next step: an air assault on the British Isles.

Through it all, Carl Spaatz was at Henry Arnold's elbow as the nation labored to help the British with one hand and to build up its own forces with the other. In May 1940, Arnold sent him to observe events in the European war. Spaatz sailed to Europe aboard the SS *Manhattan,* which made port at Naples and then at Genoa. He crossed France as the Germans were making their great drive in the west, and he departed Paris for London just before they arrived. The next four months, during the Battle of Britain, were a whirlwind of visits for him to the stations of the RAF, meetings with many of the English leaders (military and civilian), flying British planes, and getting reports back to Arnold in Washington, while enduring the frequent air raids.[12]

Though the British were not ready to share the secrets of ULTRA (the breaking of the German military codes by duplicating their coding machines), virtually all of the rest of their classified material was made available to Spaatz and the other American observers. One of the keys to the British success in frustrating Hitler's air assault on their island was radar. Spaatz visited the RAF control rooms that received the data from radar and other sources and collated it into a meaningful picture for the ground controllers of the defending fighters. He observed also that the British were finding a solution to the problem of discriminating between friendly and enemy airplanes. They had developed a device called "pip squeak": it emitted an electronic signal that showed up on the radar screens, enabling the controllers to identify and direct their own aircraft against those of the enemy. Spaatz came away with a thorough understanding of the entire reporting and command and control structure of Fighter Command, and he transmitted what he learned back to the United States. The information was useful in some of the point defense systems (such as at Pearl Harbor) that the U.S. was setting up, though the Air Corps in general remained committed to the notion that the best defense is a good offense. The need for a high volume of fire was the thing that had most impressed Spaatz about the fighters themselves.[13]

As for tactical support aviation, Spaatz got reinforcement for the Air Corps' hostility towards the dive bomber. Talks with RAF staff members and crewmen made him believe that the "suicide" region was between 50 and 5,000 feet altitude—the dive bomber flying right down the barrel of the antiaircraft gun was doomed. Though Spaatz thought that "flak" was no more accurate than in World War I, antiaircraft guns were so much more numerous and had such rapid rates of fire that the volume of fire would be deadly at low altitudes. In any event, the German Stuka impressed him as a rather inferior machine. It was lumbering and slow and had very little defensive firepower. Level bombing in the Air Corps tradition seem more effective to him.[14]

Spaatz considered the British bombers better than the German, but neither was up to the American standard in his mind. The German planes were too small, too lightly armed and armored, too short in range, and they flew too low. Neither country had a bomb sight that could compare with that of America's Air Corps. Moreover, neither side had enough bombers for formations large enough to develop the kind of mutual fire support Spaatz thought would be needed. Two signals for the improvement of heavy bombers did arise from Spaatz's experience—they should have firepower to the rear and armor plate to protect vital parts of the aircraft.[15]

Spaatz made detailed visits to the shop and supply areas of many bases and tours through aircraft factories as well. He brought home suggestions varying from the design of bomb-carrying carts, to the protection of underground command posts, to the kinds of kitchens used for the enlisted mess halls of the RAF, to designs for aircraft revetments, to temporary devices for runway surfacing.[16]

In those days, while Arnold was resisting the administration's tendency to send so many airplanes to Britain that an expansion of the Air Corps became impossible, a crucial question was whether or not Britain would survive the Luftwaffe's onslaught. The U.S. ambassador in London, Joseph Kennedy,[17] was sending back pessimistic reports on the prospects. The fear was that, were Kennedy correct, the entire British fleet and all the new American aircraft sent to Britain might fall into Hitler's hands. Spaatz gained some renown for having made an early prediction that Britain would stand, and most of the other American observers in England were of the same mind.

The Americans in England had a more intimate knowledge of airpower and of the RAF than did Kennedy. They realized that whatever the German strategy, the achievement of air superiority over southern England and the channel was a necessary prerequisite to invasion. The margin between the two air forces was not quite as narrow as many laymen imagined at the time. Though the Germans had the edge in numbers of aircraft, that edge eroded rapidly with every mile the Luftwaffe moved away from its bases and toward the British airfields. The real contest was between single-engine fighters, and the German advantage in numbers there was much smaller. The RAF's Spitfires and Hurricanes had roughly the same endurance as the Messerschmitt fighters, and since the battlefield was over their own bases they did not have to use part of their fuel to cross the channel. Thus they had more available for the air battles. Further, Spaatz thought the Germans did not use their airpower properly and would not gain control of the air. His readiness to say so not only made an impression at home, but became known in RAF circles. Two years later that helped his standing when he came back to fight.[18]

Spaatz spent his last night in London watching the Luftwaffe bomb the city. Fires were still raging when dawn came. He rode down to

Lisbon, Portugal, aboard a Dutch DC-3 with painted-over windows, expecting to proceed quickly back to the United States by air. However, space on the "clipper" out of wartime Lisbon was not easy to get, and the schedule was irregular. Though he had to hover about the Pan-American offices for a week or so, he finally got away on the 19th of September, four months and two days after leaving New York.[19]

Spaatz had witnessed the unsuccessful attempts of German fighters to escort bombers over England during the Battle of Britain. He and Arnold had never been fully convinced that unescorted bombers could succeed, but they were still faced with the old dilemma concerning escort planes: how to put enough fuel tanks on them for long-range flights while keeping them light enough for maneuverability and speed. The Germans' attempt at a solution illustrated the dilemma. The Luftwaffe bombers were loathe to wander beyond the range of their escorting fighters, and Goering himself imposed the requirement on the escorts to fly in close formation with the bombers. The results were bad. The Hurricanes and Spitfires started their attacks diving out of the sun and arrived at the formation at much higher airspeeds than the Germans. Often, they penetrated the screen of defenders, delivered the attack on the bombers, and were gone before the escorts could do much about it.[20] The Germans had developed a twin-engine fighter aircraft. It was fast and strong, but not as fast and maneuverable as the Hurricanes and Spitfires. Consequently, it was almost as vulnerable to the British fighters as were the bombers themselves. The new airplane became a liability to the attacking formations, for it could not deliver bombs and could hardly defend itself against the British. Spaatz brought these perceptions back from England, and though they did not undermine the Air Corps' preference for unescorted daylight penetrations, they stimulated renewed concern about the development of an escort fighter.[21]

For a time after his return from England, Spaatz, now a brigadier general, retained his position as chief of the Plans Division, but in the summer of 1941, he became chief of the Air Staff, and Harold George took over the planning function. His former division became one of several reporting to him. It was just at this time that President Roosevelt requested the services to estimate the materiel that would be required to defeat the Axis. The Air War Plans Division asked for and received permission to do the planning for the Army Air Forces (AAF) separately from that being done in the War Plans Division of the general staff. (On June 20, 1941, the Army Air Corps became the Army Air Forces.)

Harold George, with the aid of Haywood Hansell and Kenneth Walker, both of his office, and with the temporary help of Laurence Kuter from the General Staff's planning division, devised the plan called AWPD-1, in a very short period during the summer of 1941. The group worked under the general supervision of Carl Spaatz. Although he did not become involved in the detailed tasks, Spaatz approved the work and was present when it was briefed to higher authorities on several occasions.[22]

An article of faith for the planners was that air superiority was a fundamental prerequisite for all surface operations as well as for strategic air campaigns. Douhet had held that air superiority might best be achieved through the destruction of enemy airpower *on the ground* through attacks on his airfields and factories. By the time of the Battle of Britain, Spaatz was becoming convinced that it would be impossible to destroy the Luftwaffe on the ground. Modern dispersal and camouflage methods were too effective. Control of the air would have to be won by shooting the German planes out of the skies in air-to-air battles. He saw some indications in the Battle of Britain that destruction of an enemy air force in the air rather than on the ground had the important additional advantage of eliminating air crewmen along with the aircraft—and the lack of flyers was liable to become the "neck of the bottle," to use one of his favorite phrases.[23]

The AWPD-1 planners asserted that the mounting of a strategic air offensive *might* make unnecessary a landing on the shores of "Fortress Europe." They never made an unqualified assertion that airpower *would* win the war, only that it *might*. Even if it did not, they explained, the air campaign against German industry would weaken her ground forces and achieve the necessary air superiority to make feasible an assault on the beaches of France, if it turned out to be necessary.[24]

The planners knew from long experience that the ground officers would insist on ample air support for operations against enemy ground units. Air attacks were desired against enemy positions to interdict the flow of men and material to the battlefield, for tactical reconnaissance, and for air superiority over the battlefield. Consequently, plans for a substantial tactical air force were included to head off attempts to divert the strategic bombers away from industrial targets.[25]

Fundamental to any air campaign is a detailed knowledge of the targets to be assaulted. Thus, any daylight precision campaign against vital targets in Germany's industrial "web" required intelligence on her industrial structure. Much thought had been given to the problem at the Air Corps Tactical School in the mid-thirties, and one of the planners, Haywood Hansell, had been gathering intelligence data on German targets. As the banks of New York had funded a good deal of industrial building in Germany in the late twenties, their files contained invaluable information, and additional data from the British target folders were already becoming available to the Americans. The AWPD-1 plan identified the German electrical grid, transportation network, and petroleum industry as the most vital targets vulnerable to attack. The scheme was explicit in saying that enemy morale might at some stage become a worthwhile objective, but that was not so at the outset.[26]

The immediate concern that led to the writing of AWPD-1 was neither a desire for a statement of air doctrine nor a declaration of strategy. Rather, the purpose was to develop an overall list of production requirements for America's industrial mobilization. The airmen had found it necessary to base their figures on a strategy drawn from their own perception of a proper air doctrine. They thought that a total of 239 air groups and a little over two million men in the air arm would be necessary to assure a victory over the Axis. The number of aircraft in the Army Air Forces would have to be something over 60,000, and production plans would have to allow for aircraft going to the British and other Allies and to the United States Navy[27]—all this only two years after a time when the Air Corps consisted of fewer than 2,000 officers, flying fewer than 1,000 combat airplanes.

When AWPD-1 was completed, Arnold was in Newfoundland as a member of the American party at the Argentia conference. Spaatz, as chief of the Air Staff, was holding the fort back in Washington. George and his people briefed the plan to Assistant Secretary of War for Air Robert Lovett. He liked it and decided to push it on upstairs for the approval of the General Staff.[28] That was done, and it was duly approved all the way to the top and became the general plan for aircraft production with which America went to war—and less formally, the organizational and operational guide for the war that most Americans, by then, felt was coming. Spaatz had been near the center of two decades of theory-building upon which AWPD-1 was based, and now was associated with the writing and adoption of the scheme that applied this theory to the coming war.

Meanwhile, the air arm had undergone further reorganization. In the fall of 1940, the GHQ Air Force was again put under the control of the Army General Staff. Almost simultaneously, however, Arnold was made Deputy Chief of Staff of the Army for Air and, in that capacity, he was in the chain of command over the GHQ Air Force.[29] This arrangement was in a way a step backward; it was deemed unsatisfactory by Spaatz's office and was opposed before it was implemented.[30] Immediately after the first of the year, his division began work on the revision of Army Regulation 95–5 with a view towards increasing the autonomy of the air arm without generating a need for congressional action—which might carry the changes in unanticipated directions.[31] It was a period of buildup, and the general attitude among air officers was less radical than it had been in the days of austerity. Chief among the moderates was Arnold himself, who was advising against a drastic reorganization of the Air Corps.[32] By that time, the record of the Luftwaffe in the Polish and French campaigns was causing some of the ground officers to take a more benign view of increased autonomy for the air arm. George C. Marshall, who had replaced Craig as chief of staff in 1939, was more understanding in his attitude toward the air organization than were any of his predecessors.[33] When AR 95-5 became effective in June 1941 and the new air arm changed its name to "The U.S. Army Air Forces," it consisted of two branches: the Air Corps to handle training and logistical matters, and the Air Force Combat Command (succeeding the GHQ Air Force) to handle combat. Arnold was named chief of the Air Forces and, at the same time, retained his title as deputy chief of staff for Air. The change did not satisfy Spaatz, who had become chief of the Air Staff under the new arrangement. It still permitted the General Staff (in the eyes of the airmen) too much power to inhibit the development and employment of airpower.[34]

On the eve of Pearl Harbor, Spaatz proposed a further reorganization. His notion was not a new one for it had been discussed on occasion during the deliberations of the past several years. It sought to create three co-equal "forces" within the Army, each with its own staff, and each reporting to the chief of staff. One would be the Air Forces, already operating under that name. The others would be the Army Ground Forces and the Army Service Forces.[35] This was under discussion and being opposed by the General Staff of the Army when the bombs falling on Pearl Harbor created a whole new situation.

## Preparing the Eighth

During the first week of December 1941, Arnold was in California to see off a group of B-17 crews about to make the transpacific flight in a forlorn attempt to reinforce MacArthur and deter the Japanese from undertaking a war they were known to be contemplating. On Sunday the 7th, Carl and Ruth Spaatz were in the midst of remodeling a newly acquired house in Alexandria. During the early afternoon, a telephone call brought the stunning news of the attack on Pearl Harbor. Ruth drove Tooey across the river to the Munitions Building posthaste, and Spaatz had to grasp the reins since Arnold was out of touch. One of the first things he did was to recruit help. He called the command post at Bolling Field and had Maj. Lauris Norstad sent over to aid in handling the confusion of the first few days of the war. Spaatz's first act was to order the new Air Force Combat Command to implement its war plan, called Rainbow 5.

Soon after the Japanese attack, the commander in Hawaii was relieved, and Lt. Gen. Delos Emmons, head of the Air Force Combat Command, was sent to replace him. In February, Carl Spaatz moved to Bolling Field to take over Emmons' former command. It was a giant step for him as he was now in charge of all the USAAF's combat forces, which were growing rapidly.[36] Spaatz's role now became one of organizing and training all the combat units destined for the overseas theaters, but that did not last long. Combat Command quickly became the Eighth Air Force and was ordered to England to conduct the main air offensive against Germany. Though Spaatz remained in the United States for the next four months to get the forces moving, he was identified as the officer who would be the highest air commander in the European theater and in overall charge of the air effort. Much advance work already had been done by the Special Observer Group, which had been operating in England long before Pearl Harbor.

One of Spaatz's initial tasks was to recruit a staff and select subordinate commanders. Two of the most important posts, the VIII Bomber Command and the VIII Fighter Command, were given to his close friends Ira Eaker and Frank Hunter. Eaker was sent immediately to Britain to make preparations for the arrival of the entire force.[37] Spaatz seemed quite ready to accept people, even to recruit them, from civilian occupations to take care of staff functions related to their former work. One of these was Edward P. Curtis, who had gone through Issoudun to become, like Hunter, an ace in World War I. Curtis and many other civilians with executive experience, like Guido Perera and Barton Leach, were recruited to the Air Staff as the emergency developed. Spaatz made Curtis an assistant to the Eighth's chief of staff, Asa N. Duncan.[38] (Later Curtis was to rise to the position of Spaatz's chief of staff after

General Duncan was killed in a B-17 crash.) Other World War I veterans recruited by Spaatz from civilian life were cotton broker Everett R. Cook[39] and Harvard political scientist Bruce C. Hopper.

The Eighth Air Force had a personnel priority commensurate with the "Germany first" strategy, and Spaatz was able to attract many of the most highly regarded officers of the regular establishment to his command. Doubtless this was facilitated by a perception that Eighth Air Force would be the primary instrument of airpower throughout the war, and they wanted to be at the scene of the main attack. One of the USAAF's rising stars was Hoyt Vandenberg, serving on the Air Staff at the time. Spaatz had known Vandenberg for some time and they had been classmates at the Command and General Staff College in 1935–36. They had been working together on the Air Staff during the immediate prewar years, and now Spaatz tried to get Vandenberg for one of his key positions, G-3 (operations).[40] It did not come to pass, for a few weeks later Vandenberg was sent to Eisenhower's staff to plan for the invasion of North Africa.

Eighth Air Force had an equally high priority for equipment. But priority or no, it was still difficult to amass a force and get it across the ocean, especially with the emergency in the Pacific. The initial conception for Eighth Air Force was that it would be the air echelon for the projected invasion of North Africa. That meant it would be a "balanced" force including medium bombers, light bombers, fighters, and observation planes as well as the heavy bombers. When the plan for the landings in Africa was dropped, temporarily, in the spring of 1942, the mission of Eighth Air Force for a time was changed to one of strategic bombing of the industrial plant and air resources of Germany. Consequently, the emphasis on heavy bombers was increased at the expense of the smaller types of craft. Very soon, however, it became clear that there might be an emergency landing in France in 1942 in order to relieve pressure on the Russians, and there was a serious intent to make massive landings in 1943. For Eighth Air Force, this meant the de-emphasis of the strategic bombers and the reemphasis of the smaller aircraft used in tactical operations and mobile battles. During the three or four months preceding his departure for England, therefore, Spaatz had to cope with several changes in the projected order of battle for Eighth Air Force. There were nevertheless substantial heavy bomber formations envisioned in each of the plans.[41]

The initial equipment of the medium and light bomber units of the Eighth Air Force included Martin B-26 Marauders, North American

B-25 Mitchells, and Douglas A-20 Bostons. All were twin-engine designs of recent vintage, and all were to remain in service throughout the war. Jimmy Doolittle had flown the Mitchell in his famous Tokyo raid of April 1942, and it was to perform in many different roles throughout the war. Before the Tokyo raid, General Arnold had told Doolittle that the new B-26s were causing problems. Accident rates were higher than those of the other bombers. Arnold seemed to think that much of the difficulty was in the minds of the flyers, and he asked that Doolittle help to overcome their aversion to assignment to Marauder units.[42] The problem was bad enough that Arnold and Spaatz were wondering whether the B-26 production ought to be discontinued in favor of concentration on the B-25. The latter was of roughly the same dimensions and performance as the Marauder, but its bomb load was a bit smaller and, of course, a changeover of the Martin plants from one airplane to another would inevitably cause delays and loss of output.[43] Notwithstanding Arnold's notion that much of the trouble was with unfounded fears of the B-26 crews, the aircraft did have a higher wing loading than most others, and later versions were built with significantly larger wing areas and tail surfaces.[44] Doolittle visited the B-26 training units and put on demonstration flights for the crews with one engine feathered; that helped, but did not completely solve the problem. Still, Doolittle recommended that the USAAF continue the B-26 manufacturing program, and it went on until 1945.[45]

Throughout, first as chief of the Air Staff, and then as Commander of Combat Command, Spaatz was involved with the B-26 problem. In April 1942, Lt. Col. William Gross investigated the situation for Spaatz in an Ohio-based Marauder unit. His conclusions were that the difficulty did not arise in the panic of crew members. Rather, the airplane was one that could be safely flown by pilots with a reasonable amount of training, and the crew members he had contacted were convinced of that. Colonel Gross informed Spaatz that their greatest concern was with the mechanical unreliability of the plane. It was hard to keep enough of them in commission to maintain the combat readiness of the unit, and the frequent engine and propeller failures did reduce effectiveness and safety. Gross thought that most of the defects could be overcome through technical modifications and better maintenance procedures.[46] He may have raised Spaatz's hope enough to cause him to stick with the B-26 program a while longer.

When Spaatz was at the point of departing for England, Doolittle had just returned from his Tokyo raid and was still involved in the Marauder troubles. In a conference at Bolling Field, Spaatz advised his old friend to keep the potential of the B-26 in mind as he developed his recommendations for Arnold. He suggested that mounting numerous 50-caliber or 20mm guns in its nose might turn the Marauder into a competent ground support aircraft.[47] In any event, production of the aircraft continued, and though there were not Marauder units in the first waves of the Eighth Air Force to cross over to England, some did appear in the fall of 1942.

The first fighters assigned to Eighth Air Force were P-39s and P-38s. From the spring of 1942 onward, Arnold and Spaatz were determined that they would not be used as interceptors but rather in support of the bombers in operations over enemy territory.[48] The P-38 Lightning was thought to be qualified for the work because of its twin engines and a range somewhat longer than that of most contemporary fighters, though Spaatz knew that ultimately the bomber would have to fly beyond its range in order to penetrate German territory. The Bell P-39 Airacobra was already known to have high-altitude performance limitations that would inhibit its use against the Luftwaffe. A potential emergency arising during the Battle of Midway in June 1942 caused the Airacobra crews to be sent to England by sea without their airplanes. When the crews arrived in England without their airplanes, they were retrained in the Spitfires provided by the British, but that airplane had such a short range that it was limited in its usefulness as an escort fighter.[49]

While preparing the Eighth, Spaatz discussed attrition factors to be expected in equipping and manning the Eighth Air Force. He disagreed with Doolittle's estimate of five percent, calling it an ''appalling'' figure and stating that attacking air forces could not suffer that high a loss per mission. Rather, he thought the loss rate should be held to a maximum of two percent.[50]

About the time Carl Spaatz was getting his force under way for Britain, General Arnold paid a visit to his opposite number in the RAF, Air Chief Marshal Sir Charles Portal. The numbers of planes to be deployed to Britain had been changed several times that spring, and they were to be changed again. But in late May, Arnold told Portal that he expected to have sixty-six groups in Britain by the following March, and that nineteen of them would be made up of heavy bombers. At that point, there were no Eighth Air Force planes yet in England, and Arnold said there would be 3,469 in place ten months later. Seven hundred of them would be heavy bombers, with a slightly larger number of medium bombers and a still higher number of fighters with them.[51]

Command and control of these forces was a concern for Spaatz just as it had been for Pershing in France in World War I. Ira Eaker was writing back from England that he feared the RAF, with nearly three years of combat experience against the Luftwaffe, was showing signs of wanting to absorb American air units piecemeal as they arrived in the United Kingdom. Neither Eaker nor Spaatz was much enamored of this idea, and the latter took it up with Arnold in a conference on 20 May. Arnold's reaction was the same. He ordered Spaatz to prepare a draft letter of instructions from the chief of the USAAF to the commander of the Eighth Air Force that would detail the latter's tasks, which would be achieved in an autonomous role. The following day was the last one in Washington (for a time) for both Spaatz and Arnold. At lunch Spaatz was told that he would be going to England the next day and that he would take with him copies of the letter of instructions that asserted the autonomy of Eighth Air Force. Spaatz, who was about to depart for the north to begin shepherding his initial units across the Atlantic, must have been pleased with Arnold's approach, though the acquiescence of the British was still to be won. Arnold said that this plan had the "support of High Administration officials," and that boded well for the USAAF position.[52]

As Spaatz prepared to depart for England in the late spring, he had final conferences with the chief of staff, General Marshall, and the secretary of war, Henry Stimson. At the moment, the Russians were reeling under the German onslaught and it was feared that they would collapse, allowing Hitler to turn his full fury against Britain and the United States. In the Pacific, the Japanese tide had not yet begun to ebb. To American strategists, a sacrificial landing on the coast of France in 1942 was still a possibility—specifically to distract German airpower and armies from the Russian campaign. In any event, the Army leaders were determined to push the buildup of American ground and air forces in Britain so that even if the landings were not launched in 1942 the forces would be in place to make the assault the next year.

In his briefing to Secretary Stimson on 15 May 1942, prior to leaving for England, Spaatz emphasized that there had been a fundamental change in concepts. Earlier (in AWPD-1), the notion had been that airpower assisted by ground power would carry the day; now, the reverse was true, for the air forces being deployed would be in a role of supporting the ground forces which would later make the main attack. Still, Spaatz explained, the first part of the air campaign would be directed against German industrial targets—though the purpose now would not be the immediate defeat of Germany but rather to weaken her in order to make the invasion more feasible. Later, the purpose would become even more strongly oriented toward achieving air supremacy, again to facilitate the landings and subsequent ground campaigns. Perhaps Spaatz demonstrated during this briefing that he had learned something from his days with Benjamin Foulois and Billy Mitchell, who were prone to promise more than they could deliver. He repeated the caution that he had issued to both Arnold and Marshall: that the air forces being deployed to England should not be committed prematurely. He explained that his intention was to maintain a reserve of 100 percent of planes and men until combat experience fully established the attrition factors that would be applied to production and training schedules. He feared that political pressures might cause the premature commitment of the Eighth Air Force to action against the Luftwaffe and result in reverses that would so discourage the public that opinion would prevent attainment of full air strength. At the conclusion of the meeting Stimson promised Spaatz that he would have his "full support."[53]

## Deploying to England

While Eaker was in England making preparations for reception of the Eighth Air Force and setting up VIII Bomber Command, and Spaatz remained in Washington in overall command organizing units for the deployment, the head of VIII Fighter Command, Frank Hunter, was put in charge of the flights across the ocean. He set up temporary headquarters at Grenier Field in Manchester, New Hampshire, which was one of the final staging bases for the aircraft dispatched to England. The Ferrying Command, commanded by Hal George, was responsible for preparing the en route facilities by constructing air bases and arranging for maintenance and supply. The ground echelons were sent to Fort Dix, New Jersey, for their final processing before departing by sea from New York.[54]

The limited range of the planes made necessary a northern route across the Atlantic. Fortunately, the landing fields rimming the North Atlantic were not far from the shortest great circle route to the British Isles. The force was to be marshalled in the northeastern United States, principally at Grenier and at Dow Field in Maine. From there, the fliers would make one last stop in the U.S. at Presque Isle, Maine, to top off their tanks for the jump to Goose Bay, Labrador. For the over-water legs, convoys of P-38 Lightnings and P-39 Airacobras were to be mothered across by a Fortress which had a navigator. The longest leg was from Goose Bay to the western coast of Greenland—a cold and forbidding place. The shore there is made up of towering fjords backed by the ice cap of unmeasured thickness, thought to be around ten thousand feet. The fighters, however, could not bypass the place, so two bases were hewn out of the terrain at the end of fjords and came to be known as "BW-1" and "BW-8." The inlets were so narrow and the terrain beyond so high that the pilots were under great pressure to make the first approach a good one in order to avoid a dangerous "go around" for another pass. The next leg was to Iceland which, though also cold and forbidding, had a larger and better established population and less awesome terrain obstacles. The last part of the journey was southbound into Prestwick, Scotland, a major terminal for transatlantic traffic.[55]

Frank Hunter made the preparations for the Eighth Air Force odyssey, and Spaatz travelled north during the last week in May to inspect the units and test the route before the fledglings were committed to the trip. Just as all of the strands were coming together, the Japanese again upset things. At 8:30 on the evening of June 1, General Spaatz received an urgent telephone call from General Kuter in Washington. Although Kuter gave no reason, he ordered Spaatz to halt all movement toward the northeast. He was to have four of his units ready for takeoff by the following morning—to destinations not yet announced.[56]

Jimmy Doolittle's April 1942 raid on Tokyo, among other things, stimulated the Japanese to make yet another thrust into the central Pacific, this time with a view toward perfecting their defensive perimeter by taking new bases at Midway and in the Aleutians. This would bring Hawaii into bombing range, and might attract the American aircraft carriers into an engagement that would complete the destruction of U.S. naval power. Since the United States had broken the Japanese naval codes, Admiral Nimitz, commanding in Hawaii, knew by the middle of May that a thrust was coming in the vicinity of Midway. The Army Air Forces in Hawaii still had not recovered from the blows they had sustained the previous December. General Emmons was privy to the intelligence on the Japanese naval plans and was pleading for reinforcements from the continental United States. They were painfully slow in coming. The grand strategy operated against such reinforcement for the Pacific, which was supposed to be a defensive theater. Moreover, such reinforcements inevitably would have an impact on the training program back home. The air defense system for the West Coast was still in ragged condition, and the USAAF was trying hard to bring it up to the point where it might be able to resist a surprise air attack. The signs of the impending attack continued to mount until the pressure became too great. The USAAF had already begun to send what resources could be scraped up from domestic air units, but that was not enough, and on 1 June the decision was made to disrupt the Eighth Air Force deployment.[57]

Kuter's relayed order threw Eighth Air Force into turmoil. The C-47s of the 60th Group were fueled and loaded with cargo for the Atlantic crossing. But on the evening of the 1st, they were ordered to off-load their cargo, part of which was destined for construction of weather stations along the route to England. The planes at first were sent down to LaGuardia Field in New York to pick up airline pilots who were to fly them west. Spaatz spent the next day at Presque Isle and flew back down to Manchester, New Hampshire, during the early evening. By this time, confusion was developing over who was going to fly the transports west, and the decision was made that the USAAF pilots could and would do it.

The Japanese plan called for bombing Dutch Harbor in Alaska on the next day, the 3rd of June. It was still dark in the Pacific, of course, and the turmoil at Grenier Field continued. In the midst of it all, about the time the Japanese were attacking Dutch Harbor, Spaatz got a call from Arnold in Washington with orders that he return to the capital immediately. He arrived at Bolling just before dark and was informed that two of his units, the 97th Bomb Group with its B-17s and the 1st Pursuit Group with its P-38s, were to be sent to the West Coast immediately. A third, the 60th Transport Group, would go along with its C-47s to provide en route logistical support. The last remaining unit, the Airacobra Group, the 31st, was to go on alert pending possible orders to follow the others west.[58]

At a conference at the Munitions Building in Washington, early in the morning of 4 June, even as the Japanese and American carriers approached each other through the darkness, Spaatz was arguing that the 2 June preparatory orders for his combat units be rescinded—that they should not be sent to the West Coast but rather should depart for England as soon as possible. Some B-17s could be withdrawn temporarily from the operational training units and sent west, he said, instead of those of his own 97th Bomb Group. His 60th Transport Group C-47s could also go west—but the bombers and fighters should continue to England. Arnold seemed to agree with the plan, and took it to George Marshall to get the chief of staff's approval. He could not get it, and three hours later informed Spaatz that his Fortresses and Lightnings would have to go west. After the Doolittle raid, Marshall had been pressed by West Coast citizens, the pleas of MacArthur, the desires of the Australian allies, and the demands of Admiral King to send reinforcements westward. Little wonder, then, that he refused to go along with the recommendations of his airmen.[59]

It was late on the 4th in Washington when the decisive battles were being fought around Midway. In the capital, it was about midday on the 5th when Admiral Yamamoto decided that the loss of Japan's four greatest carriers spelled defeat and he must withdraw. Though the airmen in Washington did not yet realize the full scope of the great victory, their conferences of that day looked toward the resumption of the movement toward England.[60] The B-17s and P-38s of Spaatz's command were winging westward and would not be released from their temporary assignments for some days to come. But a great strategic victory had been won, and the naval balance in the Pacific had shifted radically back towards the United States. The shift was so great, in fact, that it weakened the arguments of both the Navy men and MacArthur for additional reinforcements and sustained supporters of the "Germany first" strategy. By the next day, 6 June, Spaatz was so reassured that he wrote to Eaker:[61]

Four groups, the 1st and 31st Pursuit, the 97th Heavy Bombardment and 60th Transport, were all concentrated at full strength about ready to move when several Japanese fishing and other boats moving in the general direction of our west coast from Japan scared everyone to death.

It probably was fortunate that this comment was private. Midway had been a much closer thing than Spaatz implied. Also, the USAAF at first made great claims for its part in the battle, but, as it turned out, its performance had been poor while that of the Navy, especially its intelligence and dive bombing forces, had been magnificent. In any case, Spaatz informed his friend that he was expecting the early return of his combat units, and he himself would start an advance trip across the ferry route in about four days.[62]

One of the by-products of the Midway crisis had been a change in plans for the Airacobra unit, the 31st Pursuit Group. It had not been sent west, but the Fortresses that were to have mothered the little P-39s across the ocean were dispatched to California. The decision was made that, unescorted, their flight to England was too dangerous, and the crews could not be kept waiting for the return of the B-17s. Thus, they were sent by sea without their airplanes and were to be equipped with Spitfires coming out of British factories.[63]

Though Spaatz was again preparing for his departure, a rash of details crowded his last days in Washington. On the 7th, he conferred with Air Marshal Sir John Slessor on the problem of getting Spitfires for the 31st Pursuit Group once it arrived in the United Kingdom. At that same meeting, Slessor informed Spaatz that a P-51 Mustang equipped by the British with a new Rolls Royce engine had achieved the startling speed of 425mph. Another subject destined later to preoccupy Spaatz also came up: the utility of RAF area-bombing attacks on German cities at night combined with U.S. precision attacks by daylight.[64]

Finally, six days after the Japanese carriers went down, Spaatz's bombers were released from their West Coast assignments, and he left Washington, arriving in New Hampshire late in the afternoon. He stayed overnight at Grenier Field, discussing final plans for the transoceanic flight with Hunter, who had remained in New England throughout the Midway crisis. Two squadrons of B-17s were to fly to the United Kingdom independently, and the remainder were retained to serve as weather scouts and navigation guides for the P-38s. Spaatz and his crew flew to Presque Isle early on the 11th, where they ran into repeated weather delays, which must have been towering frustrations, coming as they did after the Midway troubles.[65]

Spaatz spent this time wrestling with some troubling communications and personnel problems having to do with the founding of the ferry route, and it was three days before the weather permitted him to continue his trip. He finally got into Goose Bay on the evening of the 14th. The weather for the next leg to BW-1 in Greenland was unfavorable, but he nonetheless ordered his pilot to make an attempt on the 15th, feeling that he had to test the route for the fledgling crews to follow. He wrote to Hunter from BW-1 urging speed and the need to take advantage of every break in the weather. He warned of communications difficulties arising from insufficient equipment, and the strange ways in which the Greenland terrain deflected radio waves, but cited the very long daylight periods as a great asset. He also mentioned the tendency for pilots to fear the unknown more than is necessary.[66]

Spaatz remained for a day in Greenland, sending reports on the route back to Hunter and checking on conditions at the bases there. He then ordered his Liberator off for Iceland early on the 17th and found that the weather had broken. Visibility in the northern skies was unlimited, raising concern for danger of another kind: Nazi patrol planes looking for Allied convoys. The trip passed uneventfully, and the situation in Iceland seemed sufficiently under control for him to proceed to Scotland the next' day. Spitfires came up to inspect the inbound Liberator as it approached the shore. Eaker was on hand to greet Spaatz at Prestwick and then flew him down to High Wycombe, near London.[67] Spaatz had come safely over the route he expected his men to follow. He had found difficulties enough, especially with the weather and communications, but he was convinced that mass movement was possible.

The frustrations suffered by Spaatz and his crew in their Liberator were also encountered by those who followed. The first group of B-17s which went to Greenland lost three airplanes, and another a bit later lost two Fortresses and six Lightnings that landed on the ice cap. All the flyers were rescued, but those losses and the repeated weather and communications problems raised concern in Washington as to the wisdom of sending planes and crews by air. Though Spaatz had written to Arnold on 8 July commenting on the safe arrival of the first twenty planes in England, Arnold wrote back on the 16th expressing his concern and asking Spaatz for his advice on continuing to ferry aircraft over that route. He had just heard about the loss of eight aircraft on the ice cap, but still had no news about the cause of the problem.[68] Spaatz responded, saying that he thought the problems could be ironed out. Meteorologists and station personnel were gaining experience with the route, and he recommended that some lead crews be kept on the route to serve as commanders of guide ships that would show the way to the rest. This procedure might even be honed until crews would be assigned to just one segment of the route and become so expert on the terrain, facilities, and weather that efficiency and safety would be much improved.[69] In any event, the decision was made to continue operations through the fall. The first wave completed its journey before the end of July, and another was started on its way. By then, more than a hundred each of Fortresses, Lightnings, and C-47s were on hand, and by the end of the year, Eighth Air Force had flown seven hundred airplanes across the North Atlantic route. The accident rate was much lower than had been feared during the summer, and many crew members survived the crashes.[70]

## Settling In

During his first weeks in the United Kingdom, Spaatz was occupied with providing basing for a great new force, making logistical arrangements, establishing relationships with the press, creating command lines, and developing interface with the British ally. In the midst of this, Arnold ordered the USAAF to fly its first combat mission against Germany on Independence Day. Spaatz and Eaker were not happy about that.[71] None of the B-17 or P-38 units could be ready by then, so the Eighth had to hustle to get some A-20 crews in British airplanes to participate in the raid.[72]

The skies over wartime England, the base of two of the world's great air forces, were highly congested. On the ground, too, open space for airfields was limited. Most of the work of surveying sites for fields and selecting the suitable ones had been done before Spaatz and his units arrived on the scene. He had had a role in this while still back in the United States. Now he had to settle the new units on their bases and give them the needed theater indoctrination. The plan envisioned placing the fighter units at bases in southern England as close to their potential battle areas as possible. It was also desirable to place the bombers close to the channel to extend their reach into Germany. Since there would be many heavy bomber bases, located as close to one another as possible for administrative convenience, the challenge was to keep from congesting the airspace. Thus, bomber bases were in the main located to the north and northeast of London, in East Anglia.

Great maintenance and supply depots, like Burtonwood, were placed farther to the west for access to transportation and to be near places where labor and other support for maintenance operations could be found. Thus, they were sited not far from the great port cities of western England. As uncrowded airspace is desirable for training operations, Northern Ireland became a kind of way station for replacement crews headed for Eighth Air Force. Many bases were built there, where the inbound crews got their theater indoctrination before moving on to their operational bases. As a part of his own orientation, during his first two weeks in England, Spaatz visited many of the bases, flew over most of those under construction, and made two trips to the installations in Ireland, the latter in the company of Dwight Eisenhower, who became theater commander after his predecessor, Frank Andrews, was killed in a crash at Iceland. Work on the bases had begun even before Pearl Harbor. Spaatz seemed satisfied with the way Eaker and the others who preceded him to the United Kingdom had performed.[73]

Training was less satisfactory than the status of the bases, however. The crews, fresh out of the flying schools, were arriving with little flying time and with gaps in their preparation. Some of them had little or no experience at high altitude, formation practice had been neglected, and some of the gunners arrived without ever having fired their weapons in the air. The Airacobra fighter pilots from the 31st Pursuit Group were the first to arrive, and most of their training proved adequate. At first, the Spitfires with which they were equipped gave them some trouble because of the conventional landing gear: it was narrow and much more difficult to handle than was the P-39's tricycle undercarriage. Most of the accidents arising from the transition to the Spitfires occurred on the ground, but the Americans mastered the new planes soon enough. More difficult to overcome were the deficiencies in their gunnery training. The bad weather and dense population of the United Kingdom made it difficult to rectify these defects. There were few open spaces where live-fire training could be conducted, and the constant bad weather limited the time that those ranges could be used. The problem was serious enough to inspire Air Vice Marshal William Sholto Douglas, head of the Fighter Command, to write Spaatz on the subject. He offered use of the RAF gunnery school for instructors at Sutton Bridge, but suggested that other pilots get improved gunnery training in the United States before departure. Spaatz recognized the problem immediately and sent a cable to Arnold requesting that the training in America be improved and directed VIII Fighter Command to send some instructors to the RAF school.[74]

Eighth Air Force was organized into functional units: the VIII Bomber Command, a similar fighter command, another for the air support of ground units, and a logistical organization, the Eighth Air Force Service Command. The latter was responsible for handling supplies peculiar to the USAAF and for maintaining the aircraft. The British had been using American airplanes before Pearl Harbor, and a logistical support structure for these aircraft already existed in England. When the Americans arrived, they received some initial support from the British, and went on to build a massive system of their own. Each tactical base had its own maintenance and supply capability, supplemented by mobile support depots and by permanent installations one tier higher.

One of Spaatz's principal functions concerning the Service Command was recruiting personnel to manage the system. He was able to get Maj. Gen. Walter H. Frank, a man of immense drive and wide-ranging interests, to head the command. Though the two had overlapped at West Point by just a couple of months, they had been classmates for a year at the Air Service Tactical School in the mid-twenties.[75] Frank was to remain with the Eighth Air Force until November 1942, when he took over the function for the entire USAAF and was replaced by Henry Miller, one of Eisenhower's West Point classmates. Hugh Knerr was second in command. In the late thirties Knerr had been "exiled" to San Antonio as a result of his agitation for the heavy bomber program while chief of staff for the GHQ Air Force. Subsequently, he had been medically retired and had gone to work for Sperry Gyroscope Corporation. Only after a good deal of pleading on the part of Frank Andrews after the emergency began was Knerr recalled to active duty. About the time Frank Andrews was killed, Knerr was sent to Eighth Air Force, where he remained for the rest of the war.[76] The sheer massiveness of the logistical task was daunting enough, but added to that were the frequent changes of strategy that affected the numbers and kinds of airplanes to be acquired, the sensibilities of the Labour party on the kinds of people to be employed in the great logistical establishments, and the rapid change of technology stimulated by the wartime emergency.

Another major concern for Carl Spaatz in the early days of Eighth Air Force's tenure in England was the cementing of American relations with the British. The two cultures were similar enough to assure extensive mixing, yet different enough to give rise to occasional hard feelings. Under the turbulent conditions of war, the maintenance of good relations was especially difficult. One of the world's masters at the art of causing trouble, Joseph Goebbels, was doing what he could to stimulate differences between the Allies. Further, there was the perennial fear among the Americans that their growing forces would be absorbed by the more experienced RAF. It was here, perhaps, that Spaatz was on his strongest ground. He had the major advantage of having spent the summer of 1940, deemed by the British to be their "finest hour," in the United Kingdom and having made many friends among them. Now it fell to him to bring his enormous forces into their midst with a minimum of friction, to maintain the organizational and tactical autonomy of the

American air forces, and to do all this while sustaining good relations between the two peoples.

Spaatz's priorities are suggested by the large amount of time he spent with British leaders during his first couple of weeks in the United Kingdom. On his first night he had dinner with Sir Arthur Harris,[77] head of Bomber Command and one of the most powerful men in the RAF. During the ensuing half month he conferred with: the Chief of the Air Staff, Sir Hugh Portal, and his deputy, Sir Wilfred Freeman; Air Vice Marshal R. H. M. Saundby; the Fifth Sea Lord, Rear Adm. St. G. Lyster, in charge of naval air; the Secretary of State for Air, Sir Archibald Sinclair; Air Chief Marshal Sir Christopher Courtney; Air Vice Marshal William Sholto Douglas; and many others. He received an invitation to visit the king and queen on 25 June, but circumstances prevented that until several weeks later when their majesties visited an Eighth Air Force Base. Rain began to fall and Spaatz removed his coat, putting it over the queen's shoulders, and said, "This makes you a major general in the U.S. Army Air Forces, Your Majesty." The reporters present made a story of it, having never pictured the stern-visaged general in the role of Sir Walter Raleigh.[78]

Most of Spaatz's meetings with the British dealt with the thousands of housekeeping details relating to the settling of the Eighth Air Force on its new bases. But one important theme recurred throughout many of the meetings: the need to maintain the autonomy of the U.S. air arm. One dimension of this problem had to do with the pursuit groups already in the United Kingdom. Spaatz and Arnold had already determined that they would not be used to defend the island but rather would escort the heavy bombers and do their fighting over enemy territory. Eisenhower had been persuaded of the wisdom of this plan and immediately after he arrived, he met with Spaatz and confirmed the idea.

As Eisenhower reported to Arnold:[79]

He (Spaatz) and I are going to get together quickly with the British on one or two important points involving air operations. One of these concerns the responsibility of our fighter units in defensive work. Our attitude is that our own squadrons should have an emergency mission in this regard but should not be counted upon normally as an integral part of the Interceptor Command. We intend to insist that the American squadrons should be looked upon as an offensive force with the result that our fighter squadrons will be fully engaged fighting over hostile territory. If we are going out

to provoke a fight, we have got to have the close support units to fight
with, and they must not be worn out by keeping them on regular alerts.
I anticipate no real difficulty in putting over this view.

This could not have been better said by the ill-fated Billy Mitchell,
who had been court-martialed for strongly advocating the above. Eisenhower's words were entirely in harmony with the American desire for
autonomy from the RAF and with the USAAF predilection for the offensive over the defensive.

Even before his initial meeting with Eisenhower, though, Spaatz
held an off-the-record press conference during which he touched upon
the subject of autonomy from the RAF. Speaking to a group of correspondents, some of whom were British, on the day after his arrival, Spaatz
confined his remarks to a sentence or two and then opened the session
for questions. In his responses, Spaatz repeatedly made clear his intention
to cooperate closely with the British air arm, but also asserted that there
would be no overall commander, and the American operations would
be separate from those of the RAF. He was in no way rigid about the
notion that the bombers could make the deep penetrations without fighter
escort. He remarked to the reporters that the bombers would have to
try it without escort in order to reach some of the targets in Germany,
for the fighters could not fly that far. He was quite clear, however,
that unescorted deep penetrations had not yet been proven to be feasible.[80]

Having the support of both Arnold and Eisenhower on the issue,
Spaatz made the concept of the fighters as escorts a main theme of his
conferences both with his own staff and with the British. Two days
after he arrived, Eaker briefed him on what had happened in England
so far. Spaatz did not say much at that initial meeting, but he did state
that the Fortresses would have to start out with shallow penetrations
and fighter escort; they could not count on their own firepower for effective
defense of the bomber formations.[81] Two days later he conferred with
Rear Adm. St. G. Lyster, Chief of Aviation for the Royal Navy, and
made it a major point that the VIII Fighter Command existed primarily
to support VIII Bomber Command, not to become a part of the British
air defense system.[82] On the next day, Spaatz visited the Briton most
concerned with the American fighters, the head of RAF Fighter Command,
William Sholto Douglas. Spaatz told him that the American pursuit groups
were to support U.S. bombers and would back up Fighter Command
only in a defense emergency. Sholto Douglas replied that the best way

for them to be trained in air defense procedures might be to integrate them with the British units temporarily, and then perhaps the American fighters should take over their own sector—explaining that the defense of such sectors was largely accomplished with offensive tactics. Spaatz was unconvinced, and the meeting ended without definite agreement on the point.[83]

When Spaatz and Eisenhower made an inspection trip to Ireland early in July, they discussed the problems of the buildup with the U.S. Army commander there, Russell P. Hartle. On matters of organization, Ike made it clear to Hartle that, although there would be no formal order specifying the details, the fighter units were to be kept clear of any responsibilities that would tie them to the defense of any particular geographical point. They were to retain their mobility.[84] The next week, Spaatz reported to Arnold his progress on the matter. He said that he had won from Sholto Douglas agreement on the basing of the fighters in southern England, where they would be useful for the invasion still being planned for the spring of 1943 and where, in the meantime, they would be able to support bomber operations to the limits of their range. He also told of his agreement with Sholto Douglas to defer the decision as to how the U.S. pursuit groups would be related to the air defense forces of the British Isles.[85] On 11 August, again writing to Arnold, he discussed his fighter training program in some detail but still professed worry about the diversion of his units to tasks other than the attack on Germany, particularly to the attack on North Africa.[86]

Spaatz's extensive discussions with Air Marshal Arthur Harris centered on the way in which victory over the Germans could be won. Harris was firmly of the opinion that strategic bombing would be able to do it alone and was much opposed to any notion of a landing, which he thought would reduce some of the resources available to the air campaign. Spaatz argued stoutly that strategic bombing should not be expected to do it alone. He thought that a landing would be necessary, if for no other reason than to get bases for the fighters needed to escort the bombers in penetrating German air defenses.[87] Spaatz was a bit less committed to the idea that airpower with unescorted heavy bombers would win the war alone than were some of his USAAF colleagues.[88]

The repeated warnings against premature commitment to combat that Spaatz had sounded in his final briefings before leaving the United States did not seem to have the desired effect—least of all on his immediate superior and friend, Hap Arnold. Arnold was primarily responsible for generating the first mission on 4 July 1942, and the results were not good.[89] Even that did not cure the problem. Arnold sent his old friend a letter implying that Spaatz might turn out to be another "McClelland" (sic) of Civil War fame. (Neither Spaatz nor Arnold was known for any deep study of military history, but there is no chance that the misspelling of McClellan's name was a secretarial error, since he used it twice and misspelled it the same way both times.) Spaatz had the perfect answer, though, when he replied that his boss's allusion to "McClellan" (Spaatz got the spelling right) brought to mind Burnside, who had thrown away the flower of the Army of the Potomac in an ill-advised charge. Arnold was not renowned for having perfect control of his temper, and most were reluctant to trifle with him. Yet when Arnold next wrote to Spaatz, there was a contrite tone to his letter. He admitted that Spaatz, being on the scene, probably knew best, and that things were probably moving as fast as possible. He also confessed to having an impatient character, and implied that the criticism had arisen from that. (At least by the time he wrote this letter, he had learned how to· spell George McClellan's name.)[90]

What Arnold was longing for was the first Fortress mission. The press made much about the combat of the A-20 crews on the 4th, but that was not enough for the chief. Strategic bombing and the Fortress were the central theme of the whole USAAF, and nothing less than the commencement of B-17 operations over the continent would do. In a letter on 11 August, Spaatz assured him that the 97th Bomb Group was combat-ready and on the verge of a string of operations over France under the escort of Spitfires.[91] He added that the tempo of the campaign would be increased once the ground echelons of some of the other B-17 groups had arrived, but warned again that the primary question, whether the Fortresses could take care of themselves without fighter escort, was yet to be answered. He wondered whether they could cope with the four 20-millimeter cannons of the Focke-Wulf 190s and cautioned Arnold not to leap to conclusions on the evidence of the early missions because they would contain too few planes to saturate German defenses.

The next day, responding to Arnold's prodding, he added that the 97th had been combat-ready for some days, but that bad weather had prevented launching the first attack. Spaatz worried that it might be necessary to give up high-altitude for low- and medium-altitude bombing because of the frequent bad weather in northern Europe. Were that necessary, the attackers would suffer large losses to antiaircraft fire as well as to the fighters.[92] He did assure Arnold, though, that the first mission was fully prepared and waiting only for a break in the weather. It would go to France with Spitfire escort at 25,000 feet and bomb some railroad yards at Rouen. The P-38s of Spaatz's old 1st Pursuit Group would not be making the trip with the Fortresses and Spitfires because they had not yet received enough in-theater training to make them ready for that kind of penetration.[93]

Finally, on 17 August, the weather cleared enough for the first raid. Both Spaatz and Eaker had intended to go along, but British objections prevented it. Both men were privy to much secret information, and both would be hard to replace if lost, so Spaatz had to stand down from the mission. Eaker went along notwithstanding the obstacles. Spaatz saw the bombers off and waited at the field for their return. No aircraft were lost and the rail objectives were hit, but Eaker was unhappy because some bombs went astray and hit the town, though not the famous cathedral.[94] The Germans put up some antiaircraft fire, and a few enemy fighters were spotted. The battle damage was minimal, however, and none of the crew members was lost. Though the enemy rail system was far from crippled—hardly inconvenienced in fact—the target was hit and the absence of aircraft losses made the Rouen mission an auspicious start for the American strategic bombing campaign. Still, both Eaker and Spaatz were moved to again warn their superiors that nothing had been proven about the ability of the Fortresses to penetrate deep inside of Germany without help[95] and that the campaign ought to be expanded gradually and cautiously.

The caution that the leaders of Eighth Air Force issued to those back in the United States did not seem to last long in the mind of Spaatz himself. On 24 August, in a letter to Arnold aimed at heading off the depletion of his command for the needs of other theaters, he wrote:[96]

The operations of the past week, limited as they have been, have convinced me of the following:

a. That daylight bombing with extreme accuracy can be carried out at high altitudes by our B-17 airplanes.

b. That such operations can be extended, as soon as the necessary size force has been built up, into the heart of Germany without fighter protection over the whole range of operation.

c. That the operation of our air forces in close cooperation and harmony with the RAF can be accomplished without disturbing or destroying the autonomy of the Army Air Forces.

　d. That there is no other possibility left to the Allies which can have so great an effect during the coming year as the combination of night bombardment, primarily undertaken by the British, and the daylight bombing of precision objectives by our forces. With the prospective commitment of our ground forces to other theaters, the possibility of any round-up operation vanishes and this becomes a 100 percent air theater of operation . . .

Meanwhile, events were afoot that threatened to grievously weaken and delay the development of the assault on Hitler's industrial plant. Spaatz had come to Europe believing that he would mount a strategic bombing campaign to weaken the German state so it could not successfully resist the following surface assault on the coast of France. His big bombers would first attack the vital points of the German industrial plant, and then, when the date of invasion was closer, they would join the lighter bombers and fighters in attacking targets that were more directly associated with the German defense system. The earliest date contemplated for the landings was during the fall of 1942, and the more probable time would come in the spring of 1943. The American army and its air arm agreed on such a program, though many in the U.S. Navy would rather have diverted much of American strength to campaigns in the Pacific. The British, however, were even more reluctant partners in the enterprise.

Roosevelt was eager to get American troops into action against the Germans in 1942, but if the British could not be persuaded to join in an invasion of France with some enthusiasm, then something else would have to be tried. He sent Harry Hopkins and George Marshall to the United Kingdom in the latter part of July to thrash out a decision once and for all. Marshall, backed by Arnold, Eisenhower, and Spaatz, still wanted to prepare for the 1942 landing on a tentative basis with a definite commitment to make the invasion in the spring of 1943. The British, however, could not be persuaded, and when that news got back to FDR, he cabled the American delegation to secure an agreement to one of the alternatives: resurrection of the plan to invade northwest Africa, reinforcement of British troops in the Middle East, mounting an invasion of Norway, or opening a campaign through Iran—anything to get the ground forces into action before the year was gone. The plan that emerged was the invasion of North Africa, which was to be a combined Anglo-American operation with Eisenhower in charge.[97]

Spaatz spent the day prior to the arrival of Hopkins and Marshall helping prepare the arguments in favor of the fall 1942 landings in France. He argued that the German air force had been worn thin through the summer campaigns on the eastern front and in the Mediterranean campaign, and the landings in the fall would take advantage of the fact. Were the attempt to be postponed, the Luftwaffe would have the winter to recuperate and would be ready to meet the assault in the spring of 1943.[98]

By 23 July, Spaatz was beginning to see the handwriting on the wall. On that day, he and Hoyt Vandenberg (a member of Marshall's delegation) worked up an outline recommending actions to be taken if indeed the invasion of France were abandoned for 1942. The major premise of their argument, which Vandenberg was to present to the chief of staff, was that, notwithstanding the postponement of the invasion, Germany necessarily remained the main target, for she was the only decisive one. The war could not end until she was beaten. Thus, were the invasion put off, the European theater would become a wholly air theater. Consequently, the need to continue pressure on the most decisive objective meant that the air buildup in the United Kingdom should not be diminished in favor of other operations. Admitting still that the bombers would have to be escorted by fighters until they proved their ability to go it alone, the airmen argued that in the absence of the planned invasion, "air warfare may well prove to be decisive."[99]

It was all to no avail, though, for the 1942 landings were abandoned, the decision to invade North Africa was made, three different landing sites were selected, and an entirely new air force—the Twelfth—was created to support the operation. Most of it was to be taken from the body of Eighth Air Force or from units scheduled to join Spaatz. Suddenly, his task was again radically changed. Now, instead of building up a strategic bombing campaign and later a landing support operation, the goal became to put together another air force, one to be used principally in tactical support of TORCH, as the African venture was code-named. Spaatz's old friend Doolittle was appointed commander of the new force, and Spaatz's first two units, the 1st Pursuit Group and the 97th Bomb Group, among many others, were taken from the Eighth and sent to the Twelfth.[100] That, along with the effort diverted to the antisubmarine campaign, left precious little force with which to attempt to saturate the air defenses of the German homeland.

The seven months that had passed since Pearl Harbor had been hard ones for Spaatz and his bomber commander, Ira Eaker, and for everyone associated with Eighth Air Force. The plan had changed many times in that period, but through it all, the strategic bombing of Germany had remained an element. Spaatz, Eaker, Hunter, and all the rest had toiled and taken risks to build a force that could win spurs for airpower and win them early. Now that vision was postponed in favor of a more traditional campaign in support of the Army in its quest to help the British drive the Axis from the North African shore, and perhaps even from the Mediterranean basin.

# Chapter VI

## REVERSING THE TIDE IN THE MEDITERRANEAN

Rommel had come to Africa to rescue his Italian allies. In spectacular fashion, he had driven the British back to the borders of Egypt and taken the garrison at Tobruk in the process. The political leaders of the Western Allies radically changed their strategy to counter Rommel, and it fell to the military captains to create a new plan. At first, Spaatz's role was merely to aid in the planning process and to build up the air forces that would accompany Eisenhower, who had been selected to command TORCH, as the invasion of Africa had been code-named. Shortly after the beachheads were established, Spaatz was moved down to the Mediterranean first to become Eisenhower's principal air adviser and then the commander of the Northwest African Air Force. Spaatz departed the United Kingdom thinking he would be back in a few days. Instead, he was held in the Mediterranean for the next year, through the conquest of North Africa, the landings on and capture of Sicily, and the invasion of Italy.

### Planning TORCH

As with all major military operations, the goals of TORCH were complex. One objective was to partially satisfy Stalin's demand for a second front. Also, FDR wanted to get American troops into action in 1942, and the British needed to create a threat on Rommel's rear to relieve the pressure on their Eighth Army in Egypt. Marshall and Eisenhower were not enamored of the idea of invading Africa, and their airmen were even less enthusiastic. They saw Germany as the decisive target and felt that even if the North African invasion succeeded and Italy surrendered, this would not win the war.[1] However, once the decision was made, and as the weather began to worsen in England, the airmen began to think that some good might come of the North African operation, even if it did delay their strategic bombing campaign against Germany. It might give them bases in an area where the winter weather was not as bad as in England, thereby adding flexibility to their assault on German industry, and spreading the Luftwaffe's air defenses more thinly.[2]

The responsibilities of Eighth Air Force in England included not only building another entire air force, the Twelfth, largely out of its own resources, but at the same time continuing operations against Germany. These operations were to be aimed at fixing some of the Luftwaffe in place in Germany and France to keep it from participating in the defense of North Africa, and doing everything possible to lessen the submarine threat against the convoys moving TORCH forces from the United Kingdom and the United States.[3]

The environment in which Jimmy Doolittle's Twelfth Air Force was to fight was far different from that of the Eighth. There was no local industrial base in Africa, the lines of communication were primitive compared to those in England, airports were few and far between, and the aircraft had to be prepared for desert operations. The ultimate military objective was to trap the remnants of Rommel's army in Tunis, and the line to that place ran through the Straits of Gibraltar, only nine miles wide and with a potential enemy, Spain, on both sides. That created a tension in the planning between the British, who wanted to land as far to the east as possible to facilitate a quick move on Tunis, and the Americans, who wanted to make at least one landing on the Atlantic side of Gibraltar to establish a secure land line of communications in case the Spanish, or the Germans marching through Spain, interdicted the sea route at the Gates of Hercules.[4]

A further complication in the selection of landing sites had to do with airpower: place them too far to the east, and the inbound convoys would be subject to German and Italian air attacks operating out of Sicily and Italy. Sites inside the Mediterranean entailed bringing in aircraft carriers, and their vulnerability there was much greater than out in the Atlantic. The initial air cover was to be provided by naval aircraft operating from these carriers, but the vulnerability of the ships goes up rapidly with the passage of time after the landings. Thus, soon after the initial assaults, it was important to replace this airpower with land-based air units. Still, the country along the North African shore was so undeveloped, and the terrain so mountainous, that airports and sites for fields were not numerous. Also, ports had to be acquired through which to pass the sinews of war to Eisenhower's armies. In the end, enough ships were found to satisfy both the British and the American choices of landing places. Three assaults would be made, on Casablanca, Oran, and Algiers. The westernmost, at Casablanca, was to be made by Gen. George Patton's forces sailing directly from Norfolk, Virginia, and was to be an American operation. The middle site, inside the Mediterranean at Oran, was to include both American and British forces, and the eastern-most at Algiers was to be a British landing. All three sites were chosen because they had the necessary port capability and because they had airports on which land-based air power could be located quickly.[5]

Many of the air units sent their ground echelons by sea, but that could not be done with the flying echelons with any expectation that they could join the battle soon after the landings. Some of the squadrons with longer-range airplanes flew from southern England with a staging stop at Gibraltar. Other airplanes, like Spitfires, could not make that long flight and had to be shipped by sea to the "Rock" and reassembled and serviced there. They would make the rest of the trip under their own power. In some cases, paratroopers were designated to capture airports for the transport; in others, the amphibious forces would have a main objective of the early capture of an airdrome. Some substantial airborne forces were designated to be airlanded, rather than dropped, with the idea of further deploying them eastward to capture more lines of communication, airports, and perhaps even Tunis itself. As the Germans would surely see immediately, that was a serious threat to one of their main avenues of retreat. Speed was of the essence for both sides. The other air units would be concerned with air defense, convoy protection, close air support for ground troops in battle, and ultimately the interdiction of the enemy's supply lines. Gibraltar was a key point in all of this, and for Eisenhower a major worry was that the Luftwaffe would recognize this vulnerability and make an effective spoiling attack at that point.[6]

Spaatz and Arnold made a major effort to retain some Eighth Air Force strength during the TORCH buildup. The U.S. was trying to keep the USSR in the war, not only by invading Africa, but also through the shipment of war material to her, most of which moved by sea. The submarine threat was ubiquitous, having an impact not only on the TORCH invasion, but also on the effort to succor Russia and to maintain some semblance of combat power in Eighth Air Force. Countering that threat with his reduced forces in England became a major preoccupation for Spaatz in the fall of 1942. He concentrated his bombers against the submarine pens on the Bay of Biscay.[7]

Though attacks on Hitler's U-boat bases did not require deep penetrations, Spaatz was still concerned for the security of the force that would remain with him after the Twelfth Air Force deployed to Africa. On 31 October, he warned Arnold that the antisubmarine missions might not be as simple as some thought and that considerable losses might be suffered. The departure of Doolittle's forces would mean that the bombers would not have escorts over the submarine bases. The bombs available were not designed for destroying thick concrete submarine pens. One way to overcome that limitation was to bomb from lower altitudes, which would bring the Fortresses into antiaircraft artillery range and also give an additional advantage of mass to the German fighters. Concentrating on those bases would induce the Axis to increase its air defenses around them. Finally, Spaatz pointed out that the most experienced bombing groups were being dispatched to TORCH and those remaining behind would be new men in the theater and that, too, might be expected to add to the casualty rate.[8]

Unlike the American ground forces in Africa, the Twelfth Air Force did have some combat experience, though not as much as the other separate air force operating in Africa, the RAF's Eastern Air Command. Spaatz gave Doolittle his most experienced combat units, including the 97th Bomb Group, which was the first in Europe with B-17s. Both the 1st and 31st Pursuit Groups also went to Africa. The former, with its P-38 Lightnings, had not made it into combat before leaving England. The latter, the 31st, had been the first American fighter group in England, equipped with Spitfires in place of the Airacobras it had left behind in the states. During the late summer and fall, the 31st had its baptism of fire over the French coast in a series of fighter sweeps with the British and in the Dieppe raid. The 15th Bomb Squadron with its light bombers also went. This was the unit that had made the first attack on the Nazis with their raid on the fourth of July. The programmed strength of Twelfth Air Force was to be 1,244 aircraft, and the RAF Eastern Air Command was to be equipped with 454 planes. As the campaign progressed eastward, the RAF units in Malta and those coming westward with Montgomery would also have an effect on operations against Tunis. All of Spaatz's Lightnings were dispatched, which meant that the heavy bombers remaining with the Eighth would have to go it alone until their fighter escorts had been replaced.[9]

From General Arnold's point of view, the worst part of the decision to abandon landings in France for 1942 in favor of those in North Africa was that it gave Admiral King the key to loosening Arnold's hold on long-range bomber production. As long as the landings in France had been on the schedule, Eighth Air Force was deemed a part of the main effort and enjoyed the first call on the output of Liberator and Fortress factories. Once the emphasis shifted to Africa, however, the Eighth lost its priority, and King quickly succeeded in getting some additional heavy bombers diverted to the Pacific. This threatened to kill the USAAF's main project, the strategic bombing of Germany, and Arnold initiated a campaign to prevent it. He enlisted Spaatz's and Eisenhower's aid in an effort to sell the idea that the North African forces and what was left of the Eighth Air Force had the same mission; their efforts, he said, were complementary. He tried to stimulate the notion that the United Kingdom and North Africa were really one theater, since the efforts of both were directed towards a single end, the defeat of Germany. Consequently, Eighth Air Force should enjoy the same priority as the Twelfth—the highest.[10] It was a tough bill of goods to sell. Not only were King and his colleagues formidable opponents, but also the submarine campaign was at its climax and the cries for long-range airplanes in the Pacific could not be denied. Arnold kept up a constant refrain with everyone who would listen on the need to concentrate heavy bomber strength against Germany. Spaatz willingly helped him in this, and Eisenhower moved cautiously toward the one-theater concept for reasons of his own. However, the rebuilding of the strategic bomber force in the United Kingdom in the wake of the Twelfth's departure was to be a slow and painful process.

## The Landings

A combination of energy, planning competence, political expertise, and luck resulted in three successful landings at Casablanca, Oran, and Algiers—as planned—on the 8th of November, 1942. Because of the pressing concern to speedily capture northern Tunisia and trap Rommel, General Anderson's British First Army (with its "Blade Force," an armored unit) moved east from Algiers toward Tunis in mid-November.

The RAF's Eastern Air Command, under Air Marshal Sir William Welsh, was part of Anderson's force.

Initial activity for Doolittle's Twelfth Air Force was the dispatch of the 31st Fighter Group from Gibraltar on 8 November to help subdue stubborn French resistance at Oran. The group was equipped with Spitfire aircraft and had been scheduled for Casablanca, but expected resistance there did not materialize. Three of the group's Spitfires, on a reconnaisance patrol to the south, discovered a large hostile force moving on Oran. The force turned out to be the French foreign legion, which eventually turned back because its light armor was no match for the Spitfires' 20mm guns. The Spits further assisted in silencing French artillery near Oran, and their strafing attacks aided the ground forces in breaking through French defenses.[11]

By 19 November, the Twelfth's buildup of aircraft in Algeria had been rapid, and it had received approximately the number of aircraft which the plans had specified for that date. Overall effectiveness was inhibited, however, by a shortage of airdromes, the scattered locations of ground support units, and limited supplies.[12] Since the intervening country between Algiers and Tunis was broken up by mountains, and the highways and railroad that existed were poor, an orthodox land advance could not be made. Plans called for the rapid seizure of successive ports by landing-craft, motor transport and troop-carrier aircraft.

Initially, American C-47 troop carriers from the 60th and 64th Troop Carrier Groups took off from England with British paratroops and landed at Oran on 8 November and at Algiers on 9 November. Because of French resistance and some dispersion of the force, the 60th landing at Oran was unable to reservice and regroup as planned in order to move eastward the next day. The 64th landing at Algiers on 11 November took off the next morning, with escort fighters, for an airdrome southwest of Bone, and the paratroops were successfully dropped. Both troop carrier groups were immediately put into daily service supporting the move on Tunis by transporting combat troops, support personnel, guns, and munitions. This use of transport aircraft by the TORCH forces added a new mobility dimension to warfare and provided much-needed flexibility.

Other units of the Twelfth Air Force were pressed into service as soon as they were ready. By 24 November, the drive on Tunis opened with the ultimate objective of driving a wedge between Tunis and Bizerte, capturing Bizerte, and hemming in the Germans in the northernmost tip of Tunisia. Almost all Twelfth Air Force activity was in support of this operation, with the British assigning the targets.[13] German air activity was very damaging to the Allied effort, and missions against airdromes, lines of communication, and ports were assigned to the 12th Bomber Forces. The fighters flying close air support, escort, and strafing missions were in daily combat with the Axis forces, the tempo increasing as the Allied push drew nearer to Tunis.

Doolittle's tasking called for both guarding against an Axis move from Spain or its Moroccan colony and supporting the British in Tunisia. By 19 November, he was considering an organization plan more suited to the demands likely to be placed upon him. One aspect of the plan was to have a forward sector of the combat area assigned to the Twelfth Air Force.

Coincidentally, Air Marshall Welsh had chosen the Tebessa region in East Algeria, 175 miles southwest of Tunis, as a forward base area for the Twelfth. The units that went to the Tebessa area were the forerunners of the formidable 12th Air Support Command of later months.[14]

By his own admission, Doolittle got off on the wrong foot with Eisenhower in August 1942, during early planning for TORCH. He had used a less than tactful approach in replying to Eisenhower on airfield support requirements for the TORCH area.[15] Such a misstep, however, apparently had no bearing on Eisenhower's evaluation of his leadership in actual battle command and organization of the Twelfth Air Force. On 17 November, Eisenhower, with Spaatz's agreement, replied to a query from General Marshall that "Promotion of Doolittle is fully justified . . . ."[16] Doolittle was promoted on 20 November.

In late November, impressed with the boldness, courage, and stamina of General Anderson's forces, Eisenhower made the courageous decision "to take whatever additional risks might be involved in weakening our rear in order to strengthen Anderson."[17] As a beginning, the Twelfth Air Force was ordered to move as far forward to the east as possible to join in the air battle in support of General Anderson. Eisenhower now called Spaatz down from England to coordinate this American air effort with the British air forces, and Spaatz initially was given the title of Acting Deputy Commander-in-Chief for Air.[18]

The decision to move Spaatz to North Africa was Eisenhower's, but it meshed well with Arnold's thinking and concerns over preventing the demise of the strategic bombing effort against Germany. It maintained Arnold's one-theater concept in that it was the United Kingdom-North Africa campaign against Germany.

Another consideration influencing Eisenhower to transfer Spaatz was that he could be expected to get along with the British. Eisenhower insisted on harmony among the Allies, and before the campaign was over he remarked in his diary that Spaatz ". . . fits into an Allied team very well indeed."[19] Certainly, Spaatz received high marks from most of his British colleagues.[20]

It has been reported, though, that Air Vice Marshal Sir Arthur Coningham was not particularly pleased to be serving under an American general who had been in the war for less than a year.[21] Coningham commanded the Western Desert Air Force in the seesaw battles for the Suez in 1941–42. With the marrying of the Middle East and Northwest African theaters of war in February 1943, Coningham became commander of the Northwest Africa Tactical Air Force under Spaatz's Northwest African Air Force.

As the Western Desert Air Force commander, Coningham's performance was nothing less than masterful, and he played a critical role in the British successes against the Germans in Egypt and Libya. He devised tactics for coordinating with and supporting the ground forces and preserving his tactical air forces under conditions of German offensive and defensive actions. The organizational framework for providing the closest cooperation between air and ground forces used by Eisenhower's North Africa forces actually was hammered out by Coningham in the Western Desert.[22] There is no evidence that in serving with Spaatz in North Africa, Coningham did other than continue his outstanding performance and give his complete cooperation, regardless of any personal feelings he may have had toward Spaatz.

By the time Spaatz arrived on December 1, 1942, to take on the job as Eisenhower's air deputy, the initial objectives of the TORCH forces were well in hand, and the battle for Tunis was under way. His appointment was effective on 3 December 1942 and was an interim step for him while the optimum air organization was being studied and sorted out by Eisenhower and the Combined British and American Chiefs of Staff. Spaatz also was the senior commander of all of the American Air Forces in the European Theater, a position to which he had been appointed in August 1942; therefore, in addition to his air deputy responsibilities, he handled such tasks as dividing B-17 replacements between the Eighth Air Force in England and the Twelfth in North Africa.

Spaatz's immediate problem as Eisenhower's air deputy was to coordinate General Doolittle's Twelfth Air Force operations with those of the

RAF's Eastern Air Command (EAC), which was providing air support to General Anderson's Blade Force. It had not been anticipated that the Twelfth Air Force would be able to move eastward as rapidly as it did, therefore it soon was operating from the same area in central and eastern Algeria as the EAC.[23]

In addition, the available forward air forces had been subordinated to the pressing need for the drive on Tunis, thus giving the First Army practical command over USAAF and RAF aircraft. This resulted in considerable misuse, e.g., B-17s directed against airfields instead of attacking the Tunisian ports through which the German and Italian forces were being supported. Spaatz immediately switched the bomber effort from airdromes to ports and achieved a rough division of air effort between the EAC and the Twelfth.[24]

Since the Allies were operating in the mountainous areas, and the Axis forces were on the coastal plains, the former were at a disadvantage. Supply was nearly an impossible problem, and the C-47 was the only thing that prevented collapse of the forward air support. Moreover, there were few open areas in which the Allies could establish airdromes, even if the supplies were obtainable by air, whereas the Germans had greater flexibility with their airfield complex and the ability to park their Stukas on the plains when necessary. The Stukas had already had their day, but because of the supply difficulties and the need to provide bomber escort, convoy protection, and air defense, the Allied fighters and light bombers could not bring enough combat power to bear on the battlefield to sufficiently inhibit the use of the slow and vulnerable dive-bombers. In fact, Spaatz argued that the ground formations had to take care of themselves against the Stukas by using their organic antiaircraft capability, for the JU-87 had been proven extremely vulnerable to such fire in other theaters. He tried to convince the ground commanders that such combat power as the air arm could bring that far forward would do more good for the ground units if applied to other air superiority tasks and interdiction.[25] Spaatz, as well as other airmen, were saying to the ground commanders that the German air force had to be defeated first before close air support could be provided.

Expensive lessons were being learned by the TORCH forces in loss of men and materiel and in air forces support of the ground forces. These lessons had already been learned by the British in the Mediterranean and Mid-East theater in 1941. After the fall of Crete to the Germans in May, Air Marshal Sir Arthur Tedder, the Air Officer Commanding Middle

East British forces, had written to Lord Louis Mountbatten upon Mountbatten's criticism of the air support received: "I told Mountbatten that we could not conceivably afford the luxury of dividing our available air forces into penny packets and so hopelessly prejudicing our fight to attain and maintain air superiority."[26]

In early September 1941, the British prime minister, Winston Churchill, had issued a clarifying directive on the economical use of airpower that explicitly addressed controversial issues between the British air and ground forces:[27]

> Never more must the ground troops expect as a matter of course, to be protected against the air by aircraft. . . . Above all the idea of keeping standing patrols of aircraft over moving columns should be abandoned. It is unsound to 'distribute' aircraft in this way and no air superiority will stand any large application of such a mischievous practice.

Churchill went on to direct the coordination of all Army and Air commanders as to the targets and tasks to be performed and established general priorities on the use of air forces:

> The Air Officer Commanding-in-Chief would naturally lay aside all routine programmes and concentrate on bombing the rearward services of the enemy in the preparatory period. This he would do not only by night, but by day attacks with fighter protection. In this process he will bring about a trial of strength with the enemy fighters and has the best chance of obtaining local command of the air.

Anderson's Blade Force got within fifteen miles of Tunis before it was halted on 28 November 1942. Torrential rains in December turned the supply roads and Allied airfields to mud. At the end of the year, Spaatz conferred with Eisenhower on the air situation with a view toward thinning out the forces at the most forward fields. He explained that as long as there had been a real prospect of quickly taking Tunis and Bizerte, the wastage imposed on the air forces was justifiable. Now that chance seemed to be gone, however, and maintaining large air formations at the forward mud patches made them highly vulnerable and their maintenance and supply so inefficient that it would amount to the consumption of available air combat power without a commensurate gain. Eisenhower responded to that and other arguments by calling off the offensive and ordering his forces to dig in on the defensive and to regenerate themselves for another fight once the logistical systems and the weather had improved. Having missed the chance for a quick coup, if such had existed, the Allied forces settled down for the longer haul.[28]

Frustrated in the north, Eisenhower brought the American II Corps, commanded by Maj. Gen. Lloyd Fredendall, into the line well to the south of Anderson's First Army and placed some French units forming the XIX Corps between the two. For a time he was planning an offensive with the II Corps to reach the coastal ports south of Tunis and Bizerte to cut off Rommel from von Arnim. When he discovered that Montgomery would not be in the region until the middle of February, however, he ordered Fredendall's II Corps to abandon the planned offensive in favor of setting up a defensive line on the north-south mountain range well to the west of the coast. During the next six weeks, both sides built up their forces as rapidly as they could.[29]

In mid-February 1943 Rommel attacked this line, causing the flight of many green American units. The onslaught carried through Kasserine Pass and into the Allied rear areas beyond the Tunisian mountains before it began to lose steam. During the last week in February, partly because the attack had spent itself, and partly because Montgomery was approaching from the south, Rommel withdrew back through the pass, with the Americans in pursuit exacting a toll for the passage.[30]

At the moment that Rommel attacked, the Allied air forces were in the process of reorganizing. As an interim step, the RAF group supporting Anderson's First Army to the north, the 12th Air Support Command which was supporting the U.S. II Corps, and the French XIX Corps had been placed under one authority—soon to be named the Northwest African Tactical Air Force. The RAF air marshal designated to command it, Sir Arthur Coningham, had not yet arrived when the attack began, so second-in-command Brig. Gen. Laurence Kuter, USAAF, took charge of operations—insofar as communications and the state of the fields and supplies permitted. The primitive conditions along the front and the limited forces available were inhibitions enough, but in the midst of the battle, the weather closed in first with a dust storm, and then with rain and fog. Thus, Kuter could not bring the full weight of his airpower to bear on the advancing Germans and Italians.

Up to that point, the heavy bombers of Doolittle's Twelfth Air Force had been for the most part attacking the ports used by the Axis and the airfields of the Luftwaffe and Italian air force. Spaatz diverted them from these missions to meet the crisis. He assigned all of the USAAF heavy bomber strength plus some RAF Wellington units to the service of the tactical commanders fighting the battle. The "heavies," too, were limited by the weather for a time. The 12th Air Support Command had established several forward airfields to the east of the western branch of the Tunisian mountains, and Rommel's advance to Kasserine Pass was threatening to cut them off. The Allies lost several of these fields, but the retreat had been sufficiently anticipated that little in the way of equipment and supplies was left behind. Once the battle reached the far side of the pass, the weather improved and Allied airpower figured in the fighting more heavily. Allied aircraft and artillery fire harassed the Axis forces as they retreated eastward through Kasserine Pass, but that could not erase the humiliation suffered by the American army in its first large encounter with the German army.[31]

In his postmortem, General Eisenhower pointed out that Kasserine Pass was "a spot clearly indicated as one to be strongly held. But there was a local lack of appreciation of exactly what was happening and the troops assigned were neither numerous enough nor skillful enough to hold that strong position."

Contributing causes were the failure (of the TORCH forces) to quickly capture Tunis, thus dispersing units and inhibiting preparation for follow-on enemy actions; faulty intelligence about where the Germans would attack; failure to comprehend the capabilities of the enemy and the best measures for meeting them, thereby causing a dispersion of Allied mobile reserves; and, finally, the greenness of the Americans, particularly the commanders. The American divisions involved had not had the benefit of intensive training in the United States and, having been shipped quickly to the United Kingdom, had been separated from their equipment for long periods prior to their landing in North Africa.[32]

Kasserine Pass accentuated in airmen's minds the need for improved organization of airpower. They felt that the ground commanders still had too much control over tactical airpower, and that there was a strong tendency for them to misuse it. The ground commanders were prone to schedule air missions against ground targets in the immediate vicinity of their Army units or to passive overhead patrols without first having achieved air superiority. Spaatz strongly opposed such defensive use of his aircraft. Shortly before the battle at Kasserine Pass, for example, on 5 February 1943, he had visited the II Corps commander, General Fredendall, at his headquarters. Fredendall told him that in upcoming operations he wanted his troops to see American bombs falling immediately in front of their positions and, if possible, some Stukas shot down in view of the troops. He asserted that this was essential to morale. Spaatz answered that use of air assets in that way would lead to their premature consumption for insufficient return. He held that Fredendall's troops would benefit far more were American airpower to concentrate on enemy air bases and supply dumps. Spaatz argued, unsuccessfully, that the most effective defenses against the dive bombers was the organic antiaircraft of the ground units themselves.[33]

The view of airpower by Fredendall and other ground commanders led to the dispersion of Allied air resources into such small packages that the unified command of the Axis air units, though inferior in overall numbers, could mass its aircraft against a fraction of those possessed by the Allies. The consequence was that wherever the Luftwaffe was operating, it enjoyed local air superiority, and the effects were devastating.[34] Whatever the difficulties, though, Carl Spaatz (in the privacy of his own staff meeting) asserted that ". . . the air effort was probably the major effort in stopping the break-through at Kasserine."[35]

Just after the Kasserine action, the full reorganization of the air forces took place. The decision to rearrange the command and control of airpower had been made the previous month. In January some important support (from the point of view of the American airmen) came from the best possible source, Gen. Bernard L. Montgomery, himself a ground officer just then riding the crest of his fame as the victor of El Alamein. Montgomery published a pamphlet, ostensibly for the general officers serving with him in Eighth Army, which constituted a kind of primer on generalship in war. He began his instruction with some passages on the management of airpower, which gave powerful ammunition to the American airmen in their organizational struggles:[36]

5. Any officer who aspires to hold high command in war must understand clearly certain basic principles regarding the use of airpower.

6. The greatest asset of airpower is its flexibility, and this enables it to be switched quickly from one objective to another in the theater of operations. So long as this is realized, then the *whole weight* of the available airpower can be used in the selected areas in turn; this concentrated use of the air striking force is a battle-winning factor of the first importance.

7. It follows that control of the available airpower must be centralized, and command must be exercised through RAF channels.

Nothing could be more fatal to successful results than to dissipate the air resources into small packets. . . . The soldier must not expect, or wish, to exercise direct command over air striking forces.

8. The commander of an army in the field should have an Air H.Q. with him. . . . Such air resources will be in support of his army, and not under his command. . . .

Such advice flew in the face of the traditional U.S. War Department doctrine, but Montgomery's words could not have suited Spaatz more had he written them himself. According to Air Marshall Tedder, Montgomery's pronouncements were based on a speech written for him by Air Marshall Coningham.[37] The cover of the pamphlet limited its circulation to officers of the Eighth Army, but some copies were circulated among the American officers and one found its way back across the Atlantic to Arnold.[38]

In January 1943, at a meeting in Casablanca, the Allied leaders and chiefs of staff decided upon a reorganization to take place in February, of the Allied forces in the theater. Eisenhower was to be given three deputies, one each for land, sea, and air. Each of these was to be British, and the air commander appointed was Air Marshal Sir Arthur Tedder. Under Tedder would be the air forces in the Middle East, those on Malta, and the Northwest African Air Force to be commanded by Spaatz. The latter was to be reorganized along functional lines, containing British and American units in each of those subunits. The staffs of all the headquarters involved were manned by both Americans and Britons. An RAF officer, Air Vice Marshal J. M. Robb, was appointed Spaatz's deputy air commander. Another, Air Commodore A. MacGregor, became the air officer administrative and a third, Group Capt. C. L. Falconer served as Lauris Norstad's assistant in operations.[39] These combined staffs were made the norm at the next-lower level also. The commanders of the subordinate functional units were drawn from both air forces, the principal two being General Doolittle, leading the strategic air forces, and Air Marshall Arthur Coningham at the helm of the tactical support forces.[40]

Spaatz established an administrative echelon at Algiers for his Northwest African Air Force (NAAF) and set up an operational headquarters at Constantine close to Doolittle's Northwest African Strategic Air Force Headquarters. Spaatz's earlier arrival in North Africa to serve as Eisenhower's air deputy was darkened by news that the B-17 carrying his chief of staff, Brig. Gen. Asa Duncan, from England had caught fire and crashed in the Bay of Biscay. For days, it was hoped that survivors might be found, but finally Duncan and his crew were presumed dead. Col. Edward P. Curtis, assistant to General Duncan, was aboard Spaatz's aircraft on the flight to North Africa, and it was he who became acting chief of staff.

Ted Curtis, in civilian life a vice president of Eastman Kodak, was a World War I pilot who had returned to active duty at the first sign of U.S. involvement in World War II. He was one of a large number of business and professional men who left their careers and again put on uniforms to serve in any capacity needed. Because of his competence and rapport with Spaatz, Curtis soon became Spaatz's permanent chief of staff. He held that position until the end of the war in Europe and retired as a major general. Among Curtis' valuable assets was tact, and he was of great help in cementing relations with the British and with the French, whose language he spoke.[41]

Another invaluable addition to Spaatz's staff arrived early in the North African campaign. On a visit to Eisenhower's headquarters, Spaatz was impressed by a very efficient WAC secretary and immediately sent a request to his friend, Col. Oveta Culp Hobby, director of the Women's Army Corps, to please send him one of the same. Shortly thereafter, Lt. Sally Bagby arrived.[42]

When Margaret Bourke-White, the wartime photographer, visited North Africa she wrote:[43]

All business at Villa Spaatz, whether it had to do with housekeeping or the Air Force, passed through the able hands of pretty, black-haired Sally Bagby. Sally was a WAC and had one of the most interesting jobs in the Army. She had come into the General's service as a secretary and shown such intelligence and reliability that he had made her his aide . . . Sally did everything from being hostess to the many transient house-guests to keeping the General's poker scores. In addition, she knew more about each forthcoming campaign than most of the Generals knew. During my brief stay she was raised from Lieutenant to Captain, a promotion which made all of us very happy.

Reorganization did not automatically defuse the air-ground issue. Tension between airmen and ground commanders continued during the subsequent spring campaigns. After Kasserine, General Fredendall was replaced by George Patton as commander of U.S. II Corps. Patton's unit was assigned a supporting role in what was to have been the final battle to drive Rommel and von Arnim into the corner at Tunis and Bizerte. By this time, Coningham had taken command of all the tactical air forces under Spaatz. During the battle, Patton complained that the tactical air forces were not giving II Corps the close support it deserved, and he did it in somewhat immoderate terms. Coningham responded that Patton's complaints sounded like he was using the air arm as an alibi to explain away failures that arose from the want of "battle worthiness" on the part of the ground troops. This led to an uproar and, finally, to Eisenhower imposing on Coningham the requirement to make a public apology to II Corps—which, even in the words of Omar Bradley, its second-in-command, was indeed of limited battle worthiness.[44] Eisenhower sent Tedder with Coningham to talk to Patton. Peace was declared and mutual understanding achieved. Tedder adds a postscript:[45]

> When we had settled it all and the three of us were arm in arm over the odd drink, there was the sudden noise of rifle, machine-gun, and anti-aircraft fire, and three F.W. 190s scooted across about two hundred feet up. I nodded to George Patton, and said, 'I always knew you were a good stage manager, but this takes the cake.' Bradley reports that Patton's summing up was: 'If I could find the sonsabitches who flew those planes I'd mail them each a medal.'

After the reorganization, the Army and its Air Force worked out a *modus operandi* that served throughout the remainder of the war. However, in the privacy of a letter to Arnold at the end of the Tunisian campaign, Spaatz expressed his exasperation on the issue:[46]

> In so far as our relationship with the Ground Army is concerned, I would say that the "situation is normal." If it were not for the disturbance which would ensue, I would probably announce the urgent necessity of a separate Air Force. The best will, understanding, and intentions topside cannot overcome the basic difference between ground and air which permeates the entire structure.

The reorganization, nevertheless, was a giant step toward unifying control of air forces at theater level, and therefore a major step forward for Spaatz and Arnold. This was true not only in organizational terms, but also in terms of the key personnel selected for the work. Tedder and Coningham were transferred from the Middle East, where they had evolved that doctrine in the long campaigns against Rommel: they were apostles of capitalizing on the flexibility of airpower through centralizing control. But, as far as Arnold and Spaatz were concerned, it was no more than a large step in the right direction. They wanted command to include all air units deployed against the European Axis. In a sense, the new arrangements flowing from the Casablanca Conference were also a step backwards. Rather than uniting the air forces in England with those in the Mediterranean, Eisenhower was relieved of his European theater position and the two areas were made into separate theaters. Eisenhower remained the supreme commander in the Mediterranean, but Gen. Frank Andrews was called to England to become the American commander of the European theater of operations. Consequently, Spaatz no longer retained his title as the senior American air commander in the European theater—not in the formal sense at least.[47]

## Commanding the Northwest African Air Force

When Eisenhower summoned Spaatz to North Africa to coordinate air support for American forces then assisting the drive toward Tunisia, Spaatz found logistical and doctrinal confusion. Supply, communication, and intelligence problems abounded. Doolittle's Twelfth Air Force had no clear mission and was operating according to an Army doctrine that subordinated it to ground control.

These and other difficulties forced the Allied armies to grind to a halt short of Tunis in December. Writing to Arnold in January, Eaker described his visit to North Africa:[48]

The reasons for the failure to sweep the Germans and Italians out of Tunisia are primarily two:

(1) The breakdown of supply and communications; and
(2) The muddy condition of forward airdromes.

Not only was there a total lack of hangar and shop space at the forward fields, but it was also extremely difficult to bring up materiel. One of the major factors inhibiting the solution of the basing problem was the supply puzzle. Once the initial thrust toward Tunis had halted short of its goal, the whole campaign boiled down to a logistics race. The deployment of antiaircraft units, to protect the bases, competed with the bombs and gasoline of the air units themselves for transportation space on the railroads. The mud problem for runways was partially overcome by using pierced-steel planking, but enough of that for just one runway used up a fair-sized vessel by itself and much of it piled up at the depot for weeks, waiting for railcar space.

Major obstacles to air support, from Spaatz's point of view, were the restrictions imposed on airpower by the existing doctrine, which tied air missions too closely to ground armies. In December 1942 Spaatz persuaded Eisenhower to let him reorganize his air forces along functional lines. The result was the creation in January 1943, under Spaatz's command, of the Allied Air Force. Hardly had this reorganization begun than, in mid-February, as a result of the decisions reached at Casablanca a month before, Spaatz converted the Allied Air Force into a combined Northwest African Air Force (NAAF) as part of Tedder's Mediterranean Air Command. By so doing he was able to free airpower from many of the ground restrictions and allow it to perform a wide array of missions of which it was capable.

The charter for the Northwest African Air Force was to open the Mediterranean sea lanes and help drive the Axis from Tunisia and Africa. To facilitate this Spaatz rearranged his inherited air assets—the Twelfth Air Force, the British Eastern Air Command, and the Western Desert Air Force—into three functional components. His Coastal Command, headquartered at Algiers under Hugh Lloyd, was charged with defending the coastal areas, protecting the sea convoys through the Mediterranean, and striking enemy sea transports. Doolittle's Strategic Air Force was assigned the task of attacking the ports at both ends of the Axis supply route and of hitting airfields that sheltered enemy transport planes and aircraft used for convoy protection or attacks on Allied ports and sea traffic. Coningham's Tactical Air Force was concerned primarily with close support of the advancing Allied ground armies, but it also joined in the battle against the Axis flow of supplies, reinforcements, and evacuations, as well as with the campaign to gain air superiority.

For this campaign Spaatz had at his disposal an array of aircraft. The most versatile of his fighters was the P-38 Lightning. While used primarily to escort bombers, the Lightning also proved highly effective in attacking enemy shipping, in supporting ground units, and in the air-to-air struggle for air superiority.[49] The P-39 Airacobra was proving useful in ground support work, while the P-40 was having some success in air-to-air operations when used en masse.[50] A sprinkling of Spitfires rounded out Spaatz's fighter force. His bomber fleet contained B-17s, B-24s, B-25s, B-26s, and some Douglas A-20s. The B-17 Flying Fortresses and B-24 Liberators were flown against all manner of targets, from those on the battlefield to embarkation ports in Sicily and Italy, usually escorted by the P-38s.[51] The B-25 Mitchells and B-26 Marauders were both reliable aircraft and used for a variety of offensive missions. Given the austere communication lines in the theater, the importance of the C-47 Skytrain was magnified. Although this transport plane could move but a tiny fraction of the goods required, it proved critical in delivering emergency items. The C-47s also played a vital role in their troop carrier mission, and they participated in the capture of several forward airfields at critical times in the campaign.

The Allied drive resumed in February. Spaatz recognized from the outset that the success of the campaign hinged on gaining control of the air from the Luftwaffe. This his units gradually accomplished by destroying Axis forces in air-to-air battles over Africa and the Middle East and wrecking them at their bases in Sicily and Italy. The achieving of air superiority was also helped by factors outside the theater. Eaker's forces, flying out of England, were pinning down important Luftwaffe fighter and antiaircraft resources that otherwise could have been sent to the Mediterranean.[52] In addition, the Luftwaffe was suffering substantial losses in Russia—its disastrous campaign at Stalingrad coincided with NAAF's successes in Africa.[53] By May, Spaatz was able to report to Arnold that the Allies enjoyed air "domination" in the Mediterranean and that nothing he could foresee was likely to reverse that situation.[54]

Control of the skies permitted Spaatz's other forces to wreak havoc on the enemy. The Mediterranean gradually became safer for Allied shipping and more dangerous for that of the Axis. Once spring arrived, the land lines of communication and the airfields dried up, speeding the flow of materiel along the land arteries.[55] That same improvement in the weather made the campaign against the Axis shipping and the air shuttle across the central Mediterranean more successful at the very time when the Allies were beginning to overcome the enemy submarine threat. As the Axis forces contracted into the Tunis area, their supply lines became shorter, which helped them some.

Spaatz, however, had an inestimable asset in the interdiction battle because of ULTRA. Since the Allies were reading the German codes, especially those of the Luftwaffe, they often had advanced notice of impending movements across the straits. The information was so voluminous and so accurate that Spaatz's units often had to be restrained against too-quick action in response to ULTRA intelligence lest the German commander, Kesselring, suspect that the Allies had broken his codes.[56]

By April Tunisia was becoming untenable for the Luftwaffe, which moved its aerial armada, except its fighters, back to Sicily and beyond.[57] This relieved some of the threat to Allied installations and permitted the use of air defense forces in more offensive operations.

Spaatz had been watching the Luftwaffe's air shuttle between Sicily and Tunis for several months, but did not do much about it for fear of scaring off his prey.[58] He had his people continue to gather data and to plan an operation that would combine most effectively the resources of his subordinate commands. He wanted to strike a concentrated and massive blow at the German airlifters so that the shock would interdict the traffic for good. While heavy bombers attacked the JU-52 fields in Sicily, the mediums and fighters would assault the Luftwaffe transport forces over the water. Other planes would attack the receiving end of the system in Tunisia.

On 5 April the weather was good, and the slaughter was complete. In all, the Axis lost two hundred airplanes in the air and on the ground that day. Many of the crews of the JU-52s were instructor personnel for the Luftwaffe's multi-engine and instrument training programs, and their loss had a deadly long-range effect.[59] The massacre of the German airlifters continued all month. From the TORCH landings to the Axis capitulation at the end of May, the German air force, in the Mediterranean alone, lost 2,422 planes of which 371 were transports.

Just as the "domination" Spaatz enjoyed permitted his forces to play a major role in denying the Axis armies the sinews of battle, it also allowed them to overcome the initial difficulties that had been suffered in assisting the army ground units against the German and Italian troops on the battlefield. The solution of the air-ground problem arose in part out of having air superiority, partially from the coming of spring and the drying up of the airfields, in part from the lessons that the British air commanders brought with them to Tooey's command from the Middle East, and, finally, in part from the time factor which permitted the growth of the tactical air forces.

The experience afforded by the invasion of North Africa and the other Mediterranean operations doubtless improved the chances that the invasion of France would succeed once it was mounted. One of the declared objectives of the African campaign had been to reopen the Mediterranean sea lanes and thus economize on shipping, and certainly that was facilitated by the victory. Another was to undermine Italy as a German ally, and she was indeed gravely weakened by what happened in Africa. Another factor, and this was a major one, was the deployment to North Africa and subsequent destruction of major Luftwaffe forces. Though the Russians were loathe to admit it, that was a substantial benefit for them. Not only was Luftwaffe power along the eastern front gravely weakened, but, also, the Germans were forced to redeploy air strength from Norway to the Mediterranean and so release some of the air pressure they were putting on the Allied convoys going to Russia at the very time that the undersea threat was being brought under control.[60] Finally, though the numbers captured at Tunis were not huge by eastern front standards, they were substantial nevertheless—over 200,000, and von Arnim was among them.[61] There was no Axis Dunkirk, and their feeble attempt at evacuation failed almost completely, though Rommel himself got back to Germany in good time.

The North African campaign did nothing to weaken Spaatz's commitment to the idea of daylight, precision, strategic bombing.[62] In fact, there was little strategic bombing done in the sense defined by the Air Corps Tactical School. U.S. doctrine for tactical air warfare was relatively primitive at the outset of the North African operations; in the course of battle it was greatly elaborated under the guidance of the RAF, and it emerged in a form very similar to the doctrine still in force in the USAF. Spaatz was deeply involved in the development of this doctrine.

## On to Italy

The invasion of Sicily had been agreed upon in January at the Casablanca Conference, with Spaatz in attendance. The occupation of the island had much to recommend it. It would complement the acquisition of the North African shore as a step toward making the Mediterranean secure for Allied sea traffic and deny its use to the Axis maritime forces. It would provide new bases from which Allied airpower could more readily attack central and southern Italy. It would employ troops that otherwise would be idle for the latter half of 1943 for the useful purpose of holding down German ground and air units that otherwise might be sent against the Russians or United Kingdom. Finally, the Allied leaders felt that the conquest of Sicily, much more than the alternatives of Sardinia, Corsica, or the Balkans, might well put so much pressure on the Italians that Mussolini would fall and the junior Axis partner might quit—or even change sides.[63]

A special planning staff was set up for the Sicilian campaign, and the invasion was code-named HUSKY. The plan called for the British under Montgomery to land on the eastern face of the southern corner of Sicily, while the Americans assaulted the western beaches. Once ashore, the Americans would protect the left flank of the British armies as they made the main attack up the east coast to the city of Messina. That city was the embarkation point Kesselring would have to use to evacuate his forces across the two-mile strait to the toe of the Italian boot. The British thrust would pass between Mount Etna and the sea through some rough terrain that rather favored the defenders.[64]

HUSKY planners realized that any amphibious operation without adequate single-engine fighter cover would be excessively dangerous. Army and Navy alike fully accepted the USAAF thesis that air superiority over the battlefield was essential and should be the first of the air arm's missions. Sicily lay to the east of the Allied air bases in Tunisia. Though the distance is less than a hundred miles, the assault was to be made at the far end of the island; fighters would consume so much fuel getting there that they would not have sufficient endurance to provide the degree of air cover required. Malta was somewhat closer to the landing areas, but the saturated fields there could not accommodate the additional fighter units. Spaatz therefore proposed taking another island, Pantelleria, which was close enough to Sicily to serve as a base for "short-legged" fighters.[65] The difficulty was that the only feasible landing beaches on Pantelleria were immediately beneath the guns protecting the harbor, and the Axis airplanes based there were safely hangared inside a huge cave. The defenders, however, were vulnerable on one score. The island was completely garrisoned by Italian troops who were not of the first line and who had already lost what little enthusiasm they had had for the war. They were isolated from any hope of support, and it seemed possible that they might be conquered by a combined air-sea bombardment (with the air supplying the greater part of the firepower). Alexander, still Eisenhower's deputy for ground operations, was persuaded, and Eisenhower consented to the attempt. A massive bombardment was conducted during the first week of June, and the Italian garrison put up the white flag as the troops were embarking in the landing craft. The island was occupied without any Allied ground casualties.[66]

The air assault on Pantelleria was the baptism by fire for the 99th Fighter Squadron, which had been assigned to the combat-proven 33rd Fighter Group and was the first black fighter unit in aerial history to see combat. Despite some freshman mistakes in their first outings against ground targets and German bomber escorts, the determination of their commander, Benjamin O. Davis, Jr., later to rise to the rank of lieutenant general, kept them as a viable and successful unit for the rest of the war. Within a few months in Italy, the squadron was to become the nucleus of an all-black fighter group, the 332nd, which Davis would command.

The airfield on Pantelleria was promptly cleared up, and another was built on Gozo, one of the satellite islets of Malta. In this way, the HUSKY task force was assured its fighter cover. The rest of Spaatz's forces would help achieve the requisite air superiority in other ways. The bombers had been punishing the Axis airfields on Sicily and the southern parts of the Italian peninsula all through the Tunisian campaign, and the job already was partly done. Further, the German and Italian air forces had suffered substantial losses in Africa from which they had not recovered. The Sicilian campaign was to begin for the Northwest African Air Force's bombers and long-range fighters weeks in advance of the July 10th date set for the landings. The medium bombers and fighters were to continue the attacks on the Sicilian fields and the few ports there, while heavy bombers were assigned similar tasks against the airdromes and ports in Italy. Further, the plan included some long-range interdiction strikes as far north as Rome in order to inhibit Kesselring's ability to bring reinforcements and supplies down to Sicily. Finally, Spaatz's troop carrier command was to land forces behind the assault beaches to take some bridges and high ground. Spaatz expressed a note of caution, warning the ground commanders against writing a plan that would depend on such airborne strikes for success.[67] Much had been done to overcome the organizational and doctrinal problems of the young air force during the Tunisian campaign, but all of the difficulties had not yet been eliminated, and Spaatz was sensitive to the reservations of his ground and naval colleagues. In fact, he charged John K. Cannon specifically with the task of satisfying George Patton during the Sicilian landings and following battles.[68] Still, it was established everywhere within the Allied forces that the battle would be fought with centralized control of the air forces and that air superiority would be their primary mission.[69]

Though the air forces were engaged some weeks before the ground and sea forces, they were not fighting at the maximum rate. They had been going all out for several months prior to the capitulation in Tunisia, and the crews and aircraft had been used at rates higher than anticipated. They needed a period between campaigns to regenerate their units. Even as they were beginning the air battle in preparation for the invasion of Sicily, they kept operations at less than peak level to permit the consolidation of organization, the bringing in and training of replacements, the maintenance of war-weary aircraft, and some rest for the crews that had fought in North Africa. Even with this less-than-total effort, however, they pounded the airdromes of Sicily so hard that the Axis air forces had to pull more than half their strength back to the mainland even before the invading forces anchored off the coast.[70]

In the meantime, intelligence and counterintelligence had given Spaatz and the other Allied commanders two major advantages over their enemies. First, ULTRA delivered a complete picture of the enemy order of battle and revealed much about the intentions of the Axis commanders. Second, a deception scheme worked so perfectly that it not only obscured Allied intentions, but quite convinced Hitler that the main landings would be made in Sardinia and the Balkans and that any move toward Sicily would be but a feint.[71] By the time the amphibious forces were standing off the Sicilian shore on July 10, major German units had been sent to faraway places to defend against illusory threats, and those still in the vicinity of the battle had already been severely weakened by the Allied air forces.

By all accounts, the landings on the 10th were successful. Notwithstanding subsequent Navy and Army complaints,[72] out of a fleet of more than 1,400 vessels, the Axis air units sank only twelve.[73] Both the American and British forces went ashore with few losses, and the Italian coastal divisions folded without much of a fight.[74]

While all the other assigned missions of the air units were accomplished effectively and with few losses, the airborne troop delivery operations were ragged. The same weather conditions that added to the surprise of the landings (the Italians had assumed that no landing would be undertaken from such rough seas as existed on the evening of July 9th), complicated the delivery of the airborne troops. Those assigned to take a bridge beyond the British beaches to facilitate their advance were delivered by gliders. Many were released too far from shore and landed in the sea, and the troopers loaded down with combat gear had little chance to survive. Still, a tiny fragment of the force did arrive at the bridge and succeeded in holding it long enough to prevent its destruction before the seaborne troops arrived. The rest landed far and wide, but in the end did some good because they contributed to the confusion under which the Axis command had to labor.[75]

The American airborne troops were delivered by parachute, and they, too, were scattered far from their designated drop zones. That added to the confusion on both sides. Their mission had been to take some high ground behind the American beaches. The fragments that did arrive at the correct place succeeded in holding that ground and made an important contribution by delaying the Axis counterattack long enough for the Americans to build up the forces on the beaches. The German counterattack came, however, and on the second day, July 11, threatened to overrun the American beachhead. Another drop was scheduled for that evening to lend support to the beleaguered troops on the beach. The navigation this time was much better, but the planning time had been so short that the notice of the mission had not filtered down to all the units of the fleet and the army on the beach. Consequently, one of the antiaircraft gunners opened fire on the C-47s and the later waves of the airborne operation were badly punished by their own soldiers and sailors. Twenty-two of the aircraft were shot down by Allied gunners. Only a small fragment of the force landed on the airfield that was serving as their drop zone.[76]

Almost all of the troop carrier and tow planes belonged to Spaatz's 51st and 52d Troop Carrier Wings, and the experience led to much soul-searching through the summer. Part of the fault had been that the training had been inadequate before a difficult night drop was undertaken. That, in turn, had been due in part to the late delivery of the gliders. Each one had been shipped in five crates, and many individual crates were misdirected or lost en route from the United States. It took so much time to find the missing crates that there was not enough time left for the training that should have preceded the launching of the mission. In addition, the C-47 crews were at fault because their navigation and formation discipline were weak. Further, the command and control unit did not get the word of the mission to the surface units on time. They had been under attack by the Luftwaffe just a few minutes before the troop carriers arrived overhead, and it is possible that the gunner that started the panic thought that the aircraft above were the same Germans.[77]

Though there were still some details to be worked on relative to air-ground tactics, Allied troops were little bothered by the Axis air forces throughout the Sicilian campaign. The Mediterranean Air Command, of which Spaatz's Northwest African Air Force was the principal element operating in Sicily, achieved a clear air superiority, perhaps even supremacy.[78] The interdiction effort was heartening. Spaatz's fighter-bombers and medium bombers went on a rampage over the Sicilian roads and made an important contribution to the victory. They, and the naval forces, however, were unable to prevent the Axis forces from escaping to the mainland across the Straits of Messina. The straits there are only two miles wide, and Kesselring massed sufficient antiaircraft artillery to inhibit air attack. Torpedo boats prevented the naval forces from intervening as effectively as they had during the night crossing attempts of the Tunisian campaign,[79] but Spaatz's forces did some good work in close support of the troops. Air officers, equipped with jeeps with VHF radios, accompanied the ground troops; thus, in both Africa and Sicily, communication directly with the assaulting air formations to help them find their targets and to prevent mistaken attacks on Allied ground units was initiated.[80]

To a large extent, bad winter weather was the primary factor that frustrated Allied hopes for the early capture of Tunis and the trapping of Rommel. The opposite was the case in Sicily—the weather was too good! There was practically no meteorological limitation on air operations, and that led to such continuous attacks that there was little "down time" for the maintenance of aircraft. Further, even though bomber crew members in the Northwest African Air Force had a tour length twice as long as that of Eighth Air Force flyers (fifty missions versus twenty-five), their high rate of flying was threatening a crisis in manning. The rate of tour completions was exceeding the rate of replacement, and the problems with the troop carrier operations and air-ground coordination in Sicily suggested that the experience level of the force could hardly bear further reduction. Though the attrition rates in the Mediterranean were much lower than in England, the tempo of operations was higher and that, too, seemed to have some impact on crew fatigue. Neither Doolittle nor Spaatz was ready to recommend an increase in the number of missions required of an individual. Spaatz did put restrictions on the frequency with which his key personnel, commanders and operations officers, flew in combat, in the hope of maintaining the desired experience level. Beyond that there was little that he could do besides ask Arnold to increase the flow of replacements.[81]

Spaatz seemed satisfied with the organization within the Northwest African Air Force.[82] His style of command, as always, was seen by many as rather casual. He devoted much of his time to visiting combat units in the field and spent very little time in his office, preferring to do business at his living quarters—often over the supper table or during the many poker sessions.[83] Apparently his concept of what a chief of staff should be varied widely from his view of what constituted an effective commander. As Arnold's chief of staff before the war, he stayed closer to the office and often went to great lengths to make sure that none of the details were overlooked. As a commander, however, he left that kind of work to General Curtis, his own chief of staff, and traveled frequently about the theater.

Normally, Spaatz's leadership style was to give his subordinates general instructions but not hover over them during the execution. His longtime friend and companion, Ira Eaker, who with him had fought both peace and wartime battles for the Air Force, described him in a talk at the Air Force Academy in 1974:[84]

> General Spaatz's success as a military leader and manager was due primarily to his possession of two indispensable qualities, to an extraordinary degree. He possessed absolute integrity. He never vacillated, trimmed or hedged where principle was involved. Many times, when it seemed certain it would jeopardize his career, he took the unpopular course of that contrary to his military superiors, because he believed it was right and he would not compromise.
>
> The other quality was wisdom. He was always wise beyond his years. He was one of the most perceptive, quick-witted men I ever knew. Common sense dictated all his decisions and motivated his conduct . . . [He was] the wisest defense leader I ever knew . . .

The next step after the capture of Sicily was the Italian mainland. The initial objectives of the Allies were the port of Naples to provide logistical support of the forces, and the Foggia airfield complex on the eastern side of the peninsula to serve as a strategic bombing base area. Mark Clark would seize the first objective by landing his Fifth Army at Salerno, south of Naples, while the British Eighth Army under Montgomery would work its way up from the toe of the Italian boot. The Allies knew that their forces landing at Salerno were smaller than those of Kesselring, the German commander in Italy, but they counted on Montgomery's Eighth Army coming north in support and on an overwhelming naval and air superiority.

The Allies deployed more than three thousand aircraft in supporting the Italian invasion, and some seven hundred ships were used for the

Salerno landings. The Axis had hardly more than a third as many aircraft.

The Luftwaffe was able to get out sufficient reconnaissance preceding the invasion, so Kesselring knew what was going on in the marshalling ports throughout the Mediterranean. But when the various convoys got under way, he did not have enough air strength to do much about it. The convoys arrived off Salerno on the evening of 8 September having suffered only a few attacks and very few losses.[85] Things went well enough for the Allies the first day or two, but neither the requirement to disarm the Italians nor the condition of the Italian railroad system prevented Kesselring from quickly getting substantial forces to the beachhead. He launched a counter-offensive on the 13th, hoping to split the Allies at the joint between his two corps, perhaps even driving them into the sea.[86] The situation deteriorated on the Allied right flank, even to the point where Mark Clark thought of reembarking his headquarters staff and moving it to the X Corps area.

For Spaatz, this was one of the two most significant events of the fall (the other being the founding of Fifteenth Air Force at the Foggia airfield complex). The 12th Air Support Command had been committed to the direct assistance of the landing forces from the outset of the operations. As the situation became more critical, Spaatz diverted Doolittle's Strategic Air Force from its campaign against the Luftwaffe airfields and the Axis lines of communications to targets closer to the battlefield. Still, the pressure on the center of the Allied line continued, and there was not enough time to bring in reinforcements by sea. The ground situation became so critical on 13 September that, as Spaatz wrote to Arnold,[87]

an airborne operation, carrying elements of the 82nd Airborne Division was laid on for the evening of the 13th, as the result of an urgent call received at 2:30 on the afternoon of the 13th. The drop had to be made in an area not previously planned for, with the take-off at night from emergency fields. It was undertaken only because of the critical situation which existed. The operation was completely successful, with no losses of transports, and the Airborne troops placed exactly where they were wanted. They played a prominent part in holding up the enemy advance down the Sele River. The following night additional Airborne troops were dropped in the same area, as well as a battalion on Avellino. All of these drops were successfully completed, without loss in planes. Again, all take-offs were made at night.

The paratroopers helped, and the air support and naval bombardment contributed to repelling Kesselring's counterattack. After the 14th, the crisis began to subside. During the two most critical days of the counterattack, the Luftwaffe had been able to put up only about 450 sorties while Spaatz's forces alone launched 2,100 sorties on the day of the 14th. The total Allied air effort over the two days was ten times that of the Axis.[88] The German assault had been made possible in the first place by disengaging the troops in front of Montgomery and hurrying them north to help against the Salerno bridgehead. Now the British Eighth Army was approaching from the south and Kesselring had to pull away from the Salerno bridgehead and redeploy his forces on a lateral defensive line across the Italian boot.[89] When the Axis concentrated its effort against Salerno, not only did that open the way for Montgomery's march along the western shore of Italy, but it also prevented any serious opposition to landings farther east at the Gulf of Taranto. Montgomery's troops were able to move along the Adriatic coast toward the Foggia airfields rather quickly. Though Spaatz was concerned about how the forces under Rommel in the north of Italy might be used, once the counterattack had been repelled, both the Foggia airfields and the port of Naples fell into Allied hands by the end of September. Spaatz told Arnold, however, that he thought the interdiction campaign against the railroads (coastal shipping for the Axis had already been halted) would keep Rommel's troops out of the battle in the south because they simply could not be supplied there.[90] Spaatz and all other airmen took it as an article of faith that neither the close air support of the besieged beachhead, nor the tactical airlift of supplies and men to it, nor the interdiction of the enemy lines of communication leading toward the battle, could have succeeded without the air superiority that the Allies enjoyed over the "Hun."[91]

For the airmen, the chief reward of the Italian campaign, perhaps of the whole Mediterranean war, was the acquisition of new strategic bomber airfields in the Foggia area. The Ploesti raid had been flown from Africa the previous summer with tough losses, caused in part because the objective was so far from the African airdromes. The new bases in Italy were much closer to that target, and a sustained effort could be mounted that would not only help the strategic bombing campaign, but also the Russian fight on the eastern front and the coming battles in France by depriving the German war machine of its fuel. More than that, the acquisition of the new bases brought the heavy bombers into range of many strategic targets in the south of Germany, Austria, and in the Balkans that previously were out of the reach of Eighth Air Force in England. Yet some of these targets were close enough to those of the Eighth that coordinated raids were possible, with a better chance of saturating the German defenses. Major German defense units were already deployed against Eighth Air Force in the northwest. The mounting of a new threat from the south, especially one partially shielded from German radar by the Alps, would impose a further strain on Axis resources and reduce the Allied losses among both the Mediterranean and United Kingdom strategic bomber forces. Finally, the winter weather in England and northern Europe often shut down strategic bombing operations there: if the base were not "socked in," then the target would be, or so it seemed. The possession of new bases in Italy offered greater flexibility to the strategic bombers, enabling them to deny the German defenders any respite.[92]

During the summer, it had been decided to locate a major air force in the Italian boot to assist in the strategic bombing campaign against Germany, among other things. This was not achieved without opposition. Arnold favored the notion, and Spaatz and Eisenhower and Doolittle also desired to place large heavy bomber units there. However, General Eaker protested strongly that the diversion of such units to Foggia would be a mistake, a violation of the principle of mass. For a time, his arguments were supported by some RAF leaders. He pointed out that the logistical dimension of the problem would be greater than if the units were placed in England. There was already in place a major manufacturing, maintenance, and supply complex in the United Kingdom, but the same would have to be built practically from scratch in southern Italy. Further, though the Foggia area had several airfields, many of them were insufficient for heavy bombers and major improvements would be required. The engineering resources available in the Mediterranean theater were already stretched tightly. Moreover, a major land campaign was still being fought just north of the Foggia complex, and the growing strategic air forces would have to compete with the ground units for shipping and port capacity.[93] Spaatz found himself on the opposite side of this issue from Eaker for one of the rare times in their thirty-year professional association, but he insisted. In October, he flew back to Washington to state his case. He argued that the logistical problems, as severe as they were, could be overcome, and his opinion carried the day as Arnold and the JCS decided to go ahead with the project of establishing Fifteenth Air Force in southern Italy.[94]

The initial cadre for Fifteenth Air Force was created by converting the 12th Bomber Command into an Air Force and making Doolittle its commander. Its six heavy bomber groups with their escorts were put under the new air force and given orders to move from Tunis to Italy. The goal was to build up the force to twenty-one heavy groups by 15 March by diverting new units coming from the United States from their original destinations in the United Kingdom. The primary purpose of the new air force was the strategic bombing of Germany, but it also was to provide tactical support to the ground forces fighting in Italy. Eisenhower was authorized to use Fifteenth Air Force against tactical targets whenever he deemed it necessary to meet an emergency situation.[95] In the strategic realm, the top priority target was German airpower, and next came the ball bearing industry. The Fifteenth also had responsibilities to help the partisans in the Balkans and to support the advancing Russian armies headed toward that region.[96] The move was begun in the fall and, though logistics did indeed impede the buildup, attacks were begun out of Foggia even before the end of October 1943.[97]

## The Personal Side of War

Throughout these events in the Mediterranean, Tooey's thoughts never strayed for long from the personal concerns of his family and his associates. About the time of his transfer to Africa, Ruth fractured her leg. The girls, Katharine, Rebecca, and Carla, tried to make light of it with a telegram to their father, then thought to be in England, reporting the broken limb and requesting instructions as to whether their mother should be shot. One of Spaatz's aides, deeming the situation in Africa too critical to upset the general with the news, replied with a cable in his boss's name seriously mandating that the girls see to it that their mother got the best of medical attention. All involved knew that Spaatz would never have replied to the original telegram in such a serious way; they immediately inferred that it had been written by an aide and that the general was with Eisenhower in Africa.[98]

That story has survived as a family joke, but a more troubling event for Spaatz was Rebecca's marriage soon thereafter. Having fallen in love with a young USAAF pilot trainee, Emmet B. ("Red") Gresham, she agreed to marriage without consulting her father, which seems to have been a violation of a promise she had made to him before he went overseas.[99] Ruth recruited Tooey's old friend, Maj. Gen. Barton K. Yount, to stand in at the wedding and give the bride away. The ceremony was held in the chapel at Yount's training command base in

Selma, Alabama, and he later wrote to give Spaatz the father's-eye view of proceedings.[100] Spaatz, however, was not easily reconciled: he had high hopes for a musical career for Rebecca and feared that would now go to ruin.[101] Tooey's classmate, George Stratemeyer, was soon reporting on Gresham's progress in pilot school and that he would be posted to the Mediterranean theater under Spaatz's command once his training as a fighter pilot was complete.[102] By September, Gresham had arrived and was already in operations. In November, Spaatz reported to Ruth that Gresham had shot down his first German—something that surely helped establish Red's good standing with his father-in-law.[103]

Carla, the Spaatz's youngest, was still living with her mother in a Washington apartment, trying to become accustomed to her father's new fame. Hardly four years earlier, they were all members of a little-known lieutenant colonel's family living on the base down at Langley Field. Now, Carla, age 11, found her picture and those of her family in a feature article in *Life*.[104] The oldest daughter, Katharine, having been frustrated in her desire to go to Europe by the outbreak of the war in 1939, was still determined to get there. She tried all sorts of expedients. Her father even wrote to Ambassador John Winant in London in the hopes that a place could be found for Katharine on the embassy staff.[105] Finally, she went to England under the auspices of the American Red Cross and remained there and on the Continent throughout the war. Tooey had expressed a preference that she come to Africa since, in the summer of 1943, he told Ruth that he had no expectation of ever being able to get back to the United Kingdom. However, he still had plenty of friends in Eighth Air Force who could lend a hand—not that the independent Katharine would either desire it or need it.[106]

During all his years in the service, Spaatz had never been able to go very long without having to face personal tragedy. Now, more than ever, he had to live with it. Just after the victory in Tunis, he had to write what had to be one of the most difficult letters of his life to Madelaine Tinker. The Tinkers had served with the Spaatzes at March Field in the early thirties. While Spaatz had been moving Eighth Air Force across the Atlantic, Clarence Tinker had gone down into the Pacific in a B-24. Now their son, Bud, who had come into Spaatz's command, had been lost. As poignant as the letter was, Spaatz knew there was little he could say to help the bereaved mother who had lost her husband just eleven months earlier.[107]

The Tinker case was perhaps the most painful, but it was only one of a stream of tragedies that came upon him in the midst of crises. Shortly before the invasion of Sicily, one of his fighter group commanders, Lt. Col. G. W. West, crashed. He was so badly injured that both his legs were amputated in the 12th General Hospital in Africa. Even before he had regained consciousness, Spaatz had sent someone to look in on him. Four days before the landings, West had recovered enough to consider the future. He wrote Spaatz a passionate letter protesting his probable fate of being sent back to the United States to retirement and, as he saw it, a void.[108] He begged Spaatz to help him avoid the prospective retirement. He cited the case of the RAF's legless Douglas Bader, a hero of the Battle of Britain. He pleaded that what Bader had done could be done again. Apologizing to Spaatz for intruding on a busy schedule, West asked him only for a letter to carry along back to the U.S. to use in his effort to stay on active duty—or that Spaatz write to someone in authority there.[109]

Seven days after the assault on the beaches of Sicily, West, fearing that his first note to Spaatz might have gone astray in the heat of battle, wrote again along the same lines.[110] Spaatz replied the next day saying that three days earlier, immediately after the Germans had so threatened the American beachhead and his own Troop Carrier Command had lost twenty-two airplanes to friendly fire, he had written to Arnold citing West's case and asking that Hap help implement a plan to satisfy West's wishes. Spaatz had arranged that he be sent to the United Kingdom, rather than back to the homeland, and be fitted there with a pair of artificial legs.[111] He followed up on West's progress repeatedly in the ensuing months, and just three days before the Normandy invasion in 1944, he was able to entertain West at dinner. West had been promoted to colonel and arrived under his own power on his new legs.[112]

Another side of Spaatz is illustrated by his response to the continuing ostracism of black flyers. After arriving in Italy, the 99th Pursuit Squadron became part of the new black 332nd Fighter Group. Although its combat record steadily improved, its members continued to be officially segregated. Most often, this attitude spilled over into social relations. At a time when black officers were still excluded from white officers' clubs on bases in the United States, Spaatz's command created a recreation center at Capri for USAAF personnel. The officer in charge of the center banned pilots of the 99th from the island because white Red Cross women were there. Spaatz's chief of staff, General Curtis, with Spaatz's blessing, intervened and reversed the order, insisting that the blacks were fighter pilots and officers the same as any others in the USAAF and would be accorded equal treatment.[113] Although Spaatz undoubtedly shared General George Marshall's reluctance to view the Army as an instrument of social reform in the midst of a national emergency, he was determined to enforce fair treatment (by the standards of 1943) for the blacks in his units.

## Airpower Results of the Mediterranean Campaigns

During 1943, the American air forces under Spaatz developed an elaborate tactical air war doctrine and built an organization to implement it. The organization emphasized centralized control of all air assets at the theater level exercised by subordinate commands along functional lines. This was a radical departure from the geographical organization of airpower in the United States during the interwar period. Through it all, Spaatz remained in close contact with Arnold in the United States and with Eaker in England. Consequently, he had a strong impact on the development of the strategic air war against the German homeland. Though Spaatz was in command of the largest tactical campaign ever conducted by an American air force, it is clear that he never lost his desire to go back to England to join in the strategic war against the German heartland. He met Eaker frequently throughout 1943 at Gibraltar and in Africa, and their contact by the mails and electronic means was continual. He was fully versed in the mounting frustrations faced by Eighth Air Force in its daylight assaults against Germany and now his air forces were in a position, thanks to their Italian bases, to lend a hand in an important way. Finally, in the course of the Mediterranean fighting, the American air forces got their baptism of fire. They had won, and that was important morale capital, but it had not been a free ride; the combat experience they had gained was an important base on which to build for the final attack on Hitler's fortress.

For Carl Spaatz, too, it was a learning experience of the first order. He had come to the campaign with a considerable array of credentials. At the outset of the war, his experience as a tactical commander and as a high-level staff officer was hardly matched by anyone in the USAAF. During the first year of combat, as the commander of Eighth Air Force, he had been fully exposed to the problems of building and deploying a strategic air force and seeing it through its first combat trials. In Africa, Sicily, and Italy, he received valuable experience in organizing and conducting a tactical air war—and doing it in the company of a proud ally. As it included several major joint amphibious operations, and a number of important airborne assaults, his combat command experience included virtually every conceivable dimension of air warfare. The education brought important lessons in combined operations administered by the leaders of the RAF, perhaps the patriarch of modern air forces. It also incorporated some learning in joint operations administered by a Navy not at all inclined to forget its own institutional interests. Further, and perhaps most important, there were the lessons of the "school of hard knocks" delivered by a competent enemy air arm, weakened to be sure, but still not far past its prime. Finally, and not least important, Spaatz's relationship with Eisenhower was cemented. While they had worked together in England, it seems to have been the comradeship developed under trial in the Mediterranean battles that solidified the relationship and influenced Eisenhower to take Spaatz with him to England when he returned to take command of OVERLORD.

Carl Spaatz as a West Point cadet, circa 1914.

Tooey Spaatz awaits his instructor for a check ride at pilot training, circa 1916.

Maj. Carl Spaatz (*right*) in 1917 at Issoudun, France, where he was director of flying training for American aviators. *Courtesy Mrs. Carl A. Spaatz.*

Circa 1929, Maj. Carl Spaatz in his flying clothes. At this time he was with the pursuit aircraft arm of the Air Force. *Courtesy Mrs. Carl A. Spaatz.*

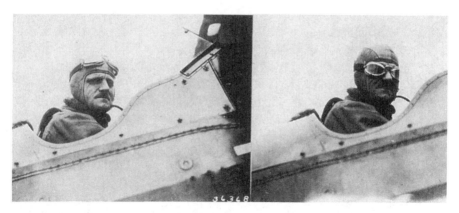

May 1929. Spaatz in his DH-4, providing support to ground forces during war maneuvers.

*Question Mark* being refueled in flight over the California coast, January 1929. Spaatz was aircraft commander; Capt. Ira C. Eaker was chief pilot.

The crew of the *Question Mark* at Bolling Field: *left to right,* Capt. Ross G. Hoyt, Capt. Ira C. Eaker, Maj. Gen. J. E. Fechet, Maj. Carl Spaatz, Lt. E. R. Quesada, Msgt. R. W. Hope. Hoyt was the tanker pilot; Fechet, then chief of the Air Corps, did not fly on the mission.

The *Question Mark* crew left its radio on the ground in order to save weight. Communication was done with flying blackboards like this one.

December 1941. Hap Arnold reviews strategic plans and operations with his staff (Spaatz to his right).

Spaatz and Arnold review support of the ground army troops by the Army Air Forces. France, circa June 1944.

General Spaatz with King George VI (*center*) at an RAF station in England, circa 1942. *Courtesy Mrs. Carl A. Spaatz.*

Lt. Gen. James Doolittle (*left*) and Lt. Gen. Carl Spaatz (*second from left*) "hangar flying" with Eighth Air Force crewmen, England, 1944.

Spaatz in front of the B-17 assigned for his personal transport during World War II. "Boops" was the family nickname for youngest daughter Carla.

Spaatz speaks with his eldest daughter Katharine (*left*) at USSTAF airfield in England, 1944. Without her father's knowledge, "Tattie" had joined the Red Cross and gone to England.

Snapshot of Spaatz, Gen. George McDonald, and Col. Julien Allen, taken by
then Col. (later Justice) Lewis F. Powell, Jr., in Normandy, France, summer
1941. Powell was in Spaatz's command. *Courtesy U.S. Supreme Court Justice
Lewis F. Powell, Jr.*

Melun, France, June 29, 1945. Spaatz (*left*) examines the German ME-262
engine, built for the first combat jet aircraft.

General Carl Spaatz (*second from right*) attends the surrender ceremonies of Germany in Berlin.

Spaatz (*third from right*) at the surrender of Japan aboard the USS *Missouri*. He was the only officer to attend the surrender ceremonies of both Germany and Japan. *Courtesy Harry S. Truman Library.*

Spaatz with Mrs. Winston Churchill on their way to receive honorary doctor's degrees from Oxford University.

Maj. Gen. Carl Spaatz pins a medal on his long-time Air Force associate, fishing pal, and friend, Brig. Gen. Ira C. Eaker.

Carl Spaatz upon becoming the last commanding general of the USAAF, January 1946.

Three of the veterans of the bombardment of Germany: Supreme Allied Commander Dwight D. Eisenhower, Commander of Eighth Air Force (and later commander of Mediterranean Allied Air Forces) Ira C. Eaker, and Commander of USSTAF Carl A. Spaatz. 13 June 1947.

First Secretary of the U.S. Air Force Stuart Symington and first Chief of Staff Carl Spaatz discuss the organization of the newly created U.S. Air Force, September 1947.

General Spaatz (*right*) with his daughter Rebecca and Col. George S. Howard, conductor of the U.S. Air Force Symphony, following a concert featuring Rebecca as piano soloist. *Courtesy Col. George S. Howard, USAF, Ret.*

Spaatz and his youngest daughter Carla on the occasion of her wedding in 1951.

Two of the *Question Mark* flyers, Carl Spaatz and Elwood Quesada, thirty years later, circa 1959. *Courtesy* Indianapolis News.

Carl and Ruth Spaatz, circa 1960. *Courtesy Mrs. Carl A. Spaatz.*

# Chapter VII

## WINNING AIR SUPERIORITY OVER WESTERN EUROPE

Late in 1943, the leaders of the Grand Alliance met at Teheran to discuss the future of the war. The commitment to invade western Europe was reaffirmed to a doubtful Stalin, and that doubt precipitated a decision on the selection of a commander for the great landings. Eisenhower was sent from the Mediterranean back to the United Kingdom to take charge and, late in December, Carl Spaatz joined him.

The first six months of 1944 were possibly the most critical in Spaatz's career. During that time he energized the flagging strategic bombing campaign, successfully resisted attempts by the Royal Air Force to gain control of the American strategic air forces, helped bring the air superiority fight to its climax, limited somewhat the tactical commitment of American strategic airpower to bombing French railroads, initiated the campaign against German resources, and provided major air support to the landings in France.

### A Commander for OVERLORD

Stalin had long been demanding that the western Allies launch a second front against Hitler's homeland. The Mediterranean campaigns and combined bomber offensive had drawn a good deal of German strength away from the Russian front, but that was not enough. Stalin wanted a landing on the coast of France. That was also the desire of Roosevelt and his military subordinates. At the Teheran conference late in November, it seemed that Churchill was trying to hedge on the commitment to land in the spring of 1944, and Stalin bore down hard to try to force the prime minister to be firm.[1] Roosevelt, to the chagrin of some of his people, did not support Churchill in his challenge of the Soviet dictator. In the end the British leader issued an unequivocal renewal of the commitment. Even so, Stalin expressed doubt of the constancy of the western Allies, for they had not yet specified a commander for the great enterprise. At that moment, it seemed the prize assignment would go to George Marshall and that Eisenhower would return to the United States as chief of staff of the U.S. Army, but FDR refused to release Marshall from Washington, declaring that he could not spare his chief military adviser. Rather, the president chose Dwight Eisenhower and announced it to him as he passed through the Mediterranean theater on his return voyage.[2]

Although Spaatz had not at first been enthusiastic about the Mediterranean assignment, he had become reconciled to serving in the south and had remarked to his family during the summer of 1943 that he saw little hope of ever returning to England. Suddenly, at the end of the year, he was sent back to the United Kingdom: General Eisenhower wanted to take "his airman" back to England for the great enterprise. Eisenhower preferred to surround himself with people he had tested in the battles of the Mediterranean and with whom he had been accustomed to working.[3]

## Reorganization of the American Air Arm for the Invasion

Even before launching the Mediterranean campaigns, Arnold had been working to create a supreme air command that would control all Allied air activities from Iceland to the Middle East. He had taken a step in that direction when he helped bring about his senior European air leader's reassignment to the African campaign. For a short time, therefore, Spaatz was the senior U.S. airman for both Africa and England. However, soon after arriving in Africa, Eisenhower was deprived of his jurisdiction over the forces in England, and Frank Andrews was sent there to command. This had the effect of taking Spaatz out of the formal chain of command in England. Thus, while Arnold and Spaatz had been trying to bring greater centralization to the airpower arrayed against Hitler, the separation of the Mediterranean and European theaters in early 1943 had the opposite effect. In practice, because of the close relationship between Eaker and Spaatz, the impact was not great. Through

1943 the Mediterranean was the main scene of action, and Eisenhower was clearly the principal power there. Arnold was partially satisfied to have his most trusted agent at Ike's elbow, but he never gave up trying to bring a greater degree of unity of command for the air forces.

Since the heavy bombers of Spaatz's Twelfth Air Force were not involved in the kind of strategic bombing that Eaker's Eighth Air Force was conducting, problems of coordination were infrequent. However, before the end of 1943, even before Eisenhower returned to England to prepare for the invasion of France (Operation OVERLORD), the Foggia airfields had been captured. This brought Arnold's and Spaatz's ambition of basing another strategic air force on Hitler's southern flank a step closer to realization. The job of the new Fifteenth Air Force, established at Foggia under Doolittle, was roughly the same as that of the Eighth Air Force, and the problems of coordinating strategic operations against the German heartland became more critical.

Throughout 1943, while Eaker was commanding U.S. Air Forces in England and Spaatz was commanding air forces in Africa, the former was well aware of what Arnold was attempting. The three were united in their desire to use the flexibility of airpower to mount threats from varying directions against Hitler's empire. The planes that survived the first of the shuttle bombing raids and the attack on the Messerschmitt factories landed at bases in Africa. During planning for the attacks, Eaker talked with Arnold about the need for a unified command, including the British forces, to manage the assault on Germany. Also, during that summer, Spaatz and Eaker were beginning to develop communication links between England and the Mediterranean that would be a prerequisite for such unification of command.[4] In his reply to Eaker's report on the conversations with Arnold, Spaatz remarked that both he and the RAF's Air Marshal Arthur Tedder agreed that the strategic air offensive would be much improved were a new threat developed from the south, and that such an offensive would best be managed by a single integrated command.[5] Thus the reorganization of the air command was being discussed by Arnold, Spaatz, and Eaker long before the end of the year, and they all knew the details of Arnold's thinking. The reorganization came about largely along the lines desired by Arnold, except that British Bomber Command was not made a part of the new command.

Before reporting to England, Spaatz made a trip back to Washington in October 1943, the only time he would see his family during the war years. He found Ruth immersed in the restoration of the federal house (built in 1810) that they had bought in Alexandria just before Pearl Harbor. This, in addition to working in the Red Cross speakers bureau and other war-related activities, kept her well occupied. Beckie was at home awaiting the arrival of the first Spaatz grandchild. Carla had entered St. Agnes Episcopal School, where she was to remain until she graduated in 1949 and went to Smith—a remarkable continuity of schooling for a service child. Eldest daughter Tattie had talked the Red Cross into letting her go overseas (though she had not attained their required age) and was serving on a clubmobile at an airdrome in England.

Having caught up with family and friends, Tooey concentrated on the main purpose of his trip, a discussion with Arnold on his ideas for reorganization. Though Spaatz had favored an integrated strategic bomber command the previous summer, he wanted it only as a subordinate part of an overall theater command. Since it was clear by October that there would be no such overall command combining the forces in the Mediterranean with those in the United Kingdom, he now opposed the creation of a bomber command. His argument was that the personal coordination between himself and Eaker was working well and ought to continue. As Spaatz remembered it a year after the war was over, Arnold was determined to create the United States Strategic Air Forces (USSTAF), principally to keep the bulk of American airpower from falling into British hands. By creating a new command to include both Eighth Air Force and Fifteenth Air Force, and giving its commander authority also over the administration of Ninth Air Force, Arnold felt he could retain the bulk of American airpower in Europe under American commanders.[6]

Immediately upon returning to England, Spaatz flew to the bomber base in East Anglia where daughter Tattie's clubmobile was stationed. It was the policy of the Red Cross not to send their people to theatres where family members were serving, so since her father was in North Africa, Tattie had been sent to England. Now, since his return to England, she was concerned she would be shipped off to India or the Pacific— especially after *Stars and Stripes* appeared with a large picture of the general and his daughter embracing, captioned "TATTY [sic] SPAATZ GREETS POPS!"

After that publicity she kept a low profile for weeks. But the Red Cross either forgot about her or was kind enough to leave her in England; her occasional weekend passes in London meant much to her father during the dark days of the 1943–44 winter. Tattie and her crewmates, Virginia Sherwood, "Doolie" Townsend, and Dorothy Myrick, stayed with the bomber groups until after the invasion, when their clubmobile was assigned to an infantry division. They accompanied the ground forces for the rest of the war, through the Battle of the Bulge and on to Czechoslovakia, where they celebrated VE Day in Prague.

In London at that time were many of Spaatz's old friends, and many new ones, serving the USAAF. Among the latter were Lowell Weicker, Sr.; Lewis F. Powell, Jr.; Walt Rostow; and Julian Allen. Allen had come from Morgan Company in Paris and had spent most of his life in France; his intimate knowledge of the country and its people was invaluable before and after the invasion. Among old friends were Bruce Hopper, an historian from Harvard; Everett Cook, a leading cotton broker from Memphis; and Howard (Hank) Stovall, a cotton planter from Mississippi and a flying companion from the old 13th Aero Squadron in World War I. Hank served on Monk Hunter's staff and his son, Howard Jr., was a fighter pilot who lost his life on a mission over France.

The Joint Chiefs of Staff took up the organizational issues in November 1943 in preparation for the upcoming Teheran conference. They favored Arnold's proposals for the organization of the strategic air forces and preferred an overall organization under one commander to govern all the forces arrayed against Hitler—on the ground, on the sea, and in the air, from the Mediterranean and the United Kingdom. Because they doubted that the British would consent to such a supreme commander, however, the Joint Chiefs of Staff conceived an alternative in which there would be two theaters, one operating from the United Kingdom and one from the Mediterranean. Under this scheme, the strategic air forces, at least, would be under a single commander, and they would include the RAF's Bomber Command. The British chose the second alternative, except they declined to place Bomber Command under any supreme strategic air commander. Thus, its commander, Arthur Harris, reported directly to the Combined Chiefs of Staff, and the new United States Strategic Air Force's commander had like status, receiving his directives through Air Marshal Portal, the Combined Chiefs' agent.[7]

The USSTAF would be made up of the Eighth and Fifteenth Air Forces, and all the tactical aviation in support of OVERLORD would be placed in an organization known as the Allied Expeditionary Air Forces (AEAF). The American contribution to the AEAF was to be the Ninth Air Force, moved up to England from the eastern Mediterranean. Though the Ninth would be under the operational control of the commander of AEAF, it was subordinate in administrative matters to the commander of USSTAF, the senior American air commander in Britain. The appointment of Carl Spaatz to command the USSTAF was almost inevitable since he was the theater's senior airman in rank, service, age, and experience, and because he was the first of Arnold's lieutenants as well as the preference of General Eisenhower.

The assignments of the air commanders subordinate to Spaatz caused some unhappiness. Nathan F. Twining was given the Fifteenth Air Force in Italy, and when the Ninth was brought up to England, Lewis Brereton came along as commander. Twelfth Air Force, which had evolved into a tactical arm, remained in the Mediterranean and was to be led by John K. Cannon. Spaatz was to bring Doolittle along with him to take command of Eighth Air Force. The supreme commander in the Mediterranean replacing Eisenhower was the Briton, Gen. H. M. Wilson. As the first commanding spot in the south had gone to the British, when Tedder came along with Eisenhower to become the deputy commander of OVERLORD, the overall air command in the Mediterranean would logically have fallen to an American. It was to this latter position that Ira Eaker was posted. On the organizational charts, it was a step up for Eaker, but he did not see it that way. Eighth Air Force was at its darkest hour just then. In the fall of 1943 it had suffered a grievous blow in the second Schweinfurt raid, making it necessary to suspend further unescorted deep penetration raids into Germany. Though there is little direct evidence that Arnold blamed Eaker for the heavy Schweinfurt losses, he did indicate his impatience with the problems in developing the strategic offensive and with the difficulty in getting a greater proportion of the heavy bombers of the Eighth into the air for truly massive raids.[8] Yet, it is easy to suppose that Eaker hoped the worst was over and that solutions were near.

Eaker mounted a considerable effort to prevent his transfer to the Mediterranean. He recruited General Devers (then the top commander in Britain following the death of General Andrews in a crash in Iceland) and some of his British friends to help him win a reversal of the decision.[9] He sent strong telegrams to both Eisenhower and Arnold to argue his case, but it was to no avail. Hap refused to reconsider his original decision. Arnold tried to put a good face on it, depicting it as a move to greater responsibility in reward for a good job done in England, and he was supported in that by Spaatz.[10] Notwithstanding Arnold's deserved reputation for impatience, and aside from the strength of Eaker's protests, there is not much concrete evidence to suggest that the transfer was anything but what Arnold insisted it was—a desire to spread his strongest commanders among the theaters. Had he responded to Eaker's protests, he would have had both Spaatz and Eaker in England. Given Eaker's strong record in developing harmonious relations between American and British air forces in the United Kingdom, it was not surprising that Arnold wanted to make him the senior Allied commander in the Mediterranean theater.

Eaker's objections seemed to have raised some heat in Washington. In a cable to Eisenhower, George Marshall was reported to remark:[11]

> I believe I was more disturbed over the pressure of Tedder and Spaatz to move Eaker to the Mediterranean because to me he did not appear particularly suited for that theater and I am forced to the conclusion that their attitude is selfish and not purely objective. . . .

That statement may have been what stimulated Eaker to write to Lovett protesting vigorously that he did not blame Tooey for his ouster, for his friend "never threw a curve ball in his life."[12] It is difficult to understand General Marshall's remark since it does seem that since his days as a "cleansleeve" (rankless) cadet, Tooey was not one who grasped for the trappings of personal power.

## The Air Order of Battle: December, 1943

Though Spaatz had been away from England a year and had been subjected to some intense experiences in a tactical air campaign, when he returned (on the 29th of December) his attitudes on strategic bombing had not changed appreciably. After the ill-fated second Schweinfurt raid, he was quite explicit, in a conversation with Harry Hopkins, in saying that the strategic bombing of German industry could bring about the collapse of the Third Reich without invasion.[13] He felt that this could best be achieved through centralized control of air assets and was quite clear on the point that enemy airpower had to be the primary target. He also asserted that the bombers would sometimes have to go beyond the range of fighter escort in order to hit airpower targets other than airdromes, such as ball bearing works and airframe factories.[14] That would be exceptional. As a general rule, Spaatz was determined to plan his good weather missions to stay within the range of escort fighter cover, which would exert the maximum pressure on the Luftwaffe at a minimum cost.[15] He also saw one other kind of mission that would contribute to that goal: the use of electronic means to bomb area targets like Berlin through the clouds. This would force the German fighters to rise in defense and suffer losses not only in combat but also in trying to make bad-weather landings which were beyond the capabilities of inexperienced German pilots.[16] Finally, Spaatz had not wavered from his commitment to precision daylight bombing of the vital centers in the enemy's industrial web. As he later recalled it:[17]

> . . . our plan was daylight bombing; precision bombing of whatever system was given top priority. . . .
> We always attacked only legitimate military targets with one exception—the capital of the hostile nation. Berlin was the administrative and communications center of Germany and therefore became a military target.
> . . . Our stand was that we would bomb only strategic targets—not areas. I believed that we could win the war more quickly that way. It was not for religious or moral reasons that I did not go along with urban area bombing.

Earlier, in the spring and summer of 1943, Spaatz was optimistic about the prospects for early victory over the Axis air forces.[18] To Arnold he was saying that the Luftwaffe was stretched thin and was likely to collapse during the coming fall. By the time he arrived back in the United Kingdom, however, his words carried a greater sense of urgency.[19] The invasion of the continent was hardly five months away, and the Luftwaffe had proven conclusively over Schweinfurt in October that it was not in a state of collapse.

The German V-1 and V-2 secret weapons programs were causing concern. The V-1 preparations were well under way, and the launching ramps were going up in western France. The Allied political leaders worried about the effects on the population of London as these flying bombs randomly hit the great metropolis. The military authorities were also thinking that these bombs might cause havoc among the enormous invasion forces being marshalled in southeast England.[20] But of more direct concern to Spaatz was the development of a German interceptor, the twin-engine jet Messerschmitt 262.[21] If air superiority were not won before appreciable numbers of these airplanes became operational, would their great speed advantage put victory over the Luftwaffe defenders beyond reach? The imminence of OVERLORD and the urgent requirement for the establishment of air superiority for the safety of the landings added a time factor to Allied calculations, and injected a note of crisis into the planning for air operations.

Allied leaders were impatient for results in the campaign against the Luftwaffe. With all the damage done to the German flyers in Russia, in the Mediterranean, and over Germany itself, why did it not affect the figures of frontline strength for Luftwaffe forces defending Germany? Some of the results were hard to see, but were real nonetheless. Intelligence showed that German aircraft production, despite the bombing of the airframe factories, continued to rise. But that rise was in numbers of airplanes, and it masked the fact that a part of it was achieved by converting from bomber production to fighter production.[22] The German aircraft industry had produced about 25,000 airplanes in 1943[23]—not even a third that of the U.S. and less than the output of planes in the USSR. When Spaatz got back to England, the German air force still had 1,732,000 personnel, but many of these were involved in antiaircraft work and some even in ground combat.[24] General Doolittle described German frontline strength based on a November 1943 report:[25]

> The current strength of the German Air Force is of extreme interest. As given in the 24 November 1943 report of the Eighth Air Force, the German Air Force had been an operational establishment of 4,854 aircraft on 19 November. Of this force, 1,968 were on the Western Front, 1,771 in Russia, and the remaining 1,115 in South Germany, Austria, and the Balkans and along the Mediterranean. Of the total of 4,854 aircraft, 1,413 are single-engine fighters, and 996 are two-engined fighters, a combined defense strength of 2,409. Of these aircraft, 207 fighters are in South Germany and Austria and 275 on the Mediterranean-Balkan front, a total of 483 operational fighters to oppose all the United Nations Air Forces in this theater (Mediterranean).

From this it can be seen that the Germans had already shifted to an emphasis on defensive aircraft, and that long before OVERLORD a good deal of the strength of the Luftwaffe had been drawn away from the Russian front. Lest it be thought that the Allied margin in numbers was greater than it actually was, it should be remembered that the defenders had the great advantage of fighting over their home fields. The German fighters could, and often did, fly as many as three sorties apiece against a single bombing raid. What is truly significant is the number of combat minutes available over the targets; that factor had weighed heavily in favor of the RAF in the Battle of Britain and was weighing heavily in favor of the Luftwaffe in the battles over the German homeland. The Eighth Air Force's escorts always had to save enough fuel to make it back to England; the German interceptors could use the equivalent amount to continue the fight against the bombers.

For his campaign against the Luftwaffe, Spaatz had in Eighth Air Force 736 heavy bombers ready to fly, with 672 fighters to support them.[26] Some of the new P-51B Mustang fighters with their large internal and external fuel tanks and Rolls Royce engines were getting into action. Most of the heavy bombers were the latest versions with chin turrets to help protect them from frontal attacks. In addition, greater numbers of H2S radar sets were available, enabling large raids in bad weather. A month earlier, Fifteenth Air Force in Italy already had 288 bombers and 320 fighters, and Doolittle was expecting that it would grow to more than a thousand heavy bombers and 560 fighters within the next two or three months.[27] The Eighth was growing at a similar pace. Thus, the two strategic air forces by themselves could hope to match the entire German air force, in numbers, by the end of the winter.

The greater part of their planes were much larger than most of those of the Luftwaffe and also the RAF, the Ninth Air Force, the Twelfth Air Force, and the Red Air Force.

Finally, the great advantage of breaking the enemy's code continued, for the Germans still did not realize that the Allies were reading their message traffic, and they were relying more heavily than they should have on their coding machines.

## Morale and Maintenance Problems

Spaatz's primary duty in the United Kingdom was to assure a unity of effort on the part of the two American strategic air forces and to coordinate their activity with that of the RAF Bomber Command. In the words of the USAAF official history:[28]

> it was clear that he [Spaatz] contemplated a small headquarters whose chief function would be to issue "broad orders and directives" to Eighth and Fifteenth Air Forces, after coordination with the Air Ministry. The new headquarters would engage in strategic planning and the selection of targets, the setting of policies with regard to combat crew tours of duty, and the movement of personnel and equipment between the two headquarters [Eighth and Fifteenth]. . . .

But that description covered only the operational dimensions of his new duties. The Ninth Air Force being redeployed to the United Kingdom for support of OVERLORD would come under a different chain of command for operations. It would be under Spaatz, however, in the administrative sense—he would direct all of the logistical support for that air force. Though it was not legally necessary to do so, Spaatz made it a point that all orders to Fifteenth Air Force would be passed through General Eaker's headquarters, possibly out of concern for the latter's unhappiness at being transferred out of the strategic bombing effort.[29]

## Compassion or Victory

As Spaatz assumed his new office, the tour length for the men in Eighth Air Force was twenty-five missions. He had on his desk an elaborate study showing rather conclusively that the average new crew member had precious little chance of surviving his tour. A sample of several thousand cases drawn from the experience of 1943 showed that more than half of the crew members were killed or had been declared missing before they reached the magic twenty-five. Fewer than a quarter of those who had started ever made it to the twenty-fifth mission. About half of those who were not shot down did not reach their twenty-fifth because of wounds, sickness, transfer, and sometimes psychological breakdown. Yet the figures also showed conclusively that the attrition among new crews was far, far higher than among those on their last five missions—once you made it to number twenty, your chances to go the rest of the distance were better than even.[30] Were Spaatz to choose to raise the tour length, morale would plunge, and attrition might well rise. Choose to lower the tour length, and the training establishment would be unable to meet the demand for pilots, the experience level in the formations would go down, attrition would go up, and the war might last longer and more people would die. The choice was complicated by the geographical reach of USSTAF. The German defenses facing westward were by far more fearsome than those to the south. How many missions should be required from those flying with Fifteenth Air Force? One of the major arguments in favor of establishing a strategic air force in the Mediterranean had been to give the commander the flexibility of shifting his forces from one flank to the other. How many missions should be demanded of the crewmen who flew part of their tour from the United Kingdom and another part from Italy?

The pace of operations would go up rapidly with the coming of the spring weather and with the diversion of the bomber forces to the tactical support of OVERLORD. During the invasion period sorties would be short, but much more frequent. Were USSTAF to stick with the policy of releasing crew members from combat duty at the end of twenty-five missions, many of them might finish their tours within a month.[31] Not only would the training commands in the U.S. find it impossible to keep up with that turnover, but it would lead to a rather dramatic decline in the level of experience of the crews flying missions during the summer.

In the course of the spring, Arnold made it a policy that the air officers in their respective theaters would establish the tour length criteria for their own commands, which put the burden squarely on Spaatz. With Washington's approval, Spaatz decided to undertake a program of giving crews a thirty-day leave back in the United States for rest and recreation, but then returning them to their duties in England and Italy.[32] The hope was that it would be possible to raise the experience level of the bomber formations and get longer service out of each crewman without causing a disastrous decline in morale and mission effectiveness. As the evidence suggested that there was a direct relationship between experience and survival on any given mission, there was also hope that overall losses would be less. One can well imagine the impact on the individual flyer who had finished his twenty-five missions or was nearing that mark: instead of a release from the terror, he would get only temporary relief and then return to the battle.

Gen. Barney Giles, Arnold's chief of staff, dispatched back to Spaatz a discouraging report on the first crews sent to Atlantic City for their rest and recreation. He remarked that the fighter pilots were ready to return and even fearful that they would not make it back in time for OVERLORD. The bomber crews, however, were glum, and Giles was not at all sure that the program would have the desired effect with them—and the bomber crews were Spaatz's chief concern.[33] As more crews returned, it appeared to Arnold that the effort was not having the desired morale effects, and the procedure was discontinued. USSTAF then went back to the original criteria. The situation improved because of the impact of declining attrition, the obvious advances of the ground armies towards victory, and the growing ratio of crews to aircraft—the crewmen felt they had better prospects for survival.[34]

Another sticky problem that Spaatz inherited was the difficulty in keeping his airplanes in commission. The discrepancy between the numbers of aircraft Arnold had sent to Eaker and the numbers that got over the target had been a running source of friction between the two.[35] Spaatz was aware of this and understood that one of his major charges was to get a larger proportion of the planes in England airborne for each raid.

Some of the measures that finally resolved the difficulty had already been initiated before Spaatz arrived on the scene. A team under Maj. Gen. Follett Bradley had been sent to Eighth Air Force during the summer of 1943 to study logistical affairs and recommend a system to keep up with the demands that were bound to grow at an exponential rate.[36] One of its members was Hugh Knerr, who soon after was transferred to England as the second-in-command of Eighth's logistical organization, the Air Service Command. He soon became the commander and implemented many of the recommendations of the Bradley Committee. This allowed Knerr to establish units for assembling new aircraft arriving from the U.S., for repairing the ever-growing amount of battle damage, and for routine overhaul of aircraft.

All this was facilitated by Spaatz's adoption of new command arrangements on his arrival in England. He selected a "double deputy" system in which Fred Anderson became his deputy commander for operations, and Hugh Knerr his deputy for administration (including everything except operations). This separated the functions of staff and command work, and when they were unified under Spaatz, Knerr considered it a great improvement.[37]

The problem of raising the operationally ready rate of aircraft was less intractable than the stimulation of crew morale. By the time Spaatz took over in England, there were 5,133 combat aircraft there. There had been but 3,061 just three months earlier at the time of the second Schweinfurt raid. By May 1944, the figure had risen to 8,351,[38] yet the logistical system was able to keep up with the requirements. The percentage of aircraft ready for operations and the time required for both modification and battle-damage repair all improved during the period.[39] Still, Spaatz's friendship with Arnold did not protect him from the chief's impatience. Before he had been in England a month, Arnold wrote:[40]

I cannot understand why, with the great number of airplanes available to Eighth Air Force, we continually have to send a boy to do a man's job. In my opinion, this is an uneconomical waste of lives and equipment. In the first place, it allows the Germans to rebuild their only partially demolished facilities, and in the second place, we have to expose our youngsters and our aircraft a second and sometimes a third time to the German fighter and anti-aircraft defenses. These defenses, we all know, are not getting any less effective.

To this prod Spaatz replied four days later. He suggested to Arnold that the airplanes involved in a recent raid were far greater in number than was reported in the newspapers. He told his boss that he had launched fifteen hundred airplanes including nine hundred bombers (compared to fewer than three hundred on the second Schweinfurt raid), but they had to be recalled because of frontal weather conditions. This had to be done to ensure that they could get back while bases were still open for landing. Moreover, he pointed out to Arnold that the force had gone far enough toward Germany to engage some German fighters and to provoke others into taking off under very bad weather conditions. The low ceilings and heavy icing conditions made Spaatz confident that the inexperienced German fighter pilots had suffered losses even when they had not attacked the bombers. He further tried to reassure Arnold by saying that progress was being made in overcoming the effects of weather through development of shuttle bombing tactics where the bombers would land at another field—usually to the south—when their home bases were closed by weather, and by radar scope photography that would aid in bombing targets through the clouds. As for the maintenance problem, Spaatz told Arnold:[41]

(I) visited depot activities during (the) week and feel that Knerr has (the) situation under control. He will have processed more than one thousand airplanes through his depots this month as compared to four hundred last month. Most of this increase is due to (the) organization he has established which is getting into stride.

## Command Relations with the Royal Air Force

The reorganization that had taken place among the American air units at the end of 1943 had stabilized and was to serve for the rest of the conflict. Questions remained, however, about how the new American air command structure would relate to that of the British and the Allied forces designated to invade the continent. As Spaatz viewed it, one of the chief obstacles to his plans for the strategic bombing of Germany would be the command structure set up for the invasion—particularly putting the strategic bombing forces under the Allied Expeditionary Air Forces (AEAF) commander. Spaatz thought that the war might be winnable by strategic bombing alone, but he realized that his theory would not be tested because the invasion would take place in any case. He recognized that at some point his strategic bombers would have to support the invasion forces, but hoped that his commanders would have a large say in the selection of targets. He further hoped that this diversion to the invasion would be neither complete nor long-lasting.[42]

The man chosen to command AEAF was Air Marshal Trafford Leigh-Mallory. He was not uniformly admired in his own service and had participated in (perhaps even precipitated) an unbecoming internal squabble at the height of the Battle of Britain. Since practically all of his experience had been in fighters, particularly in their air defense role, that did not recommend him to Spaatz as suitable for the direction of strategic bombing forces—especially now that there were indications of achieving the air superiority that would permit them to put the strategic bombing theory to its decisive test in the destruction of German industry.[43] The question was complicated by the British refusal to incorporate the RAF Bomber Command into an overall strategic air organization. That made the Americans reluctant to give complete control of their tactical air forces to Leigh-Mallory and later to accede to an OVERLORD arrangement that would also place their strategic forces under his command.[44] Bomber Command also was headed by a strong personality, Arthur Harris. Harris was equally reluctant to place his organization under the command of someone with no strategic bombing experience, who might try to use the force in ways for which it had not been designed.[45]

From the beginning Eisenhower was determined that *he* would command all the air resources during the vital period of the invasion. Before returning to England from the Mediterranean, he had gone back to the United States and made the point with George Marshall that he *had* to have control of the strategic bombers as well as tactical forces. Arnold was present during the consultations and assured Eisenhower that Spaatz's forces would come under him for the period of the landings.[46] In the end, Eisenhower was satisfied that the American heavy bombers would eventually be available, though the time when control would be transferred to him was not specified. The agreement, however, did *not* assure that Harris's forces would come under Eisenhower's authority. That proved to be one of the more troublesome problems for Eisenhower during the early days of his tenure in England, as the Air Ministry and even Churchill were reluctant to give Bomber Command over to Eisenhower without qualifications. The question was argued vigorously for some weeks and, in the end, Eisenhower was prepared to resign unless he received the authority he wanted.[47] He had his way, though the definition of the time span of his control remained undefined. He mollified Spaatz and Harris and the Britons who had opposed him by assuring them that the strategic forces would not be reporting to Leigh-Mallory. They would be subordinate to Air Marshal Sir Arthur Tedder, the deputy commander of the Supreme Headquarters Allied Expeditionary Forces (SHAEF).[48]

As spring wore on, Eisenhower satisfied the British that the heavy bombers would not be frittered away on small tactical targets, and that diversions from their campaigns against the German air force, cities, and industries would be short. Leigh-Mallory had first indicated that USSTAF and Bomber Command should come under SHAEF control on 1 March,[49] but by the time the command arrangements and a plan for the employment of air forces had been agreed upon, six weeks had passed, during which the Fortresses and Liberators had continued pounding away at their original objectives.

For Spaatz the outcome of these changes was mixed. He had been unsuccessful in preventing the placement of a strategic air organization under a tactical commander. Yet, he did delay that development for a crucial period, and when it came to pass on 14 April, he was not subordinated to Leigh-Mallory, a man he mistrusted—one who had appalled Spaatz with his assertion that it was not necessary to win air superiority before the invasion was launched, but rather that the battle could be won over the beaches.[50] Instead, he was to work with Tedder, a man with whom he had been closely associated in the Mediterranean and whose grasp of airpower employment inspired his confidence.

## The Gaining of Air Ascendancy

When Spaatz arrived in the United Kingdom, his marching orders were clear enough. On 27 December 1943 Arnold had written one of his more terse letters to "Dear Tooey:"[51]

> You know my apprehensions over our not destroying the German Air Force. I believe that we must use every effort to secure the maximum use of our tremendous airpower—an airpower so vastly superior to that of the Germans.
>
> Without destroying the German Air Force, we can never secure the

maximum benefits of our Air Force in their operations against objectives assigned. As a matter of fact, we may reach a stalemate in the air.

Hence, we must use our initiative and imagination with a view of seeking out, destroying the German Air Force in the factories, depots, on the ground, or in the air, wherever they may be. . . .

The letter took a while to catch up with Spaatz, and if he had needed any instruction in the matter, he showed in his 21 January 1944 response that he had gotten the word:[52]

. . . Destruction of remaining fighter factories and ball bearing plants is entirely dependent on few days of visual bombing. Losses will be heavy but we must be prepared to accept them.

All other attacks will be made on basis of destroying enemy air force in air and on ground. Such attacks will be made so far as possible under conditions most favorable to ourselves and normally will be against objectives which force German fighters into combat action within range of our fighters. . . .

Spaatz was doubtless speaking of a counterair plan that had been devised by Eaker's staff before he left for the Mediterranean and that was being held in abeyance pending the arrival of good weather. The plan called for a concentrated, one-week series of deep-penetration assaults by large formations of the Eighth Air Force, the Fifteenth Air Force, and the Bomber Command against the German aircraft industry and the Luftwaffe. But, all through the month of January and into February, Spaatz's meteorologists could not give him a forecast of a week of good weather. The weather did break occasionally, but no more than twenty-one heavy bomber attacks were mounted from England during the first six weeks of Spaatz's tenure at USSTAF. Of these, just six aimed their bombs by visual means, and only two of those strikes were against targets in Germany. Of the twenty-one raids, thirteen were directed on the new V-1 weapon launch sites along the channel coast.[53]

Spaatz seldom gave public vent to any sort of exasperation, but as the gloomy weather kept him from his goals, he expressed it in his headquarters diary. On the 25th of January, 1944, he wrote that it seemed impossible to put together a large enough formation to achieve the destruction required and then get it back home within the short spells of flyable weather.[54] Eleven days later he lamented to Arnold that he could not get the kind of weather that was needed, but rather Eighth was forced to bomb by radar (which was still quite inaccurate) most of the time.[55] Then, four days later, he complained in his diary: "Today is to go on record as completely wasted. Good weather at bases, good weather over target and Doolittle sent *no* bombers."[56] General Doolittle recalls that during this period Spaatz was very upset about the Eighth's failure to get a single mission through to the target because of the weather. Later, Doolittle and Spaatz were aboard a B-17 going from one base to another in England when all the fields within reach became fogged in, and their pilot had to go down through a hole in the fog and land in a farmer's field. That made Doolittle's point: were the same thing to happen to the whole force, it would be a disaster. After that, the tension between them lessened.[57]

By this time, Spaatz was beginning to realize that the USSTAF would not be able to cripple German airpower solely by destroying their airframe plants. The upcoming assault would also have to strike the Luftwaffe in the air and smash it at its bases. As he saw it in January, this would have to be accomplished by choosing targets that were vital enough to force the Luftwaffe to come up and fight, and yet be within the range of American and British escort fighters. Spaatz believed that it would be possible for the Allied airmen to choose their targets to secure the maximum possible advantage for themselves—preferably far from antiaircraft concentrations.[58]

The battle plan was not aimed at German airpower in general, but rather at air defense. Though engine plants were left out, ball bearing factories were included as critical and concentrated enough that their destruction would have a direct effect on fighter output. Beyond that, the targets were associated with the kinds of airplanes being used against the bomber formations trying to penetrate German airspace: Me-109s, Me-110s, Ju-88s, and FW-190s. These attacks were to be mounted simultaneously by various air divisions of Eighth Air Force and by Fifteenth Air Force in order to spread the enemy's defenses as much as possible. Bombers going against several targets deep in Germany would penetrate along a single axis. This would keep the defending controllers guessing, as long as possible, about the objectives and also would maximize the benefit of any escort available for Eighth Air Force. The Fifteenth Air Force's fighters did not yet have the range for deep penetrations with the bombers.[59]

The Luftwaffe had not come out unscathed by battles during the autumn of 1943. Spaatz and Eaker had sought a way to keep the pressure on the German air force to prevent its recuperation during bad weather.[60] The British had developed an airborne radar system called H2S, which would help them with finding and hitting nighttime targets that lay beyond the range of electronics devices. They gave it to the Americans, who had shipped some samples back to the United States. A priority effort was mounted to improve it and manufacture some sets to serve in path-finder aircraft for USSTAF. The British had all they could handle to produce enough sets of H2S for the RAF and were able to deliver only a few for Spaatz's bombers. By November, the American version, manu-factured virtually by hand, was beginning to arrive in small numbers. The need was so urgent that the radar bombardiers received their training in combat over Europe.

The sets were so primitive and the training so hasty that the official USAAF historian was moved to lament that the bombers flying over the clouds seldom hit their targets during the dreary days of January and February 1944.[61] But Spaatz saw another advantage in continuing the raids, even though they did not have the precision sought by American air doctrine. The radar-guided raids were forcing the Luftwaffe aloft. When this was done in bad weather, there was an important by-product. Many of the crews Goering had sent so recklessly into the Stalingrad resupply operation had been made up of instrument flight instructors, most of whom did not come back. Many more were killed trying to succor the Afrika Korps in Tunisia. The German training system was designed for a short war, and it could no longer keep up with demands. Thus the training time given to new pilots had already declined radically. As mentioned earlier, if Spaatz's forces could draw them aloft in bad weather, those who were not shot down by the more experienced American pilots stood an excellent chance of killing themselves trying to find their landing fields.[62]

German pilots, on the average, were going into combat with around 170 hours total flying time against American adversaries who had had about 310. They were committed to the fight with about 40 hours of training in combat-type aircraft, while the Americans were getting about 170 hours in fighters before entering the fray.[63] Moreover, since the attrition was so much higher among the German flyers, most of them had far less posttraining flying experience than did the USAAF and RAF fighter pilots. During the last half of 1943, the Germans had lost almost as many aircraft to accidents as to combat. In the first six months of 1944, 6,259 airplanes were lost in battle, and half that many were destroyed in noncombat-related crashes.[64] Noncombat losses were contributing to Spaatz's ultimate goal of air superiority just as surely as were those planes that went down in flames. Even without firm data, Spaatz saw the opportunity. In late January, he told Arnold that he intended to launch some raids without escort on days when Germany was fogbound, with the explicit purpose of imposing "heavy operational losses to their fighters."[65]

USSTAF was entering its most critical hour with a stable of aircraft that remain among the most esteemed in USAF history: the Fortress, Thunderbolt, Lightning, and Mustang. The B-24 Liberator was there, too, but it did not get the same high marks from people flying out of the United Kingdom that it earned in other theaters, where its range advantage was more important. The airplane was uncomfortable to fly, but in the environment of western Europe it was more a question of survival than comfort, since its altitude capability was less than that of the Fortress. Following along in the trail of a Fortress formation, it was terrifying for Liberator crews to watch the B-17s being mauled by the Luftwaffe, knowing that it would be all the easier for the German fighters when they turned their attention to the lower-flying Liberator unit.[66] Liberator crew morale was so critical at the outset of the 1944 campaigns that General Doolittle wrote to Arnold through Spaatz, pleading for "major modifications" to make it a more suitable craft for combat in his theater.[67] But the supply system had too much momentum to be deflected from its course quickly. The flow of Liberators continued, and more of them were produced during the war than any other combat aircraft, including fighters. Many of them went to other nations and to the U.S. Navy, but the USAAF inventory during the summer of 1944 contained more Liberators than Fortresses.[68]

Finally, the weeks of waiting ended. On the 19th of February 1944, the forecasters predicted a spell of good weather over the continent beginning the following day. Ordinarily, Spaatz's function as USSTAF commander was that of policymaking; the day-to-day operations were in the hands of the strategic air forces commanders. However, in the case of the offensive against German airpower, the operation was to be an integrated one, code-named ARGUMENT, and it would include Eighth and Fifteenth plus some aid from the RAF and the Ninth Air Force. Thus, the final decision was Spaatz's. It was not an easy one to make. It was predicted that the bomber losses on the first day might reach two hundred, and Spaatz had tried to prepare Arnold for that possibility.

Moreover, though USSTAF's weather forecasters were optimistic about the visibility in the target areas, Doolittle's weather scouts were sending down reports of a thick cloud deck, with icing conditions, over his fields.

The winter days are so short in those latitudes that the forces would have to be launched before daybreak. The danger of collision on the climb-out was great. The rendezvous promised to be most difficult and to take more time than could be afforded.

Fred Anderson, Spaatz's deputy commander for operations, ordered Eighth Air Force to prepare to launch just before dawn. A heated argument broke out between him and Doolittle over the factors that could make the mission too costly in relation to its potential benefits. Doolittle out-ranked Anderson, and it fell to Spaatz to choose between the arguments advanced by his two subordinates. Typically, in marginal weather the command would proceed as if the mission would be launched on schedule. A decision to launch or cancel could be delayed until the last minute. But the moment of truth could not be postponed past late evening. When it arrived, Spaatz, who had been uncertain through the day, decided to take the risk. The mission would be flown as ordered.[69]

About a thousand bombers took off for Germany on the 20th of February. The main thrust penetrated the German heartland before it broke up into multiple attacks at different targets. A second wave flew across the North Sea and over southern Denmark. Its route was longer, but away from the German air defenses. The planners hoped that this second thrust would not be intercepted by the defenders, who would be preoccupied with the others. The plan worked. The main attack so occupied the Luftwaffe that the northern group went to and from its distant targets with little trouble. The air defense had been worn down during the night of the 19th by a substantial RAF Bomber Command raid on Leipzig, in the same general area as the Eighth Air Force main attack targets. As it happened, Eaker's bombers could not fly their support-ing mission from the south because the ground commanders in the Mediter-ranean deemed the situation at the Anzio beachhead to be crucial. The Fifteenth's heavy bombers had to be reserved for support there. Still, General Brereton's Ninth Air Force medium bombers were able to get off and fly diversionary attacks mainly against airports in France and the low countries. His fighters were deployed as a part of the escorting force in support of the main attack.

The first day of the offensive was blessed with visual bombing conditions in several of the German locations, and the destruction was substantial—so great that it led to the dispersal of the German aircraft production plants. Over nine hundred heavy bombers got credit for a combat sortie that day. Only twenty-one of them did not come back, hardly one-tenth the worst-case prediction! According to one report, Spaatz was so elated with the results that it was his "highest" day of the war to that point.[70]

"Big Week" was off to a smashing start. The raids went on until the 26th. The role of the Fifteenth was limited by the requirements of the battle in Italy, but it did participate on some days. The weather interfered with the accuracy of some of the later raids. Twining's force, not yet as amply provided with escort or radar as was Eighth Air Force, took especially grievous losses on the 26th. On that day, both air forces were assigned to strike the aircraft plants at Regensburg at nearly the same time in the hope of dividing the German defenses and holding down losses. Unfortunately, the Fortresses coming from the south were well beyond the range of escorts based in Italy, and the Luftwaffe concentrated on them. Of the 176 that reached the target area, 33 were shot down—a loss rate in the same category as the Schweinfurt raids.[71] Still, the overall loss rate for the week—5.9 percent—was lower than that of the RAF night attacks of the same period.[72]

For the month of February 1944, Eighth's loss rate was 3.5 percent, in contrast to October 1943, when it had been 9.2 percent of the bombers attacking targets.[73] That was small comfort for the survivors, for even at the lower rate it was still far from "a milk run" to fly to Germany. To apply the February percentage to a group of 1,000 crews that were not reinforced by replacements during the campaign would leave but 411 of them still flying after the twenty-fifth mission. That is an oversimplification, to be sure, but more complex calculations were likely to be seen as sophistry by combat crew members.

The calculus was further complicated by overestimates of the numbers of German aircraft shot down and of the damage done to the Reich's aircraft industry. The former was due in part to exaggerated claims on the part of the crews, the latter to intelligence errors often arising from photo interpretation that deemed destroyed buildings as tantamount to the destruction of the machine tools they contained. In any case, the Germans did not run out of airplanes during Big Week or in the months that followed, though the experience level of its crews continued to slide.[74]

The average strength of the Luftwaffe in fighter pilots that spring was about 2,200. During February of 1944 alone, 434 of them were lost. (USSTAF had lost more airmen, partly because of the larger aircrews involved.) The German losses remained fairly typical for the entire spring and substantially higher than they had been during the fall of 1943.[75] Gen. Adolf Galland, commander of the German Fighter Forces, remarked long after the war that the Allied media made much more of Big Week than it should have, especially in the matter of damage done to the aircraft factories, and the official history of the USAAF agrees.[76] Still, Galland admits that his pilots were being killed off through the spring, and that there was not much he could do to stop it.[77]

One major factor that kept the Luftwaffe losses on the upward trend was a change in tactics. As Spaatz had observed in the Battle of Britain, the Germans misused their fighter escorts. This had been the big issue between the Luftwaffe's bomber pilots and escort flyers. The former wanted to keep their protectors in close formation; the latter wanted to be turned loose to pursue more offensive tactics against the Hurricanes and Spitfires. Goering had sided with the bomber pilots, and that has often been seen as a major factor in the British victory. The same issue surfaced in the American air force during 1943. Gen. Frank Hunter, the first leader of 8th Fighter Command, had tried to get more freedom of action for his escort fighters, but General Eaker had never permitted it. Hunter was replaced by William E. Kepner during the summer of 1943. For a time, the old escort tactics were continued, but after Spaatz and Doolittle came up from the Mediterranean they permitted a part of the fighter force to go after the enemy interceptors whenever they were sighted, not just when they were an immediate threat to the formation being escorted. This was so successful that more and more of the escort force was given such freedom.

More or less by trial and error, it also was discovered that great good could be done by fighters on their way home from escort missions. The bombers were much slower than the fighters, so the escorts protected their charges in relays. When a group of escorts was relieved by another while it still had ammunition, it would go down to low level on the return to its home field and shoot up the German airfields along the way, often attacking Luftwaffe fighters that were landing or taking off. The work was especially effective for a time, because when the P-51 was traveling at high speed at very low levels its outline so resembled that of the Messerschmitt 109 that it inhibited the antiaircraft gunners around the German airfields from opening fire for fear of hitting their own planes.[78] Adolf Galland credits this change in tactics more than Big Week or the other bombing attacks as decisive in weakening his pilot force. He and many others also have cited a decrease in the quality of Luftwaffe aircrews as a decisive factor in the Allies' achievement of air superiority.[79]

By April, when the shift in targeting and command took place, the air battle was practically won. The Luftwaffe had as many airplanes as ever, but the strategic bombing so strongly advocated by Spaatz had taken its toll. The destruction of German oil refineries and storage tanks had caused a critical shortage of fuel for the airplanes. In addition, the Luftwaffe replacement pilots were young men with no experience and little training. Air superiority, if not air supremacy, had been achieved; now the problem became one of holding it while exploiting the freedom of the skies. The Allied air forces now could turn to the relatively unhindered destruction of those targets that were the foundations of German military power; landings on the French coast were feasible; British and American airplanes could safely drop supplies to partisans fighting behind German lines; and the delivery of airborne troops became thinkable. But it was still uncertain how long that condition would last. The German aircraft industry was hard at work to restore their country's air strength, and no one could be certain that Hitler's fabled secret weapon would not come along to upset things.

If Spaatz's high spirits at the beginning of Big Week had any tendency to turn into long-lasting euphoria, he must certainly have been blasted out of it by tragedy of a personal nature. On the next-to-the-last day of the offensive, his new son-in-law was downed. On a mission near the head of the Adriatic on the 25th, "Red" Gresham's starboard engine caught fire. His wing man urged him to jettison his external tank, which dropped away cleanly, but soon after turning back towards the base in Italy, Lieutenant Gresham's plane went into a flaming dive. His wingman followed him down as far as he could but as he was pulling out, Gresham's plane crashed and exploded on a small island. No parachute was seen. Rebecca and Red had been married hardly a year, and their daughter, Edith, was but a month old. There followed a frantic exchange of cables between England and Eaker's headquarters in the Mediterranean, but there seemed to be no doubt that Gresham was gone. The tragic news was brought to Ruth and Rebecca by Everett Cook, who was flying back to Washington from England at that time.[80]

Then, less than two weeks later, came the news that Gresham was alive.[81] Spaatz had to be sure that the news was authentic, that there could be no mistake. After a series of cables from his friends in the Mediterranean, Eaker and Cannon and others, he became convinced that they had indeed seen the young pilot. Gresham had bailed out at a very low altitude after his wingman had already pulled out. He had been captured immediately and for a time was held on the island. When his German sentry let down his guard for a careless moment, Gresham pounded him on the skull with a rock and escaped. He was picked up by partisans on the island and returned to Allied territory in Italy. Once he was sure of his facts, Spaatz relayed the good news to Ruth and Rebecca.[82]

## OVERLORD and the Targeting Controversy

Planning for the cross-channel invasion had begun while Eisenhower and Spaatz were still in the Mediterranean. Months before they returned to England, Leigh-Mallory had been appointed as the commander of the Allied Expeditionary Air Force. Before the end of the year, he was deeply immersed in the planning and gathering of forces. Meanwhile, Tedder had on his staff a scientific adviser, Professor Solly Zuckerman, trained as a physician and a researcher in biology and animal behavior. Zuckerman had been investigating bomb effects in the ruins of Tripoli, Libya, planning for the Pantelleria raid, and evaluating the air attacks on Sicily.[83] According to Zuckerman, his relationship with Spaatz during these days was a good one.[84] Applying the empirical methods of a biologist to the problems of air war, Zuckerman came away from the Mediterranean convinced that air attacks on railroad yards and repair facilities were more productive than attempts to cut the lines at bridges and tunnels.[85]

Zuckerman returned to the United Kingdom about the same time Eisenhower and Spaatz came north and was assigned as the scientific adviser to Leigh-Mallory to examine the air plan for OVERLORD. At that moment, the plan called for a relatively moderate air attack by the airpower of AEAF for a few weeks prior to the landings, aimed at inhibiting the movement of German reserves to the lodgement area during the first weeks. The landings were to be made on a five-division front on the Normandy coast between the estuary of the Seine and the Cherbourg Peninsula. Two divisions of the British army would assault the beaches on the east, and three U.S. Army divisions would land on those to the west. There would be fighter patrols overhead and a fighter barrier set up in a semicircle some distance inland to prevent German planes from penetrating the airspace above the landing area. Meanwhile, the tactical air forces would suppress Axis air activity at all the airfields within fighter range of the beachheads. The RAF Coastal Command was to protect shipping on the way across the channel. The airlift forces would make two airborne attacks, one behind the American beaches to prevent rapid German reinforcement of the shore defenses, and another near the east end of the line to capture bridges over the river.[86] As the ground forces would have to be supplied and reinforced over the beaches until the port of Cherbourg was captured and cleared, the process promised to be a tedious one. There was a strong and well-fortified German garrison in the city, and in order to give the Allied buildup a chance of increasing at a higher rate than that of the Germans, airpower would have to put a toll on Wehrmacht communications both before and after the landings.

When Zuckerman looked over the air plan, he quickly concluded that it was inadequate. In his view it counted too much on good weather in the period before the landings, and the forces assigned to Ninth Air Force and 2d Tactical Air Force (RAF), which made up Leigh-Mallory's command, did not have the strength to do the job. Zuckerman also thought the target selection wrong, for it looked toward cutting the lines of communication more than to wrecking the rail yards and repair facilities. He persuaded Leigh-Mallory, Eisenhower, and Tedder of the correctness of his views. His remedy was to extend the preinvasion period of attacks on French communications and to also include major air strikes against the rail yards in northern France, even some in Germany. This would require the participation of the RAF's Bomber Command and USSTAF's Eighth Air Force for a substantial period prior to the early June landings. These conclusions and prescriptions were being made in January 1944, at a time when the Luftwaffe fighter forces were yet unbowed and when Spaatz had little assurance that air superiority was truly in the offing.[87]

When the strategic bomber commanders and staffs discovered what was afoot, they immediately raised objections on several grounds. Air Marshal Harris pointed out that his forces were trained for night area bombing, not for hitting small targets. He was then in the midst of his "Battle of Berlin," which he hoped would win the war without the need for an invasion, and looked upon any directive to hit railroad yards in France, or even Germany, as diversions from his main mission. Though the role envisioned for Bomber Command was somewhat less than AEAF proposed for Spaatz's forces, it was important to involve Harris, for that would make it easier to get control of USSTAF. But it was a difficult problem in that Harris was in a semiautonomous position, because of what was perceived as his special relationship with the prime minister.[88]

For Spaatz, the issue came to a head in the middle of February, just before Big Week. At a meeting on the 15th of February that included Tedder, Leigh-Mallory, Harris, Spaatz, Fred Anderson, Zuckerman, and their staffs, the AEAF commander briefed his proposal to use Spaatz's heavy bombers and all the other air forces that would be involved in OVERLORD. The meeting became more than a little acrimonious. Spaatz argued that Leigh-Mallory's plan was at loggerheads with his present directives under the POINTBLANK plan, namely to defeat the Luftwaffe and gain air superiority before the landings. He insisted that the strategic air forces had to continue hitting vital targets in the interior of Germany to force the Luftwaffe to come up and fight so that it could be defeated before OVERLORD. Leigh-Mallory retorted that attacks on the rail yards in France would make the German fighters come aloft. Aside from the fact that such battles would not drive the Reich's surviving fighters back to their homeland and far away from the OVERLORD beaches, Spaatz asked his adversary what he thought would happen if the Luftwaffe chose *not* to come aloft. Leigh-Mallory answered that it would make no difference, for the great battle for air superiority would take place over the beaches on D-Day and the Allies would win it then. That was outrageous to Spaatz, who then asked the RAF air marshal *when* he proposed to take control of the American strategic bombers. When the latter replied March 1, Spaatz said no more.[89]

Harris was not silent through all this. He seconded Spaatz's assertion that whatever targets were attacked, they must be chosen to make the Luftwaffe fight. He argued that Leigh-Mallory's scheme was fundamentally wrong for two reasons. First, the attacks on the yards would not sufficiently inhibit German military movements. Second, the RAF Bomber Command could not deliver the kind of accuracy that would be demanded of it. For a time, the seconds of the main actors argued about these points, but it was clear that no decision could be reached. Finally, Harris asserted that the plan had no chance to succeed. He said that the Army would then grasp the chance to blame the Air Force for the failure, and Harris was prepared to give a written guarantee that that would happen if Leigh-Mallory's plan were implemented.[90] Tedder then stepped in with a proposal that a committee of representatives from each of the interested commands be assigned to work out a plan satisfactory to all of them. The others agreed and the meeting broke up.[91]

Nothing had been settled at Leigh-Mallory's Tuesday meeting. By

Saturday, the 19th, Spaatz was still seething when he sent off his weekly cable to Arnold. Usually the update contained a full page of remarks about the week's fighting with the Luftwaffe, and a second page addressing the ways in which USSTAF was tackling its other problems. This time it was much shorter. The section on operations contained but two sentences, and the rest of the message was a complaint about the OVERLORD air plan, especially its failure to seek air superiority *before* the landings were attempted.[92] Spaatz well knew that Arnold had promised control of USSTAF to Eisenhower. There was no changing that. Though he did not directly ask Arnold to intervene, it was clear that he hoped his boss would help delay the change until the Luftwaffe was defeated. Even as he composed the cable to Arnold, the weather over the continent was clearing, and Spaatz stayed up late that night listening to the arguments about whether or not the force should be launched on Big Week. Finally, he issued the go order, and on Sunday he flew down to Eaker's headquarters to observe the proceedings from there.

The Americans in England knew that the force was growing rapidly and that long-range escorts were coming on the line. They hoped these things meant real air superiority was in the offing. While USSTAF had been girding for the great battle, some of its planners, along with others attached to the U.S. Embassy, were pondering what should be done with that air superiority if indeed it were soon obtained. At the outset of the war, the RAF had seen the German oil industry as a potential "vital center": the targets were few, but were vulnerable to air attack and not easily reparable. Even before the U.S. entered the war, AWPD-1 had included petroleum as one of the targets to be hit in Germany.[93] The imperatives of defeating submarines, gaining air superiority, and fighting Rommel had driven oil off Allied target lists, but now that some of the threats were receding, the strategic bomber people were showing renewed interest.

The Fifteenth Air Force was now in a position to make telling attacks against the Reich's principal source of natural petroleum: Ploesti. Hitler had seen the vulnerability of the Wehrmacht's fuel supply and had set the advanced German chemical industry to solving the problem through synthetic products well before he invaded Poland. The industry did well. The synthetic plants turned out high-quality aviation gasoline (along with a number of vital by-products) and produced enough of it to keep the war machine going. However, the machinery was complex, very expensive, not at all mobile, and difficult or impossible to hide. Most of the plants were out in the open where young navigators could find them and where stray bombs would not kill a lot of people needlessly. The gasoline demands of fighting mechanized war on two fronts were high, and that made it certain that the Luftwaffe would try to protect the oil plants. This latter factor was the handle Spaatz needed to prevent AEAF from getting control of his forces.[94] He could offer it as an option to Eisenhower, one that might do more than the transportation plan to defeat Germany, and, more importantly in Spaatz's mind, one that would guarantee the destruction of the Luftwaffe.

Solly Zuckerman perceived his own plan as being the logical one and tried to explain away Spaatz's vehement opposition as arising in part from the political imperatives of interservice rivalry. The implication is, of course, that Spaatz preferred not to come under the tactical commander and wanted to pursue independent targets in Germany in order to build the case for an independent air force.[95]

While it is true that the airmen had put the agitation for a separate service on the back burner for the duration of the war, it is also clear that the thought was seldom far from Spaatz's mind. Not only was it a topic for private discussion within the USAAF establishment, but Spaatz occasionally spoke to others about the future of the air arm. During the African campaign he had lamented to Arnold that he was inclined to get away from Army control and was inhibited from starting a campaign to do so only by the great stir it would cause in the midst of a war. That summer he spoke to Senator Henry Cabot Lodge about a separate service when the latter visited his headquarters in August.[96] He and Secretary Lovett often brought up the subject in their correspondence.[97] There is little doubt that Spaatz had a continuing concern for the future health of his own organization. Zuckerman's implication, however, that independence was the primary motivator discounts the fact that Spaatz had been wrapped up with notions of air superiority ever since the days of World War I, and that that was one of the main themes of his Mediterranean campaign. Spaatz did not leave much in the way of memoirs, but in the few interviews he granted after the war, his passing references to this episode declare his primary motive as being a concern for air superiority. It is therefore obvious that his decision processes were just as logical as those of Zuckerman.

During March 1944, the ad hoc committee met but arrived at no consensus. There was much behind-the-scenes pushing and shoving, again without progress. It was in this month that the problem of putting

USSTAF under the direct control of Leigh-Mallory was resolved,[98] but the targeting issue remained open. OVERLORD was approaching, however, and the bombers had not yet been put to the tasks conceived by Zuckerman and Tedder. Finally, Portal proposed developing a consensus through another meeting among all the interested parties. The issue came to a head on March 25, 1944,[99] and this time, Spaatz came to the meeting fully armed with an alternative proposal.

The USSTAF alternative plan had been reduced to writing and circulated to the other parties prior to the meeting on the 25th. In it, Spaatz argued that the primary goal remained the establishment and the maintenance of "air supremacy." He pointed out that there was no argument on that point. In all plans, it remained the first priority; thus the current question was over the second priority. Tedder's rail plan was deemed defective for two reasons. First, it would not make the German air force come up and fight, and therefore the first priority goal could not be achieved. Second, Spaatz argued that there was so much "cushion" in the northern European rail system that an attack on it would not prevent the movement of military units and supplies to the invasion area. The forces at hand and the time allowed would permit substantial damage to the transportation net, but since military traffic was such a small part of the whole, its first-priority status would guarantee that it would move, and only nonessential civilian traffic would be hampered. He did not propose that the attempt to isolate the battlefield through interdiction of rail traffic be abandoned—only that the tactical forces organic to AEAF be used to achieve that goal. Only later would USSTAF join in that work. Spaatz felt that meanwhile the American strategic forces could be used more effectively on other targets. The destruction of a rail yard, he argued, required the same weight of bombs as the obliteration of an oil plant. Since there were far fewer oil plants, the number of attacks that could eliminate the entire petroleum system would barely make a dent on the northern European rail system.

The alternative target was identified as the petroleum industry in Germany. Spaatz held that it was vulnerable and that the German reserve stocks were so low already that the effect of the bombing would be felt immediately. His brief suggested that the Germans would not wait to make changes in their plans and military dispositions, but rather would take action in *anticipation* of a shortage arising from the successful bombing of the synthetic plants. But more importantly, he argued: "We believe attacks on transportation will not force the German fighters into action. We believe they will defend oil to their last fighter plane."[100]

The crucial meeting on Saturday, March 25, was chaired by Marshal of the RAF, Sir Charles Portal, chief of the Air Staff, who was the agent of the Combined Chiefs of Staff. Tedder and Leigh-Mallory were there from AEAF and were accompanied by their boss, General Eisenhower. Air Chief Marshal Harris came alone, but Spaatz was seconded by his deputy for operations, Fred Anderson. There were also representatives of the Joint Intelligence Staff, the Ministry of Economic Warfare, the War Office, and a couple of Portal's assistants from the Air Ministry. Zuckerman was not at the meeting.[101]

One of the great barriers to consensus during the month of March had been lack of agreement on the condition of the Luftwaffe. General Kepner has claimed that by that stage of the war, his 8th Fighter Command pilots could claim no air victory that was not recorded on their gun cameras.[102] But how many of those "probables," not confirmed by the cameras, actually crashed before getting home? How many of those planes that the Luftwaffe did lose had been survived by their pilots? Though it could not be known then, the limiting factor was the number of competent pilots—there were always more than enough airplanes for the German defenders. By 1944, aircrew reports were so notorious for their inaccuracy that few intelligence officers would accept them without a massive discount. Besides the fighters shot down and recorded on the gun cameras, how many went down under the guns of the bombers or could not penetrate the weather to find a safe field? How many of the green Luftwaffe pilots crashed on the slippery runways of wintertime Germany?

ULTRA had achieved wonders before the spring of 1944, and the Luftwaffe had been one of its most lucrative sources, since its communications security discipline had been less stringent than that of the other German military services. But by the spring of 1944 even the Luftwaffe was learning better communications discipline. The great contraction of the territory held by the Axis also meant that much of its internal communications now went over land lines or was done in person and was thus not vulnerable to the radio intercepts that ULTRA depended upon. Consequently, during the period leading up to Eisenhower's decision, the magic of ULTRA could not develop an order of battle on the Luftwaffe—or at least not one that would win the agreement of all the intelligence agencies involved in building the estimate.[103] Even as late as April 24, 1944, Arnold was to say to Spaatz that the pressure on the German air force had to be "uninterrupted," and he was still anticipating that there might be a great air battle over the beaches on D-Day.[104]

Thus, though everyone at the meeting on March 25 agreed that the goal was complete aerial supremacy, no one really knew the starting point: there was no agreement about how far along the road the Allies were at that time.

Spaatz's main argument at the meeting depended heavily on the fact that the Luftwaffe was not yet defeated and that strong measures were required to put it down and keep it down. All his remarks to the inter-Allied, interservice representatives adhered to that notion. The press had made a big thing of Big Week, and many accounts since then have described the USSTAF effort as the one that broke the back of the Luftwaffe. In the privacy of his communication with his own staff, Spaatz thought that he saw signs of hope, but he still behaved as though the battle was far from complete. In a March 4 letter to Eaker, Doolittle, and Twining, the subject of which Spaatz described as "Exploitation of Air Supremacy," his outlook was optimistic but not complacent. First he asserted that though air supremacy was within reach, the job was not yet complete. He thought that the Luftwaffe was in such condition that it had to conserve its resources for defense of only the most sensitive targets. He told his subordinate commanders that USSTAF was now close enough to the goal of air supremacy that it was time to think of the exploitation phase. The situation was still dangerous, but it had improved enough to permit the strategic bomber air forces to send out more smaller raids against a wider variety of targets rather than to concentrate all resources in one main attack for the sake of the security of the penetrating force.[105] In his undated report to Arnold at the end of Big Week, Spaatz did say that the Luftwaffe had taken a serious blow, but did not make any claim that air superiority or supremacy had been won.[106]

Arnold had been pressing him and Eaker for quick results, and we can suppose that Spaatz would not have been hesitant to report the achievement of goals to Arnold.[107] His weekly message was upbeat on the issue of air fighting, but defensive on problems of maintenance—another sore point with Arnold:[108]

> In two attempts to reach Berlin, weather has prevented all but a small force from getting there. The enemy has been unable or unwilling to send his fighters in strength against these operations. I believe he will withhold them except when weather conditions over Germany indicate good visual bombing over vital areas. We will take every opportunity to hit German installations by visual bombing of vital targets when possible, by bombing vital areas through the overcast and by bombing targets of

opportunity through breaks in the overcast. Missions such as the operations against Brunswick and Frankfort (sic), which brought practically no reaction this week, would have been subjected to violent enemy opposition several months ago. . . .

Thus, what Spaatz was saying to his own people in their private correspondence was not inconsistent with what he was telling the British and Eisenhower. He felt that the Luftwaffe had been hurt and was perhaps on the road to collapse, but there still was work to be done. Besides, the recuperative ability of the Germans was well known, and Spaatz was much too cautious to jump to conclusions.

Marshal of the RAF Sir Charles Portal opened the March 25 meeting with a résumé of the events that had led up to it and then turned the floor over to Eisenhower's deputy, Tedder. Tedder rehashed the arguments that had been advanced by Zuckerman and Leigh-Mallory for many weeks past, but showed signs that he had read and tried to react to Spaatz's written proposals. He began his remarks with a strong statement that air superiority comes first, and with the assurance that he understood that the ball bearing plants were to be classified as airpower targets—a continuing concern of USSTAF headquarters. He also addressed another of Spaatz's main arguments by proclaiming that the SHAEF staff did not expect that the attack on the rail yards would shut off all German military traffic. No more was expected than to reduce its volume and efficiency in order to make the interdiction campaign of the tactical air forces more feasible when the time came to mount it and to inhibit German military operations during the first five weeks after the landings.[109]

Spaatz was not alone in arguing against the Zuckerman plan. Even before their turn came to speak, Maj. Gen. Sir John Kennedy of the War Office and Sir Andrew Noble of the Joint Intelligence Service both rose to speak against the railroad plan. They argued that the complete shutdown of the northern European railroad system was indeed out of the question, and the fraction of the traffic that was devoted to the military was so small that no amount of bombing would have a significant impact on operations. They denied that the experience in Sicily and Italy was a good guide because the situation there had been very different from the one in northern Europe. Eisenhower, they felt, was about to make a decision based on the findings of one *civilian* investigator who had not consulted the War Office's military transportation experts.[110]

General Eisenhower interjected a restatement of the problem to be solved and laid great emphasis on the notion that whatever plan was adopted, its effects would have to be felt within the first five weeks. He was reported to have remarked that if the preparatory bombing would help this task (tactical interdiction) sufficiently to justify hopes that enemy movement would be hampered and delayed, then it was worthwhile; and, in default of an alternative plan that would produce greater results, he thought the present one should be adopted. Perhaps that suggests he had come to the meeting with his mind already made up, for he had been aware of the oil plan for some time before March 25.

Later, but still before Spaatz spoke, Eisenhower remarked that ". . . everything he had read convinced him that apart from the attack on the GAF [German air force], the transportation plan was the only one which offered a reasonable chance of the air forces making an important contribution to the land battle during the first vital weeks of OVERLORD; in fact, he did not believe that there was any other real alternative." These comments must have been a blow to Spaatz, as he still had not had his chance to speak.[111] Eisenhower did seem, however, a little taken aback by the fact that the military transportation experts of the British army had not been consulted, and he promised to do so.

When Spaatz's turn came, he reiterated the points made in his paper that were in direct contradiction of those just made by Eisenhower. He did not promise immediate decisive results from the oil plan, but insisted that the rail plan would not impede the movement of military units and supplies sufficiently to have an impact on operations. He further insisted that the attack on rails would not cause the German air force to stand and fight. He tried to reassure the soldiers that his position did not imply any notion of denying the help of the strategic bombers to the landing operations, and he fully intended that in the period immediately prior to the landings, the full weight of the USSTAF be joined with the tactical air forces in a massive interdiction campaign and in hitting the military installations and airfields within reach of the battlefield. What he was arguing for was not independence from the battle on the ground, but only that the targets selected were wrong and the time was premature. In neither Spaatz's written brief, nor in the minutes reporting his comments at the meeting of March 25, is there expressed a moral concern for the threat the rail plan posed to the French civilians in the communities surrounding the rail centers and shops (this subject was discussed late in the meeting and was brought up by Portal). But in Spaatz's remarks at the meeting, he was quite explicit on one point:[112]

Strategic attacks on the enemy railway system with the forces and the time available would not affect the course of the initial battle and would not prevent the movement of German reserves from other fronts. On the other hand, the execution of the oil plan would force the enemy to decide to reduce oil consumption in anticipation of an impending shortage and consequent reduction of fighting power.

In other words, though there would be reserve stocks in France, the Allies would not have to wait until they were exhausted to see the effect. Rather, the Wehrmacht commanders would be forced to ration fuel stringently from the moment they knew that the synthetic plants would not be producing replenishment supplies. This would, in turn, have immediate effect on the "fighting powers" of the forces that would face the Allies on the beaches.

At this point, Portal may have implied that his mind, also, was already made up, but that the oil plan was certainly something that should be kept in mind. A representative of the Ministry of Economic Warfare had supported the notion that the oil attack would not have early effects and gave some data on the large oil stocks the Axis had been holding in the west. Portal then asserted that that was conclusive and the rail plan was the better for the short run, but that the oil plan ought to be studied for the future. Eisenhower agreed. It appeared clear that Spaatz had lost the case. Both Eisenhower and Portal had their minds set on the rail plan, and there was no dissuading them from it.[113]

Air Chief Marshal Harris had not played much of a part in the drama up to that point, and now his remarks were confined mainly to cautioning the others on the limitations of Bomber Command. He doubted that his organization could do what it would be asked to do, and he backed Spaatz in the hope that alternative plans would be considered.[114] Though the support of Harris, on paper at least, was not that impressive, it is apparent that Spaatz was not alone, for both the War Office and Bomber Command were skeptical of the plan created by Zuckerman, Leigh-Mallory, and Tedder.

The matter of killing French civilians was brought up only very late in the meeting and was introduced by Portal. Even then, it appears that there was more concern for the political than the moral aspects of the issue, for Portal suggested that the civilian casualty factor made it advisable to bring the British cabinet into the plan to make sure that the political leaders knew about the impact on the French living near the rail yards. Eisenhower promised to take it up with the British government leaders.[115]

When the meeting ended, Spaatz had suffered one of the toughest defeats of his official life. He and the other airmen had long looked upon the Mediterranean campaign, the submarine attacks, and the bombing of the V-weapon launching sites as diversions from their main purpose—as obstacles to the bombing of the vital centers of Germany. Now Spaatz felt that air supremacy was finally in his grasp, that the road to the vital centers seemed clear, and the target that would have the most deadly effects had been identified. It seemed that the Luftwaffe was on the ropes and USSTAF was poised on the brink of victory— and just at that moment, the great weapon in Spaatz's hands was taken from his control to be used against the railroad yards of France. The Luftwaffe would be given a reprieve just as the end came in sight.

On an official level, Spaatz did not let his disappointment creep into his report to Arnold. On Sunday, March 26, he signaled Hap that the meeting had chosen the rail plan over the oil scheme and asserted that the time was now at hand to turn to the support of OVERLORD in full force.[116] Though in the legal sense the control of USSTAF was not to pass from Portal to Eisenhower until both had formally approved the operational plan for striking the rail yards, Spaatz's forces immediately started responding to Eisenhower's requirements. For a time, Spaatz continued to receive directions from Portal, but when Eisenhower found out about that, he brought it to an end through discussions with the British.[117]

If Eisenhower thought that his decision of March 25 was final, he was mistaken. The commitment to bring the British political leaders back into the drama complicated his life for a while longer. The cabinet considered the problem in early April and balked. They did not want to accept a plan that entailed many thousands of French casualties, some estimates reaching above 100,000. But Eisenhower was firm in his decision and resisted Churchill. Ultimately, the prime minister appealed back to the United States for aid, but Roosevelt, Marshall, and Arnold declined to intervene. DeGaulle was not yet in England, but when the commander of the French forces in the United Kingdom, Gen. Pierre Joseph Koenig, was consulted on the matter, he brusquely dismissed the problem with the comment that lives are lost in wars and that would be the price the French people would have to pay to escape their bondage.[118] In the end, the prime minister ceased his opposition.

Thus, it was the early part of April before the last of the obstacles to the railroad plan was removed and the operations could begin in earnest—a full month after the date that had been cited by Leigh-Mallory for beginning the campaign. Only sixty days remained before the landings, and Zuckerman had asserted that the rail attack should prepare the way for ninety days. However, Spaatz had an extra month, at least, to carry out his strategic operations against the Luftwaffe, and during the month following Big Week, the Luftwaffe lost more flyers than it had in February. After March, there were 511 fewer fighter pilots to oppose the landings.[119] Although Spaatz and Arnold were not deliberately trying to delay the transition to the railroad operation, the extra month for attacks on German factories could hardly have been unwelcome.

Though the arguments of March had an unhappy outcome for Spaatz, they did have some hidden benefits. His oil plan had had a thorough airing before the highest officials of both the Air Ministry and SHAEF; both Portal and Eisenhower proclaimed that there was merit in the plan and that it ought to be further pursued, once the armies were firmly ashore. Thus, their minds may have been biased in favor of Spaatz's goals once a little more time had passed.

Before the end of March, Spaatz made it clear that he had not yet given up. While he fully accepted the task of bombing the French railroads, in a March 31, 1944, memorandum to Eisenhower, he began to explore the question of which was to take priority *within Germany,* the transportation or petroleum targets. Spaatz gave further arguments in favor of the oil targets and also proposed attacking transportation targets in Rumania. When Tedder's directive finally came out in mid-April, there were no oil targets listed at any level of priority. It did list the Rumanian rail yards at Ploesti, however, and the Fifteenth Air Force, which had already made some attacks on them, continued to choose aiming points there. "Coincidentally," many of these small yards happened to be adjacent to oil refineries, and the spread of the Fifteenth's bomb patterns turned out to be somewhat wider than theretofore. Many of the "stray" missiles came down in the oil works instead of the rail yards which were the aiming points.[120]

It was harder to clear the way for Eighth Air Force attacks against synthetic plants in Germany. Spaatz's case was strengthened when very few German fighters rose to contest the early attacks on French rail yards. Still, it was not until Spaatz threatened Eisenhower with resignation that he was able to get permission to use two good-weather days for attacks on the synthetic oil works. Even then, Eisenhower made a strong point that the main purpose of those two attacks would be to test the proposition that the Luftwaffe would rise to defend such plants more than they had for the rail yards.[121] Two attacks were made in the middle of May.

From Spaatz's point of view, the results of the May attacks on oil were outstanding. The Luftwaffe came up in strength, and Eisenhower soon got feedback through ULTRA that the effects on the Germans were dramatic. The military leaders of the Reich reacted immediately. They redeployed antiaircraft defenses hurriedly from the aircraft factories to those synthetic plants that had not yet been bombed. In addition, they changed the training programs of some of the ground units to conserve fuel and modified additional vehicles to wood-burning propulsion systems.[122] Though USSTAF could not at that moment be relieved of its responsibilities in the preparatory phases of OVERLORD, the combination of effects seems to have so impressed Eisenhower that later in the summer he permitted additional oil attacks.[123]

Underlying the original Zuckerman plan were notions that the bombing of rail yards in Sicily and Italy had been much more economical than cutting the lines at bridges and tunnels. The latter were so hard to hit, the argument went, that a much greater bomb tonnage had to be assigned to each one than would be the case to achieve comparable effects through attacks on rail yards and repair facilities. In an attack on a bridge, many bombs would fall into the water and on the banks without any effect at all. Rail yards were such large targets, compared to bridges, that every bomb falling would achieve some worthwhile effect.

Spaatz's staff had investigated the validity of this proposition well before the decision on the rail yards had been made. Their conclusions were that Zuckerman had based his assumptions on a faulty sample and that more current information from Italy showed that the line cuts were not nearly so difficult to achieve as Zuckerman had supposed. Therefore, the counterargument went, the isolation of the Normandy battlefield would be much more easily achieved by bridge busting than by yard bombing. This could be best achieved by light and medium bombers or fighters. Spaatz's staff pushed this argument because it would release the strategic forces to continue the destruction of the Luftwaffe and especially to mount a sustained assault on the German oil industry.[124] Spaatz did not bring the "bridge-busting" proposition into his arguments at the meeting of March 25, because he was hesitant, perhaps, to tell the tactical air commanders their business.[125] On April 22, however, he wrote to Eisenhower that the transportation campaign, as envisioned in the directive he had just received, would cause too many casualties among our Allies. He voiced doubt that the attacks on the rail yards were achieving much and urged Eisenhower to consider shifting to targets cutting the rail lines outside populated areas.[126] On May 7, some of Brereton's P-47s were sent to test the ideas coming from the Italian interdiction campaign against a bridge at Vernon on the Seine River. The test was a spectacular success, and the air effort in that direction was immediately increased.[127] During the preparatory phase, all the bridges over the Seine up to Paris were knocked down, and many others along rivers further to the east were also destroyed. Those across the Loire were left standing until D-Day lest the location of the landings be given away to German observers, but they too were almost completely destroyed on D-Day.[128]

## D-Day: The Primary Outcome

The air element of D-Day began in the late evening of June 5, 1944. Three full divisions of paratroopers and glider-borne soldiers were launched from the airfields of southern England, headed for drop zones at both ends of the beachhead areas. Their landings were scheduled shortly after midnight, and the drop zones were to be marked by pathfinders preceding the main force. The initial reports on these operations were optimistic;[129] however, the paratroopers came down in anything but precise military order. They were scattered far and wide, and only a few of their objectives were achieved. Some of the targeted bridges and crossroads were taken, and in some cases, the troopers were able to prevent a quick Wehrmacht response to the landings. There were unintended benefits too, for the appearance of paratroopers over such a wide area did confuse the German response. Gen. Omar Bradley, in command of the American landing, judged that the operation, for all of its disorder, was worth the cost. Casualties among the paratroopers were far lower than had been predicted by Leigh-Mallory, who had cautioned Eisenhower against the use of the airborne, fearing it would turn into a massacre.[130] Among the troop carrier forces casualties also were light. Out of approximately a thousand airplanes that had been launched, only twenty-four were missing on the following day.[131] All went down to enemy ground fire, and there were no accidental losses to Allied gunners. The Allied aircraft were painted with thick, white "zebra stripes" to help avoid mistakes, and the routing carried the troop carrier forces far away from the track of the surface fleet then bound for Normandy.

By daylight, there were twenty-four thousand Allied troops on the ground trying to consolidate their organizations. The Luftwaffe was nowhere in sight. The Allies flew fourteen thousand sorties in support of the landings on the first day—nearly nine thousand by the Eighth and Ninth Air Forces.[132] Against this the Luftwaffe was able to get only three hundred nineteen aircraft aloft during the whole day. Most of the ground forces at the beaches did not see any of these, and the few German aircraft that did penetrate had insignificant effect. One formation of twelve JU-88 bombers was among the larger units reported to have approached the lodgement area; four of them were shot down, while the bombs of the others had no serious effect.[133] Spaatz drafted his initial report to Arnold at noon on D-Day:[134]

Enemy air activity almost negligible and limited to reconnaissance flights. Activity of enemy shore batteries reported light. Full details of our fighter and bomber losses to cover this period not fully reported, but are believed very light.

There were several reasons for Allied air supremacy over the beaches. A large part of the surviving Luftwaffe was pinned down in Germany by the threat of deep penetrations by Eighth Air Force and Bomber Command. Luftwaffe losses had continued to rise in the spring while those of the Allies had taken a decided turn for the better. On D-Day, the 8th Fighter Command set up a cordon around the beachhead area that was maintained all day long. Twelfth Fighter Command and the RAF maintained a patrol of fighters over the beaches in like fashion. The P-38s were assigned to cover the convoys traveling toward Normandy. Their distinctive shape made them readily identifiable to the greenest gunner in the fleet. The Luftwaffe had long had a plan to redeploy its fighters from the home defense force to forward fields to counter the invasion. But in the several weeks before D-Day, the bombers of both the strategic and tactical air forces in England had pounded those fields, and the pounding continued during and after the landings. Luftwaffe fighter forces bound for the lodgement area had no place to land. Their inexperienced pilots often were given new destinations while en route, and when they landed they were of limited utility because they had never operated at any but a fully developed airfield. Not only did the Allied air defense protect the troops and the ships, and make the air safe for the troop carriers, but it also opened the way for unhindered preparatory bombardment.[135]

Leigh-Mallory, controlling the heavy bombers for D-Day and a few days before and after, ordered both Bomber Command and Eighth Air Force to attack the beach defenses just before the landings were scheduled to hit the shore. Their purpose was to destroy defenses, make the surviving defenders keep their heads down, and detonate the mines that the Germans had planted everywhere. Spaatz thought this an improper use of heavy bombers for they did not have the accuracy required for such work and, in his mind, could have been more profitably used elsewhere. There was an argument over the possibility of some of the bombs falling short. Spaatz wanted the boats to stand farther off shore during the bombardment, but the ground commanders did not want to give the Germans an opportunity to recover between the time the bombing halted and the boats made it to the beach. In the end, it was necessary to instruct the bombardiers to hold their bombs a few seconds beyond their aiming point; the result was that the effectiveness of the preparatory bombardment suffered. The missiles fell too far inland, often behind the beach defenses, and did not set off the mines as extensively as had been intended. This was little understood by the ground commanders, who were generally disappointed with the results of the air bombardment.[136]

The use of medium bombers and fighters for close support work in front of the troops was not prominent on D-Day itself, although they were on call overhead through the day. Methods of coordination were not yet as fully practiced as they were to become and, of course, the Germans had not yet had time to react. Some German tanks managed to break through the lines between two English divisions and get to the beach, but the Germans could not get supporting infantry to the tanks.[137]

One reason Rundstedt could not then or later get enough infantry to the scene was the crushing air interdiction campaign fought in the days before and following the landings. Bridges over the Seine had been shut down by Ninth Air Force before the landings, while those across the Loire were destroyed by Eighth on D-Day and later. Overwhelming air superiority allowed many Allied fighters to attack military traffic along roads and railroads. By D-Day, the Germans had banned civilian traffic from railroads in the vicinity, giving the American and British fighter pilots a blank check to fire upon anything they saw moving on the rails. In many cases, the German troops had to go to the battlefield on foot, carrying their ammunition and rations with them.

In short, the Normandy campaign still provides the classic case of air supremacy and isolation of the battlefield that results from it.[138] The official history of the RAF described it all:[139]

> Thus ended "D-Day," the most momentous in the history of war since Alexander set out from Macedon "to ride in triumph through Persepolis." To say that the Allied air forces were omnipotent, overwhelming, is no more than the truth. That was precisely what they were. Leigh-Mallory swept the skies and carried all before him. From dawn till long after dusk, the Norman air was vibrant with the sound of aircraft passing to and fro. "The sky seemed to be full of our fighters the whole time, even in weather which was scarcely fit for flying. It was a most inspiring and comforting sight," said a sailor on the deck of one of the hundreds of ships. . . .

An American historian was more generous to USSTAF in his evaluation:[140]

> Air superiority for OVERLORD had been won early in 1944 when the great bomber fleets, escorted by long-range fighters, assaulted critical targets on the continent and the Luftwaffe rose to the challenge, to be beaten back and finally defeated. General Carl Spaatz had been insistent—and correct. The enemy would fight for oil, and the enemy would lose his fighters, his crews, *and* his fuel.

But perhaps a better witness on that subject than either of those was Generalfeldmarschall Gerd von Rundstedt. Replying passionately to a question as to whether he had been satisfied with his deployments on D-Day he said:[141]

> No, unfortunately not. Had I been able to move the armored "divisionen" which I had behind the coast, I am convinced that the invasion would not have succeeded. Always assuming your air force . . . away. If I had been able to move the troops, then my air force would also have been in a position to attack your ships. You would first of all have sustained losses on disembarkation, and you would not have been able so undisturbed to bring up your large battleships so near the coast to act as floating gun batteries. That is all a question of air force, air force, and again air force. . . .

With the beachheads established, Carl Spaatz was anxious to renew the assault on German industry. At the end of the month he wrote to Eisenhower asking for a revision of priorities. He held that air superiority in the west was so secure that it was time to return to the attack on the Reich. He recommended that on good-weather days the first priority for USSTAF be the targets in Germany, with the reservation that major tactical emergencies and attacks on the V-2 rocket sites would take precedence. Spaatz argued that the normal number of days of bad weather over Germany would automatically assure enough weight of attack for the rocket sites and the lesser tactical crises.[142] Spaatz was impatient to get on with the full exploitation of hard-won air supremacy.

# Chapter VIII

## THE TACTICAL EXPLOITATION

By May 1944, the RAF and USAAF had won air superiority over Europe. It now fell to the British and American airmen to exploit this supremacy. There were two main dimensions to the task: pressing the battle on the ground and striking directly at the German homeland from the air. The tactical exploitation in support of the surface war is the subject of this chapter. The strategic exploitation to dry up the sources of fuel in the German homeland and to break down its transportation system will be examined in the next chapter.

Lt. Gen. Carl Spaatz played a key role in both of these efforts. In the tactical campaign, though his legal authority did not extend to the operations of the tactical air forces assigned to AEAF, he was in constant contact with its leaders and had some influence on their thinking. At the same time, he directed the tactical operations of the heavy bombers as they supported the ground campaign. Through it all he strove to keep some strategic pressure on Germany to deny the Reich time for recuperation. He was also the policymaker for both personnel and materiel matters not only for the Eighth Air Force but also for the American air organizations assigned to Eisenhower under Ninth Air Force.

### Summer Battles: The Breakout

For several reasons the German response to Allied landings was to concentrate the main Wehrmacht strength against the British end of the line around Caen. First, Rundstedt still was not sure that the Normandy attack was the main assault. The Allied deception that the biggest strike would come at a site farther north was still working. Thus, he did not want to engage the Allies so far to the west that his forces could not be brought back to face another attack. Second, the British forces at Caen, if unmolested, would have a straight shot at Paris and the German borders, so they represented the most dangerous threat to the Germans. Finally, with transportation paralyzed in western France, it was easier for the Germans to bring their forces into the line facing Montgomery than farther west in front of the American forces. Still, the German organizations in front of the U.S. Army were tough enough to make things difficult. It was not until the end of June that the Americans captured the port of Cherbourg after stiff resistance. By the time the Germans surrendered, they had so completely destroyed the port facilities that it would be a long time before the port again reached full capacity. Even after the fall of Cherbourg, the summer weeks were slipping by and the German line still held. Though Montgomery was making no dramatic advances in the east, he was tying down the major part of the German army, so, as the plan evolved by early June, the Allies would attempt a breakout on the American flank, driving to the south to open some of the ports along the Brittany Coast, and then turning eastward to threaten the rear of the German units facing Montgomery.[1]

## Carpet Bombing at St. Lo

Eisenhower was always consistent in asserting that the whole OVER-LORD plan was based on the fundamental assumption of overwhelming air superiority, and there is little evidence that he was swayed by the argument of his friends in the USAAF that strategic bombing of German industry or cities could win the war by itself. The belief remained strong in the American army that airpower could be most useful as an auxiliary to the operations of the ground units. One dimension of this was the notion that the American-style blitzkrieg might be most effective if the heavy bombers, rather than the infantry and artillery, blasted a hole in the enemy line and provided a carpet over which the mobile units would roll into the enemy's rear areas. Such ''carpet bombing'' had been tried earlier in the war. At Pantelleria, saturation bombing made the assault a ''walk-in'' for the amphibious troops. It could be argued, however, that the Italian defenders were already so demoralized that it was not much of a contest from the beginning. At Monte Cassino, earlier in 1944, Eaker's heavies had obliterated everything in sight, but the German defenders did not give way.[2] Even larger attacks were carried out in July in front of Montgomery at Caen by the combined weight of RAF Bomber Command and the USSTAF Fortresses and Liberators. The minimum objectives of these assaults were to fix the German units in position, to capture the town of Caen, and to gain some ground to the south towards Falaise, where airfields could be built to increase the effectiveness of the tactical air arms supporting the armies.[3] Ultimately, some small advances were made, but the results of Montgomery's efforts were disappointing to the Americans and even to some of the British leaders.[4] By July, the plan was to use the eastern end of the Allied line in Normandy as a pivot for a large wheeling movement in a counterclockwise direction. It was hoped that this would pin the German armies against the Seine River west of Paris. In July 1944, then, the Allied commanders expected to make a breakout on the American front followed by an exploitation of the U.S. Army's mobility to carry it on a broad sweep first to the south and then to the east.[5]

One of the purposes of fixing the German armies in front of Montgomery was to facilitate the breakout on the American part of the front. The combination of British ground attacks and heavy bombings accomplished this. In some instances, though, the bombings were counterproductive, for they threw so much rubble down and created so many craters that it slowed the ground advance, while the constant rains of late July turned the whole area into a sea of mud.

Planning for the American breakout was the charge of Omar Bradley. He was in Normandy initially as the commander of the U.S. First Army and, later, as head of the U.S. Twelfth Army Group. There had been a strategic bomber operation in preparation for the Normandy landings that resembled what later became known as ''carpet bombing'' and Bradley was critical of the lack of results of that attack.[6]

By the second week in July, the situation began to look like a stalemate. From the infancy of the Grand Alliance, the British had been most reluctant to undertake a cross-channel attack because of the bitter memories of the long stalemate on the western front in World War I.[7] Now, even some of the American generals were becoming uneasy about such possibilities.[8] Bradley's forces had tried a thrust directly down the west coast of France, but that had not done much to change the situation. The hedgerows of the bocage country so added to the defensive strength of the Wehrmacht that the mobile American forces could not generate the necessary momentum.

When it became clear to Bradley that the strike down the coast road would not work, he devised an alternative plan. Somewhat farther east, to the south of St. Lo, the country was more suitable for mobile warfare than in other parts of the front.[9] Bradley's scheme was to capture the country down to St. Lo and the road from that town towards Periers to the east. Then, he would gather all available forces behind that road in preparation for the breakthrough and exploitation. At the appointed time, a massive bombing assault would be sent in immediately south of the St. Lo-Periers road to destroy and demoralize as many of the defenders as possible. This air attack would be made by a combined force of more than 2,000 aircraft including fighter-bombers and medium bombers from Ninth Air Force and the "heavies" of the Eighth. Once the fighter-bombers had made their attack immediately south of the road, the "heavies" would drop their light fragmentation bombs in the area immediately to the south of that, and the mediums would follow into the area still farther south. At that moment, there was a bit of an ammunition shortage in Normandy, so the artillery forces could not supplement the bombing as heavily as might have been hoped. Still, the sequence and weight of the attack envisioned by Bradley did resemble the rolling artillery barrages of the First World War.[10]

Bradley's plan was one that would be sure to make the old theorists of the Air Corps Tactical School wince. It was no more acceptable to Spaatz.[11] On 15 June, he had complained to Eisenhower that Montgomery and Leigh-Mallory had so little imagination that they could not conceive of any other use for Fortresses than to "plough up" the ground in front of the lines.[12] At the very time Bradley was conceiving additional tactical uses for his heavies, Spaatz conferred with Tedder and reported that both agreed that the Allies had been doing too much ploughing up of the Normandy terrain with their strategic bombers.[13] Before he had ever been briefed on Bradley's plan, then, Spaatz was skeptical about using his heavy bombers in this fashion.

Bradley sold Eisenhower on his operation, named COBRA, and Montgomery raised no objection to it. Bradley went to Leigh-Mallory's headquarters at Stanmore, back in England, to make the final arrangements for the attacks with the airmen. Spaatz and Brereton, among others, were at the meeting. Bradley later maintained that he had stipulated that the axis for attack be east-west (or the reverse) along the St. Lo-Periers road, but south of it. He maintained that the bombers could blunt the effectiveness of the antiaircraft fire by attacking in the early morning or late afternoon so the sun would be in the eyes of the gunners. The airmen of Eighth Air Force, however, insisted that the axis of attack be north to south, perpendicular to the lines. This, they argued, was necessary because they had to attack the target at its widest point because of the vast number of airplanes involved. To attack the narrow part would cause unacceptable congestion and delay. Moreover, the accuracy of the strikes would be enhanced by north-to-south strikes because the aircraft would not be under fire as they approached their bomb release points. Were they to come at the targets along the lines rather than across them, the planes would be under fire long before they reached the release point, which would interfere with their accuracy and endanger their own troops. The bomber men argued that the lateral accuracy was less reliable than that along the flight path and therefore the parallel attack track would be the more dangerous to their own men.[14] Bradley came away from the meeting believing that he had won the agreement of the airmen to the parallel attack, but the strategic bomber people said that had not been the case. They later insisted that they would not have accepted the plan had it required such an attack.[15]

COBRA was to have come immediately after one of Montgomery's attacks on the eastern flank on 19 July. However, the rainy weather caused repeated postponements until finally the mission was scheduled for the 24th. Leigh-Mallory was the impresario on the scene, and at the very last minute he aborted the mission, once more on account of the bad weather. His recall order did not go out in time to stop all of the attacks, and because of the smoke and bad weather, some of those who did not receive the message dropped bombs on their own troops. Most of the erroneous strikes were made by USSTAF bombers.[16] Some Americans were killed, and the prospect for achieving tactical surprise was lost. Bradley was outraged upon discovering that the attack had been made perpendicular to the lines, and that his troops had suffered from the bombs. He demanded that the Air Force revise the plan to attack parallel to the lines, but was informed that such an attack could not be arranged in time for an assault the next day. It was to be another perpendicular attack or nothing. Fearing that the slim remaining chance for surprise would elude him, Bradley ordered the attack to be flown as planned on the next day.[17]

The weather on 25 July was somewhat better, and no recall went out. Spaatz was at the front to witness the beginning of the offensive. Over two thousand airplanes passed over the target area and nearly four thousand tons of bombs were dropped. Despite the additional safety precautions that had been promised to Bradley, more bombs fell on the American lines, some on the same division that had taken the hits the previous day. Over a hundred Americans died, among them one of the most senior generals in the U.S. Army, Lt. Gen. Leslie J. McNair.[18]

Eisenhower was in France with Bradley when COBRA was launched on the 25th, and the initial reports indicated that the units hit by their own bombs were so badly shaken that they could not jump off as scheduled. One battalion command post, for example, had taken a direct hit. It had to be replaced by an entirely new unit before that part of the force could go forward. The first reports also indicated that the Germans had not been severely affected. Their artillery seemed as formidable as it had been before the bombing. Consequently, when Eisenhower went back to England that evening, things looked bleak. Once the initial shock wore off, however, the troops began to make progress, and as early as the 26th, it was becoming clear that the effects of the bombings on the Wehrmacht had been much more serious than they had at first appeared. Finally, the hard German crust cracked.[19] Bradley's First Army moved south, and soon Patton's Third Army poured through the gap for the pursuit across France. The Americans swung around to an easterly direction and began to form the Falaise Pocket around the German armies caught between Montgomery in the Caen vicinity and the Americans farther south. The Allies did not close the mouth of the pocket in time to trap the entire German force, but the Wehrmacht suffered substantial losses and retired in such disarray that the pursuit did not stop until the overextension of the Allied supply lines pulled it up short of the Rhine.

Before the end of July the outlook for both Bradley and Eisenhower had brightened considerably. In spite of the tragic losses among their own troops, both rated the mission of USSTAF and Ninth Air Force in support of the breakout a success. Eisenhower, especially, proclaimed that the carpet bombing had been absolutely essential to the successful penetration of the German defense lines.[20] Still, that did not prevent an investigation or recriminations. The former showed that all of the bombing errors had been due to human error—each one understandable, but collectively adding up to tragedy. Spaatz thought the losses were less than might have been expected under those conditions, but that did not ease the pain. He confided to his headquarters diary that future attacks should be flown parallel to the front.[21] Some soldiers also tried to console themselves that the deaths from their own bombs were far fewer than would have occurred had the armies tried the penetrations without the help of the heavy bombers. The airmen agreed that the bombers had been a decisive factor in the breakout.[22]

Eisenhower at first came away from France vowing he would never again use heavy bombers in close support of troops,[23] but after the success of the breakthrough became apparent, he changed his mind. By the 27th Eisenhower was beginning to regain his enthusiasm for the use of strategic air forces for the penetration of enemy lines, but Spaatz and the other airmen still were reserved in their attitudes. In the words of Lewis Brereton:[24]

> In a talk with General Spaatz and myself, General Eisenhower stated that he was pleased with the air attack at St. Lo and that he considered heavy bombers an indispensable weapon to keep our army moving when they (sic) bogged down. General Eisenhower's idea is sound, but the use of heavies in close support is in direct contradiction to what General Spaatz, Doolittle, Eaker (also visiting the front in France) and I feel is the proper employment of heavy bombardment. General Spaatz expressed this by pointing out that if the heavies were diverted too long from their strategic program, it would allow targets inside Germany to be rehabilitated. . . .

As for enemy opinion on carpet bombing, ULTRA picked up the following words from a Panzer Lehr Division:[25]

> Since 0750 hours very heavy bombing attacks on main defense and rearward areas.

> Following took part:
> About 800 four-engined aircraft, 100 Thunderbolts and Lightnings, followed by 80 Marauders. In addition fighter protection . . . fighter-bomber attacks on main defense zone were continuous. Presumably the enemy intends to break through in division area; in area of right and left neighbor no attacks. GAF support is urgently requested.

After the war, Gerd von Rundstedt cited the attack at St. Lo as the single most effective use of air power in tactical support in his experience.[26]

By the end of the month the threat of a stalemate was disappearing. The American armies were making for the Brittany ports and finding the open country that was necessary for the full exploitation of Allied superiority in mobility and airpower. Still, the great victory was flawed for everyone on the Allied side by the deaths sustained due to their own bombs. For the airmen, it was also flawed by what was seen as excessive reliance on strategic bombers for tactical purposes, and Spaatz feared that it would become a narcotic.[27] But whatever the flaws, the crust was broken.

Toward the latter part of the summer, Spaatz's enthusiasm for carpet bombing seemed to be warming. Conferring with Eisenhower, he was arguing that Montgomery's contention that the heavies could not be used effectively in tactical support was wrong, but when Spaatz took it up with Monty, the latter agreed it had been crucial to his progress.[28] At the onset of winter, whatever his remaining doctrinal reservations, Spaatz's enthusiasm was greater still. On 13 December he wrote to Doolittle saying that it might be necessary to do more carpet bombing in support of Patton's planned offensive. He argued that the quality of German troops had degenerated to the point where such bombing might turn out to be decisive. Spaatz felt that if the Eighth Air Force could itself achieve the breakthrough, it would do wonders for USAAF prestige.[29] He did not then suspect that those apparently deteriorating German troops would soon sting the Allies again in Rundstedt's imminent Ardennes offensive and the Luftwaffe's last great surge on New Year's Day.

## ANVIL: The Invasion of Southern France

In the original planning for the secondary landings in southern France that were to have supported the Normandy attack, ANVIL was selected as the code name to suggest that they would serve as the firm base against which the hammer of OVERLORD would smash the Wehrmacht. It did not work out that way. From the strategic or tactical point of view, a secondary attack should be made with the minimum force required and should be so timed as to distract attention from the main attack to create surprise or to attract enemy forces away from the main attack. ANVIL was originally to have taken place almost simultaneously with OVERLORD, but the lack of landing craft, among other things, prevented that from happening. Thus the surprise value was lost.

Churchill was not enthusiastic about ANVIL, preferring greater efforts in northern Italy or a landing at the head of the Adriatic. Though Spaatz was not much involved in the argument between Eisenhower and Churchill over the advisability of continuing with the ANVIL plan, he was to be affected by the landings in the south of France in various indirect ways. If the potential strategic or tactical benefits to be derived from such landings were disappearing as the summer wore on, the logistical imperatives were growing to buttress Eisenhower's position that ANVIL should go forward. Cherbourg was not cleared as quickly as had been hoped, and the channel ports farther to the north and east were not falling into Eisenhower's hands as rapidly as he wanted. Once the St. Lo breakout had been achieved, some of the Brittany ports became available, but they were small and farther from the fighting and from Germany than was Cherbourg.

After the Allies had broken out of the beachhead and were moving to the east, their consumption rose rapidly, and the pulverized French railroads could not bring up the needed fuel and ammunition. The limiting factor on the thrust to the east was logistical rather than tactical. It is fundamental that once an enemy is on the run the pursuit be maintained with all the power available. Thus, the great attraction for Eisenhower was that ANVIL held the promise of substantially improving his logistical position. After a tough struggle on the issue, he had his way, and the final orders for the landings in southern France went out only a few days before they were scheduled to take place.[30]

As the execution of the landings involved the forces under Wilson and Eaker in the Mediterranean, Spaatz did not have a formal operational role in either the planning or the attack. Since the Luftwaffe was even further emaciated in August than it had been at the time of OVERLORD, the air support needed for ANVIL was not nearly as massive as it had been for the Normandy assault. The greater part of it was conducted by the tactical units of Twelfth Air Force under Generals Eaker and Cannon. Eaker's Fifteenth Air Force played a part, but it was also involved in shuttling its bombers to Russia, in supporting the campaign in northern Italy, in bombing oil and transportation targets in the Balkans, and in the logistical support of partisan groups. Thus, though Eaker's Fortresses and Liberators did help with ANVIL, the greater part of the load was carried by Cannon's organization. Spaatz made a trip to the Mediterranean shortly before the landings to arrange last-minute coordination.[31] The possibility of moving Fifteenth Air Force to France to improve its potential against German targets was to be considered and rejected later on, but in July 1944, the difficult task of transferring Twelfth Air Force from the Mediterranean command to Eisenhower's authority had to be planned.

Further, a substantial part of the C-47 force assigned to Ninth Air Force was to be lent to Eaker for an airborne assault on the French coast just before the amphibious landings. This took the airlifters out of the resupply mission just at the time that Patton was driving across France and his needs were at their greatest. That, in turn, increased demands on Spaatz's heavy bombers to serve as airlifters, thereby diverting them from the strategic bombing of the German heartland which Spaatz so ardently desired.[32]

When the ANVIL landings came in the middle of August, the Luftwaffe was no longer a factor in those regions, and the air defense dimension of the airpower problem was of little concern. A few attacks were made against airfields in the region, and Spaatz sent some heavies from Eighth Air Force to help hit enemy airdromes on an arc around the battle area.[33] The rest of the air operation, however, was similar to that of OVERLORD, though somewhat less prolonged and massive. If anything, the aerial part of ANVIL worked even better than it had for OVERLORD. The airborne operation in particular was one of the best in the entire war. Most of the parachutists and gliders landed on target, few men or aircraft were lost, and their objectives were achieved. The interdiction campaign seriously hampered those German forces still in the south. It was so effective that the American ground commander had to ask Twelfth Air Force to stop attacking the bridges because their destruction was hurting the advancing Americans more than the retreating Germans. Before the summer was gone, the Americans and French coming from the south joined hands with the Allies headed for Germany from the west. ANVIL had been a model operation and showed that the Allies had learned much from the amphibious attacks they had conducted in the Mediterranean.[34]

For Spaatz, ANVIL was good news and bad news. The good news was that the severe logistical problems in the north that gave rise to the requirement for aerial resupply were helped by ANVIL, and then finally solved by the capture and clearing of the channel ports. The bad news was that it diverted some bombing power from Germany and toward the south of France. Worse, it distracted a major part of the Ninth Air Force airlift capacity to the Mediterranean and that, in turn, caused too many of Spaatz's bombers to be diverted from bombing and used for trucking. But this trucking was only one of the distractions that was limiting what he could do with his Fortresses and Liberators against Germany.

## Trucking: The Air Line of Communications

One thing even more likely to arouse the ire of strategic bombing purists than the use of heavies in close air support was their diversion to aerial logistics missions. Spaatz's USSTAF had long had the mission of providing long-range resupply to partisans in various parts of Europe and even had units especially organized for the purpose.[35] After the breakout, though, additional requirements were levied to use bombers in a logistical role to support the Poles in their uprising in Warsaw, Patton in his dash across France, and Montgomery in his attempt to breach the Rhine barrier at Arnhem. Spaatz expressed discontent with these missions, and some of the big bomber men in his command, like Fred Anderson and Jimmy Doolittle, were even more outspoken.

Eighth Air Force's 801st Bomb Group had been trained to drop supplies to resistance fighters and had been doing so for some time before the OVERLORD landings. After the invasion, the requirement surged from time to time beyond that group's capability. In July and August the planes of the 3d Bomb Division were drafted on two occasions to fly resupply missions to the "Maquis" in southern France. Another specialized unit of B-17s and B-24s under Spaatz, the 406th Bombardment Squadron, at Cheddington, was trained for night delivery of propaganda leaflets and warnings of impending bombing attacks to French civilians.[36] Spaatz's aircraft had longer range and a greater payload than any others in the American air forces. Moreover, they had a better defensive capability than any of the other larger airplanes and because of that were called upon for special missions much more frequently than the aircraft of other commands. It was a built-in conflict, for the airmen in USSTAF perceived these things as less important than striking at the heart of German industry, a target no other military arm could reach.

## Trucking for Warsaw

At Teheran in November 1943, before Spaatz arrived in England from the Mediterranean, Stalin had approved a plan to build shuttle bases in western Russia which would give USSTAF access to targets otherwise beyond its reach. In February 1944, after Spaatz was in England, he became involved in the creation of some of the bases. The first shuttle bombing flights were flown from Italy four days before the Normandy invasion. Eighth Air Force flew the second mission later in June, dispatching over a hundred bombers with seventy P-51 escorts. Although the mission was successful and the planes landed safely at Poltava, the

German air force raided the bases two days later, destroying forty-three Fortresses and fifteen Mustangs.

Attempts to win Russian agreement to stationing an American air defense unit at Poltava had not succeeded by the time the ANVIL forces were moving up the Rhone Valley and Patton's Third Army was sweeping across France. By August, Spaatz was beginning to doubt that the strategic results of these shuttle missions would be decisive and whether they were worth the cost.[37] In the spring, Spaatz had been optimistic about working with the Russians. They had cooperated at the time of the Normandy landings, but by July signs of hostility had arisen. One example was the harassment of Russian women who had fraternized with American airmen in Poltava. Another was the Soviet failure to approve the deployment of the air defense unit.[38]

By August Spaatz had become somewhat disillusioned while still entertaining hopes that he could use the bases there for reconnaissance missions and ground electronic bombing aids, if not as staging sites for bombers and fighters. He knew, too, that Roosevelt and other leaders in Washington were still optimistic about Russian cooperation against Japan, even if Spaatz himself did not hold much hope for mounting a massive strategic bomber attack from bases in the maritime provinces. Further, the Red Army was seizing some places where the Germans had been conducting advanced scientific research. There had already been some Russo-American cooperation in investigating these centers, and Spaatz hoped that it could be continued. As winter approached, Spaatz and his commander at Poltava, Brig. Gen. Robert L. Walsh, faced the choice of either preparing the base for the cold weather or withdrawing the units to more benign climes.

Just as the logistics problem in northern France was approaching its crisis, and as the troop carrier units of Ninth Air Force were being repeatedly withdrawn from the aerial resupply operation to prepare for airborne strikes, a crisis in Soviet-Polish-British relations threatened to involve Spaatz's strategic forces in yet another trucking operation. In the beginning of August, as the Russian armies approached Warsaw from the east, the Polish Home Army staged an uprising in the city. Though within sight of the capital, the Red Army halted on the east bank of the Vistula. The decision to stage the uprising had been made by the local commander in Warsaw without the authority of the Polish government in exile in London. The commander's forces were associated with that government, but the USSR had set up a rival one at Lublin and therefore was hostile to the Polish troops fighting the Germans in Warsaw. Thus, the Russians had political reasons for halting on the outskirts of the city and permitting their enemies to kill each other.[39] However convenient the decimation of the London Poles in Warsaw, it also was probable that the Red Army was not militarily capable of entering the city in early August.[40]

Notwithstanding the humanitarian aspects of the problem in Warsaw, it was clear to Spaatz and his staff that aerial delivery did not offer much promise of real relief to the Poles. They had assured Spaatz that the antiaircraft defenses the Germans had posted around the city were weak, but to make the deliveries accurate, the planes would have to come down very low where they were most vulnerable to ground fire. Moreover, the airmen most practiced in air drops were those of the troop carrier units, and their airplanes had neither the range nor the defensive capability for this task. The flyers of the Liberators and Fortresses had airplanes perhaps double the size of the C-47s, but they could not deliver larger loads because of the space limitations of their bomb bays where the parachute loads had to be slung. Further, their crews had been trained for bombing from very high altitudes, not the low altitude work required of the Warsaw resupply missions. Finally, such shuttle missions would tie up the bombers for as long as five days— days in which they would not be pounding the German railroads and refineries. In the end, Spaatz was sufficiently aware of the political imperatives of the situation to consent to do the job, but certainly he was not enthusiastic, for he did not want to get involved in it for any lengthy period.[41] He was quite sure that the drops could never be massive nor accurate enough to save the Poles.[42]

Once Spaatz had passed on information about the operational feasibility of the Warsaw airlift missions and his political superiors had ordered them to be carried out, the problem remained of getting Russian permission to use the shuttle bases. The heavy bombers had the range for a round trip from England to Warsaw, but the escort fighters did not. Consequently, without the USSR's permission to stage through Poltava, a dangerous mission would become all the more perilous for the want of fighter escort. Spaatz's people in Russia, and those at the U.S. Embassy in Moscow, sought permission, but Soviet foot-dragging prevented them from getting it until the middle of September,[43] when the Warsaw uprising had already been on its own for six weeks.

The Warsaw resupply mission was flown on 18 September. The

losses were low, but the battle damage considerable. By then, the Poles were too far gone to be saved, even had the drops been perfect. They were far from perfect, and only a tiny fraction of the total bundles dropped wound up in the hands of the insurgents. Ambassador Harriman sent overly optimistic mission reports back to the United States, and for a time there was a prospect of launching further resupply missions. For Spaatz that development was undesirable in two ways. First, it tied down some of his bomber forces in anticipation of such a mission. Second, the uncertainty prevented him from shutting down his ground operations in Russia before the cold weather set in. The second mission was ordered despite the poor results of the first, and permission was obtained from the Russians. The weather prevented an immediate launch, however, and by the time it cleared, the Soviets had rescinded permission. Soon after, the Warsaw insurgents gave up, and for USSTAF it became a dead issue. A caretaker unit was kept at Poltava through the winter, but neither major bombing raids nor resupply missions requiring the use of that base were ever again sent there.

Three hundred thousand Poles died in the uprising, and when the Red Army finally marched into Warsaw in the beginning of January, more than 90 percent of it lay in ruins.[44] It had been a major worry for Spaatz, but only a small fraction of the combat power available to him had been expended on the effort. The Warsaw mission was only one of many trucking missions that diminished the weight of his assault on the German homeland.

## Trucking for Patton

The air logistical doctrine that governs today's Air Force was born of the practical necessities of the battlefield, and nowhere did it get greater impetus than in the battles of northern France in the summer and fall of 1944. Spaatz, as the administrative commander of the Ninth Air Force airlifters and the operational commander of the strategic bombers in Europe, had a significant role in this development. Once Hodges' and Patton's armies were free of the beachhead area, they charged southwards in the hope of liberating the Brittany ports before turning eastward across the German rear. While they were still driving to the south, the German army, at Hitler's insistence, mounted an offensive toward the coast through Mortain in the hope of cutting the Allied communications. The offensive failed, and Bradley, armed with good ULTRA intelligence on Hitler's intentions, had resisted the temptation to bring all his forces to bear at the main point of danger. Rather, he had directed some of them eastward on the southern flank of the attacking Germans. Aided by Hitler's no-retreat order, the Allies were able to face their enemy on three sides by Americans, Englishmen, and Canadians. Montgomery mounted an offensive southward from Caen, and Patton turned northwards to Argentan. The Germans were faced with complete envelopment. Though the Falaise Pocket, as it came to be called, was not completely closed in time to gather up all of the Germans, the enemy was routed, a substantial part of his force captured, and a greater part of his equipment left behind. The German situation was so bad and their crossing of the Seine so difficult that they could not set up a defense along the far bank of the river. Rather, they continued to retreat helter-skelter for the border of the Reich.

All this happened at the time of both the Warsaw uprising and the ANVIL landings.[45] Gasoline consumption by the Allied armies on the move had soared, and ammunition requirements were still substantial. Meanwhile, the Allies liberated Paris in late August, but in so doing, transferred the logistical burden of feeding its millions from the German to the Allied accounts. As the Germans retreated to their Siegfried Line, they provided a classical demonstration of the way in which the side falling back on its lines of communication tends to redress the balance of power with its enemies by the simplification of its logistical problems and the complication of those of its foes. Thus, when Spaatz lamented to Arnold that it had been the logistical tail of the Allied armies that had dragged them to a stop, and not the tactical power of the Germans, he was quite correct.[46]

The battle had moved too fast for several reasons. First, it was clear that the combination of the speed of the movement and the slowness of opening up new ports made it impossible for the surface supply system to sustain the pursuit aimed at denying the Germans the time they needed to reconstitute their defenses along the Siegfried Line or the Rhine River. Second, the line and the river constituted such formidable obstacles to the ground commanders, and they had so much invested in the First Airborne Army, that they were continually seeking ways to use that Army to get behind the German offenses and disorganize enemy attempts to build a new defense line. The trouble was that by the time the airlifters and the airborne troops got a mission planned and organized, the ground battle had moved so fast that it was beyond the objectives that were to have been seized from the air. Thus, planned operations were repeatedly cancelled, and preparations were renewed for assaults that themselves would be overtaken by events.

For Spaatz, this meant that the Ninth Air Force transports were too often called away to support the advancing ground units for no profit. Rather, the overall impact was negative, for he had to substitute heavy bombers for the cargo planes. They were thus taken from their bombing role for a logistical one that they could not perform as well as the airlifters. Bombers could not carry any more than the C-47s, and their configuration was such that loading and unloading was much more cumbersome and lengthy than it would have been for the cargo planes. Therefore, what was gained by their speed advantage over the airlifters was lost by the long turnaround times on the ground. Moreover, the Liberators and the Fortresses were much heavier, and yet their tires were not proportionally larger, than the C-47. That meant they damaged the temporary fields on which they had to land. Lastly, their weight and wing configuration made their takeoff runs, loaded and unloaded, much longer than those of the airlifters, which imposed greater burdens on the engineers in airfield construction and prevented them from delivering their cargoes as close to the front as was possible for the C-47s. In September, Spaatz's heavy bombers flew 2,488 supply missions for the thrusting armies. Spaatz heard the loudest complaints from his bomber commanders, who were unhappy about being taken away from the mission of striking German industry, but the airlifters, the ground commanders, and the logistics managers also had grounds for complaint.[47] Still, the work had to be done, for all concerned hoped that keeping up the pressure during the pursuit would end the war in 1944.

Most of Eisenhower's leading commanders, including Spaatz, thought they had the answer to ending the war. Each thought that if "the boss" would only supply him with the means, he could deliver the knock-out blow. Patton wanted the gasoline and ammunition that would permit him to charge through the German border on the south. Montgomery was sure that a "full-blooded thrust" in the north would do the trick. Either of these moves would cause distractions for the big bombers. If they were not used in carpet bombing or other tactical support, then they would be drafted into logistics work. Spaatz still hoped that the USSTAF would be left alone to bomb the Germans into submission.[48] But he was too much of a realist to suppose that Eisenhower would ever choose such an option to the exclusion of others.

## Arnhem: An Attempt at Aerial Envelopment

Finally, Eisenhower chose to make the thrust in the north, to provide Montgomery with the means he hoped would carry the Allies across the Rhine and turn the north end of the Siegfried Line. His principal force was to be the First Airborne Army consisting mainly of two U.S. parachute divisions, one English division of jumpers, and a Polish brigade also trained for parachute work. These troops were to be dropped at various places along a sixty-four-mile corridor that spanned several rivers and canals. The function of the parachutists was to seize the bridges and defend them until the ground element, the 30th Corps of Montgomery's 2d Army, had advanced the length of the corridor to set up the permanent defenses. Time was of the essence because the airborne divisions were only lightly armed and had neither tanks nor heavy vehicles. They could not be expected to hold off the Germans once the latter had recovered from their surprise. Therefore, according to the plan, the 30th Corps had to reach the farthest bridge, the one at Arnhem, on the third day of the operation.[49]

The aerial part of Montgomery's thrust was firmly in the tactical domain, so Carl Spaatz had little direct involvement in planning or executing it. The operation was code-named MARKET-GARDEN, the first part of which referred to the aerial delivery, and the latter part to the ground advance. General Brereton was the commander of the First Allied Airborne Army, and his subordinate for the air part of the planning and execution was Maj. Gen. Paul Williams of the U.S. IX Troop Carrier Command. Though Williams had fifteen hundred transport planes and nearly five hundred gliders at his disposal, the insertion could not be made in one wave. Since the troops had to be put in on several consecutive days, the whole plan was highly dependent upon the September weather in the vicinity of the English Channel. Eighth Air Force's role was to provide a large share of the fighters for flak suppression before the insertion and for escorting the troop carriers during the deployment. Spaatz's bombers were assigned to hit some of the Luftwaffe airfields within striking distance of the battle area. They also were committed to participate in aerial delivery of supplies in the days following the initial strikes.[50]

The whole plan was a daring one, especially for Montgomery who had a reputation among the Americans for excessive caution.[51] The aerial part of the operation came off fairly well. Though there has been a good deal of recrimination about the execution, little of it has had to do with the role of the air forces, and still less with the role of those under the control of Spaatz. Montgomery put the main blame on the deterioration of the weather, and the degree to which that interfered with the air support by the fighter-bombers and the aerial resupply that was supposed to have come from the troop carriers and bombers. It did come, though sometimes the weather had caused it to be late. Montgomery's detractors have complained that the GARDEN part of the operation was not pressed with sufficient vigor—that the ground forces under Gen. F.A.M. Browning simply did not move fast enough to relieve the British 1st Airborne Division at the Arnhem bridge before the Germans had overwhelmed it. Still others complained that Montgomery's fixed ideas prevented him from utilizing the good ULTRA intelligence he had on the presence of the Panzers around Arnhem. In any event, the main object—to breach the Rhine barrier and turn the Siegfried Line—was not accomplished; it therefore should have come as no surprise when General Doolittle bemoaned losing the potential for four major and two minor bombing attacks on the heart of Germany for no purpose.[52] Nor was it surprising that Spaatz privately laid the blame for the great disappointment at Montgomery's door.[53]

## Flying Bombs: Round II

After the collapse of the Warsaw uprising, and after the halt of the Allied armies at the German border because of their logistical chains, and after the failure at Arnhem, it is understandable that the so-called "bomber barons" like Doolittle, Spaatz, and the others should weary of their "trucking" operations and long to apply their full force to the vital centers of the German industrial system.

But trucking was not the only distraction they had to contend with that summer. The launching areas of the new German missiles V-1 and V-2 also absorbed a large effort that Spaatz would rather have applied to targets in Germany for Operation CROSSBOW. The V-1 program, to some extent, was aimed at becoming a decoy for the more vital targets back in Germany, and it had achieved that purpose sufficiently to evoke the protests of Spaatz's deputy commander for operations, Fred Anderson, long before the first missile was launched. As the summer wore on, though the Germans never reached their production goals, the V-1 attacks on England increased in tempo. It became an increasing irritant for Spaatz. He could understand the psychological impact on the English people, who had come to believe the worst was in the past just at the time the Nazis renewed their attack on the British Isles. He knew also that the political imperatives made countermeasures inevitable. Yet, his concern was that the heavy bombers were the wrong instruments, for they could have but little effect on the launching sites, and their power would be much more effective were it applied to the interior of Germany. Late in June he wrote to Eisenhower:[54]

> I do not consider that operations against pilotless aircraft firing sites can be sufficiently decisive on any one day to justify the diversion of the Strategic Air Forces from their primary tasks on the few days which are favorable over Germany. In the absence of a major ground force emergency, I do not believe that the results obtained from the tactical use of heavy bombers will constitute as much support to OVERLORD as the use of the same force against critical German targets . . .

The very next day Eisenhower directed Tedder to inform Spaatz that the priority for attacks on the launching sites would have to stand no matter what the weather over Germany. He did direct, though, that when the entire force of USSTAF could not be used against the V-1 targets, then it would be permissible to use the remainder against aircraft, oil, ball bearing, and motor manufacturing targets in Germany. He included also the qualifier that land battle emergencies would take priority over all other conceivable targets.[55]

Though Spaatz had been denied, he did not give up trying to reduce the impact of CROSSBOW on the weight of his attack on Germany. On 10 July he wrote again to Eisenhower. This time he was critical of the actions of Leigh-Mallory. The latter had published a CROSSBOW target list that assigned thirty sites to the RAF Bomber Command, six to his own tactical air forces, and sixty-eight to Spaatz's USSTAF. Not only was this unfair, in Spaatz's opinion, but it also was inefficient. Almost all of the targets on the list were within range of both Bomber Command and AEAF, whereas USSTAF was the only one among the three that could operate freely over the German homeland. A better policy, he argued, would be to publish the CROSSBOW target list without assigning any particular objective to any particular air force. He maintained that Harris' and Leigh-Mallory's forces, because neither could operate against Germany in daylight, should be assigned a mandatory proportion of their daily effort to be applied against the V-1 targets.

For its part, USSTAF would attack with whatever forces were left over from the strikes on Germany.[56]

For the time being, however, Spaatz was butting his head against a stone wall. Britons were dying in London, and there was serious talk about increasing, not decreasing, the strategic bomber attacks on the V-weapon sites. Inside the British government, some suggested retaliatory attacks against German towns—that a series of specified and announced cities be exterminated until the Germans discontinued their V-bomb attacks. Others proposed that the Allies retaliate with gas attacks against the launching sites! Neither of those options was chosen, the first because it would be another major diversion away from German targets and there was little assurance that it would work, and the latter because it would open a Pandora's box. Spaatz did have one ally within British circles. Harris was arguing that the heavy bombers could not hit the launching sites accurately enough to be decisive and, worse, that the work accomplished in all the previous campaigns against the German homeland was being rapidly undone. The distractions of OVERLORD and CROSSBOW, he argued, were giving the Germans inside the Reich the respite they desperately needed to build their defenses and restore their faltering air force and industry.[57] Neither Spaatz's nor Harris' arguments prevailed. The CROSSBOW priority was retained until it was overtaken by events.

The impact of the V-weapons on England was reduced somewhat during the middle of the summer by the air defenses. It is true that a lot of effort was put on the concrete emplacements, which the Germans continued to give the appearance of repairing, but it did not have much to do with the reduction of the attack. While they were trying to deceive the Allies into believing that the ski sites from which the V-1s were launched were indeed important, the Germans had been developing mobile launchers much less vulnerable to bombing, and it was from these that most of the V-1s were sent on their way.[58] Tedder thought that the attack on transportation had slowed deliveries to the point where it had a more important effect on the missile attack than did the bombing of the launching sites.[59] Finally, the original deployment of the antiaircraft artillery around London had been on the periphery of the city. By the summer of 1944, the weapons were good and the gun-laying systems were becoming quite sophisticated. The V-1 had a speed that was substantially less than that of the latest fighters, and it was guided on its track by gyroscopes that had to be set during the preflight procedure. Thus, the track was a straight line and could be predicted very quickly. The trouble at first was that when the AAA was able to damage one of the V-1s, it did so on the outskirts of London, and the weapon did just as much damage to the city as if it had come in unhindered. Consequently, the British moved the guns down to the Channel shore, with the result that the flying bombs when hit started falling into the open countryside to the south and east of the metropolis. Moreover, the air defense fighters learned to cope with the new missile. Their aircraft could overtake the German intruders, and they could count on the fact that the V-1s would neither fight back nor take evasive action. Thus, one tactic was to fly up next to the missile and use the fighter's wing to tip that of the missile, causing its gyros to tumble.[60] Tedder himself thought that the V-1s in their current state were not that much of a threat, though they had serious implications for the future of war. In the end, even though Eisenhower scoffed at the notion of diverting his ground forces against the V-weapon threats, it was the army that finally solved the problem by taking over the launching sites. But that happened in the summer—after the V-1 had already absorbed a good deal of USSTAF's effort and when the bad weather of the fall was in the offing. If the Germans had not actually killed a great number of civilians in London, at least their V-1s had postponed the application of some of the force of both Bomber Command and the USAAF to their homeland.

One hundred thousand tons of bombs were used against the launching sites between the summer of 1943 and that of 1944. According to the United States Strategic Bombing Survey, this may have delayed the beginning of the V-1 campaign by "three or four" months. That may have been valuable time, for it was during the period when the final preparations for OVERLORD and the landings themselves were carried out. The survey says that the attacks had no effect on the V-2 program, and that the bombing of the plants engaged in V-weapon work in Germany also had little effect.[61] The USSTAF attack on German oil began in May 1944, and it was not until November of that year that the total weight of bombs put on that industry exceeded the total that had been expended on the launching sites.[62]

## Manpower

Spaatz's charter was not only to visit as much destruction as possible on the sinews of German military power, but also to build up and conserve the sources of USSTAF and Ninth Air Force strength. During the spring of 1944 the B-29 program for the Pacific was getting into full gear, and the requirement for air crews there was immense. Eighth and Fifteenth Air Forces were still building up, while their attrition, though lower than it had been in 1943, remained substantial. The individual airman's chances of surviving a tour of twenty-five missions at the onset of 1944 remained less than even.[63] The average rate of attrition for the Eighth Air Force's heavy bombers between May and August 1944 was slightly over 1.5 percent of the sorties launched.[64] On the surface that appears quite low, but to the crew member at the outset of his flying tour, the view was different. There was necessarily a lag in learning of this decline in attrition rates, and those doing the flying based their perceptions on the losses during the spring months, which had been above 3 percent. To the ordinary crewman, it meant that he had less than an even chance to survive, and according to at least one official judgment, the most fundamental factor that affected USAAF morale was the threat to one's survival.[65] Even if the man in the cockpit understood that the attrition rate was falling to 1.5 percent, had he applied that discount to a thousand crews starting a tour that summer, he would discover that only 589 of them were likely to survive if the tour length were increased to thirty-five missions. It is clear now that the influx of replacements improved those odds, and once a crew was past the first few missions, it improved further. This information was hard to sell to the flyers, however, especially in an environment where horror tales of the Luftwaffe's massacre of certain units were rampant. The German air force was husbanding its resources, launching them only periodically and concentrating on one part of an attack, especially an unescorted bomber formation. When that happened, attrition was far, far in excess of the 1.5 figure. Notwithstanding that living conditions, food, and recreational facilities were better for USSTAF than they were in many other theaters,[66] this fundamental threat to survival lowered the crew members' morale appreciably. Yet, were the tour length left at twenty-five sorties, in a good-weather situation where many of the missions in support of OVERLORD and against the V-2 launching sites were but short hops across the Channel and back, Spaatz's force would melt away, and the air superiority so dearly bought would melt away with it. The best compromise solution, then, and the one adopted by Spaatz, was to raise the tour length to thirty-five missions.

One thing gnawing at the USSTAF commanders was the number of crews that were landing their heavy bombers in Sweden or Switzerland because battle damage or mechanical difficulties made it impossible for them to make it back to their bases in England. By mid-summer 1944, there were 94 such crews interned in Sweden alone, and Arnold wrote to Spaatz on the subject. Spaatz thought he saw in the letter an implication of cowardice on the part of the crews, for rumors had it that life for the internees in both Switzerland and Sweden was idyllic.[67] Spaatz was aroused and replied to his boss, labelling it as "slander"; he demanded that military representatives go to Sweden to check the hearsay evidence that was being passed largely through diplomatic channels.[68]

Arnold was not to be dissuaded from his effort to investigate the morale aspects of the difficulty, and his response, though he did phrase it to mollify Spaatz's anger, still proposed sending a field grade officer, Lt. Col. James Wilson, to Spaatz's command. Wilson ostensibly would have some other purpose, but he was to mingle with crews at the bases in England to get some insights through informal contacts in social and operational settings. Arnold insisted that this officer would not be a "spy" and would report his findings to Spaatz before he returned to the U.S. Whatever the definition of "spy" might have been, the officer did go to England and made his reports to Spaatz and to Arnold without any remarkable results. As Eaker reported, there could be no doubt that the crew members of USSTAF had a fear for life and limb, and that this was a healthy and normal response, which did not indicate that the whole command was on the verge of collapse.[69] A military investigation concluded that cowardice was not involved, and that the airplanes in Sweden were indeed incapable of flying on to England.

An official U.S. Air Force historical study in the years right after World War II suggests that one positive morale factor generally operative in all parts of the U.S. Army Air Forces was that no matter how bad things got, at least the airmen could console themselves with the thought that they "were not in the infantry."[70] But the experiences of Carl Spaatz's USSTAF suggest that this smugness was not as secure for the airmen as it was for their brothers in the Navy. The original estimates for attrition among the airmen turned out to be higher than that which actually occurred; for the infantry, the estimates turned out to be too low. As the infantry did not get into combat on the soil of France until only eleven months before the end of the war, America was already near the end of her manpower resources (given the decision to maintain the U.S. economy and to serve as the arsenal of the democracies) when a crisis in infantry manning developed. It was too late then to adjust manpower policies at the source, and efforts were made to find additional potential soldiers within the combat theaters—which was bad news for some of Spaatz's airmen.[71] The overall manpower standing in the theater was good; many of the occupational specialties in the armies were actually overmanned, including some in the USSTAF. The great shortage was within the infantry and especially among the riflemen.[72]

The shortage grew through the summer of 1944 as casualties mounted among the advancing divisions. Most of the shipping space was occupied by new divisions and could not have transported replacements even if they had been available in the right specialties. Beginning in the summer, efforts were made to transfer excess Army ground personnel within the theater for retraining as infantrymen. After the disappointments of MAR-KET-GARDEN and the great casualties of the Battle of the Bulge in December,[73] even the most optimistic came to realize that the end of the war was not in the offing and that more serious measures were needed to provide infantrymen.

Even before the Germans aggravated the infantry crisis with their Ardennes Offensive, the problem had begun to touch USSTAF. The transition of the Ninth Air Force from fixed-base operations in England to mobile work on the continent, for example, created additional personnel problems for Spaatz and his administrative deputy, General Knerr. Some of these had not been fully anticipated, and the rapid rate of airdrome construction and the basing of some of the Eighth Air Force fighters on French bases increased the need for airport security troops. The Army ground forces could not provide these, and if the operational group commanders took them from among their own maintenance and service troops, then the efficiency and rate of their air operations would suffer.[74]

In mid-December, Barney Giles, Arnold's chief of the Air Staff, wrote to Spaatz explaining that the total personnel authorized the USAAF had been drastically reduced during the past year and that was one of the main reasons why some of the worthy projects of Spaatz and other theater air commanders had to be disapproved. Giles warned that things would get worse:[75]

The overall manpower situation is made considerably tighter by the fact that the Army ground forces have a pressing need for infantry replacements. The Army Air Forces is at present transferring to the infantry 55,000 men physically qualified for infantry combat duty. This week the Deputy Chief of Staff (War Department) sent us a memorandum proposing to cut our troop basis by an additional 100,000 by taking from us 20,000 troops a month and transferring them directly into the infantry as combat replacements. The final decision on this is not yet at hand.

Spaatz replied after the Ardennes crisis had passed, assuring Giles that he understood the problem and would economize wherever the military situation permitted.[76]

By January 1945, the effort to comb out all noninfantry units in Europe for potential riflemen had reached USSTAF. Spaatz set his West Point classmate, Col. Benjamin Weir, to doing a survey of the command to discover manpower spaces that could be eliminated, and ways in which people could be transferred to reduce overall requirements.[77] The following excerpt is from notes taken during his staff meeting on 7 January:[78]

General Spaatz requested that a figure of 3,000 to be used as a goal for the number of bodies that we can turn over to the Army as replacements. In effecting these transfers, only the bodies are lost—not the grades and ratings. This program should be drawn up very carefully for presentation to the organization commanders. The personnel to be considered should be: first, volunteers—particularly from the Aviation Engineers, where many of the men are itching to get into combat; secondly, personnel that the organization commanders would like to have transferred. . . .

It did not seem to Spaatz that the problem was likely to go away by itself. On the same day, the 7th, he wrote to Arnold that he did not think the Germans would crack any time soon. "Even though the hope of victory may be remote, the Germans will resist to the bitter end."[79]

Nor was help likely to come from the United States. George Marshall had been fighting the attitude of Congress, the bureaucracy, and industry to assume that the war was won and to start thinking about the postwar readjustment.[80] This was reflected in Robert Lovett's remark to Spaatz:[81]

The battle for manpower is still continuing and the Air Forces over here (in the U.S.) have so far given up 101,000 men to the ground troops. I think we have made our last contribution but I cannot be certain of it. The way the new draft call has gone out will affect us adversely. . . .

The adverse effect that Lovett feared was that some of the engineers working on America's first jet plane, the P-80, were about to be drafted.

American and British jet developments were still many months behind the Germans, and Spaatz and the rest of the high command in Washington and Europe feared that the German jet program might yet wipe out the Allied air superiority. Likewise, there was a growing shortage of bombs in the European theater that could hardly help but be aggravated by changing the criteria for exemption from the draft for farm and industrial work.[82]

The shuffling of people went on in USSTAF through the early months of 1945. Those not physically qualified for infantry combat were retrained where possible for ground support jobs being held by fit people. Some technical specialists simply could not be replaced in the time available. Still, by the middle of February, several thousand of the USSTAF ground personnel were finding that they did indeed have to "march like the infantry," and the flow of men from Spaatz's command to the ground units was scheduled to continue until the middle of March.[83] Spaatz replied to Lovett with a report on the manpower crisis on his side of the Atlantic:[84]

> Currently we are contributing to the reinforcement program for furnishing personnel to the ground forces. Four thousand men have already been assigned to infantry training during January. Fifteen thousand more will be committed to infantry training by 20 March in order to fulfill the ground forces requirements. You are undoubtedly well aware that this contribution cuts our manpower resources to the bone.

One would naturally wonder about the effect of General Spaatz's encouragement to his organization commanders to ship out their problems (not that the typical commander needed any encouragement on that score),[85] but Eisenhower at least thought the USSTAF contribution substantial enough to remark on it in *Crusade in Europe*.[86]

These tour-length and infantry manpower developments were major concerns and consumed a good bit of Spaatz's attention. There were also many smaller problems having to do with individuals. One of these concerned Fred Castle, one of the USAAF's rising stars and descendant of an old army family. Just at the time he was being sought out by USAAF headquarters for an assignment back in the U.S., Spaatz had to report that he had been killed on a mission over Europe.[87] Another had to do with the president's family. Col. Elliott Roosevelt had been under the direct command of Spaatz since the beginning of the African campaign. For all the competence with which he performed his functions as commander of the photoreconnaissance wing, the fact that he was the president's son caused complications. Spaatz had recommended the promotion of Roosevelt to the rank of brigadier general the previous summer, but George Marshall vetoed it in view of the pending election campaign. Soon after the first of the year, word got back to Washington that the younger Roosevelt was discontented and had requested a transfer back to the United States to other work. The president took the initiative and ordered the promotion of his son. Another source of discontent on the part of Elliott Roosevelt was that he did not have pilot wings, and Spaatz was ordered to award him that rating. Meanwhile, Spaatz had reported his reconnaissance wing commander's desire for transfer and that proved so exasperating to Arnold that the salutation on his next letter was "My Dear Spaatz" instead of the normal "Dear Tooey." He asked his old friend for the "lowdown" on the motivations of the president's son so that he could decide on the next step. Spaatz replied on the 29th that he thought the younger Roosevelt had been disturbed more by the absence of wings than of the star, and now that both had been awarded the tempest was subsiding.[88]

## Materiel

Though the United Kingdom had reached the limits of her personnel capacity, and the United States was approaching hers, the western Allies still had an overwhelming materiel advantage over the Germans in both numbers and quality. The industrial plant of the United States by mid-1944 was in full stride, and whatever equipment and supply shortages existed were only spot problems arising from unforeseen requirements. Most often they were overcome without too much delay. There was not much chance that the Reich could reverse the quantitative edge, but the durability of the Allies' qualitative advantage was not quite as secure. By the fall, Spaatz and the other American commanders were convinced that Hitler's V-1 and V-2 missiles would not be the war-winning secret weapons that the Fuehrer desired. But the performance of these missiles was enough to cause some uneasiness that the Reich might indeed come up with an innovation that could have decisive effects. For a time, Spaatz gave serious consideration to talk that the Germans were working on some kind of "death ray" that would halt the ignition of the reciprocating engines powering his airplanes.[89] Although this never materialized, a new generation of German submarines did pose a real threat. The earlier ones had been defeated largely by radar. New snorkel devices, however, promised to decrease the effectiveness of electronic detection by allowing the U-boats to stay underwater almost indefinitely, using their diesel engines while submerged and exposing only a small breathing apparatus to the Allies' prying radar antennae. While this was a concern to Spaatz, it was overshadowed by the rising threat of the new German jets. They were a potential threat to command of the air upon which attacks on all other targets relied.

The ME 262 jet had first flown in 1942 after it had finished a long wait for the development of the engines. The earliest versions had conventional landing gear, and suggestions for equipping the plane with tricycle gear were rejected partly because that was an "American" innovation. The trouble with the conventional configuration was that the rudder and elevator surfaces were masked by the wing on the takeoff roll and did not get enough airflow to give the pilot good control. The first takeoffs were made by tapping the brake pedals with the toes just as the airplane was reaching flying speed, thereby forcing the tail up into the slipstream where it could take hold. But that procedure required a lot of finesse and added to the length and the danger of the takeoff roll, which was already long enough for the fields in use in those days.[90] The Germans had not yet been seriously threatened by Allied airpower, and there was little urgency about increasing their fighter defenses. Adolf Galland, the Luftwaffe's premier fighter commander, first flew the jet the following spring (on 22 May 1943) and came away so enthusiastic that he strongly recommended to the Air Ministry that the 262 be pushed for mass production.

Soon after Galland's flight, however, Hitler directed that the airplane not go into mass production but be continued in a test status. After a flight demonstration in November 1943, the Fuehrer reversed that decision, but ordered that it be developed as a bomber to be used against the Allies during the expected invasion. Professor Messerschmitt too facilely assured the dictator that this could be done, and thus the jet fighter program suffered a setback. This decision was not fully implemented for a time. When the Fuehrer discovered several weeks before OVERLORD that none of his jets could carry bombs, he went into a fury. The result was that the whole 262 program was transferred to the supervision of the bomber leaders—who had not even asked for it. That led to a host of technical and training delays through the summer of 1944.[91]

One of the first considerations was the landing gear, by then a tricycle arrangement. Would it support the weight of the bombs? The answer turned out to be negative, and the undercarriage had to be redesigned, which also caused delay. Next came the requirement to add hard points from which to sling the bombs. Then the ability to hit a target had to be considered. The maximum speed limitation made it impossible to aim the bombs by diving the whole aircraft at the target, for the jet would soon have exceeded the permissible stresses. Level bombing was tried with poor results. Finally, the wing was redesigned to permit a shallow dive for a bomb run, and the accuracy improved.[92] Once Hitler had decided that the 262 would be a bomber, no more was heard from Goering about its potential for the defense of the fatherland. Rather he forbade his generals from referring to the plane, even in private, as a fighter or a fighter-bomber. All this was going on during the last half of 1943 and the first half of 1944.

Meanwhile, Spaatz was getting some excellent intelligence about the potential of the German jet, but not much about the political inhibitions against its deployment as an interceptor for his bombers. He was receiving plenty of news about the difficulties in the development of an American jet fighter. Before the summer of 1944 was over, the German jets, though not yet deployed in substantial numbers, were a serious concern for Spaatz. He knew that they had a large performance advantage over the American fighters and that their production was being done "from repaired and underground facilities."[93] Already the 262s had made the Allied air reconnaissance over the Reich a dangerous proposition. Though Spaatz thought that technical advances on the American side might help, only the deployment of a long-range jet fighter would be decisive. He urged nonetheless the development of higher-rate-of-fire bomber guns, improved sights for both bombers and fighters, stabilized and more effective gun turrets, larger-caliber guns, and more effective adverse-weather bombing equipment—but he emphasized to Arnold that the most important counter-measure would remain the development of a jet that could match the ME 262.[94] Arnold replied three weeks later saying that he had put many of the technical suggestions into practice and that the P-80 program was being pushed at a maximum rate. But he did not make any specific promises as to early delivery and remarked that the combat radius of that airplane would be 600 miles.[95]

German technological progress was only one of Spaatz's worries about the perishability of Allied air superiority. At the time of OVER-

LORD, there had been great satisfaction among both ground and air commanders about the completeness of the American and British command of the air. The Germans had hoarded some of their air strength to use against the invasion, but when they tried it, they threw it away on a fruitless quest. Through the summer of 1944 the Luftwaffe did not much interfere with either air or ground operations, and there was a concern that the Germans were conserving and rebuilding their strength for a new contest to try to reverse the air decision of the spring.

## The "Resurgence" of the Luftwaffe

Though it was hard to be sure, Spaatz's intelligence people had told him that the USSTAF had made inroads into German aircraft production during the winter and spring of 1944. Though the blows administered during Big Week were not as complete or as decisive as the media then imagined, they were nonetheless quite enough to shake the German leaders. Theretofore, all armaments production, except aircraft, had been under the direction of Albert Speer. The Luftwaffe, and specifically Ehrhard Milch, had been responsible for producing its own armaments. Immediately after the American air offensive of the last week of February, the Reich reorganized its aircraft production and put it in the charge of Speer's Armaments Ministry. By then, it was generally recognized that there was an air defense emergency, and Speer and his staff took drastic measures to make sure the Luftwaffe had all the defensive airplanes it needed. A special "Fighter Staff" was created to concentrate on this need, and the results were early and impressive. Bomber production was further curtailed in favor of fighters.

The manufacturers had already undertaken some dispersal on their own initiative, but now it was ordered by the government. The production units were scattered far and wide in small organizations all over Germany, and a significant part of the operations was put in underground shops. Meanwhile, Spaatz's forces were not doing much to interfere. When they were not fully committed in support of the land battle or hitting the V-weapon sites, they were being sent after the oil industry. Though some attacks continued, the aircraft industry received a respite compared to what it had suffered during the previous winter. The results were dramatic, and German fighter production reached its all-time peak in September 1944. Allied intelligence had been following all this and had a very good grasp of what was happening. Thus, through the summer, Arnold, Spaatz, Doolittle, and Eaker worried that the Luftwaffe might somehow be able to stage a comeback. Certainly, the German air force was not suffering from any shortage of new airplanes.[96]

ULTRA was giving Spaatz a fairly good picture of the resurgence of German aircraft production. But he also had good information on the decline of the petroleum industry, and especially on the declining production of aviation gasoline. Although he was somewhat uneasy about a possible revival of German airpower, he was not sufficiently worried to let go of the oil campaign in favor of a return to one against aircraft factories. He knew that the factories had been so dispersed and buried that he could not get at them as effectively as he had in earlier campaigns.[97]

There was more than just the technical advance of jets and the increase in numbers of conventional fighters that was strengthening a weak Luftwaffe. The Germans had at first attempted to aid their ground armies in opposing OVERLORD, but the reserves they had built up for the purpose were quickly decimated and had to be pulled back to Germany for refitting.[98] By the end of the summer, some of these units were increasing their combat capability, with new aircraft and with partially trained replacement pilots—partially trained primarily because of the gasoline shortage. But the Luftwaffe, too, benefited somewhat by the German retreat on their own line of communications. Since the beginning of the year, the area to be defended had contracted greatly, and the ground support and bomber missions had been virtually abandoned in favor of concentration on defense against USSTAF and Bomber Command.[99] This enabled the flak units to build up a greater density of guns around vital targets.

Besides the jets and rocket airplanes, the Germans also were casting about for other technical and tactical solutions to their mounting problems. Ramming was conceived and actually practiced against USSTAF, but it never went as far as it did with the Japanese, for it was always intended to give the pilot a chance to bail out and survive.[100] In September 1944, the Germans adopted a plan for the production of the HE 162 jet, not only because of the superior performance to be expected, but also because they thought it could be produced from materials not vital to other aircraft programs, it would consume factory capacity that would otherwise be idle, and it would be flown by youngsters who otherwise could not be used as air defense pilots because of their youth and the time available for training.[101] According to the commander of the fighter arm, Adolf Galland, the project never had much potential from the technical or tactical points of view and was to a large extent a morale booster. He has asserted, though, that it did divert resources that would have been useful for the more promising 262 program.[102]

Another thing aiding the defenders was a redirection of the defensive strategy. By the summer of 1944, Hitler's obsession with the offense and bombers had largely vanished, and the bomber units were being raided for their personnel to be trained for the defense organization. The bomber production program had come to a virtual halt. Further, the Luftwaffe went over to a strategy of conservation and concentration. The remaining strength would be massed in the homeland. It was not to be frittered away in piecemeal attacks to meet every incoming Allied raid, but rather conserved for concentrated attacks against selected formations on selected days when the conditions were particularly favorable to the defenders. Allied raids during bad weather, for example, were to be ignored. The limited experience of the defending pilots in instrument flying and the absence of gasoline for such training meant that the number of Allied air crewmen killed per German loss would be higher were operations confined to days when the weather over the Luftwaffe bases was good enough to permit the young pilots to return under visual flying conditions. In concentrating the available force against certain Allied air units, the idea was to cause periodic losses so serious that it would make the Allied commanders more cautious about exploitation of their air superiority over the Reich.[103] Most of the German decision makers were well enough agreed on this disposition of air defense resources; the question that remained was whether it should be concentrated against the incoming American and British bombers, or against the Allied armies in cooperation with the German ground forces in one last, great shot for a decisive blow against them.[104] During the early fall of 1944, it seemed that the decision was in favor of operating against the bombers, sporadically, but in force.

Some other variables had changed in favor of Allied air superiority. If the Germans benefited from having a smaller area to defend and shorter communications lines to service, they also lost ground as the Allies captured the sites for the antennae of their air defense radars. The Luftwaffe was partially blinded, for it could no longer spy on the assembly of the massing bomber formations as they were leaving their bases in England. Though the bombers had to fly as far as ever, since the conquest of France they did not have to run the gauntlet of the defenders for as long. Moreover, Spaatz was able to bring various ground-based electronic aids to sites in France, which increased the accuracy of

USSTAF bombing and gave better guidance to the escort fighters who were seeking their rendezvous or the German enemy. Damaged bombers no longer had to make it back across the Channel or go into internment. Rather, they could, and often did, land at bases in France or beyond the Russian lines.[105]

The numerical balance had continued to shift in the Allied direction. Frontline fighter strength of the Luftwaffe had been 1,604 on the 1st of January; six months later it was 1,523.[106] Before the end of the year, Eighth Air Force alone launched 2,074 heavy bombers and 923 fighters on a single raid.[107] Added to that were the bombers and fighters of Fifteenth Air Force, Ninth Air Force, 2d Tactical Air Force, and Twelfth Air Force, many of which had been moved to France, where their fields were much closer to the battle. Notwithstanding all these advantages and the good intelligence enjoyed by Spaatz and Arnold, there were still enough imponderables and grievous losses to make both uneasy. The memories of Poltava, not to mention their disappointment that the great surface victories of the summer had not resulted in Hitler's collapse, were too fresh in their minds to permit complacency. Arnold wrote to Spaatz in a concerned tone near the end of September:[108]

> I am disappointed, to say the least, that the ground campaign has not moved along much more rapidly than it has. . . . Within the last few days, the German air has made a strong comeback. I have not as yet gotten your report as to what happened and there must be some explanation for it. . . . I am looking forward to a letter from you in this regard, for according to my recollection, losses for the last three days were all above forty and hit fifty as a high.

Forty or fifty out of thousands being launched is a far cry from the sixty lost out of the fewer than three hundred that had attacked Schweinfurt the previous October. Still, it hurt, and Spaatz too showed his concern in a letter written before he had received Arnold's:[109]

> You have, of course, noted the heavy increased losses we have suffered during the last week's operations into Germany, . . . but I am very much concerned over the possibilities involved. There is every chance, I think, that the Germans may be using proximity fuses or an improved type of radar control for their flak. We can't prove this yet and our increased flak losses may be due simply to the fact that they are concentrating all their available flak in a smaller area. We are watching this situation

closely as well as the possibility that the Germans may have adopted our armor piercing incendiary type of ammunition. We had reports on the raid of the 28th that 17 heavy bombers were seen on fire in the air in the Cologne area. We are also watching carefully the development of the jet-propelled boys which will be a constant potential threat, even though their numbers have been too small to be very effective so far. This all adds up to the fact that the Hun has still got a lot of fight left in him, even in the air, and we must concentrate to kill him off if possible before he can develop those new threats against us.

After a few more days, Spaatz had received Arnold's letter and accumulated more facts about the losses. By then he felt that the increases came from the greater concentration of German flak and a lucky break on the 27th that had enabled the Luftwaffe to stumble upon a bomber formation that had lost contact with its fighter escort. As for his earlier worries about possible technological surprises, he remarked: "I am reasonably sure that, at the present time, the Germans have no new weapons that are causing our losses, although I am not overlooking the possibility of proximity fuses, and better ammunition and sights for their fighters."[110]

These interchanges between Spaatz and Arnold took place in the aftermath of the disappointments at Arnhem. The mood was not much more optimistic a couple of weeks later when Spaatz went down to Bari, Italy, to hold a conference on the subject of the enemy air defense with his commanders of the Fifteenth Air Force.[111] He opened it by remarking that the threat of German antiaircraft artillery and air interceptors was increasing, and he asked what the commanders of the units in Italy were doing to overcome it. Most of the options open to them were tactical solutions. In the discussions that followed, Twining's wing commanders remarked that new formations were being tried, the bomb runs were being flown downwind to decrease the time of exposure to the flak, the escort fighters were being used to spread chaff to interfere with enemy gun-laying radar, and attacks were being made on gun concentrations.

Spaatz could not then offer any dramatic new ideas. He did warn them about the new tactics that the German air force had been using against the bomber attacks coming from England, and he spoke of experiments being run with rockets fired backwards from the tail positions of B-17s. He told the Fifteenth commanders that he did not think an attack on aircraft factories would do much good just then, but if they wanted to go after German airpower on its airfields for a couple of weeks, they would not be criticized for somewhat neglecting their primary target—still the oil industry. The Germans, he said, could put up 600 or 700 fighters when they had the fuel for it, but that jets were still feeling their way and had not yet had any impact. He expected that the opposition would get worse; therefore the air crews of the Fifteenth would have to maintain their vigilance and the pressure on the Germans. There would have to be as many coordinated missions as possible between Fifteenth and Eighth Air Forces in order to "split the German defense." In closing remarks, Eaker agreed that a temporary diversion from the oil targets would do some good in that it would draw off some of the flak batteries and make the initial resumption of the assault on the petroleum installations less costly.

After he came back to England, Spaatz summed up the air situation for Arnold. Though USSTAF had achieved a major tactical victory on the preceding Thursday, Spaatz was still not optimistic. He said, ". . . I still feel that the build-up of the GAF defensive strength is a growing threat. Presently the GAF is using every possible means to attain a strength extremely dangerous to our strategic forces."[112] He told Arnold that this was being achieved through the complete conversion of bomber crews to fighters, the forced-draft build-up of conventional fighter forces, the first-priority production of jet units, and the conservation of fuel and forces for dramatic and decisive strikes against selected deep-penetration raids. A part of the difficulty arose from the fact that his heavy bomber forces had been increased much more rapidly than had the number of escorts. Thus, the escort-bomber ratio was not nearly as favorable as when air superiority had been won the previous spring. He saw as one possible solution a reduction of the size of deep-penetration raids to improve the escort ratio, and an increase of the bomber formations going against peripheral targets without any escort at all. Spaatz did not want to do that because it would give some respite to the vital targets in Germany just as they might be approaching the point of collapse.

Another way in which the density of escort fighters could be increased was to move the bases of the Eighth Air Force P-51s to the continent. There were great obstacles to that. First, there were not enough bases available, and the supply lines were already choked with material for the armies and Ninth Air Force. The communications for the bases that potentially could be used were undeveloped. Here was one of the indirect costs of the failure of MARKET-GARDEN—or rather, a cost of undertaking it in the first place. The port of Antwerp was still not open because of the German occupation of Walcheren Island at the mouth of the estuary. Spaatz promised Arnold that once that terminal was available, communications could be improved and units could be supported on the continent. When the armies got moving again, the Ninth Air Force would move forward with them, vacating bases that could then be occupied by the fighters of the Eighth Air Force, which would greatly increase the time that the Mustangs would be able to stay with the bombers over the target areas in Germany.[113]

Notwithstanding ULTRA, the American air commanders did not seem to feel that the situation of the German air force was quite as desperate as it appeared to the leaders of the Luftwaffe.[114] Spaatz seemed to understand fully that the foe was amazingly resilient and much too clever to be left unwatched. He knew he could no longer get at German airpower in the factories and that it would have to be held down through indirect means by attacks on oil, and more directly through continuing the pressure in the aerial battles. The exception was the jet problem: they could not be handled in the air and could not be attacked in the factories. Countermeasures would have to include limiting the supply of trained pilots for the jets through attacks on the oil industry and training fields, bombing the airfields where the final assembly of the jets took place, and hoping that the war would end before the Luftwaffe could get truly significant numbers of jets into action.

At the onset of the fall of 1944, then, the Allies still enjoyed air superiority over France and Germany. But the German air force was showing enough signs of life to make the Allied commanders uneasy and all the more eager to end the war before the enemy could find a solution to the air problem. One of the means by which the end might be hurried was to bring the strategic exploitation of air superiority to its fruition by drying up the sources of strength not only of the Luftwaffe but of all the other German armed forces as well.

# Chapter IX
## THE STRATEGIC EXPLOITATION

The main preoccupation of Spaatz and USSTAF during the summer of 1944 had been tactical support of the battle on the ground. By the fall, however, the emphasis had shifted to attacks on the vital centers of the German industrial system. While Charles Portal believed in the primacy of the oil target, advocates of attacking the transportation system inside Germany continued to raise that issue. This time, however, no choice between the two was necessary. A torrent of bombs fell on Germany through the fall, and there was disappointment on the Allied side that the Reich did not collapse from the pressure. The disappointment was greater still when, just before Christmas, the fuel-starved Wehrmacht launched a massive offensive against the Western Allies which severely upset their timetable. Yearning for the end of the war, despite the astonishing resilience of the Reich, made many believe that the Germans were on the verge of collapse, and some dreamed of a knockout blow that would bring the peace. The single dramatic blow never occurred, and Hitler staggered on until May 1945 before the German state capitulated.

### Keeping the Pressure on Oil
Before the Normandy landings, Spaatz had threatened Eisenhower with resignation in order to win the latter's consent to some attacks on oil targets in the German homeland.[1] After the Allies were ashore, Eisenhower was so pleased with the air superiority his forces had achieved that he allowed the bombing of oil targets to continue, but only on the

condition that they not interfere with CROSSBOW and tactical emergencies.

Together, the Eighth and Fifteenth Air Forces had the power to maintain pressure on oil facilities despite the best efforts of the enemy. Moreover, ULTRA gave immediate confirmation of the effectiveness of the oil raids, and it provided Spaatz with data increasing his confidence that he was pursuing the right path.[2]

For the time being, at least, the transportation network was not consuming the bulk of the bombs. The main advocate of hitting transportation targets, Tedder, still had a powerful voice in affairs, but as the Allied armies swept across France, they captured most of the rail yards that had been the targets before OVERLORD. Although CROSSBOW, carpet bombing, and trucking used more bombers than Anderson and Doolittle would have liked, there were enough left for effective work against the German oil system. By July, Harris was sending part of the Bomber Command against it, bringing the total USAAF and RAF force to some 4,400 heavy bombers.[3] On those occasions when the Eighth and the Fifteenth mounted coordinated raids, the Luftwaffe found about two thousand bombers and one thousand escorts coming from different directions. In addition, Ninth Air Force in France outnumbered the entire Luftwaffe on all its fronts and was accompanied by the RAF 2 ATAF, while to the east was the Soviet air force.

One of the original reasons for creating Fifteenth Air Force had been to make raids on the Ploesti oil refineries easier than they had been from African bases. Spaatz had been one of the chief proponents of that plan. In April 1944, even before he won Eisenhower's consent for the pre-OVERLORD Eighth Air Force raids on oil, the Fifteenth Air Force had returned to the offensive against Ploesti. By August, the Romanian field's output was all but eliminated, and the Russians marched in to terminate what little production still existed. Meanwhile, there was so little opposition to the ANVIL landings that the Fifteenth could concentrate on oil targets in Austria and Czechoslovakia. Thus, while Eighth Air Force was supporting the landings, its partner kept enough pressure on oil to prevent the German recovery. Once Ploesti fell, the potential for attacks on the Reich's synthetic oil industry was greatly enhanced.[4] On top of that, the Wehrmacht was fully engaged on three fronts, and Spaatz learned from ULTRA that its petroleum demands were higher than ever.

Through the summer, Spaatz was concerned with maintaining

USSTAF's independence, not so much from the ground commanders as from the RAF. He wanted to run an American strategic bombing campaign undiluted by RAF or Bomber Command values. As he wrote to Arnold in August:[5]

> We [USSTAF] feel very strongly that under no conditions should RAF Bomber Command be consolidated with the U.S. Strategic Air Forces. We feel that British night bombers will find it extremely difficult to operate during daylight and that their use in daylight operations will jeopardize fighter cover for our own bombers. If the consolidation of strategic air forces is effected with either an American or a RAF officer in command, the consequences are easily foreseen . . . It may not be fully appreciated by you how strongly our American Air Force personnel feel about serving under British command.

Part of his concern arose from the fear that even then, a year and a half after the Casablanca Conference, the British would yet succeed in deflecting the Americans away from their precision bombing doctrine. He further added:[6]

> I have been subjected to some pressure on the part of the Air Ministry to join hands with them in morale bombing. I . . . have maintained a firm position that our bombing will continue to be precision bombing against military objective (sic). So far my stand has been supported by Eisenhower. I feel that a case may be made on the highest levels for bombing the city of Berlin. I personally believe that any deviation from our present policy, even for an exceptional case, will be unfortunate. There is no doubt in my mind that the RAF wants very much to have the U.S. Air Forces tarred with the morale bombing aftermath which we feel will be terrific . . .

Spaatz was anticipating increased pressure for some sort of knockout blow that would deflect him from his course. The Air Ministry continued a campaign to persuade Arthur Harris to concentrate a greater portion of Bomber Command's power on oil targets. The Ministry's insistence on removing the American strategic air forces from Eisenhower's control was designed principally to strengthen its hand against Harris in order to increase Bomber Command's concentration on the oil complex in the Reich. At the same time, there were currents in American political and military circles tending to erode Spaatz's commitment to the precision bombing of military targets. When the exhilaration of the summer offensives resulted not in victory, but rather in an apparent stalemate along the western borders of Germany, it stimulated the longing for a knockout blow of some kind that would finish Hitler before the grind of another wartime winter became necessary.[7]

Late in September, after Harris had been placed under the Combined Chiefs of Staff, Spaatz and the deputy chief of staff of the RAF, Air Marshal Sir Norman Bottomley, coordinated a policy on bombing that gave oil the top priority and singled out gasoline production within that industry for special attention.[8] But by then the bombing had greatly reduced production, and the new front in the west increased the consumption so that the reserve stocks that the Germans held early in the summer were gone by the end of the month. The Luftwaffe's use of aviation gasoline had declined to less than a third of what it had been three months earlier during OVERLORD, and the decrease in both production and reserve stocks had been equally dramatic.[9] What is more, Spaatz knew well that the weakened condition of Germany's air defense arose from the shortage of gasoline and lack of trained pilots. Spaatz instructed his commanders on these points: "The German Air Force, ground forces, and economy are all imminently faced with collapse for the lack of fuel. . . . Pilot and gasoline shortages have become the limiting factors in G.A.F. operations, *not* aircraft. . . . the attack on oil [should] be further intensified."[10] In short, Spaatz thought peace might be at hand if only he were permitted to freely swing the instrument that would give Hitler a USSTAF knockout blow.

## The End of SHAEF Control

Since April, when USSTAF was first put under Eisenhower's control, Spaatz was never far from his side, and there were no great conflicts between them. The heavy bombers were used from time to time in roles at odds with USSTAF air theory, but never to the extent that it caused an open break between the airmen and the soldiers. There was the fear among some of the air leaders that the soldiers might become "drugged" on the use of heavy bombers to penetrate the enemy's lines, and the soldiers were rather extravagant in crediting the carpet bombing at St. Lo for the success of their breakthrough. Further, Doolittle and Anderson were impatient with the bombing constraints. It fell to Spaatz to soften the impact of that impatience on those outside the command and to limit the demands of outsiders on the resources of the Fifteenth and Eighth Air Forces.[11]

Late in the summer of 1944, Spaatz and Eisenhower became aware of a movement to return the strategic air forces to the control of the Combined Chiefs of Staff and, in practice, to the control of Portal. Neither liked the idea. The initiative arose in the RAF as a part of an effort to improve control over Harris.[12] But Spaatz was reluctant to leave Eisenhower because things were going well and he feared RAF interference with his strategic campaign more than that of Eisenhower, to whom he was subordinate.[13] Eisenhower for his part still preferred what he deemed to be unified control and the responsiveness to the requirements of the ground battle that he had as supreme commander.[14]

At first, Arnold seemed to agree with the positions of Spaatz and Eisenhower. At a conference of the political leaders and the Combined Chiefs of Staff held at Quebec in September,[15] he reversed himself, however, under the weight of the British arguments and agreed to yet another revision of command arrangements. He did impose one provision that protected the interests of USSTAF (as perceived by Spaatz) in that he, not Portal, would now be the agent for the Combined Chiefs with respect to USSTAF.[16] Thus, Harris would be reporting to Portal and, theoretically, Spaatz would be directly subordinate to Arnold. In practice, Arnold delegated his authority to Spaatz and permitted him more or less to run his own war against the German homeland.

It was still necessary to give Eisenhower authority to call upon both Bomber Command and USSTAF when he needed their assistance for ground emergencies, and indeed he did so in later crises.[17] In the end, it did not seem to matter. There was so much airpower available as 1944 waned that so-called diversions did not prevent striking those targets Spaatz and his staff thought most important. Moreover, Arnold was thinking of the legislative battles to come in the postwar world.[18] When that day arrived, it would be important to have allies among the soldiers in the debates over budgets and the creation of a separate Air Force. There was no doubt that the war would be won—only the victory date remained uncertain—and it was obvious that Marshall and Eisenhower would be heavyweights in the political bouts to follow.

## Return to the Rail Yards

There was substantial evidence early in the fall of 1944 that great physical damage was being done to Germany and the German army. Pressure on the Reich was immense, and it was hard to understand how the Germans continued to fight. In late October, the search intensified for means to make the tightly stretched country snap. George Marshall informed Eisenhower that a Combined Chiefs of Staff directive might be forthcoming to increase the pressure to cause the break before the end of the year. The directive, it was suggested, might include orders to the strategic bombers to give up their long-term objectives in favor of targets whose destruction would have more immediate effects on the ground battle.[19] This appeared to signal abandonment of the oil target in favor of carpet bombing in front of the troops.

Eisenhower replied to Marshall that maximum pressure was being kept on the Wehrmacht. He insisted that the campaign against oil was paying off handsomely, and that air assistance to the ground troops was readily forthcoming from the strategic bombers. He also pointed out that the Fortresses and Liberators could not be used in close support of the troops in overcast conditions. Radar aiming was not accurate enough for that—and there was an overcast in the region of the front almost constantly.[20]

Meanwhile, Portal had informed Tedder of the trend of thought among the Combined Chiefs. Tedder quickly prepared a new plan for greater coherence in the air effort and more effective support of the ground offensive.[21] Perhaps an additional unspoken purpose was to head off a directive from above that would undermine the oil campaign so favored by Spaatz and Portal, and now even Tedder.

As soon as the strategic forces were released from Eisenhower's command, Spaatz met with Bottomley to coordinate separate directives for their heavy bomber organizations. They established oil targets as a first priority. In the second category, they placed three target systems: "The German rail and waterborne transportation systems; tank production plants and depots, ordnance depots; and M. T. (motor transport) production plants and depots."[22] According to Tedder, Spaatz's forces directed more than half their bombs at transportation targets during the following weeks—a far greater tonnage, in fact, than they dropped on oil installations.[23]

Tedder quickly drew up for Portal a proposal which retained the oil system in first position, but more clearly placed Germany's rail system in second priority. According to the plan, commanders would concentrate on that part of the rail system that serviced the Ruhr, the objective of the ground forces. The Ruhr was so close to the front lines that the tactical air forces, subject directly to the orders of Tedder himself, could also be sent against targets in the same general area. Not only would the weight of the attack on German transportation be increased, but it also would be concentrated (according to Tedder) as never before, and would support the ground battle sufficiently to satisfy Marshall's desires.[24]

A meeting was held at Eisenhower's headquarters on 28 October to discuss Tedder's proposal. As Spaatz's oil targets remained the top priority in Tedder's plan, he had no objection to it. As he reported to Arnold, in the preceding months rail targets had been in the second category along with tank and truck factories. He told Arnold that the rail program tended to take a back seat, however, in favor of the armament factories and depots because that had been the way Eisenhower had wanted it. Spaatz agreed that Tedder's plan would elevate the priority of the transportation attack, concentrate the bombing in the vicinity of the Ruhr, tie the air strikes more closely to the land battle, and automatically provide greater coordination between the strategic and tactical air forces.[25]

Meanwhile, objections to Tedder's scheme were being raised in other quarters. Portal had sent a copy to Arthur Harris, who immediately responded that the force had been concentrating for some years against the Ruhr, which practically was reduced to impotency. He complained to Portal that there were too many cooks in the strategic act and that they were likely to spoil the broth—comments which did not endear him to Tedder. He added some remarks about the past and potential value of "city-busting," remarks that were no more likely to endear him to Tedder than to his superiors at the Air Ministry.[26] Additional worries surfaced at the Air Ministry, where it was feared that the new emphasis on rails might weaken the thrust against the oil industry[27] and among some American target planners who thought it would not work as quickly as its proponents anticipated.[28] However, with Tedder, Spaatz and Eisenhower behind the plan, and with the Combined Chiefs of Staff restless about strategic targeting policy, these objections were overruled. On 1 November, the Combined Strategic Targets Committee approved Tedder's proposal, and it went into effect, for the time being.

By November 1944, then, hopes were high among the Allied leaders that the war would be over by Christmas. Tedder hoped that the increased bombing of transportation targets in the same region as Allied ground attacks might constitute the blow that would precipitate the German crash. Spaatz still had full license to pursue his oil objectives, and if Tedder's ideas resulted in early victory, so much the better.

## Disillusionment: The Battle of the Bulge

Throughout the fall of 1944, while the Allied generals were hoping for an imminent German collapse, Hitler was planning an offensive to turn the tide. He envisioned another strike in the vicinity of his great victory of 1940, the Ardennes Forest. Though the Allies well remembered that experience, the Fuhrer thought they would not expect him to strike in the same place a second time—particularly in winter weather. His generals, especially Rundstedt, told him it would not work and the offensive should be scaled down, but Hitler persisted. He gathered twenty-four divisions, ten of armor and fourteen of infantry, into two Panzer armies and one infantry army at a point opposite the Ardennes, which was being held by four American divisions, some battle-weary and others lacking combat experience.[29] The Luftwaffe massed about a thousand airplanes for the offensive, most of them single-engine fighters manned by ill-trained pilots.[30] Hitler's scheme duly recognized Allied air superiority, for it was to be the weather—a forecast for a long spell of bad weather—that would determine the time for launching the counterattack.

Most of the Allies did not believe that the Germans could mount an offensive and felt that the remainder of the war would be characterized by Allied offensives and ever weaker German counterattacks. In September, for example, Air Marshal Coningham in command of 2d ATAF supporting Montgomery in the north, had directed that antiaircraft units no longer be deployed around the RAF airfields in the Low Countries and that camouflage netting was no longer required.[31] Eisenhower's armies were then preparing to mount two offensives, a major one in the north under Montgomery and another to be led by Patton farther south toward the Saar. One of the main reasons for the weakness in the Ardennes sector was that the Americans were concentrating their forces for the coming offensives and practicing economy of force elsewhere.

Though there was a striking similarity between Hitler's new plan and the original Ardennes Offensive, few Allied leaders gave thought to the possibility of a second strike through the Ardennes.[32] Plenty of German message traffic was being read by ULTRA, but security measures on the Nazi side had improved. So few people knew the purpose of Hitler's buildup and redeployments that the decoded traffic might equally have suggested that Hitler was preparing for the Allied thrusts he knew would soon be launched towards the Rhine.[33] Spaatz, who was now spending most of his time on the Continent and taking part in many of Eisenhower's staff meetings, shared the views of most other Allied senior officers. As he confessed to Arnold in early January:[34]

> The offensive undertaken by the Germans on 16 December undoubtedly caught us off-balance. We had planned an offensive which was to have

been preceded by air blitzes of the type mentioned in one of your letters. The concentration of the German forces in the area of Ardennes, chosen for attack, was very cleverly accomplished. For quite some time they habitually moved into the area their new Volks Grenadier divisions, apparently for a brief period of orientation, and then moved them to other parts of the front. During a period sometime prior to the attack, three or four divisions were noticed to have moved into the area and no movement out. At about the same time, the Fifth and Sixth German Panzer armies were ordered to observe complete radio silence. During this period, Vandenberg kept his tactical reconnaissance on all parts of the battlefront, in front of our armies to the extent that weather would permit. The weather favored the enemy in that only occasionally could portions of the area be covered. . . .

The German weather forecast was a good one. The attack jumped off early in the morning of 16 December and made dramatic progress for the first several days. The American line broke, and Eisenhower put Montgomery in charge of the two armies on the northern shoulder of the break, the U.S. First and Ninth. Omar Bradley was left in command of those to the south—mainly Patton's Third Army. Until the 23d, the miserable winter weather of northern Europe protected the Germans. A few Allied sorties were flown by tactical planes, but most of the time the Allied air forces were grounded. Eisenhower moved his reserves in fairly quickly, and the 101st Airborne Division arrived in time to help the defenders of Bastogne hold out throughout the battle. Another group of Americans was surrounded at St. Vith, but in the end had to give way, though the delay it imposed on the German advance was vital.[35]

The German drive was aimed at Antwerp, as the Allied generals deduced. Eisenhower quickly decided that every effort should be made to hold the shoulders of the growing salient to cling to the road centers at St. Vith and Bastogne, and to stop the Wehrmacht before it reached the Meuse River. As soon as it became clear that the German offensive was a major one, Eisenhower advised his commanders to aim at making it a disaster for the Germans, as it had been at Mortain and the Falaise Gap.[36]

Spaatz gathered his assistants on the 20th, instructing them to aim at halting the German offensive before it made too deep a penetration. The heavy bombers would concentrate on targets whose destruction (within twenty-four hours at the most) would have an immediate effect on the battle. This meant that they would have to strike targets on the near side of the Rhine in the neighborhood of the battlefield. He also cautioned that excessive battle damage to the heavies be avoided. The weather at the moment was too bad to hope for truly decisive results, and Spaatz was concerned lest, when the weather broke, he have so many bombers grounded for battle damage that he could not achieve good results.[37] In general, Spaatz's heavy bombers would be assigned to interfere with communications from Germany to the battle area along an outer ring, as far away as Saarbrucken. The bombers and fighter-bombers of Ninth Air Force and 2d ATAF would handle interdiction targets along an inner ring closer to the action. Still, the heavies might be called upon to attack objectives even on the battlefield where appropriate.[38] USSTAF's fighters were still based in England, far from the action. Spaatz offered two groups of P-51s to Vandenberg if he could find space for them on Ninth Air Force airfields.[39] As it turned out, Ninth Air Force was crammed into the few available airdromes, and space was located for only one of the Mustang groups from England.[40]

Meanwhile, George Patton had been ordered to drop his plans for an offensive through the Saar and to wheel his forces northward toward the southern flank of the German salient. This he did quickly and soon was in contact with the exposed wing. Sepp Dietrich's 6th Panzer Army had been charged to make the penetration on the north flank, but its progress fell behind schedule on the first day. Hasso von Manteuffel commanded the 5th Panzers in the center, and his thrust made the best progress, notwithstanding the siege at Bastogne. His left flank (south) was protected by the 7th Army under Gen. E. Brandenberger. Even before the jump-off, however, he had worried about the lack of supplies, especially fuel and bridging equipment, and this did not speak well for his prospects of keeping up on the left flank. Manteuffel had to dispatch some of his units to meet Patton's northward attack. This diversion of troops, added to those left behind to reduce the 101st at Bastogne, seriously slowed his march.[41] The German thrust ran out of steam only four miles short of the Meuse, and the Allies soon knew that the Germans had been frustrated.

On the 23d, the weather broke. This released 241 C-47s that had been waiting in England loaded with supplies and ammunition for the beleaguered troops at Bastogne. With a heavy escort of fighters, they made good drops in broad daylight and returned with light casualties. At the same time, the bombers and fighters had a field day. The Luftwaffe was greatly outnumbered, and soon ULTRA was relaying messages of GAF commanders threatening to court-martial pilots who fled from battle.[42] The Germans had started the battle with a shortage of fuel, and Manteuffel, at least, knew it. He had objected that the stocks were not nearly adequate for an offensive and demanded replenishment. The levels were not raised, however, and tanks and trucks had to be abandoned on the battlefield for want of fuel.[43] The German operational plan counted on capturing Allied fuel stocks, but not nearly enough were seized.[44]

Before the battle, some German ground formations were ordered to demechanize and to organize horse-drawn supply columns.[45] Adding to their general fuel shortage was the crushing interdiction that struck them when the weather cleared. Starvation of the men and engines on the leading edge of the German offensive arose not only from the general shortage caused by the Bomber Command and USSTAF offensive against oil, but also from their inability to transport what supplies they did have. By Christmas, the Luftwaffe was driven back and Allied fighters and bombers roamed the skies at will, hitting roads, knocking down bridges, cutting rail lines, blasting locomotives, and bombing rail yards and stations well back into Germany. Secretary Lovett thought that the airpower employed in the battle was the only "true strategic reserve" we had (because of the inadequate replacement system of the ground army). Hitler understood that his main chance was to mask his offensive with bad weather which would deny the Allies the benefit of their airpower. When the mask evaporated, the flexibility which airmen had lauded throughout the interwar period paid dividends as the German armies, up to that point making steady progress, came to a halt.

Spaatz reported to Arnold shortly after the crisis passed:[46]

On the second day of the attack the Ninth Air Force stopped the onslaught in the direction of Spa and Liege by some of the most remarkable flying and control of flying from the ground that has, in my opinion, been effected in this war. Under conditions of almost zero/zero (no visibility, no ceiling) flying, the Panzer column was detected by one of our fighter reconnaissance planes, kept under observation, and attacks directed by (radar) . . . control. The net result of the attack was some fifty to sixty tanks destroyed . . . Thereafter, for several days, the Germans were favored by weather conditions which prevented our operations in strength. Unfortunately for the German plan, the weather broke in our favor on the fourth day which gave us three days in succession of almost perfect flying conditions . . . during which time full and effective use was made of the Air Forces. The extent to which the enemy was set back by this air onslaught is evidenced by his inability to maintain his offensive.

As for the Eighth Air Force, it was in an agonizing position. At that time of the year, there was a tendency for the fog to "burn off" over the bases in England late in the morning and to set in again simultaneously at all the bases early in the evening. In the midst of the battle, the bomber pilots felt an urgency to take off in marginal conditions in the hope of helping the ground forces and in the hope of returning to their home bases before the white mist closed them down. Spaatz marvelled that the young Fortress and Liberator pilots were taking off with visibilities as low as seventy-five yards and doing it day after day. USSTAF's bombers in England were launched on twelve consecutive days commencing on the 23d and threw 30,000 tons of bombs into the battle with telling effect.[47] Much of this bombing was done with radar, and both the effects of the attack and the continuity of operations showed that giant strides had been made in just one year.

Curiously, one of Spaatz's old antagonists in the rail yards versus oil plants controversy was at his headquarters during the Battle of the Bulge. Though Lord Tedder in his memoirs does not complain of being slighted at the time, Zuckerman remarks that Generals Vandenberg and Quesada, the two principal American tactical commanders, were consulting by telephone with Spaatz at a hectic pace throughout the battle, although their formal superior was then Arthur Tedder. Zuckerman was annoyed enough, by his own account, to suggest that the Americans might at least give the tactical air commander a call.[48] He also reported that "Tooey did not appear to view the situation gravely . . . ," yet he offered all his strategic forces for the use of the tactical commanders![49]

The 6th Panzer Army was supposed to carry out the main attack, but it bogged down early in the battle and the 5th Panzer made the largest advances. Its drive reached the high-water mark on the 26th, just shy of the Meuse, when the U.S. 2d Armored Division attacked and stopped it. Some of the German vehicles were running out of fuel, and the divisions behind it tried to extricate them. On the same day, Patton's forces made contact with the besieged Americans in Bastogne, increasing the pressure on the German left flank. Hitler's generals urged a withdrawal, but he insisted that they hold their ground. That facilitated the attacks of both Allied ground and air forces and increased German losses. Finally, in the second week of January, Hitler gave way, and the Germans pulled out of the salient. The Battle of the Bulge was over.[50]

Hitler gained perhaps six weeks by delaying the offensives Eisenhower had poised on 15 December. He also gained a one-month respite for his domestic oil and transportation industries as Spaatz's USSTAF and Harris's Bomber Command were diverted to the Ardennes battle. The German army inflicted 76,890 casualties on the Allies.[51] But the price was steep. German casualties in the battle amounted to 81,834 men, and the Wehrmacht could not afford to trade on a man-for-man basis with enemies who so greatly outnumbered it.[52] Moreover, what little usefulness was left in the Luftwaffe had been squandered with few meaningful results.

On the morning of 1 January 1945, the German air force launched its last large raid. The mission had been planned and ready for two weeks. Pilots were gathered from as far away as eastern Europe while an armada of about eight hundred airplanes was assembled. Most of the flyers were novices and most of the airplanes were single-engine fighters, led to their targets by more experienced crews in twin-engine JU-88s. Allied tactical air forces were packed onto their airfields. There were none too many fields in the first place, and weather conditions had caused more than the normal concentration. In addition, all the tactical units that could be located were crammed onto forward fields to meet the emergency on the Ardennes battlefield. The Germans learned of these lucrative targets from aerial intelligence obtained by their new jets and realized that it would be easier for them to destroy the Allied planes on the ground than in the air.[53]

The attack on New Year's Day caught the Allies off guard. Nearly two hundred American and British planes were destroyed on bases in Belgium and Holland. Few of the Allied pilots were able to take off in time to counter the intrusion. The Germans approached the fields below radar coverage, and some even flew a part of the route through valleys.[54] According to the RAF official history, Britain alone lost 144 aircraft and 46 men. But the Luftwaffe lost at least 211 airplanes, which could be replaced, and 100 pilots, who could not.[55] The German air force, in losing, had shown a flash of its old brilliance, even arousing some grudging admiration from Carl Spaatz:[56]

> The German fighter force had been concentrated to a large extent in forward areas during the period [before the end of the year]. They [the Germans] have become increasingly aggressive, but not strikingly effective. . . . The major portion of our fighter losses are still due to flak. The German Air Force is operating under [Major General Dietrich] Peltz,

whom I consider the most competent air commander the Germans have. He gives every evidence of being not only aggressive, but intelligent. . . . On 1 January, Peltz launched a full-out attack on our airdromes with some 800 fighters. Of the attacking planes, our air, including the RAF, shot down 140 and the anti-aircraft at least as many (it was in the region where the AAA had been deployed against the V-1) and possibly more. This attack was well planned. JU-88s acting as leaders for the formations, all attacks on the deck, with complete radio silence and no warning . . . we lost about 20 P-47s and several P-51s; on RAF airdromes we lost some 12 B-17s and B-24s. . . . On one airdrome which Jimmy [Doolittle] and I visited the same day, . . . a group of P-51s of the Eighth Air Force, which has been moved temporarily over here, engaged the enemy on take-off. . . . Colonel [John C.] Meyers (sic), the group commander, shot down one plane with his landing gear still extended.

On the day of the Luftwaffe's raids, Spaatz almost became an Allied casualty—to friendly fire. He and Jimmy Doolittle were flying to various bases visiting units, and on the way their misidentified twin-engine plane was fired upon by some of Patton's antiaircraft gunners. For a time, they were under heavy fire, but fortunately the aim was poor and they survived.[57] Patton was presently informed by Spaatz of both the poor aircraft identification and the faulty aim.

## Searching for the Knockout Blow

The idea that an enemy structure contained a keystone, or vital center, whose destruction would topple the entire edifice is as old as the initial theorizing attempts at the Air Corps Tactical School in the 1930s.[58] By early 1945, the notion that enemy civilian morale might be that keystone was being severely questioned almost everywhere except at Bomber Command. It was also evident that USSTAF had not halted German aircraft production and the Luftwaffe had more airplanes than it could fly. There were signs that the oil shortage was hurting the German system, but still the structure stood. Throughout the fall of 1944, Spaatz had clung to the notion that oil was the vital center, though he warned Arnold that the growing threat of jets might force him to turn again to a campaign against Nazi airpower, at least temporarily.[59]

One result of the Ardennes Offensive was to intensify the stream of alternative strategic bombing proposals coming from all quarters. Among these was renewed pressure for civilian morale bombing. As early as the previous August, Spaatz had reported to Arnold that he was again being subjected to pressure from the Air Ministry to join in a great strike against Berlin. He opposed this and told Arnold that he still believed he had to continue precision attacks against military targets. He was worried, however, that Eisenhower might be persuaded to approve an attack on Berlin.

The probable cause of Spaatz's concern was a staff meeting the British Chiefs had held on 5 July 1944. Though in the conference Portal had tried to move Harris away from area bombing to join in the attacks on oil, the chiefs nonetheless concluded that there might be a time when an all-out attack on German civilian morale might be decisive.[60] They mulled over several options: strafing attacks all over Germany, numerous obliteration attacks on small towns, or an announced attack on all movement in Germany. Each of these was deemed defective, and the recommendation that emerged was a gigantic attack on Berlin when the right psychological time arrived.[61]

The Air Ministry memorandum arrived in Washington as an attachment to a letter from Spaatz's deputy commander for operations, Fred Anderson. It was circulated to some staff members for comment before going to Arnold. Both Kuter and Col. Charles D. Williamson, who staffed the proposal, took a dim view of the British idea. They did not like it because it flew in the face of declared U.S. doctrine, it did not square with the American national will, and it was considered unlikely to succeed.[62] They nonetheless thought it prudent to have plans ready should an obvious occasion arise. If it did, Williamson and Kuter both believed it would be better to spread the attacks all over Germany so that the maximum number of people would witness the Allied command of the air. They felt that such multiple raids should still be directed at precision military targets similar to those that had been sought in the larger cities.[63]

Arnold agreed and directed USSTAF to prepare a plan for an all-out effort that might turn out to be the decisive blow. It was to be another Big Week where all the air forces would go after German targets for six or seven consecutive days at a specially chosen psychological moment. But Arnold, too, did not then think that the target should be Berlin, and he rejected notions of a direct attack on the German people. He wanted widespread roving attacks against targets of military value so that all Germans could witness the ease with which Allied airpower roamed through the airspace of the Reich. Arnold recognized that no single commander in Europe had the authority to order all the air units into action, but informed Spaatz that he thought the Combined Chiefs of Staff could issue orders to implement a USSTAF plan among all the air commands operating against the Reich.[64]

By early October, Spaatz had reacted to Arnold's directives and had two versions of an all-out contingency plan in the works: one that might be flown in conjunction with ground army operations, and another that would be independent and directed farther into Germany. He promised Arnold that the latter version would provide roles for all the air forces in Europe and that it would strike at every nook and cranny of Germany while still keeping oil facilities as the paramount target. The plan required good weather throughout Germany and passable conditions over the bases in Italy, France, and England.[65] In the same vein, he had written to Lovett three days earlier:[66]

> I have urged and have started the development of a plan for the full-out beating up of Germany with all the Air Forces at our disposal if and when we have a proper weather break. . . . Whether or not such an operation can be decisive may be open to question, but to my mind it represents the only means of terminating the war this year with our forces. The types of targets to hit on such an effort have been the subject of much discussion. Whatever system of targets is selected [the attack] must be widespread and cover much of Germany to be effective.

Just three days before the outbreak of the Ardennes Offensive, Spaatz gave Arnold a less guarded progress report:[67]

> There is increasing evidence that the attacks on rail communications and industrial areas in Germany are having a cumulative effect. There is [a] possibility that the breaking point may be closer at hand than some of us are willing to admit.

In the same letter he added that he had the all-out plan, called HURRI-CANE #2, ready to exploit the break. It would send small packets of attackers all over Germany with the objective of causing a complete and widespread breakdown of the Reich's rail system.[68]

The Ardennes Offensive interrupted Spaatz's personal search for the knockout blow, but it did not end it. By the day after Christmas he was telling Barney Giles that destruction of the German fighters during the Battle of the Bulge may actually have paved the way for the great strike. He said that he was waiting for the right psychological instant to launch the all-out strike at the transportation system, and for the first time he suggested that he was considering following it up with a blow at Berlin itself. Before the end of 1944, then, he had reversed himself on the opposition he and Arnold had expressed just four or five months earlier toward bombing the city of Berlin.[69]

On the day of the Luftwaffe's last full-out attack on Allied fighter fields in the Low Countries, Spaatz's old friend Ira Eaker expressed opposition to the USSTAF plan for an attack on the whole German rail system. He was a little miffed because the plan, now called CLARION, had gone to Fifteenth Air Force directly from Fred Anderson, and it was only through the Fifteenth that Eaker had learned of the new scheme. He said he could not think that Spaatz himself was fully committed to it. Rather, he said, "My personal belief is that the idea stems from the Zuckerman crowd, which has gone nuts on transportation." Eaker complained that CLARION would give credence to German assertions that the Allies were barbarians, for 95 percent of the casualties were sure to be civilians. He reemphasized the point by adding, "I personally . . . am completely convinced that . . . we should never allow the history of this war to convict us of throwing the strategic bomber at the man in the street."[70]

Impassioned as he was about the moral implications of CLARION, Eaker was equally upset about its utility, arguing that it would have no practical effect. The German transportation system was too massive and had so much redundancy built in that it could not be destroyed by a knockout blow. Further, the methods suggested were inadequate. To bring the heavy bombers down to lower altitudes, and to dispatch them in small units in clear weather, day after day, would play into the hands of the defense. He offered up the low-level raids on Ploesti to prove his point. Though the Liberators then had been led by experienced group commanders, they had difficulty finding their way, many formations missed their mark, and the losses were much too high. In the end, Eaker conceded that if an attack on German civilian morale were mandated from above, perhaps the CLARION scheme might be the most desirable of the options.

Meanwhile, in Washington, Assistant Secretary of War for Air Robert Lovett proposed a special outfit made up of five hundred new P-47Ns to be called a "Jeb Stuart unit." The new organization would be created immediately under Spaatz to take advantage of the increased dependence of recently dispersed German industry on the transportation system. As

Lovett saw it, the "Germany first" strategy still applied, and these new fighters could be provided to Spaatz from other theaters. The new planes would be equipped with the latest bomb-aiming devices and weapons. Some P-38s would serve as formation leaders. The Lightnings would have the most sophisticated bombing radar available to enable the Jeb Stuart planes to operate under the worst weather conditions. Similarly, the units' home fields would be provided with the latest in electronic approach devices so that recoveries could be made with low ceilings and visibilities. Lovett thought the need for such a unit was urgent. The Germans had shown in the Ardennes Offensive that they were far from dead. Besides, they had captured some secret proximity fuses during that battle, and their jet fighter force appeared to be developing rapidly. The secretary maintained that the new Thunderbolts would be much less vulnerable to the German countermeasures than were the Fortresses and Liberators. Moreover, they could complement the activities of the heavy bombers and at the same time act as one more reserve for the ground forces when they got into trouble. This new Jeb Stuart unit would engage in CLARION-type operations on a permanent basis.[71]

The secretary's memo received immediate attention by the harried wartime Air Staff. Its response was that the five hundred airplanes could not be had from USAAF sources, but would have to be drawn from the fighters already in Spaatz's theater. Its recommendation was to refer Lovett's memorandum to USSTAF with the caveat that the airplanes for a Jeb Stuart unit would have to come from Spaatz's own organizations.[72]

Arnold sent the whole package off to Spaatz with a cover letter revealing some of his own frustration in the search for the blow that would finish Hitler. He marvelled that with a five-to-one superiority in the air, the Allies seemed unable to find the stroke that would break the Germans. He assured Spaatz that he was not criticizing the work of the people in the theater, but only trying to help find the new idea that would open the road to Berlin.[73]

Spaatz replied that the idea was not a new one, and on marginal weather days the kind of operations envisioned by Lovett were approximately what his Eighth Air Force fighters were already doing. He cited the CLARION plan as one that fully incorporated the strategic and tactical notions of Lovett's memorandum. Since Arnold had remarked that he could not provide Spaatz with the five hundred fighters in question, and Spaatz did not see any possibility of drawing them from the air forces already in the theater, there was not much that could be done in fielding the Jeb Stuart unit. He closed with what might easily be deemed a lecture to his bosses in Washington:[74]

> Your comment on the decisiveness of results achieved by airpower leads me to believe that you might be following the chimera of one air operation that will end the war. I have concluded that it does not exist. I also feel that in many cases the success of our efforts is unmeasurable, due to our inability to exploit the decisive results achieved. For example, I am convinced that much of the Russian advance has been due to the immobility conferred on the German ground forces by our attacks on oil. On the other hand, the results achieved by the POINTBLANK program were sufficiently decisive to give us at least a year of definite air supremacy. Both the strategic and tactical air forces have operated with virtual immunity, and the success of the ground forces, including the invasion of the Continent was assured. Likewise, the results attained by the tactical air commands have been decisive from a short-term point of view. Their effect on the German offensive during the recent Ardennes operation is an example. . . . I am certain the results have been decisive in the past, and in my opinion, they will again be decisive when weather ceases to handicap our own ground forces and gives our air forces a better opportunity to fully exploit their capabilities.

Doubtless it was unintentional, but his comments about the "chimera" were quite at variance with the old Air Corps Tactical School assumption that there were indeed vital targets that were keystones to the enemy edifice. Still, if his desire to bring the misery to an end and the impatience from Washington were not enough, Spaatz was also being gnawed by the thought that if the break did not come soon, the new technical threats from submarines, still-unknown secret weapons, or the jet program might come along to reverse the tide.

In January 1945, the idea of a knockout blow against Berlin and some other east German cities began to gain momentum. The Allies had not looked good during the Ardennes Offensive, and by mid-January the Red Army was making substantial progress in the east. The Yalta Conference was in the offing, and it may have been that some of the impetus for attacking the east German cities came from a desire to compensate for the Ardennes humiliation and the strong hand that Stalin would hold at the conference. The idea was revived in the Air Ministry and received added support from the prime minister. When it was presented to Harris, he agreed, adding to Berlin the idea of hitting Leipzig, Dresden, and some other eastern cities. These additions were made known to the Air Ministry and to Churchill, and neither raised objections.[75]

Spaatz and USSTAF were brought into the proceedings through discussions with Air Marshal Bottomley. Spaatz agreed to a plan whereby USSTAF would participate in the city raids, but in which the aiming points would be military targets.[76] Odds were high that the weather would require radar bombing, and Spaatz must have known that many stray bombs would fall outside the areas of the rail yards. Nevertheless, the program was undertaken with repeated references to preventing the movement of reinforcements through the transportation centers to the Russian front and to creating confusion in the areas immediately behind the German armies.[77]

Meanwhile, the Combined Chiefs of Staff (CCS), en route to the Yalta Conference, gathered at Malta for consultations on the progress of the war in the West. According to Lewis F. Powell, Jr., then an intelligence officer on Spaatz's staff, Tooey was a sincerely modest man who tried to stay out of the limelight. He had never gone to Russia in connection with FRANTIC (shuttle bombing by Fifteenth Air Force between its Mediterranean bases and the USSR). He had remained in the background at the Casablanca Conference while Eaker argued the case for daylight bombing, and now he sent his deputy commander, Fred Anderson, to Malta and Yalta to represent USSTAF and provide any information the decision makers required about the American strategic bombing strategy.[78] Anderson reported back to Spaatz by letter before the conference ended. During the proceedings at Malta, it seems clear that George Marshall was as eager as any of the airmen to hit the cities in eastern Germany. Not only did he explicitly approve of the attacks, but the CCS was also fully informed and gave its approval. The announced motives were to interdict any reinforcements on the way to the eastern front and to create confusion in the rear of the German armies.[79] When the group moved on to Yalta in early February for the talks with the Russians, the subject came up again. Though Dresden was not mentioned explicitly, Berlin and Leipzig were. Not only were the Russians informed of the plan, but General Antonov specifically requested that the heavy bombers make the strikes in support of the Red Army.[80]

The first of USSTAF's attacks came against Berlin on 3 February. The bombing was done visually, and accuracy was good, with the bombs hitting the rail yards and administrative centers in the city. One thousand

Fortresses took part in the operation that day and twenty-five thousand Berliners lost their lives. Four hundred Liberators from Eighth Air Force simultaneously struck other targets on a diversionary raid. The Luftwaffe did not respond, and Allied losses were light.[81]

On the night of 13 February, the British Bomber Command flew two raids against Dresden. The target was marked with precision, and both waves dropped their huge bomb loads into the city through a thin overcast of clouds. The city was filled with refugees, and the regular residents, because of their longtime exemption from bombing attacks, were somewhat complacent about the threat of raids. Less complacency could not have made much difference. A fire storm was started, creating hurricane-force winds which swept all in their path into the inferno. There were no regular air raid shelters in Dresden, and many of those who fled to cellars were asphyxiated. Even Dresden's famous zoo was hit and the animals escaped, only to succumb to the fires that followed.

The USSTAF force assigned to Dresden was launched at 8 A.M. the following morning. When it arrived, the smoke was still so dense that the air crews could not see the city. Bombing was done by radar. Three hundred and eleven Fortresses unloaded their bombs into the inferno. On the next day, 210 bombers from the Eighth returned, and on the fifteenth, the RAF followed up with another attack on the hapless city. Because of the many refugees in the city and the wartime turbulence of the period that followed, it is uncertain how many Germans died in the Dresden bombings. The lowest estimates are thirty-five thousand and the highest around one hundred thirty-five thousand.[82]

The Dresden attack quickly became a political issue. When the news reached England, criticism arose in the Parliament and the newspapers against the barbarities of terror bombing. The aftermath was a particularly emotional one. It was aggravated for Spaatz by reports coming out of a SHAEF news conference on 18 February. The Canadian air commodore presiding had commented that Allied bombing policy had now been changed and implied that in the future the strategic air forces would conduct a deliberate campaign of terror.

This quickly made headlines in the United States and caused Arnold much grief. He immediately wanted to know what was happening in England. The SHAEF spokesman was not representing Spaatz's headquarters, but he nevertheless asserted that USSTAF had been adhering rigidly to its operating directives.[83] The attacks on the eastern European cities had been made under exactly the same orders and conditions that had governed the previous raids on Berlin. Arnold quickly replied that the explanation satisfied him, but the exchange has been dismissed as "cant" by at least one author.[84]

There was such a political uproar in Parliament and in the newspapers, and Communist propaganda has made so much of it while studiously ignoring the Russian role in it all, that one must suspect those who would condemn the morality of the American planners. Spaatz himself, long afterwards, denied that he had rejected area bombing in the first instance on moral grounds. One of his contemporaries, Gen. Charles P. Cabell, was unrepentant about it in a letter written after Spaatz's death. Cabell argued that there was nothing immoral, after five years of experience with the horrors perpetrated by the Nazis, in seeking the most effective ways of bringing them to an end without further slaughter of Allied citizens, military and civilian alike.[85] One reason why the Dresden raids were so devastating was that they went practically unopposed. Perhaps the estimates of the previous month had been unduly pessimistic. Perhaps the collapse of the Reich was not far off after all. But if Dresden did not precipitate it, what would?

At the same time that George Marshall had given his approval to Fred Anderson for the concentrated blows on the east German cities, he also expressed his interest in CLARION (which he called the Quesada Plan). He told Anderson at Malta that he had never understood why his Air Staff in Washington opposed it, and that now perhaps the conditions for a diffuse assault all over Germany might be the catalyst that the Allies had been seeking.[86] Eaker had been appalled at the notion on both moral and utilitarian grounds, but Marshall was now behind it— even enthusiastic about it—and Spaatz, who had seen some merit in the plan right along, decided to give it a try.

The weather promised to be clear all over Germany on 22 February, and SHAEF Headquarters requested that CLARION be launched that day. Tedder was somewhat uncomfortable with the plan, for it sent forces all over Germany rather than concentrating them in a region where they could complement the ground effort. Nonetheless, nine thousand airplanes were dispatched far and wide. The physical damage wrought was impressive. Losses were extremely light: Eighth Air Force launched over one thousand bombers and only two failed to return.[87] The results were good enough for Spaatz and Doolittle to launch a second raid the following day. This, too, suffered little battle damage and roamed far and wide with practically no interference from the defenders. But the great physical damage did not translate into a crack in enemy morale. The German people plodded on, and the damage to locomotives, bridges, stations, and tracks was so scattered that the Germans were able to work around it. In short, Tedder had been right.[88] It seemed clear from the weakness of the resistance that the end could not be far off, but where was the stroke that would bring it about?

If Spaatz's command enjoyed a string of tactical victories with low casualties, his losses in the public relations campaigns were much higher. No sooner had the flap over the Dresden affair subsided than Spaatz became personally embroiled in a diplomatic crisis of the first order. One of the CLARION strikes had lost its way, wandered over Switzerland, and attacked the wrong target. Forty Swiss were killed, and the U.S. had given Switzerland assurances that it would not happen again. Stern measures were taken within the air forces to prevent it, yet, less than two weeks later, two more small formations of heavy bombers strayed over Switzerland and bombed Basel and Zurich, with repercussions all the way to the White House.[89]

The Swiss had a case. They had been between the mill-stones of war for a long time and their borders had been violated again and again by both sides. Spaatz knew that a storm was coming. The bombers had no sooner landed than he sent a message both to Arnold and the American military attache in Switzerland.[90] He told them that he was investigating the tragedy, but he probably knew that would not be enough to head off the reaction. Two days later George Marshall sent Spaatz a stern signal: ''The successive bombings of Swiss territory now demand more than expressions of regret.'' The chief of staff then directed Spaatz to go to Switzerland in person and in secret to make the unabashed apology now required. He did so in the company of his chief of staff Brig. Gen. E. P. Curtis; both in civilian clothes. They flew to Lyons and drove into Bern to meet with the Swiss authorities on the 8th of March. Spaatz made the necessary apologies to the minister of war and later explained to the military authorities, in very great detail, the lengths to which he was going to prevent a recurrence. Radar-aimed attacks in the future would be prohibited within 150 miles of the Swiss border. He asked them to keep this information secret lest the Germans take advantage of the sanctuary.[91]

When the meetings were over, according to Curtis, Spaatz was much relieved. As they motored out of Switzerland, they stopped at a country inn for a meal. The place was crowded with people of various nationalities, it was warm, the food was good, and the atmosphere congenial. Spaatz wanted to prolong this respite from the war by staying overnight, but Curtis, fearing the presence of Axis agents in Switzerland, dissuaded his boss.[92] On his return, Spaatz reported to Marshall that the mission had been accomplished and that the Swiss had been extremely cordial.[93] Nothing was said in the report about an indemnity for the injured parties. On the next day, however, Spaatz wrote to Arnold telling him the Swiss had proposed that some Mustangs be provided to their air force in lieu of a part of the cash compensation for diplomatic settlement. Spaatz recommended that course to Arnold, but warned he would not have enough P-51s for that purpose for the next six weeks or so.[94]

By the time Spaatz returned to France, Germany lay at the feet of USSTAF, the Bomber Command, and the Allied armies, a heap of smoldering ruins, incapable of reacting to further attacks. But still the collapse did not come. Arnold's intelligence chief commented on 16 March that the Luftwaffe was finished as a fighting organization. American soldiers had crossed the Remagen Bridge and the German air force was hardly able to muster fifty airplanes in an attempt to destroy the span. The Reich's air defense was no better. Though the density of fighter escort for USSTAF was hardly half what it had been a year earlier, its heavy bombers crossed the German skies virtually unchallenged. The intelligence chief was able to report:[95]

AAF heavy bomber losses to GAF fighters have declined almost to the vanishing point. This fact is emphasized by the recent statement of . . . General Spaatz . . . that only one bomber gunner had an opportunity to shoot down a German fighter in the entire month of February when 20,700 heavy bomber sorties were flown over Germany. Our bomber losses to fighters amounted to .09 percent in January 1945 as compared with 2.2 percent in January 1944. . . .

## The Waning of the Reich

After the failure of the Ardennes Offensive, the Allied ground forces continued their eastward march. The bulge was flattened in January 1945, and the Germans began transferring units to the eastern front, where the Russians had launched a new offensive. The ensuing Anglo-American offensives brought the western armies up to the Rhine and one of them, the U.S. First, seized intact the Remagen Bridge across the river. It was necessary to gain another crossing over the Rhine at a more northerly location, in front of the British 21st Army Group. Once that was done, the Allied armies could encircle the Ruhr Valley from the north and deny the Reich its last, great industrial area.[96]

The Ruhr had been a principal target of Bomber Command for years and it was already fairly devastated. In the wake of CLARION, Tedder persuaded Spaatz and the others to concentrate their air attack against German communications in the area around the Ruhr. In that way, the efforts of the tactical and strategic air forces would be more complementary both to one another and to the ground forces. Moreover, the Russians had recently deprived the Germans of the great Silesian coal fields, and since those in the Ruhr were the principal alternative source, a campaign against the Ruhr's communications would yield important strategic, as well as tactical, results. There was already a coal shortage in other parts of Germany, and that commodity was fundamental to the whole economy. If the Ruhr could be isolated from the rest of the country, the coal shortage would add to the effects of the oil campaign and hasten the end.[97] That plan was adopted, and in the ensuing months the Ruhr Valley was progressively cut off from the rest of Germany.

The next step was to get the northern wing of the attack, under Montgomery, across the Rhine. The main attack would be made on a four-division front during darkness on the night of 23–24 March. It would go over the lower Rhine at a spot so wide that Monty likened his operation to an amphibious landing. Two of the assault divisions would come from the British 21st Army group; two others would come from Gen. William H. Simpson's U.S. Ninth Army. There was some high ground beyond the landing sites, and two airborne divisions would be used to take those commanding heights. These jumps, code-named VARSITY, were to be the largest single-day aerial assault during World War II. Unlike those in Sicily and Normandy, they would be made *after* the amphibious landings had started, and unlike the jumps at Arnhem, they would be made within supporting artillery range of the ground forces. One of the lessons of Arnhem was thought to be that airborne divisions were too light to stand up against the heavier surface divisions of the enemy once the element of surprise had worn off. Thus, the theory went, they had to be dropped within supporting range of the conventional surface divisions coming across the river.[98]

USSTAF's role was to join the other air forces in the preparatory phase, striking at communications on the far side of the Rhine and around the Ruhr; to neutralize enemy airfields in the region of the assault;

to fly diversionary strikes against the interior of Germany on the day of the attack; and to provide aerial resupply to the paratroopers on the day of the drops. Though air defense over the battlefield would be the responsibility of Ninth Air Force and the British 2d ATAF, USSTAF fighters would set up an outer screen to the east of the assault zone to prevent the movement of Luftwaffe airplanes to the scene of the action.[99] The aerial resupply mission was assigned to the Liberators of Doolittle's 2d Air Division.[100]

As the hour for the crossing approached, the Navy brought forward the landing craft, partly by road, and partly by river and canal. The assault was preceded by a massive artillery bombardment, and both British and American casualties were very light. The armada of transports and gliders approaching from fields in England and France found the assault areas much more easily than they had at Sicily and Normandy, and the casualties at the drop zones were lighter than anticipated. There was considerable German antiaircraft artillery on the far bank, however, which took a large toll of the airlift planes as they departed the drop areas. They had arrived seven minutes early, which caused premature curtailment of flak suppression by the fighters. Fortunately, many of the crews bailed out, while others steered their stricken planes to safe crash landings on the west side of the river. Personnel casualties were few. For the most part the paratroopers landed on or near their assigned drop zones and quickly organized for action. German opposition was not nearly as formidable as it had been at Arnhem, and the paratroopers quickly achieved most of their objectives despite sporadic fierce resistance.[101]

So far the role of Spaatz's command in VARSITY had been a supporting one: bombing communications lines, air defense to the east of the battle area, a Fifteenth Air Force raid against Berlin all the way from Italy, and the suppression of the Luftwaffe on its airfields.

While the Ninth Air Force's transports were flying to the drop zones, 240 USSTAF Liberators warmed up in England for their supply drops on the far bank of the Rhine. It was a mission that would make strategic bombing dogmatists shudder—the use of heavy bombers in logistical support for a tactical operation that itself was a secondary attack! The aircrews at Bungay and the other East Anglian bases of the 2d Air Division showed little enthusiasm for the mission. They were trained for high-altitude precision bombing, but those who had participated in the Arnhem resupply drops knew that buzzing around a drop zone at very low altitudes could be just as dangerous as soaring high over Berlin.

When they arrived at the drop zones, their premonitions proved accurate. Each bomber carried ten thousand pounds of supplies, stored not only in the bomb bay, but also in the rear of the plane, making the touchy aircraft tail-heavy and more difficult to fly. Each had its load packed in about twenty bundles, some of which had to be pushed by hand out of the rear of the aircraft.

Eisenhower later called VARSITY the ". . . most successful airborne operation we carried out during the war."[102] No doubt in casualties among the paratroopers and their effectiveness after landing, it was. Some have questioned that judgment, however, in strategic results. Though the casualties were low, they were higher than among the infantrymen who had crossed the river in boats, and by the time the parachutists were on the ground, the surface units were already well established on the east bank. The airborne assault did not do much to ease the way for Monty's armies.[103] For Spaatz's Liberators, it was a bloody business. Fourteen of the 240 Liberators failed to return, a loss rate of 5.8 percent of the force launched. The average heavy bomber losses for the year of 1943 had been 5.1 percent[104]—and that had been the year of Regensberg, Ploesti, and Schweinfurt. Germany was staggering on her feet, but she still could bite hard, and neither VARSITY nor Monty's great crossing were to be the blows that would bring her down.

## The Last Act

The crossing of the Rhine opened the flood gates. In Eisenhower's next news conference, four days after VARSITY, he told the correspondents that the Germans were a "whipped" enemy.[105] Within a week of the Rhine crossing, the U.S. Ninth and First Armies dashed around the Ruhr and linked hands on the far side. The USSTAF bombers kept striking the oil, rail, and jet airplane targets, but it was becoming less and less productive. For safety's sake, a "bomb line" was maintained to the east of the American and British front and another to the west of the Russian front. As the armies continued their march, these two lines which defined the area in which the Fortresses and Liberators could bomb freely came closer and closer together. Between them, most targets had been reduced to rubble. Portal in early April argued that the time had come to think about the difficulty in taking care of the defeated population: he wanted to prevent further damage to those facilities that would aid the Allies in doing this.[106] Further, one bomb group had already been redeployed to the U.S. en route to the Pacific, and the need to move the others was very much on Spaatz's mind.[107] On the ground, the armies were moving so fast that their tactical air support was hard pressed to keep up with them. They were getting so far away from the air bases that the Thunderbolts could not carry enough fuel to loiter long above the columns they were protecting.

In mid-April, Carl Spaatz proclaimed that the strategic air war was over, that the heavy bombers and their escorts had finished their job. The Luftwaffe was gone and there was nothing left in Germany for USSTAF to hit. From then on, the task would be tactical support of the rampaging armies. On 30 April 1945, Adolph Hitler and Eva Braun committed suicide. Still, the fighting went on.

Even after the remains of the Nazi dictator and his mistress had been cremated, his successors still procrastinated, trying to reduce the full impact of Germany's defeat. A few still thought they could somehow divide the Western Allies from Russia and that the fight would go on against the Bolsheviks. Goering had fallen from grace during the last days of the Reich and Adm. Karl Doenitz inherited the ruins. During these last days, Spaatz was at Eisenhower's headquarters in a schoolhouse in Rheims, a witness to the final drama. It was the first weekend in May 1945. The individual Wehrmacht commanders, with their world crumbling around them, were surrendering their units piecemeal to the various Allied leaders on the western front. There was a general movement in Germany from east to west to escape the advancing Red Army. During the early hours of Monday, May 7, the Allied commanders, Spaatz among them, gathered in the war room in Rheims amid the situation maps and under the hot lights for the cameras. Col. Gen. Alfred Jodl and other German generals marched in, and Jodl signed the document of unconditional surrender. Gen. Walter Bedell Smith signed for the Allies. The war was over.[108]

Or was it? The ceremony in Rheims did not satisfy the Russians. Although they had a representative at the signing, Maj. Gen. Ivan Suslaparov, the Soviets feared that the ceremony at Rheims might encourage the Germans to believe that a separate peace had been made with the West and that the fight against the USSR was to continue.[109] They insisted on a second signing ceremony, in Berlin, with full Soviet participation. Eisenhower wanted to go to Berlin, but his staff feared that the invitation to him was a propaganda ploy for internal Russian consumption. Further, the staff suggested that the prestige of the West was at stake, since Marshal Zhukov, the ranking Soviet representative, was of a lesser rank than Eisenhower.[110] It was decided to send his deputy, Air Marshal Arthur Tedder. The senior American on the delegation was General Spaatz.[111]

On Tuesday, with hardly two hours' notice, Tedder gathered a task force to go to Berlin for the "ratification." The group flew to Stendahl, a staging point where they were to pick up the German delegation and an escort of Russian fighters for the flight to Tempelhof Airdrome in Berlin.[112] Spaatz, a part of his staff, and Soviet General Suslaparov travelled in a C-47.[113] When they arrived, the Red Air Force was nowhere in sight. Soon, an RAF airplane arrived carrying Field Marshal Wilhelm Keitel, the chief of the German surrender delegation. A misunderstanding of time zones led to the mix-up on the rendezvous with the Soviet escorts. They landed exactly on time, according to their own watches. The air fleet then made the short hop to Berlin.

Tedder's group arrived in Berlin expecting the formalities would proceed with dispatch and they would return to their own headquarters that same day. From the outset, however, it became clear that things would not proceed quickly. The contingent was driven to the other side of Berlin and it was already well into the afternoon when they arrived. More time passed as they were served a sumptuous lunch. The Soviet political representative, Andrei Vishinsky, had not yet arrived, and the ceremony could not start without him.[114] In addition, in the excitement of the Rheims surrender, General Smith forgot the copy of the surrender instrument that had been agreed upon previously by the Big Three, and he had made the Germans sign one of his own design. The Russians were not satisfied with that and insisted on writing a new one.[115]

While Tedder and Zhukov contemplated these problems, time moved very slowly. Spaatz and Tedder were in and out periodically as they went to and from their conferences with Zhukov. One of the sticking points involved Spaatz. The Western Allies desired that General de Lattre de Tassigny be permitted to sign the surrender document in the name of France and that Spaatz sign for the United States. Tedder would sign both as Eisenhower's deputy and as the British representative. Vishinsky, however, did not want either the French representative or Spaatz to sign as an equal to Marshal Zhukov. Tedder, as Eisenhower's deputy, could sign for both Britain and America. The protocol problem was overcome, however, by letting Spaatz and de Lattre sign the document, but at a level lower than that of Zhukov and Tedder and in the capacity of witnesses, not principals.[116]

Still, the time had not come. The monotony was partially relieved by sending back to Tempelhof for the baggage, for it was plain they would be staying overnight. Some time was passed in listening on the German radios to the victory announcements of Truman and Churchill. Spaatz went for a stroll in the compound and was deluged by Russians seeking snapshots. When he passed the cottage of the German delegation, Keitel and the others emerged on a balcony for a moment, apparently to take a look at the man supposed to have laid waste to their homeland.[117] One of the last items of delay was the acquisition of a French flag for the surrender room—de Lattre was not to be snubbed this time. One was hastily manufactured from the remnants of a Nazi flag, a bed sheet, and a set of overalls—but, according to John Toland, the first version was sewn together with the stripes going in the wrong direction and had to be reassembled correctly.[118]

It was near midnight before the participants filed into the surrender room. At one end was a long head table; perpendicular to it were several others at which the press and the staffs were seated. One of the perpendicular tables was shorter than the others, and it was for the German representatives. The whole scene was illuminated by bright lights for the photographers. Marshal Zhukov was at the center of the head table with Air Marshal Tedder on his right and General Spaatz on his left. On the flanks of the head table were Andre Vishinsky and Jean de Lattre de Tassigny.[119] When all was ready, Zhukov called the meeting to order, and the German delegation was ordered into the room.

Field Marshal Wilhelm Keitel entered, followed by the Luftwaffe's Generaloberst Hans Jurgen Stumpff and the navy's Adm. Hans Friedeburg. Keitel came to a halt and saluted his antagonists with his field marshal's baton. The Germans were, according to Major Sally Bagby, ". . . smartly dressed and bedecked in ribbons. Good looking, intelligent men, with a dignity becoming a conqueror rather than the defeated."[120] Tedder asked Keitel if he was ready to sign, and when the German said yes, he moved to the head table to put his signature on the several copies of the surrender instrument. Keitel quibbled for a moment over the timing of the surrender, but Zhukov silenced him. While Keitel was signing, the photographers crowded forward, blocking the view of others in the room. One assistant elbowed a path for his cameraman, and someone in the mob hit him in the face. This started a melee which marred the solemnity of the occasion.[121] Once the crowd had calmed down, the other Germans were called forward to add their names to Keitel's, and then the Allied generals had their turn. Zhukov and Tedder led the way. Spaatz signed next, and de Lattre last. The European war was over—it was time for the celebration.[122]

The Russians converted the ceremonial hall into a banquet room, setting bottles of beer, red wine, white wine, cognac, vodka, and champagne at every other place. The dinner began with caviar, salads and soups, then proceeded to courses of chicken and fish with fresh vegetables. Dessert was a white cake.[123] But more remembered than the food was the continuous stream of toasts. Participants started dropping out—some by departing the room and others by falling asleep at the table. Spaatz offered the sixth toast to the ". . . soldiers, sailors, and airmen who gave their lives to make peace possible."[124] His turn came again on the twenty-fifth drink, and this time he ". . . had run out of toasts, so he toasted the women of Russia." Notwithstanding the exhilaration of the moment, Spaatz did not dispense with his usual economy of words. His last salute was to the United States of America with the words, "We stand for honesty—justice—and the rights of the individual."[125]

Dawn was approaching when the dinner ended. The staid Tedder later remembered: "It was not surprising that there were a number of alcoholic casualties. I was glad to note that none of them were British."[126] Spaatz walked back to his cottage after the banquet only to find all the cots, chairs, and floors occupied by newsmen in various states of disarray. Sally Bagby "routed" one of them out of a cot, and the general lay down. Barely an hour later, however, he was roused for a tour of downtown Berlin en route back to Tempelhof.[127] The forlorn sights of the crushed city that Wednesday dawn were in stark contrast to the revelry of the previous night. There was no card playing on the three-hour flight to Rheims, and after landing, Spaatz spent the rest of the day sleeping. Wednesday evening, he flew back to the USSTAF headquarters at St. Germain.[128] It was time to think about the tasks that lay ahead.

## Anticlimax: "Those Were Wonderful Times"

On his first day back at St. Germain Spaatz flew to Gen. Alexander Patch's Seventh Army headquarters to interview Hermann Goering. Accompanying Spaatz were his chief of staff, Maj. Gen. E. P. Curtis, and the commander of the Ninth Air Force, Lt. Gen. Hoyt Vandenberg, as well as Alexander de Seversky,[129] the famous Russian pilot who became an American airplane designer.

Insofar as Goering's testimony could be counted as reliable, Carl Spaatz was able to get a rare insight into the view from the other side of the lines. Unfortunately, while Spaatz tried through questioning to ascertain Goering's views on the causes for the Luftwaffe's failure, Germany's second-ranking Nazi tried to diminish his own blame by heaping it on the head of his fallen leader. Spaatz's first question to his erstwhile foe was why the Luftwaffe had failed, and Goering immediately accused Hitler, saying that the Fuehrer had interfered with the sound plans of the German air force from 1940 onward—a theme to which he returned time and again throughout the interview.[130]

They also discussed the Battle of Britain. Spaatz, even in 1940 doubtful of rigid German escort tactics, now asked Goering about the reasons for the British victory. Goering was unclear on the point, responding differently at various times. First, he said that the retarded state of German long-range bomber technology made it necessary to use the fighters for support of the bombers. Later he asserted that he would have won the Battle of Britain, had it not been for Hitler's diversion of the force to the Russian campaign, which he, Goering, consistently opposed. At another time, he claimed that he was always for precision bombing of military targets but was forced to go to urban area bombing by the Fuhrer, who understood very little about airpower. Goering accepted no responsibility for prematurely dropping the Luftwaffe's attacks on the RAF and its installations and redirecting them on the city of London. At another time, the Reichsmarschall told Spaatz that the conquest of Germany by airpower alone was out of the question, but that the conquest of England by the Luftwaffe alone had been feasible if only Hitler had not interfered.

According to Goering, the jet program had the real potential for reversing the tide of events, if only he had been allowed another ". . . four to five months more time." He claimed that the Allied bombing of the production facilities and training establishments would not have prevented it. The airframe plant was underground and could not be reached. The production of the low-grade fuel for the ME-262 was also well along underground. General Vandenberg asked Goering if the oil shortage would have prevented adequate training of jet pilots, but the Reichsmarschall dismissed the problem, asserting that the transition to jets ". . . was very easy training." He said nothing about sheer numbers, the damage that the USSTAF was doing to his airfields, and the fact that both the British and American jet programs were progressing (albeit behind that of the Luftwaffe by a substantial distance).

General Curtis questioned Goering on the effectiveness of Allied target selection, but the answers were of little help. There were no RAF men in the room. At one point, he told Curtis that the oil attacks had been the utmost in deadliness and that the target selection had been excellent: at another, he asserted that the rail yard attacks had been very successful, but the assaults on the bridges and lines of communications only slightly so. He added, too, that the British and American airmen were the equal of the German flyers, but that the Russians were inferior to all.

Spaatz asked Goering why the attack on Poltava had been so successful. The Luftwaffe's chief replied, ''Those were wonderful times,'' and suggested that it was only by chance that the Fortresses' destination was discovered. The Germans mounted the attack by diverting planes that were heading for a nearby railroad target.[131]

Spaatz came away from the meeting with a feeling of skepticism. It was so full of contradictions and mistakes that it appeared as either a deception or a display of remarkable ignorance about the affairs of one's own organization. Spaatz, after all, had had a rather good picture of the Luftwaffe through ULTRA, derived from the words of German air force commanders.

Throughout the last year of the European war, Spaatz's headquarters had become increasingly involved in developing plans for redeploying to the Pacific and, once the job was done there, for settling the postponed question of the air arm's future. Given little time to savor the victory in Europe, Spaatz was quickly thrust into these issues.

# Chapter X

## AN END AND A BEGINNING

Even before the Germans surrendered in Berlin, Spaatz and his staff had begun planning for redeployment to the Pacific and then for a postwar air force. Hard on the heels of the Nazi capitulation, Spaatz was sent to the Pacific to command the strategic air forces in that theater. At the time Arnold made the decision to send him there, in May 1945, it was not yet fully apparent that the Japanese were on the verge of defeat. Plans had been prepared to invade the southern island of Kyushu that fall and to land on the main island of Honshu the following spring. Spaatz's stay in the Pacific was short, however. He was there just over a week when the first atomic bomb was dropped and had been there just a month when he attended his third surrender ceremony of the year, this one on the deck of the USS *Missouri* in Tokyo Bay. With Arnold's health failing, Spaatz was called home immediately after the surrender to prepare for the legislative battles that were shaping up over revamping America's military organization.

### Redeployment Planning

In his victory message to his airmen in USSTAF, Spaatz had rejoiced in the Nazi defeat, but cautioned that there was still another war to be won. Since the battles against Hitler were much more ground campaigns than those that faced them in the Pacific, most of Eisenhower's ground forces would be demobilized, but many of his sailors and airmen were needed in the Pacific to fight Japan.

According to the redeployment plan, some of Spaatz's strategic air forces would remain in Europe for the occupation. The rest would return to the United States, some for demobilization and some to be sent to the Pacific. Spaatz preferred that units, rather than individuals, be redeployed, but Army planners overruled him on the grounds that that would create inequities intolerable to the American public. Some men with much combat time would be sent against Japan while others who had not fought would be demobilized with their units. Instead, an elaborate point system was devised that rated each individual according to his time in the service, time in overseas theaters, time in combat, and status as a family head. Once the complex formula had assigned points to each individual, those with the highest scores would be discharged in the United States, while those with lower scores would go on with their units to the Pacific.[1]

The carrying capacity of Spaatz's bombers was not wasted on their trips back to the United States. Ten airmen (in addition to the crews) were aboard each B-17 and B-24 to return them home quickly without placing an extra burden on the Air Transport Command. In addition to the heavy bombers, the A-26s, the C-46s, and some of the C-47s were flown home under their own power. By 20 May 1945, when the redeployment began, the routes were much better developed than they had been in 1942 when Spaatz brought over the leading elements of the Eighth Air Force. Losses on the return trip were far fewer than they had been three years earlier. More than four thousand heavy bombers and close to two thousand twin-engine airplanes made the trip with just five fatal crashes.

Many aircraft were delayed along the way, especially on the southern route through North Africa and by way of the Azores and Newfoundland or Dakar and Brazil to the terminal at Savannah, Georgia. This route did not contain as many maintenance and supply facilities as did the northern one. The problems were cleared up by the time the summer was over, however, and the move was completed in three months.[2]

While the USSTAF portion of the redeployment went well, the plan faltered in getting the units through the United States and on to the Pacific. The USAAF had won partial exemption of its officers and crew members from the point system, hoping that it could retain half of its experienced people in each unit as it passed through the states. That proved impossible, however, and most squadrons were rebuilt with new men from training bases, led by only two or three veteran commanders.

The plan called for reconstituting Eighth Air Force on Okinawa, by year's end, with B-29s in strength equal to that of the Mariana-based Twentieth Air Force. There were numerous delays in manning and training, however, and the war against Japan was over before many of the flyers from Spaatz's old command could reach the Far East to serve under him again. One exception was Doolittle, who arrived in Okinawa before the fighting in Europe stopped and was preparing a B-29 unit for combat as the war ended.

## Planning for the Postwar Air Force

Two conceptually separate but historically connected organizational issues, that of a separate air force and that of a unified military establishment, lay just below the surface throughout the war. Early in the war, Arnold and Marshall agreed tacitly that the Army Air Forces did not have enough trained staff men to be independent and that the question of autonomy should be postponed until after peace had been won. Inherent in this was the understanding that Marshall would support an independent air force when that day arrived.[3] The issue of unification, however, which had been associated with that of autonomy for the air arm since the days of Billy Mitchell, refused to stay in the background ''for the duration.'' In 1943, Marshall had proposed to the Joint Chiefs of Staff the idea of a unified Department of National Defense.[4] Soon after, a committee of Congress, the Woodrum Committee, held hearings on the proposal. Although the committee's report was inconclusive, it led to the suggestion that opinions should be solicited from the combat commanders who were fighting the war. Since these commanders were too heavily committed in battle to travel to Washington, a JCS group led by Rear Adm. J. O. Richardson visited the commanders in their theaters.[5] The group's charge was to evaluate the relative merits of one, two, or three military department systems and to render a report to the Joint Chiefs.

Admiral Richardson's committee reached USSTAF headquarters at St. Germain in early November 1944. Spaatz told Richardson he thought that a single department would be the best, but that even a three-department structure would be better than the present arrangement of two. He believed the civilian secretaries should be identified with a unified military establishment rather than with the individual services. Although he advocated a separate intelligence organization for each service, it was still imperative that a single, unified intelligence agency of great sophistication be created at the highest level. Great benefit would be derived, he added, from a unification of both supply and services.[6]

Meanwhile, the issue of postwar autonomy for the air force was not completely dormant. While some considered it a foregone conclusion that there would be a separate air force as soon as the war ended, Arnold was not among them. During the final two years of the war, he spent considerable time building a case for an independent air arm.

Much of Spaatz's involvement with the issue of autonomy during the war years took place orally. He made a trip to Washington in October 1943 to talk with Arnold and others on the Air Staff. Arnold came through the Mediterranean the next month where they met again, and his deputy, Lt. Gen. Barney Giles, visited Spaatz's headquarters two months later. Arnold flew to Europe again at the time of the Normandy invasion.[7] After his heart attack in early 1945, Arnold travelled again to Europe, where he discussed postwar organization with Eisenhower and Spaatz.[8] Three months later, in early June, Spaatz was in the United States briefly and, after several weeks back in Europe, he returned to Washington for his briefing on assuming command in the Pacific and on dropping the nuclear weapons. Thus, there were many occasions for the two to discuss plans for the postwar air force.

Both Arnold and Spaatz knew well from experience the importance of public relations in realizing their goals. During World War I, while Spaatz was in France, Arnold had been in Washington as an information officer. Both had been educated in the subject by a master, Billy Mitchell, and both had observed the success of the Navy League in the 1920s in advocating naval power. In the fall of 1944, a movement was afoot to found an organization dedicated to the strengthening of national security through air power, and Arnold was fully behind it. In October he wrote to Spaatz:[9]

This letter, which will be presented to you by Colonel Trubee Davison [already well-known to Spaatz as former Assistant Secretary of War for Air], is to bring to your attention a program which has been undertaken by a group of substantial, public-spirited citizens in this Country. . . .

There is enclosed a list of groups of citizens (including the likes of Lawrence Bell, Donald Douglas, Eddie Rickenbacker, and Clark Gable, to name only a few) comprising the Organization Committee of an organization to be known as the Air Forces League, the object of which is briefly to promote and develop public understanding of the influence of airpower on international relations and national security and the importance to our Country of adequate United States Air Forces. . . .

Arnold's letter went on to ask that Spaatz cooperate with Davison in recruiting an officer eligible for retirement to leave the service and serve as a full-time executive officer for the new organization. The recommendation was his chief of staff, E. P. Curtis. Spaatz fully shared Arnold's goals and helped with the founding of the organization that was the predecessor of the present Air Force Association.

Assistant Secretary of War Robert Lovett also supported independence, and at about the same time he wrote to Spaatz:[10]

Naturally, everything must be subordinated to the goal of winning the war at the least cost and at the earliest possible date. However, the whole future security of this country depends, I believe, on a proper recognition of Air Power in our national defense setup and the acceptance of the demonstrated fact that its striking power is at least equal to that of land or sea forces and probably is greater than either since it is a prerequisite to successful offensive operations.

In the same letter, Lovett voiced his concern that, because all the theater commanders were either ground or naval officers, their role would be dramatized, and the light of the air forces would be dimmed. He also expressed interest in developing a strategic bombing survey to bring into public view the role of the air forces in the defeat of the Axis.

## Going Home

Shortly after the German surrender, General Marshall ordered Eisenhower to send several fifty-man delegations back to the U.S. for victory celebrations around the country in June. The groups were to be a cross section of ranks. Carl Spaatz was one of those sent, but his homecoming would not be permanent.[11] He participated in a gala parade in Philadelphia and in another even closer to home, in Reading, Pennsylvania. From among the dignitaries he met in Reading came a request and an offer. Omar Bradley had already been tapped to become the head of the Veterans Administration, and the local congressman and a judge asked Spaatz to approach Bradley about getting the VA to locate a new veteran's hospital in the district. In addition, the congressman and judge asked Carl Spaatz to become the Democratic candidate for the governorship of

Pennsylvania![12] Spaatz sent the hospital proposals on to Bradley with a tepid recommendation; he dismissed the gubernatorial offer out of hand.[13] But the victory tour was soon over, and Spaatz was back in Europe before the end of the month. For a time he had thought that his postwar assignment would be at the head of the Continental Air Command with responsibility for managing the demobilization, but, in May, Arnold had decided to send him, as well as Doolittle and Twining, to the Pacific instead. Consequently, he turned around in Europe almost immediately and returned to the United States.

Spaatz's last act in the European war in 1918 had been to run out of fuel and land in no-man's-land. It almost happened again in World War II. He, his USSTAF chief of staff, Maj. Gen. E. P. Curtis, his aide, Major Bagby, his daughter Katharine, and some others came back to the U.S. aboard his assigned B-17, named "Boops," his youngest daughter's nickname. The Fortress could not make it all the way across the Atlantic against the prevailing winds without stopping for fuel, so they went by way of the Azores. The distance from there to Gander, Newfoundland, is about 1,500 miles, which is not an excessively long trip for a B-17, but the bases in Newfoundland were few and far between. Inbound to Gander, they learned that fog had closed the field. Spaatz's pilot turned toward Goose Bay, far to the north, but soon heard by radio that that field, too, "had gone below minimums." There was nothing left but to try to stretch the fuel to reach the southern shore of the Gulf of St. Lawrence, where the airfield at Sydney was still open. Katharine had been enjoying her ride in the plastic nose of her father's Fortress, but now the pilot, Maj. Robert Kimmel, told the generals they had better get the passengers ready for ditching, just in case. He was not sure he had enough fuel to reach Sydney. As it happened, they barely made it, with the tanks running dry just as they were taxiing across the field toward the parking apron.[14] After refueling, they continued their journey and arrived in mid-morning at what is now Washington National Airport. Ruth and Carla met them there with a joyous reception before they all went home to Alexandria for a celebration.[15]

Tooey was home again, but not for long. Hap Arnold did not like the way things had been going in the Pacific and wanted to send Spaatz immediately to take over the growing strategic air forces. But he did allow him a week of rest at Miami Beach with the whole family, including Rebecca and the two grandchildren. The USAAF had taken over a hotel on the shore for a recuperation center, and they all were given quarters there. There was time for plenty of sun and even a little fishing.

In mid-July, the family returned to Washington. On the 16th, while President Truman was in Potsdam, the atomic bomb was tested successfully at Alamagordo, and plans were made to use it against Japan. The Army's chief of the project, Maj. Gen. Leslie M. Groves, came to Washington to brief Spaatz on the new weapon and to help work out the directive for its employment.[16] Spaatz insisted on receiving a written order for using the bomb. Since General Marshall was at Potsdam with the president, his deputy, Lt. Gen. Thomas Handy, wrote it. The wording of the directive was cleared with Marshall and the president in Germany. Although the letter explicitly stated that Spaatz was to order the dropping of the bomb "after about 3 August . . . ," there was an arrangement whereby the president could countermand the order were the Japanese to respond favorably to the Potsdam ultimatum.[17]

Following these briefings, Tooey left Washington. He and Ruth flew across the country where she saw him off from Hamilton Field. After their goodbyes she went south to visit her mother, still living in California, while Spaatz winged his way to his new headquarters on Guam.[18] Arriving there on 29 July, he found the Superfortress organization under a full head of steam and growing fast.[19]

## Reorganization in the Pacific

The arena into which Spaatz flew was one that required the utmost of diplomatic as well as military skill. Command of the American forces in the Pacific was divided between Admiral Nimitz in the center and General MacArthur in the south. By the time Spaatz landed on Guam, both commanders had completed successful thrusts across the Pacific. Nimitz's forces had taken Okinawa a month earlier, while MacArthur's liberation of the Philippines preceded Spaatz's arrival by three weeks. There was some apprehension among naval leaders that the soldiers, who had their way in Europe, would now try to change the rules in the Pacific. Spaatz, located in Nimitz's area and dependent on the Navy for much of his logistical support, would have to deal with these sensitivities. In addition, MacArthur and some of his staff resented those units coming from Europe. For years, they felt, they had taken second place to the fight against Hitler. To make matters worse, most of the big names in the European theater—Eisenhower, Bradley, Spaatz, Patton— had been junior officers in the thirties when MacArthur was chief of staff.

One of Hap Arnold's main goals since the 1930s had been to establish central control of airpower, ideally in the form of a separate service but, short of that, at least at the theater level. Spaatz had shared that goal all the way, but it was an uphill struggle. The GHQ air force in the thirties had gathered most of the Army's air combat power under one commander, but that experiment collapsed when the war started. All through the war, Arnold and Spaatz had been resisting pressures for further fragmentation. They thought they had made some progress in the African and Mediterranean campaigns with the creation of the Northwest African Air Force and the Mediterranean Allied Air Forces, but when the scene of the main action shifted to the north and to OVER-LORD, it proved impossible to push centralization as far as Arnold would have liked. In fact, the organization for OVERLORD appeared to be a step backward. The best that Arnold could achieve in Europe was a single commander for the American strategic forces operating out of Italy and England, and even at that, both the European and Mediterranean theater commanders were entitled to call for the aid of the heavy bombers whenever they deemed that a tactical emergency existed. Arnold hoped that he would enjoy greater success in the Pacific.

In November 1944, before the Ardennes counteroffensive had dashed Allied hopes for a pre-Christmas victory, Spaatz presented his ideas to Arnold on reorganizing the air effort in the Pacific. Notwithstanding the limitations of USSTAF in Europe, Spaatz thought the organization had been effective and a similar arrangement would work well in the Pacific. He proposed a new headquarters in the Pacific to centralize control of all the strategic land-based airpower and to coordinate its use against strategic targets in Japan with the carrier attacks against the same objectives. Spaatz envisioned a command that would not only handle the operations of the new B-29s coming into action, but that would also gather together all the Fortresses and Liberators from the theater commanders and the RAF heavy bombers that would be deployed to the Pacific once Hitler was gone. The theater commanders would retain operational control of their tactical aircraft, but administrative functions would be handled by the new centralized air headquarters, as had been the case with USSTAF and Ninth Air Force operating in France.[20]

Arnold agreed with Spaatz's ideas and proposed to the Joint Chiefs a similar arrangement. He asked that one supreme commander be placed in charge of all the Allied forces deployed against Japan. Under that supreme commander would be three subordinates, one each for ground, sea, and air forces. All U.S. Army airpower, tactical and strategic, would come under one man at the theater headquarters.[21]

Conditions in the Pacific, however, presented some obstacles that had not been experienced in the European theater. One problem was that the theater commander for both the Mediterranean and OVERLORD campaigns had been an American. If there were to be a supreme commander in the Far East, the British would have a strong argument that he be a Briton, even though most of the forces being used against Japan were American.[22] An even greater barrier to Arnold's proposal was posed by the existing divided command. Nimitz and MacArthur were both stout-hearted men. Which of them should be the supreme commander? The invasion of Japan was approaching, and the glory accruing to the supreme commander, whoever he was, would do much for the future of his service. If the existing geographical division continued unchanged, the top job would go to Nimitz since Japan lay within his theater. But the invasion of the Japanese home islands would be quite different from the seizure of the numerous atolls which Nimitz had accomplished in his drive across the central Pacific. The bulk of the men for the invasion would be soldiers rather than Marines, and it was unlikely that George Marshall, Douglas MacArthur, or anyone else in the Army would agree to placing Nimitz in charge of the final attack.

The Joint Chiefs chose to retain the existing division of command, singling out neither MacArthur nor Nimitz for the top position. As a result, there continued to exist seven separate air forces fighting the Japanese, each reporting to a different commander through separate channels—an anathema to Arnold and Spaatz. Both MacArthur and Nimitz would have liked to add the B-29s to his own air force, but the airmen were convinced that the potential of the Superfortresses would be frittered away through such piecemeal commitment.[23] While Arnold was unable to achieve total centralization of air resources, he did succeed in keeping the B-29s out of the hands of either MacArthur or Nimitz by persuading the Joint Chiefs that he should control the Superfortresses directly from Washington.

The instrument for this control was the Twentieth Air Force, which began operations from the Marianas in November, 1944. There was a feeling among ground officers in Washington that the operational control of Twentieth Air Force from the capital was too cumbersome, and the day-to-day work of that organization should be controlled on the scene of the action, as was the case with all the other military organizations in the theater. But the chief obstacle to overall reorganization remained the Joint Chiefs' hesitancy to designate a single commander for the whole theater. Throughout the winter of 1944–45, George Marshall had tried to resolve these problems, and though Arnold's staff had fashioned an air reorganization plan, Arnold could not press it until action had been taken on Marshall's proposals.[24]

Meanwhile, one of Spaatz's old friends from Ellington and Selfridge days, Lt. Gen. Millard F. Harmon, was serving as Arnold's agent in the central Pacific and his on-scene manager of the B-29 program. Harmon held two positions. First, as commander of the Army Air Forces Pacific Ocean Area (AAFPOA), he was Nimitz's land-based air commander, principally for Seventh Air Force. At the same time, he was Arnold's deputy commander of Twentieth Air Force, charged with getting things ready for the inbound Superfortress units.

In the first months of 1945, two events hastened the need for organizational change. First, the war had moved westward from the central Pacific, and it was becoming harder for Seventh Air Force to carry out its logistical responsibilities in the rear while it was operating far to the west. Second, Harmon, who had become the keystone of the whole Pacific B-29 program, was killed in an air crash near Kwajalein in February 1945.[25]

At about the time of Harmon's death, Arnold suffered a heart attack, creating a command crisis in the USAAF. Arnold's Chief of the Air Staff, Barney Giles, was sent to replace Harmon, and Eaker was called back from the Mediterranean to fill Giles's post.

Giles's assignment was not altogether satisfactory. He lacked the combat experience that would justify putting him over men like LeMay (and later Doolittle and Twining), and he had neither the rank nor the prestige to hold his own with Nimitz and MacArthur. This latter factor was important, for Arnold was trying to build up the image that the air branch of the armed forces ought to be equal to the sea and ground forces at all levels. Arnold recovered from his heart attack fairly quickly and in May decided to send Spaatz out as head of a new command to consolidate at least the strategic air operations against Japan. Robert Lovett travelled to Europe in May and so informed Spaatz.[26]

In June, Arnold flew to Manila to enlist the support of MacArthur and Nimitz for his reorganization plan. Nimitz raised no objection, but MacArthur was not as easy. He was never one given to letting parts of his empire slip through his fingers, but Arnold sensed that his objection was not so much to the proposed organization of a new strategic air headquarters at Guam as it was to the notion of Carl Spaatz commanding it.[27] MacArthur's relationship with his airman, George Kenney, was good, and the latter was senior to Spaatz by a few days. It is likely that MacArthur was concerned lest Spaatz's reputation dim the lustre of his own protege. It is certain that there was resentment around his headquarters toward those coming from Europe to help defeat Japan. Also, Spaatz was closely identified with Eisenhower, and it is possible that did little to enhance his standing with MacArthur. Whatever the source of the opposition, it is doubtful that it arose from any particular personality conflict. MacArthur had been a member of the court during the trial of Billy Mitchell, and though Spaatz had been rather outspoken in his testimony on Mitchell's behalf, MacArthur many years later said that he himself had favored Mitchell.[28]

Returning from the Pacific, Arnold won JCS concurrence for a reorganization, but for one substantially weaker than that originally envisioned by Spaatz. There would be a strategic headquarters on Guam, to be known as the U.S. Army Strategic Air Forces (USASTAF) with Spaatz in command and reporting directly to Arnold. This new headquarters was not to control all the strategic air operations against Japan, but rather only those conducted by the B-29s. MacArthur and Kenney would retain their Fortresses and Liberators, and Spaatz would have to coordinate his operations with them. The Navy, too, would be making carrier strikes against strategic targets, and here again Spaatz was given only a coordinating function. The proposal that USASTAF would be responsible for the administrative command functions of all the air forces in the Pacific was not accepted. The logistical arrangements were left vague and unsatisfactory. USASTAF would be responsible for its own "internal" logistics, and the theater command would provide the "external" logistics. Nimitz would bring in the bombs and the fuel for the B-29s, but beyond that, the definitions of "internal" and "external" were not very clear.[29]

Spaatz's new command would be composed of Twining's Twentieth Air Force of five B-29 wings and a fighter command based in the Marianas, and Doolittle's redeployed Eighth Air Force, with an identical structure, located on Okinawa. Each of these air forces was to have 720 B-29s, but the crews of one group of bombers in the Twentieth (the 509th Composite Group) were to be especially trained to deliver atom bombs. The USASTAF was to be responsible for[30]

> . . . the conduct of land-based strategic air operations against Japan with the object of accomplishing the progressive destruction and dislocation of Japan's military, industrial, and economic system to a point where her capacity for armed resistance is fatally weakened.

A great deal of airpower in the Pacific remained outside Spaatz's control. But the B-29s, which both he and Arnold considered the critical striking force, were centralized in USASTAF. Further, the arrangement was an achievement in a negative sense, keeping the Superfortresses out of the hands of MacArthur and Kenney. Arnold and Spaatz hoped that Japan would be brought down without an invasion. Should that occur, the Superfortresses would be one of the principal elements in her surrender, strengthening the case for a separate air force.

## The Superfortresses

The initial decision to acquire the B-29 Superfortress was made before the war while Spaatz was still on Arnold's Air Staff. First, as Chief of Plans Division and later as Chief of the Air Staff, he recognized both the promise and the problems of the airplane. The initial specifications were provided to Boeing in January 1940, and the prototypes flew in 1942. The first seven production aircraft were delivered in the summer of 1943. The B-29 was twice as heavy as the B-17, but its engines did not have quite double the horsepower. Yet its performance was substantially superior because of improved aerodynamic design. The program consumed immense resources in a time of extreme scarcity. Though the airplane held great promise, the development program had troubles. It was the first pressurized bomber, and its fire control system was advanced beyond those of any of the other bombers of World War II. All of its guns, except those in the tail, were fired by a remote control system and aimed by advanced sights. In some versions, there were twin 20-millimeter guns in the tail, and the best model had a range of over five thousand miles.[31] The engines were larger and more complex than any used before, and the fuel injection system for a time was prone to cause fires that were difficult for the crews to extinguish.[32]

Arnold had gambled and was banking heavily on the success of the B-29s. He gave Boeing a very large order before the airplane had gone through its conventional flight tests. By 1944, he was working hard to make sure that the Superfortresses got into combat and demonstrated the value of airpower.[33] He saw their success as providing valuable ammunition in the coming battle for an independent air force. In September 1944, he expressed this concern in a letter to Spaatz in Europe:[34]

> I want you to know that I am very appreciative of the way that you have handled my request for additional personnel over here for the B-29s. There will be additional requests from time to time, for the B-29s are coming out quite rapidly, and if we are to get a place in the sun at

all in the Pacific war, in my opinion, it will have to be through the B-29s. As I wrote to you before, everything coming out of the Pacific now is "Navy, Navy, Navy." It will be a long time before we will have bases sufficiently close to make direct attacks on Japan with the heavy bombers—Fortresses or the 24s. Accordingly, I must create the strongest possible Very Heavy Bomber [B-29] force that we can get . . .

The first B-29s were delivered to the USAAF in the summer of 1943 and, pending the seizure of Pacific islands closer to the Japanese homeland, were sent to bases in India the following spring. From there they were to stage through fields in China for strikes against steel facilities in Kyushu and Manchuria.[35] A few missions were flown against Japan, but the bombing accuracy was poor, the damage light, and the losses higher than they should have been. In January 1945, the Superfortresses were pulled out of India and sent to join those on the Mariana Islands of Guam, Tinian, and Saipan. The initial B-29 campaign had failed, increasing even further Arnold's eagerness for good results.[36]

Soon after the Marianas were seized in the summer of 1944, the first B-29s arrived there from the U.S., commanded by Brig. Gen. Haywood Hansell, an author of AWPD-1 and experienced in strategic bombing against Germany. Their first missions were launched against Japan in November 1944. The number of bombers was still small and, since Iwo Jima was still in Japanese hands, the B-29s had to make their attacks without fighter escort—something contrary to the lessons learned in the battles against the Luftwaffe.[37]

The Japanese defenses were not nearly as formidable as had been the German, but they were still troublesome. The B-29s were operating too close to their range limits to make long detours around Iwo Jima, giving the Japanese warning of inbound attacks. The cloud cover over Japan was troublesome, and the weather offered some surprises as well. The existence of the jet stream, unknown at the time, made precision bombing from high altitudes impossible with the bombsights then in use. At times, wind speeds at altitude reached 200 knots. If the crews tried to bomb downwind, the target went through the sight so fast that the bombardier could not get set up quickly enough. If they tried it upwind, they were moving so slowly over the ground that they exposed themselves to the enemy counteraction too long. If they tried it crosswind, the drift caused by the high winds exceeded the limits of the bomb sights.[38] Although they were flying above the reach of Japanese antiaircraft artillery and fighters, the strain on the complex and new engine was substantial. Aircraft that had mechanical breakdowns or battle damage had a long way to go to get home. Despite these adverse circumstances, Arnold was impatient for results. When the B-29s arrived from India in January 1945, their commander, Maj. Gen. Curtis E. LeMay, replaced Hansell at the head of the XXI Bomber Command, the Superfortress unit on Guam.[39] Prior to Spaatz's July arrival on Guam, LeMay had abandoned attempts at precision bombing in favor of mass incendiary attacks on major Japanese cities, with devastating results.

## The Coming of the Atom Bomb

Spaatz was to show MacArthur and Nimitz his letter of instructions on dropping the first atom bomb, which he did immediately upon his arrival in the theater. He flew down to Manila on 1 August 1945. As Spaatz remembered it later, MacArthur reacted by saying that atom bombs would change warfare—with no particular explanation of what he meant by that.[40] Spaatz was back in the Marianas before the appointed hour for launching the first nuclear mission.

The unit charged with delivering the atom bomb was Col. Paul Tibbetts' 509th Bombardment Group, which had been training on Tinian for the mission since June 1945. Several practice strikes were made under actual combat conditions using TNT bombs shaped and weighted to resemble the atom weapon that was to be used on the second nuclear mission. The results of those practice attacks were good, and by 31 July, the first atom bomb was in place on the island and assembled so it could be employed on order (the final assembly was to be done in flight, to eliminate any explosion at the base in case of a crash on takeoff).[41]

There was some sentiment among airmen that the nuclear weapons ought not be used. Arnold is recorded as having raised doubts about the wisdom of doing so, at least partly because he felt that the conventional bombing campaign combined with the blockade would be sufficient to bring about Japan's capitulation without a costly invasion of the Japanese homeland and the attendant casualties.[42] As soon as he arrived on Guam, Spaatz toured the command and was briefed on the campaigns just past. He concluded that the Japanese were in a bad way and would soon give in, unless they were inclined to national suicide.[43] According to the recollections of his family, a part of the reason for his reluctance to take command of USASTAF in the first place arose from his revulsion over what had happened to the cities of Germany and his expectation of doing even worse to the Japanese.[44] As Spaatz later recalled, he agreed with Arnold that the invasion should be avoided if possible, but that conventional bombing would be enough to bring about that result.[45] Spaatz was not in on the decision to drop the first bomb, and his opinion had not been sought by either the Interim Committee, which the president had put together to advise him on the issue, nor by the president, who himself made the final decision.[46] In a 1962 interview, Spaatz said:[47]

> I told General Handy that I would not go out to the Pacific for the purpose assigned without notifying both Admiral Nimitz and General MacArthur with regard to the atomic bomb. That was relayed to General Marshall (at Potsdam) and the President and it was agreed that I should notify them. I also made further notification that I would not drop an atomic bomb on verbal orders—they had to be written—and this was accomplished.

He did not make clear in that interview his grounds for insisting on written orders and that MacArthur and Nimitz be advised, but he was explicit that his objections to the area bombing of German cities were technical rather than moral:[48]

> We always attacked only legitimate military targets (in Germany) with one exception—the capital of the hostile nation. Berlin was the administrative and communications center of Germany and therefore became a military target. Other than that, our targets were always military targets. Our stand was that we'd bomb only strategic targets—not areas. I believed that we could win the war more quickly that way. It wasn't for religious or moral reasons that I did not go along with urban area bombing.

Yet within the context of the entire interview a somewhat different image emerges. Spaatz implied that he thought it legitimate to use atom bombs, or any other weapons if necessary, for survival, but short of that, no more force than required should be used. Since his preference was to finish the war with conventional bombing, it is likely that he insisted on the written orders to emphasize that the moral choice was not his.

On 6 August 1945, Carl Spaatz ordered the *Enola Gay* (the name Tibbetts had given his B-29) and its crew to Japan to drop the bomb.[49] The mission was accomplished with more than the usual precision and a gun-type atom bomb was dropped on Hiroshima. Early in the afternoon, the crews were back at Tinian, where Spaatz pinned a Distinguished Service Cross on Colonel Tibbetts' flying suit and Silver Stars on those of the other crew members.[50]

During the next couple of days there was no word from the Japanese. Spaatz continued to send out small-to-moderate-sized bombing forces against Japan. Some of them dropped six million leaflets on the cities, and the message of hopelessness was also sent to the Japanese by radio transmitters on Tinian. During this waiting period, he called Washington and suggested that the next bomb be delivered on the outskirts of Tokyo or at some other spot where the damage would not be as devastating as it would be in the center of the urban areas still on his target list.[51] That did not bring about any changes. Instead, he received orders to proceed against one of the targets on the list, and the second atomic bomb mission was launched in the early hours of 9 August. It did not go as smoothly as the first because of the weather. Finally, however, the first implosion bomb exploded over Nagasaki. It was somewhat off its mark, but the results were nonetheless awesome.[52] Still, there was no answer from Tokyo.

On 10 August, the weather over Japan was poor enough that the bombing would have had to be done with radar. Spaatz cancelled the mission, feeling that bombing inaccuracy might upset whatever negotiations or deliberations were taking place among the Japanese decision makers. Although it was only a weather stand-down, speculation was widespread in the news media that it was a cease-fire associated with secret negotiations. On the next day, the 11th, the weather improved, and Spaatz released his force for more conventional bombing raids. The mission was recalled, however, after President Truman, reacting to speculation in the media on the cease-fire, ordered that any future missions as well as those already en route be cancelled. He did not want renewed speculation that the negotiations had broken down. As crowded as things were in the Marianas, this recall caused a good deal of confusion. Finally, on the 14th, Spaatz got the word that his force was released for more conventional bombing and that Arnold desired the grandest possible "finale." USASTAF put up 828 B-29s and 186 fighter escorts for attacks on Japan on the last day of the war, and all of them came home.[53] At long last, the militants within the Japanese elite had been overcome, and the fighting was ended.

## Wind-Up Operations

There was still much to be done before USASTAF could go home. There were demonstrations to be flown in support of the occupation troops going into Japan and in connection with the surrender ceremonies. Kenney had to requisition 250 C-54s from the Air Transport Command to move the 11th Airborne Division from the Philippines to the Atsugi airport on Honshu. The B-29s were also pressed into service in an airlift role. Kenney's troop carrier C-47s and C-46s could not be used because they did not have the fuel capacity to make the round trip to Japan, and there was no fuel to be had at Atsugi.[54]

As had been the case in Europe, the most urgent requirement was to get succor to the prisoners. However, intelligence on their locations and conditions was far from complete, and some of the work had to be postponed until the information was acquired from the Japanese themselves, who turned out to be generally cooperative on that and other points. Food and medicine were sent in, and even some beer and ice cream were air delivered. It was a wholly unaccustomed role for the B-29 crews, and the shortage of parachutes forced them to deliver some of the goods by "free-fall." Eight B-29s were lost in the course of this aerial resupply operation and one of them was a portent of things to come: it was fired upon by Russian fighters and was so badly damaged it crash-landed (fortunately without the loss of life).[55] The Russians claimed that the attack had been a mistake, which in those days was reasonable enough, since the same thing had happened over Germany in the closing hours of that war.

Numerous transport missions were flown by the Superfortresses from the Marianas in support of the people going to Japan for the surrender ceremony and for occupation duty. In the early days of peace, it was thought necessary to make a show of force over Japan, and B-29 formations with ammunition but no bombs were dispatched for that purpose. Many morale flights were flown during which the ground crewmen from the bases were given sightseeing trips around Japan. Finally, plans were drawn up for an aerial parade to take place immediately after the surrender was signed on the deck of the *Missouri*.

## The Surrender

Planning for the surrender was a complex affair. Appointment of the supreme commander, which had proved impossible during the war, was necessary when peace came. MacArthur was designated for the post and was immediately swamped with the protocol details of the ceremony. Both the British and the Russians were determined to get as impressive a delegation as possible onto the quarterdeck of the *Missouri*,[56] and every American on the far side of the International Dateline wanted to be there too.

MacArthur's party gathered in Okinawa on 29 August 1945, and

Spaatz arrived there from Guam that same day. The Allied delegation flew to Atsugi, an airport serving Yokohama, on the 30th in the company of planeloads of paratroopers, with B-29 formations passing overhead. The group drove to the New Grand Hotel in Yokohama along a route lined with Japanese guards, their backs to the road, not only as a security measure, but also as a sign of respect.[57] As with the route from Tempelhof to the surrender site in Berlin, the surrounding bomb devastation was awesome.[58]

The capitulation ceremonies were set for the morning of Sunday, 2 September 1945. The day was cool, the sky overcast. Spaatz and the rest of those invited to witness the ceremony were picked up from the quay at Yokohama before 8 A.M. and taken several miles to the anchorage of the battleship *Missouri,* flagship of Halsey's fleet. About 260 Allied ships crowded into the harbor. The Allied leaders came up the gangway on the starboard side, most of them gathering on the quarterdeck. MacArthur and Nimitz went into Halsey's cabin to pass the time until the arrival of the Japanese delegation from Tokyo. The ship's crew members were draped from various parts of her superstructure, overlooking the surrender site.[59]

Around 9 A.M., the destroyer carrying the Japanese delegation came alongside, and someone called the Allied generals to attention. There were some awkward moments as Foreign Minister Mamoru Shigemitsu, who had lost a leg in an assassination attempt before the war, struggled up the gangway. The enemy delegation was lined up in a box formation with their backs to the sea as MacArthur, Nimitz, and Halsey emerged from their cabin. Shigemitsu was the first to sign the surrender document, followed by the reluctant chief of the Japanese General Staff, Yoshioiro Umezu, who had been as militant as any in Japan's army and who had attended only at the insistence of the emperor himself. The reporters were better behaved here than they had been in Berlin, but one of the Allied officers, who had begun the victory celebration too early, marred the ceremony by making faces at Shigemitsu.[60] MacArthur then signed (using five different pens) as supreme allied commander, followed by Admiral Nimitz as the representative of the United States. They were followed by officers of each of the Allied countries. MacArthur then gave a short, eloquent speech, and, according to some reports, just at that point, the clouds parted and the sun shone through,[61] whereupon an air armada of 1,500 USN carrier planes and 462 Superfortresses roared by overhead to punctuate the end of World War II.[62]

## Evaluation of the Air Wars

Two months after the surrender ceremony on the *Missouri,* Arnold submitted a report on the activities of his command to the secretary of war.[63] Throughout, Arnold was careful not to claim too much. He never asserted that strategic airpower, or even airpower in general, was the decisive factor in either the European or the Pacific wars. When speaking of airpower in the war against Japan, he repeatedly emphasized that the term included both land- and carrier-based airplanes. But even as he tried to disarm his potential critics in that way, he built a major theme that if airpower cannot be said to have won the war alone, it nonetheless was critical to the success of surface battles. No land or sea campaign could be won without command of the air.[64]

Arnold made much of the effects of the oil attack and the destruction of the German railroads. While granting that the submarines had crippled the Japanese merchant marine before the fall of 1944, he nonetheless emphasized the importance of the B-29 attacks on the Japanese homeland. Arnold was strong in his insistence that the atomic bombs had not beaten Japan, but rather that the conventional bombing and blockade had already eliminated the need for an invasion before Hiroshima was destroyed. This critique of airpower stressed that the air arm should be reorganized as a separate service equal to the Army and the Navy, and that, for essential coordination, all three services be placed under a unified defense organization.

In one sense, Arnold's report was the "swan song" of a great airman. In another, it was the opening round in the legislative battle for air autonomy. As he had during the war, Arnold then sent out his most trusted agent, Carl Spaatz, to wield the weapons he himself had fashioned to achieve their common ends. Although Arnold was still in office, he had suffered several heart attacks and announced in November that he would retire in three months. Eaker had been in Washington since the spring, shouldering some of the burden, and now Spaatz was back in the capital to assume many of the responsibilities.

What was Spaatz's evaluation of the events just past? The long answer is contained in Arnold's report, with which he was in agreement. The short answer can be found in his article "Strategic Air Power: Fulfillment of a Concept," which he wrote just after Arnold retired in February 1946.[65] Spaatz was careful not to claim that strategic airpower alone had won the war and to give credit to the combined arms team. In his view, airpower "sparked" the victory of combined arms in Europe and, after the Army and Navy had conquered bases close enough to the vital targets in Japan, the B-29s administered the knockout blow:[66]

> Strategic airpower could not have won this war alone, without the surface forces. The circumstances of timing did not permit. The full potential of sufficient striking power was attained only in the winter of 1943–44. By 1944 much of German war industry was going underground. Further, the invasion by land was necessary. Thus, this war was won by the coordination of land, sea, and air forces, each of the Allies contributing its essential share to the victory. Airpower, however, was the spark to success in Europe. And it is interesting to note that Japan was reduced by air power, operating from bases captured by the coordination of land, sea, and air forces, and that she surrendered without the expected invasion becoming necessary.

In June 1947, Spaatz wrote:[67]

> In our victory over Japan, airpower was unquestionably decisive. That the planned invasion of the Japanese home islands was unnecessary is clear evidence that airpower has evolved into a force in war co-equal with land and sea power, decisive in its own right and worthy of the faith of its prophets.

For both Arnold and Spaatz, then, airpower had been decisive both in independent operations and in support of the Army and Navy. Both men emphasized the importance of time, asserting that the mistakes that the Germans had made could not be counted upon to be repeated in the future. The capabilities of aviation would continue to lessen the amount of time available for mobilization. The United States would be vulnerable, and instantly vulnerable. The implication of these air leaders was that the air arm had to be the first line of defense, ready on the first day of any future war.

These assertions by Arnold and Spaatz were not just idle rhetoric. Both leaders were so confident of what they said that they proposed establishment of the United States Strategic Bombing Survey (USSBS), an evaluation of their work by an agency outside the USAAF and not under their control.[68] The proposal for the survey was made early in 1944 to obtain unbiased data upon which to base attacks on Japan and organize a postwar national security system.[69] They would hardly have taken the initiative were there much doubt in their minds about the outcome.

Looking back on it two decades later, General Spaatz displayed limited enthusiasm for the survey, claiming that he had never read it. Had the United States lost, it would have meant more, but victory had been justification enough.[70] Nevertheless, the survey's evaluation of his work was in the main favorable. It explicitly favored precision bombing of vital targets and used strong words in saying an advanced industrial society could not long endure the loss of control of the air over its homeland. It claimed that airpower had been a decisive factor in the war against Hitler and in the one against Japan.[71]

The Strategic Bombing Survey was just as convinced of the importance of air superiority as were Spaatz and Arnold. The survey held that no operations on the ground, at sea, or in the air could hope to succeed in the long run without it.[72] Japan had understood at the outset that air superiority was needed for local campaigns, but she never realized the need for a coordinated and massive campaign to win general air superiority. In the end, Japan's military impotence was demonstrated to its citizens by the freedom with which the B-29s roamed the skies over Nippon.[73] Though the survey concluded that the surrender had been caused by the bombing, the blockade, the previous defeats of Japan, and the shock of the nuclear weapons, it was explicit in saying that the blockade and the bombing alone would have brought about the capitulation without the dreaded invasion,[74] as Arnold and Spaatz had asserted before the atom bombs were dropped.

The conclusions of the USSBS on the correctness of the precision bombing theory matched those of Spaatz: in general, precision bombing was to be much preferred over area bombing; the oil plan had been the best of the precision attacks (this pronouncement could hardly have been displeasing to Spaatz); the railroad assault, reaching its climax later, was also devastatingly effective; some of the other precision attacks had not had much of an effect for varying reasons; the rubber industry had been damaged severely in an incidental way, but that never became a bottleneck for the Germans; the ball-bearing attacks had had the potential for decisiveness, but would have required more massive attacks repeated more frequently in order to succeed; the attacks on the V-weapon launching sites and the concrete submarine pens were ineffective (again, Spaatz was probably not displeased by this conclusion).

As for Japan, the survey was not as enthusiastic as were some of the airmen about the incendiary raids, asserting that some of the precision attacks had been more effective than had been believed at the time.

Though Hansell's strikes against the aircraft plants and engine factories had been unimpressive in the amount of physical damage, they did provoke the Japanese into a dispersal program that was poorly planned and executed. This dispersal resulted in a reduced aircraft production from which the Japanese never recovered. This was not critical, however, because in Japan, as in Germany, the limiting factor was the shortage of trained pilots, not aircraft.[75]

In both Europe and Japan, the USSBS saw some missed opportunities. The German electrical power system, it said, had been vulnerable and potentially vital.[76] Some airmen responded that the targets were so small and hard to hit that it was not as vulnerable as the survey directors supposed. In Japan, the railroad system, vital to the functioning of the Japanese war machine, should have been attacked. Some of the survey members had come back to the U.S. during the summer of 1945 to advise the targeting people in Washington and to brief Spaatz on their findings and recommendations. They brought up the railroad suggestion to Spaatz, but Eaker saw a defect in the recommendation. At the moment, B-29s were the only planes that had sufficient range to hit the railroad system. The campaign in Europe, Eaker said, showed that the proper instruments for such targets were the medium and fighter bombers, which could not be used until they were in place on Okinawa.[77] In any event, the war ended before Spaatz could act on these recommendations.

Another major point made by the survey was that targets of potential decisiveness had to be hit accurately and repeatedly in order to realize the full effects[78]—something that was beyond the capability of Eighth Air Force in Eaker's time, but which was done under Spaatz in the case of the oil installations.

As for the nuclear weapons, the USSBS agreed that they had not been necessary for victory over Japan. It also said, however, that they may well be decisive in future wars. It recommended the creation of a separate air force coequal to the Army and Navy. The survey writers felt that a proper air force, nuclear-armed, might be enough to prevent the outbreak of war in the first place. This air force, they argued, should be integrated into a unified national security organization, supported by a comprehensive national system of intelligence.[79]

Planning for this independent air force, and getting it launched, would occupy Carl Spaatz for the remainder of his military career.

# Chapter XI

## CREATING THE AIR FORCE

In early September 1945 when Carl Spaatz returned to the United States from the Pacific aboard his B-17, the great air forces he had commanded in the battles against Germany and Japan were already beginning to disintegrate. Another kind of battle, over the independence of the Air Force and the unification of the armed forces, was brewing. Now came the task of transforming what had been a superbranch of the Army into an autonomous service with new institutions of its own. It had been almost thirty years since Spaatz had returned from the Pacific to attend pilot school at Rockwell Field. The Air Force that he was helping to shape would be to a large degree the organizational expression of his experiences during those three decades.

### The USAAF in 1945

In September 1945, when Spaatz got back to his home in Alexandria, Virginia, just a few miles from Washington, D.C., he was "bone tired" and wanted to retire.[1] Arnold's health continued to deteriorate, however, and it was clear that he could not continue in office for long. It was equally evident that critical changes were in the offing and that the nature of these changes would depend upon who was at the helm of the USAAF. Who, besides Spaatz, was available to succeed Arnold? George Kenney had four stars, was Douglas MacArthur's airman, and outranked Spaatz by a few days. He had the backing of MacArthur, but he was more experienced in the field of tactical than strategic aviation.

In addition, he was not as close to Arnold as Spaatz was. Eisenhower was slated to take over from Marshall as Chief of Staff of the Army; he and Kenney were not well acquainted, but Spaatz had long been a comrade in arms. Joseph McNarney also had achieved four stars and was on good terms with George Marshall, but he was more a staff man than a commander and had not had much experience with strategic bombing during the war. That experience was important since it formed the keystone of the quest for an autonomous air force.

Arnold persuaded Tooey to postpone retirement until the battle for autonomy was won.[2] McNarney remained for awhile as Allied air commander in the Mediterranean and then returned to the U.S. to head the logistical element of the Air Force. Kenney received a consolation prize:[3]

> The prospects for a United Nations force were considered so good that ambitious General George Kenney, Air Force commander under MacArthur in the Pacific, wanted General Marshall and General Arnold to make a commitment for him to be commander of the United Nations air forces in return for his "letting" General Spaatz take command of the Army Air Forces after the war.

Whatever Kenney's perception of his own power, the advocacy of Eisenhower and Arnold, along with Spaatz's reputation as the most experienced practitioner of strategic bombing in the American air forces, carried much weight. On 12 December, Secretary of War Robert Patterson informed the president that Eisenhower wanted Spaatz to replace Arnold, adding his own concurrence.[4] Though Arnold was not to retire officially for two months, Spaatz had been acting as the commanding general since September. But what was he commanding? The U.S. Army Air Forces were demobilizing so rapidly it seemed they would disappear entirely before they could stabilize at some undefined peacetime level.

At the time of the Japanese surrender, the USAAF had 2,253,000 men. During October 1945 alone, the service discharged 439,093 of them. The slide was to continue until, by the end of May 1947, its total strength was down to 303,614![5] By December 1946, Spaatz was to complain that because of the loss of so many trained personnel, only two of the AAF's groups were combat-ready, down from a force that only eighteen months earlier had been striking the enemy with more than two hundred groups.[6]

During the last year of the war, Arnold had part of his staff busy planning for the peace. They had at first envisioned an air force of more than a million men and over a hundred combat groups. By the time Spaatz returned from Japan, George Marshall had imposed more realistic budget figures on the air planners, and the goal had been reduced to seventy combat groups, but even that had not been accepted by the political authorities. Still, that was to be the figure that Spaatz adopted as the minimum to maintain national security. Even before he officially took over the USAAF, however, the actual figure had fallen far below that.

The numbers and conditions of planes were equally discouraging. By October 1946, only 18 percent of the aircraft in the Army Air Forces were in condition to fly, and the number on hand was radically smaller than it had been a year earlier.[7] Although there were numerous surplus airplanes stored in Arizona and elsewhere, which could have been brought back into service in an emergency, the problem of obsolescence remained. The jet revolution was underway, and airmen were thinking of interconti-nental and transpolar flight, reviving the escort problem. The only potential adversary in the foreseeable future was the USSR, whose vital targets were so far inland that even the B-29 could not hope to cover them all from bases in the American homeland. The jet bombers coming along might be able to overcome the penetration difficulty with their speed, but their fuel consumption was so high that they could not develop the necessary reach.[8]

It was more than just changing aviation technology, however, that brought into question the worth of the Liberators and Fortresses waiting in reserve in the Arizona sun. There was the question of what effect the advent of the atomic bomb would have on air strategy, in general, and on the nature of the new Air Force. Spaatz many years later admitted that neither the meaning of the nuclear weapons nor that of missiles had been assimilated by the air planners at the time they drew up their initial programs for the size and organization of the postwar air force.[9] Events had tumbled upon them so rapidly in 1945 that it was beyond human ability to assimilate *all* of the implications of the atom bomb in time for the demobilization and initial peacetime legislative battles. For the airmen, the coming of nuclear weapons only confirmed the validity of the strategic bombing doctrine, and if the B-29 were the only vehicle that could possibly deliver them, then that was all to the good.[10]

The U.S. capability for nuclear war was far less when Spaatz took over than most laymen realized. The bombs were not numerous, and the control measures were such that the assembly and dispatch of the weapons would have been cumbersome indeed. During the winter of 1945–46, only a few B-29s had been modified to carry atomic bombs, and crews qualified for that mission were in equally short supply. The Superfortresses were incapable of reaching vital targets in the USSR from bases in the U.S., and those equipped for atomic bombs were prohibited from leaving the national territory. Strategic plans for the employment of atomic bombs simply did not exist at the time Spaatz became the commanding general.[11]

It is to his everlasting credit that Hap Arnold understood the urgency of codifying for the coming Air Force a set of basic ideas about airpower which incorporated jet aircraft, guided missiles, and nuclear weapons. No sooner had Spaatz returned to Washington than the chief of staff put him to work heading a committee to determine the meaning of the atom bomb to America and the USAAF. That Lauris Norstad and Hoyt Vandenberg were two other members of the group is another indication of the importance that Arnold attached to the issue. Two of the three were to serve as Chief of Staff of the U.S. Air Force and the third as the only airman ever placed in command of NATO's armed forces. The board met through September and October, 1945. It produced a report that provides insight into the notions that governed the initial organization and equipping of the autonomous air force.[12]

Spaatz, Norstad, and Vandenberg explicitly assumed that: the secret of atomic bombs could not be preserved; other nations would soon have delivery systems comparable to that of the United States; no one would risk war with the U.S. unless they possessed an equal or greater number of weapons; America could find overseas bases for her planes; the heavy bomber would continue as the main delivery vehicle for ten years or so; a stockpile of nuclear weapons would be available for war; and *there would be no time for mobilization after the onset of future wars.*[13]

One of the items listed by the Spaatz Board draft report as a "Fact Bearing on the Problem" was really an assumption that was not to hold up. It held that "The minimum weight and dimensions of the atomic bomb are not generally fixed for technical reasons and no major changes are expected in the near future." Another such "fact" was "The bomb is enormously expensive and definitely limited in availability." Though it was not so stated in the draft, one of the implicit assumptions was that any future wars would commence with an unannounced attack, and that it would come by air. Another that was not explicit in the report, but was well understood in the Army, was the notion that the U.S. could not or would not maintain a large standing army.[14]

Although the Spaatz Board report did not address doctrine directly, nothing in its report questioned the validity of the doctrine that had evolved from the battle against Germany. The authors thought the bomber could penetrate enemy air space, escorts would be necessary to make it economical to do so, and precision methods would have to be used in striking targets. The atom bombs were assumed to be so few and so expensive that conventional bombing would still be necessary against many categories of targets. Notwithstanding the fire bombing of Tokyo and other Japanese cities, there was little indication in the report that area bombing had gained favor among its writers.

Because future wars would commence without declaration, and because air attack would come suddenly, the board concluded that the peacetime Air Force would have to be a standing one—there would be no time for mobilization and training of reserves. Though the notion of deterrence was not yet clearly delineated, the idea was germinating among the members of the Spaatz Board even in the fall of 1945.[15] Their assumptions on the size and expense of nuclear weapons practically precluded discussion of tactical airpower from their proceedings.

Although the marriage of the facts and assumptions about the postwar world with ideas on air theory and doctrine did not produce a strategy, the Spaatz Board did make some explicit recommendations to Arnold. First, the board told him that the invention of the atomic bomb "does not at this time warrant a material change in our present conception of the employment, size, organization, and composition of the post-war Air Force." Seventy groups would still be the goal. The atom bomb, it said, only enhances the validity of the strategic bombing doctrine. The requirement for World War II-type conventional strategic bombing forces would continue because there were many targets not appropriate for atomic weapons. Overseas bases were a "must" for the combat effectiveness of the air arm and for the security of the United States. Though Spaatz and his colleagues were not explicit, they also concluded that alterations to the organization for national defense were needed to make it more adaptable to future changes in weapons technology. They emphasized strongly that vast improvement was needed in the American system for producing timely intelligence and that the United States must stay ahead of the rest of the world in research and development. The need for this latter was so urgent that the immediate appointment of a senior officer to take charge of the Air Force's part in nuclear development and all other research and development was proposed[16]—and when implemented, the man selected was Curtis E. LeMay, who became the Deputy Chief of Staff for Research and Development. That was about as far as the Spaatz Board could go with specific recommendations. The political leaders had yet to provide the armed forces with national objectives upon which to base their strategic planning.[17] It was not even politic yet for officers in responsible positions, including Spaatz, to suggest publicly that the USSR might be a potential enemy.[18] Operating under those limitations and preoccupied with the struggles over unification, an independent air force, and the division of a radically declining defense budget, it was little wonder that no strategic plan emerged for quite some time after World War II.

## Unification and Autonomy

While he was chairing this board, Spaatz was appointed by Arnold to head another committee to handle affairs related to unification. As officer-in-charge, he became the single point of contact in the AAF for all unification items. At the same time, a group of important civilians was organizing to promote unification and an autonomous air force. Arnold also designated several different committees to handle the USAAF's relationships with various elements of the media on subjects related to the reorganization of the defense structure.[19]

Views on unification and a separate air force were shaped along service lines. The U.S. Navy was on the defensive at the outset. At first it opposed change more than did the Army and the USAAF. The Navy feared that if a third service were created, there would be a strong tendency for the Army and the new Air Force to combine against the interests of the sea service and be able to continually win with a 2:1 majority. The result for the Navy might be the loss of its air arm and the U.S. Marine Corps.[20]

George Marshall, on the other hand, thought that the Army would inevitably be in the inferior position for the budget wars of the postwar years if there continued to be just two branches, because of the glamor of the Navy and the strength of its position in Congress. Marshall, therefore, hoped to organize all the armed forces into a single department so that the defense budget could be hammered out inside the services before it became an issue for the politicians. He felt that the ground Army would have a better chance of getting its fair share of appropriations under those circumstances.[21] For the same reason, the Army would have liked to limit the size and the functions of the Marine Corps and to deny it armor and artillery units altogether.[22]

The main goal of Arnold and Spaatz was to achieve a separate Air Force equal to the Army and Navy. They preferred that it come about as part of a single national military establishment; but, if necessary, would have settled for a system of three different military departments in order to achieve their main goal. As a corollary to the autonomous Air Force, Spaatz and Arnold wanted the strategic air mission to be assigned exclusively to the emergent Air Force.[23] Those items were not much subject to compromise for the airmen. They did assert publicly that they did not intend to deprive the Navy of its air arm, but in their statements the division between the naval and air functions was somewhat hazy. The declared goal for the airmen was that the new Air Force would control all land-based aviation to include antisubmarine warfare and overwater reconnaissance, but the Navy would retain all its waterborne and shipborne aviation. Generally, whether for tactical reasons or otherwise, the officers of the AAF supported the Army positions on strengthening the new national military establishment and on abolishing the Marine Corps.[24]

The airmen argued that the strategic air mission would become ever more crucial in the future and that it must therefore be unified under one command. So unified, it would be the single user of large, long-range aircraft. This being so, the desire for economy through the avoidance of duplication meant that all land-based aviation should be under the centralized control of a new and equal Air Force.[25]

In the fall, the Navy and Army each prepared a reorganization proposal reflecting its own position. The Navy's Eberstadt Plan advocated a separate Air Force, a centralized intelligence function, and legalization of the Joint Chiefs of Staff. It opposed a strong single military department, however, arguing that a strong defense secretary would repress initiative and tend to be antidemocratic. The Army's counterproposal, prepared under the direction of Lt. Gen. J. Lawton Collins, called for a single military department composed of three branches and headed by a strong secretary. Although it allowed the Navy to retain its air arm and the Marine Corps, it recommended that the new Air Force control all land-based aviation.

Marshall was adamant in his contention that a strong national military agency was needed to unify the efforts of the services, and Spaatz supported that notion along with Collins' plan. The Collins Plan was clearly much closer to the position of the president, and it received a big boost from Eisenhower, who was returning from his occupation duties in Europe. He was foursquare behind the Army position on unification and was one of the strongest advocates the airmen had outside their own ranks.[26]

Little progress was made through the fall, and President Truman grew impatient. In December, he tried to accelerate the process by sending his own proposal directly to Congress.[27] The president's message was a cause of satisfaction for Spaatz and the rest of the USAAF, but for chagrin among the Navy leaders. The president had given Navy Secretary James Forrestal little chance to comment on the draft of his message before it was delivered, and its strong tone and the degree to which it favored the Army-USAAF position upset the Navy leaders.

By April, Senator Elbert Thomas, assisted by Maj. Gen. Lauris Norstad and Rear Adm. Arthur Radford, had drafted and introduced into the Senate a unification bill along the lines of Truman's message. The debate quickly reached the pitch of the previous fall, and it was clear that Forrestal and the Navy were not yet ready to throw in the towel.

By this time, some of the principal actors had changed. Marshall was replaced as Chief of Staff of the Army by Eisenhower in the fall of 1945, and Arnold had officially retired in February and gone to California to live. Spaatz was Commanding General of the Army Air Forces. W. Stuart Symington, Assistant Secretary of War for Air, had been charged by Secretary of War Robert Patterson to present the War Department's case for unification to Congress and the public. Symington delegated Spaatz and his staff to define the goals of the new Air Force and fashion detailed plans for their achievement so he could take them into the congressional arena and, before the president and the Bureau of the Budget, argue the case for the air arm.[28]

Spaatz had plenty to think about besides winning independence for the air arm. To aid him in building the case for Symington to carry into the legislative fray, he created an Air Board in the spring of 1946, placing at its head Maj. Gen. Hugh Knerr, who had graduated from the Naval Academy well before Spaatz and Eisenhower had emerged from West Point. Assisting Knerr were some operations commanders, important civilians, and some retired officers. Spaatz felt that policy should be decided at the senior levels and not always percolate up from the staffs below. He tried to include rapid advancement possibilities in the initial personnel policy of the new USAF, but his attitude was not a "knee-jerk" obsession with youth. He could take good ideas wherever he found them. He charged the Air Board to develop policy for execution by the Air Staff and commands. Although the priorities were unification and the organization of an independent air force, he also directed Knerr to examine the history of the Second World War to develop some "lessons" for the future.[29]

Forrestal was still unhappy with the draft bill. The president made another attempt to break the deadlock with a 13 May White House conference with Patterson and Forrestal. Spaatz was present and, in his view, little was settled. Notwithstanding his assurances and those of the president that the Navy would retain its fleet air arm, the question of the control of land-based reconnaissance and antisubmarine organizations was still beyond settlement. The Army and Navy failed to find common ground on the issue of the Marine Corps. Truman did not give ground on the strong powers he wanted for the secretary of defense,[30] and Spaatz also remained firm on that issue. By this time, it was plain that there would be a separate Air Force, but it was equally obvious that there would be large elements of airpower outside its jurisdiction. There was little doubt that there would also be a single department as desired by the Army and USAAF, but the powers to be exercised by its head were still undefined, and it seemed likely that they would be much weaker than Spaatz and Symington desired.

While Congress was in adjournment for the November election campaign, Forrestal called an informal meeting of the principals at his home, during which the way was cleared for agreement. General Norstad and Admiral Sherman were appointed to work out the details concerning the powers of the new secretary of defense and the exact definition of service roles and missions. The scheme they worked out was for upcoming legislation to define the organization of defense, while the roles and missions of the services would be set down separately by executive order simultaneously with the passage of the unification act. There would be a separate Air Force and a single National Military Establishment. But the Navy had its way on the land-based aviation issue almost completely, and had so limited the powers of the secretary of defense that they amounted to the "coordination" Forrestal had been demanding. If Spaatz had been despondent, he would not have been likely to let it show, even to his inner circle of friends. But neither did he betray much of a sense of triumph. From his retirement, Arnold wrote to him complaining that the USAAF appeared to have done most of the compromising in the Norstad-Sherman agreement. Spaatz replied:[31]

> With reference to the unification compromise, I suppose there will always be a controversy over who-got-what out of the agreement. The fact that each interested party feels that the other got the best break is probably the strongest argument in favor of the soundness of the agreed scheme. So far as the Air Force is concerned, we will, under the proposed arrangement, achieve the position of independence and parity with the other services. I feel that the aircraft, air facilities, and air functions not under the Air Force are at least under a top authority who can insure that they are not misapplied or used to establish a basis of encroachment on the proper activities of the Air Force. We believe that the agreement, when implemented by legislation, will be a forward step for the Air Force and will represent marked progress in the operating efficiency and economy of our Armed Forces.

If Spaatz had felt this latest proposal a great triumph, even as taciturn as he was, one would have expected stronger terms than "a forward step" and "marked progress."

As the draft act worked its way through Congress, little was done to strengthen the prospective National Military Establishment, or widen the scope of the new Air Force, but Symington and Spaatz did what they could to prevent weakening them. Forrestal was one of the early witnesses in the Senate, and he warned that the draft compromise was a delicately balanced thing and the whole structure might be wrecked by changes to any part of it.[32]

Eisenhower and Spaatz both went up to Capitol Hill to testify for the bill on 25 March 1947. Both were very much in favor of it in their testimony. Some of the senators worked on Eisenhower during the questioning with respect to the absence of explicit and detailed provisions on roles and missions in the draft bill. Clearly interested in protecting the status of the U.S. Marine Corps and naval aviation, the senators tried to lead Eisenhower into saying that such details ought to be included in the legislation. But he persistently held that general statements on the functions of the various services would not be objectionable, but that they ought to be limited to the "basics"—flexibility should be retained.[33]

Spaatz followed Eisenhower, and his prepared statement was substantially shorter. It was along the same lines, with perhaps more emphasis on the need for an autonomous Air Force (though Eisenhower had been stalwart on that point). In both his statement and in the questioning that followed, Spaatz repeatedly asserted the importance of not weakening the powers of the prospective secretary of defense. He held that were the powers outlined in the bill retained, then the security of the United States would be improved and, over the long run, it would be maintained at a lower cost than would otherwise be possible.

Some of the senators asked both Eisenhower and Spaatz to specify the economies that would immediately arise from the bill before the legislature, and neither would do so. Spaatz was questioned about whether the assignment of some of the research and development responsibilities to agencies of the proposed National Military Establishment would not fly in the face of the rationale for a separate Air Force. Hadn't one of the complaints during the 1930s been that airpower could not be properly developed as long as the War Department controlled the function and was made up of people who could not understand war in the air? Spaatz explained that the Air Force would be allotted its research and development funds and through control of these monies would be able to supervise research and development done by outside organizations. The example he used was the need for a hypothetical new fuse for bombs. The Air Force would not set up an agency that would duplicate munitions research and development in the Army, but rather arrange for such a fuse to be developed in an existing organization. It would be able to negotiate with that agency to get the proper service because of its control of funds.[34]

One of the senators tried to lead Spaatz into criticizing the Army's General Staff. Spaatz replied that he had been actively engaged in the promotion of aviation since 1915 and that from 1924 onward, from the time of Mitchell, he had believed that airpower would be the "most effective arm of offense and defense . . ." Spaatz said that the Army General Staff had not been sold on an expansion of the air arm until 1939. Senator Mahoney asked, "Is it not a fact that the development of aviation was retarded for the simple reason that the War Department and the General Staff did not really comprehend what it could do for many years?" Spaatz well understood that whatever the situation before 1939, the War Department and the airmen were *now* on the same side of the argument. He was reluctant to be too critical, but the Senator pressed him, and he finally avowed that, "I do not believe that the

General Staff in the days before the war had a proper appreciation of the role that airpower was going to play in World War II.'' The questioner then asked Spaatz if that were the reason he was supporting the present bill and the general replied: ''I feel that I would be negligent in my duty to the country if I did not say that if the air force is not set up on an autonomous basis that the country may well go back in future years to where it was before World War II with the air neglected.'' That satisfied the senator, who ended the discussion with, ''I thought that would be your answer. Thank you, General.''[35]

Though some opposition to the proposed act was still voiced by retired naval officers, and even some active duty ones, no radical change was made during the legislative process. Such amendments as there were generally were designed to protect the U.S. Marine Corps' functions and size, to preserve naval aviation, and to limit the powers of the new secretary of defense. Some of the individuals associated with the Navy still testified that the Air Force ought not be created because it would ''institutionalize'' the strategic bombing mission and that mission was not a viable one. But Congress persisted in that and most of the other parts of the Norstad-Sherman agreement. It also resisted pleas that the roles and missions be written into the law and, if Spaatz had to face the fact that the Navy had kept its land-based aviation, at least the way it would be used had not been set in concrete by law. By midsummer, the testifying and amending were over, the National Security Act was passed, and Truman signed it in July.[36]

Once the National Security Act of 1947 became the law of the land, it fell to Truman to staff the new structure. He offered the post at the apex of the National Military Establishment* to Patterson, who refused it. Instead, James Forrestal was appointed. He had, of course, been doing everything he could to limit or weaken the powers of the prospective office, while W. Stuart Symington and Carl Spaatz would have liked to have made it stronger. In September, Symington and Spaatz were appointed as Secretary and Chief of Staff of the Air Force, respectively.

The president had issued the executive order on roles and missions at the same time as he signed the act, but the order was not precisely worded and differing interpretations soon arose. The problem was further complicated by Truman's determination to limit the size of the defense budget and Forrestal's determination that the few funds allotted would

---

*It would become the Department of Defense two years later.

be split more or less evenly among the three services. President Truman's Air Policy Commission (Finletter Commission) met that fall and gave very strong support to the need for a seventy-group Air Force, and the congressional Brewster Committee seconded the conclusions that same winter. That fueled Spaatz's determination to get more than the "balanced" one-third of the defense budget for the Air Force, which he now deemed to be the new first line of defense. But the admirals were far from prepared to concede that point.

Forrestal found that his office lacked the power to mandate solutions to these problems, so in exasperation he ordered all the service chiefs to meet with him in early March, 1948, at Key West, Florida, to reach agreements. Spaatz attended, seconded by Vandenberg. For the Navy, Adm. Louis Denfeld was the principal backed by Arthur Radford. Omar Bradley had just taken over as Chief of Staff of the Army and he was there, but the argument turned into Air Force versus Navy over the issue of the strategic bombing mission and its limits.[37]

The Joint Chiefs were in Florida from the 11th to the 14th, and an agreement of sorts was hammered out. Admiral Radford, in his memoirs, explicitly gives Spaatz much of the credit for the agreement, saying that he was one of the few with an open mind, capable of making new decisions.[38] The USAF's claim to the strategic bombing mission was explicitly recognized, but the agreements allowed that the Navy would participate in any all-out air campaign, that it would be permitted a new supercarrier, and that it would also be allowed to have nuclear bombs. Further, naval aviation was to have a collateral role in both close air support on the battlefield and interdiction and the USAF was to have one in antisubmarine warfare and mine laying. Spaatz insisted on including provisions that the Navy would not build up a second strategic air force, and that it would not use its collateral missions to justify procurement of airplanes and ships.[39] Spaatz lacked enthusiasm for the Key West agreements. Rather he came back to Washington believing that much remained unresolved and, soon after he retired, he was writing in national magazines that the building of the supercarrier was a duplication of the Air Force's capability for strategic attack and therefore a questionable use of the taxpayer's money.[40] But whatever these limitations, the main goal that Mitchell and Arnold had bequeathed to Spaatz, the winning of Air Force autonomy, had been achieved. Now it fell to him to establish the initial institutions and procedures that would set the course for the new service.

## Launching a New Service

Immediately after he took over from Arnold, in February 1946, Spaatz announced his goals for the USAAF, goals toward which he worked throughout the period of the unification and autonomy struggle. One goal was to reorganize the service along functional lines instead of the geographic scheme that had existed before World War II. Another was to reshape the headquarters that presided over the force to make its decisions more timely and, presumably, more effective. A third was to build up the force to seventy active duty groups and sixty-one Air National Guard and Air Reserve units. Finally, he was determined to press scientific research and development and ensure planning for the industrial bases of airpower.[41]

Arnold had been directing the USAAF with a staff similar to that of the Army precisely to make it easier to conduct business with the parent service. Called a horizontal staff organization, it was made up of a series of numbered sections—A-1 for Personnel, A-2 for Intelligence, A-3 for Operations, and A-4 for Logistics—to conform to the traditional Army method. Spaatz had organized his United States Strategic Air Forces in Europe (USSTAF) along different lines, through the "deputy commander system." He had had just two deputy commanders, Hugh Knerr for "Administration" (everything except intelligence and operations) and Fred Anderson for "Operations." In theory, the deputy commander system so reduced the number of people reporting to Spaatz that he could focus his attention on the larger issues to a greater degree than permitted by the traditional Army scheme. Knerr and Anderson had the authority to make most of the decisions themselves, which left Spaatz free to ponder the higher questions of policy and strategy.[42]

As early as April 1946, anticipating autonomy, Spaatz had set Knerr to studying the problem of headquarters structure, and he also ordered the Air War College to consider the problem. The collective decision was that the old Army General Staff system was too cumbersome for the postwar world because decisions would have to come more rapidly in the future. Knerr, who had retired and worked in the business world for a time before the war, argued that the Air Force should adopt some of the methods of big business—especially to simplify the lines of authority and responsibility wherever possible. Spaatz agreed and decided to use deputy commanders, or "Deputy Chiefs of Staff" as they were finally called. At first, it was deemed necessary to have three such deputies instead of the two that had been used in Europe: one each for personnel, material, and operations.[43] At the suggestion of Symington, a comptroller was added to the staff to advise the commanding general on financial matters and apply statistical analysis to the work of the USAAF in many different areas.[44] When the new USAF organization became effective in October 1947, then, there were in effect four deputies: one each for the operations, personnel, material, and comptroller functions, though the latter was not titled a "Deputy Chief of Staff." Under the old USAAF scheme, Spaatz had thirteen people reporting directly to him; now the figure had been reduced to seven.[45]

The arrangement of subordinate commands, both combat and support, with which the Air Force began its existence in 1947 was a continuation of the organizational structure Spaatz had installed a year earlier. In the spring of 1946, he had divided the combat force into three commands reporting directly to his headquarters: the Strategic Air Command, Tactical Air Command, and Air Defense Command. Five other support commands, most of which also had flying missions of one sort or another, were also established.[46]

That division, and especially the establishment of the Tactical Air Command with a status apparently equal to that of the Strategic Air Command, led to speculation about Spaatz's reasons for seeming to fly in the face of Air Corps tradition of strategic bombardment. Some suggested that was the price Spaatz had to pay for Eisenhower's support in attaining a separate Air Force. There is no doubt that that support was stalwart and very valuable, but Eisenhower had long been a strong supporter of airpower, and Spaatz in later life denied he had been coerced. Rather, he and Eisenhower had discussed the matter early in 1946 and decided that would be the best way to organize the Air Force.[47] A much stronger influence on Spaatz in organizing the subordinate commands appears to have been his experiences during the war. When he had arrived in England as the head of Eighth Air Force in 1942, he found the RAF organized in a way very similar to that structure he chose for the USAF after the war. The RAF had its fighter, bomber, army support, and coastal commands. Likewise, when Spaatz had taken Twelfth Air Force into combat in Africa, it learned its trade from the British Desert Air Force, which was organized along similar functional lines. During the Normandy invasion, separate tactical and strategic air forces had attacked both of Hitler's flanks. There was much precedent by 1946 for the way in which Spaatz structured his combat commands. Moreover, it was clear to him that he could preempt any movement among the officers of the Army to build a tactical air force of their own by looking to their needs within the ranks of the U.S. Air Force.[48]

At first, Spaatz and his staff made a half-hearted attempt to incorporate the antiaircraft artillery forces of the Army in the Air Defense Command. When the Army resisted, however, the airmen did not strongly contest the point since they were receiving good support from the soldiers for the separate air force. Neither the Army nor the Air Force had a great deal of enthusiasm for air defense in the late forties because the emerging deterrence theory held that the best defense against any possible nuclear attack would be the maintenance of an offensive counterthreat.[49]

Since early in his career, Spaatz had been a strong proponent of research and development. His attempts to start off the Air Force in a strong technological direction were aided by the American preference to expend technology in battle, rather than the bodies of its youth. One of the things the Air Force had going for it during the unification debates was that it was perceived far and wide as the epitome of modernity—as the ultimate expression of American excellence in science and technology. The Navy theretofore had the first claim on the hearts and minds of many citizens, for it won its points with steam power, not muscle power. Now steam was only slightly less antiquated than muscle power. The future lay in atomic power.[50]

During the war, Arnold had built a good foundation for postwar research and development. In November 1944, he commissioned Theodore von Karman to analyze the air arm's scientific prospects in the years ahead. The scientist submitted a thirty-volume study that tried to chart the scientific future of American security. At war's end, Arnold spent ten million dollars to get the Douglas Aircraft Company to start a research organization, the RAND Corporation. When Germany collapsed, many of her surviving scientists came to the United States. The technological scares they had given to Arnold, Spaatz, and many others with their jets, rockets, and guided missiles provided the American airmen with substantial motivation to keep up the momentum of research and development in their own country.

All this was a substantial legacy for Spaatz when he replaced Arnold in 1946, but there were many factors working against the momentum Arnold had built up. One of these was uncertainty about the level at which national security research and development should be conducted. The USAF was claiming to be the new first line of defense, and many citizens agreed. Yet the weapons that were to be the backbone of that security were the products of many different lines of scientific research, and Spaatz's command did not have much control over any of them. One of the main arguments of the Army and the USAAF for unification had been that it would bring economies through the elimination of expensive duplication—and research and development was among the most expensive of activities. Many different governmental and civilian agencies had vital interests in aeronautical, electronic, and nuclear research, and that was a powerful argument for the escalation of the management of that function to a level higher than Headquarters, USAF. As a result, the National Security Act provided for a Research and Development Board at the Department of Defense level.[51]

Another factor complicating Spaatz's quest for a strong USAF research effort was the secrecy surrounding nuclear weapons. The Manhattan Project, which had developed the atomic bomb, controlled information so closely that the air units charged with delivering weapons did not control their storage, did not know how to assemble them, and often did not know what they looked like. One of the reasons Spaatz had recommended LeMay as Deputy Chief of Staff for Research and Development was to charge him with building relations with the nuclear people, so the bomber units could get at least enough nuclear information to carry out their mission. Though some progress was made in this during Spaatz's time as chief of staff, the problem continued after his tenure.[52]

Budget cuts presented the greatest obstacle to Spaatz's vision of long-term research for the Air Force. He was to lament at the end of his service that the American capital in basic research had been used in applying it to the practical problems of war and now it was imperative to resume spending more for pure research.[53] However, throughout his time as chief, the funds for research and development were so scarce that the bulk of them had to be diverted to perfecting the current capability of the Air Force, with little left over for work that looked to the future.[54] That neglect of scientific advance during the late forties was later deemed by some to be the most serious mistake of the Truman years, but the fault cannot be laid at Spaatz's door, for his warnings were clear enough.[55] That same financial stringency was preventing the buildup of conventional forces and, consequently, was driving the U.S. in the direction of adopting a nuclear strategy,[56] which would be the bane of the very groups who had done the most to impose the stringency in the first place.

About the best that can be said is that Arnold gave the postwar Air Force a good start in building a system to keep up its technological base, and his successor, Spaatz, well understood the importance of that dimension of the work. Ably assisted by Secretary Symington, he did what he could to inform the people and their decision makers of the problem and the recommended solutions. But in a democracy tired of depression and war, it was beyond their powers to make the point to their masters.

The same factors that weakened Spaatz's drive for a strong research and development program also stood in the way of achieving his force structure goals. If the military instruments of foreign policy are to achieve political objectives, the political authorities must specify to the military planners and leaders the military goals that will contribute to the desired political outcomes. The military staffs will then (ideally) prepare a strategy for the deployment and employment of forces, and the logistical plans necessary to support such action. These force and logistical requirements are then made known to the political leadership, which will either provide them or change the objectives. In theory, then, a force structure is derived from a grand strategy, specified objectives, and a military strategy. Seldom have the U.S. military services been farther from the ideal than they were during Spaatz's tenure as chief of staff. There was no grand strategy, no objectives had been identified, no enemy or potential enemy had been publicly specified, no joint strategy had been written, and the great military forces that had been deployed against Japan and in Europe in 1945 were wasted away by the beginning of the following year. Spaatz and the other members of the Joint Chiefs did not even know whether President Truman considered it probable or even possible that he would release atom bombs for use in any future war.[57]

Spaatz had always argued that a healthy aircraft manufacturing industry was a vital element of national airpower. That was a widely accepted notion while the unification debate approached its climax, but in reality the aircraft industry was staggering along. The large orders that had been predicted from an expanding airline industry were not materializing. The orders of the services were so small that the aircraft manufacturers were coming on hard times. The same month the National Security Act was signed into law, Senator Owen Brewster convened his Aviation Policy Board to examine the situation. Almost simultaneously, Truman created the President's Air Policy Commission, headed by Thomas F. Finletter, to conduct a similar examination.[58]

Symington and Spaatz appeared before both groups during the fall of 1947. The air leaders drove hard to persuade the country to accept the seventy-group goal for the emergent Air Force. Although most of the witnesses before both committees agreed that the United States should increase its security forces, they disagreed over the methods for achieving this. The air leaders, and many civilian supporters, argued that the Air Force was the first line of defense and should receive priority treatment. Many agreed with Spaatz's testimony that this required a balanced aerial force that could: defend the United States, deliver an immediate retaliatory blow, support the ground forces in tactical operations, and establish air superiority that would permit sustained operations against the enemy heartland. Spaatz testified that this required a seventy-group Air Force, backed up by adequate research and development along with a healthy aircraft manufacturing industry. It further required ample civil airlines and a fully developed industrial mobilization scheme.[59] The cutting edge of such a force, according to Spaatz, would be nearly seven thousand first-line combat aircraft in the regular Air Force backed up by nearly that many more planes in the Reserves and Air National Guard.[60] Many of the Army witnesses, including former Secretary of War Robert Patterson, supported Spaatz's position. Not so the Navy witnesses.

Forrestal, by now the secretary of defense, took a neutral position, testifying that a substantial air buildup was required, but suggesting that a defense buildup would have to be balanced and that the Navy (and Army) should share in any growth mandated by Congress and the president.[61] In the main, he left it to the Navy representatives to plead their own case before the Finletter Commission and the Brewster Board.

The testimony of the principal naval witnesses, Secretary of the Navy John L. Sullivan and Admirals Chester Nimitz and William Leahy, made it clear that the Unification Act and its accompanying executive order on roles and missions had not ended the strife between the services. They were less concerned with developing a comprehensive air policy for the United States than in sustaining the Navy's position in the continuing political struggles. While agreeing with the other witnesses that the defenses of the United States had been weakened too much in the aftermath of the Second World War, their prescription for the restoration of the situation was a Navy of half a million men with six thousand aircraft at its core.[62]

The attitudes of the Navy men did not have much influence on the Finletter Commission and the Brewster Board. The reports of both groups solidly supported the Air Force position. Both asserted that the safety of the United States depended upon maintaining an aerial retaliatory capability that would be so fearsome that no enemy would be so bold as to attack the American homeland or to even threaten U.S. vital interests. Both reports asserted that to achieve this, the minimum force required would be the seventy-group Air Force that had been Spaatz's goal for the past two years. The creation of such an air force would bring health to the ailing aviation industry. The Finletter Commission estimated that the earliest possible nuclear attack against North America could be at the onset of 1953. Consequently, it would be necessary to complete the buildup by the end of 1952, and the seventy groups of the regular Air Force should be in place by the beginning of 1950.[63]

The President's Air Policy Commission rendered its report in December 1947; Senator Owen Brewster's Board published its conclusions about the time of the Key West Conference of March 1948. As Spaatz approached the end of his Air Force career, this strong support for his principal force structure goal from congressional sources and a group commissioned by the president was welcome indeed. President Truman, however, avoided making any specific commitment on a force of seventy groups. His mandatory compliments on the reports were so general they evaded any such contract. Congress moved quickly, though, to put its stamp of approval on the Air Force's goal and to take steps to implement it. It passed a supplemental authorization of 2.3 billion dollars to begin the climb to seventy groups.

In the spring of 1948, the prospect looked bright for Spaatz's seventy groups. The Secretary of the Air Force had been stalwart in its defense, the president's Air Policy Commission had explicitly recommended it, Senator Brewster's Board had seconded that move, the JCS supported the goal, and Congress had made a supplemental authorization that seemed to be the first step on the way to fulfillment of the objective. President Truman, however, imposed a ceiling on defense spending for the subsequent fiscal year that was just over fourteen billion dollars; the bright hopes of the Air Force quickly withered away, since that was not nearly enough to support the desired seventy groups.[64] Spaatz and Symington and the rest of the Air Force, along with the civilian groups that supported them, had persuaded practically the whole country that their goals were valid, but the president resisted the pressure, and the force structure goals were not to be reached until the onset of the Korean War. By the time he retired, Spaatz's Air Force did not have its seventy groups, but it did have a good deal of public relations capital, in both Congress and among the people, that would stand it in good stead for years to come.

When Spaatz had first tried to retire in 1945, he had been dissuaded from doing so on the condition that he would remain at the head of the air arm only until autonomy had been won and the new service was established on the road of independence. By the spring of 1948 that time had come. Right after the Key West Conference, on 30 June, he turned the reins over to Hoyt Vandenberg. According to his wishes, there were no parades or massive fly-overs for him. Following a small ceremony in the Pentagon, he remained in uniform long enough for a farewell visit to the Royal Air Force in England. When he returned to Fort Myer (where the Wright brothers had first demonstrated their airplane for the Army), the problem of family relocation was a primary concern. But, characteristically, he told Ruth that whatever she did about moving would suit him: he was off on a month-long deep-sea fishing trip in Mexico[65] with one of his favorite fishing pals, Erik Nelson.

It had been almost thirty-eight years to the day since Cadet Spaatz had turned his eyes skyward from the plain at West Point to gaze in wonder at Glen Curtiss' aerial flivver. He could now take enormous satisfaction in knowing that he had been one of the principal architects of the technological and strategic revolution that had produced the United States Air Force.

The qualities that carried a not-very-promising West Point cadet to the top of his profession have been pondered by military historians. Some of those qualities—among them an irreverence toward military custom, tradition and official dogma—would have destroyed the careers of many officers, particularly in the more conservative senior services. But Carl Spaatz had the saving grace of a sense of humor and proportion that perhaps kept him from self-destruction. He was objective about his own strengths and weaknesses, and he was not driven by self-aggrandizement. His ambition, rather, was for the recognition of airpower as a new and, until World War II, relatively untested force in military affairs. Freedom from the bonds of overweaning ambition gave him a sense of personal security and hence the courage to make difficult decisions that often were not popular with his peers or his superiors, but that proved to be right.

Tooey Spaatz also was fortunate in the friendships he made at West Point and later among officers of the Army's air arm who were destined for important assignments. The ability that he showed early in his career augmented those friendships to give him a range of experience in several facets of airpower and in the military-political arena where he was universally respected for his unfailing ability to work with others. He reflected the essence of teamwork. He probably was the most widely experienced officer in the air arm when this country entered World War II. There was, therefore, some element of luck in the juncture of character and events that opened the path for this quiet, wise, and patient man. But luck aside, the essence of his genius lay in one of the rarest of all gifts—an unerring sense of what would work.

# EPILOGUE

No one will deny that when Carl Spaatz retired in 1948 there still were many problems, including the Berlin Airlift, facing the recently created United States Air Force. He had every right to feel "bone tired," for he had just survived the trials of war and the storms of unification. He was exhausted, in fact, both physically and emotionally.

Not long before, the Yugoslavians had shot down an American C-47, killing its crew. When the bodies were brought home, Secretary of the Air Force Stuart Symington and Spaatz went together to Arlington Cemetery for the burial. Symington later confessed to feeling stricken by the sight of the widows and orphans, and he wondered at Spaatz's apparent calm as Spaatz watched his men being lowered into the ground. The short ride back to the Pentagon was silent. The pair walked through the halls and came to the secretary's office. Symington finally broke the silence.

"You know something, Tooey," he said. "You are a cold bastard, aren't you?"

Spaatz, not much given to strong language, turned white.

"God damn it!" he replied. "My life has been nothing but one long attendance at the burials of my friends!"[1]

Spaatz had been looking forward to retirement for a long time, and when the day finally came, he reviewed the options before him. There had been some talk in 1945 of a career as governor of Pennsylvania, but he quickly turned that aside. His friends, Dwight Eisenhower and

Omar Bradley, did well during those years writing their memoirs of the war, and publishers were after Spaatz to do the same.[2] He discussed the prospect in a half-hearted way with his historian friend, Bruce Hopper, but nothing ever came of it because Spaatz had always felt that memoirs, in their very nature, were self-serving. His friend Ira Eaker took a position with Hughes Aircraft, and many of his other colleagues did similar work after retirement, but that was not for him. *Newsweek* offered him a position as its military editor, and that was an offer with built-in appeal.[3] With his background as the son of a country editor, Spaatz had considered going to Boyertown to buy back his father's newspaper. Also, he had gotten along very well with members of the press corps in Africa and England, so the *Newsweek* position would keep him among people congenial to him and would give him a forum in which to continue his support of the cause of preparedness and airpower. The duties would not be so onerous that they would prevent him from fulfilling his long-held dreams of fishing and travel. Without much deliberation, he accepted the offer and then went to Mexico on a month-long deep-sea fishing trip with his friend, Erik Nelson.[4]

The *Newsweek* activity was hard work for Spaatz. Notwithstanding his boyhood experience on his father's newspaper, the written word never came as easily to him as it seemed to come to his friends Henry Arnold and Ira Eaker. He had an office at *Newsweek* where he spent much time when he was in Washington. According to his closest colleague there, Kenneth Crawford, Spaatz typically would develop a set of ideas and discuss them with him. Crawford would then knock out a draft and bring it back to the general, who would edit it, and together they would hammer out a final draft. Mrs. Spaatz says that it was a difficult process for Spaatz, but one he worked hard at, in order to further his ideas on defense.[5]

There were few surprises in the articles Spaatz wrote for *Newsweek* over a period of thirteen years. He was consistently in favor of more service unification, almost always on the side of strong, land-based airpower and against building supercarriers. As a close friend of Eisenhower, he was identified with the Europe-first-pro-NATO side of the officer corps as opposed to those associated with MacArthur and others who supported an Asia-first foreign policy.

Spaatz was at his most prolific during the Korean War, which he covered for a time as a war correspondent, arguing for bombing China and unleashing Chiang's forces against the mainland. He also wrote of the need for economy in defense spending and the limitations of the national economy in its ability to support military forces. He often proposed large air forces and airpower solutions.[6] In fact, his good friend at the White House, Eisenhower, once felt compelled to privately ask Spaatz to go a little easier in promoting larger funds for the Air Force.[7]

When Tooey accepted the position with *Newsweek,* he gave Ruth carte blanche in the choice of a new home. She indulged her interest in restoration and bought an old house in Georgetown. It had been built around the turn of the century and needed remodeling. The remodeling was not completed in time, however, for Tattie's wedding in September to Walter Bell, whom she had met when he was serving at the British Embassy. They were married, instead, at the home of close friends, Connie and Lyle Wilson. The Spaatzes moved into their new home in 1948, and Carla was married in 1951 to a Washingtonian, Francis Thomas. In 1953, Beckie became a widow with three little girls to support. She had left the music conservatory to marry before she graduated and did not have a diploma to help procure a good teaching position. She yearned to study at the Royal Academy of Music in London, so her parents took her three daughters to live with them while she pursued her degree and made her professional debut in England. With the arrival of three young granddaughters, the Spaatzes needed a larger house. They moved to Chevy Chase, Maryland, and lived happily there for the rest of Tooey Spaatz's life.[8]

In 1950, Spaatz and Ira Eaker built a fishing cabin in the Oregon wilds along the Rogue River and, thereafter, made annual pilgrimages into this wilderness. The cabin was built high on a cliff overlooking the river, and the view from the deck was magnificent. There was no electricity or telephone; heat came from a large fireplace and a wood-burning stove in the kitchen; but, fortunately, the cabin boasted indoor plumbing.

Originally, the site could be reached only by water, but later a rocky field (known as the Rogue River International Airport) was cleared sufficiently to allow a helicopter or small plane to land. After that, fishing pals like Nate Twining and Curt LeMay were able to visit. Ruth Spaatz and Ruth Eaker were granted one trip to the cabin, and Walter Bell, Spaatz's English son-in-law, considered it a major compliment to be invited one year.

For Tooey, the weeks on the Rogue were as much social occasions as sporting events. He treasured the companionship of old friends and the conviviality of the evening card games. He and Ira were seldom alone, but when they were, the two old flyers relaxed in the most perfect peace they had ever known.[9]

Another annual pilgrimage, each January, was to J. H. "Jock" Whitney's plantation in Thomasville, Georgia. Whitney would send his plane down from New York to Washington, D.C., where it would pick up Spaatz and Eaker and a few of the other old-time airmen. Ted Curtis and Fred Anderson were frequent passengers, and Monk Hunter would drive over to the "Greenwood Plantation" from Savannah. Hank Stovall, too, was a participant; he and Everett Cook would fly down from Memphis. For the most part, their friendships dated back to the First World War. Several of them, in fact, were aces: Hunter, Cook, Curtis, and Stovall all had the five air victories necessary to place them in the "ace" category. The visit to the plantation was a hunting trip, and, according to Cook, a considerable social event, too. After the day's shooting, the men would change to dinner jackets for the evening. Then, naturally, would come the after-dinner drinks and cards.

With the passing years, Spaatz had become an avid bird-watcher. Though he enjoyed the companionship of daily shooting expeditions, his binoculars finally became more important to him than his shotgun. On one occasion, he was pursuing his bird-watching near the hunt when he became convinced he had seen the legendary ivory-billed woodpecker. His uncharacteristic excitement over this unbelievable sighting caused great merriment among his irreverent companions, who dubbed the fabulous bird "Tooey's ivory-peckered woodbill." The male camaraderie of those days at Thomasville and on the Rogue River, says Ruth Spaatz, possibly were the happiest times of Tooey's life.[10] Gradually, however, the hunting and fishing trips became less frequent and Spaatz spent more and more of his time in the study of nature, especially bird-watching.

One of General and Mrs. Spaatz's retirement dreams had been to take trips together. Some of their travel after his retirement was pure recreation, such as a memorable camera-safari in Kenya where Tattie's English husband, Walter Bell, was posted in Nairobi. Much of the travel, however, was done in conjunction with government business. Spaatz was appointed to the Battle Monuments Commission, which meant travel to Europe, and it was on one of these trips that the Spaatzes drove to the site of the World War I Issoudun School where Spaatz had been posted to his first command. The flying fields were all gone by then and the land returned to agriculture, but there was a clearing where the

French had erected a small monument to the flyers who had died while in training. Now, even so long after the First World War, the monument was well cared for and flowers were at its base. That was a poignant moment for Spaatz.[11]

Shortly after the United States Air Force was created as a separate service, the secretary of defense appointed a board headed by Dwight Eisenhower to consider the problem of acquiring regular officers for the new service. The board reported in favor of a third academy. When Eisenhower became president, he appointed Harold E. Talbott as secretary of the Air Force, and Talbott made the creation of the Air Force Academy one of his highest priorities.[12] The Air Force Academy Site Selection Commission received its formal charter from Talbott on April 6, 1954, and Spaatz was appointed to the commission, along with Dr. V. M. Hancher, General Harmon, Charles A. Lindbergh, and M. C. Meigs.

Selection of a site for the academy was much more complex than it might at first appear. By 1954, the older academies had been in existence for more than a century, and their traditions colored the thinking of everyone involved with the third academy. The news that there was to be a new academy stoked the fires of ambition within practically every chamber of commerce in the U.S. By the deadline, the commission had received 580 proposals for sites! The weeks that followed were hectic ones for Spaatz and the other members. They traveled by air to all corners of the United States, making ground inspections of thirty-four promising locations and examining thirty-three others from the air.

There were three final contenders. One encompassed Lake Geneva, Wisconsin. Another was a site on a high bluff overlooking the Mississippi River near Alton, Illinois. The third was a large tract on the eastern face of the Rampart Range just north of Colorado Springs, Colorado.[13] After lengthy consideration of the pros and cons of each of the three sites, none was a clear favorite. Consequently the Site Selection Commission submitted a list of three without any expression of preference, and the secretary chose the Colorado location.[14] Spaatz understood that the air academy must, first of all, be an educational institution and not a flight training school, but he did insist that it should attract an "airfaring" group. He asserted that every graduate, no matter what his specialty, should get enough flight training at the institution to know what flying is about. To Spaatz, that meant flight training beyond the point of soloing and up to the winning of the private pilot's license. No doubt, he saw the academy as an institution that would provide the graduates with the basic tools, not one that would produce finished engineers or scientists. The time for specialization, said General Spaatz, was after graduation—and that was as true for scientists and engineers as it was for tactical experts. He thought that the military and naval academies had been too specialized in their approaches and that the Air Force Academy should place greater emphasis on the liberal arts. Among these studies he saw a continuing need for Spanish instruction and an increasing requirement for studies in the Russian language.[15]

Spaatz was associated with the Air Force Academy during its formative years. He was a member of the Board of Visitors for several years in the late fifties and its chairman for part of that time.[16] He demonstrated his backing for the fledgling academy by his participation on the Board of Directors of the Air Force Academy Foundation, Incorporated.[17] His work on that board was not extensive, but he was being deluged with requests to participate on the boards of a host of charitable and service organizations and was quite capable of saying "no" to many of them. He seldom said "no" to any associated with the academy or with airpower preparedness.

Arnold had taken the initial steps that led to the foundation of the Air Force Association even before the end of World War II, but from the beginning Spaatz and Doolittle were among its stalwarts and both served as the chairman of its board of directors.[18] Somewhat later, in the early fifties, Spaatz was among the fathers of the Air Force Historical Foundation and more consistently attended its meetings than he did those of other organizations to which he lent his name.[19]

Carl Spaatz's involvement in the development of security through airpower continued in countless other ways. He was the national chairman for the Civil Air Patrol, lent his name to the Air Force Aid Society,[20] helped with Columbia University's Arnold Oral History Project,[21] tried with the Air Force Association to reverse the verdict of the Mitchell court-martial, succeeded in helping to have Mitchell's statue put in a place of honor in the National Air Museum of the Smithsonian, and was a frequent witness before Congress where he consistently argued in favor of more unification and better airpower preparedness.[22] To many organizations not directly connected with airpower, he readily lent his name because of their various service efforts: International Rescue Committee, cancer drives, the March of Dimes, and multiple sclerosis campaigns.

It was a busy life well into the 1960s, and Spaatz seemed content. There were many trips to Los Angeles where Ruth's mother and sister still lived and where Spaatz was a member of the Board of Directors of Litton Industries. There were trips to San Francisco where he was on the board of U.S. Leasing. Most California trips included a week at the Cochran-Odlum Ranch where, according to Ruth Spaatz, Tooey and Jacqueline Cochran, director of the women's pilot training program during World War II and, in later years, a record-breaking woman pilot, would sit up half the night playing backgammon. Ruth and Tooey drove across the continent by every known route and felt that they had missed nothing in the United States worth seeing, but it was always a joy to them to return home to Chevy Chase and family life. Beckie's girls were now at college—Swarthmore, Bryn Mawr, and Colorado College—but Carla's large family lived just a few blocks away. So, Daddy Tooey, as they called him, saw much of this brood of grandchildren, and he enjoyed his game-playing with them—chess with the oldest and go-fish with the youngest. He had never really had the time to devote to his own children and now he was finding great delight in this new generation.[23]

Spaatz suffered his first heart attack on a trip to the Air Force Academy in 1972 and was never the same after that. A massive attack sent him to Walter Reed Army Hospital on the 13th of June, 1974, and he lingered there, sometimes conscious and sometimes not, for a month and a day. The doctors had offered no false hope, and everyone knew for several weeks what was ahead.

Memorial services for General Carl Spaatz were held at the Andrews Air Force Base Chapel on the 16th of July, 1974. It was certain to be a long day for those who loved him because interment was to be at the Air Force Academy Cemetery, entailing a 2,000 mile flight from Maryland to Colorado. The jet cortege was airborne on schedule and more than just the family grandchildren had cause to recall memories of Carl Spaatz. As they winged westward toward the Rockies, Ruth Spaatz, Stuart Symington, Ira Eaker, and others aboard the plane realized that they were saying a final farewell to a beloved husband and friend and to a quiet, unpretentious man whose contributions to his country and to the Air Force he loved were beyond counting.

This was a man whose courage and daring during the first quarter of the twentieth century helped advance the capabilities of aircraft so that man could realize his dream of flying long distances and attaining ever-improving aircraft performance. And, surely, his role in the Allied victory of World War II was an eminent one. Under a commander with less stature and force of character, the air superiority over the Normandy beaches might not have been as assured. It is hard to think of another commander in the USAAF who had enough influence with General Eisenhower to hold off, as well as Spaatz did, the diversions proposed by Leigh-Mallory. Neither is it easy to think of any other who had both the perception to identify the oil targets as decisive and the strength to conserve a part of the U.S. strategic air striking power for them.

Spaatz's name is inexorably connected with the United States Air Force as a military service separate from the Army and the Navy. Both Billy Mitchell and Hap Arnold put their careers at risk in their battles for recognition of the importance of airpower, but their personalities were very different from that of Spaatz. Their outspoken and impetuous characteristics were best for the accomplishment of some of their goals, but it was Spaatz's low-profile leadership and his more pragmatic, healing approach, his strength and his flexibility that helped bring about unification and define the initial institutions of the Air Force that Spaatz, Arnold, and Mitchell had so earnestly desired.[24]

Spaatz had told his wife that he did not want to be buried at Arlington. Rather, he said, make it West Point or the Air Force Academy. Ruth had chosen the latter, and it was a choice in harmony with her husband's character. The modern architecture symbolizes the faith of airmen everywhere in the potency of airpower and new ideas. The mountain vastness and the endless views of surrounding terrain are fitting to Spaatz's love of nature.

It was past noon when the mountains appeared on the western horizon and the descent of Air Force jet 86972 was beginning. Two Air Force bands, one from Lackland AFB and another from the academy, waited on the ramp as the funeral plane taxied in. There would be no chapel ceremonies here. The mourners immediately went to their cars, and the procession wound up the road toward the mountains and the academy cemetery a thousand feet above.

Family and friends disembarked and walked to the grave site. An honor guard of cadets, paced by a slow drum cadence, carried the casket to its resting place. The quiet was shattered for a moment by a flight of four F-4 Phantoms that hurtled by with the lead plane pulling away, symbolically, from the rest. Chaplain Charles Carpenter read from the *Psalms* and a choir sang Spaatz's favorite song, "Battle Hymn of the Republic." An honor guard fired a salute of twenty-one rounds. From a nearby hill, the mournful strains of "Taps" filled the air and then slowly faded away. One of America's greatest airmen had made his last flight.

# AUTHOR'S ACKNOWLEDGMENTS

Many people and agencies played an important role in gathering material for this book. To mention all of them would be to write yet another book. All are identified in the footnotes. They all have my gratitude, but I wish to single out a few agencies and people for special notice.

Brig. Gen. Thomas Griess, U.S. Army, is one of America's leading military historians. I wish to thank him for his example, inspiration, and confidence. Mrs. Marie T. Capps, USMA Library and Archives, provided outstanding assistance. Col. Roger H. Nye, U.S. Army, provided me with insights on Carl A. Spaatz, the military academy, and officer education. The Air University Library at Maxwell Air Force Base, Alabama, is a unique institution and a fine place to do research on any dimension of the history of airpower. I wish to thank Mr. Robert Lane and his staff for their help, which was essential to the completion of this book.

Located with the Air University Library is the USAF Historical Research Center, a subordinate unit of the Headquarters USAF Office of Air Force History. Mr. Harry Fletcher, whose long experience with the archives and deep knowledge of the Luftwaffe were crucial to me, is worthy of special note. The oral history collection at the USAF Historical Research Center was an indispensable asset. It has been long served by two historians whose status in the profession is inadequately noted, Dr. James C. Hasdorff and Mr. Hugh N. Ahmann. The center is especially well served by Mrs. Judy G. Endicott, Mr. Pressley Bickerstaff, and

Mrs. Margaret C. Claiborn, who assist users of the center. Their industriousness, expertise, patience, and courtesy provide worthy models of career civil service members.

Dr. David MacIsaac of the Airpower Research Institute at Maxwell AFB, who is an authority on strategic bombing in World War II, provided valuable information and counsel to me.

I did research for the biography of Carl Spaatz at numerous other libraries and archives, almost all of them operated by arms of the U.S. government. They are collectively a priceless national asset and should be jealously preserved. At the head of this array is the Manuscripts Division of the Library of Congress, in Washington, D.C. Located now in the new Madison Building, the facilities are comfortable and efficient, and the staff is a credit to the U.S. Civil Service. So, too, is the staff at the Franklin D. Roosevelt Library, headed by Dr. William B. Emerson, himself an expert on the history of airpower. Equally impressive were the staffs at the Harry S. Truman Library, the Dwight D. Eisenhower Library, the Naval Historical Center at the Washington Navy Yard, and the Office of Air Force History at Bolling AFB, headed by Dr. Richard H. Kohn. At the latter place, Mr. Herman S. Wolk, Dr. Wayne W. Thompson, and Dr. George M. Watson were particularly helpful. The Air Force Academy Library has grown in its excellence; Mr. Duane Reed, who is in charge of special collections there, was especially helpful.

Air Comdr. H. A. Probert of the RAF is to be thanked for the fine work he did in facilitating both my access to the archives of the Ministry of Defence in London and interviews with Dudley Saward, Dennis Richards, and Air Vice Marshal S. O. Bufton, who provided me with one of the most memorable experiences of the entire project.

A host of people allowed me to interview them and provided me with additional information and insights by correspondence, telephone, and conversations. All are identified in the footnotes. Only a few who were most central to the story can be individually cited here. Mrs. Ruth Spaatz is one. In a way she is a walking history of the U.S. Air Force almost back to the very beginning. She is articulate, has a fine memory, and is a most gracious lady. Without her interviews, letters, and suggestions there could be no Spaatz book.

Interviewing Gen. James Doolittle was an impressive experience. His contribution was substantial and I thank him for it. For a pilot who once was a Strategic Air Command aircraft commander, interviewing Gen. Curtis LeMay was equally awe-inspiring. He went far out of his way to help me, and I thank him for it. General LeMay's predecessor at the helm of XXI Bomber Command was Maj. Gen. Haywood S. Hansell, himself a major asset to airpower history. He granted me two extended interviews and has answered many other questions through the mails. His books have been invaluable, and his contribution to the Spaatz biography has been a major one. Justice Lewis F. Powell, Jr. was a member of General Spaatz's staff in England in World War II. Earlier, he was a participant in the North African campaign. Not only has Justice Powell contributed with a major interview and material from his personal files, but he has continually supplied encouragement with his interest and correspondence as well.

As for the scholars who helped with this book, Dr. Forrest C. Pogue not only gave me an entire evening to discuss the problem of writing a biography, but he also provided a model for all biographers in his work on Gen. George C. Marshall. I thank him for his help and his inspiration. Dr. Irving B. Holley, Jr. also had a major hand in shaping this book.

The efforts of Lt. Gen. John B. McPherson, USAF (Ret.), past president of the Air Force Historical Foundation, were absolutely vital to this book. He helped with administration, fundraising, and took a major hand in the final editing. It is notable that in addition to its own funds, the Foundation received significant financial support for the Spaatz biography from the Eighth Air Force Historical Society, through its Eighth Air Force Memorial Museum Foundation. Equally important was the help rendered by the Air Force Association's Aerospace Education Foundation. Hopefully this book will be a step toward the goals of both those fine organizations and I wish to thank them for their assistance.

Col. Edward Rosenbaum, USAF (Ret.), arranged a stay at Carl Spaatz's birthplace, Boyertown, Pennsylvania. Mr. James Boyer of that city was most helpful with all the arrangements and his continual encouragement ever since. Col. John Schlight, USAF (Ret.), was appointed to edit the second draft. He did it with a sure hand and in record time. He reduced its length by a full forty percent and yet was able to retain the coherence of its substance and preserve what I believe is a respectable academic level. Ms. Jo Ann Perdue keyboarded the second draft swiftly and yet produced a remarkably clean and accurate manuscript. She did it with unfailing good spirit, and I thank her for both her industriousness and her patience.

Lastly, I thank the members of the Air Force Historical Foundation and the Aerospace Education Foundation for the opportunity to undertake this project. It has been a profound learning experience.
DAVID R. METS

# NOTES

## CHAPTER I

[1] Katherine Gresham, granddaughter, interview, Washington, D.C., 19 September 1982.

[2] Ira C. Eaker, *AIR FORCE Magazine,* Sept. 1974, "General Carl A. Spaatz, USAF," June 28, 1981; July 14, 1974, p 46.

[3] Alfred Goldberg, "General Carl A. Spaatz," *The War Lords,* ed. Field Marshal Sir Michael Carver, Little Brown and Company, Boston, 1976.

[4] Richard H. Kohn and Joseph P. Harahan, "Air Leadership Conference, April 13–14, 1984," Government Printing Office, Washington, D.C.

[5] Mrs. Carl A. Spaatz, interview, Washington, D.C., 25 March 1982. Though Air Service and Air Corps records use the single "a" from 1910 to 1937, the double "a" is used in this book from the beginning for clarity and to distinguish General Spaatz from his grandfather, Carl Spatz. In Germany, the family always spelled the name as "Spatz," and Gen. Carl Spaatz's grandfather and father retained that spelling through their lifetimes. During the late 1930s, the general's daughters and wife were annoyed with the tendency for the girls' playmates to pronounce the name "spats," which were the men's short ankle leggings still in use at the time. The family prevailed upon him to add an "a" to the spelling to induce others to pronounce the name as "spots" in order to end the embarrassment. (See p. 104) There seems to have been a branch of the family in Belgium that did use that spelling, but the general's family clearly had its origins in Germany, not Belgium.

[6] Passport, King of Prussia, King's Government of Duesseldorf, Town of Eberfeld, dated 14 March 1965, issued to Carl Spatz, copy and translation in the possession of author.

[7] Notes, undated, Library of Congress, Manuscript Division, Spaatz Collection, Box 28. (Hereafter cited as "Spaatz Papers")

[8] Mrs. Carl A. Spaatz, interview, Washington, D.C., 25 March 1982.

[9] "Charles B. Spatz," *Book of Biographies—Berks County, Pennsylvania* (Buffalo, NY: Biographical Publishing Company, 1898, copy of extract in the possession of the author).

[10] "Boyertown Newspaper Marks 125 Years of Publication," *Boyertown Area Times* (3 June 1982), Sec. A, p. 1.

[11] *Berks County Democrat,* (1908–1910).

[12] "Charles B. Spatz," *Book of Biographies.*

[13] Letter, Mrs. Ruth Steinmiller to Mrs. Carl A. Spaatz (August 1942).

[14] "Charles B. Spatz," *Book of Biographies.*

[15] Letter, Mrs. Ruth Steinmiller to Mrs. Carl A. Spaatz (August 1942?); *Berks County Democrat,* 25 January 1908; Mrs. Carl A. Spaatz, interview, 25 March 1982.

[16] Letter, Mr. William Baker, Office of the Headmaster, Perkiomen School, Pennsburg, PA, to David R. Mets, 17 March 1983.

[17] Letter, Mrs. Ruth Steinmiller to Mrs. Carl A. Spaatz (August 1942?); U.S. Military Academy Form 189, "Personal and School History." USMA archives

[18] Mrs. Ann Spatz, interview, Boyertown, PA, 11 July 1982.

[19] *Boyertown Area Times,* (3 June 1982), Section B, p. 3.

[20] Edgar F. Puryear, *Stars in Flight* (Novato, CA: Presidio, 1981), p. 47, citing a 1959 interview as indicating that Carl Spaatz wanted to go to West Point; Lt. Gen. Ira C. Eaker, "Memories of Six Air Chiefs," *Aerospace Historian* (December 1973), p. 194.

[21] *Berks County Democrat,* (26 February 1910), p. 1.

[22] Roger H. Nye, "The United States Military Academy in an Era of Educational Reform, 1900–1925," unpublished Ph.D. dissertation, Columbia University, 1968, pp. 214–16.

[23] Robert Priest, Terrence Fullerton, and Claude Bridges, "Personality and Value Changes in West Point Cadets," *Armed Forces and Society* 8 (Summer 1982), pp. 629–42.

[24] United States, U.S. Military Academy, "Headquarters Correspondence, 1904–1917, So-Tho," Document #8397–28, Summaries, USMA Archives.

[25] Mrs. Carl A. Spaatz, interview, 25 March 1982.

[26] Ibid.

[27] United States, U.S. Military Academy, "Register of Delinquencies," Vol. 48½, Class of 1914, August 1910–May 1913; Mrs. Carl A. Spaatz, interview, 25 March 1982.

[28] USMA, "Register of Delinquencies."

[29] Maj. Gen. Robert L. Walsh, USAF (Ret.), interview, Washington, D.C., 31 March 1982. General Walsh was two classes behind Spaatz and was then in his first semester at West Point. Normally, the connection was not a close one between "plebes" and "cows" (Juniors), but in this case they marched near one another in the ranks. West Pointers spent a good deal of their time in the ranks, for they averaged two parades a day, especially in the summertime.

[30] Mrs. Carl A. Spaatz, interview, 25 March 1982; DeWitt S. Copp, *A Few Great Captains* (Garden City, NY: Doubleday, 1980), p. 26; Association of Graduates USMA, *Register of Graduates—1982* (West Point, NY, 1982), p. 312. F. J. Toohey graduated last in the class of 1913 and retired as a major in 1933.

[31] Brig. Gen. Hume Peabody, USAF (Ret.), interview, Chaptico, MD, 13–16 September 1975, AFSHRC.*United States, U. S. Air Force, Albert F. Simpson Historical Research Center (Hereafter cited as AFSHRC).

[32] William E. Simons, *Liberal Education in the Service Academies,* (New York: Teachers College, Columbia University 1965), p. 39.

[33] Form D, "Class Graduation Standing Cards."

[34] *Howitzer,* 1914, p. 84.

[35] Ibid.

[36] Mrs. Carl A. Spaatz, interview, 25 March 1982; Ms. Katharine Gresham, interview, 19 September 1982.

[37] Nye, "United States Military Academy," pp. 176–77.

[38] Ira C. Eaker, interview with David R. Mets, Washington, D.C., 26 March 1982.

[39] James Parton, interview, New York, NY, 29 July 1982; Maj. Gen. E. P. Curtis, USAF, (Ret.) interview, Small Point, ME, 3 August 1982; Maj. Gen. Everett R. Cook, USAF (Ret.), *A Memoir,* Joseph Riggs and Margaret Lawrence, eds. (Memphis, TN: Memphis Public Library, 1971), pp. 68–71.

[40] Lt. Gen. Ira C. Eaker, USAF (Ret.), "Memories of Six Air Chiefs," *Aerospace Historian* (December 1973), pp. 188–96.

[41] Mrs. Carl A. Spaatz, interview, Washington, D.C., 27 June 1982.

[42] Association of Graduates USMA, *Register of Graduates—1981* (West Point, NY, 1981), pp. 312–14.

[43] Ibid., pp. 314–18.

[44] E. P. Curtis, interview, 3 August 1982; Letter, Col. Thomas H. Monroe, USA (Ret.), Eureka, CA, 2 September 1982, to author. Curtis was Spaatz's chief of staff through the African and European campaigns; Mrs. Carl A. Spaatz, interview, 25 March 1982.

[45] Sherwood Harris, *The First to Fly: Aviation's Pioneer Days* (New York: Simon and Schuster, 1970), pp. 168–73; Alvin M. Josephy, Jr. (ed.), *The American Heritage History of Flight* (New York: American Heritage, 1962), p. 124.

[46] Harris, *First to Fly,* p. 175.

[47] Ibid., p. 173.

[48] "General Carl Spaatz, Sidelights," document #K-141.2421 Spaatz, 1919–1974, AFSHRC; Gen. Carl A. Spaatz, interview, USAF Academy, CO, 27 September 1968, Oral History Interview #583, document #K-239.0512–583, hereafter cited as "Spaatz Interview #1." At that moment, Spaatz could not remember that Curtiss had been the pilot, and he was mistaken about the year, citing it as 1912, but he was quite clear that his desire to fly started while witnessing that flight and said it was a greater motivation than any desire for a military career. Also, Gen. Carl A. Spaatz, interview, place not given, published 19 May 1965, United States, U.S. Air Force Oral History

Interview, AFSHRC document #K-239.0512–755, hereafter cited as "Spaatz Interview #2."

49 Spaatz Interview #1.

50 Eaker, "Memories of Six Air Chiefs," p. 195; Spaatz Interview #1; Mrs. Carl A. Spaatz, interview, 25 March 1982. The 25th was one of the army's black regiments.

51 Puryear, *Stars in Flight,* p. 53.

52 Mrs. Carl A. Spaatz, interview, 21 May 1985.

53 Letter, Mrs. Ruth Steinmiller to Mrs. Carl A. Spaatz (August 1942?).

54 Mrs. Carl A. Spaatz, interview, 25 March 1982; Mrs. Carl A. Spaatz, interview, 27 June 1982.

55 Letter, Mrs. Carl A. Spaatz to author, 29 January 1983.

56 Thomas M. Coffey, *Hap: The Story of the U.S. Air Force and the Man Who Built It, General Henry H. "Hap" Arnold,* (New York: Viking, 1982), p. 3.

57 Alfred Goldberg (ed.), *History of the United States Air Force* (Randolph AFB, TX: Air Training Command, 1 June 1961), pp. 1–7 to 1–10; Maj. Thomas D. Milling, "A Short History of the United States Army Air Service," unpublished manuscript, December 1923, AFSHRC, #167.401–11A, 1861–1917, pp. 29–32.

58 Milling, "Short History," p. 30.

59 Ibid., pp. 52–53. It never did, for it has remained in the hands of the government ever since, though it is now a naval air station.

60 Milling, "Short History," pp. 29–32; Goldberg, "History of the USAF," pp. 1–7 to 1–10; Dr. Maurer Maurer, "The 1st Aero Squadron, 1913–1917," *Air Power Historian,* Vol. 4 (October 1957), pp. 207–12.

61 Maj. H. H. Arnold, "The History of Rockwell Field," unpublished ms., 1923, USAFHRC, #288, 12–1, p. 55.

62 Spaatz Interview #1.

63 Arnold, "History of Rockwell Field," pp. 46–58.

64 Milling, "Short History," p. 30.

65 Mary J. Schneider, "Boyertown's Famous Flier; Carl A. Spaatz," *Boyertown Area Times* (June 1982), Sec. B, p. 3; Milling, "Short History," p. 29.

66 Arnold, "History of Rockwell Field," p. 56; Copp, *A Few Great Captains,* p. 27; Goldberg, "History of the USAF," pp. 1–9 to 1–10.

67 Goldberg, *History of the USAF,* p. 1–10.

68 Arnold, "History of Rockwell Field," p. 57; Maj. Joseph T. McNarney, Corps Air Service Commander, VI Corps, "Lessons Learned," undated, report to chief of air service, AEF (Fall 1918), in Maurer Maurer (ed.), *The U.S. Air Service World War I, Vol IV, Post War Review* (Washington, D.C.: Government Printing Office, 1979), pp. 98–105. Shows that the problems were not solved even at war's end.

[69] Milling, "Short History," p. 31.

[70] Arnold, "History of Rockwell Field," p. 49.

[71] Ibid., p. 74.

[72] Col. Frank P. Lahm, U.S. Army, *The World War I Diary of Colonel Frank P. Lahm,* Air University, Aerospace Studies Institute, Historical Research Division, Maxwell AFB, AL, December, 1970; Brig. Gen. Frank P. Lahm, USAF (Ret.), "Early Flying Experiences," *Air Power Historian,* Vol. 2 (January 1955), p. 1–10.

[73] Arnold, "History of Rockwell Field," p. 55.

[74] United States, War Department, Special Order No. 131, 5 June 1916, Spaatz Papers, Library of Congress, Box 2, JMA rating.

[75] Frank E. Vandiver, *Black Jack: The Life and Times of John J. Pershing,* Vol II (College Station, TX: Texas A&M Press, 1977), pp. 602–4; Calvin W. Hines, "First Aero Squadron in Mexico," *American Aviation Historical Society Journal* 10 (Fall 1965), pp. 190–97; Juliette Hennesy, *The United States Army Air Arm, April 1961 to April 1917,* United States, USAF, Air University, Research Studies Institute, Historical Division, May 1958, p. 167.

[76] Hines, "First Aero in Mexico," p. 191.

[77] Maurer, "The 1st Aero Squadron," p. 209; Maj. Clayton Bissell, USA, "History of the Air Corps and its Late Development," United States, Army, Air Corps Tactical School, unpublished mimeograph, January 1927, Air University Library, #U 746, p. 15; James L. Crouch, "Wings South: The First Foreign Employment of Air Power by the United States," *Aerospace Historian* 19 (Spring, March 1972), p. 28.

[78] Crouch, "Wings South," pp. 27–31; Herbert Molloy Mason, Jr., *The Great Pursuit* (New York: Random House, 1970), pp. 219–33; Milling, "Short History," pp. 38–40; D. M. Fox, "A Fighting Air Force Was Born," *Flying* 58 (March 1956), pp. 30–31, 64–65.

[79] Hennesy, *Army Air Arm,* pp. 167, 173.

[80] Hennesy, *Army Air Arm,* p. 174.

[81] Spaatz Interview #1.

[82] Davidson, interview, 25 March 1982.

[83] United States, USAF, Air University, Historical Division, "Selected Case Histories," USAF Historical Study 491, 1953, hereafter cited as "Case Histories."

[84] Benjamin Foulois, Diary, 31 August 1916, mentions Spaatz by name, Foulois Papers, Manuscript Division, Library of Congress, Box 1.

[85] Maj. Gen. Benjamin Foulois and Col. C. V. Glines, USAF (both retired), *From the Wright Brothers to the Astronauts: The Memoirs of Major General Benjamin D. Foulois,* (New York: McGraw-Hill, 1968.)

[86] Hennesy, *Army Air Arm,* pp. 167–68. It is possible that Dargue and Spaatz

had met earlier, at Rockwell. Dargue was a senior at West Point when Spaatz was a plebe and there is also a good chance that they knew each other there. On Dargue's death, see Dewitt S. Copp, *Forged in Fire* (Garden City, NY: Doubleday, 1982), p. 219.

[87] Mrs. Carl A. Spaatz, interview, 25 March 1982.

## CHAPTER II

[1] Maj. Carl A. Spaatz, USA, Air Service, to Col. Wirt Robinson, secretary, Cullum Biographical Register, West Point, NY, 12 December 1919, in files of the Association of Graduates, U.S. Military Academy, West Point, NY.

[2] Alfred Goldberg (ed.), *History of the United States Air Force*, USAF, Air Training Command Pamphlet, 190–1, 1 June 1961, p. 2–6.

[3] Majorie Stinson, "Wings for War Birds: How a Girl Taught Fighters to Fly," *Liberty* (28 December 1929), pp. 25–27, copy located in Marjorie Stinson Papers, Manuscript Division, Library of Congress, Box 18; Mrs. Carl A. Spaatz, interview with Dr. James C. Hasdorff, 3 March 1981, U.S., Air Force, Office of the Chief of Air Force History, USAFHRC, USAF Oral History No. 1266, 3 March 1981.

[4] Letter, Spaatz to Robinson, 19 December 1919.

[5] Mrs. Carl A. Spaatz, interview, 25 March 1982.

[6] "Personal Report—Officers," Signal Corps Form 213, August 1917, Carl Spaatz, Major Aviation Section. Apparently Spaatz was prevented from naming the ship in "Personal Report" by censorship, but Frank Lahm was aboard the same vessel and wrote of it in his diary (p. 2).

[7] Lahm, *Diary*, pp. 2–6; John E. Tynan, "U.S. Air Service: Emerging from Its Cradle," *Airpower Historian* 10 (July 1963), pp. 85–7.

[8] Maurer Maurer (ed.), *The U.S. Air Service in World War I*, Vol. I, *Final Report of the Chief of Air Service, AEF and A Tactical History of the Air Service, AEF* (Washington, D.C.: Government Printing Office, 1978.), p. 77 (hereafter: Maurer, *Final Report*).

[9] Goldberg, *History of the USAF*, p. 2–7; "Making Aviators Man Uncle Sam's Big Air-Fleet," *The Literary Digest* 22 (January 19, 1918), pp. 56–60; Hiram Bingham, *An Explorer in the Air Service* (New Haven, CT: Yale University, 1920), pp. 126–27.

[10] Wesley Frank Craven and James Lea Cate (eds), *The Army Air Forces in World War II*, 7 vols., Vol. I, *Plans and Early Operations, January 1939 to August 1942* (Chicago, IL: University of Chicago Press, 1948), p. 5.

[11] Edward V. Rickenbacker, *Rickenbacker* (Greenwich, CT: Fawcett, 1967), p. 93.

[12] Maj. Gen. Edward P. Curtis, USAF (Ret.), interview with Dr. James C. Hasdorff, 22–23 October 1975, USAF Oral History Interview, USAFHRC No. 875, General Curtis was a cadet at the 3d AIC at the time; John Francisco

Richards II, *War Diary and Letters of John Francisco Richards II, 1917–18* (Kansas City, MO: Lechtman Printing Co., 1925), p. 55, copy in the papers of Maj. Gen. Ralph Royce, USAFHRC #168.609–1, 1917–1918; Tynan, "US Air Service Emerging From its Cradle," pp. 85–89; Gen. George C. Kenney, USAF, interview with Dr. James C. Hasdorff, 10–21 August 1974, USAF Oral History #806, USAFHRC.

[13] United States, Army, Air Service, American Expeditionary Forces ("Gorrell History"), Series J, Volume 9, "The Third Aviation Instruction Center, Issoudun, France," pp. 9, 10, 18, Microcopy No. T-619. This work, known as the "Gorrell History," served as a basis for Maurer Maurer's splendid published version cited above. Col. Edgar Gorrell was given the task of assembling the history of the air service at war's end. He was a tough, intelligent, and thoroughgoing man. The result was a massive collection of valuable data now held in the National Archives. There is a microfilm copy of the entire collection held at the USAFHRC, Maxwell AFB, and it is this source from which this account draws. It and its attachments will hereafter be cited as "Gorrell *History*," Also, Personal Reports, Signal Corps, Carl Spaatz, November 1917–August 1918.

[14] Gorrell, *History*, pp. 9, 10, 18.

[15] Bingham, *Explorer in the Air Service*, p. 130; Gorrell *History*, pp. 16, 178; James J. Hudson, *Hostile Skies: A Combat History of the American Air Service in World War I* (Syracuse, NY: Syracuse University Press, 1968), p. 32; 1st Lt. Charles D'Olive, U.S., Army, Air Service, AEF, interview, 16 June 1969, USAF Oral History Interview, USAFHRC 612, 16 June 1969; Maj. Gen. Leigh Wade, interview, Washington, D.C., 2 April 1982.

[16] Gorrell *History*, p. 202; Maj. Gen. Leigh Wade, interview, 2 April 1982.

[17] Maj. Gen. Robert Walsh, interview, 31 March 1982; Maj. Gen. Leigh Wade, interview, 2 April 1982.

[18] Maurer, *Final Report*, pp. 110–11; Hudson, *Hostile Skies*, pp. 35–6.

[19] Gorrell *History*, p. 202.

[20] Col. Walter C. Kilner, "Lessons Learned #117," in Maurer Maurer (ed.), *The U.S. Air Service in World War I*, Vol IV, *Postwar Review* (Washington, D.C.: Government Printing Office, 1979), pp. 319–32. (Hereafter: Maurer, *Postwar Review*.)

[21] Hudson, *Hostile Skies*, p. 33.

[22] Maurer, *Final Report*, p. 110.

[23] Maurer, *Final Report*, pp. 93–94.

[24] Maj. Gen. Robert Walsh, interview, 31 March 1982; Maj. Gen. Leigh Wade, interview, 2 April 1982.

[25] Rickenbacker, *Rickenbacker*, pp. 93–95; Hudson, *Hostile Skies*, p. 36, says that Rickenbacker's acrobatics over a football crowd was the thing that finally stimulated Spaatz to release Eddie, but Rickenbacker himself said that Tooey

grounded him for that demonstration and does not relate it to his release from Issoudun.

[26] Kilner, "Lessons Learned," p. 331.

[27] Bingham, *Explorer in the Air Service*, p. 202.

[28] Maurer, *Final Report*, p. 99.

[29] Bingham, *Explorer in the Air Service*, p. 193.

[30] These reports have been conveniently reprinted in Maurer, *Postwar Review*, under the general title of "Lessons Learned" with an individual number for each report: #116, Lt. Col. Philip A. Carroll, Assistant Chief, Training Section Air Service, AEF, pp. 313–18; #117, Col. Walter C. Kilner, Chief, Training Section Air Service, AEF, pp. 319–32; #118, Lt. Col. Carroll, pp. 332–35; #119, Maj. Thomas G. Lanphier, OIC Training, 3d AIC, pp. 335–36; #120, Maj. Howard S. Curry, CO, Hq Det., 3d AIC, pp. 337–38; #121, 1st Lt. Lewis A. Smith, Police, Prison and Labor Office, 3d AIC, p. 338; #122, Capt. Harry L. Wingate, Executive Officer, 3d AIC, pp. 338–39; #123, Capt. Lester E. Cummings, Adjutant, 3d AIC, p. 340; #124, 1st Lt. Louis H. Kronig, Jr., CO, Field Three, 3d AIC, pp. 341–43; #126 L. H. Byam, Engineering Officer in Charge of Construction, 3d AIC, p. 344; #127, 1st Lt. George W. Eypper, OIC Aerial Gunnery, 3d AIC; #1238, 1st Lt. Richard H. Merkel, OIC, Field No. 10, 3d AID, p. 345.

[31] Richards, *War Diary*, pp. 61, 73.

[32] Maurer, *Postwar Review*, pp. 323–46; Gorrell, *History*, pp. 22, 28, 248, 256–65, 277–79; Arthur Sweetser, *American Air Service* (New York: Appleton, 1919), p. 301; Bingham, *Explorer in the Air Service*, pp. 200–14; Benjamin Foulois, Diary, 22 February 1918, Foulois Papers, Library of Congress, Box 3.

[33] Tynan, "U.S. Air Service," p. 89; Maurer, *Final Report*, p. 106; Foulois, Diary, 16 March 1918, Foulois Papers, Library of Congress, Box 3.

[34] Alfred F. Hurley, *Billy Mitchell: Crusader for Air Power* (Bloomington, IN: Indiana University Press, 1964 and 1975), pp. 22–38.

[35] Maurer, *Final Report*, p. 106.

[36] Goldberg, *History of the USAF*, p. 2–18.

[37] Letter, Carl A. Spaatz to Col. Wirt Robinson, 12 December 1919; Personal Report, Signal Corps Form 213, Carl A. Spaatz, August and September, 1918. The popular literature of the 1930s and Boyertown legend today holds that Spaatz went AWOL to get in his shots at the front, but it is quite clear that he went to gunnery school on orders in July (Personal Report, July, 1918, cites Special Order 118, Hq., SOS, date 8 July 1918) and went initially to the 1st Pursuit Group and then to the 2d also on official orders (Special Orders 236, 3d Aviation Instruction Center, 27 August 1918, citing telegraphic orders from higher headquarters for authority to send Spaatz to the front for 3 weeks of temporary duty, in Spaatz Papers, Library of Congress, Box 3).

[38] Brig. Gen. Vincent J. Esposito, USA (Ret.), ed., *The West Point Atlas of American Wars,* Vol II, 1900–1953 (New York: Praeger, 1959), plate 62.

[39] Capt. B. H. Liddell Hart, *The Real War* (Boston: Little Brown, 1930), pp. 449–58; Esposito, *West Point Atlas,* plate 68.

[40] Esposito, *West Point Atlas,* plate 68; Liddell Hart, *The Real War,* pp. 449–55; Hurley, *Billy Mitchell,* pp. 35–37; Maurer Maurer, *The U.S. Air Service in World War I,* Vol III, *The Battle of St. Mihiel* (Washington, D.C.: Government Printing Office, 1979), pp. 713–17. (Hereafter: Maurer, *St. Mihiel.*)

[41] Forrest C. Pogue, *George C. Marshall: Education of a General* (New York: Viking, 1963), pp. 174–75.

[42] Maurer, *St. Mihiel,* pp. 5–6.

[43] Personal Reports, Signal Corps Form 213, July 1918, Carl Spaatz, on file at USAFHRC.

[44] Personal Reports, Signal Corps Form 213, February and August and September, 1918, Carl Spaatz, on file at USAFHRC.

[45] Lahm, *Diary,* p. 231; Maurer, *St. Mihiel,* pp. 129–30.

[46] Spaatz Interview #1, Spaatz Interview #2, Lahm, *Diary,* p. 211.

[47] Battle Orders #1, American Expeditionary Forces, Headquarters Air Service, First Army, 11 September 1918 (signed by Mitchell), in Maurer, *St. Mihiel,* pp. 137–38.

[48] Operations Orders #12, Hq First Pursuit Wing, Air Service, AEF, 12 September 1918, in Maurer, *St. Mihiel,* pp. 146–47.

[49] Operations Orders #12, Hq First Pursuit Wing, 12 September 1918; Lt. Col. Davenport Johnson, "Lessons Learned," in Maurer, *Postwar Review,* pp. 39–40.

[50] Hurley, *Billy Mitchell,* pp. 35–36.

[51] Report of Operations #76, 2nd Pursuit Group, First Pursuit Wing, AEF, 12 September 1918, in Maurer, *St. Mihiel,* pp. 193–94.

[52] Lt. H. G. Armstrong, Reconnaissance Report, 13th Aero Squadron, 2d Pursuit Gp., 1st Pursuit Wg, AEF, 13 September 1918 and Lt. J. Dickinson Este, Reconnaissance Report, 13th Aero Squadron, 2d Pursuit Group, 1st Pursuit Wg., AEF, 13 September 1918 in Maurer, *St. Mihiel,* pp. 306–8.

[53] Report of 1st Lt. R. R. S. Converse, undated, 13th Pursuit Sq., 2d Pursuit Group, 1st Pursuit Wg., AEF, in Maurer, *St. Mihiel,* pp. 310–12.

[54] Capt. Charles J. Biddle, Reconnaissance Report, 13th Aero Squadron, 2d Pursuit Gp., 1st Pursuit Wg, AEF, 14 September 1918, in Maurer, *St. Mihiel,* pp. 409–10.

[55] Lt. Charles W. Drew, Statement, 13th Aero Squadron, 2d Pursuit Gp., 1st Pursuit Wg, AEF, undated, in Maurer, *St. Mihiel,* pp. 413–15; Maj. Charles J. Biddle, *Fighting Airman: The Way of an Eagle* (Garden City, NY: Doubleday, 1919 and 1968), p. 189.

[56] Report of Operations, #78, Hq 2d Pursuit Gp., 1st Pursuit Wg, AEF, 14 September 1918, in Maurer, *St. Mihiel,* pp. 419–20.

[57] Lt. William Stovall, Reconnaissance Report, 13th Aero Squadron, 2d Pursuit Group, 1st Pursuit Wg., AEF, 15 September 1918, in Maurer, *St. Mihiel*, pp. 521–22, Maj. Carl A. Spaatz, Pilot Report, 13th Pursuit Squadron, 2d Pursuit Gp., 1st Pursuit Wg., AEF, 15 Sep 1918, in Maurer, *St. Mihiel*, p. 523.

[58] Maj. C. J. Biddle, *Fighting Airman* (Garden City, New York: Doubleday, 1968), p. 193.

[59] William Mitchell, *Memoirs of World War I* (New York: Random House, 1960), pp. 250–53.

[60] Hudson, *Hostile Skies*, p. 258.

[61] Mitchell, *Memoirs*, p. 257.

[62] Spaatz Interview #1, Spaatz Interview #2; Hudson, *Hostile Skies*, p. 261; Copp, *A Few Great Captains*, p. 28.

[63] Biddle, *Fighting Airman*, p. 195.

[64] Personnel Records, Carl A. Spaatz, AF 577–42–4886, NPRC F O 722–659, filed at National Personnel Records Center, St. Louis, MO (hereafter cited as "Spaatz 201 File"), Citation, Distinguished Service Cross; Copp, *A Few Great Captains*, p. 27.

[65] Mrs. Carl A. Spaatz, interview, 3 March 1981.

[66] Letter, Col. Ralph A. Harrison, Adjutant General of the Army to Quartermaster General of the Army, 24 December 1918, in Spaatz 201 File.

[67] D'Olive, interview, 16 June 1969.

[68] Richards, *War Diary*, pp. 54–56, 63.

[69] Gen. George C. Kenney, interview with Dr. James C. Hasdorff, 10–21 August 1974, Bay Harbor Islands, FL, United States Air Force Oral History #806, USAFHRC.

[70] Gorrell, *History*, p. 45.

[71] D'Olive, interview, 16 January 1969.

[72] Maurer, *Final Report*, p. 106; William Henry Harbaugh, *Power and Responsibility: The Life and Times of Theodore Roosevelt* (New York: Farrar, Straus & Cudahy, 1961), pp. 510–11.

[73] Maj. Gen. Leigh Wade, interview, 2 April 1982.

[74] Letter, Carl A. Spaatz to Col. Wirt Robinson, 12 December 1919.

[75] Hurley, *Billy Mitchell*, pp. 24–37; Lt. Gen. Ira C. Eaker, USAF (ret.), "The War in the Air," in Vincent J. Esposito (ed.) *A Concise History of World War I* (New York: Praeger, 1961), pp. 262–64; Dr. Thomas Greer, *The Development of Air Doctrine in the Army Air Arm, 1917–1941*, United States, Air Force, Air University, USAF Historical Study #89, September 1955.

## CHAPTER III

[1] Interview, Mrs. Carl A. Spaatz with Dr. James Hasdorff, 3 March 1981, Washington, D.C., USAF Oral History #1266, USAF Historical Research Center, Maxwell AFB, Alabama.

[2] Ibid.

[3] Arnold, "History of Rockwell Field," p. 83.

[4] Officer Classification Card, Spaatz 201 File.

[5] Hurley, *Billy Mitchell*, pp. 40–41.

[6] Hurley, *Billy Mitchell*, pp. 40–41; Glenn L. Martin, "Lessons of the Transcontinental Race," *US Air Service* 2 (November 1919), pp. 12–13; Maj. John C. P. Bartholf, USA, Air Service, "From Pacific to Atlantic in an SE-5," *US Air Service* 2 (November 1919), pp. 14–17; Capt. J. O. Donaldson, USA, Air Service, "Twice Across the Continent in a Single-Seater," *US Air Service* 2 (November 1919), p. 26.

The *US Air Service* magazine was published between the wars by the Army and Navy Air Service Association of Washington, and its membership included both navy flyers and air service men, but probably more of the latter than of the former. The magazine and its parent association were somewhat similar to the *Air Force Magazine* and the Air Force Association of today.

[7] Bartholf, "Pacific to Atlantic," p. 15; Lt. B. W. Maynard, USA, Air Service, "Most Dramatic Incident of My Flight," *US Air Service* 2 (November 1919), p. 26.

[8] Raymond Landis Bowers, "The Transcontinental Reliability Test: American Aviation After World War I," unpublished Master's thesis, University of Wisconsin, 1960, pp. 60–69.

[9] "Double Derby," p. 8; Copp, *A Few Great Captains*, p. 28; Martin, "Lessons," p. 12.

[10] Bowers, "Transcontinental Reliability Rest," pp. 149–59; Officers Classification Card, December 1919, Spaatz 201 File.

[11] Arnold, "History of Rockwell Field," pp. 84–86.

[12] Ibid., pp. 87–93; Thomas M. Coffey, *"Hap,"* (New York: Viking, 1982), p. 101–5.

[13] Henry H. Arnold, *Global Mission* (New York: Harper, 1949), p. 99; Coffey, *Hap*, p. 105; War Department, Air Service Form 94, Spaatz 201 File.

[14] Spaatz Interview #1; Air Service Form 100, Personal Report, November 1921, AFSHRC. He had temporarily commanded the group for a few months the previous spring while it was still at Kelly Field.

[15] Goldberg, *History of the USAF*, p. 3–1.

[16] Mrs. Carl A. Spaatz, interview, 20 June 1985.

[17] Supply Officer, First Pursuit Group to Surgeon, 8th Corps Area, 5 June 1922, Spaatz Papers, Library of Congress, Box 2.

[18] "Group History," *The Flyer* (Selfridge Field, 12 July 1957), p. 1, copy on Spaatz Papers, AFSHRC, Reel 23156, Frames 492–97; Maj. W. C. McChord, USA, Air Service, Hq 6th Corps Area, to Maj. Carl Spaatz, 1st Pursuit Group, 19 June 1922, and Maj. H. A. Dargue, USA, Air Service, Office of the Chief of Air Service to Maj. Carl A. Spaatz, 1st Pursuit Group, 19 June 1922, in Spaatz Papers, Library of Congress (LOC) Box 2.

[19] "Tactical History of Corps Observation," in Maurer, *US Air Service in World War I*, Vol. I, *The Final Report and a Tactical History*, p. 229; Col. Thomas DeWitt Milling, USA Chief of Air Service, First Army, "Lessons Learned," in Maurer (ed.) *The US Air Service in World War I*, Vol. IV, Postwar Review, pp. 10–11.

[20] Dargue to Spaatz, 19 June 1922.

[21] Spaatz to Maj. E. H. Brainard, USA, Medical Corps, Walter Reid (sic) Hospital, Washington, D.C., 8 July 1922, in Spaatz Papers, LOC, Box 2; Spaatz to Maj. Frank D. Lackland, USA, Air Service, Air Officer, 8th Corps Area, 18 July 1922, in Spaatz Papers, LOC, Box 2; Brig. Gen. William Mitchell, USA, Air Service, at Selfridge Field to (Maj.) Gen. Mason N. Patrick, Chief of Air Service, Washington, 3 August 1922, in Spaatz Papers, LOC, Box 2.

[22] Letter, McChord to Spaatz, 19 June 1922.

[23] 1st Lt. C. G. Brenneman, USA, Air Service, Hq Temporary Storage Depot, Selfridge Field, Michigan to Maj. Carl Spaatz, Hq First Pursuit Group, Ellington Field, TX, 19 June 1922, in Spaatz Papers, LOC, Box 2.

[24] Letter, McChord to Spaatz, 19 June 1922.

[25] Letter, Dargue to Spaatz, 19 June 1922.

[26] Mrs. Carl A. Spaatz, interview with John B. McPherson, 20 June 1985.

[27] Letter, Maj. Horace Hickam, USA, Air Service, Office of the Chief of Air Service, Washington, to Maj. Carl Spaatz at 1st Pursuit Group, 18 July 1922, in Spaatz Papers, LOC, Box 2.

[28] Letter, Maj. Gen. Mason Patrick, in Washington, to Spaatz, 5 October 1922, in Spaatz Papers, LOC, Box 2; Brig. Gen. William Mitchell, in Washington, to Spaatz, 11 September 1922, asking Spaatz to arrange to have a good, big, fast car available for Mitchell during the period of the races, in Spaatz Papers, LOC, Box 2; Rear Adm. W. A. Moffett, in Washington, to Maj. Gen. Patrick, in Washington, 20 October 1922, commending Spaatz's work in races, Spaatz Papers, LOC, Box 2; Letter, Secretary of War John W. Weeks in Washington to Spaatz, 21 October 1922, commending Spaatz's work on the races, Spaatz Papers, LOC, Box 2.

[29] Letter, Patrick, in Washington, to Spaatz, 20 October 1922, Spaatz Papers, LOC, Box 2.

[30] Maurer, *The Final Report and a Tactical History*, p. 110.

[31] Letter, Spaatz to Maj. Thurman H. Bane, USA, Air Service at McCook Field, 13 July 1922, in Spaatz Papers, LOC, Box 2; Spaatz to Patrick in Washington, 26 October 1922, in Spaatz Papers, LOC, Box 2.

[32] Letter, Spaatz to Mitchell in Washington, 8 September 1922, in Spaatz Papers, LOC, Box 2.

[33] Letter, Spaatz at Selfridge to Capt. B. V. Baucom, USA, Air Service, at Kelly Field, San Antonio, TX, 14 March 1924 in Spaatz Papers, LOC, Box 3; Lt. T. W. Blackburn, USA, Air Service, at Selfridge to Spaatz at

Fort Sam Houston, San Antonio (on temporary duty), 16 May 1923, Spaatz Papers, LOC, Box 2.

34 Spaatz to Arnold at San Diego, 6 February 1924, in Spaatz Papers, LOC, Box 3; Letter, Spaatz to Capt. B. V. Baucom, at Kelly Field, San Antonio, TX, 14 March 1924; Spaatz to Maj. H. S. Martin, USA Air Service, Hq 6th Corps Area, Chicago, IL, 3 March 1924, in Spaatz Papers, LOC, Box 3.

35 "Personal Report," Carl Spaatz, War Department Form 100, April 1930, reported that Spaatz served on a board of officers to make recommendations on the improvement of maintenance procedures on file at AFSHRC; "Personal Report," Carl Spaatz, War Department Form 100, July, 1923, reported that he was a member of an " 'Airplane Specification Board' " at Dayton.

36 Spaatz to Patrick in Washington, 26 July 1923, reporting on recruiting and desertion problems, in Spaatz Papers, LOC, Box 2; Dargue to Spaatz, 19 June 1922, on problems of initial manning; Spaatz to Maj. W. C. McChord, USA, Air Service, 6th Corps Area Hq, Chicago, 8 July 1922, on manning the pursuit school and shortage of troops at Selfridge, in Spaatz Papers, LOC, Box 2; "Frank" (Maj. Frank W. H. Frank), Office of the Chief of the Air Service, Washington, to Spaatz, 27 July 1922, on the moratorium on army recruiting, in Spaatz Papers, LOC, Box 2.

37 Mitchell at Selfridge to Patrick in Washington, 3 August 1922, complaining that he found on inspecting Selfridge that there were but 25 officers assigned and indicating that there were supposed to be 100, in Spaatz Papers, LOC, Box 2; Spaatz to Mitchell at Washington, 22 August 1922, lamenting orders for four more officers to go to various schools without replacement bringing him down to a force of 21, in Spaatz Papers, LOC, Box 2.

38 Baucom at Kelly to Spaatz, 30 July 1922; Spaatz to Baucom, 7 August 1922; Baucom to Spaatz, 12 August 1922; Baucom to Spaatz, 3 December 1922; Spaatz to Baucom, 8 December 1922; Spaatz to Baucom, 21 December 1922, Spaatz Papers, LOC, Box 2.

39 Spaatz at Langley Field, Air Service Tactical School to Judge Lee E. Skeel, Cleveland, OH, 27 October 1924; Capt. Burt E. Skeel, USA, Air Service, at Selfridge, to Patrick, in Washington, 30 November 1923, in Spaatz Papers, LOC, Box 3.

40 Gen. Dwight Eisenhower in the midst of World War II lamented in his diary that Spaatz was not tough enough on the discipline of his bases, but did allow that perhaps a different style of leadership was required there than in other parts of the army, in David MacIsaac, "Eisenhower: A Reputation in Transition," *Air University Review* 33 (September–October 1982), p. 89.

41 Puryear, *Stars in Flight*, p. 66, based on an interview with Lt. Gen. Ira C. Eaker, 4 October 1977.

[42] I. D. Schulze, Adjutant, Headquarters Selfridge Field, Memorandum to all personnel, 15 December 1923, in Spaatz Papers, LOC, Box 3.

[43] Letter, Spaatz to Lingle, 24 November 1923, in Spaatz Papers, LOC, Box 3.

[44] E. A. Pasha, Greiling Brothers Co., Detroit, Michigan, to Spaatz, 12 June 1923; Milton G. Goff, Detroit, to Spaatz, undated, and Spaatz to Goff, 3 May 1923; Henry B. Joy (Mt. Clemmens, Michigan?), 9 November 1923 to Patrick in Washington, copies in Spaatz Papers, Box 2.

[45] Mrs. Carl A. Spaatz, interview, 20 June 1985.

[46] Maj. Gen. Harry G. Hale, Commander, 6th Corps Area, to Adjutant General, Washington, D.C., 22 November 1924, with endorsements in Spaatz 201 File; Letter, Adjutant General, U.S. Army to Maj. Carl Spaatz, 6 August 1925, in Spaatz 201 File.

[47] Craven and Cate, *Plans and Early Operations,* pp. 18–24; Archibald D. Turnbull and Clifford L. Lord, *History of United States Naval Aviation* (New Haven, CT: Yale, 1949), pp. 176–201; Hurley, *Billy Mitchell,* pp. 66–69.

[48] Mitchell at Selfridge to Patrick in Washington, 3 August 1922, Spaatz Papers, Box 2; Mitchell at Harford Hunt in Monkton, Maryland, September 1922, taking time in the midst of a fox hunt to warn Spaatz of his coming and asking that a room and a car be arranged; Spaatz at Kelly Field, San Antonio on temporary duty, 15 May 1923, to Mitchell in Washington, in Spaatz Papers, Box 3; Spaatz at Kelly to Mitchell at Washington, 21 May 1923, same location; Mitchell in Washington to Spaatz at Selfridge, 1 June 1923, asking for help in caring for his horses, same location; Telegram from Mitchell in Chicago to Spaatz, 12 October 1923, thanking Selfridge officers for participation in Mitchell's wedding, same location; Letter, Mitchell in Washington to Spaatz at Selfridge, 6 September 1924, asking Spaatz to "Please send me that document I left in your safe about 1½ years ago."

[49] Capt. H. W. Cook, USA, Air Service, at the Air Service Tactical School at Langley Field, VA, to Spaatz, 22 and 31 January 1923, in Spaatz Papers, LOC, Box 3.

[50] Spaatz to Maj. Lewis H. Brereton, USA, Air Service at Kelly Field, San Antonio, TX, 4 August 1923, in Spaatz Papers, LOC, Box 2.

[51] Telegram, Air Service Hq, Washington to Spaatz at Boyertown, 9 November 1922, ordering Spaatz to come off leave for a day to attend a "Meeting of Air Service Technical Committee"; War Department Form 100, "Personal Report Officers," Carl Spaatz, July, 1923, twelve days temporary duty at McCook Field as member of "Airplane Specification Board," on file AFSHRC.

[52] Spaatz to Brereton, 4 August 1923.

[53] Hurley, *Billy Mitchell,* pp. 56–60.

[54] U.S. Army, Adjutant General 319–12, to the Chief of the Air Service, 25 November 1922, with attachments, in Spaatz Papers, LOC, Box 2.

[55] Maj. Barton K. Yount, USA, Air Service, Office of the Chief of Air Service, Washington, to Spaatz, 16 January 1923, in Spaatz Papers, LOC, Box 3.

[56] Ibid.; Spaatz to Yount at Washington, 10 January 1923, in Spaatz Papers, LOC, Box 3.

[57] Spaatz to Yount, 10 January 1923; Capt. H. W. Cook, USA, Air Service, Air Service Tactical School, Langley Field, VA, to Spaatz, 22 January 1923, in Spaatz Papers, LOC, Box 3.

[58] Cook to Spaatz, 31 January 1923, in Spaatz Papers, LOC, Box 3.

[59] Spaatz 201 File.

[60] Spaatz to Maj. George E. Stratemeyer, USA, Air Service, at Luke Field, Territory of Hawaii, 17 August 1923, Spaatz Papers, LOC, Box 3; Letters, Stratemeyer to Spaatz, 9 July 1923, same location; Stratemeyer to Spaatz, 20 July 1923, same location.

[61] Stratemeyer to Spaatz, 1 March 1924, same location.

[62] United States, Air Force, *History of the Air Corps Tactical School*, Air University, USAF Historical Study #100, March 1955, p. 7.

[63] Raymond R. Flugel, "United States Air Power Doctrine: A Study of the Influence of William Mitchell and Giulio Douhet at the Air Corps Tactical School, 1921–1935," unpublished Ph.D. dissertation, University of Oklahoma, 1965, pp. 185–201; Frank Futrell, *Ideas, Concepts, Doctrine: A History of Basic Thinking in the United States Air Force, 1907–1964* (Maxwell AFB, AL: Air University, 1955), pp. 8–28; Dr. Thomas Greer, *Development of Air Doctrine* (Maxwell AFB: Air University, 1955) pp. 8–28.

[64] Greer, *Development of Doctrine*, p. 14.

[65] Hurley, *Billy Mitchell*, p. 128.

[66] Spaatz Papers, Box 31.

[67] Telegram, War Department to Commandant, Air Service Tactical School, Langley Field, VA, 6 January 1925, ordering Spaatz to Washington for temporary duty; Special Orders #45, 20 February 1925; Headquarters Langley Field, VA, 20 February 1925, ordering Spaatz to report to the capital for testifying for the Lampert Committee; both in Spaatz Papers, Box 3.

[68] Futrell, *Ideas, Concepts, Doctrine*, p. 25; Greer, *Development of Doctrine*, pp. 26–28.

[69] *Air Corps Tactical School*, p. 54.

[70] Ibid., p. 67.

[71] Handwritten diary, Spaatz Papers, Box 31.

[72] Adjutant General to Maj. Carl Spaatz, 6 August 1925; Spaatz 201 File.

[73] Handwritten diary, Spaatz Papers, Box 31; Carl Spaatz to Bert Atkinson, Office of the Adjutant General, State Arsenal, St. Augustine, FL, 9 September 1925; Spaatz to Atkinson, 6 November 1925, Spaatz Papers, Box 3.

[74] Commander, 6th Corps Area, to Adjutant General, U.S. Army, 22 November 1924, in Spaatz 201 File.

[75] War Department, Adjutant General Form No. 67, 18 June 1925, Spaatz 201 File.

[76] Turnbull and Lord, *Naval Aviation*, pp. 193–204; Craven and Cate, *Plans and Early Operations*, pp. 24–26; Hurley, *Billy Mitchell*, pp. 64–70; Spaatz Interview #1 remarks that the bombing experiments convinced many people inside the air service that bombing in the coastal defense mission had an important future; Henry H. Arnold to Brig. Gen. William Mitchell, 10 August 1921. Arnold, writing from San Francisco, said that he believed that Mitchell's bombing tests had been a complete success and that they had ". . . put the Air Service on the map as a real offensive arm." In Mitchell Papers, Manuscript Division, Library of Congress, Box 9.

[77] James P. Tate, "The Army and its Air Corps: A Study of the Evolution of Army Policy towards Aviation, 1919–1941," unpublished Ph.D. dissertation, Indiana University, 1976, pp. 20–29; Futrell, *Ideas, Concepts, Doctrine*, pp. 20–26.

[78] Personnel Orders No. 142, Office of the Chief of Air Service, 18 June 1925; Memo, Chief of Training and War Plans Division, 18 June 1925, Spaatz Papers, Box 3.

[79] Greer, *Development of Doctrine*, p. 28.

[80] Hurley, *Billy Mitchell*, p. 101; Lt. Gen. Ira C. Eaker, interview with Arthur Marmor, January 1966, USAF Oral History #626, USAF Historical Center, Maxwell AFB, AL. (See next footnote.)

[81] Turnbull and Lord, *Naval Aviation*, names as other members of the board Senator Hiram Bingham, Congressman Carl Vinson, Howard E. Coffin, an admiral and an army general, p. 251; Greer, *Development of Doctrine*, p. 28; R. Earl McClendon, *Autonomy of the Air Arm* (Maxwell AFB, AL: Air University, 1954), pp. 65–66.

[82] Craven and Cate, *Plans and Early Operations*, pp. 21–22, 28; Greer, *Development of Doctrine*, p. 28.

[83] Craven and Cate, *Plans and Early Operations*, pp. 19–28; Futrell, *Ideas, Concepts, Doctrine*, pp. 26–27; Greer, *Development of Doctrine*, p. 28; McClendon, *Autonomy of the Air Arm*, pp. 68–70; Tate, "Army and its Air Corps," pp. 58–63; General Patrick set out his views on the proper role of airpower in a memorandum to his staff dated 19 December 1924, a copy of which is in Mitchell Papers, Manuscripts Division, Library of Congress, Box 16. It gives his concept of a marine corps-like organization for the air service, and it appears to be the view voiced by almost all of the airmen to the Lampert Committee, the Morrow Board, and to the court at the Mitchell trial, all in 1925.

[84] William Mitchell, *Winged Defense* (New York: Putnam's, 1925).

[85] Hurley, *Billy Mitchell,* p. 103; Isaac Don Levine, *Mitchell: Pioneer of Air Power* (New York: Duell, Sloan and Pearce, 1943), pp. 334–35; Tate, The Army and Its Air Corps, p. 66.

[86] Arnold, *Global Mission,* p. 157.

[87] Tate, "The Army and Its Air Corps," pp. 67–68.

[88] Burke Davis, *The Billy Mitchell Affair* (New York: Random House, 1967), p. 253; Lt. Gen. Ira C. Eaker, USAF (Ret.), interview, 26 March 1982.

[89] "Mitchell Adds to Air Service Charges; Sees Perjury Plot in Shenandoah Case; Three Officers Back Him Before Court," *New York Times* (10 November 1925), p. 1.

[90] Ibid.

[91] Copp, *A Few Great Captains,* p. 51; Tate, "The Army and Its Air Corps," p. 70.

[92] Ira C. Eaker, interview, 26 March 1982.

[93] Coffey, *Hap,* pp. 113, 123–24, 130, paints Coolidge as lacking in foresight and wanting in understanding of national security needs; Isaac Don Levine in *Mitchell,* p. 319, suggests that Coolidge was against progress in aviation almost automatically; Thomas H. Buckley, "The United States and the Washington Conference," unpublished Ph.D. dissertation, University of Indiana, 1961, p. 138.

[94] Futrell, *Ideas, Concepts, Doctrine,* p. 29.

[95] Tate, "The Army and Its Air Corps," pp. 92–99.

[96] Ira C. Eaker, "Major Gen. James E. Fechet: Chief of the Air Corps, 1927–1931," *Air Force* 61 (September, 1978), pp. 94–97; Lt. Gen. James H. Doolittle, interview by R. Burch and R. Fogelman, 26 September 1971, #239–0512–793, (hereafter, Doolittle Interview #1.)

[97] Craven and Cate, *Plans and Early Operations,* pp. 28–29; Futrell, *Ideas, Concepts, Doctrine,* p. 29.

[98] Greer, *Development of Doctrine,* pp. 12–14.

[99] Spaatz to Arnold at Fort Riley, 9 November 1926, Spaatz Papers, Box 4; Letter, Spaatz to Maj. Thomas Lanphier at Selfridge Field, 15 December 1926, Spaatz Papers, Box 4, are examples.

[100] Maj. John F. Curry, McCook Field, Ohio, to Spaatz, 3 August 1926, Spaatz Papers, Box 4; Memorandum, 1st Lt. Harold L. George, at Office of the Chief of the Air Corps to Spaatz, 30 November 1926, Spaatz Papers, Box 4.

[101] Since the end of World War II, airplanes and units specialized for that function have reappeared, though standard fighter wings still retain a ground attack role as one of their missions. Those wings equipped with A-10s, A-7s, and the Special Operations Wings with AC-130s have the principal mission of ground attack in close air support and interdiction roles.

[102] Spaatz to Capt. Oliver W. Broberg at the Canal Zone 3 August 1927, Spaatz Papers, Box 4.

[103] Greer, *Development of Doctrine,* p. 37.

[104] 1st Lt. Clayton Bissell at the Air Corps Tactical School, to Spaatz, 21 February 1927, Spaatz Papers, Box 4.

[105] Mr. M. H. Gillett, Wright Field, OH, to Spaatz, 1 October 1927, and Letter, Spaatz to Gillett, 4 October 1927, Spaatz Papers, Box 4. These letters suggest ideas related to Operations Research and Systems Analysis which are generally thought to have had their roots in World War II.

[106] Maj. Gen. Leigh Wade, interview, 2 April 1982; Ernest A. McKay, *A World to Conquer* (New York: Arco, 1981), p. 39. Spaatz was one of those under consideration to command that flight, but Maj. Frederick Martin was selected instead.

[107] Spaatz to Lewis Brereton, at Langley Field, 15 February 1927, Spaatz Papers, Box 4.

[108] Spaatz to Maj. John F. Curry at McCook Field, Dayton, OH, 21 August 1926 and letter, Spaatz to Maj. Thomas Lanphier, Selfridge Field, MI, 21 August 1926, in Spaatz Papers, Box 4.

[109] Maj. John C. McDonnell, AC, in Philadelphia to Spaatz, 13 September 1926, Spaatz Papers, Box 4.

[110] Paul E. Garber, "The 1926 National Air Races," *U.S. Air Services* (October 1926), pp. 13–20.

[111] Carl A. Spaatz, Report of the Flight of the *Question Mark,* January 1–7, 1929, Box 110, Spaatz Papers.

[112] Charles F. McReynolds, "The Refueling Flight of 'Question Mark,' " *Aviation* 26 (January 19, 1929), 158–62.

[113] Ibid.; Maj. J. B. Welsh, USAF, "Never a 'Question Mark,' " *Airman* (March 1976), pp. 24–29; Brig. Gen. Ross G. Hoyt, USAF (Ret.), "Reflections of an Early Refueler," *Air Force* 57 (January 1974), pp. 55–59.

[114] Spaatz, Report of the Flight of the *Question Mark.*

[115] Welsh, "Never a 'Question Mark,' " p. 26; Eaker, "Memories of Six Air Chiefs," p. 195.

[116] When the Air Force got back into the air refueling business right after World War II, its standard tanker was the Boeing KC-97, which had a maximum wartime equivalent gross weight at takeoff of over 180,000 pounds and of course the latterday KC-135s and KC-10s far exceed that. Eaker explained the weight problem in an interview in Washington, D.C., 26 March 1982.

[117] Spaatz, Report of the Flight of the *Question Mark;* Hq. Rockwell Field, CA, Refueling Operations Order No. 1, 20 December 1920, Spaatz Papers, Box 110.

[118] Hoyt, "Reflections of an Early Refueler," pp. 55–59; Bradley Jones, "The Questions Are Answered," *U.S. Air Service* 14 (February 1929), pp. 19–27.

[119] 1st Lt. Ray G. Harris, Air Corps, Engineer Officer, to Chief, Material Divi-

sion, Wright Field, Dayton, OH, 30 January 1929, in Box 4, Spaatz Papers; Jones, "The Questions Are Answered," pp. 19–27.
[120] Spaatz, Report of the Flight of the *Question Mark.*

## CHAPTER IV

[1] Letter, Collector of Internal Revenue, Baltimore, MD, to Spaatz, 12 February 1931, Spaatz Papers, Box 5; Letter, Spaatz to Collector of Internal Revenue, Baltimore, MD, 24 February 1931, Spaatz Papers, Box 5.
[2] "Pilot's Book No. III," 13 August 1929, Spaatz Papers, Box 31.
[3] Letter, Capt. Ira C. Eaker, AC, in Washington to Spaatz, 3 March 1930; Letter, Spaatz to Capt. F. O. D. Hunter, AC, in Washington, 13 July 1929, Spaatz Papers, Box 5.
[4] Letter, Spaatz to Mr. Randall Henderson, Calexico, CA, 13 November 1929; Letter, Spaatz to Mr. Erik Nelson, Seattle, WA, 26 September 1932, Spaatz Papers, Box 5.
[5] Letter, Spaatz to General Foulois at Washington, 9 July 1929; Letter, Spaatz to Captain Hunter, 13 July 1929; Letter, Capt. H. M. Elmendorf, AC, in Washington to Spaatz, 23 December 1930, on Foulois's support for squash court building at March Field.
[6] Letter, Maj. Delos C. Emmons, AC, in Washington to Spaatz, 19 June 1929; Letter, Spaatz to Foulois in Washington, 9 July 1929; Spaatz to Maj. J. B. Brooks, General Staff, at Washington, 23 August 1929; Letter, Elmendorf in Washington to Spaatz, 23 December 1930, in Spaatz Papers, Box 5.
[7] Maj. George Brett, at Selfridge Field, to Spaatz, 11 February 1933; Spaatz to Brett, 14 February 1933; Proceedings, Pursuit Board, Wright Field, Dayton, OH, 12 January 1933, in Spaatz Papers, Box 6.
[8] Letter, Spaatz to Hunter, at Washington, 13 July 1929; Temple N. Joyce, of Berliner-Joyce Aircraft Corporation, Baltimore, MD, to Spaatz, 23 October 1929. Spaatz held some stock in this company for a time and was a personal friend of both Joyce and Henry Berliner. In their frequent correspondence, they exchanged technical information and Spaatz therefore had a direct input to the technical end of the aviation industry itself. The corporation was absorbed by North America in the early thirties, but Spaatz maintained his contact with Berliner until well after World War II. Also, letter, Spaatz to Foulois, 4 February 1930.
[9] U.S., Army Air Corps, Pursuit Board, Proceedings, Wright Field, OH, 12 January 1933, in Spaatz Papers, Box 6.
[10] Ibid.
[11] Letter, Brett to Spaatz, 11 February 1933; Letter, Spaatz to Brett, 14 February 1933, in Spaatz Papers, Box 6.

[12] Letter, Maj. "Jan" (Clinton W.) Howard, Air Corps, at Wright Field, to Spaatz, 5 February 1930; Letter, Howard to Spaatz, 28 February 1930; Letter, Spaatz to Howard, 10 March 1930, in Spaatz Papers, Box 5.

[13] U.S., Army Air Corps, Accident Classification Committee, 7 January 1932, #200.3912–1, 4 January 1932, at Albert F. Simpson Historical Research Center, Maxwell AFB, AL.

[14] John W. R. Taylor (ed.), *Combat Aircraft of the World from 1909 to the Present* (New York: Paragon, 1969), p. 510.

[15] Letter, Spaatz to Howard at Wright Field, 19 November 1931, Spaatz Papers, Box 5.

[16] U.S., Army Air Corps, 7th Bombardment Group, "History of the 7th Bombardment Group (1st Bombardment Wing)," in "History of Organization of Aero Squadrons," Vol I, #168–65011–7, 1913–1936, Albert F. Simpson Historical Research Center, Maxwell AFB, AL, pp. 23–29.

[17] Taylor, *Combat Aircraft,* p. 474.

[18] Letter, Spaatz to Howard, 19 November 1931, Spaatz Papers, Box 5.

[19] "History of the 7th Bombardment Group," p. 24.

[20] Ibid., p. 25.

[21] Ibid., p. 26.

[22] Ibid., p. 33; Letter, Spaatz to Foulois in Washington, 19 November 1931, Spaatz Papers, Box 5; Letter, Spaatz to Capt. H. M. Elmendorf, Air Corps, in Washington, 16 March 1931, Spaatz Papers, Box 5; especially ltr., Spaatz to Capt. H. R. McClelland, Air Corps, in Washington, 10 March 1931, in Spaatz Papers, Box 5.

[23] Letter, Spaatz to Arnold at Wright Field, 6 July 1931; Spaatz to Arnold, 20 July 1931, in Spaatz Papers, Box 5; R. Bruce Harley, *The March Field Story (March AFB, California: Directorate of Information, Fifteenth Air Force, 1968)*, pp. 35, 62.

[24] Mrs. Carl A. Spaatz, interview, 25 March 1982.

[25] Ibid.

[26] Letter, Spaatz to Commanding Officer, Headquarters Detachment, 7th Bombardment Group, 24 January 1930, with endorsements; Letter, Spaatz to Commanding Officer, Headquarters Detachment, 7th Bombardment Group, 29 January 1930; Letter, Spaatz to Commanding Officer, Rockwell Field, 12 May 1930, with attached efficiency report, in Spaatz Papers, Box 5.

[27] Letter, Spaatz to Mr. Harold T. Lewis, Boeing Airlines, Cheyenne, WY, 6 August 1932, in Spaatz Papers, Box 5.

[28] Spaatz to Maj. L. W. McIntosh, Air Corps, at Crissy Field, San Francisco, CA, 27 October 1930, in Spaatz Papers, Box 5.

[29] Letter, Norman H. Ives at Fitzsimons General Hospital to Spaatz, 10 August 1930, in Spaatz Papers, Box 5.

30 Letter, Robert J. Pritchard, ed., *Western Flying*, Los Angeles, to Spaatz, 30 August 1930, Spaatz Papers, Box 5.

31 Letter, Spaatz to Pritchard, 10 September 1930, in Spaatz Papers, Box 5.

32 "History of the 7th Bombardment Group," pp. 18–19.

33 Telegram, "Longanecker" (Lt. Col. Ira Eaker), Washington D.C., to Spaatz, 4 October 1930; Letter, Spaatz to Mrs. Muriel A. Casey in Los Angeles, 6 October 1930, in Spaatz Papers, Box 5.

34 Copp, *A Few Great Captains*, pp. 107–8.

35 Letter, Kraus to Spaatz, 29 September 1930; Letter, Spaatz to Kraus, 3 October 1930, in Spaatz Papers, Box 5.

36 Turnbull and Lord, *History of Naval Aviation*, p. 280.

37 Alfred Thayer Mahan, *The Influence of Seapower Upon History* (New York: Hill and Wang, 1890 and 1957), pp. 116–21, explains it as a principle that the defensive or secondary uses of naval power, such as commerce raiding, cannot be decisive in the absence of the control of the sea—and can be disastrous. The correct strategy, he asserts, must be the prior destruction of the main units of the enemy battle fleet, and then the naval power can be turned to commerce raiding, shore bombardment, or any other function at its own leisure—and consequently can do a thorough and decisive job.

38 Craven and Crate, *Plans and Early Operations*, pp. 60–61; Turnbull and Lord, *History of Naval Aviation*, p. 280; Futrell, *Ideas, Concepts, Doctrine*, p. 34.

39 Letter, 1st Lt. Kenneth Walker at Maxwell Field, AL, to Spaatz, 23 November 1932, Spaatz Papers, Box 5, and related correspondence is particularly significant, for Walker was one of four of the Maxwell instructors who were assigned to Washington immediately before the onset of World War II to write the fundamental document that was used as the army air force's guide to the development of the strategic bombing attack on Germany and the building of the entire air component of the U.S. Army. Spaatz, at the time of the writing of the plan, was at least theoretically in charge of the effort as the officer of the air staff directing the plans function. He was present on several occasions when Walker and the others (Hansell, Kuter, and George) briefed the scheme to other decision makers. Later, as we shall see, Spaatz was the chief executor of the plan as it applied to Europe.

40 Letter, Spaatz to Maj. Millard F. Harmon, Air Corps, Command and General Staff School, Fort Leavenworth, KS, 2 January 1931, is an answer to Harmon's request for ideas.

41 Letter, Spaatz to Harmon, 2 January 1931, Spaatz Papers, Box 5.

42 Letter, Spaatz to Howard, 19 November 1931, Spaatz Papers, Box 5.

43 Letter, Spaatz to Walker, 5 December 1932, Spaatz Papers, Box 5.

44 Ibid.

45 Letter, Spaatz to Walker, 5 December 1932, in Spaatz Papers, Box 5.

[46] Letter, Spaatz to Capt. Hugh M. Elmendorf, Air Corps, in Washington, 16 March 1931, in Spaatz Papers, Box 5.

[47] Letter, Spaatz to Maj. W. H. Frank, Air Corps, in Washington, 12 September 1932, Spaatz Papers, Box 5.

[48] Letter, Spaatz to Elmendorf, 16 March 1931, in Spaatz Papers, Box 5.

[49] Letter, Spaatz to Maj. Thomas D. Milling, Air Corps, in Fitzsimons General Hospital, Denver, CO, 20 August 1930, in Spaatz Papers, Box 5.

[50] Letter, Spaatz to Maj. H. Conger Pratt, Air Corps, in Washington, 23 August 1930, in Spaatz Papers, Box 5.

[51] Letter, Spaatz to Milling, 20 August 1930, in Spaatz Papers, Box 5.

[52] Letter, Spaatz to Maj. Walter G. Kilner, Air Corps, in Washington, 23 August 1930, in Spaatz Papers, Box 5.

[53] Efficiency Report, War Department Form No. 67, 10 June 1933, in Spaatz 201 File.

[54] War Department Form No. 121, Personal Report—Officers, 30 June 1933, on file at AFSHRC.

[55] Letter, Spaatz to Arnold, 18 July 1933, in Spaatz Papers, Box 6; Memorandum from Lt. Col. J. H. Pirie, Air Corps, Chief, Training and Operations Division, Office of the Chief of the Air Corps to the Chief of the Air Corps, 15 February 1933, in the Papers of Maj. Gen. Benjamin Foulois, Manuscripts Division, Library of Congress, Washington, D.C., Box 22; Memorandum, Capt. H. A. Halverson, Air Corps, Chief Training Section, Operations and Training Division, to Spaatz, 6 July 1935, Spaatz Papers, Box 7.

[56] Letter, Lt. Col. Frank M. Andrews, Air Corps, at Selfridge Field to Brig. Gen. Oscar Westover, AC, in Washington on instrument equipment and training, 21 September, in Spaatz Papers, Box 6; Memorandum from Capt. Harold M. McClelland, Air Corps, Operations Section, Operations and Training Division of Office of Chief of Air Corps to Spaatz on overwater training, 19 January 1934, Spaatz Papers, Box 6; Arnold to Spaatz, on the desirability of the big bombers, 5 February 1935, in Spaatz Papers, Box 7; Mr. Erik Nelson (of Boeing), in Seattle, WA, to Spaatz on the crash of the first B-17 and the development of the even larger B-15, 8 November 1935, in Spaatz Papers, Box 7.

[57] Futrell, *Ideas, Concepts, Doctrine,* pp. 37–40.

[58] Tate, ''The Army and Its Air Corps,'' p. 176.

[59] Maj. John F. Shiner, USAF, ''General Benjamin Foulois and the 1934 Air Mail Disaster,'' *Aerospace Historian* 25 (Winter, December 1978), pp. 221–30; Lt. Col. Eldon Downs, USAF, ''Army and the Air Mail—1934,'' *The Air Power Historian* 9 (January 1962), pp. 35–51.

[60] ''Statement of Brigadier General J. E. Chaney,'' February 1934, in Spaatz Papers, Box 6; Shiner, ''Foulois and the Air Mail Disaster,'' pp. 221–30.

[61] Maj. John F. Shiner, USAF, *Benjamin Foulois and the U.S. Army Air*

*Corps* (Washington, D.C.: Government Printing Office, 1984), pp. 125–27; "Statement of Brigadier General J. E. Chaney," February 1934, in Spaatz Papers, Box 6; Copp, *A Few Great Captains,* pp. 160–66.

[62] Downs, "Army and the Airmail—1934," pp. 35–46; Capt. William M. Crabbe, USAF, "The Army Airmail Pilots Report!" *The Airpower Historian* 9 (April 1962), pp. 87–94, for first person accounts by crew members.

[63] Norman E. Borden, Jr., *Air Mail Emergency, 1934* (Freeport, ME: Bond, Wheelwright, 1968), pp. 121–24, 136; Shiner, "Foulois and the Air Mail Disaster," pp. 227–28.

[64] Shiner, "Foulois and the Air Mail Disaster," p. 229; Copp, *A Few Great Captains,* pp. 162–66.

[65] Copp, *A Few Great Captains,* p. 163.

[66] United States Air Force, *Selected Air Force Case Histories,* USAF Historical Study, No. 91, Air University, 1953.

[67] Copp, *A Few Great Captains,* pp. 47–48; Futrell, *Ideas, Concepts, Doctrine,* p. 18.

[68] Tate, "The Army and Its Air Corps," p. 195; Copp, *A Few Great Captains,* pp. 147–48; Greer, *Development of Air Doctrine,* p. 104.

[69] Greer, *Development of Air Doctrine,* p. 73; Tate, "The Army and Its Air Corps," p. 185.

[70] Tate, "The Army and Its Air Corps," pp. 186–88; Futrell, *Ideas, Concepts, Doctrine,* pp. 36–37.

[71] Greer, *Development of Air Doctrine,* p. 72–73, in an official USAF study, was moderate in his criticism of the Baker Board, pointing only to its conservatism; Carroll V. Glines in *Jimmy Doolittle: Master of the Calculated Risk* (New York: Van Nostrand Reinhold, 1972) said that the report "reflected the thinking of those on the committee who did not visualize the potential of the airplane as a military weapon," p. 116; Lowell Thomas and Edward Jablonski, in *Doolittle: A Biography* (New York: Doubleday, 1976), pp. 134–36, explicitly criticize the board for failing to see a threat of "an aerial attack on the United States . . ." and go on to say that Doolittle's minority report was vindicated in the next decade.

[72] Greer, *Development of Air Doctrine,* p. 75; Goldberg, in *History of the USAF,* pp. 3–15 (an official USAF publication) says: "Air leaders had accepted the GHQ Air Force, but they were not enthusiastic about it as a solution to their problems. It was a compromise of what most of them really wanted, . . . At best it was a step toward a more fundamental change, and General Andrews as well as the successive chiefs of the Air Corps . . . accepted it as such, sincerely."

[73] Greer, *The Development of Air Doctrine,* p. 74; Shiner, *Foulois and the US Army Air Corps,* pp. 226–30.

[74] Futrell, *Ideas, Concepts, Doctrine,* pp. 37–40; Greer, *The Development of Air Doctrine,* p. 74.

[75] Memorandum, Spaatz to the chief of the air corps, 14 July 1934, Spaatz Papers, Box 6.

[76] Futrell, *Ideas, Concepts, Doctrine,* p. 40.

[77] Memorandum, Spaatz to "Executive," 5 January 1935, Papers of Frank M. Andrews, Manuscripts Division, Library of Congress, Washington, D.C., Box 16.

[78] Greer, *Development of Air Doctrine,* p. 74; Shiner, *Foulois and the US Army Air Corps,* p. 228.

[79] Ibid.

[80] Letter, Spaatz to Arnold at March Field, 5 February 1935, in Spaatz Papers, Box 7; Letter, Spaatz to Kilner at Maxwell Field, AL, 11 March 1935, in Spaatz Papers, Box 7.

[81] Letter, Spaatz to Arnold at March Field, California, 5 February 1935, in Spaatz Papers, Box 7.

[82] Letter, Col. William A. Stofft, U.S. Army, Director, Combat Studies Institute, Fort Leavenworth, KS, to author, 30 August 1982.

[83] Puryear, *Stars in Flight,* pp. 79–81.

[84] Efficiency Report, War Department Form 67, 1 July 1936, Spaatz 201 File; Gen. Laurence Kuter, interview, 30 September–3 October 1974, remembers a "story" that Spaatz so ridiculed their teachings that the school almost refused to graduate him, p. 129.

[85] United States, Army Air Corps, "History of Langley Field, 1 March 1935 to 7 December 1941," AFSHRC, No. 285–49–2, pp. 24–30.

[86] Mrs. Carl A. Spaatz, interview, 25 March 1982.

[87] USAF Historical Study, No. 91.

[88] Hurley, *Billy Mitchell,* p. 128.

[89] Knerr, "Autobiography," p. 126.

[90] Ibid, pp. 125–30.

[91] Gen. Curtis LeMay, USAF (Ret.), interview with David R. Mets, Babson Park, Florida, April 1982.

[92] Greer, *The Development of Air Doctrine,* pp. 44–47; Tate "The Army and Its Air Corps," pp. 116–25.

[93] Lt. Gen. Barney M. Giles, interview with Dr. James C. Hasdorff and Brig. Gen. Noel F. Parrish, USAF (Ret.), San Antonio, TX, 20–21 November 1974, AFSHRC, K239.0512–814, pp. 19–20.

[94] Goldberg, *History of the USAF,* pp. 3–17.

[95] Tate, "The Army and Its Air Corps," pp. 178–80, 216–22; Greer, *Development of Air Doctrine,* pp. 97–106, explains that the usual argument of the airmen on the experience of the foreign wars of the thirties was that none was a valid test of airpower.

[96] Curtis E. LeMay with MacKinlay Kantor, *Mission with LeMay* (Garden City, NY: Doubleday, 1965), pp. 154, 169–75.

[97] Gen. Laurence S. Kuter, USAF (Ret.), interview with Hugh N. Ahmann and Tom Sturm, Naples FL, 30 September–3 October 1974, AFSHRC No. K239.0512–810, pp. 148–52.

[98] MGEN F. M. Andrews, "The GHQ Air Force," 1937, USAFHRC No 248.211–62G; MGEN D. C. Emmons, "The GHQ Air Force," 1939, USAFHRC No 248.211–62A.

[99] Robert W. Krauskopf, "The Army and the Strategic Bomber, 1930–1939," *Military Affairs* 22 (Summer 1950), p. 89.

[100] U.S., Army Air Corps, "History of Langley Field, 1 March 1935 to 7 December 1941," AFSHRC No. 285.49–2, pp. 23–25; Greer, *Development of Doctrine,* pp. 105–6.

[101] Mrs. Ruth Spaatz, interview, 20 June 1985.

[102] Spaatz 201 File.

## CHAPTER V

[1] Mrs. Carl A. Spaatz, telephone conversation with David R. Mets, 16 July 1983.

[2] Spaatz 201 File; Mrs. Carl A. Spaatz, telephone conversation, 16 July 1983.

[3] Ibid.

[4] Greer, *Development of Air Doctrine,* pp. 93–100; H. H. Arnold, *Global Mission,* pp. 167–68; Mark Skinner Watson, *United States Army in World War II: Chief of Staff: Prewar Plans and Preparations* (Washington, D.C.: Historical Division, Department of the Army, 1950), pp. 45–46.

[5] James MacGregor Burns, *Roosevelt: The Lion and the Fox* (New York: Harcourt Brace & World, 1956), pp. 286–87; Rene Albrecht-Carrié, *Diplomatic History of Europe,* (New York: Harper, 1958) pp. 525–28.

[6] Burns, *The Lion and the Fox,* pp. 388–89; Greer, *Development of Doctrine,* pp. 100–101; Arnold, *Global Mission,* p. 177.

[7] Spaatz 201 File. Spaatz made a contribution to the program writing because Arnold called him to Washington on a temporary duty status in mid-November.

[8] Arnold, *Global Mission,* pp. 176–80; Craven and Cate, *Plans and Early Operations,* pp. 104–5.

[9] Craven and Cate, *Plans and Early Operations,* p. 104; Greer, *Development of Doctrine,* p. 101; Alfred Goldberg, *History of the United States Air Force* (Randolph AFB, TX: Air Training Command, ATC Pamphlet 190–1, 1961), pp. 3–22.

[10] Craven and Cate, *Plans and Early Operations,* p. 89.

[11] Arnold, *Global Mission,* pp. 181–82; Goldberg, *History of the USAF,* pp. 3–22.

[12] "Diary of Brigadier General Carl Spaatz on Tour of Duty in England," 17 May 1940 to 19 September 1940, in Spaatz Papers, Manuscripts Division, Library of Congress, Box 7.

[13] Spaatz England Diary; Letter, Spaatz at U.S. Embassy in London to Arnold in Washington, 4 June 1940, in Spaatz Papers, Box 7; Letter, Spaatz in London to Arnold in Washington, 31 July 1940, Spaatz Papers, Box 7.

[14] Spaatz England Diary; Letter, Spaatz at the U.S. Embassy in London to Arnold in Washington, 4 June 1940.

[15] Spaatz England Diary; Letter, Spaatz to Arnold, 4 June 1940.

[16] Spaatz England Diary; Letter, Spaatz to Arnold, 31 July 1940; Spaatz in London to Arnold in Washington, 27 August 1940, in Spaatz Papers, Box 7.

[17] Father of President John Kennedy.

[18] Spaatz England Diary; Letter, Spaatz to Arnold, 31 July 1940. Already at the end of July he was signalling Arnold that the chances for the Germans were not good.

[19] Spaatz England Diary.

[20] Futrell, *Ideas, Concepts, Doctrine,* p. 53; Adolf Galland, *The First and the Last,* (New York: Ballantine, 1954) pp. 25–29.

[21] Arnold, *Global Mission,* p. 199; Futrell, *Ideas, Concepts, Doctrine,* pp. 53–61.

[22] Arnold, *Global Mission,* p. 245; James C. Gaston, *Planning the American Air War: Four Men and Nine Days in 1941* (Washington, D.C.: NDU Press, 1982), pp. 13–17; U.S. Strategic Air Forces in Europe, "Outline of History by Periods," undated, Spaatz Papers, Box 295; one of the briefings was done for the president on 15 September 1941, "Notes on Preparation of AWDD," in Spaatz Papers, Box 7.

[23] Letter, Spaatz in London to Arnold in Washington, 27 August 1940, in Spaatz Papers, Box 7.

[24] Maj. Gen. Haywood S. Hansell, USAF (Ret.), *The Air Plan that Defeated Hitler* (Atlanta, GA: Higgins-McArthur/Longino and Porter, 1972), pp. 78–89.

[25] Ibid, p. 87.

[26] Ibid, pp. 49–55; David MacIsaac, *Strategic Bombing in World War II: The Story of the United States Strategic Bombing Survey* (New York: Garland, 1976), pp. 10–12.

[27] MacIsaac, *Strategic Bombing,* p. 12; Hansell, *Air Plan that Defeated Hitler,* p. 88.

[28] Gaston, *Planning the American Air War,* pp. 85–91.

[29] Greer, *Development of Doctrine,* p. 127.

[30] Watson, *Prewar Plans and Preparations,* p. 288.

[31] Guido R. Perera, *Leaves from My Book of Life,* Vol II, *Washington and War Years* (Boston: privately printed, 1975), pp. 17–31.

[32] Watson, *Prewar Plans and Preparations,* p. 285.

[33] Gen. Laurence S. Kuter, USAF (Ret.), "George C. Marshall, Architect of

Airpower," *Air Force* 61 (August 1978), pp. 65–67; Watson, *Prewar Plans and Operations,* p. 280, are only two of many.

[34] Greer, *Development of Doctrine,* p. 127; Craven and Cate, *Plans and Early Operations,* p. 115; Watson, *Prewar Plans and Preparations,* pp. 292–93.

[35] Watson, *Prewar Plans and Preparations,* pp. 295–97; Futrell, *Ideas, Concepts, Doctrine,* p. 63.

[36] Letter, Edgar S. Gorrell, 31 January 1942, in Washington to Carl Spaatz at Bolling Field and letter, James Fechet, Laguna Beach, CA, 5 February 1942, both in Spaatz Papers, Box 8, are two examples among many from the "old greats" of the air service and air corps who recognized the magnitude of the step and sent congratulations to Spaatz.

[37] Lt. Gen. Ira C. Eaker, USAF (Ret.), interview with David R. Mets, Washington, D.C., 26 March 1982.

[38] Letter, Spaatz to Curtis, 23 July 1942, in Spaatz Papers, Box 8.

[39] Cook, *A Memoir,* pp. 6, 58. Cook passed through Issoudun on the way to the front in World War I and though he did become friends with the commander, of course, he did come away with a cadet's-eye view of Spaatz similar to that of Curtis.

[40] Letter, Spaatz to Arnold, 23 July 1942, in Spaatz Papers, Box 8.

[41] Craven and Cate, *Plans and Early Operations,* pp. 616–50.

[42] Carroll V. Glines, *Jimmy Doolittle* (New York: Van Nostrand Reinhold, 1972 and 1980), pp. 125–26; Arnold, *Global Mission,* pp. 299–300; Lt. Gen. James Doolittle, USAF (Ret.), interview with David R. Mets, Washington, D.C., 19 May 1982.

[43] Roger A. Freeman, *The Mighty Eighth: Units, Men, and Machines* (Garden City, NY: Doubleday, 1948 and 1961), p. 55; Taylor, *Combat Aircraft,* pp. 529–30.

[44] Taylor, *Combat Aircraft,* pp. 529–30.

[45] Glines, *Jimmy Doolittle,* pp. 125–26.

[46] Memorandum, Lt. Col. William M. Gross, U.S. Army, Air Corps, at Dayton, OH, to Spaatz, 3 April 1942, in Spaatz Papers, Box 8.

[47] Diary, HQ Eighth Air Force, 20 May 1942, recording conference with Doolittle at Bolling Field, in Spaatz Papers, Box 8.

[48] Craven and Cate, *Plans and Early Operations,* p. 607.

[49] HQ Eighth Diary, Washington, D.C., 4 June 1942, Spaatz Papers, Box 8; Letter, Spaatz in Washington to Eaker in UK, 6 June 1942, Spaatz Papers, Box 8.

[50] HQ Eighth Air Force, Daily Diary, Bolling Field, D.C., 20 May 1942, in Spaatz Papers, Box 8.

[51] Craven and Cate, *Plans and Early Operations,* p. 652.

[52] HQ Eighth Air Force, Daily Diary, 21 and 22 May 1942, Spaatz Papers, Box 8.

[53] HQ Eighth Air Force, Office of the Commanding General, Daily Diary, 15 May 1942, "General Spaatz and Staff–Secretary of War Stimson," in Spaatz Papers, Box 8.

[54] Memorandum, Spaatz in Manchester, NH, to M. F. Harmon in Washington, 25 May 1942, in Spaatz Papers, Box 8.

[55] Ibid.; Letter, Spaatz at base BW-1, Greenland, to Frank O. Hunter at Dow Field, ME, 16 June 1942, in Spaatz Papers, Box 8; HQ Eighth Air Force, Daily Diary, various locations, 10–18 June 1942, in Spaatz Papers, Box 8.

[56] HQ Eighth Air Force, Daily Diary, 23 May–1 June 1942, at various locations, in Spaatz Papers, Box 8.

[57] Craven and Cate, *Plans and Early Operations,* pp. 298–99, 451–54; HQ Eighth Air Force, Daily Diary, 1 June 1942, in Spaatz Papers, Box 8.

[58] HQ Eighth Air Force, Daily Diary, 3 June 1942, in Spaatz Papers, Box 8.

[59] Forrest C. Pogue, *George C. Marshall, Ordeal and Hope* (New York: Viking, 1966), pp. 323–36; HQ Eighth Air Force, Daily Diary, Washington, D.C., 4 June 1942, in Box 8, Spaatz Papers.

[60] HQ Eighth Air Force, Daily Diary, 5 June 1942, Washington, D.C., in Spaatz Papers, Box 8.

[61] Letter, Spaatz in Washington to Eaker in England, 6 June 1942, in Spaatz Papers, Box 8.

[62] Ibid.

[63] HQ Eighth Air Force, Daily Diary, 4 June 1942, Washington D.C., in Spaatz Papers, Box 8; Letter, Spaatz to Eaker, 6 June 1942; Craven and Cate, *Plans and Early Operations,* p. 642.

[64] HQ Eighth Air Force, Daily Diary, 7 June 1942, Washington D.C., in Spaatz Papers, Box 8.

[65] HQ Eighth Air Force, Daily Diary, 10–11 June 1942, Manchester, NH and Presque Isle, ME, in Spaatz Papers, Box 8.

[66] Letter, Spaatz in Greenland to Hunter in Bangor, ME, 16 June 1942, in Spaatz Papers, Box 8.

[67] HQ Eighth Air Force, Daily Diary, 16–18 June 1942, in Spaatz Papers, Box 8.

[68] Letter, Spaatz in England to Arnold in Washington, 8 July 1942; Letter, Arnold in Washington to Spaatz in England, 16 July 1942, both in Spaatz Papers, Box 8.

[69] Letter, Spaatz in England to Arnold in Washington, 20 July 1942, in Spaatz Papers, Box 8.

[70] Craven and Cate, *Plans and Early Operations,* pp. 644–45; Letter, Spaatz in England to E. P. Curtis in Washington, 15 July 1942, and Arnold to Spaatz, 16 July 1942, in Spaatz Papers, Box 8; the initial P-38s across were of the 1st Pursuit Group, the unit which had been Spaatz's earliest tactical command back in the early twenties.

[71] Copp, *Forged in Fire,* p. 266.

[72] Craven and Cate, *Plans and Early Operations,* pp. 658–60; Arnold, *Global Mission,* p. 329.

[73] Letter, Spaatz in England to Arnold in Washington, 5 July 1942, and HQ Eighth Air Force, Daily Diary, 23, 24, and 25 June 1942 in Spaatz Papers, Box 8.

[74] Craven and Cate, *Plans and Early Operations,* pp. 655–56; Letter, Arnold in Washington to Spaatz in London, 9 August 1942; Letter, Air Marshal Sir William Sholto Douglas to Spaatz, 25 July 1942, and Spaatz to Sholto Douglas, 28 July 1942, in Spaatz Papers, Box 8.

[75] Copp, *A Few Great Captains,* p. 42; *Register of Graduates* (West Point, NY: Association of Graduates, USMA, 1982), p. 306; Letter, Spaatz in England to Arnold in Washington, 5 July 1942, in Spaatz Papers, Box 8; Letter, Spaatz to Arnold, 8 July 1942, in Spaatz Papers, Box 8; Craven and Cate, *Plans and Early Operations,* pp. 628–39, 648.

[76] Hugh Knerr, "Autobiography," unpublished manuscript, AFSHRC, Maxwell AFB, Alabama, pp. 141–53, 171; Letter, Andrews in Panama to Spaatz in Washington, 28 July 1941, Andrews Papers, Library of Congress, Manuscripts Division, Box 6; Letter, Spaatz to Andrews, 11 July 1941, in Andrews Papers, Box 6.

[77] HQ Eighth Air Force, Daily Diary, 18 June 1942, in Spaatz Papers, Box 8.

[78] HQ Eighth Air Force, Daily Diary, 19 June–4 July 1942, in Spaatz Papers, Box 8; Letter, Dwight D. Eisenhower in England to Arnold in Washington, 26 June 1942, in Pre-Presidential File, Box 5, Eisenhower Library, Abilene, KS; Mrs. Carl A. Spaatz.

[79] Letter, Eisenhower to Arnold, 26 June 1942, in Pre-Presidential File, Box 5, Eisenhower Library, Abilene, KS.

[80] Notes on an informal off-the-record press conference to meet General Spaatz in Col. H. B. Hinton's office, 4:30 P.M., 19 June 1942, in Spaatz Papers, Box 8.

[81] HQ Eighth Air Force, Daily Diary, London, 20 June 1942, in Spaatz Papers, Box 8.

[82] Ibid., 22 June 1942.

[83] Ibid., 23 June 1942.

[84] Ibid., 1 July 1942.

[85] Letter, Spaatz in London to Arnold in Washington, 8 July 1942, in Spaatz Papers, Box 8.

[86] Letter, Spaatz to Arnold, 11 August 1942, in Spaatz Papers, Box 8.

[87] HQ Eighth Air Force, Daily Diary, 26 June 1942, in Spaatz Papers, Box 8.

[88] Letter, Maj. Gen. Haywood S. Hansell to David R. Mets, 25 August 1983. General Hansell says that Spaatz was fully convinced of the effectiveness

of the strategic bombing idea, but he may have doubted that the people of the United States would be willing to wait long enough for it to have its effect. Thus, though Spaatz asserted to Harris that the landings were necessary, Hansell thinks that it would be more accurate to say that he felt that they were "likely" because of political pressure.

89 Copp, *Forged in Fire,* pp. 266–69; Lt. Gen. Ira C. Eaker with Arthur Marmor, January 1966, AFSHRC #K238.0512–626.

90 Letter, Arnold in Washington to Spaatz in England, 9 August 1942; Letter, Spaatz to Arnold, 12 August 1942; Letter, Arnold to Spaatz, 19 August 1942, all in Spaatz Papers, Box 8.

91 Letter, Spaatz to Arnold, 11 August 1942, in Spaatz Papers, Box 8.

92 Letter, Spaatz to Arnold, 12 August 1942, Spaatz Papers, Box 8.

93 Ibid.

94 Wilbur H. Morrison, *Fortress Without a Roof: The Allied Bombing of the Third Reich* (New York: St. Martin's, 1982), pp. 47–49.

95 Craven and Cate, *Plans and Early Operations,* pp. 660–65.

96 Letter, Spaatz to Arnold, 24 August 1942, in Spaatz Papers, Box 8.

97 Robert E. Sherwood, *Roosevelt and Hopkins* (New York: Grosset and Dunlap, 1948 and 1950), pp. 605–12; Stephen E. Amrose, *Eisenhower,* Vol. I, *Soldier, General of the Army, President-Elect, 1890–1952* (New York: Simon and Schuster, 1983), pp. 179–83; Letter, Arnold to Spaatz, 3 September 1942, in Spaatz Papers, Box 8.

98 HQ Eighth Air Force, Daily Diary, 17–21 July 1943, Spaatz Papers, Box 8.

99 Untitled Notes, annotated in pencil "This worked up by Craig, Vandenberg, Spaatz–prepared by Van to give to General Marshall on 7/23/42," in Spaatz Papers, Box 8.

100 Letter, Arnold to Spaatz, 30 July 1942, in Spaatz Papers, Box 8; Denis Richards and Hilary St. George Saunders, *Royal Air Force, 1939–45,* Vol. II, *The Fight Avails* (London: HMSO, 1954), pp. 244–46; Craven and Cate, *Plans and Early Operations,* pp. 573–75; Robert H. Ferrell, ed., *The Eisenhower Diaries* (New York: Norton, 1981), pp. 72–76.

## CHAPTER VI

1 Ferrell, *The Eisenhower Diaries,* pp. 72–76; Pogue, *George C. Marshall: Ordeal and Hope,* pp. 327–49.

2 Morrison, *Fortress Without a Roof,* p. 70; Notes, Meeting October 30 in General Spaatz's office with General Duncan, General Hansell, General Doolittle, General Craig, and Colonel Vandenberg, in Spaatz Papers, Box 9; Letter, Spaatz in England to Arnold in Washington, 31 October 1942, in Spaatz Papers, Box 9; Memorandum, Eisenhower to Spaatz, 13 October 1942, in Spaatz Papers, Box 9.

3 Letter, Spaatz to Arnold, 31 October 1942; Memorandum, Eisenhower to

Spaatz, 13 October 1942, in Spaatz Papers, Box 9; Letter, Eisenhower in London to Arnold in Washington, 31 October 1942, in Pre-Presidential File, Box 5, Eisenhower Library, Abilene, KS.

[4] Ambrose, *Soldier, General of the Army, President-Elect*, p. 183.

[5] Lt. Gen. Fred M. Dean, USAF (Ret.), interview with Maj. Richard H. Emmons, USAF, 25–26 February 1975, Hilton Head, SC, AFSHRC #K239.0512–834, Maxwell AFB, AL, p. 20; Wesley Frank Craven and James Lea Cate, eds., *The Army Air Forces in World War II*, Vol. II, *Europe: Torch to Pointblank, August 1942 to December 1943* (Chicago, IL: University of Chicago, 1949), pp. 47–49.

[6] Craven and Cate, *Torch to Pointblank*, p. 56; Dwight D. Eisenhower, *Crusade in Europe* (Garden City, NY: Doubleday, 1948 and 1961), pp. 82, 84.

[7] "Conference with General Eisenhower," HQ Eighth Air Force Daily Diary, 21 October 1942, in Spaatz Papers, Box 9; Peter Calvocoressi and Guy Wint, *Total War: The Untold Story of World War II* (New York: Random House, 1972), pp. 415–32.

[8] Letter, Spaatz in England to Arnold in Washington, 31 October 1942, in Spaatz Papers, Box 9.

[9] Craven and Cate, *Torch to Pointblank*, pp. 51–54; HQ Eighth Air Force Daily Diary, 21 October 1942 in Spaatz Papers, Box 9; Message, Arnold in Washington to Eisenhower in England, 10 September 1942, in Pre-Presidential File, Box 5, Eisenhower Library, Abilene, KS.

[10] Letter, Arnold in Washington to Spaatz in England, 19 August 1942, in Spaatz Papers, Box 8; Letter, Spaatz to Arnold, 24 August 1942, in Spaatz Papers, Box 8; Letter, Arnold to Spaatz, 25 August 1942, in Spaatz Papers, Box 8; Letter, Arnold in Washington to Eisenhower in Africa, 15 November 1942, in Pre-Presidential File, Box 5, and especially Letter, Arnold to Eisenhower, 12 December 1942, in Pre-Presidential File, Box 5, Eisenhower Library, Abilene, KS; Craven and Cate, *Torch to Pointblank*, pp. 61–62.

[11] Craven and Cate, *Torch to Pointblank*, p. 73.

[12] Craven and Cate, *Torch to Pointblank*, p. 82.

[13] Thomas Maycock, USAF Historical Study #114, *The Twelfth Air Force in the North African Winter Campaign*, 11 November 1942–18 February 1943, p. 23.

[14] Maycock, *Air Force in North Africa*, p. 21.

[15] Lowell Thomas and Edward Jablonski, *Doolittle* (Garden City, NY, Doubleday, 1976), p. 208.

[16] Thomas, Jablonski, *Doolittle*, p. 219.

[17] Eisenhower, *Crusade in Europe*, p. 121.

[18] Eisenhower, *Crusade in Europe*, p. 122.

[19] Ferrell, *Eisenhower Diaries*, p. 94; Gen. Carl Spaatz, interview with Bruce C. Kopper, et al., Washington, D. C., 8 November 1946 in Spaatz Papers, Box 269.

[20] Air Vice Marshal Sidney Bufton, RAF, interview with David R. Mets, Riegate, United Kingdom, 18 March 1983; Solly Zuckerman, *From Apes to Warlords* (New York: Harper and Row, 1972), p. 173.

[21] Zuckerman, *From Apes to Warlords,* p. 204.

[22] Sir Arthur Tedder, *With Prejudice* (Boston: Little, Brown & Company, 1966), p. 394.

[23] Craven and Cate, *Torch to Pointblank,* p. 107.

[24] Craven and Cate, *Torch to Pointblank,* p. 108.

[25] Letter, Spaatz to Arnold, 23 November 1942, in Spaatz Papers, Box 10; Daily Diary, 3 January 1943, Spaatz Papers, Box 10 (Spaatz's title at this time was a little uncertain and the diary for this date is untitled. The letters from Eaker are addressed with varying titles, and one from Arnold in January still addresses Spaatz as commander of Eighth Air Force; General Orders, No. 23, Allied Force HQ, 5 December 1942, officially Spaatz's Acting Deputy Commander in Chief for Air, in Spaatz Papers, Box 9; Ferrell, *Eisenhower Diaries,* 15 December 1942, 25 February 1943; "The Plotters of Souk-el-Spaatz," *Time* (22 March 1943), pp. 20–25; Craven and Cate, *Torch to Pointblank,* pp. 85–91.

[26] Arthur Tedder, *With Prejudice,* p. 108.

[27] Arthur Tedder, *With Prejudice,* p. 169.

[28] Craven and Cate, *Torch to Pointblank,* pp. 85–91; Ferrell, *Eisenhower Diaries,* 15 December 1942, 25 February 1943; Omar N. Bradley and Clay Blair, *A General's Life: An Autobiography by General of the Army Omar N. Bradley* (New York: Simon and Schuster, 1983), pp. 122–24.

[29] Brig. Gen. Vincent J. Esposito, USA (Ret.), ed., *The West Point Atlas of American Wars,* Vol. II (New York: Praeger, 1959), Section 2, plates 83–85.

[30] John Strawson, *Battle for North Africa* (New York: Scribner's and Sons, 1969), pp. 204–10; Esposito, *West Point Atlas,* plates 85–86.

[31] Lt. Gen. Fred M. Dean, USAF (Ret.), interview, 25–26 February 1975, Air University, AFSHRC #K239.0512–0834, pp. 25–27, General Dean remembers that much equipment was lost, but Craven and Cate, *Torch to Pointblank,* pp. 153–61, hold that the greater part of it was removed and that the stocks at the forward fields had deliberately been kept low in any event.

[32] Eisenhower, *Crusade in Europe,* pp. 143, 147.

[33] Lt. Gen. Fred M. Dean, interview, 25–26 February 1975.

[34] Gen. William W. Momyer, USAF (Ret.), *Airpower in Three Wars* (Washington, D.C.: Government Printing Office, 1978), pp. 41–42; Gen. Laurence S. Kuter, interview, 30 September–3 October 1974, p. 297.

[35] Notes, Staff Meeting, Northwest African Air Force, 4 March 1943, in Spaatz Papers, Box 11.

[36] Gen. Bernard L. Montgomery, "Some Notes on High Command in War," Tripoli, Libya, January 1943, p. 2, copy in Spaatz Papers, Box 10.

[37] Tedder, *With Prejudice*, p. 397.

[38] Letter, Spaatz in Africa to Arnold in Washington, 19 February 1943, in Spaatz Papers, Box 10.

[39] HQ Northwest African Air Forces, GO 2, 20 February 1943, in Spaatz Papers, Box 10.

[40] Air Headquarters, Mediterranean Air Command, GO 1, 18 February 1943, in Spaatz Papers, Box 10; Allied Force Headquarters, GO 20, 17 February 1943, in Spaatz Papers, Box 10; Letter, Spaatz in Africa to Arnold in Washington, 19 February 1943, in Spaatz Papers, Box 10; Craven and Cate, *Torch to Pointblank*, pp. 161–65; Notes on Reorganization, "dictated by Colonel Cook," undated (February 1943), in Spaatz Papers, Box 10.

[41] Mrs. Ruth A. Spaatz, notes and interview, 18 June 1985; Copp, *Forged in Fire*, p. 321.

[42] Mrs. Ruth A. Spaatz, notes and interview, 18 June 1985.

[43] Margaret Bourke-White, *Purple Heart Valley* (New York: Simon and Schuster, 1944).

[44] Omar Bradley, *A Soldier's Story* (New York: Henry Holt & Co., 1954), p. 62.

[45] Tedder, *With Prejudice*, p. 411.

[46] Letter, Spaatz to Arnold, 24 May 1943, in Spaatz Papers, Box 11.

[47] Craven and Cate, *Torch to Pointblank*, p. 115.

[48] Letter, Eaker to Arnold, 2 January 1943, in Eaker Papers, Box 16.

[49] Letter, Spaatz to Arnold, 24 May 1943; Craven and Cate, *Torch to Pointblank*, pp. 130, 134.

[50] "Notes for General Cannon" from Maj. Vincent Sheean, AC, 16(?) January 1943, in Spaatz Papers, Box 10; Letter, Spaatz to Arnold, 24 May 1943.

[51] Letter, Spaatz to Arnold, 24 May 1943; Craven and Cate, *Torch to Pointblank*, pp. 123–24.

[52] Letter, Spaatz to Eaker in England, 9 April 1943, in Spaatz Papers, Box 11.

[53] Williamson Murray, *Strategy for Defeat: The Luftwaffe 1933–45* (Maxwell AFB, AL: Air University Press, 1983), pp. 159–63.

[54] Letter, Spaatz to Arnold, 24 May 1943, in Spaatz Papers, Box 11.

[55] Lt. Gen. Fred M. Dean, interview, 25–26 February 1975, p. 30.

[56] F. W. Winterbotham, *The Ultra Secret* (New York: Dell, 1974), p. 152.

[57] Letter, Spaatz to Eaker in England, 9 April 1943, in Spaatz Papers, Box 11.

[58] Ibid.; Craven and Cate, *Torch to Pointblank*, p. 189.

[59] Ibid.

[60] Murray, *Strategy for Defeat*, pp. 165–66.

[61] Gen. Laurence S. Kuter, interview 30 September–3 October 1974, pp. 321–23.

[62] Letter, Spaatz to Arnold 24 May 1943, in Spaatz Papers, Box 11.

[63] Ferrell, *The Eisenhower Diaries*, 1 July 1943; Bradley, *A Soldier's Story*, p. 113; Eisenhower, *Crusade*, pp. 169–71; Winston S. Churchill, *The Second World War*, Vol. IV; *The Hinge of Fate* (Boston, MA: Houghton Mifflin, 1950), pp. 670, 693.

[64] Eisenhower, *Crusade*, pp. 171–74; Bradley, *Soldier's Story*, pp. 120–22, Esposito, *West Point Atlas*, Section 2, Plate 90.

[65] HQ Northwest African Air Force, Daily Diary, 7 April 1943, in Spaatz Papers, Box 11.

[66] Letter, Eisenhower to Arnold, 18 June 1943, in Pre-Presidential File, Box 5, Eisenhower Library, Abilene, KS; HQ NWAAF, Daily Diary, 7 April 1943, in Spaatz Papers, Box 11; Maj. Gen. E. P. Curtis, interview, 23 October 1975, p. 87.

[67] HQ NWAAF, Daily Diary, 7 April 1943, in Spaatz Papers, Box 11; Craven and Cate, *Torch to Pointblank*, pp. 415–19.

[68] HQ NWAAF, Daily Diary, 10 May 1943, in Spaatz Papers, Box 11.

[69] Craven and Cate, *Torch to Pointblank*, pp. 415–19.

[70] Bradley, *Soldier's Story*, p. 124; Craven and Cate, *Torch to Pointblank*, p. 439.

[71] Winterbotham, *Ultra Secret*, pp. 155–60; Anthony Cave Brown, *Bodyguard of Lies* (London: W. H. Allen, 1977), pp. 278–89.

[72] Vice Adm. George C. Dyer, USN (Ret.), for example, remarked in 1973 on the air support provided in the Mediterranean campaigns: "You should realize that the Army Air Force was so independent of the Army and so little interested in the combat activities of the Army and the Navy, in this amphibious operation (Sicily), that the orders from on high provided that requests for air support after D-Day had to be submitted 12 hours in advance to a committee located back in North Africa, where presumably they would be given consideration . . . It was an impossible arrangement and, in my opinion, an indication of the arrogance of the United States Army Air Force commander in that theater of the war, Lieutenant General Carl Spaatz, . . . Under him (Coningham) was a United States XII Air Support Command who must have conceived his mission to be to avoid at all costs providing any air support . . . the air support it gave was worse than pitiful. No change of moment was made as a result of this very poor showing for the Salerno operation . . ." "Reminisces" prepared for the U.S. Naval Institute, Annapolis, MD, 1973, on file at Naval Historical Center, Operational Archives Division, Washington Navy Yard, Washington, D.C., quoted with permission. As for the army, the latest "autobiography" of General of the Army Omar N. Bradley has him saying: "The air support provided us on Sicily

was scandalously casual, careless, and ineffective." (Bradley and Blair, *A General's Life*, p. 178.) But in *Soldier's Story* (published in 1951) we find Bradley saying: "Of all the terrors we faced, however, none seemed more menacing than the threat of German air. For our Army, huddled on a narrow beachhead, could be severely mauled should the Luftwaffe break through in strength. And a Naval force concentrated offshore would offer Goering a tempting target . . . I was not to learn how groundless those fears were until after the invasion. During May and June the Allied Air Force had decimated the enemy's Mediterranean air strength . . ." , p. 123. Blair's "autobiography" also has Bradley implying arrogance on Spaatz's part, and his footnotes indicate a reliance on Samuel Eliot Morison's *The Two Ocean War* (Boston, MA: Little, Brown, 1963), which itself asserts: "This was a poor strategic plan, better calculated to push the Axis forces out of Sicily than to trap them in Sicily. But its chief weakness lay in the refusal of the United States Army Air Forces to cooperate, largely because General Tooey Spaatz was wedded to the concept of strategic air operations—which meant the A.A.F. fighting its own war. He planned to devote practically his entire strength to fighting the Luftwaffe and the Royal Italian Air Force . . . the amphibious expedition sailed and landed with no promise of tactical support from the air, and almost none did it obtain," pp. 247–48, and later: "The enemy had almost complete control of the air over the beachhead, while the A.A.F. and R.A.F. flew strategic [missions]," p. 255.

[73] Craven and Cate, *Torch to Pointblank*, p. 452, say that but twelve vessels were lost on the day before D-Day, notwithstanding the fact that "friendly" antiaircraft fire from the fleet required the protecting aircraft to fly their patrols at heights above the optimum altitudes.

[74] Bradley, *Soldier's Story*, p. 138.

[75] Lee Brown et al., *USAF Airborne Operations: World War II and Korean War* (Washington, D.C.: HQ USAF, Directorate of Operational Requirements, USAF Historical Division Liaison Office, 1962), pp. 9–22.

[76] Ibid.; Letter, Spaatz to Arnold, 14 July 1943, in Spaatz Papers, Box 11.

[77] Letter, Spaatz to Arnold, 14 July 1943; Letter, Arnold to Spaatz, 25 July 1943 and 20 August 1943, in Spaatz Papers, Box 11.

[78] Letter, Spaatz to Arnold, 14 July 1943, in Spaatz Papers, Box 11; F. W. Deakin, *The Burial Friendship: Mussolini, Hitler, and the Fall of Italian Fascism* (New York: Harper, 1962), p. 379, reports that Mussolini tried to assuage Hitler's anger at the poor performance of Italian troops on Sicily by blaming the disaster on the hegemony that the Allied air forces enjoyed.

[79] Letter, Spaatz to Arnold, 14 July 1943, in Spaatz Papers; Spaatz to Arnold, 30 July 1943, in Spaatz Papers, Box 11; Kenneth Macksey, *Kesselring: The Making of the Luftwaffe* (New York: David McKay, 1978), p. 171.

[80] Bradley, *Soldier's Story*, pp. 156–57.

81 Letters, Spaatz to Arnold, 4 July 1943, 16 July, 30 July, and to Maj. Gen. Walter B. Smith, USA, at HQ Allied Forces, 1 August 1943, all in Spaatz Papers, Box 11.

82 Letter, Spaatz to Arnold, 14 July 1943, in Spaatz Papers, Box 11.

83 Gen. Laurence S. Kuter, interview 30 September–3 October 1974, pp. 283–86.

84 *8th Military History Symposium,* U.S. Air Force Academy, 18–20 October, 1978, recollection of LGEN J. B. McPherson, USAF, ret.

85 Samuel Eliot Morison, *The Two Ocean War* (Boston, MA: Little, Brown, 1963), p. 351, Admiral describes the approach as peaceful and calm and giving the "illusion of a pleasure cruise . . ."; Craven and Cate, *Torch to Pointblank,* pp. 520–21.

86 Eisenhower, *Crusade,* pp. 198–99.

87 Letter, Spaatz to Arnold, 18 September 1943, in Spaatz Papers, Box 12. Spaatz, of course, was writing to Arnold based on the initial combat reports. As it turned out, they were about as successful as he thought at that moment, for indeed all three drops were made without the loss of any of the troop carrier airplanes, and the 82d soldiers delivered to the drop zones within the beachhead landed on target in good order, though later reports showed that those sent to Avellino were more scattered; Craven and Cate, *Torch to Pointblank,* pp. 531–33.

88 Kenneth Macksey, *Kesselring: The Making of the Luftwaffe* (New York: David McKay, 1978), p. 180; Spaatz to Arnold, 18 September 1943, in Spaatz Papers, Box 12.

89 Macksey, *Kesselring,* pp. 180–83; Liddell Hart, *History of the Second World War,* pp. 463–67.

90 Letter, Spaatz to Arnold, 18 September 1943, in Spaatz Papers, Box 12; Eisenhower, *Crusade,* pp. 192–202.

91 Letter, Spaatz to Eaker, 18 September 1943, in Spaatz Papers, Box 12.

92 Eisenhower, *Crusade,* pp. 199, 201; Richards and Saunders, *The Fight Avails,* p. 348; Capt. Harry C. Butcher, USNR, *My Three Years with Eisenhower, The Personal Diary of Captain Harry C. Butcher* (New York: Simon and Schuster, 1946), pp. 446–47, wherein is related Spaatz briefing Harry Hopkins on the value of strategic bombing out of Italy and explicitly asserting his belief that strategic bombing could win the war without the need of the Normandy landings; Doolittle to Arnold, 7 December 1943, in Spaatz Papers, Box 13; Craven and Cate, *Torch to Pointblank,* pp. 123–27.

93 Craven and Cate, *Torch to Pointblank,* pp. 563–65, 723–27; Richards and Saunders, *The Fight Avails,* p. 348; Message, Arnold to Spaatz, 31 October 1943, in Spaatz Papers, Box 12.

94 Message, Spaatz to Arnold, 1 November 1943, in Spaatz Papers, Box 12; Craven and Cate, *Torch to Pointblank,* pp. 563–65, 723–27; Mrs. Carl A.

Spaatz, interview, 25 March 1982. Tooey got a taste of home-front problems when Ruth was out of gas on the way home from the airport.

[95] Message, Spaatz to Arnold, 10 November 1943, in Spaatz Papers, Box 12; Message, Spaatz to Arnold, 1 November 1943; Craven and Cate, *Torch to Pointblank,* pp. 465–66.

[96] Message, Spaatz to Arnold, 10 November 1943; Craven and Cate, *Torch to Pointblank,* pp. 572–73; "Notes on Strategic Bombardment Conference, Gibraltar, 8, 9, 10 November 1943," 11 November, in Spaatz Papers, Box 12.

[97] Denis Richards and Hilary St. George Saunders, *Royal Air Force, 1939–45,* Vol. II, *The Fight Avails* (London: HMSO, 1954), p. 348.

[98] Mrs. Carl A. Spaatz, interview, 25 March 1982; Telegram, Katharine Spaatz to Maj. Gen. Carl Spaatz, 20 November 1942, in Spaatz Papers, Box 10.

[99] Ibid.; Letter, Spaatz to Mrs. Carl A. Spaatz in Alexandria, VA, 7 March 1943, in Spaatz Papers, Box 10.

[100] Mrs. Carl A. Spaatz, interview, 25 March 1982; Letter, Maj. Gen. Barton K. Yount, USA, to Spaatz, 17 February 1943, in Spaatz Papers, Box 11.

[101] Letter, Spaatz to Mrs. Carl A. Spaatz, 7 March 1943; Mrs. Carl A. Spaatz, interview, 25 March 1982.

[102] Letter, Maj. Gen. George Stratemeyer, USA, in Washington to Spaatz, 19 March 1943, in Spaatz Papers, Box 11.

[103] Letter, Spaatz to Mrs. Carl A. Spaatz, 1 September 1943 and 1 November 1943, in Spaatz Papers, Box 11.

[104] Lincoln Barnett, "General 'Tooey' Spaatz," *Life* (14 April 1943), pp. 72–84.

[105] Letter, Spaatz to Ambassador John Winant in London, 1 May 1943, in Spaatz Papers, Box 11.

[106] Letter, Eaker in England to Spaatz, 19 July 1943, in Spaatz Papers, Box 11.

[107] Letter, Spaatz to Mrs. Madelaine Tinker, 26 May 1943, in Spaatz Papers, Box 10; Copp, *A Few Great Captains,* p. 396.

[108] Letter, Lt. Col. G. W. West, USA, at 12th General Hospital to Spaatz, 5 July 1943, in Spaatz Papers, Box 10.

[109] Ibid.

[110] Letter, West to Spaatz, 16 July 1943, in Spaatz Papers, Box 10.

[111] Letter, Spaatz to West, 17 July 1943, in Spaatz Papers, Box 10.

[112] HQ USSTAF, Daily Diary, 3 June 1944, in Spaatz Papers, Box 15.

[113] Gen. Laurence S. Curtis, interview, 23 October 1975, pp. 80–84.

**CHAPTER VII**

[1] Charles E. Bohlen, *Witness to History, 1929–1969* (New York: Norton, 1973), pp. 145–49.

2 Ibid.; James MacGregor Burns, *Roosevelt: The Soldier of Freedom* (New York: Harcourt Brace Jovanovich, 1970), pp. 115–16.

3 Eisenhower, *Crusade,* pp. 230–31. Ike himself described it that way without taking up any of the complications.

4 Letter, Eaker to Spaatz, 21 July 1943, in Eaker Papers, Library of Congress, Manuscripts Division, Box 17.

5 Letter, Spaatz to Eaker, 30 July 1943, in Eaker Papers, Box 17.

6 Gen. Carl Spaatz, interview with Brig. Gen. A. R. Maxwell, Bruce C. Hopper, Maj. W. R. Livingston, Lt. M. W. McFarland, and Miss Monica S. Weber, 8 November 1946, in Spaatz Papers, Box 269.

7 Pogue, *Organizer of Victory,* pp. 318–22; Craven and Cate, *Torch to Point-blank,* pp. 740–42.

8 Copp, *Forged in Fire,* p. 448; Gen. Carl A. Spaatz, interview with Bruce C. Hopper et al., 8 November 1946, Washington, D.C., in Spaatz Papers, Box 269.

9 Lt. Gen. Ira C. Eaker, interview with Arthur Marmor, January 1966, USAF Oral History #626, USAF Historical Center, Maxwell AFB, Alabama, in which Eaker recalls his unhappiness, but says that he later became reconciled to the work in the Mediterranean; Copp, *Forged in Fire,* pp. 446–51.

10 HQ NWAAF, Daily Diary, 23, 25 December 1943, in Spaatz Papers, Box 13; Message, Arnold to Eaker, 18 December 1943; Message, Eaker to Arnold, 19 December 1943, and Message, Devers to Arnold, 20 December 1943, all in Eaker Papers, Box 16, Manuscripts Division, Library of Congress; "The Reminiscences of General Carl Spaatz," Arnold Project, Oral History Research Office, Columbia University, 1961, cited with permission; Spaatz, interview, 8 November 1946.

11 Alfred D. Chandler, Jr., ed., *The Papers of Dwight David Eisenhower, The War Years: III* (Baltimore, MD: Johns Hopkins Press, 1970), p. 1614n.

12 "Butcher Diary," Eisenhower Papers, Pre-Presidential File, Box 167, Eisenhower Library, Abilene, KS, 28 December 1943; Letter, Eaker in England to Lovett in Washington, 8 January 1943, in Spaatz Papers, Box 14.

13 Butcher, *My Three Years with Eisenhower,* pp. 446–48. Here Spaatz is reported as being explicit that OVERLORD is not necessary to the President's confidant and in the presence of Eisenhower's personal aide.

14 Letter, Spaatz to Assistant Secretary of War for Air Robert Lovett, 23 January 1944, in Spaatz Papers, Box 14.

15 Letter, Spaatz to Arnold, 23 January 1944, in Spaatz Papers, Box 14.

16 Gen. Carl A. Spaatz, interview with Brig. Gen. Noel F. Parrish, USAF (Ret.), and Dr. Alfred Goldberg, 21 February 1962, AFHRC #105.5–12. Years later Spaatz implied that his commitment to escort fighters was not just a reaction to the heavy losses on the deep penetration raids of 1943. Rather he pointed to his insistence that the initial deployment of the Eighth

Air Force in 1942 include a fighter command as well as one for bombers and that it be dedicated to the support of the bomber force and not just a supplement to the air defense of the British Isles.

17 Ibid.

18 Letter, Spaatz to Arnold, 21 April 1943, in Spaatz Papers, Box 11, for example remarks: "There is no indication how much the German (sic) is prepared to continue air operations in the Mediterranean area, but it is very evident that at present possibly as much as 40% of his fighter and certain other types of production are being sent here for replacements. If further operations here can force him to continue at this rate, I can foresee the end of his air force by next fall if we are supported by heavy bomber attacks from the U.K. against his aircraft industry."

19 Message, Spaatz to Arnold, 21 January 1944; Letter, Arnold to Spaatz, 27 December 1943; Letter, Spaatz to Arnold, 23 January 1944; Letter, Col. R. D. Hughes of Spaatz's HQ, to Spaatz, 15 February 1944, Conference Held at AEAF Headquarters, Stanmore, 15 February 1944, which details Spaatz's differences with Air Chief Marshal Leigh-Mallory on the urgency of achieving air superiority before OVERLORD was to be undertaken; Message, Spaatz to Arnold, 19 February 1944: all in Spaatz Papers, Box 14.

20 Eisenhower, *Crusade,* pp. 275–76.

21 David Irving, *The Rise and Fall of the Luftwaffe: The Life of Field Marshal Erhard Milch* (Boston, MA: Little, Brown, 1973), pp. 217–19; Morrison, *Fortress without a Roof,* pp. 289–91.

22 Wesley Frank Craven and James Lea Cate, eds., *The Army Air Forces in World War II,* Vol. III, *Europe to V-E Day* (Chicago, IL: University of Chicago, 1951), pp. 9–10; Thomas Anthony Julian, "Operation Frantic and the Search for American-Soviet Military Collaboration, 1941–1944," unpublished Ph.D. dissertation, Syracuse University, 1968, p. 84.

23 Werner Baumbach, *The Life and Death of the Luftwaffe,* trans. by Frederick Holt (New York: Ballantine, 1949 and 1960), p. 257.

24 Ibid.

25 Letter, Maj. Gen. James H. Doolittle, USA, in Italy (commanding Fifteenth Air Force temporarily), to Commanding General, USAAF, 7 December 1943, in Spaatz Papers, Box 13.

26 "Report of Activities of HQ Eighth Air Force for the Year 1944, Summary of Activities of Operations Echelon for the Year 1944," 11 January 1945, in Spaatz Papers, Box 325.

27 Letter, Doolittle to CG, USAAF, 7 December 1943, in Spaatz Papers, Box 13.

28 Craven and Cate, *Torch to Pointblank,* p. 752.

29 Notes, ". . . points were discussed by Generals Spaatz, Eaker, and Giles on 9 January 1944," in Spaatz Papers, Box 14.

[30] Carrier Sheet, by Lt. Col. Dudley H. Fay, "Loss Rate by Combat Crew Experience," 10 January 1944, with attachments, in Spaatz Papers, Box 14.

[31] Letter, Arnold to Spaatz, 28 March 1944, in Spaatz Papers, Box 14.

[32] Letter, Spaatz to Commanding General, Eighth Air Force (Doolittle), 11 April 1944, in Spaatz Papers, Box 14.

[33] Letter, Maj. Gen. Barney Giles in Washington, to Spaatz, 28 May 1944, in Spaatz Papers, Box 15.

[34] Craven and Cate, *Argument to V-E Day*, p. 307.

[35] Morrison, *Fortress Without a Roof*, p. 108, passim.

[36] Craven and Cate, *Torch to Pointblank*, pp. 635–48.

[37] Ibid.; Oral History Interview of Maj. Gen. Hugh J. Knerr by A. Goldberg, 24 November 1947, typed transcript, pp. 1–3, K239.0512–616, in USAF Collection, AFSHRC.

[38] Craven and Cate, *Torch to Pointblank*, p. 663.

[39] Ibid., pp. 657–64.

[40] Letter, Arnold to Spaatz, 24 January 1944, in Spaatz Papers, Box 14.

[41] Message, Spaatz to Arnold, 26 January 1944, in Spaatz Papers, Box 14.

[42] Morrison, *Fortress Without a Roof*, pp. 214–16.

[43] Russell F. Weigley, *Eisenhower's Lieutenants: The Campaign of France and Germany, 1944–1945* (Bloomington, IN: Indiana University Press, 1981), pp. 58–59; Ferrell, *The Eisenhower Diaries*, pp. 114–15; HQ USSTAF, Daily Diary, 14 February 1944, in Spaatz Papers, Box 14.

[44] Craven and Cate, *Torch to Pointblank*, pp. 735–40.

[45] Hilary St. George Saunders, *Royal Air Force: 1939–1945*, Vol. III, *The Fight Is Won* (London: HMSO, 1954), p. 85.

[46] Eisenhower, *Crusade*, pp. 236–38; "Butcher Diaries," 16, 20, 23 January 1944, Eisenhower Papers, Pre-Presidential File, Box 168, Eisenhower Library, Abilene, KS.

[47] Ferrell, *The Eisenhower Diaries*, 114–15.

[48] Ibid.; Letter, Eisenhower to Tedder, 29 February 1943, in Chandler, *The Papers of Dwight David Eisenhower*, p. 1755.

[49] Letter, "Conference Held at A.E.A.F. Headquarters, Stanmore 15 February 1944," Col. R. D. Hughes, USA, to CG, USSTAF (Spaatz), 15 February 1944, in Spaatz Papers, Box 14.

[50] Ibid.

[51] Letter, Arnold to Spaatz, 27 December 1943, in Spaatz Papers, Box 14.

[52] Message, Spaatz to Arnold, 21 January 1944, in Spaatz Papers, Box 14.

[53] Craven and Cate, *Argument to V-E Day*, p. 21.

[54] HQ USSTAF, Daily Diary, 25 January 1944, in Spaatz Papers, Box 14.

[55] Letter, Spaatz to Arnold, 5 February 1944, in Spaatz Papers, Box 14.

[56] HQ USSTAF, Daily Diary, 9 February 1944, in Spaatz Papers, Box 14.

[57] Lt. Gen. James H. Doolittle, USAF (Ret.), interview with David R. Mets, Washington, D.C., 19 May 1982.

[58] HQ USSTAF, Daily Diary, 4 January 1944, in Spaatz Papers, Box 14.

[59] Craven and Cate, *Argument to V-E Day*, pp. xii, 13.

[60] Letter, Eaker to Spaatz, 10 October 1943, in Spaatz Papers, Box 14.

[61] Craven and Cate, *Argument to V-E Day*, pp. 13–26.

[62] Letter, Spaatz to Arnold, 23 January 1944, in Spaatz Papers, Box 14.

[63] The United States Strategic Bombing Survey, Overall Report (European War), 30 September 1945, p. 21.

[64] Murray, *Strategy for Defeat*, p. 304.

[65] Letter, Spaatz to Arnold, 23 January 1944.

[66] Col. H. A. Yoder, USAF, Retired, interview with David R. Mets, Boyertown, Pennsylvania, 9 July 1982.

[67] Letter, Doolittle to Arnold, 14 February 1944, in Spaatz Papers, Box 14.

[68] Wesley Frank Craven and James Lea Cate (eds.), *The Army Air Forces in World War II*, Vol. VI, *Men and Planes* (Chicago: University of Chicago Press, 1955; Reprint, Office of Air Force History, 1984), pp. 206–8.

[69] "Discussions with Colonel C. G. Williamson (Assistant Deputy Commander for Operations)," 14 June 1944, with "BCH" (probably Bruce C. Hopper, USSTAF historian), in Spaatz Papers, Box 136; Hansell, *The Air Plan that Defeated Hitler*, pp. 180–81.

[70] "Discussion with Williamson," 14 June 1944; Hansell, *Air Plan*, pp. 180–82.

[71] Craven and Cate, *Argument to V-E Day*, p. 41.

[72] Letter, Spaatz to Arnold, undated (late February 1944?), in Spaatz Papers, Box 14, reports the offensive as a "conspicuous success."

[73] Murray, *Strategy for Defeat*, p. 345.

[74] Adolf Galland, *The First and the Last* (New York: Balantine, 1954), pp. 199–207; Craven and Cate, *Argument to V-E Day*, pp. 59–66.

[75] Murray, *Strategy for Defeat*, p. 240.

[76] Galland, *First and the Last*, p. 205; Craven and Cate, *Argument to V-E Day*, pp. 43–8.

[77] Galland, *First and the Last*, p. 202–3.

[78] Maj. Paul F. Henry, USAF, "From Airships to the Nuclear Age: A History of Lieutenant General William E. Kepner," unpublished student research report, Air Command and Staff College, Air University, Maxwell AFB, AL, May 1981, pp. 33–35.

[79] Ibid.; Galland, *First and the Last*, pp. 205–6; Boylan, "Long-Range Escort Fighter," dissertation pp. 227–28; William R. Emerson, "Operation Pointblank: A Tale of Bombers and Fighters," Harmon Memorial Lecture, USAF Academy, 27 March 1962.

[80] Message, Brig. Gen. P. W. Timberlake, USAAF, to Eaker, 26 February

1944, in Spaatz Papers, Box 14; Letter, "Larry" (Kuter?) to Spaatz, 28 February 1944, in Spaatz Papers, Box 14; Message, Eaker to Timberlake, 26 February 1944, in Spaatz Papers, Box 14; Letter, Maj. Gen. Barney Giles to Spaatz, 6 March 1944 in Spaatz Papers, Box 14.

81 Message, "Caserta 091716 A to AWW 091753 A," 9 March 1944, in Spaatz Papers, Box 14; Message, from "Hinton" to Eaker and Spaatz, 9 March 1944, in Spaatz Papers, Box 14; Message, Maj. Gen. John K. Cannon, USAAF, in Italy to Spaatz, 9 March 1944, in Spaatz Papers, Box 14.

82 Message, Arnold to Spaatz, 10 March 1944, in Spaatz Papers, Box 10; Letter, Spaatz to Mrs. Spaatz, 17 March 1944; Letter, Spaatz to Mrs. Spaatz, 27 March 1944, in Spaatz Papers, Box 14.

83 Zuckerman, *Apes to Warlords,* pp. 177, 182, 201.

84 Ibid., p. 173.

85 Ibid., p. 210.

86 Eisenhower, *Crusade,* pp. 233–68; Henry, "Airships to the Nuclear Age," pp. 35–37.

87 Zuckerman, *Apes to Warlords,* p. 217–19.

88 Saunders, *The Fight Is Won,* p. 85; Gen. Carl Spaatz, interview with Dr. Bruce C. Hopper, location not given, 20 May 1945, in Spaatz Papers, Box 136.

89 Col. R. D. Hughes, Air Corps, notes, "Conference Held at A.E.A.F. Head-quarters, Stanmore, 15 February 1944," 15 February 1944, in Spaatz Papers, Box 14.

90 Ibid.

91 Ibid.; Tedder, *With Prejudice,* pp. 507–8; Saunders, *The Fight Is Won,* pp. 85–86.

92 Message, Spaatz to Arnold, 19 February 1944, in Spaatz Papers, Box 14.

93 Hansell, *Air Plan that Defeated Hitler,* p. 80; Tedder, *With Prejudice,* p. 502.

94 W. W. Rostow, *Pre-Invasion Bombing Strategy: General Eisenhower's Decision of March 25, 1944* (Austin, TX: University of Texas Press, 1981), pp. 30–35; Craven and Cate, *Argument to V-E Day,* pp. 76–77.

95 Zuckerman, *Apes to Warlords,* pp. 195, 235–36, 350.

96 HQ NAAF, Daily Diary, 13 August 1943, in Spaatz Papers, Box 14.

97 HQ USSTAF, Daily Diary, 12 February 1944, 13 April 1944, in Spaatz Papers, Box 14.

98 Letters, Sir Charles Portal to Eisenhower, 7 and 9 March 1944, with attachments, in Eisenhower Papers, Pre-Presidential Files (PPF), Box 93, Eisenhower Library, Abilene, KS.

99 Letter, Portal to Eisenhower, 20 March 1944, in Eisenhower Papers, PPF, Box 93.

[100] Carl Spaatz, "Employment of Strategic Air Forces in the Support of OVER-LORD," 24 March 1944, in Spaatz Papers, Box 14.

[101] "Final Minutes of a Meeting Held on Saturday, March 25, to Discuss the Bombing Policy in the Period Before 'OVERLORD'," in Spaatz Papers, Box 14.

[102] Henry, "Airships to the Nuclear Age," pp. 22–33.

[103] Cave Brown, *Bodyguard of Lies*, p. 523.

[104] Letter, Arnold to Spaatz, 24 April 1944, in Spaatz Papers, Box 4.

[105] Letter, Spaatz to Doolittle, Eaker, and Twining, 4 March 1944, in Spaatz Papers, Box 14.

[106] Letter, Spaatz to Arnold, undated (late February 1944?), in Spaatz Papers, Box 14.

[107] Message, Arnold to Spaatz, 2 February 1944, in Spaatz Papers, Box 14.

[108] Message, Spaatz to Arnold, 4 March 1944, in Spaatz Papers, Box 14.

[109] "Final Minutes," 25 March 1944.

[110] Ibid.

[111] Ibid.

[112] Ibid.

[113] Ibid.

[114] Ibid.

[115] Ibid.

[116] Message, Spaatz to Arnold, 26 March 1944, in Spaatz Papers, Box 14.

[117] "Memorandum for Diary," 12 April 1944, in Chandler, *The Papers of Dwight David Eisenhower*, p. 1642.

[118] Eisenhower, *Crusade*, pp. 247–49; Letter, Eisenhower to Churchill, 5 April 1944, in Chandler, *The Papers of Dwight David Eisenhower*, pp. 1809–10; Message, Spaatz to Arnold, 9 April 1944, in Spaatz Papers, Box 14; Tedder, *With Prejudice*, p. 528.

[119] Murray, *Strategy for Defeat*, p. 240.

[120] Rostow, *Pre-Invasion Bombing Strategy*, pp. 54–55, Appendix C.

[121] Ibid., p. 56; Craven and Cate, *Argument to V-E Day*, p. 153; Letter, Maj. Gen. Fred Anderson, AC, in England to Kuter in Washington, 22 April 1944, and Message, Spaatz to Arnold, 8 May 1944, in Spaatz Papers, Boxes 14 and 15.

[122] "ULTRA History of US Strategic Air Force Europe vs. German Air Force," 6 June 1945, copy supplied to author by Justice Lewis F. Powell.

[123] Weigley, *Eisenhower's Lieutenants*, p. 61; Eisenhower, *Crusade*, p. 249.

[124] Rostow, *Pre-Invasion Bombing Strategy*, pp. 57–60; Craven and Cate, *Argument to V-E Day*, pp. 157–62.

[125] Rostow, *Pre-Invasion Bombing Strategy*, pp. 43–44, 65.

[126] Letter, Spaatz to Eisenhower, 22 April 1944, in Spaatz Papers, Box 14.

[127] Craven and Cate, *Argument to V-E Day*, pp. 157–62; Weigley, *Eisenhower's Lieutenants*, pp. 66–68.

[128] Ibid.

[129] Draft Message, Spaatz for Arnold, 6 June 1945, in Spaatz Papers, Box 15, Lt. Gen. Lewis H. Brereton, USA, *The Brereton Diaries* (New York: Morrow, 1946), pp. 178–81.

[130] Bradley and Blair, *A General's Life*, p. 247.

[131] Draft Message, Spaatz for Arnold, 6 June 1945, in Spaatz Papers, Box 15.

[132] Weigley, *Eisenhower's Lieutenants*, p. 94.

[133] Brereton, *Diaries*, p. 279.

[134] Draft Message, Spaatz for Arnold, 6 June 1944, in Spaatz Papers, Box 15.

[135] Letter, Spaatz to Giles, 27 June 1944, in Spaatz Papers, Box 15.

[136] Bradley and Blair, *A General's Life*, p. 249; Message, Eisenhower to Combined Chiefs of Staff, 8 June 1944, in Chandler, *The Papers of Dwight David Eisenhower*, p. 1916.

[137] Ibid., p. 1917; Brereton, *Diaries*, pp. 280–83; Saunders, *The Fight Is Won*, pp. 112–14.

[138] Weigley, *Eisenhower's Lieutenants*, pp. 67–68, 94; Saunders, *The Fight Is Won*, pp. 94–96.

[139] Saunders, *The Fight Is Won*, p. 114.

[140] Herman S. Wolk, "Prelude to D-Day: The Bomber Offensive," *Air Force* (June 1974), p. 65.

[141] Generalfeldmarschall von Rundstedt, interrogation, 2 September 1945, p. 3.

[142] Memorandum, Spaatz to Eisenhower, 28 June 1944, in Pre-Presidential File, Box 115, Eisenhower Library, Abilene, KS.

## CHAPTER VIII

[1] Russell A. Buchanan, *The United States and World War II*, Vol. II (New York: Harper, 1964), pp. 371–89.

[2] Esposito, *West Point Atlas*, Sec. 2, Plate 103.

[3] Chandler, *The Papers of Dwight David Eisenhower*, pp. 2000–2004, letters, Eisenhower to Bernard Montgomery, 13, 14 July 1944.

[4] Tedder, *With Prejudice*, pp. 562–65.

[5] Weigley, *Eisenhower's Lieutenants*, pp. 116–20.

[6] Bradley and Blair, *A General's Life*, p. 249.

[7] Buchanan, *US and World War II*, pp. 360–62.

[8] Bradley and Blair, *A General's Life*, p. 272: Omar N. Bradley, *A Soldier's Story*, (New York: Holt, Rinehart and Winston, Eagle Books edition, 1951), p. 317.

[9] Bradley and Blair, *A General's Life*, pp. 272–76.

[10] Weigley, *Eisenhower's Lieutenants*, pp. 107, 151; Craven and Cate, *Argument to V-E Day*, pp. 228–31.

[11] Hansell, *Air Plan*, p. 239.

[12] Hq USSTAF, Daily Diary, 15 June 1944, in Spaatz Papers, Box 15.

[13] Ibid., 10 July 1944.

[14] David Irving, *The War Between the Generals* (Hammondsworth, Middlesex, England: Penguin, 1981), pp. 211–12; Bradley and Blair, *A General's Life*, pp. 276–77; Brereton, *Diaries*, p. 313.

[15] Bradley, *Soldier's Story*, pp. 329–45; Brereton, *Diaries*, pp. 312–13; Weigley, *Eisenhower's Lieutenants*, p. 151.

[16] Brereton, *Diaries*, p. 314.

[17] Bradley, *Soldier's Story*, pp. 345–48; Weigley, *Eisenhower's Lieutenants*, pp. 152–53.

[18] Craven and Cate, *Argument to V-E Day*, pp. 232–34.

[19] Esposito, *West Point Atlas*, Sec. 2, Plate 53; Craven and Cate, *Argument to V-E Day*, pp. 234–38; Weigley, *Eisenhower's Lieutenants*, p. 156.

[20] Weigley, *Eisenhower's Lieutenants*, p. 162; Brereton, *Diaries*, p. 317; Craven and Cate, *Argument to V-E Day*, p. 237.

[21] HQ USSTAF, Daily Diary, 26 July 1944, in Spaatz Papers, Box 15.

[22] Letter, Spaatz to Arnold, 4 October 1944, in Spaatz Papers, Box 16.

[23] Bradley, *Soldier's Story*, p. 347.

[24] Brereton, *Diaries*, p. 317.

[25] "ULTRA History of US Strategic Air Force Europe vs. German Air Force," 6 June 1945, copy supplied author by Justice Lewis F. Powell, Jr.

[26] Craven and Cate, *Argument to V-E Day*, p. 236.

[27] Tedder, *With Prejudice*, p. 572.

[28] HQ USSTAF, Daily Diary, 9 August 1944, in Spaatz Papers, Box 15.

[29] Letter, Spaatz to Doolittle, 13 December 1944, in Spaatz Papers.

[30] Ferrell, *The Eisenhower Diaries*, 6, 7 August 1944, 5 September 1944, pp. 123–29; Buchanan, *US and World War II*, pp. 399–412.

[31] Memorandum, HQ USSTAF, 30 July 1944, in Spaatz Papers, Box 15; Craven and Cate, *Argument to V-E Day*, pp. 415–20; Weigley, *Eisenhower's Lieutenants*, pp. 224–26.

[32] Ibid.; Memorandum, HQ Mediterranean Allied Air Forces, 29 August 1944, in Spaatz Papers, Box 15.

[33] Memorandum, HQ USSTAF, 30 July 1944; Craven and Cate, *Argument to V-E Day*, pp. 421–32; Buchanan, *US and World War II*, pp. 404–5.

[34] Weigley, *Eisenhower's Lieutenants*, pp. 224–26; Craven and Cate, *Argument to V-E Day*, p. 434.

[35] HQ Eighth Air Force, "Summary of Activities for Director of Operations for the Year 1944," 9 January 1945, in Spaatz Papers, Box 325; HQ USSTAF,

Daily Diary, 9 June 1944, and Letter, from Gen. Walter B. Smith, SHAEF, to Spaatz, 3 June 1944, in Spaatz Papers, Box 15.

[36] Ibid.

[37] Julian, "Operation 'Frantic'," pp. 262–65.

[38] Ibid., p. 269.

[39] Calvocoressi and Wint, *Total War,* p. 458.

[40] Alexander Werth, *Russia at War, 1941–1945,* (New York: Avon, 1964), pp. 798–801.

[41] Anderson, "Conference with Hopkins," 7 September 1944; Letter, Spaatz to Arnold, 4 October 1944, in Spaatz Papers, Box 16.

[42] Anderson, "Conference with Hopkins," 7 September 1944; Julian, "Operation 'Frantic'," pp. 280–82, 294.

[43] Julian, "Operation 'Frantic'," p. 307; Craven and Cate, *Argument to V-E Day,* pp. 316–17.

[44] Julian, "Operation 'Frantic'," p. 323–25; Werth, *Russia at War,* p. 801.

[45] Buchanan, *US and World War II,* pp. 393–99; Ronald Lewin, *ULTRA Goes to War,* (New York: Pocket Books, 1978), pp. 405–9.

[46] Letter, Spaatz to Arnold, 4 October 1944, in Spaatz Papers, Box 16.

[47] Letter, HQ Eighth Air Force, Doolittle to Spaatz, 29 September 1944, in Spaatz Papers, Box 15; Craven and Cate, *Argument to V-E Day,* pp. 275–77; Letter, Spaatz to Arnold, 4 October 1944, in Spaatz Papers, Box 15; "Summary," Eighth AF Director of Operations, 9 January 1945, in Spaatz Papers, Box 325; HQ AEAF, Versailles, France, "Minutes of Commanders Conference," 15 September 1944, in Spaatz Papers, Box 15.

[48] Letter, Spaatz to Arnold, 4 October 1944, in Spaatz Papers, Box 16.

[49] Weigley, *Eisenhower's Lieutenants,* pp. 288–96; Esposito, *West Point Atlas,* Vol. II, Sec. 2, Plate 58.

[50] Craven and Cate, *Argument to V-E Day,* pp. 600–605; Weigley, *Eisenhower's Lieutenants,* pp. 288–96; "Summary," Eight AF Director of Operations, 9 January 1945.

[51] Weigley, *Eisenhower's Lieutenants,* pp. 286–89.

[52] Craven and Cate, *Argument to V-E Day,* p. 609; Lewin, *ULTRA Goes to War,* p. 418.

[53] Draft letter, Spaatz to Lovett, 1 October 1944, in Spaatz Papers, Box 16, with handwritten annotation that the paragraph relating to Montgomery's role in MARKET-GARDEN was not included in the letter sent to Lovett.

[54] Letter, Spaatz to Eisenhower, 28 June 1944, Pre-Presidential File, Box 115, Eisenhower Library, Abilene, KS.

[55] Memo, Eisenhower to Tedder, 29 June 1944, in Pre-Presidential File, Box 115, Eisenhower Library, Abilene, KS.

[56] Letter, Spaatz to Eisenhower, 10 July 1944, in Spaatz Papers, Box 15.

[57] Tedder, *With Prejudice,* p. 584.

[58] Bernard and Fawn M. Brodie, *From Crossbow to H-Bomb*, (Bloomington, IN: Indiana University, 1973), pp. 230–32.

[59] Tedder, *With Prejudice*, p. 584.

[60] Brodie, *Crossbow to H-Bomb*, pp. 230–32.

[61] The United States Strategic Bombing Survey, *Overall Report*, (*European War*), September 30, 1945, pp. 87–89.

[62] Ibid., p. 41.

[63] Craven and Cate, *Argument to V-E Day*, pp. 306–7; Air University, Historical Division, "Morale in the AAF in World War II," 1953, #M-27218, No. 78, copy in Fairchild Library, p. 23.

[64] Murray, *Strategy for Defeat*, p. 345.

[65] Air University, "Morale in the USAAF," pp. 33, 41.

[66] Ibid., p. 26.

[67] Craven and Cate, *Argument to V-E Day*, p. 307.

[68] Ibid.; Letter, Arnold to Spaatz, 14 August 1944, in Spaatz Papers, Box 15.

[69] Craven and Cate, *Argument to V-E Day*, p. 307.

[70] Air University, "Morale in the USAAF," p. 5.

[71] Weigley, *Eisenhower's Lieutenants*, pp. 370–75.

[72] Ibid., p. 373.

[73] Ibid.

[74] Letter, Spaatz to Giles, 3 January 1945, in Spaatz Papers, Box 20.

[75] Letter, Giles to Spaatz, 16 December 1945, in Spaatz Papers, Box 20.

[76] Letter, Spaatz to Giles, 3 January 1945.

[77] HQ USSTAF, Staff Meeting Notes, 5 January 1945, in Spaatz Papers, Box 20.

[78] HQ USSTAF, Staff Meeting Notes, 7 January 1945, in Spaatz Papers, Box 20.

[79] Letter, Spaatz to Arnold, 7 January 1945, in Spaatz Papers, Box 20.

[80] Pogue, *Organizer of Victory*, pp. 489–98.

[81] Letter, Lovett to Spaatz, 12 February 1945, in Spaatz Papers, Box 20.

[82] Letter, Spaatz to Brig. Gen. R. C. Coupland, USA, in Washington, 1 February 1945, in Spaatz Papers, Box 20; Letter, Knerr to Giles, 14 March 1945, in Spaatz Papers, Box 21; Letter, Spaatz to Giles, 26 March 1945, in Spaatz Papers, Box 21; Letter, Eaker to Spaatz, 31 March 1945, in Spaatz Papers, Box 21.

[83] HQ USSTAF, Staff Meeting Notes, 14 February 1945, in Spaatz Papers, Box 20.

[84] Letter, Spaatz to Lovett, 21 February 1945, in Spaatz Papers, Box 20.

[85] Weigley, *Eisenhower's Lieutenants*, p. 373.

[86] Eisenhower, *Crusade*, p. 354, reports that during the comb-out of the noninfantry ground units the previous summer very few of the people offered

for transfer to the infantry proved suitable for training as combat riflemen.

87 Letter, Spaatz to Brig. Gen. Lauris Norstad, USA, in Washington, 12 January 1945, in Spaatz Papers, Box 20.

88 Letters, Giles to Spaatz, 21 January 1945; Arnold to Spaatz, 15 January 1945; and Spaatz to Arnold, 29 January 1945, all in Spaatz Papers, Box 20; Pogue, *Organizer of Victory*, p. 127; Message, Marshall to Eisenhower, W-23384, 19 January 1945, in Spaatz Papers, Box 23.

89 Letter, John G. Trump, Advisory Specialist Group, USSTAF, to Spaatz, 15 January 1945, in Spaatz Papers, Box 23.

90 Cajus Bekker, *The Luftwaffe War Diaries*, trans. Frank Ziegler (New York: Ballantine, 1964), pp. 476–79.

91 Galland, *The First and the Last*, pp. 261–62.

92 Bekker, *Luftwaffe Diaries*, pp. 485–87.

93 Craven and Cate, *Argument to V-E Day*, p. 715.

94 Letter, Spaatz to Arnold, 3 September 1944, in Spaatz Papers, Box 15; Lewin, *ULTRA Goes to War*, pp. 424–28.

95 Letter, Arnold to Spaatz, 21 September 1944, in Spaatz Papers, Box 15.

96 Albert Speer, *Inside the Third Reich* (New York: Avon, 1970), pp. 427, 448–49, 517–20; The United States Strategic Bombing Survey, *Overall Report (European War)*, September 1945, pp. 17–19; Ralph Bennett, *ULTRA in the West*, (New York: Charles Scribner's Sons, 1979), pp. 175–78.

97 "ULTRA History of US Strategic Air Force Europe vs. German Air Forces," June 1945, pp. 229, 234, 236, 243.

98 "USSTAF ULTRA History," p. 206; Galland, *First and the Last*, pp. 216–19.

99 Galland, *The First and the Last*, pp. 216–19; Murray, *Strategy for Defeat*, pp. 280–91.

100 Galland, *The First and the Last*, p. 276.

101 Ibid., pp. 268–69; Baumbach, *The Life and Death of the Luftwaffe*, p. 202; Speer, *Inside the Third Reich*, p. 524.

102 Galland, *The First and the Last*, pp. 268–69.

103 Ibid., pp. 229–30, 238; Craven and Cate, *Argument to V-E Day*, pp. 657–59.

104 "USSTAF ULTRA History," p. 264.

105 HQ USSTAF, Staff Meeting Notes, 2 February 1945, in Spaatz Papers, Box 20.

106 Murray, *Strategy for Defeat*, p. 308.

107 HQ Eighth Air Force, Director of Operations, "Summary of Activities for Director of Operations for the Year 1944," 9 January 1945, in Spaatz Papers, Box 325.

108 Letter, Arnold to Spaatz, 29 September 1944, in Spaatz Papers, Box 16.

109 Letter, Spaatz to Arnold, 30 September 1944, in Spaatz Papers, Box 16.

[110] Letter, Spaatz to Arnold, 4 October 1944, in Spaatz Papers, Box 16.

[111] "Notes on Conference-Bari-15 October 1944," in Spaatz Papers, Box 16.

[112] Letter, Spaatz to Arnold, 5 November 1944, in Spaatz Papers, Box 16.

[113] Ibid.

[114] Galland, *The First and the Last,* pp. 213–270; Bekker, *Luftwaffe Diaries,* pp. 475–539; Speer, *Inside the Third Reich,* pp. 464ff; Bennett, *ULTRA in the West,* pp. 175–78.

## CHAPTER IX

[1] Hansell, *Air Plan* p. 235; Alfred Goldberg, "Spaatz," in Field Marshal Sir Michael Carver, ed., *The War Lords: Military Commanders of the Twentieth Century* (Boston, MA: Little, Brown, 1976), p. 574; Rostow, *Pre-Invasion Bombing Strategy* p. 56. Rostow cites Hansell and Goldberg as two of his sources on the resignation threat, and adds that Noble Frankland told Rostow personally that General Spaatz had told Frankland that he had remarked to Eisenhower that he would have to give up command of USSTAF if he were not permitted to attack the oil targets along with the rail yards and battlefield objectives.

[2] "ULTRA History of U.S. Strategic Air Force Europe vs. German Air Forces," SRH-013, prepared by Lt. Col. William Haines, 1945, at the direction of Maj. Gen. George C. Macdonald and Spaatz, copy provided to author by Justice Lewis F. Powell, Jr. Another copy is in the National Archives, pp. 206, 212–13, 219, 235, 236, and 244.

[3] Craven and Cate, *Argument to V-E Day,* p. 280.

[4] Draft, Chapter 7, "Spaatz Report: The Final Attack Against the German Military Economy," USAF HRC #168.04–24, 1941–1945, Maxwell AFB, AL, p. 13.

[5] Spaatz to Arnold, 27 August 1944, in Spaatz Papers, Box 15.

[6] Ibid.

[7] Memorandum, Maj. Gen. Laurence S. Kuter to Arnold, both in Washington, 9 August 1944, and letter, Kuter in Washington to Anderson in United Kingdom, 15 August 1944, both in Spaatz Papers, Box 15.

[8] "Directive Agreed by DCAS, RAF, and Lieutenant General Carl Spaatz," 23 September 1944, in Spaatz Papers, Box 15.

[9] The United States Strategic Bombing Survey, *Overall Report (European War),* September 30, 1945, pp. 42–44, hereafter cited as "USSBS."

[10] USSTAF ULTRA History, pp. 243–45; Lewin, *ULTRA Goes to War,* pp. 290–92.

[11] Doolittle to Spaatz, 28 September 1944, and "Background Material Illustrating the Need for a Unified U.S. Air Command," unsigned and undated (written by Anderson ?), both in Spaatz Papers, Box 15.

[12] Anthony Verrier, *The Bomber Offensive,* (New York: Macmillan, 1969); Denis Richards, *Portal of Hungerford,* (New York: Holmes and Meier, 1977), p. 322; Saunders, *The Fight Is Won,* pp. 258–60.

[13] Spaatz to Arnold, 1 September 1944, in Spaatz Papers, Box 16.

[14] Chandler, *The Papers of Dwight David Eisenhower,* Message, Eisenhower to Marshall, 2 September 1944, pp. 2111–12.

[15] Arnold to Eisenhower, 6 September 1944, in Spaatz Papers, Box 16.

[16] Arnold to Spaatz, 29 September 1944, in Spaatz Papers, Box 16.

[17] Craven and Cate, *Argument to V-E Day,* p. 319; Spaatz to Arnold, 30 September 1945, in Spaatz Papers, Box 15; Arnold to Spaatz, 23 October 1944, and Eisenhower to Spaatz, 18 September 1944, both in Spaatz Papers, Box 16.

[18] Craven and Cate, *Argument to V-E Day,* p. 320.

[19] Chandler, *The Papers of Dwight David Eisenhower,* Message, Eisenhower to Marshall, 23 October 1944, pp. 2247–48.

[20] Ibid.

[21] Tedder, *With Prejudice,* pp. 610–11; Air Chief Marshal A. W. Tedder, RAF, "Notes on Air Policy to be Adopted with a View to Rapid Defeat of Germany," 26 October 1944, in Spaatz Papers, Box 16.

[22] "Directives Agreed by DCAS, RAF, and Lieutenant General Carl Spaatz," 23 September 1944, in Spaatz Papers, Box 15.

[23] Tedder, *With Prejudice,* p. 605.

[24] Tedder, "Notes on Air Policy" and *With Prejudice,* pp. 610–11.

[25] Spaatz to Arnold, 28 October 1944, in Spaatz Papers, Box 16.

[26] Tedder, *With Prejudice,* p. 612.

[27] Ibid., p. 611.

[28] Rostow, *Bombing Strategy,* p. 67.

[29] Saunders, *The Fight Is Won,* pp. 205–6; Liddell Hart, *History of the Second World War,* pp. 642–43.

[30] Craven and Cate, *Argument to V-E Day,* pp. 672–73; Tedder, *With Prejudice,* pp. 624–25.

[31] Saunders, *The Fight Is Won,* p. 208.

[32] Bennett, *ULTRA in the West,* pp. 177–99; Weigley, *Eisenhower's Lieutenants,* pp. 320–21.

[33] Bennett, *ULTRA in the West,* pp. 177–81; Ferrell, *The Eisenhower Diaries,* 23 December 1944, pp. 129–31; Esposito, *West Point Atlas,* Section 2, plate 61.

[34] Spaatz to Arnold, 7 January 1945, in Spaatz Papers, Box 20.

[35] Esposito, *West Point Atlas,* Sec. 2, Plates 60–61.

[36] Ibid., plates 61–63; Chandler, *The Papers of Dwight David Eisenhower,* cable, Eisenhower to Bradley and Lt. Gen. Jacob Devers, both in France, 18 December 1944, pp. 2356–57; Tedder, *With Prejudice,* p. 625.

[37] USSTAF Staff Meeting notes, 20 December 1944, in Spaatz Papers, Box 16.

[38] Craven and Cate, *Argument to V-E Day,* pp. 691, 696.

[39] USSTAF Staff Meeting notes, 20 December 1944.

[40] USSTAF Staff Meeting notes, 22 December 1944, in Spaatz Papers, Box 20.

[41] B. H. Liddell Hart, *The German Generals Talk* (New York: Morrow, 1948), pp. 288–90; Esposito, *West Point Atlas* Sec. 2, Plates 62–63.

[42] Bennett, *ULTRA in the West,* p. 217.

[43] Liddell Hart, *German Generals Talk,* pp. 290–91.

[44] Esposito, *West Point Atlas,* Plates 62–63.

[45] Liddell Hart, *German Generals Talk,* pp. 290–92; Tedder, *With Prejudice,* p. 638; Bennett, *ULTRA in the West,* p. 218.

[46] Spaatz to Arnold, 7 January 1945, in Spaatz Papers, Box 20.

[47] Ibid.

[48] Zuckerman, *Apes to Warlords,* p. 312.

[49] Ibid., p. 315.

[50] Esposito, *West Point Atlas,* Plates 62–63.

[51] Buchanan, *US and World War II,* p. 439.

[52] Ibid.

[53] Saunders, *The Fight Is Won,* pp. 208–10.

[54] Ibid.

[55] Ibid.

[56] Spaatz to Arnold, 7 January 1945, in Spaatz Papers, Box 20. Meyer was an ace in World War II and later became a four-star general.

[57] HQ USSTAF, Daily Diary, 1 January 1945, in Spaatz Papers, Box 20; Lt. Gen. James H. Doolittle, USAF, Retired, interview, USAF Oral History #793, 26 September 1971, USAF Historical Center, Maxwell AFB, AL.

[58] Thomas A. Fabyanic, *Strategic Air Attack in the United States Air Force: A Case Study* (Manhattan, KS: Military Affairs/Aerospace Historian Publishing, 1976), p. 178.

[59] Spaatz to Arnold, 7 January 1945, in Spaatz Papers, Box 20.

[60] Memorandum, Brig. Gen. Laurence Kuter to Arnold, both in Washington, 9 August 1944, quoting Air Ministry memorandum, in Spaatz Papers, Box 15.

[61] Ibid.

[62] Kuter to Anderson, 15 August 1944, and memorandum, Williamson to Kuter, 4 September 1944, both in Spaatz Papers, Box 15.

[63] Ibid.

[64] Memorandum, Williamson to Anderson, 12 September 1944, in Spaatz Papers, Box 15.

[65] Spaatz to Arnold, 4 October 1944, in Spaatz Papers, Box 16.

[66] Spaatz to Lovett, 1 October 1944, in Spaatz Papers, Box 16.
[67] Spaatz to Arnold, 13 December 1944, in Spaatz Papers, Box 16.
[68] Ibid.
[69] Spaatz to Giles, 26 December 1944, in Spaatz Papers, Box 16.
[70] Eaker in Italy to Spaatz, 1 January 1945, in Spaatz Papers, Box 20.
[71] Memorandum, Lovett to Arnold, 9 January 1945, in Spaatz Papers, Box 20.
[72] Memorandum, Brig. Gen. R. C. Lindsay, USA, in Washington to Arnold, with excerpt from a Kuter memorandum, 11 January 1945, in Spaatz Papers, Box 20.
[73] Arnold to Spaatz, 14 January 1945, in Spaatz Papers, Box 20.
[74] Spaatz to Arnold, 5 February 1945, in Spaatz Papers, Box 20.
[75] Pogue, *Organizer of Victory*, pp. 540–46; Craven and Cate, *Argument to V-E Day*, pp. 725–32.
[76] Spaatz to Eaker with attachment, 2 February 1945, in Spaatz Papers, Box 20.
[77] Craven and Cate, *Argument to V-E Day*, pp. 624–31; Pogue, *Organizer of Victory*, pp. 540–46; Spaatz to Eaker, 2 February 1945.
[78] Justice Lewis F. Powell, Jr., interview with David R. Mets, 21 October 1982, Washington, D.C.
[79] Anderson in Malta to Spaatz in France, 2 February 1945, in Spaatz Papers, Box 20.
[80] Pogue, *Organizer of Victory*, pp. 540–45; Anderson to Spaatz, 2 February 1945; Justice Lewis F. Powell, interview, 21 October 1982.
[81] Craven and Cate, *Argument to V-E Day*, p. 725.
[82] Ibid., pp. 731–32; Saunders, *The Fight Is Won*, pp. 269–71; John Toland, *The Last 100 Days* (London: Arthur Barker, 1966), pp. 135–47.
[83] Message, Spaatz to Eaker, 20 February 1945; Arnold to Spaatz, 18 February 1945; Spaatz to Arnold, 18 February 1945; Arnold to Spaatz #2, 18 February 1945; Spaatz to Arnold, 19 February 1945; and Spaatz to Lovett, 21 February 1945, all in Spaatz Papers, Box 20.
[84] Max Hastings, *Bomber Command* (London: Pan, 1979), pp. 414–15.
[85] David MacIsaac, *Strategic Bombing*, p. 81.
[86] Anderson at Malta to Spaatz, 2 February 1945, in Spaatz Papers, Box 20.
[87] Craven and Cate, *Argument to V-E Day*, pp. 733–34.
[88] Ibid.; Tedder, *With Prejudice*, pp. 666–67.
[89] Craven and Cate, *Argument to V-E Day*, pp. 734–36.
[90] Message, Spaatz to Arnold and to Brig. Gen. B. R. Legge, USA, in Switzerland, 4 March 1945, in Spaatz Papers, Box 23.
[91] Spaatz to George C. Marshall in Washington, 10 March 1945, in Spaatz Papers, Box 23.

[92] Maj. Gen. E. P. Curtis, interview, 23 October 1975, in USAF HRC #K239.0512–875, Maxwell AFB, AL.

[93] Spaatz to Marshall, 10 March 1945.

[94] Spaatz to Arnold, 11 March 1945, in Spaatz Papers, Box 21.

[95] Maj. Gen. J. P. Hodges, USA, in Washington, to Arnold, 16 March 1945, in Arnold Papers, Manuscripts Division, Library of Congress, Washington, D.C., Box 287.

[96] Eisenhower, *Crusade,* pp. 410–13.

[97] Tedder, *With Prejudice,* pp. 666–67.

[98] Weigley, *Eisenhower's Lieutenants,* pp. 647–49; Eisenhower *Crusade,* pp. 411–12.

[99] Craven and Cate, *Argument to V-E Day,* pp. 746–47.

[100] Freeman, *The Mighty Eighth,* p. 222.

[101] Eisenhower, *Crusade,* pp. 412–13; Weigley, *Eisenhower's Lieutenants,* pp. 647–49; Saunders, *The Fight Is Won,* p. 285.

[102] Eisenhower, *Crusade,* p. 413.

[103] Weigley, *Eisenhower's Lieutenants,* p. 649.

[104] Murray, *Strategy for Defeat,* p. 345.

[105] Butcher, *My Three Years,* p. 783.

[106] Tedder, *With Prejudice,* p. 681.

[107] Giles to Spaatz, 4 March 1945, in Spaatz Papers, Box 21.

[108] Butcher, *My Three Years,* pp. 832–33; Eisenhower, *Crusade,* pp. 452–53; Toland, *Last 100 Days,* p. 474.

[109] Toland, *Last 100 Days,* p. 576.

[110] Ibid., pp. 576–78.

[111] Butcher, *My Three Years,* pp. 834–35; Tedder, *With Prejudice,* p. 683.

[112] Ibid.

[113] Maj. Sarah Bagby in France to "Dearest Mother" (Mrs. Robert Bagby in New Haven, MO?), 10 May 1945, copy provided author by Mr. John Dry, Kutztown, PA.

[114] Tedder, *With Prejudice,* p. 685.

[115] Ibid.; Toland, *Last 100 Days,* p. 561.

[116] Toland, *Last 100 Days,* pp. 588–89.

[117] Cook, *A Memoir,* p. 97.

[118] Toland, *Last 100 Days,* p. 588.

[119] Butcher, *My Three Years,* p. 843; Bagby to Mother, 10 May 1945; Toland, *Last 100 Days,* p. 588.

[120] Bagby to Mother, 10 May 1945.

[121] Tedder, *With Prejudice,* p. 686; Butcher, *My Three Years,* p. 844.

[122] Bagby to Mother, 10 May 1945; Tedder, *With Prejudice,* p. 686.

[123] Bagby to Mother, 10 May 1945.

[124] Ibid.

[125] Ibid.
[126] Tedder, *With Prejudice,* p. 686.
[127] Bagby to Mother, 10 May 1945.
[128] Ibid.
[129] Ibid., p. 388; Spaatz in France to Arnold, 23 May 1945, with interrogation of Hermann Goering, 10 May 1945, attached, in Spaatz Collection, USAF Historical Research Center, Maxwell AFB, AL (hereafter cited as Goering Interrogation).
[130] Goering Interrogation.
[131] Ibid.

## CHAPTER X

[1] Wesley Frank Craven and James Lea Cate, eds., *The Army Air Forces in World War II,* Vol. 7, *Services Around the World* (Chicago, IL: University of Chicago Press, 1958), pp. 549–52.
[2] "Post War Strategic Operations," in draft, "Report by General Carl Spaatz to the Joint Chiefs of Staff, U.S. Strategy in World War II, Part I, European Operations, and Part II, Pacific Operations," in USAF Historical Center, #106–90, 1947, Maxwell AFB, AL (hereafter cited as "JCS Report").
[3] Herman S. Wolk, "The Establishment of the United States Air Force," *Air Force* 65 (September 1982), p. 79.
[4] Demetrios Caraley, *The Politics of Military Unification* (New York: Columbia, 1966), p. 23.
[5] Futrell, *Ideas, Concepts, Doctrine,* p. 96.
[6] "Committee for Reorganization of the National Defense Hearing held on 6 November 1944, St. Germain, France," in Spaatz Papers, Box 16.
[7] HQ USSTAF, Daily Diary, 18 June 1944, in Spaatz Papers, Box 15.
[8] Arnold, *Global Mission,* p. 247.
[9] Letter, Arnold to Spaatz, 27 October 1944, in Spaatz Papers, Box 58.
[10] Letter, Lovett to Spaatz, 18 September 1944, in Spaatz Papers, Box 16.
[11] Eisenhower, *Crusade,* pp. 459–60.
[12] Letters, Representative Daniel K. Hoch, in Washington to Spaatz in Alexandria, VA, 13 June 1945, and Honorable Paul N. Schaeffer, Reading, PA, to Spaatz in Virginia, 11 June 1945, both in Spaatz Papers, Box 20.
[13] Letters, Spaatz at Guam to General Omar Bradley, USA, in Washington, D.C., 4 August 1945, and Spaatz to Schaeffer, 4 August 1945, and Spaatz to Hoch, 4 August 1945, all in Spaatz Papers, Box 20.
[14] Maj. Gen. E. P. Curtis, USAF (Ret.), interview with James C. Hasdorff, 22–23 October 1975; Letter, USAF Oral History #875, USAF Historical Center, Maxwell AFB, AL; letter, Mrs. Walter Bell to David R. Mets, 6 February 1984.
[15] Letter, Mrs. Walter Bell, 6 February 1984.

[16] Leslie R. Groves, *Now It Can Be Told: The Story of the Manhattan Project* (New York: Da Capo, 1962 and 1983), p. 308.

[17] Wesley Frank Craven and James Lea Cate, eds., *The Army Air Forces in World War II*, Vol. V., *The Pacific: Matterhorn to Nagasaki, June 1944 to August 1945* (Chicago, IL: University of Chicago Press, 1958), p. 714.

[18] Letter, Mrs. Carl A. Spaatz to David R. Mets, undated (January 1984).

[19] Gen. Curtis E. LeMay with MacKinlay Kantor, *Mission with LeMay* (Garden City, NY: Doubleday, 1965), p. 386; Craven and Cate, *Matterhorn to Nagasaki*, p. 700.

[20] JCS Report, Part III.

[21] Craven and Cate, *Matterhorn to Nagasaki*, p. 676; JCS Report, Part III.

[22] Ibid.

[23] Futrell, *Ideas, Concepts, Doctrine*, p. 82.

[24] Craven and Cate, *Matterhorn to Nagasaki*, p. 680.

[25] JCS Report, Part III; Gen. George C. Kenney, USAF (Ret.), *General Kenney Reports* (New York: Duell, Sloan, Pearce, 1949), pp. 544–45.

[26] Craven and Cate, *Matterhorn to Nagasaki*, p. 684; JCS Report, Part III.

[27] D. Clayton James, *The Years of MacArthur*, Vol. II, *1941–1945* (Boston, MA: Houghton, Mifflin, 1975), p. 725.

[28] William Manchester, *American Caesar: Douglas MacArthur, 1880–1964* (Boston, MA: Little, Brown, 1978), p. 147.

[29] Craven and Cate, *Matterhorn to Nagasaki*, pp. 684–88; JCS Report, Part III.

[30] Ibid.

[31] John W. R. Taylor, ed., *Combat Aircraft of the World* (New York: Paragon, 1969), pp. 455–56; Maj. Gen. Haywood S. Hansell, USAF, (Ret.), *Strategic Air War Against Japan* (Maxwell AFB, AL: Airpower Research Institute, Air War College, 1980), p. 99.

[32] Hansell, *Strategic Air War*, p. 33.

[33] Ibid., p. 48.

[34] Ibid.

[35] Craven and Cate, *Matterhorn to Nagasaki*, pp. xiv–xvi.

[36] Ibid.

[37] Hansell, *Strategic Air War*, pp. 25–31; Craven and Cate, *Matterhorn to Nagasaki*, pp. xviii–xx.

[38] Gen. Curtis E. LeMay, USAF (Ret.), interview with David R. Mets, Babson Park, FL, 30 April 1982.

[39] Maj. Gen. Haywood S. Hansell, Jr., interview with David R. Mets, 14 December 1982, Hilton Head, SC; LeMay, *Mission With LeMay*, p. 339.

[40] Gen. Carl A. Spaatz, interview with Brig. Gen. Noel Parrish and Dr. Alfred Goldberg, 21 February 1962, USAF Oral History #754, USAF Historical

Center, Maxwell AFB, AL; interview, 27 September 1968, at USAF Academy, Colorado, USAF Oral History #583, USAFHRC.

[41] Groves, *Now It Can Be Told,* p. 317; JCS Report, Part III.

[42] Arnold, *Global Mission,* pp. 259–60; Kenney, *Kenney Reports,* p. 557.

[43] Craven and Cate, *Matterhorn to Nagasaki,* p. 732.

[44] Letter, Mrs. Walter Bell to David R. Mets, 6 February 1984; Ms. Katharine Gresham, interview with David R. Mets, 19 September 1982, Washington, D.C.

[45] Spaatz, interview, 21 February 1962.

[46] Craven and Cate, *Matterhorn to Nagasaki,* p. 713.

[47] Spaatz, interview, 21 February 1962.

[48] Ibid.

[49] JCS Report, Part III.

[50] Paul W. Tibbetts, *The Tibbetts Story* (New York: Stein and Day, 1978), p. 231.

[51] Spaatz, interview, 21 February 1962.

[52] Groves, *Now It Can be Told,* pp. 341–53.

[53] Craven and Cate, *Matterhorn to Nagasaki,* pp. 728–35.

[54] Kenney, *Kenney Reports,* p. 572.

[55] Craven and Cate, *Matterhorn to Nagasaki,* p. 734; Memo, Brig. Gen. Thomas Power to Lt. Gen. Barney Giles, both at Guam, 20 August 1945, in Spaatz Papers, Box 24.

[56] James, *MacArthur Years,* II, p. 781.

[57] Kenney, *Kenney Reports,* p. 574; James, *MacArthur Years,* II, p. 785.

[58] "The AAF Inside Japan," *Air Force* 28 (November 1945), p. 8.

[59] John Toland, *The Rising Sun: The Decline and Fall of the Japanese Empire* (New York: Random House, 1970), p. 867; Toshikazu Kase, *Journey to the Missouri* (New Haven, CT: Yale, 1950), p. 6; "The Surrender," *Time* (10 September 1945), pp. 28–31.

[60] Toland, *Rising Sun,* p. 869.

[61] Kase, *Journey to the Missouri,* p. 10; James, *MacArthur Years,* II, p. 791.

[62] Craven and Cate, *Matterhorn to Nagasaki,* p. 734.

[63] United States, Army Air Force, "Third Report of the Commanding General of the Army Air Forces to the Secretary of War," 12 November 1945, copy in Air University Library, Maxwell AFB, AL.

[64] Ibid., p. 63.

[65] Gen. Carl Spaatz, "Strategic Air Power: Fulfillment of a Concept," *Foreign Affairs* 24 (April 1946), pp. 385–96.

[66] Ibid., p. 396.

[67] Gen. Carl Spaatz, "Evolution of Air Power," *Military Review* XXVII (June 1947), pp. 3–13.

[68] MacIsaac, *Strategic Bombing,* pp. 22–28.

[69] Ibid., p. 52.

[70] Gen. Carl A. Spaatz, USAF, interview, 27 September 1968, USAF Academy, Colorado, USAF Oral History, #583, USAF Historical Center, Maxwell AFB, AL.

[71] United States, Strategic Bombing Survey, "Summary Report (Pacific War)," in David MacIsaac, ed., *The United States Strategic Bombing Survey,* Vol. VII (New York: Garland, 1976), p. 27 (hereafter cited as "USSBS VII").

[72] MacIsaac, *Strategic Bombing,* pp. 19, 76, 77.

[73] USSBS VII, p. 22.

[74] Ibid., p. 26.

[75] USSBS VII, p. 17; United States, Strategic Bombing Survey, "Summary Report (European War)," in David MacIsaac, ed., *The United States Strategic Bombing Survey,* Vol. I (New York: Garland, 1976), pp. 8–10, 16 (hereafter cited as "USSBS I").

[76] USSBS I, p. 14.

[77] Lt. Gen. Ira C. Eaker, USA, to Arnold, 18 July 1945, in Arnold Papers, Box 180, Manuscripts Division, Library of Congress.

[78] USSBS I, pp. 8, 17.

[79] MacIsaac, *Strategic Bombing,* p. 147; USSBS VII, pp. 31–32.

## CHAPTER XI

[1] Mrs. Carl A. Spaatz, interview, 25 March 1982.

[2] David MacIsaac, "The Air Force and Strategic Thought, 1945–51," unpublished paper, presented at a colloquium of the Woodrow Wilson International Center for Scholars, Washington, D.C., 21 June 1982, pp. 1, 17.

[3] Noel Francis Parrish, "Behind the Sheltering Bomb: Military Indecision from Alamogordo to Korea," unpublished Ph.D. dissertation, Rice University, 1968, p. 137.

[4] Robert P. Patterson to President Harry S. Truman, 12 December 1945, in Official File, Box 157, Folder 25 U, Harry S. Truman Library, Independence, MO.

[5] U.S. Air Force, "Report of the Chief of Staff of the United States Air Force to the Secretary of the Air Force," 30 June 1948, copy in Air University Library p. 10 (hereafter cited as "Spaatz Report").

[6] Ibid., p. 13.

[7] Alfred Goldberg, ed., *History of the United States Air Force,* ATC Pamphlet 190–1, Randolph AFB, TX, 1 June 1961, p. 9–1.

[8] Futrell, *Ideas, Concepts, Doctrine,* pp. 110, 118–19.

[9] Gen. Carl A. Spaatz, interview with Brig. Gen. Noel Parrish, USAF, and Dr. Alfred Goldberg, 21 February 1962, USAF Oral History #754, USAFHRC.

[10] John T. Greenwood, "The Emergence of the Post-War Strategic Air Force," in Alfred F. Hurley and Robert C. Ehrhart, eds., *Air Power and Warfare* (Washington, D.C.: Office of Air Force History and United States Air Force Academy, 1979), pp. 218–20.

[11] Ibid., pp. 215–20; the authority on this subject is Harry R. Borowski, *A Hollow Threat: Strategic Air Power and Containment Before Korea* (Westport, CT: Greenwood, 1982), pp. 4–6. Borowski thinks that the Kremlin probably had a better understanding of our true nuclear strength than did the American public. Also see Parrish, "Behind the Sheltering Bomb."

[12] Draft, "Spaatz Board Report," 23 October 1945, in Spaatz Papers, Box 22, hereafter referred to as "Spaatz Board Report."

[13] Ibid.

[14] MacIsaac, "Air Force and Strategic Thought," p. 15.

[15] Ibid., p. 19.

[16] Draft "Spaatz Board Report."

[17] Perry McCoy Smith, *The Air Force Plans for Peace* (Baltimore, MD: Johns Hopkins, 1970), p. 104.

[18] Futrell, *Ideas, Concepts, Doctrine,* p. 113, remarks that neither Spaatz nor the other leaders could openly say that the Russians might become enemies until the spring of 1947.

[19] Demetrios Caraley, *The Politics of Military Unification* (New York: Columbia University, 1966), p. 220.

[20] Clark Clifford, interview with Jerry N. Hess, 23 March, 13 and 19 April, 10 May, 26 July 1971; 16 March 1972; 14 February 1973, all in Washington, D.C., copy in Truman Library, Independence, MO, p. 113.

[21] Caraley, *Politics of Unification,* pp. 58–69; Louis Gambos, ed., *The Papers of Dwight David Eisenhower: The Chief of Staff,* Vol. VII (Baltimore, MD: Johns Hopkins, 1978), pp. 976–78.

[22] Ibid.

[23] Herman S. Wolk, "Independence and Responsibility: USAF in the Defense Establishment," in Paul R. Schratz, ed., *Evolution of the American Military Establishment Since World War II* (Lexington, VA: George C. Marshall Research Foundation, 1978), pp. 58–60.

[24] Ibid.; Caraley, *Politics of Unification,* pp. 77–82.

[25] Ibid.

[26] Herman S. Wolk, *Planning and Organizing the Post-War Air Force, 1943–1947* (Washington, D.C.: Office of Air Force History, 1984), p. 36; Gambos, ed., *Papers of Eisenhower,* Vol. VII, pp. 928–30; 976–78.

[27] Harry S. Truman, *Memoirs,* Vol. II, *Years of Trial and Hope* (Garden City, NY: Doubleday, 1956), p. 49.

[28] Senator W. Stuart Symington, interview with David R. Mets, 4 August 1982, Camden, ME.

[29] Wolk, *Planning and Organizing,* pp. 106–107; Spaatz Report, p. 44.

[30] Walter Millis, ed., *The Forrestal Diaries* (New York: Viking, 1951), pp. 167–70; Caraley, *Politics of Unification,* pp. 139–40.

[31] Letters, Arnold to Spaatz, 17 January 1947, and Spaatz to Arnold, 5 February 1947, in Spaatz Papers, Box 256.

[32] Caraley, *Politics of Unification,* pp. 160–65.

[33] Memorandum, Spaatz to All Major Commands and All Staff Sections, HQ, Army Air Forces, 1 April 1947, with attached testimony on Senate Bill 758, copy in Air University Library, Maxwell AFB, AL, pp. 1–62.

[34] Ibid., pp. 63–88.

[35] Ibid., pp. 86–88.

[36] Caraley, *Politics of Unification,* pp. 160–70.

[37] Greenwood, "The Emergence of the Post-War Strategic Air Force," pp. 232–33.

[38] Stephen Jurika, ed., *From Pearl Harbor to Vietnam: The Memoirs of Admiral Arthur W. Radford* (Stanford, CA: Hoover, 1980), pp. 113–14.

[39] Ibid., p. 114; Greenwood, "The Emergence of the Post-War Strategic Air Force," pp. 231–33.

[40] Futrell, *Ideas, Concepts, Doctrine,* pp. 99–100.

[41] Spaatz Report.

[42] HQ, United States Strategic Air Forces in Europe, "Conference on historical development of USSTAF between Major General Hugh J. Knerr and Captain A. Goldberg, Historical Branch, on 12 June 1945," in Box 136, Spaatz Papers, Manuscripts Division, Library of Congress.

[43] Wolk, *Planning and Organizing,* pp. 187–91.

[44] Senator W. Stuart Symington, interview, 4 August 1982.

[45] Wolk, *Planning and Organizing,* pp. 192–93.

[46] Herman S. Wolk, "The Establishment of the United States Air Force," *Air Force* 65 (September 1982), pp. 76–87; Spaatz Report, p. 19.

[47] Futrell, *Ideas, Concepts, Doctrine,* pp. 100–105; Gen. Carl A. Spaatz, interview with Brig. Gen. Noel Parrish and Dr. Alfred Goldberg, 21 February 1962, USAF Oral History #754, USAF Historical Research Center, Maxwell AFB, AL.

[48] Ibid.; Maj. Gen. Haywood S. Hansell, interview, 23 March 1984; Wolk, *Planning and Organizing,* pp. 125–29.

[49] Wolk, *Planning and Organizing,* pp. 105–8; Futrell, *Ideas, Concepts, Doctrine,* pp. 104–5.

[50] Wolk, *Planning and Organizing,* p. 40, relates that Arnold was convinced that the U.S. would have to put its primary reliance for security on technology, not on manpower.

[51] Futrell, *Ideas, Concepts, Doctrine,* p. 98.

[52] John T. Greenwood, "The Emergence of the Post-War Strategic Air Force,"

pp. 215, 219–29; Noel Francis Parrish, "Behind the Sheltering Bomb: Military Indecision from Alamogordo to Korea," unpublished Ph.D. dissertation, Rice University, 1968, pp. 130–36.

[53] Harry R. Borowski, *A Hollow Threat: Strategic Air Power and Containment Before Korea* (Westport, CT: Greenwood, 1982), pp. 18–20.

[54] Spaatz Report, p. 71.

[55] Ibid.; Futrell, *Ideas, Concepts, Doctrine*, p. 112.

[56] Parrish, "Behind the Sheltering Bomb," p. xiv.

[57] Borowski, "A Narrow Victory," pp. 18–30.

[58] Futrell, *Ideas, Concepts, Doctrine*, p. 115.

[59] Ibid., p. 116; Donald Edward Wilson, "The History of President Truman's Air Policy Commission and Its Influence on Air Policy 1947–49," unpublished Ph.D. dissertation, University of Denver, 1978, pp. 74–77, 87–89.

[60] Wilson, "Truman's Air Policy Commission," pp. 90–91.

[61] Ibid., p. 81.

[62] Ibid., pp. 79–80.

[63] Futrell, *Ideas, Concepts, Doctrine*, pp. 117–18.

[64] Wilson, "Truman's Air Policy Commission," p. 228; Borowski, *Hollow Threat*, pp. 117, 122.

[65] Mrs. Carl A. Spaatz, interview, 12 April 1984.

## EPILOGUE

[1] Sen. W. Stuart Symington, interview with David R. Mets, 4 August, 1982, Camden, Maine.

[2] Omar N. Bradley and Clay Blair, *A General's Life: An Autobiography by General of the Army Omar N. Bradley* (New York: Simon and Schuster, 1983), pp. 9, 467; Letters, Representative Daniel K. Hoch, in Washington to Spaatz in Alexandria, VA, 13 June 1945, and Honorable Paul N. Schaeffer, Reading, PA, to Spaatz in VA, 11 June 1945, both in Spaatz Papers, Box 20; James K. Boyer, interview with David R. Mets, 10 July 1982, Boyertown, PA.

[3] Mrs. Carl A. Spaatz, interview with David R. Mets, 25 March 1982, Washington, D.C.

[4] Ibid.; Kenneth Crawford, interview with David R. Mets, 25 March 1982, Washington, D.C.

[5] Ibid. Ed. note: Henry Arnold wrote *Global Mission* (New York: Harper, 1949), a series of boys' books in the late twenties, and coauthored some others with Ira Eaker. Ira Eaker coauthored *This Flying Game* (New York: Funk, 1936), with Arnold and wrote more articles than perhaps any other flyer of the interwar period. In fact, he took a graduate course in public relations in California in the early thirties and gave substantial help to his

friend Carl Spaatz in the conduct of the latter's correspondence in their later years. Spaatz authored the column for *Newsweek* for many years after his retirement, but, according to Kenneth Crawford, also of the *Newsweek* editorial staff, Spaatz would often provide a set of ideas, Crawford would work up a draft, and the two of them would edit it for publication. (Kenneth Crawford, interview, Washington, D.C., 30 March 1982). Spaatz published only a very few newspaper articles prior to World War II and never produced a book—though some New York publishers and Professor Bruce Hopper repeatedly urged him to do an autobiography. After the end of World War II, several rather prominent articles appeared under his name, the most important one being "Strategic Air Power: Fulfillment of a Concept," *Foreign Affairs* (24 April 1946), pp. 385–96. Since he was Commanding General of U.S. Army Air Forces and deeply involved in demobilization and the unification struggle at the time, he very probably received substantial help from his staff on the preparation of that article. Mrs. Spaatz, speaking of the time when her husband was a general, said that he "loathed" writing (Mrs. Carl A. Spaatz, interview, 25 March 1982).

6 Gen. Carl A. Spaatz, "The Era of Air-Power Diplomacy," *Newsweek* (20 September 1948), p. 26; "Strategic Thinking and Western Civilization," *Newsweek* (18 October 1948), p. 42; "An Open World: Imperative of Air Mobility," *Newsweek* (13 December 1948), p. 28; "Budgeting for Land-Sea-Air Power," *Newsweek* (10 January 1949), p. 24, and many others.

7 Stephen E. Ambrose, *Eisenhower,* Volume II, *The President* (New York: Simon and Schuster, 1984), p. 90.

8 Mrs. Carl Spaatz, interviews, with David R. Mets, 25 March 1982 and 12 April 1984, Washington, D.C.

9 Ibid.; Mr. Walter Bell, interview with David R. Mets, 7 March 1983, London, United Kingdom.

10 Mrs. Carl A. Spaatz, interview, 12 April 1984.

11 Ibid.

12 Alfred Goldberg, ed., *A History of the United States Air Force* (Princeton, NJ: Van Nostrand, 1957), p. 158.

13 Air Force Academy Site Selection Committee, Report to the Secretary of the Air Force, 3 June 1954, in Spaatz Papers, USAF Historical Center, Maxwell AFB, AL, Reel 23149, Frame 0321.

14 Gen. Carl A. Spaatz, interview with Maj. Edgar A. Holt, USAF, 13 June 1956, Washington, D.C., in Spaatz Papers, USAF Historical Center, Maxwell AFB, AL, Reel 23149, Frame 286.

15 Ibid.

16 Board of Visitors to the United States Air Force Academy, 1957, Report, in Spaatz Papers, USAF Historical Center, Maxwell AFB, AL, Reel 23149, Frame 0040; Board of Visitors to the United States Air Force Academy,

1958, in Spaatz Papers, USAF Historical Center, Maxwell AFB, AL, Reel 23149, Frame 0150.

[17] Letter, J. E. Manning, President, The Air Force Academy Foundation, Inc., in Colorado Springs to Spaatz in Chevy Chase, MD, 4 May 1959, in Spaatz Papers, USAF Historical Center, Maxwell AFB, AL, Reel 23149, Frame 0220.

[18] James H. Straubel, *Crusade for Airpower* (Washington, D.C.: Aerospace Education Foundation, 1982), pp. 34, 41ff.

[19] Letter, Maj. Gen. Benjamin D. Foulois, USAF (Ret.), President, Air Force Historical Foundation, offices at Maxwell AFB, AL, to Spaatz at Chevy Chase, MD, 28 September 1961, in Spaatz Papers, USAF Historical Center, Reel 23149, Frame 321.

[20] Letter, Spaatz in Washington to Doolittle in New York, 19 May 1950, in Spaatz Papers, Library of Congress, Box 30.

[21] Letter, Spaatz in Washington to Maj. Gen. Benjamin D. Foulois in Ventnor City, NJ, 21 November 1958, in Spaatz Papers, USAF Historical Center, Reel 23150, Frame 21.

[22] Draft, "General Spaatz' remarks to Eberstadt Commission," 16 September 1948, Spaatz Papers, Library of Congress, Box 28.

[23] Mrs. Carl A. Spaatz, interviews, 25 March 1982 and 12 April 1984.

[24] Lt. Gen. James H. Doolittle, USAF (Ret.), interview with David R. Mets, 19 May 1982, Washington, D.C.

# SELECTED BIBLIOGRAPHY

**PRIMARY SOURCES: BOOKS**

Arnold, Gen. of the Air Force Henry H., *Global Mission*. New York: Harper, 1949.

————. *Third Report of the Commanding General of the Army Air Forces to the Secretary of War*. Washington, DC: GPO, 1945. Copy in Air University Library, Maxwell AFB, AL.

Bekker, Cajus. *The Luftwaffe War Diaries*. Trans. Frank Ziegler, New York: Ballantine, 1964.

Bingham, Lt. Col. Hiram. *An Explorer in the Air Service*. New Haven, CT: Yale University Press, 1920.

Bradley, Gen. of the Army Omar N. and Clay Blair, *A General's Life: An Autobiography by General of the Army Omar N. Bradley*. New York: Simon and Schuster, 1983.

————. *A Soldier's Story*. New York: Holt & Co., 1954.

Brereton, LGEN Lewis H., USAAF, *The Brereton Diaries*. New York: Simon and Schuster, 1983.

Butcher, Capt. Harry C, USNR. *My Three Years with Eisenhower, The Personal Diary of Captain Harry C. Butcher*. New York: Simon and Schuster, 1946.

Chandler, Alfred D., Jr., ed., and Stephen E. Ambrose, assoc. ed. *The Papers of Dwight David Eisenhower: The War Years*. 5 Vols. Baltimore, MD: Johns Hopkins, 1970.

Churchill, Winston S. *The Second World War,* 6 Vols. Boston, MA: Houghton Mifflin, 1948–54.

Cook, Maj. Gen. Everett R, USAF Ret. *A Memoir*. Memphis, TN: Memphis Public Library, 1971.

Eisenhower, Gen. of the Army Dwight David. *Crusade in Europe*. Garden City, New York: Doubleday, 1948, 1961.

————. *The Eisenhower Diaries*. Edited by Robert H. Ferrell. New York: Norton, 1981.

Foulois, Maj. Gen. Benjamin D., USAF, Ret., and Col. C. V. Glines, USAF (Ret.) *From the Wright Brothers to the Astronauts: The Memoirs of Major General Benjamin D. Foulois*. New York: McGraw-Hill, 1968.

Galland, Adolf. *The First and the Last*. New York: Ballantine, 1954.

Groves, Gen. Leslie R., USA, Ret. *Now It Can Be Told: The Story of the Manhattan Project*. New York: Da Capo, 1962, 1983.

Hansell, Maj. Gen. Haywood S., Jr., USAF, Ret. *The Air Plan that Defeated Hitler*. Atlanta, GA: Higgins-McArthur/Longina & Porter, 1972.

————. *Strategic Air War Against Japan.* Maxwell AFB AL: Airpower Research Institute, 1980.

Kenney, Gen. George C., USAF, Ret. *General Kenney Reports.* New York: Duell, Sloan, Pearce, 1949.

Kesselring, Generalfeldmarschall Albert, Luftwaffe. *Kesselring: A Soldier's Record.* New York: Morrow, 1954.

Lahm, Col. Frank P., US Army. *The World War I Diary of Colonel Frank P. Lahm.* Maxwell AFB, AL: Aerospace Studies Institute, 1970.

Lee, Maj. Gen. Raymond, USA. *The London Journal of Raymond E. Lee.* Boston: Little, Brown, 1971.

LeMay, Gen. Curtis E., USAF, Ret., with MacKinlay Kantor. *Mission with LeMay.* Garden City, New York: Doubleday, 1965.

Maurer, Maurer, ed. *The U.S. Air Service in World War I.* 4 Vols., Washington: Government Printing Office, 1978–79.

Mitchell, William. *Memoirs of World War I.* New York: Random House, 1960.

————. *Winged Defense.* New York: Putnam's, 1925.

Momyer, Gen. William W., USAF, Ret. *Airpower in Three Wars.* Washington: Government Printing Office, 1978.

Perera, Guido R. *Leaves from My Book of Life,* Vol. II, *Washington and the War Years.* Boston, MA: privately printed, 1975.

Rickenbacker, Edward V. *Rickenbacker.* Greenwich, CT: Fawcett, 1967.

Rostow, W. W. *Pre-Invasion Bombing Strategy: General Eisenhower's Decision of March 25, 1944.* Austin, TX: University of Texas, 1981.

Speer, Albert. *Inside the Third Reich.* New York: Avon, 1970.

Tedder, Sir Arthur. *With Prejudice.* Boston, MA: Little, Brown & Company, 1966.

Truman, Harry S. *Memoirs.* 2 Vols., New York: Doubleday, 1956.

United States, Strategic Bombing Survey. *Overall Report (European War),* 30 September 1945.

————. "Overall Report (Pacific War)" in David MacIsaac, ed., *The United States Strategic Bombing Survey.* 10 Vols., New York: Garland, 1976.

Winterbotham, F. W. *The ULTRA Secret.* New York: Harper & Row, 1974.

Zuckerman, Solly. *From Apes to Warlords.* New York: Harper and Row, 1972.

## PRIMARY SOURCES: ARTICLES

Arnold, Gen. of the Army Henry H. "Air Power for Peace." *National Geographic,* Feb., 1946.

Eaker, Gen. Ira C., USAF, Ret. "General Carl A. Spaatz." *Air Force,* Sept., 1974.

————. "Major General James E. Fechet: Chief of the Air Corps, 1927–1931." *Air Force,* Sept., 1978.

————. "Memories of Six Air Chiefs." *Aerospace Historian,* Dec., 1973.

————. "The War in the Air." In Vincent J. Esposito, ed., *A Concise History of World War I*. New York: Praeger, 1964.

Goldberg, Alfred. "Spaatz" in Field Marshal Sir Michael Carver, ed., *The War Lords: Military Commanders of the Twentieth Century*. Boston, MA: Little, Brown, 1976. (This item is classified among the primary sources as Goldberg was serving as a captain in Spaatz's USSTAF headquarters during World War II.)

Hopper, Bruce C. "When the Air was Young." *Airpower Historian*, 4, Apr., 1957.

Hoyt, Brig. Gen. Ross, USAF, Ret. "Reflections of an Early Refueler." *Air Force*, Jan., 1974.

Kuter, Gen. Laurence S., USAF, Ret. "George C. Marshall, Architect of Airpower." *Air Force*, Aug., 1978.

McFarland, Marvin W. "The General Spaatz Collection." *Library of Congress Quarterly Journal of Current Acquisitions*, 6, May 1949.

Spaatz, Gen. Carl A. "Air Power in the Atomic Age." *Colliers*, 8 Sept. 1945.

————. "The Airpower Odds Against the Free World." *Air Force*, Apr. 1951.

————. "Air Warfare." *Life*, 5 July 1948.

————. "Atomic Warfare." *Life*, 16 Aug. 1948.

————. "Evolution of Air Power." *Military Review*, XXVII, June 1947.

————. "Faith in Air Power." *Air Force*, Vol. 30, Nov. 1947.

————. "The Future of the Army Air Forces." *Military Review*, Vol. 26, July 1946.

————. "Leaves from My Battle-of-Britain Diary." *Airpower Historian*, Vol. 4, Apr. 1947.

————. "Strategic Air Power: Fulfillment of a Concept." *Foreign Affairs* 24 (Apr. 1946).

————. *Newsweek* magazine. Spaatz was the military editor for many years after retirement and authored numerous columns. (See footnotes.)

Stinson, Marjorie. "Wings for War Birds: How a Girl Taught Fighters to Fly." *Liberty*, 28 Dec. 1929.

## PRIMARY SOURCES: ARCHIVAL MATERIALS

Andrews, Lt. Gen. Frank M. The Papers of Lt. Gen. Frank M. Andrews, Manuscripts Division, Library of Congress, Washington, D.C.

Arnold, General of the Air Force. The Papers of Gen. Henry H. Arnold, Manuscripts Division, Library of Congress, Washington, D.C.

Doolittle, Gen. James H. The Papers of Gen. James H. Doolittle, Manuscripts Division, Library of Congress, Washington, D.C.

Eaker, Gen. Ira C. The Papers of Gen. Ira C. Eaker, Manuscripts Division, Library of Congress, Washington, D.C.

Eisenhower, Dwight David. The Papers of Dwight D. Eisenhower, Eisenhower Library, Abilene, KS.

Mitchell, Maj. Gen. William. The Papers of William Mitchell, Manuscripts Division, Library of Congress, Washington, D.C.

Spaatz, Gen. Carl A. "Report of the Chief of Staff of the United States Air Force to the Secretary of the Air Force." 30 June 1948, bound copy in the collection of the Air University Library, Maxwell AFB, AL.

————. The Papers of General Carl Andrew Spaatz, Manuscripts Division, Library of Congress, Washington, D.C.

Truman, Harry S. The Harry S. Truman Library, Independence, Missouri, contains the papers and oral history interviews of many of the political leaders who affected Spaatz during the unification debates and his tenure as chief of staff.

United States, Air Force, USAF Academy Library, Special Collections Division, has some valuable collections of papers (like those of Generals Kuter and Hansell) and interviews. Many of the latter have been copied and are on file at the USAF Historical Research Center.

United States, Air Force, USAF Historical Research Center, Maxwell AFB, Alabama, archives, contains the most comprehensive collection of the private and official papers of figures connected with Spaatz's career. It also includes the transcripts of hundreds of oral history interviews done by Center personnel with many of Spaatz's associates. All of the existing unit histories of air units in which he served are held at the Center. It is collocated with the Air University Library, which has the country's best collection of published materials on airpower history.

United States, Army Air Forces, US Strategic Air Forces Europe, "ULTRA History of US Strategic Air Force Europe vs. German Air Force," 6 June 1945. Copy supplied to author by Justice Lewis F. Powell, Jr.

United States, Military Academy, USMA Archives, West Point, New York.

United States, National Archives, Modern Military Records Center, Washington, D.C., is the repository of many documents bearing on Spaatz's career.

United States, National Records Center, St. Louis, MO, holds Spaatz's personnel file.

## PRIMARY SOURCES: INTERVIEWS

Bell, Mrs. Walter (Spaatz's oldest daughter). Interview with David R. Mets, 7 March 1983, London.

Bufton, Air Vice Marshal Sidney, RAF, Ret. Interview with David R. Mets, 18 March 1983, Reigate, United Kingdom.

Burke, Adm. Arleigh, USN, Ret. Interview with David R. Mets, 23 March 1983, Fort Myer, VA.

Crawford, Kenneth. Interview with David R. Mets, 30 March 1982, Washington, D.C.

Curtis, Maj. Gen. E. P., USAF, Ret. Interview with Dr. James Hasdorff, 22–23 October 1975, on file at USAF Historical Research Center, Maxwell AFB, AL.

————. Interview with David R. Mets, 3 August 1982, Small Point, Maine.

Davies, R. Adm. Thomas, USN, Ret. Interview with David R. Mets, 12 Sept. 1983, Arlington, VA.

Doolittle, Gen. James H., USAF, Ret. Interview with Ronald Fogleman and Robert Burch, 26 Sept. 1971, on file at USAF Historical Research Center, Maxwell AFB, AL.

————. Interview with David R. Mets, 19 May 1982, Washington, D.C.

Dyer, V. Adm. George C., USN, Ret. "Reminisces" prepared for the US Naval Institute and on file at Naval Historical Center, Washington Navy Yard, along with the interviews and papers of many other naval figures with roles in the events of Spaatz's life.

Eaker, Gen. Ira C., USAF, Ret. Interview with Arthur Marmor, Jan. 1966, on file at USAF Historical Research Center, Maxwell AFB, AL.

————. Interview with David R. Mets, 26 March 1982, Washington, D.C.

Gresham, Katharine. Interview with David R. Mets, 19 Sept. 1982, Washington, D.C.

Hansell, Maj. Gen. Haywood S., Jr. Interview with David R. Mets, 14 Dec. 1982, Hilton Head, SC.

————. Interview with David R. Mets, 23 March 1984, Maxwell AFB, AL.

Hull, Brig. Gen. Harris B, USAF, Ret. Interview with David R. Mets, 11 July 1982, Washington, D.C.

Kenney, Gen. George C., USAF, Ret. Interview with Dr. James Hasdorff, 10–21 Aug. 1974, Bay Harbor Islands, FL, on file at USAF Historical Research Center, Maxwell AFB, AL.

Knerr, Maj. Gen. Hugh J., USAAF. Interview with Alfred Goldberg, 24 Nov. 1974, on file at USAF Historical Research Center, Maxwell AFB, AL.

Kuter, Gen. Laurence S. Interview with Hugh Ahmann, 30 Sept.–3 Oct. 1975, Naples, FL.

LeMay, Gen. Curtis E., USAF, Ret. Interview with David R. Mets, April 1982, Babson Park, FL.

Leo, Steve. Interview with David R. Mets, 11 Aug. 1982, Harpeswell, Maine.

McKee, Gen. William F., USAF, Ret. Interview with David R. Mets, 23 March 1983, Washington, D.C.

Musgrave, Maj. Gen. Thomas, USAF, Ret. Interview with David R. Mets, 24 March 1983, Washington, D.C.

Parton, James. Interview with David R. Mets, 29 July 1982, New York.

Peabody, Brig. Gen. Hume, USAF, Ret. Interview, Chaptico, MD, 13–16 Sept. 1975, filed at USAF Historical Research Center, Maxwell AFB, AL.

Powell, Justice Lewis F., Jr. Interview with David R. Mets, 21 Oct. 1982, Washington, D.C.

Quesada, Lt. Gen. Elwood, USAF, Ret. Interview with David R. Mets, 14 Sept. 1983, Washington, D.C.

Spaatz, Gen. Carl A. Interview with Bruce Hopper, 8 Nov. 1946, in Spaatz Papers, Library of Congress, Box 269.

———. Interview with Bruce Hopper, 20 May 1945, location not given, in Spaatz Papers, Library of Congress, Box 136.

———. Interview with Brig. Gen. Noel F. Parrish, USAF, Ret. and Dr. Alfred Goldberg, 21 Feb. 1962, Washington, D.C., on file at USAF Historical Research Center, Maxwell AFB, AL.

———. Interview, 19 May 1965, on file at USAF Historical Research Center, Maxwell AFB, AL.

———. Interview 27 Sept. 1968, USAF Academy, CO, on file at USAF Historical Research Center, Maxwell AFB, AL.

———. Interview 24 April 1972, on file at USAF Historical Research Center, Maxwell AFB, AL.

Spaatz, Mrs. Ruth. Interview with David R. Mets, 25 March 1982, 27 June 1982, 12 April 1984, Washington, D.C.

———. Interview with Dr. James Hasdorff, 3 March 1981, Washington, D.C., on file at USAF Historical Research Center.

Symington, Secretary of the Air Force W. Stuart. Interview with David R. Mets, 4 Aug. 1982, Camden, Maine.

Wade, Maj. Gen. Leigh, USAF, Ret. Interview with David R. Mets, 2 April 1982, Washington, D.C.

Walsh, Maj. Gen. Robert, USAF, Ret. Interview with David R. Mets, 31 March 1982, Washington, D.C.

## SECONDARY SOURCES: BOOKS

Ambrose, Stephen E. *Eisenhower*, Vol. I, *Soldier, General of the Army, President-Elect, 1890–1952*. New York: Simon and Schuster, 1983.

Association of Graduates, U.S. Military Academy. *Register of Graduates, 1981*. West Point, New York, 1981.

Baker, William. *Perkiomen: Here's to You: A Centennial History of Perkiomen School*. North Wales, PA: North Wales Press, 1975.

Baumbach, Werner. *The Life and Death of the Luftwaffe*. New York: Ballantine, 1949, 1960.

Bennett, Ralph. *ULTRA in the West*. New York: Scribner's, 1979.

Borden, Norman E., Jr. *Air Mail Emergency, 1934*. Freeport, Maine: Bond, Wheelwright, 1968.

Borowski, Harry R. *A Hollow Threat: Strategic Air Power and Containment Before Korea*. Westport, CT: Greenwood, 1982.

Boylan, Bernard L. *Development of the Long Range Escort Fighter*. Maxwell AFB, AL: Research Studies Institute, 1955.

Brodie, Bernard and Fawn M. *From Crossbow to H-Bomb*. Bloomington, Indiana: Indiana University, 1973.

Brown, Anthony Cave. *Bodyguard of Lies*. London: W. H. Allen, 1977.

Buchanan, Russel A. *The United States and World War II*. 2 Vols., New York: Harper, 1964.

Calvocoressi, Peter and Guy Wint. *Total War: The Story of World War II*. New York: Random House, 1972.

Caraley, Demetrios. *The Politics of Military Unification*. New York: Columbia University, 1966.

Coffey, Thomas M. *Hap: The Story of the U.S. Air Force and the Man Who Built It, General Henry H. "Hap" Arnold*. New York: Viking, 1982.

Copp, Dewitt S. *A Few Great Captains*. Garden City, NY: Doubleday, 1980.

———. *Forged in Fire*. New York: Doubleday, 1982.

Craven, Wesley Frank and James Lea Cate, eds. *The Army Air Forces in World War II*, 7 Vols. Chicago, ILL: University of Chicago Press, 1948–53.

Davis, Burke. *The Billy Mitchell Affair*. New York: Random House, 1967.

DeBuque, Jean. *The Development of the Heavy Bomber*. Maxwell AFB, AL: Air University, 1951.

Dugan, James and Carroll Stewart. *Ploesti: The Great Ground-Air Battle of 1 August 1943*. New York: Random, 1962.

Earle, Edward M., ed., *Makers of Modern Strategy: Military Thought from Machiavelli to Hitler*. Princeton, NJ: Princeton University, 1944.

Esposito, Brig. Gen. Vincent J., USA, Ret., ed. *The West Point Atlas of American Wars*, 2 Vols. New York: Praeger, 1959.

Fabyanic, Thomas A. *Strategic Air Attack in the United States Air Force: A Case Study*. Manhattan, KS: Military Affairs/Aerospace Historian Publishing, 1976.

Freeman, Roger A. *The Mighty Eighth: Units, Men, and Machines*. Garden City, New York: Doubleday, 1970.

Futrell, Frank. *Ideas, Concepts, Doctrine: A History of Basic Thinking in the United States Air Force, 1907–1964*. Maxwell AFB, AL: Air University, 1965.

Glines, Col. Carroll V., USAF, Ret. *Jimmy Doolittle: Master of the Calculated Risk*. New York: Van Nostrand Reinhold, 1972.

Goldberg, Alfred, ed. *History of the United States Air Force*, USAF, Air Training Command Pamphlet 190–1, 1 June 1961.

Greer, Dr. Thomas. *The Development of Air Doctrine in the Army Air Arm, 1917–1941*. Maxwell AFB, AL: Air University, 1955.

Gropman, Col. Alan L., USAF. *The Air Force Integrates, 1945–1964*. Washington: Government Printing Office, 1978.

Harris, Sherwood. *The First to Fly: Aviation's Pioneer Days*. New York: Simon and Schuster, 1970.

Hastings, Max. *Bomber Command*. London: Pan, 1979.

Hennesy, Juliette. *The United States Army Air Arm, April 1961 to April 1917*. Maxwell AFB, AL: Research Studies Institute, 1958.

Holley, Irving B., Jr. *Ideas and Weapons*. New Haven, CT: Yale, 1954.

Hudson, James J. *Hostile Skies: A Combat History of the American Air Service in World War I*. Syracuse, New York: Syracuse Univ., 1968.

Huie, William Bradford. *The Fight for Air Power*. New York: L. B. Fischer, 1942. Reportedly, this work had been written by MGEN Hugh Knerr but he had been recalled to active duty by 1942 and it was published under Huie's name.

Huntington, Samuel P. *The Soldier and the State*. Cambridge, MA: Harvard, 1957.

Hurley, Alfred F. *Billy Mitchell: Crusader for Air Power*. Bloomington, Indiana: Indiana Univ., 1964, 1975.

Irving, David. *The Destruction of Dresden*. London: Kimper, 1963.

―――. *The Rise and Fall of the Luftwaffe: The Life of Field Marshal Erhard Milch*. Boston, MA: Little, Brown, 1973.

―――. *The War Between the Generals*. Hammondsworth, Middlesex, England: Penguin, 1981.

James, D. Clayton. *The Years of MacArthur*. 2 Vols., Boston, MA: Houghton, Mifflin, 1975.

Janowitz, Morris. *The Professional Soldier: A Social and Political Portrait*. Glencoe, IL: Free Press, 1960.

Josephy, Alvin M. Jr., ed. *The American Heritage History of Flight*. New York: American Heritage, 1962.

Jurika, Stephen, ed. *From Pearl Harbor to Vietnam: The Memoirs of Admiral Arthur W. Radford*. Stanford, CA: Hoover, 1980.

Kase, Toshikazu. *Journey to the Missouri*. New Haven, CT: Yale, 1950.

Levine, Isaac Don. *Mitchell: Pioneer of Air Power*. New York: Duell, Sloan and Pearce, 1943.

Lewin, Ronald. *ULTRA Goes to War*. New York: Pocket Books, 1978.

Liddell Hart, B. H. *The German Generals Talk*. New York: Morrow, 1948.

―――. *History of the Second World War*. New York: Putnam's, 1970.

McClendon, R. Earl. *Autonomy of the Air Arm*. Maxwell AFB, AL: Air University, 1954.

MacIsaac, David. *Strategic Bombing in World War II: The Story of the United States Strategic Bombing Survey.* New York: Garland, 1976.

Manchester, William. *American Caesar: Douglas MacArthur, 1880–1964.* Boston, MA: Little, Brown, 1978.

Maurer, Maurer. *US Air Service Victory Credits, World War I.* Maxwell AFB, AL: Albert F. Simpson Historical Research Center, 1969.

———. ed. *The U.S. Air Service in World War I,* 4 Vols. Washington: Government Printing Office, 1978.

Millis, Walter, ed. *The Forrestal Diaries.* New York: Viking, 1951.

Morison, Samuel Eliot. *The Two Ocean War.* Boston, MA: Little, Brown, 1963.

Morrison, Wilbur H. *Fortress without a Roof: The Allied Bombing of the Third Reich.* New York: St. Martin's, 1982.

Murray, Williamson. *Strategy for Defeat: The Luftwaffe 1933–45.* Maxwell AFB, AL: Air University, 1983.

Overy, R. J. *The Air War, 1939–1945.* London: Europa, 1981.

Pazek, Lawrence. *United States Air Force History: A Guide to Documentary Sources.* Washington: Government Printing Office, 1973.

Pogue, Forrest C. *George C. Marshall,* 4 Vols. New York: Viking, 1963–87.

Puryear, Edgar F., Jr. *Stars in Flight: A Study in Air Force Character and Leadership.* Novato, CA: Presidio, 1981.

Quester, George H. *Deterrence before Hiroshima.* New York: Wiley, 1966.

Richards, Dennis. *Portal of Hungerford.* New York: Holmes and Meier, 1977.

———. and Hilary St. George Saunders. *Royal Air Force, 1939–1945,* 3 Vols. London: Her Majesty's Stationery Office, 1954.

Shiner, Col. John F., USAF. *Benjamin Foulois and the U.S. Army Air Corps.* Washington: Government Printing Office, 1984.

Simons, William E. *Liberal Education in the Service Academies.* New York: Columbia University, 1965.

Smith, Maj. Gen. Perry McCoy, USAF, Ret. *The Air Force Plans for Peace.* Baltimore, MD: Johns Hopkins, 1970.

Taylor, John W. R., ed. *Combat Aircraft of the World from 1909 to the Present.* New York: Paragon, 1969.

Thomas, Lowell and Edward Jablonski. *Doolittle: A Biography.* New York: Doubleday, 1976.

Toland, John. *The Last 100 Days.* London: Barker, 1966.

———. *The Rising Sun.* 2 Vols., New York: Random House, 1970.

Toulmin, H. A., Jr. *Air Service, American Expeditionary Force.* New York: Van Nostrand, 1927.

Turnbull, Archibald D. and Clifford L. Lord. *History of United States Naval Aviation.* New Haven, CT: Yale Univ., 1949.

Vandiver, Frank E. *Black Jack: The Life and Times of John J. Pershing,* Vol. II. College Station, TX: Texas A & M Univ., 1977.

Verrier, Anthony. *The Bomber Offensive*. New York: Macmillan, 1969.

Watson, Mark S. *The U.S. Army in World War II: Chief of Staff: Prewar Plans and Preparations*. Washington: Government Printing Office, 1950.

Weigley, Russell F. *Eisenhower's Lieutenants: The Campaign of France and Germany, 1944–1945*. Bloomington, Indiana: Indiana University, 1981.

Werth, Alexander. *Russia at War, 1941–1945*. New York: Avon, 1964.

Wolk, Herman S. *Planning and Organizing the Post-War Air Force, 1943–47*. Washington, D.C.: Office of Air Force History, 1984.


## SECONDARY SOURCES: ARTICLES

Barnett, Lincoln. "General 'Tooey' Spaatz." *Life*, 14 April 1943.

*Berks County Democrat*, January, 1908–December 1911, on file in the offices of the *Boyertown Area Times*, Boyertown, PA.

Crabbe, William H. Jr. "The Army Air Mail Pilots Report." *The Air Power Historian*, April 1962.

Downs, Lt. Col. Eldon, USAF. "Army and the Air Mail—1934." *The Air Power Historian*, Jan. 1962.

Emerson, William R. "Operation Pointblank: A Tale of Bombers and Fighters." Harmon Memorial Lecture, USAF Academy, 27 March 1962.

Erickson, H. A. "The Flight of the Question Mark." *Popular Aviation and Aeronautics*, March 1929.

Futrell, Robert F. "Preplanning the USAF." *Air University Review*. XXI, 1971.

Greenwood, John T. "The Emergence of the Post-War Strategic Air Force." In Alfred F. Hurley and Robert C. Ehrhart, eds., *Air Power and Warfare*. Washington, D.C.: Office of Air Force History and the United States Air Force Academy, 1979.

Holley, Irving B., Jr. "Of Saber Charges, Escort Fighters and Spacecraft." *Air University Review*, XXXIV (Sept.–Oct. 1983).

———. "An Enduring Challenge: The Problem of Air Force Doctrine," Harmon Memorial Lecture, USAF Academy, 1974.

McReynolds, Charles F. "The Refueling Flight of 'Question Mark'." *Aviation*, 19 Jan. 1929.

Maurer, Maurer. "The 1st Aero Squadron." *Air Power Historian*, October, 1957.

Middleton, Drew. "Boss of the Heavyweights." *Saturday Evening Post*, 20 May 1944.

Parrish, Noel L. "Hap Arnold and the Historians." *Aerospace Historian*. Vol. 20, Sept. 1973.

Priest, Robert; Terrence Fullerton and Claude Bridges. "Personality and Value Changes in West Point Cadets." *Armed Forces and Society* 8 (Summer, 1982).

Shalett, Sidney. "Nerveless Master of our Superfortresses." *New York Times Magazine*, 5 Aug. 1945.

Shiner, Maj. John F., USAF. "General Benjamin Foulois and the 1934 Air Mail Disaster." *Aerospace Historian*, Dec. 1978.

Simpson, Albert F. "The Attack on Ploesti." *Military Review*, Vol. 29, Jan. 1952.

Welsh, Maj. J. B., USAF. "Never a 'Question Mark'." *Airman*, March 1976.

Williams, T. Harry. "The Macs and the Ikes: America's Two Military Traditions." *American Mercury*, LXXV, Oct. 1952.

Wolk, Herman S. "The Establishment of the United States Air Force." *Air Force*, Sept. 1982.

————. "Independence and Responsibility: USAF in the Defense Establishment." In Paul R. Schratz, ed., *Evolution of the American Military Establishment Since World War II*. Lexington, VA: George C. Marshall Research Foundation, 1978.

————. "Men Who Made the Air Force." *Air University Review*, XXIII, Sept.–Oct. 1972.

————. "Prelude to D-Day: The Bomber Offensive—the Overlord Air Dispute." *Air Force*, Vol. 57, June 1974.

## SECONDARY SOURCES: DISSERTATIONS AND THESES

Buckley, Thomas H. "The United States and the Washington Conference." Indiana University, 1961.

Bowers, Raymond Landis. "The Transcontinental Reliability Test: American Aviation after World War I." Master's thesis, University of Wisconsin, 1960.

Eppley, Samuel M. "General Carl A. Spaatz." Air Command and Staff College, 1965 copy in Air University Library, Maxwell AFB, AL.

Flugel, Raymond R. "United States Air Power Doctrine: A Study of the Influence of William Mitchell and Giulio Douhet at the Air Corps Tactical School, 1921–1935." University of Oklahoma, 1955.

Henry, Paul F. "From Airships to the Nuclear Age: A History of LGEN William E. Kepner." Air Command and Staff College, 1981, copy in Air University Library, Maxwell AFB, AL.

Julian, Thomas A. "Operation 'Frantic' and the Search for American-Soviet Military Collaboration, 1941–1944." Syracuse University, 1968.

Nye, Roger H. "The United States Military Academy in an Era of Educational Reform, 1900–1925." Columbia University, 1968.

Parrish, Brig. Gen. Noel F., USAF, Ret. "Behind the Sheltering Bomb: Military Indecision from Alamogordo to Korea." Rice University, 1968.

Tate, James P. "The Army and its Air Corps: A Study of the Evolution of Army Policy towards Aviation, 1919–1941." Indiana University, 1976.

Wilson, Donald Edward. "The History of President Truman's Air Policy Commission and Its Influence on Air Policy, 1947–1949." University of Denver, 1978.

# Index

A-20s, 118, 127, 133, 157
AEF, 23–30, 37
Aerobatics, 21–22, 26, 40
Africa, in World War II, 10, 117, 132–59
  passim, 176, 203, 296
Agua Caliente, Mexico, 76
AIC, 3d, 23–30, 36
Airacobras (Bell P-39s), 119, 122, 125, 142,
  156
Air Board, 318–19
Air Corps, 66–112, 115
  aircraft of, 66, 67–68, 75, 77–79, 85–86,
    90, 98–111 passim
  and GHQ Air Force, 102–3
  name of, 64, 66
  personnel of, 66, 83, 109
Air Corps Act (1926), 66
Air Corps Tactical School, 96, 97, 109, 114,
  273
Aircraft, 66
  in air races, 41–42, 69
  pursuit, 24–25, 67, 75, 78
  transport of, 45–46, 47, 125–27, 290
  in World War I, 31, 33 (see also Fokkers;
    Spads)
  See also Bombers; Industries; Jets; individ-
    ual names of planes
Air Force, U.S. See United States Air Force
Air Force Academy, 14, 337–38, 339, 340
Air Force Association, 293, 338
Air Force Combat Command, 115
Air Force Historical Foundation, 3, 338
Air forces
  British, see Royal Air Force
  German, see Luftwaffe
  U.S., see United States Air Force
  U.S. Army, see Army, U.S.

Air Forces League, 292–93
Airlines, and mail, 91–92, 93, 94, 95
Airmail crisis, 75, 91–95
Air Policy Commission (Finletter Commis-
  sion), 323, 328–30
Air Service, 13–66, 70
Air Service Tactical School (ASTS), 54, 55,
  56–60
Air superiority, 55, 96
  Strategic Bombing Survey on, 309
  in World War I, 31
  in World War II, 111, 113, 151, 157,
    182–83, 190–220 passim, 247–48, 250,
    254, 255–56, 262, 272, 273
Air War College, 324
Alexander, Harold R.L.G., 160
Allen, Julian, 179
Allied Expeditionary Air Forces (AEAF),
  179–80, 189, 199–219, 237
American Expeditionary Force (AEF), 23–
  30, 37
Anderson, Fred, 195, 201, 205, 269, 324
  and CLARION, 271, 276
  at Malta and Yalta conferences, 274, 276
  retirement activities with, 336
  and trucking, 229
  and V-1s, 236
Anderson, Frederick L.
  General, 143–44, 145, 147, 148, 149
Anderson, Muriel, 83
Andrews, Frank, 99–100, 103–4, 128, 129,
  155, 176, 180
Annual maneuvers, 88–89
Antonov, General Alexei, 274
ANVIL, 226–28, 233, 256
Appearance, Spaatz's, 9

Ardennes battles, 226, 242–43, 262–68, 270, 272, 273, 296
ARGUMENT, 194
Armstrong, H. G., 33–34
Army, U.S.
    Air Corps of, 66–112, 115
    Air Service of, 13–66, 70
    Aviation Section of, 20, 21–23
    standing army of, 315
    and unification of armed forces, 316–17, 327
    and USAF organization, 326
    World War II preparedness of, 107–9, 114
    World War I preparedness of, 21, 24
    See also United States Army Air Forces
Army Ground Forces, 115
Army-Navy Preparatory School, 5
Army Regulation, 95–5, 115
Army Service Forces, 115
Army War College, 109
Arnhem battle, 235–36, 279
Arnold, Henry "Hap", 98–111 passim, 340
    and atomic bomb, 302, 303, 314, 315
    health failing, 289, 292, 298, 307, 311
    at March Field, 81
    and Mitchell, 62, 64, 66, 100, 340
    report evaluating air wars by, 307, 308
    and research and development, 326, 327–28
    retirement of, 311–12, 318, 324
    in San Diego, 16
    in San Francisco, 40, 42–43
    and separate air arm, 259, 291, 292–93, 295–96, 307, 312, 317, 323
    Spaatz characterized by, 89
    training of, 13
    and unification of armed forces, 296, 307, 316, 317, 320
    at West Point, 10
    and World War II European theater, 111–35 passim, 155, 176–94 passim, 202–14 passim, 233, 241–78 passim
    and World War II Mediterranean theater, 141–142, 143, 154, 164–81 passim
    and World War II Pacific theater, 115–16, 289, 294–304 passim
Atomic bomb, 295, 302–4, 307, 309, 310, 313–16, 327, 328
Attack aviation (close air support), 54, 66, 87, 113
Autonomy. See Independence
Aviation Policy Board (Brewster Committee), 323, 328–29
AWPD-1, 113–14, 120–21, 202

B-15 bombers, 98
B-17s. See Fortresses
B-24s. See Liberators
B-25s, 117–18, 157
B-26s, 117–19, 157
B-29 Superfortresses, 240, 295–314 passim
B-2s, Curtiss Condor, 78, 79
B-9s, Boeing, 79
Bader, Douglas, 171
Bagby, Sally, 153, 284, 285, 294
Baker, Newton D., 17, 29, 57–58, 95
Baker Board, 95–98
Baltic, S.S., 22–23
Bari, Italy, conference in, 252
Barksdale Field, Louisiana, 67
Battle of the Bulge, 261–68, 270
Baucom, Bryne V., 44, 50, 54
Bell, Walter, 335, 336
Bell P-39 Airacobras, 119, 122, 125, 142, 156
Benedict, Charles C., 10, 36, 59
Berks County Democrat, 4–5, 15
Berlin Airlift, 333
Berlin attack, 269, 271, 272, 274–75, 303
Biddle, Charles, 32, 34, 35–36
Big Week, 196–98, 202, 206
Bingham, Hiram, 36–37
Black, Hugo, 91–92
Black flyers, 160–61, 171–72
Boeing B-9, 79
Boeing P-12s, 78
Boeing Thomas Morse aircraft, 48–49
Bombers
    AEF, 37
    Air Corps, 67–68, 75, 78–79, 85–86, 90, 98–111 passim
    Allied (World War II), 110–27 passim, 132–36 passim, 142–43, 147, 156–57, 181–82, 184, 187–88, 194, 215, 222–36 passim, 256, 258, 263–64, 296–305 passim (see also Fortresses; Liberators)
    British, 110–11, 112 (see also Spitfires)
    dive, 110
    escorts for, 56, 77–78, 85, 106, 112, 119, 130–31, 136, 142–43, 181–82, 197, 253–54, 301
    German, 108–9, 112, 183, 193–94, 246–47, 250 (see also Messerschmitts)
    jet, 31, 246–47
    Martin, 41, 78, 117–19, 157
    refueling of, 72, 73
    transport of, 125–27, 290
    trucking by, 228–34, 236, 274
    in World War I, 31, 33
    See also Bombing

Bombing
    atomic, 295, 302–4, 307, 309, 310, 313–
        16, 327, 328
    carpet, 220–26, 258, 260
    early experiments in, 16
    independent missions of, 38, 57–58, 90,
        96–98, 115, 152 (see also Separate air
        arm; Strategic bombing)
    by pursuit planes, 54
    precision, 67, 182, 257–58, 302, 309
    See also Targets
"Bomb line," 281
Bottomley, Norman, 258, 260, 274
Bourke-White, Margaret, 153
Bowen, Thomas, 23
Boyertown, 4
Boyertown Area Times, 4
Boyertown Democrat, 4
Boyertown High School, 5
Bradley, Follett, 100, 187
Bradley, Omar, 10, 154, 213, 221–24, 232–
    33, 263, 293–94, 295, 323, 333–34
Bradley Committee, 187
Branch, Harlee, 92
Brandenberger, E., 264
Braun, Eva, 282
Brereton, Lewis, 54, 58–59, 68, 99, 180,
    195, 213, 222, 225, 235
Brett, George, 77, 78
Brewster, Owen/Brewster Committee (Avia-
    tion Policy Board), 323, 328–30
Brindley, Oscar, 14, 15, 16
Britain
    Battle of, 109–12, 113, 286
    See also United Kingdom
Browning, F. A. M., 236
Budgets, military, 45, 68, 259
    Air Force (USAF), 323, 327, 330, 335
    and annual maneuvers, 88
    Army air arm, 20, 21, 45, 54–55, 60, 64,
        65, 90, 100–101, 108
    and coastal defense, 55, 68, 84
    after National Security Act, 322–23
    Navy, 65, 84, 90
    and unification of armed forces, 316–17
"Buzzing," 51–52
BW-1, 122, 125
BW-8, 122

C-46s, 305
C-47s, 123, 126, 144, 147, 157, 163, 228,
    231, 234, 264, 305
C-54s, 304–5
Cabell, Charles P., 276
Campbell, Douglas, 37
Cannon, John K., 44, 45, 161, 180, 227

Card playing, 9
Carpenter, Charles, 1, 340
Carpet bombing, 220–26, 258, 260
Carranza, Venustiano, 12, 17
Carriers, in annual maneuvers, 88–89
Carver, Michael, 2
Casablanca Conference, 152–55, 156, 159,
    274
Casey, William R., 83
Castle, Fred, 244
Casualties
    in World War II European theater, 213,
        242, 267, 281
    See also Death
Centralization. See Organization; Separate air
    arm; Unification, of armed forces
Chaney, James E., 59, 92
Chennault, Claire, 44, 77
Churchill, Winston, 148, 176, 189–90, 210,
    226–27, 274, 284
Circuses, flying, 40
Cities, bombing of, 57–58, 86, 87, 97, 220,
    268–69, 271, 273–77, 302, 303, 304
CLARION, 271, 272, 276, 277
Clark, Mark, 165, 166
Clothing, flight, 18, 51, 62
Coal shortage, 279
Coastal defense, 55, 58, 65, 68, 73, 84, 85,
    91, 96, 101
Coast Artillery, 84
COBRA, 222–24
Cochran, Jacqueline, 339
Code interception, in World War II, 110,
    157–58, 162, 184
Collins, J. Lawton/Collins Plan, 317–18
Columbus, New Mexico, Pershing expedi-
    tion, 16, 17–20
Combat
    aerobatic, 21–22, 26, 40
    training in, 24, 43 (see also under Train-
        ing)
    See also World War I; World War II
Command and General Staff College, Fort
    Leavenworth, 56–57, 85, 98–99, 109,
    117
Communications
    air-to-ground, 15–16, 71, 80
    Question Mark, 71, 80
    in transport over Greenland, 125–26
    See also Radar
Communist revolution, in Russia, 23–24
Condors (Curtiss B-2s), 78, 79
Conduct record, Spaatz's school, 5, 7
Conduct. See Discipline
Congress, U.S.
    and airmail crisis, 93

Congress, U.S. (*continued*)
appropriations for aviation by, 20, 21, 64, 95, 100, 108, 330
and appropriations for Navy, 90
and coastal defense, 84
Department of Aeronautics considered by, 41
separate air force considered by, 41, 57, 60, 321, 322
and unification of armed forces bill, 318–22
Coningham, Arthur, 146, 149, 152, 154, 155, 156, 262
Converse, Lieutenant Rob Roy, 34
Cook, Everett R., 117, 179, 198, 336
Cook, Harvey W., 54, 55, 56, 58
Coolidge, Calvin, 61, 64, 66
Coronado Beach Corporation, 14
Courtney, Christopher, 130
Cousins, Ralph, 10
Craig, Malin, 101, 103, 107, 115
Crawford, Kenneth, 334
CROSSBOW, Operation, 236, 237, 238, 256
*Crusade in Europe* (Eisenhower), 244
Cuddihy, C. T., 69
Curry, John, 69
Curtis, Edward P. (Ted), 36, 116–17, 153, 165, 277–78, 285, 286–87, 293, 294, 336
Curtiss, Glenn, 10–11, 13–14
Curtiss aircraft, 17, 18, 19, 78, 79
Czechoslovakia, 107

Dargue, Herbert A., 16, 20, 47
Davidson, Howard, 20
Davis, Benjamin O., Jr., 161
Davison, Trubee, 292–93
D-Day, 201, 205, 213–17
Death, 333
in airmail crisis, 93–94
in carpet bombing, 223, 224–25, 226
in 1st Pursuit Group, 50
in Issoudun training program, 26
at March Field, 82–83
San Diego flying school and, 14
Spaatz's, 1–2, 339, 340
in World War II, 170–71, 185, 223, 224–25, 226, 240
"Death ray," 245
DeGaulle, C., 210
de Lattre de Tassigny, Jean, 283, 284, 285
Denfeld, Louis, 323
Depression, 75–76, 83
Dern, Walter, 92, 94

de Seversky, Alexander, 285
Devers, General Jacob L., 180
DH-4s, 41–42, 45–46
Dialectic Society, West Point, 10
Dickinson Este, L. J., 34
Dietrich, Sepp, 264
Discipline
air arm, 28, 44, 48, 49, 50–52, 55–56, 59, 64, 81–82
Spaatz's school, 5, 7
Distinguished Service Cross, 36
Doctrine, airpower, 83–89, 91
Allied World War II, 107, 113, 120–21, 130–32, 150–61 passim, 167, 172, 181–82, 257–58
German World War II, 197
precision bombing, 67, 182, 257–58, 302, 309
pursuit, 54–56
War Department, 57, 95–97, 152
*See also* Offense; Strategic bombing
Doenitz, Karl, 282
D'Olive, Charles, 36
Doolittle, Jimmy, 177, 180
and Air Force Association, 338
on Baker Board, 95–96
and European theater, 183, 192, 194, 195, 197, 206, 226, 229, 236, 248–49, 258, 268, 276, 280
and MARKET-GARDEN, 236
and Mediterranean theater, 136–56 passim, 164, 166, 168, 169, 184
and Pacific theater, 118–19, 122, 291, 294, 299
"Double deputy" system, 187
Douglas A-20 Bostons, 118, 157
Douglas Aircraft Company, 326
Douglas biplanes, 70, 72
Douhet, Giulio, 57, 113
Dow Field, Maine, 121–22
Dresden attack, 275, 276
Drew, Charles, 34
Drinking, 9, 50–51, 82
Drum, Hugh/Drum Board, 91, 92, 95
Duncan, Asa N., 116–17, 153

Eaker, Ira, 64, 65, 185, 202, 206, 307
and European theater, 116–37 passim, 157, 177, 180, 191, 192–93, 195, 241, 248–49, 253, 271, 274, 276
with Hughes Aircraft, 334
at March Field, 81
and Mediterranean theater, 137, 155, 168, 172, 176–77, 178, 180–81, 195, 197, 198, 199

and Mitchell, 62
in Pacific theater, 298
and *Rex* interception, 101
on Rogue River, 335–36
Spaatz described by, 165
and USSBS, 310
Eaker, Ruth, 335
Eberstadt Plan, 317
Economics
Depression, 75–76, 83
*See also* Finances
Education
Spaatz's, 5, 6–11
*See also* Schools, military; Training
Eighth Air Force, 172
in European theater, 116–34 passim, 140,
143, 168, 180–96 passim, 211–29 passim, 235, 240, 242, 251–58 passim,
266, 272, 275, 276
in Mediterranean theater, 117, 136–43
passim, 164, 177
organization of, 116–17, 178, 179–80,
325
in Pacific theater, 291, 299
Eisenhower, Dwight, 292, 299, 312, 318,
333–34
and Air Force Academy, 337
and Arnold replacement, 312
and budget for Air Force, 335
and European theater, 128–35 passim,
155, 173–80 passim, 189–90, 199–227
passim, 234–35, 237, 244, 255–67 passim, 281, 295, 340
in Mediterranean theater, 10, 117, 135–56
passim, 168, 173, 177
and Pacific theater, 289
and separate air arm, 321, 325
and surrenders, 282
and unification of armed forces bill, 318,
320, 321
and victory celebrations, 293
at West Point, 10
Electrocardiograph, 106
Ellington Field, Texas, 43–45
Elmendorf, Hugh, 83
Emmons, Delos, 103, 116, 122
England. *See* United Kingdom
*Enola Gay,* 303
European theater, World War II, 106–43
passim, 155, 157, 167–68, 173–282
passim, 295, 340
Expenditures. *See* Budgets, military

Falaise Pocket, 224, 233
Falconer, C. L., 152

Family
Spaatz's, 3–6, 22, 76, 104, 105, 169–70,
177–78, 198–99, 294–95, 331, 335,
339
*See also individual family members*
Farmer, Howard, 52, 59, 81
Fechet, James, 39, 65, 70, 77, 80, 82
Ferdinand, Archduke, 12
Ferrying Command, 121
Fickel, Jacob, 59
"50 mission crush," on garrison cap, 9
Fifteenth Air Force, 240, 251, 258
and European theater, 192, 194, 195, 196,
202–3, 211, 227, 252–53, 256, 271,
274, 280
in Mediterranean theater, 166, 168–69,
177–85 passim, 195, 196, 252
Finances
military pay, 15, 62
of Spaatz's family, 5–6
*See also* Budgets, military
"Finishing schools," 24
Finletter, Thomas F. (Finletter Commission),
323, 328–30
1st Aero Squadron, 14, 15, 16, 17–20, 32
1st Bombardment Wing, 77, 81, 83
1st Pursuit Group, 19, 31–32, 39, 43–56,
66, 123, 134, 136, 142
Foch, General Ferdinand (France), 30–31
Focke-Wulf 190s, 133, 192
Fokker, Anthony, 25
Fokkers, 34–35, 41, 70, 72, 80
Forest Service, U.S., 42
Forrestal, James, 318, 319, 320, 322–23,
329
Fort Leavenworth, Kansas, 56–57, 85, 98–
99
Fortresses (B-17 Flying), 107–8, 296
for European theater, 125, 126, 131, 133–
34, 143, 194, 196, 221, 231, 260, 272,
275, 281
at Langley Field, 75, 100–102
in Mediterranean theater, 142, 147, 157
for Pacific theater, 123–24, 125
after World War II, 313
Fort Sam Houston, 43
Fort Sill, Oklahoma, 14, 15
Fosnes, Carl E., 9, 11, 13
Foulois, Benjamin, 17–20 passim, 30, 65,
76, 81, 92–94, 95, 100, 102, 121
France, 134, 135–36, 140, 142, 143, 158,
167, 219–33 passim, 250–51
OVERLORD in, 173–89 passim, 199–220
passim, 226, 228, 238, 239, 247–48,
249
and surrender, 283, 284

Frank, Walter H., 59, 129
FRANTIC, 274
Fredendall, Lloyd, 149, 150–51, 154
Freeman, Wilfred, 130
French language, Spaatz and, 28
Friedeburg, Hans, 284
FW-190s, 133, 192

Galland, Adolf, 197, 198, 246, 249–50
Garros, Rolland, 24–25
General Headquarters (GHQ) Air Force, 68,
    75, 91, 95–98, 99–104, 114–15, 296
"General Headquarters Reserve," 38, 90
George, Harold (Hal), 77, 112, 113, 114,
    121
Germany
    scientists from, 326
    surrender by, 282–85
    in World War II, 106–21 passim, 132–282
        passim, 309
    See also Goering, Hermann; Industries;
        Luftwaffe
"Germany first" strategy, 124, 272
Gibralter, in World War II, 141
Giles, Barney, 186, 242–43, 270, 292, 298
Global Mission (Arnold), 62
Goebbels, Joseph, 129
Goering, Hermann, 112, 184, 193, 197,
    247, 282, 285–87
Goldberg, Alfred, 2–3
Gorrell, Edgar, 20, 37, 38, 95
Greenland route, 125–26
Grenier Field, Manchester, New Hampshire,
    121–23, 125
Gresham, Emmett B. (Red), 169–70, 198–99
Gross, William, 118
Ground campaigns, 219
    See also Tactical units and missions
Groves, Leslie M., 295
Gunnery training, 31, 128

H2S, 184, 193
Hale, Anne, 104
Hale, Dudley, 104
Hale, Harry, 56, 59
Halsey Admiral William (USN), 306
Halvorsen, Harry, 70
Hancher, V. M., 337
Handy, Thomas, 295
Hansell, Haywood, 113, 114, 301, 302, 310
Harmon, General Hubert, 337
Harmon, Hubert, 10
Harmon, Millard, 20, 77, 298
Harriman, A., 232
Harris, Arthur, 130, 132, 179, 189, 190,
    200–201, 259

and Battle of the Bulge, 267
and bombing targets, 200, 256, 257, 258,
    261, 269, 273–74
and CROSSBOW, 237, 238
and OVERLORD, 200, 205, 209
Harrison, Edith, 13, 22, 295
Harrison, Ralph, 13, 22, 44
Harrison, Roger B., 9, 22
Harrison, Ruth. See Spaatz, Ruth Harrison
Hartle, Russell P., 132
Hawaii, Schofield Barracks in, 11–13
Hazing, West Point, 6, 7
HE 162s, 249
Heart disease, 106, 339
Hines, J. L., 56
Hiroshima bombing, 303, 307
Hitler, Adolph, 107–11 passim, 232–33,
    250, 251, 255, 258
    and aircraft industry, 246, 247
    and Battle of the Bulge, 261–62, 265,
        266–67
    fabled secret weapon of, 198
    and fuel industries, 202
    and Goering interview, 286
    and Mediterranean theater, 162
    suicide of, 282
    See also Germany
Hobby, Oveta Culp, 153
Hodges General Courtney H., 232
Holley, I. B., Jr., 3
Hooe, R. W., 70, 72
Hoover, Herbert, 66, 91–92
Hopkins, Harry, 135, 181
Hopper, Bruce C., 117, 179, 334
House, Edwin, 92
Houston, Texas, 44
Howard, Jan, 85–86
Hunter, Frank O'D. (Monk), 83
    in 1st Pursuit Group, 44, 50, 55
    at Issoudun, 37
    on Pursuit Board, 77, 83
    in retirement, 336
    in World War II, 116, 121, 122, 125,
        126, 179, 197
HURRICANE 2, 270
Hurricanes, 111, 112
HUSKY, 160–61

Ideology. See Doctrine, airpower
Independence
    of air missions, 38, 57–58, 84, 90, 96–98,
        115, 152 (see also Separate air arm;
        Strategic bombing)
    of American World War II air arm, 129–
        32, 189, 257, 259

Industries
  bombing of (general), 57–58, 85, 87–88, 90
  bombing of German (general), 113–14, 117, 121, 135, 140, 181, 182, 217, 220, 237, 255, 309
  bombing of German aircraft, 177, 181, 191, 192, 194–96, 248, 268, 286
  bombing of German ball bearing, 169, 181
  bombing of German missile, 237–38
  bombing of German oil, 202–12 passim, 239, 248–61 passim, 286, 287, 307, 340
  German aircraft, 177, 181, 183, 191, 192, 194–96, 198, 248–50, 268, 286
  intelligence re, 87–88, 113–14, 248, 249
  U.S., 28, 114, 245, 328
Intelligence, 278
  on carpet bombing, 225
  German aerial, 267
  German code interception, 110, 157–58, 162, 184
  on German reaction to oil industry bombings, 212, 256
  industrial, 87–88, 113–14, 248, 249
  on Luftwaffe, 205, 212, 254, 287
  U.S. agency organization of, 291–92
  See also Reconnaissance; ULTRA
"Interdiction," 33
International Pulitzer Air Races (1922), 47–48, 69
Ireland, in World War II, 127–28
Issoudun, 23–30, 36–37, 40, 336–37
Italy, 213
  and Africa, 139, 140, 158, 159
  Fifteenth Air Force in, 166, 168–169, 177–85 passim, 195, 196, 252
  invasion of, 159–69, 207, 212, 220–21

Japan
  surrender of, 304–7
  and World War II, 109, 115–16, 120, 122–24, 230, 289–310 passim
"Jeb Stuart unit," 271–73
Jennies, 17, 18
Jets, 16, 243–44, 246–47, 249–50, 254, 268, 286, 313
Jodl, Alfred, 282
Johnson, Davenport, 32, 33
Jones, B. Q., 16
Jouett, John H., 9
Joy, Henry B., 52
JU-52s, 158
JU-87, 147

JU-88s, 192, 214
Jutland, Battle of, 80

Keitel, Wilhelm, 283, 284
Kelly Field, San Antonio, Texas, 43, 49, 50, 54
Kennedy, John, 207
Kennedy, Joseph, 111
Kenney, George, 36, 100, 298, 299, 304–5, 311–12
Kepner, William E. (Bill), 104, 197, 205
Kesselring, Albert, 158, 160, 164, 165, 166, 167
Keystone LB-7s, 78–79
Key West Conference, 323, 330
Kilbourne, Charles E., 96, 97
Kilner, Mike, 20, 26, 29, 106
Kilner, Walter G., 25
Kimmel, Robert, 294
King, Admiral Ernest J. (USN), 124, 143
Knerr, Hugh, 100, 103, 129, 187, 242, 318, 324
Koenig, Pierre Joseph, 210
Korean War, 330, 334–35
Kraus, Walter F., 83
Kuter, Laurence, 113, 122, 149, 269

Lahm, Frank P., 16, 23
Lampert, Lester, 9
Lampert Committee, 58, 60, 61, 63–64
Landings, World War II, 117, 132–55 passim, 165–66, 200, 213–17, 227–28, 279
Langley Field, Virginia, 43, 54, 56–60, 66, 75, 99–104
Language studies, 28, 338
Lanphier, Thomas, 9, 28, 36
Lassiter Board, 60
Leach, Barton, 116
Leahy, William, 329
"The Lecture," 12–13
Leigh-Mallory, Trafford, 189, 190, 199–215 passim, 222, 223, 237, 340
LeMay, Curtis, 100, 298, 302, 316, 327, 335
Letchell, Charles, 44
Lexington, 88
Liberators, after World War II, 313
Liberators (B-24s), 107, 296
  in European theater, 126, 143, 194, 221, 231, 260, 271, 272, 275, 280–8
  in Mediterranean theater, 157
Life, 170
Liggett, Hunter, 43
Lightnings (P-38s), 119–26 passim, 134, 142–43, 156, 157, 194, 272

Lima (Peru) conference and Declaration, 108
Lindbergh, Charles A., 93, 95, 337
Lingle, D. G., 51
Lloyd, Hugh, 156
Lodge, Henry Cabot, 203
Logistics, of basing, 66–67, 229–34
*Los Angeles,* 69
Lovett, Robert, 114, 181, 203, 243, 244,
    265, 270, 271–72, 293, 298
Ludendorff, General Erich (Germany), 30
Luftwaffe, 136, 282
    aircraft of, 108–9, 112, 183, 193–94,
        246–47, 250 (*see also* Messerschmitts)
    and European theater, 22, 108–15 passim,
        182–84, 191–216 passim, 227, 228,
        235, 248–56 passim, 262–80 passim
    Goering interview on, 286
    and Mediterranean theater, 136, 140, 141,
        151, 157–59, 163, 166, 167
    personnel of, 183, 193–94, 196–97, 211
    ULTRA on, 157–58, 205, 212, 254, 287
Luke, Frank, 37
Lutheran faith, 4
Lyster, St. G., 130, 131

MacArthur, Douglas, 84, 96–97
    and airmail crisis, 92, 93, 94
    and Asia-first policy, 334
    and atomic bomb, 302, 303
    and Kenney, 36, 298, 299, 311
    in Pacific theater, 115–16, 124, 295, 297,
        298–99
    and surrender, 305–6
McClellan, George, 133
McCook Field, Dayton, Ohio, 43, 48, 49,
    54, 56
MacGregor, A., 152
McNair, Leslie J., 224
McNarney, Joseph, 10, 58, 81, 312
Mahan, Alfred Thayer, 84
Mails, crisis with, 75, 91–95
Malta conference, 274, 276
Maneuvers, annual, 88–89
Manhattan Project, 327
Manteuffel, Hasso von, 264, 265
Marauders, 117–19, 157
March Field, Riverside, California, 7, 66,
    77–89
Marine Corps, U.S., 61, 316, 317, 319,
    320, 322
MARKET-GARDEN, 235–36, 253–54
Marne, Battle of, 12
Marshall, George C., 115, 120, 172, 176,
    189, 243, 245, 293, 312
    and atomic bomb, 295

and European theater, 135, 136, 140, 210,
    259–60, 274, 276, 277, 278
and Mediterranean theater, 139–40, 145,
    181
and Pacific theater, 124, 297–98
and separate air arm, 291, 313
and unification of armed forces, 316–
    18
Martin B-26 Marauders, 117–19, 157
Martin bombers, 41, 78, 117–19
Materiel
    at Issoudun, 28
    in World War II, 245–48
    *See also* Aircraft; Missiles; Submarines
Mather Field, 43
Maynard, B. W., 41
ME-109s, 192
ME-110s, 192
ME-262s, 182, 246–47, 250, 286
Mediterranean theater, 139–85 passim, 195–
    99 passim, 228, 296, 297
    in North Africa, 10, 117, 132–59 passim,
        176, 203, 296
    *See also* Italy
Meigs, M. C., 337
Menoher, Charles, 40, 41, 53
Messerschmitt, Professor Willy, 246
Messerschmitts, 111, 177, 182, 192, 197,
    246–47, 250, 286
Mexico, 11, 12, 17–20, 42, 76
Midway, Battle of, 119, 124–25
Miller, Betty, 53
Miller, Henry, 10, 129
Miller, James, 25
Milling, Thomas DeWitt, 58, 60
Missiles, German, 182, 191, 236–37, 238–
    39, 245
*Missouri,* 305–7
Mitchell, Billy, 39, 40, 53, 57, 121, 292,
    340
    at air races, 48
    Andrews and, 99–100
    and coastal defense, 55, 68
    court-martial of, 62–64, 65, 66
    MacArthur and, 299
    Martin bombers used by, 78
    and separate air arm, 53, 58, 60–61, 62,
        291, 323
    training manuals ordered by, 55
    Transcontinental Reliability Test of, 41,
        60
    in World War I, 30–37 passim
Mitchell bombers, 117–18, 157
Mobility, air, 45, 68, 88, 102, 132
Moffett, William A., 3

Montgomery, Bernard L., 142–43, 149, 151–52, 160, 165, 167, 220–36 passim, 262, 263, 279, 281
Morale
 attack on civilian, 114, 268–77 (see also Cities)
 at Issoudun, 26–27, 29
 World War II military men, 185–88, 194, 240–41
Morality, of city bombing, 275–76, 303
Morrow, Dwight/Morrow Board, 61–62, 64
Mountbatten, Louis, 148
Music, 4, 19
Mussolini, B., 159
Mustangs (P-51s), 125, 184, 194, 197, 264, 278
Myrick, Dorothy, 178–79

Naiden, Earl, 58
National Air Races, 69
National Defense Act, 60
National Guard, 87
National Military Establishment, 320, 321, 322
National Security Act (Unification Act), 318–22, 327, 329
NATO, 314, 334
Navy, U.S., 87, 326, 329
 in air races, 69
 in annual maneuvers, 88–89
 budget for, 65, 84, 90
 and coastal defense, 65, 84, 101
 and North Island, 76–77
 and separate air arm, 61, 84, 316, 317, 322, 323
 and unification of armed forces, 316, 318, 319
 and World War II, 107, 124, 135, 173, 241, 280, 299
Navy Department, 57, 61
Nazis. See Germany
Nelson, Erik, 331, 334
New Mexico, Pershing expedition, 16, 17–20
Newsweek, 334–35
New York Times, 36, 62–63
New York World, 10
Nieuports, 26, 28, 32
Nimitz, Chester, 122, 295–306 passim, 329
97th Bomb Group, 123–24, 133, 136, 142
Ninth Air Force, 178, 179–80, 185, 219, 239, 242, 251, 254, 256, 264
 in ANVIL, 228, 230
 in ARGUMENT, 194, 195
 in COBRA, 224
 on D-Day, 214

in OVERLORD, 185, 200
 trucking by, 234
Noble, Andrew, 207
Norstad, Lauris, 116, 152, 314, 318, 319–20
Norstad-Sherman agreement, 319–20, 322
North American B-25 Mitchells, 117–18, 157
North Island, San Diego, 13–16, 76
Northwest African Air Force (NAAF), 152–57, 156, 163–65, 296

Offense
 airpower as, 32–33, 55, 57–58, 101, 110, 113, 130–31
 See also Strategic bombing
Oil industry, Germany, 202–12 passim, 239, 248–61 passim, 268, 286, 287, 307, 340
Olds, Robert, 100, 104
One-theater concept, World War II, 143, 145
Organization
 Allied Expeditionary Air Forces, 179–80
 of Army air arm, 90–91, 102–3, 114–15
 Jeb Stuart unit, 271–72
 of military aviation, 37–38, 90–91 (see also Independence; Separate air arm)
 of Northwest African Air Force, 152–55, 156
 of unified armed forces, 57, 316–23, 327
 USAAF staff, 324–25
 USAF, 325–26
 USASTAF, 299–300
 USSTAF, 178, 179–80, 296, 324
 of World War I forces, 31
 of World War II forces, 116–17, 152–55, 156, 172, 176–81, 188, 271–72, 295–300, 324–26
Ortiz, Robert M., 101
Ostfriesland, 60
OVERLORD, 173–89 passim, 199–220 passim, 226, 228, 238, 239, 247–48, 249, 258, 296, 297

P-12s, Boeing, 78
P-38 Lightnings, 119–26 passim, 134, 142–43, 156, 157, 194, 272
P-39s (Bell P-39 Airacobras), 119, 122, 125, 142, 156
P-40s, 156
P-47s (Thunderbolts), 107, 194, 213, 271–272, 282
P-51s (Mustangs), 125, 184, 194, 197, 264, 278
P-80s, 243–44, 247

Pacific theater, World War II, 109, 115–25
    passim, 143, 230, 289–310 passim
Panama Canal, 12
Parachutes/Paratroopers, 15, 16, 26, 48,
    213–14
Patch, Alexander, 285
Patrick, Mason, 26, 37, 39, 46–65 passim,
    77, 82, 84
Patterson, Robert, 312, 318, 319, 322, 329
Patton, George, 141, 154, 161, 224–34 pas-
    sim, 262–68 passim, 295
Pay, military, 15, 62
Pearl Harbor, 115–16
Peltz, Dietrich, 267–68
"Penguins," 26
Pennsylvania Assembly, 4–5
Pennsylvania governor offer, 293–94, 333
Perera, Guido, 116
Perkiomen Preparatory School, 5
Pershing, John J., 16, 17–20, 25, 29–31,
    38, 90
Personnel problems, 49–52, 81–83, 109,
    240–45
    See also Casualties; Death; Discipline;
    Morale; Training
"Pip squeak," 110
Ploesti raids, 167, 202–3, 211, 256, 271
POINTBLANK, 201, 273
Poland, in World War II, 109, 230–32, 233,
    251, 287
Poltava, 229–30, 231, 232, 251, 287
Portal, Charles, 119–20, 179, 204–11 pas-
    sim, 255, 259, 260, 261, 269, 282
Portal, Hugh, 130
Powell, Lewis F., Jr., 179, 274
Pratt, H. Conger, 60, 99, 100
Pratt, William V., 84, 90, 91, 101
Precision bombing, 67, 182, 257–58, 302,
    309
Pulitzer races, 47–48, 69
"Punitive Rag" (Spaatz), 19
Pursuit, 24–25, 75, 77, 87, 100
    planes for, 24–25, 67, 75, 78
    training in, 24–25, 26, 40, 54, 55–56, 57
    in World War I, 31, 32–33
Pursuit Board, 77, 83
Pursuit Group, 1st, 19, 31–32, 39, 43–56,
    66, 123, 134, 136, 142
"Pushers," 15

Quesada, Elwood, 65, 70, 266
Question Mark, 70–72, 80

Races, air, 41–42, 47–48, 60, 68, 69
Radar, 78, 110, 184, 192, 193, 260, 266
Radford, Admiral Arthur (USN), 318, 323

Radio communications, air-to-ground, 15–
    16, 71, 80
RAF. See Royal Air Force
Rail transport system
    attacks on, 204, 207–13, 215–16, 227,
        260–61, 270–71, 274, 287, 307, 309,
        310
    for moving planes, 45
Rainbow 5, 116
Ramming, 249
RAND Corporation, 326
Randolph Field, Texas, 109
Range, aircraft, 48–49, 72–73, 90
Reconnaissance, 12, 16, 17–18, 31, 33, 56,
    100
Recreation, 9, 76, 103–4, 106, 335–39
Red Cross, 29, 170, 171, 178–79
Reformed (Lutheran) Church, 4
Refueling, air-to-air, 69–73
Research and development, U.S., 15–16,
    77–78, 315–16, 326–28
Retirement, Spaatz's, 331, 333–39
Rex, 101
Rhoads, Thomas, 6
Richards, John Francisco III, 36
Richardson, J. O., 291
Rickenbacker, Eddie, 25, 27, 37, 93
Robb, J. M., 152
Rockwell Field, San Diego, 40, 73, 75–77,
    83
Rogue River, 335–36
Rommel, Erwin, 139, 140, 143, 149, 150,
    154, 155, 159, 167
Roosevelt, Elliott, 244–45
Roosevelt, Franklin D., 90–94 passim, 107,
    108, 109, 112, 135, 139, 175–76, 210,
    230, 245
Roosevelt, Quentin, 37
Roosevelt, Theodore, 37
Rose Bowl game, 70–71
Rostow, Walt, 179
Rothermel, John H., 6
Royal Air Force (RAF), 57, 109–11, 168,
    173, 184, 259
    aircraft of, 111, 112 (see also Spitfires)
    Goering interview and, 286, 287
    gunnery school of, 128
    organization of, 179, 189, 325
    U.S. air arm's independence from, 129–
        32, 189, 257, 259
    in World War I, 30, 31
    in World War II European theater, 119–
        20, 125, 194, 195, 200, 201, 202, 214,
        215, 216, 219, 221, 237, 256, 257,
        262, 267, 275

in World War II Mediterranean theater,
142–50 passim, 156, 159
and World War II Pacific theater, 296
Royce, Ralph, 9, 20
Ruhr Valley, 279–80
Rundstedt, Gerd von, 215, 216, 219–20,
225, 226, 262
Russians. *See* USSR

Safety standards, 49, 93–94
*See also* Death
St. Lo carpet bombing, 220–26, 258
St. Mihiel offensive, 30–31, 33–35
San Diego
flying school at, 13–16, 24
Rockwell Field at, 40, 73, 75–77, 83
San Francisco Presidio, 40–42, 83, 88
*Saratoga*, 88
Saundby, R. H. M., 130
Schofield Barracks, Hawaii, 11–13
Schools, military, 24, 56–57, 109
Air Corps Tactical, 96, 97, 109, 114, 273
Air Force Academy, 14, 337–38, 339,
340
Air Service Tactical, 54, 55, 56–60
Army flying, 13–17, 24
Command and General Staff College/
School, 56–57, 85, 98–99, 109, 117
*See also* Training
SE-5s, 41, 45–46
Second Wing, GHQ Air Force, 75, 99–104
Selfridge Field, Michigan, 45–56, 66, 81, 82
Separate air arm, 57–58, 292–93, 311–23
Arnold and, 259, 291, 292–93, 295–96,
307, 312, 317, 323
Congress and, 41, 57, 60, 321, 322
establishment of, *see* United States Air
Force
Mitchell and, 53, 58, 60–61, 62, 291, 323
Navy and, 61, 84, 316, 317, 322, 323
strategic bombing and, 38, 57–58, 307,
317, 322, 323
USSBS and, 310
War Department and, 57, 60, 61–62, 95–
96
World War I and, 31, 38
World War II and, 203, 259, 291
7th Bombardment Group, 73, 77–83, 88
SHAEF, 190, 258–59, 275
*Shenandoah*, 61
Sherman, Admiral Forrest (USN), 319–20
Sherwood, Virginia, 178–79
Shigemitsu, Mamoru, 306
Sholto Douglas, William, 128, 130, 131–32
Shuttle missions (trucking), 229–34, 236,
274

Simpson, William H., 279
Sinclair, Archibald, 130
Skeel, Burt E., 50
Slessor, John, 2, 125
Smith, Lowell, 42
Smith, Walter Bedell, 282, 283
Smoking, 9
Somervell, Brehon B., 9
Somme, Battle of, 20
Spaatz, Carl Andrew (personal)
birth of, 4
character/personality of, 2, 8–9, 46, 63,
164–65, 331–32, 339–4
death of, 1–2, 339, 340
family of, 3–6, 22, 76, 104, 105, 169–70,
177–78, 198–99, 294–95, 331, 335,
339, (*see also individual family members*)
health of, 106, 339
retirement of, 331, 333–39
Spaatz, Carla (Boops), 76, 104, 105, 169,
170, 178, 294, 335, 339
Spaatz, Katharine (Tattie), 76, 104, 105,
169, 170, 178–79, 294, 335, 336
Spaatz, Rebecca (Becky), 76, 104, 105,
169–70, 178, 198–99, 294, 335, 339
Spaatz, Ruth Harrison, 9, 13, 44, 81, 340
homes of, 116, 177–78, 335
at Langley, 59, 103–4
and retirement period, 331, 334, 338–39
at Rockwell, 75–76
and Spaatz spelling, 104
during World War II, 116, 169–70, 177–
78, 294, 295
and World War I, 36
Spaatz Board, 314–16
Spaatz spelling, 104
Spads, 32–35, 41, 45–46, 47
Spanish-American War, 84
Spatz, Anne (Muntz) (mother), 4, 6
Spatz, Anne (sister), 4
Spatz, Auguste, 3
Spatz, Carl (grandfather), 3–4
Spatz, Charles B., 4–6
Spatz, Flora, 4
Sptaz, Frederick, 4
Spatz, Juliana Amalie Busch, 3–4, 6
Spatz, Julie, 3
Spatz, Ruth (sister), 4
Speer, Albert, 248
Spitfires, 111, 112, 119, 125, 128, 134,
141, 142, 144, 156–57
Stalin, J., 139, 175–76, 229, 273
Standardization, aircraft, 28
Stimson, Henry, 120, 121
Stinson, Marjorie, 22

Stinson family, 22
Stock market, 76
Stovall, Howard, Jr., 179
Stovall, Howard (Hank), 32, 34, 179, 336
Strategic Air Command, 72
"Strategic Air Power" (Spaatz), 307–8
Strategic bombing, 38, 57–58, 85–88, 90–
     91, 97, 101, 312
   atomic bomb and, 302–4, 313, 314, 315
   and separate air arm, 38, 57–58, 307,
     317, 322, 323
   Spaatz's article on, 307–8
   and USAF organization, 325
   USSBS evaluation of, 308–10
   in World War II, 117, 132–37 passim,
     143, 159, 168, 169, 172, 181–82, 188–
     220 passim, 228, 255–82, 307–8
   See also Targets
Stratemeyer, George, 9, 56, 98–99, 170
Stripes, 28–29
Stukas, 110, 147
Stumpff, Hans Jurgen, 284
Submarines
   in World War I, 20, 22, 23, 140, 141–42,
     143
   in World War II, 245–46, 307
Sullivan, John L., 329
Superfortresses (B-29s), 240, 295–314 pas-
     sim
Supreme Headquarters Allied Expeditionary
     Forces (SHAEF), 190, 258–59, 275
Surrenders, World War II, 282–86, 304–7
Suslaparov, Ivan, 282, 283
Sweden, 240–41
Switzerland, 240–41, 277–78
Symington, W. Stuart, 318, 319, 320, 322,
     325, 328, 330, 333
Synchronizers, 25

Tactical units and missions, 33, 60–73, 110,
     113, 169, 172–73, 219–54, 256, 325–
     26
   See also Attack aviation
Taft, William Howard, 6
Talbott, Harold E., 337
Taliaferro Field, Fort Worth, Texas, 40
Targets
   in air campaigns, 113–14, 199–213, 260–
     61, 268–74, 286–87, 340
   See also Cities; Industries; Transport sys-
     tem
Technical improvements
   aircraft, 18–19, 24–25, 48–49, 67, 68, 69,
     71–73, 77, 78–79, 90, 102, 217–18
   (see also Jets)
   airfield, 68

communications, 15–16, 71, 80 (see also
     Radar)
   refueling, 69–73
   research and development for, 15–16, 77–
     78, 315–16, 326–28
Tedder, Arthur
   and European theater, 180, 190, 199–211
     passim, 222, 237, 238, 256, 260, 261,
     266, 276, 277, 279
   and Mediterranean theater, 147–56 passim
   and surrender, 283, 284–85
Teheran conference, 175–76, 179, 229
Theory. See Doctrine, airpower
Thomas, Elbert, 318
Thomas, Francis, 335
Thomas Morse aircraft, Boeing, 48–49
Thunderbolts (P-47s), 107, 194, 213, 271–
     72, 282
Tibbetts, Paul, 302, 303
Tinker, Bud, 170
Tinker, Clarence L., 59
Tinker, Madelaine, 170
Toland, John, 284
Toohey, F. J., 7
TORCH, 136, 139–59
Tour length, in World War II, 185–86, 240
Townsend, "Doolie," 178–79
"Tractors," 15
Training, 13, 21–22, 54
   at Air Force Academy, 337–38
   in 1st Pursuit Group, 43
   gunnery, 31, 128
   in Issoudun, 24, 25–30
   manuals for, 55–56
   pursuit, 24–25, 26, 40, 54, 55–56, 57
   at Randolph Field, 109
   in San Diego, 13–16, 24, 40
   Spaatz's, 5, 6–11, 13–17, 21–22, 31, 56–
     60, 98–99
   of World War II crews, 128
   See also Doctrine, airpower; Schools, mil-
     itary
Training Regulation, 440–15, 97–98
Transcontinental Reliability Test, 41–42, 60,
     68
Transport system
   for aircraft from European theater, 290
   for aircraft to European theater, 125–27
   for aircraft to Selfridge Field, 45–46, 47
   attacks on, 204–20 passim, 227, 238, 255,
     256, 260–61, 270–71, 274, 287, 307,
     309, 310
   shuttle mission, 228–34, 236, 274
Trenchard, Hugh, 31
Trucking (shuttle missions), 228–34, 236,
     274

Truman, Harry S., 284, 295, 304, 318, 319, 322–23, 327, 328, 330
Tunner, William, 81
Twelfth Air Force, 136–56 passim, 177, 180, 227, 228, 251, 325
Twentieth Air Force, 297–98, 299
Twining, Nathan F., 180, 196, 206, 252, 294, 299, 335

ULTRA, 232
    and Battle of the Bulge, 262, 264–65
    on carpet bombing, 225
    code interception by, 110, 157–58, 162
    on German aircraft industry, 249
    on Luftwaffe, 157–58, 205, 212, 254, 287
    and MARKET-GARDEN, 236
    and Mediterranean theater, 162
    and oil industry bombing, 212, 256
Umezu, Yoshioiro, 306
Unification, of armed forces, 57, 291, 296, 307, 316–23, 327
Uniforms, military, 51, 62
United Kingdom, 127–39
    American relations with, 129–32, 140, 146, 154, 178, 181, 188–90, 257, 259
    German attacks on, 109–12, 113, 236–39, 286
    and surrenders, 282–86 passim, 305
    in World War II, 109–12, 113, 119–20, 135–93 passim, 199–286 passim, 296, 297
    See also Royal Air Force
United States Air Force (USAF), 322–31
    Chief of Staff of, 99, 314, 322, 331
    establishment of, 322
    Secretary of, 322
    staff organization of, 325
United States Army Air Forces (USAAF), 9, 112, 115–325
    manpower of, 240–45, 312–13
    planes of, 114, 117–20, 187–88, 194, 256, 313 (see also Bombers)
    USASTAF of, 299–305
    USSTAF of, see United States Strategic Air Forces
United States Army. See Army, U.S.
United States Navy. See Navy, U.S.
United States Strategic Air Forces Europe (USSTAFE), 291, 299–305
    aircraft available to, 187–88, 194
    in European theater, 178, 179–80, 184–289, 296
    organization of, 178, 179–80, 296, 324
    Pacific redeployment of, 290
United States Strategic Bombing Survey (USSBS), 239, 308–10

USSR, 120, 159, 175–76, 183, 273, 274
    and city bombing, 276
    future adversary, 313, 316
    and landings in France, 117
    Mediterranean theater and, 141–42, 157, 167, 175–76
    in Pacific theater, 305
    and Ploesti oil fields, 167, 256, 279
    and surrenders, 282–85, 305
    and trucking missions, 229–32

V-1s, 182, 191, 236–37, 238–39, 245
V-2s, 182, 236, 239, 245
V-1400 high-compression engine, 69
Vandenberg, Hoyt, 99, 117, 136, 264, 266, 285, 286, 314, 323, 331
VARSITY, 279–81
Veterans Administration (VA), 293–94
Victory celebrations, 293
Villa, Pancho, 12, 16, 17–18
Vishinsky, Andrei, 283, 284
von Arnim, Juergen, 149, 154, 159
von Falkenhayn, Erich, 20
von Karman, Theodore, 326
Count Alfred von Schleiffen's plan, 12

Wade, Leigh, 37
Walker, Kenneth, 85, 86, 113
Walsh, Robert L., 7, 230
War Department, 57–66 passim, 95, 152, 318, 321–22
War Lords (Carver), 2
Washington, Spaatz in, 60–73, 89–98, 104, 105–20, 121, 335
Washington Post, 1
Watergate affair, 1
Weather
    in air race, 41
    Selfridge Field, 49
    in transport over Greenland, 125–26
    United Kingdom, 128
    in World War II, 164, 188–200 passim, 217, 223, 236, 250, 262–70 passim, 304
Weaver, Walter, 99
Weeks, John W., 48
Weeks, Sinclair, 60
Weicker, Lowell, 179
Weir, Benjamin, 243
Welsh, William, 144, 145
West, G. W., 171
Western Desert Air Force, 146, 156
Western Flying, 82
Western Flying Circus, 40, 45

Westover, Oscar, 58, 91, 93, 94–95, 99–100, 103
West Point, 5, 6–11
Wheeler, Sheldon H., 9, 11, 12–13, 20
Whitney, J. H. "Jock", 336
Williams, Paul, 235
Williamson, Charles D., 269
Wilson, H. M., 180, 227
Wilson, James, 241
Wilson, Woodrow, 12, 17
Winant, John, 170
*Winged Defense* (Mitchell), 62
Woodring, Harry H., 103
Woodrum Committee, 291
World Disarmament Conference, 101
World War I, 20–38, 294, 336
    aviation in, 12, 14, 22–38, 54, 55–56, 101
    communications in, 80
World War II
    Air Board and, 319
    Allied bombers in, 101, 110–27 passim, 132–36 passim, 142–43, 147, 156–57, 181–82, 184, 187–88, 194, 215, 222–36 passim, 256, 263–64, 296–305 passim (*see also* Fortresses; Liberators)
        end of, 306
    European theater, 106–43 passim, 155, 157, 167–68, 173–282 passim, 295, 340
    Mediterranean theater in, *see* Mediterranean theater
    Pacific theater, 109, 115–25 passim, 143, 230, 289–310 passim
    preparedness for, 107–9, 114
    surrenders, 282–86, 304–7
Wright, Orville, 95
Wright brothers, 13
Wright Field, 68, 85

Yalta Conference, 273, 274
Yamamoto, Admiral Isoroku, 124
Yount, Barton K., 169–70

Zhukov, Marshal Georgi K. (USSR), 282–83, 284–85
Zuckerman, Solly, 199–212 passim, 266, 271